The World of Work

AN INTRODUCTION TO INDUSTRIAL / ORGANIZATIONAL PSYCHOLOGY

To the memory of my parents
*   Jackson and Leonora,*
and to my sister Annice—
*   all of whom taught me language*

ABOUT THE AUTHOR

Born in the United States and educated in Canada, Alan Auerbach has been teaching personnel and I/O psychology for over 25 years at Wilfrid Laurier University, Waterloo, Canada, where he is Associate Professor. He has served as a personnel consultant to many local businesses and governmental agencies and has published book reviews in the *Journal of Personnel Psychology.* His interest in teaching led to his reviewing many books and audiovisual aids for *Contemporary Psychology.* To experience the role of ergonomics in equipment design he earned a pilot's license. He's written almost two hundred consumer-advice newspaper columns, held many offices in the Consumers' Association of Canada, and in 1992 was named *Consumer Educator of the Year* by the Province of Ontario.

The World of Work

AN INTRODUCTION
TO INDUSTRIAL / ORGANIZATIONAL PSYCHOLOGY

ALAN AUERBACH

Wilfrid Laurier University

Brown & Benchmark
PUBLISHERS

Madison   Dubuque, IA   Guilford, CT   Chicago   Toronto   London
Caracas   Mexico City   Buenos Aires   Madrid   Bogota   Sydney

Book Team

Publisher *Edgar J. Laube*
Acquisitions Editor *Steven Yetter*
Managing Editor *John S. L. Holland*
Production Manager *Brenda S. Filley*
Managing Art Editor *Pamela Carley*
Development Coordinator *Alan M. Sturmer*
Editor *Ava Suntoke*
Designers *Harry Rinehart, Charles Vitelli*
Art Editor *Elizabeth L. Hansen*
Permissions Coordinator *Janice M. Ward*
Typesetting Supervisor *Libra Ann Cusack*
Typesetter *Juliana Arbo*
Proofreader *Diane Barker*
Graphics *Shawn Callahan, Lara M. Johnson, Laura Levine*
Marketing Manager *Carla Aspelmeier*

President and Chief Executive Officer *Thomas E. Doran*
Vice President of Production and Business Development *Vickie Putman*
Vice President of Sales and Marketing *Bob McLaughlin*
Director of Marketing *John Finn*

A Times Mirror Company

The credit section for this book begins on page lxxii
and is considered an extension of the copyright page.

Cover ©*Frank Herholdt/Tony Stone Images*
Cover design *Harry Rinehart*
Research by *Elizabeth L. Hansen*

Copyright © 1996 Times Mirror Higher Education Group, Inc.
All rights reserved

Library of Congress Catalog Card Number: 94-062137

ISBN 1-56134-185-1

Printed in the United States of America
by Times Mirror Higher Education Group, Inc.
2460 Kerper Boulevard, Dubuque, IA 52001

10 9 8 7 6 5 4 3 2 1

Preface

When I am forgotten, . . . say I taught thee.

(Shakespeare, *Henry VIII*)

Writing this textbook raised many considerations. Students who often wonder why they have to learn this or that want relevance, brevity, and clarity in an interesting package. Some potential adopters prefer staid writing that emphasizes historical background and classical research; others want the future accentuated with innovation and panache. Reviewers look for some improvements on existing alternatives. Academics with an eye for scholarly research want a book to reflect the discipline thoughtfully, accurately, currently, and comprehensively. Purchasers want a low price, but publishers are in business to make a profit. And of course, authors want to please everybody; I hope the compromise I struck is a happy one.

1. Student orientation

Any instructor who gives lectures and writes books knows how much more student-oriented the lectures seem. This is to be expected; communications to a live audience, here and now, create a different set of implied demands than an author's communicating to a keyboard. The main objective of this book is to maintain the *immediacy* and the *student orientation* of the lecture. With this intent I have introduced the following considerations and features:

• Students bring high expectations to a book on industrial/organizational (I/O) psychology. They may not expect a book on cognition or physiology to captivate their interest, but since the world of work is familiar and important to them, they expect a text on this subject to be user-friendly as well as worthwhile. I have tried to make the contents integrated, brief, and balanced, in a writing style at once unadorned, palatable if not engaging, and sometimes personalized.

• The subject matter is explained in a clear and interesting way, with occasional attention to simplifying the concepts. Sentence construction and paragraph length are designed for readability.

v

- Each chapter begins with a carefully chosen quotation, a set of learning objectives, and an overview. Other pedagogical aids within the textual material include explanatory illustrations, examples, and "Brief Cases." To satisfy students' interest in relevance, "So What" boxes, which show the practical value of the topics under discussion, are located throughout the chapters. Each chapter ends with a Study Guide comprising terms to be learned (especially discipline-related terminology), issues to consider, and a sampling of five multiple-choice questions.

- I/O psychology ranges across wide and diverse areas. To add cohesiveness, interrelationships are emphasized through frequent cross-references within the book.

- Citations, which can seem intrusive, irrelevant, and cluttering to an undergraduate student, are minimized. I chose equal thirds of those that are basic and classic, those that exemplify the topic under discussion, and recent citations that represent current research. Because novices may find citations extraneous due to their unfamiliarity with the complex and arcane system of academic literature, I have outlined this in chapter 2. Moreover, Appendix C shows a recent title page from the most important journal in I/O psychology, as well as a sample paper.

2. A comprehensive approach

A second objective is to provide coverage that is *comprehensive*. This stems from a conviction that an introduction to a discipline should serve as a sampler. A broad coverage also permits instructors to select sections that they deem appropriate to their course.

- The broader the topic range, the more disjointed a book may appear to the learner. To give coherence, the topics are organized into a carefully designed sequence. The rationale is detailed in chapter 1. Notwithstanding the attempt at comprehensiveness, limiting the length was a challenge. I/O psychology is so central to human experience and so related to psychological research that only a small fraction of its theories and findings can be represented in any one book.

- All I/O psychology textbooks deal mainly with people-related topics, as does the present offering. But here, personnel is interpreted broadly, to include ergonomics and consumer psychology, both of which stem from and deal with the needs and concerns of people. In addition, there is coverage of timely topics such as robotics, computers (as workplace tools, communication devices, and research instruments), program evaluation, occupational health and safety, quality of work life, the consumer movement, and current legal, social, and ethical issues.

- I have attempted to present contrasting perspectives such as those of the employee and employer, union and management, and buyer and seller. There are allusions to topics such as archaeology, music, evolution, and world history.

- Most I/O psychology data derive from the United States, but taking into account the global nature of today's marketplace, I also address internationalism, particularly some problems, advances, and practices associated with Canada and Mexico, Great Britain, Scandinavia, and the Far East.

- Some readers and adopters will bring strong and incompatible opinions to certain topics. For instance, students may want PMS to be recognized as a sometimes debilitating event, but not one that should permit employment discrimination against women. Those with management experience or aspirations may be opposed to unions; others who have seen the benefits of unions may want them championed. A treatment of employment equity that pleases one group of readers may trouble another. I attempted to be even-handed, balanced, and inoffensive.

3. Some distinctive features

Despite the need to control length, another objective is to present some content not found in other texts.

- The chapter on communication ergonomics is unique and, given the importance of effective communication in industry, worthy of inclusion.

- All technical terms are defined in the glossary, which also contains brief biographies of the discipline's founders.

4. Book design

The final objective is to provide a book that is meritorious apart from the manuscript contents:

- One type-font is used to emulate the emphasis that is occasionally given the spoken word, and another font designates terminology that is to be learned. (The system is explained in chapter 1.)

• In terms of *value*, the book includes a built-in Study Guide as well as the glossary. There's also a rich array of appendices designed to serve many students' needs and interests. Issues of prices affected this book from its earliest stages. Generally, the more features, the higher the cost, but our objective was to create an offering that is much less expensive than most, yet more fully featured. A book that covers communication, the pros and cons of using textual material as a training medium, and consumer advocacy should itself model good principles.

This book is written for undergraduates who have minimal exposure to academic psychology. It is hoped, however, that its mixture of theory and application will also serve others who participate in the world of work, whether as assembler, manager, cleaner, or purchaser. The contents are designed to be clear, realistic, current, and helpful, so that they may serve as both textbook and brief handbook. As well, the "how to" appendices are designed to serve a practical purpose for many readers. This title was designed for a second-year undergraduate course comprising 36 lecture-hours, with minimal term assignments. With appropriate term projects that include supplementary reading, the book could be used as a basis for a 72-hour course. An Instructor's Resource Guide and accompanying materials are available to adopters.

No first edition can be guaranteed free of teething problems, but in this case the manuscript and supplements were class-tested over four years, and all of the chapters were reviewed by academics and in some cases by practitioners.

Acknowledgments

A lot of work by others has preceded this volume. As a starting point, my prime mentor has been Anne Anastasi, whose combination of clarity and scholasticism has been a model to follow. At the end point, Trudy Trudel would calmly read the computer manuals at every "Unrecoverable Application Error"; she served as first-level manuscript reader, and she let me work late. I am particularly indebted to John F. Binning of Illinois State University, and Karen G. Duffy of State University New York, Geneseo, for their insightful reviews. The professionals at Brown & Benchmark Publishers listed on the copyright page taught me that a publisher does vastly more than just "publish." Finally, to the many past students who read chapters as course handouts, and to the recent ones who used the manuscript as a textbook, all the while providing the kind of sharp, eager feedback that every author yearns for, much is owed.

Alan Auerbach
Wilfrid Laurier University

Contents in brief

Contents

Part two
The people 73

Part three
The workplace 309

Chapter 10

OCCUPATIONAL HEALTH AND SAFETY 310

Chapter 11

INTRODUCTORY ERGONOMICS 340

Chapter 12

APPLICATIONS OF ERGONOMICS 370

Part four
The product 435

Chapter 14

CONSUMER PSYCHOLOGY 436

Part one

CHAPTER 1 **Orientation**

CHAPTER 2 **Methodology**

The introduction

We start with two orientation chapters. The first chapter tells you what industrial/organizational (I/O) psychology is, how it affects your life, where it came from, and what it's good for. You may be surprised at what you'll learn about industrial revolutions, the meaning of "work," and the contributions of academia to warfare. It also tells you how this book is designed to serve you in your course (and beyond it), and how it relates to what is known as "the literature." The second chapter shows you *how* we know what we know. It outlines I/O methodology in general, and covers the important survey techniques in particular. It also touches on how I/O research relates to the literature, and how principles of ethics always guide and sometimes limit the researcher.

Write to express, not impress.
Hewlett-Packard style guide.

Bird's-eye view of the chapter

The many advantages that we associate with civilization are largely the products of industry. Industrial/organizational (I/O) psychology, the study of industry's psychological aspects, has a short, interesting history. Because it is a problem-solving discipline, the history of I/O psychology is linked to the history of war. The scope and the literature of I/O psychology, as well as the meaning of "work," are explained in this chapter. It also outlines the other parts of the book: methodology (the science of research procedure); the main topic, personnel psychology (the science of people at work); human factors engineering (the design of equipment to suit the user); and consumer psychology (the psychology of the marketplace).

Chapter 1
Orientation

The payoff from chapter 1 You will:

1. Learn some basic terminology of industrial/organizational (I/O) psychology
2. See how your own life has been influenced by the work of other people
3. See how the world of work is interconnected
4. Understand how your educational institution is part of this network
5. Appreciate the changing role of "work" in human development
6. Understand the impact of the first industrial revolution
7. Realize that a second industrial revolution is taking place right now
8. Learn the varied meanings of the concept of "work"
9. Appreciate the typical attitudes toward "work" today
10. Find the history section to be unexpectedly interesting and vibrant
11. Know the founder of psychology's connection with I/O psychology
12. Identify the three founders of I/O psychology
13. Know the founders of ergonomics
14. See the role of warfare in the development of I/O psychology
15. Understand the combined contribution of Wundt and Binet
16. Discern the role of the Hawthorne research
17. See the changing connection between social and I/O psychology
18. Grasp the importance of ergonomics in World War II
19. Learn the synonyms for I/O psychology
20. Know the history of major workplace legislation
21. Recognize the present status of I/O psychology
22. Appreciate the practical value of the discipline
23. Differentiate between academic and nonacademic periodicals
24. See the design, format, and value of this book

A book is of value only if it tells you what you don't already know. You may be surprised to learn how broad the topic of industrial/organizational (I/O) psychology is, and how pervasively it affects your life. You will learn that the word "work" has complex and far-reaching meanings and that industrial revolutions aren't limited to the distant past. You will also learn that a history can sometimes be fascinating and brief.

THE SCOPE OF I/O PSYCHOLOGY

Has any area of study had a greater impact on your life than I/O psychology? Consider what has happened to you already. You probably entered this world in a building that represents the height of industrial technology and organizational efficiency, the hospital. Your hospital functioned in connection with thousands of other industries, indirectly if not directly.

When you left your first institution a few days after your arrival, you were probably carried to a car for the first trip home. That vehicle was produced in a factory that made it available for a tiny portion of the cost it would have borne if it had been designed and produced by any one individual. In fact, no individual would have been able to produce any major component of the car single-handedly. Nor could the transportation network on which it traveled have been constructed by any one person.

When your proud parents announced your safe arrival home, they no doubt did so on the telephone. This communication device is part of a "person-machine system" comprising thousands of employees and millions of components. Your house, crib, playthings, and diapers all were products of a myriad of interlocking industries. Throughout your early years you learned to accommodate yourself to society's institutions like school or church to such an extent that you do not think of them as institutions or **organizations**.

Now, as a member of the college or university community, you are part of an elaborate institutional complex. A university's interconnecting organization touches every facet of the nation. Through its library, for instance, you have access to any book or periodical that's ever been published. (You may be pleased to know that along with medical and social care, U.S. states, Canadian provinces, and other technologically advanced countries spend most of their revenues on education, and that next to salaries the biggest budget item for most colleges and universities is their library.)

In short, although I/O psychology focuses on people at work, every aspect of our world is touched by the problems and solutions studied in this engaging topic. You should find the subject matter vital, the treatment of it vibrant, and the course valuable. We'll start by looking at where "work" comes from, and what the word means.

A BRIEF HISTORY OF "WORK"

For tens of thousand of years, our ancestors made their living by hunting for edibles, and probably did not think of it as work. With the development of civilization, livelihood was based mostly on agriculture. A few artisans pursued their crafts within a cashless, illiterate community, and most households were self-sufficient. Few people traveled from their homes to serve an employer for pay during specific hours each day; the concept of work time, which so governs work today, was largely unknown or irrelevant.

"Remo! Lift with your knees, not your back!"

Collective effort was introduced to work life in the last ten thousand years. The Great Wall of China, England's Stonehenge, and Roman and Greek cities and culture all show that some ancient civilizations used organizational principles to weld hundreds of thousands of workers into a highly organized, hierarchical team. Machinery and tools did exist back then, as did some central power sources, usually rivers and streams. Even so, most work continued to be individual and customized. Each stone block in the Egyptian pyramids, each window in a medieval church, and each suit of armor was a unique product that had been fashioned by hand. Nothing really changed until the **industrial revolution**.

The industrial revolution

A revolution is a sudden, major change. Watch what happened over a span of only one hundred years. In 1700, goods were "manufactured" (from *manus facere*, or hand make) by artisans who performed all or most of the steps themselves. For instance, a cobbler would convert a piece of leather into a pair of boots by himself. But by 1800, the cobbler's descendants were working in shoe "factories" (a word that derives, ironically, from "manufacture"). Each worker repeated the same small task throughout a 12-hour workday, usually operating a machine. The shoe factory purchased components (heels, insoles, laces, eyelets, and so on) from other factories, whose workers repeated their little tasks all day. It is largely the mass-production factory that has formed our current view of the meaning of work.

The industrial revolution of the mid-1700s started in England and rapidly spread to the Western world, changing the nature of daily activity. With centralized factories funded by the few who inherited wealth, work became something one did under strict instructions from somebody else. Work also became much more hierarchical, bringing prestige and power to a few.

The industrial revolution resulted from several forces. With the invention of the steam engine in Great Britain, an efficient, central power source

Many modern assembly lines show sophisticated technology. Here the equipment has been designed to suit a sightless assembler.

could be located wherever a fire could be maintained. This led to the rise of mass-production factories, which originally concentrated on textile weaving.

In the United States the industrial revolution reached a high point due largely to Henry Ford. Ford borrowed two earlier concepts:

1. Around 1800, Eli Whitney invented the cotton gin, a machine that extracted cotton fibers from the seeds. (The word "gin" is at the root of "ingenuity" and "engine.") Inherent in the invention was a more important though less celebrated advance. Whitney's gins used *interchangeable parts*. Instead of skilled craftsmen having to custom-make each component to produce the machine, unskilled assemblers did so by fitting together identical parts from a central supply. For the customer, if a part wore out in use, it was simple to replace it from the parts stock.

2. Traditionally, even in the early factories, the item being made stayed put, and the workers toiled around it. In the mid-1800s, a Cincinnati meat plant changed the procedure for cutting up carcasses. Instead of workers standing around an animal on a chopping block, the carcass was hung from a steadily moving conveyor belt. In this "disassembly line," each worker had a single, specialized task to perform on animal after animal. Now the workers stood still and the work was brought to them.

So what Imagine that in the 1790s, your forebear said, "I'm in the middle of an industrial revolution. This means production will never be the same. Knowing what's happening, I can adjust and benefit, and ensure that my progeny a couple of centuries from now will inherit more than I did." You are very much in that same position now. The world of work is undergoing another revolution. If you understand it, you'll be in a position to benefit from it. Let's see what changes you are in the midst of.

In the early 1900s Henry Ford combined these two advances to assemble cars. Conveyors brought the growing car to assemblers, each of whom added one more interchangeable part. This *assembly line* had two effects. The assembly process became so efficient that the cost of cars dropped from thousands of dollars to a few hundred. And the nature and pace of factory work was taken from the workers and determined entirely by the plant managers. This led to conflict between assemblers and managers, and the rise of unionism.

Many factors then combined to make the United States the world's most productive, powerful, and envied country in the first half of the twentieth century. Ford's 15 million early cars encouraged the development of road transportation, and the inventions of Edison and Bell did the same for a communication system. Natural resources were abundant. The new opportunities and freedoms, plus unrest in Europe, brought millions of immigrants, many of whom were young, healthy, adventurous, and entrepreneurial. A massive public education system, universal and secular, ensured a literate population sharing a common language. And unlike countries in Europe or Asia, no bomb would fall on American factories, and no invading army would destroy its people or its power. The American industrialist had become the new monarchy.

The current industrial revolution

The original industrial revolution took place in the mid-1700s. The last three quarters of the 1900s have brought another revolution, one as profound and fundamental as the original one. The new one is again changing our attitudes to work and the way we perform it.

Brief case

In 1930, when a major depression was beginning, the Kellogg cereal plant in Michigan changed the system of three 8-hour work shifts to four 6-hour ones. The 6-hour workday ended in 1985. The women workers liked the shorter hours, but the men wanted the extra money for working the extra two hours a day, and management preferred dealing with the smaller workforce possible with an 8-hour day.

The changing job   New jobs, once abundant in manufacturing, are becoming scarce. For instance, as recently as 1980, all writing was done by pen or typewriter; reading matter was composed by skilled typesetters. Now there are around 100 million computers in business use in the United States alone.

Good new jobs with major employers are rare. Most new job opportunities are found in service rather than manufacturing, and most service openings are for low-skill, dead-end positions. Much new work is self-generated by entrepreneurs, mostly women, starting in their own homes.

What jobs there are offer less security than they used to, as managers talk of flexibility and global competitiveness. Employees are being replaced by robots or losing their positions as a result of restructuring, in which companies close down or relocate. Employers may also eliminate positions by using microelectronic and satellite technology to transfer work like programming and routine data entry to workers in Ireland or India. Governments, while deploring the lack of jobs, are leading the way in replacing salaried employees with external contract workers.

Once, men would learn the factory procedures to work a 40-hour week; now women are learning WordPerfect to work 80 hours at home, if they get a contract. Electronic mail allows instant and efficient communication within an organization, between businesses, and from home to office. Factories concentrate on high-tech efficiency. Instead of stockpiling components, they rely on computer communication with suppliers and customers, and "just-in-time" delivery of components. In the same way, they use temporary or contract workers ("just-in-time personnel") where they can.

The changing union   Unions have lost much of their power and continue to lose it, as governments give employees more basic rights under the law than the unions did at their height. Because unions once controlled job classification, seniority brought relief from physically demanding, repetitive work, which would be turned over to young newcomers. Now plants aren't hiring, and to keep their jobs employees have to work harder and longer at the same types of work they were hired to do a quarter century earlier.

Youngsters are either unemployed or hired for minimum-wage, part-time, dead-end, service jobs.

The preindustrial workday lasted through the hours of daylight, and many people worked at home or lived on the job site. With the industrial revolution the workweek increased to 70 or 80 hours, with virtually no holidays, and the major goal of unions was to reduce it to 40 hours. Now the workweek is defined in law, but employers, faced with expensive fringe benefits and training costs, would rather induce an existing employee to work overtime than hire an additional staffer.

The changing equipment   There has long been tension between workers and their workplace machinery, but it's taken on a new face. Computers do not work very intuitively, and workers feel that the machines control them more than vice versa. Jobs that were once described in terms of prerequisite skills or knowledge required are now defined in terms of the apparatus to be operated.

A job posting, instead of recruiting a car painter, now specifies familiarity with a specific paint robot. The group of six switchboard operators, who had to know the firm, the clients, and telephone diplomacy, has become a single "telecommunications coordinator," perhaps with longer hours and less pay. The employer is prouder of the capabilities of machinery than the skills of the operator, who can be offered low-tech pay to run high-tech equipment. The company that once lauded its friendly and knowledgeable switchboard personnel now extols its user-friendly, automated voice mail. Machines are anthropomorphized; humans are automated.

"Labor-saving" machinery hasn't reduced the workers' labor as much as it has lessened the employer's costs. The employer who has replaced six workers with a costly machine wants it to be operated efficiently and continuously, preferably while the machine is automatically reporting to management how it's being operated. Machines are still driving the operators.

No equipment has changed more radically than that for *communicating*. At the time of the very first commercial enterprises, messages could travel as fast as a horse could gallop or a ship could sail. Those speed limits didn't change with the first industrial revolution; the changes didn't begin until the mid-1800s, and they approached maturity only a century after that.

Now watch what might happen when you buy a broom at a hardware store. The bar code at the cash register signals a computer in the store's office; the computer detects a need for more brooms. The computer signals the warehouse computer, which decides it's time to place a factory order, and signals the factory's computer. The factory's computer analyzes stock on hand and supplier data, and signals the handle maker to prepare a shipment. The handle maker sends a fax to the lumber supplier, who phones the lumberjack. Hours after you bought a broom in Toronto, a tree is felled in a Swedish managed forest, sparked by your simple purchase (Figure 1.1).

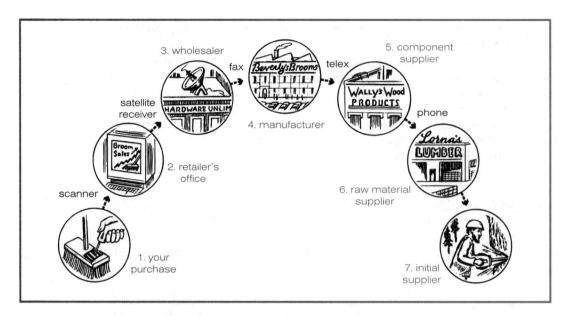

FIGURE 1.1 Modern communications equipment

> The purchase of a broom in your local hardware store could trigger a chain of signals that results in a tree being felled in a managed forest.

The changing marketplace With the reduction of political trade barriers and more efficient transportation, the marketplace is becoming global. A new motion picture or computer program can be sold in a hundred countries rather than in one or two, and fads can quickly spread across the world. A global marketplace justifies the investment of huge sums of development resources but also makes it harder to predict demand and to serve consumers. Errors are more likely and more costly; decision makers must be fast and accurate.

Retailing is also changing, with today's trends including specialized catalogs at one end and huge warehouse stores at the other. Advertisers are targeting more specific types of prospects. There are new forms of marketing, and more sophisticated approaches to customer service.

The changing employee The North American employee of the previous century was typically a white male. He had stable work, and his wife stayed home (putting in more hours at housework than he did on the job). Today's job applicants represent vastly more diversity in education, work experience, ethnicity, age, sex, and lifestyle.

Employees are also consumers, and it's the employment that permits the purchase of goods. In the past, people's needs were simple, and there were few goods for sale. Workers were paid by the day (the hourly wage was uncommon until the industrial revolution), and if they didn't need anything they could take days off. Now there's a limitless range of goods that people want, and both spouses, if they have work, have to put in longer hours to pay for these.

The changing management   Management style is modifying to reflect, on the one hand, the increasing emphasis on humanizing the workplace and improving the quality of work life. On the other hand, sophisticated machinery, often involving computers as well as surveillance technology, give managers more information about, and control over, employees.

The changing organization   Workers' social structure has altered. Jobs were once rigidly classified by training, formal designations, the apprenticeship system, custom, and union contract. If the factory's power failed, the plant electricians would have a cigarette break or a card game; if the assembly line stopped, the assemblers could enjoy a break together. Now employers are increasingly gaining the right to move workers where they are needed and to have them do whatever's assigned. This removes the job classification barriers, the opportunities for downtime, and the human interaction associated with them.

Employers argue that workers are given more variety, and that consequently there is less likelihood of repetitive strain injuries (page 329). Employees are finding, however, that they have fewer opportunities to make friends, to take a break, and to engage in human interaction. And they have to work harder, replacing one repetitive task with a series of repetitive tasks.

Management is also being influenced by the Japanese method of altering workers' attitudes toward the employer. To foster feelings of solidarity and loyalty, Japanese workers and managers share common uniforms, cafeterias, parking places, work locations, and, to a large extent, pay. Through pre-work rituals of songs, slogans, and calisthenics, workers are trained to think of themselves as part of a large team, and to focus on ***kaizen***, which is the search for ways of improving productivity and quality.

But North American workers are finding that kaizen reduces the number of their jobs and increases their workloads, and that they're acquiring an ability for multitasking rather than for multiskilling. These attitudes—that they're being made to work harder rather than smarter—reduce their commitment to the employer and increase employee turnover.

The above types of workplace changes (in jobs, unions, equipment, marketplace, employees, and the organization) are more sudden and far-reaching than you are probably aware. They add up to the second industrial revolution, offering both opportunities and challenges to those engaged in the world of work.

So what What's the value of understanding the meaning of the word "work"? It's that work is always with us. Reading and learning the material in this book and others is work. Every year, your teachers have given you homework. Some of you are working your way through college. When you graduate, finding the right kind of work may be uppermost in your mind. The kind of work you do will help to define your image and lifestyle, and indirectly your friends and perhaps your spouse too. Most of your waking hours will be spent at work-related activities. If offered a blind date, surely one of your first questions would be, "What does the person do?" If two similar people want to marry you, one known to be a hard worker and the other to be a hard sleeper, whom would you choose? If your tombstone were to give a comment about you, would you like the word "work" included? The title of this book is *The World of Work*. It is because work so dominates our lives and thoughts that it's important to understand exactly what the term means.

TODAY'S MEANING OF "WORK"

Like many common words, work is a hard term to define; dictionary editors struggle with a dozen meanings of the word as both a noun and a verb. The nature and meaning of work has long attracted philosophers, clerics, revolutionaries, and political scientists, but not so much psychologists.

Physicists call work the application of force over distance. (According to this definition, the only work performed in writing this book was pushing pencils sideways and computer keys down.) Animal researchers such as ethologists and sociobiologists apply the word to much of the behavior of animals like squirrels and beavers, and even to some insects.

Work, as addressed by the present book, is a recent concept forged by the two industrial revolutions outlined above. Work dominates human thought, and nine-tenths of North American workers sell their labor for wages. Only a few of them have total control over the conditions of their work, generally through the operation of franchises and small, independent businesses.

In modern I/O psychology, **work** refers to human behavior that is usually

- purposeful or goal-directed

- motivated and skillful

- disciplined, demanding, and prolonged

- structured by task and by time

- social or cooperative

- requiring some combination of physical and mental capabilities, and

- paid for by someone else.

- Work has a *societal* aspect to its definition. For instance, a rancher riding a horse to round up cattle is working, whereas a suburbanite who rides a horse does so as a costly and prestigious leisure activity.

On one hand, work is seen as something that *must* be done; on the other, it is often seen as a noble endeavor, a source of pride, even having a spiritual quality. Testimonials, eulogies and character references, for instance, laud people for being hardworking, but never for being hard-eating or hard-playing.

Finally, our overall attitudes toward work are curiously ambivalent. Millions of unemployed people desperately seek work. A steady job not only has monetary benefits, it also confers status, dignity, and self-definition; unemployment often brings depression, anxiety, frustration, and lowered self-esteem. Yet, many people view their work negatively, as an undervalued and unpleasant activity they have to do so that they can afford to live without working during vacations and retirement. The first question often asked of major lottery winners is whether or not they are going to keep working. One objective of this book is to help change the perception and definition of work in a more positive direction.

THE HISTORY OF I/O PSYCHOLOGY

Students are rarely interested in starting a course of study with names and events from previous generations. But a short history of a discipline like I/O psychology can be fascinating in its own right. The following account focuses on the history of **personnel psychology**. Relevant historical backgrounds are included in the chapter on organizational psychology, as well as in the two other main sections, ergonomics and consumer psychology.

I/O psychology is quite modern. It's one of the most recent branches of psychology, which itself has been a separate discipline of study for only the last hundred years. The history of any science is really an account of the advances in its theories as supported by the arguments and evidence provided by its researchers. As an applied branch of psychology, I/O psychology has a problem-solving orientation, and its two spurts of growth were associated with the two world wars of this century. (The meaning of applied, as opposed to basic, research will be covered in chapter 2.)

Let's start with an overview of what I/O psychology is. Psychology is the study of *behavior*; I/O psychology is the study of behavior in the *work setting*. It looks at how individuals are affected by the structure and practices of the work organization, by colleagues and managers, and by the physical and social environment of the workplace. The main area is *personnel psychology*, which deals with recruiting, selecting, training, evaluating, and helping employees in the context of the organization's present and future needs. *Ergonomics* deals with modifying the tools and other aspects of the physical environment of the work, so that the job can be performed as easily, effectively and safely as possible. *Organizational psychology* looks at how people relate with each other and within the organization, and how their emotional and social needs are identified and respected. Finally, *consumer psychology* studies how the end product can be tailored to the needs and wants of those who purchase the goods or services provided by the organization.

The earliest years

As an art, I/O psychology reaches back to the beginning of civilization, but as a formal science, it started only within the present century. As an academic discipline, psychology began as an outgrowth of philosophy, which had been systematically studied for many centuries. That's why the early psychologists were more likely to ask how the mind operates, and what is the meaning of consciousness, than to deal with applied issues like increasing productivity.

Between 1900 and 1915 there were only two people in North America who could be termed industrial psychologists. They were Hugo **Münsterberg** and Walter **Scott**. Both had received their doctorates in Germany from Wilhelm **Wundt**, generally acknowledged to be the founder of modern psychology.

The title of the founder of industrial psychology is generally accorded to Scott, on the basis of his books on advertising written during the early 1900s. They helped to establish psychology as not only an academic, but also an applied, dollars-and-cents discipline. Walter Dill Scott (not to be confused with the writer Sir Walter Scott) also founded the first consulting firm that specialized in industrial personnel problems.

The early practitioners, influenced also by Münsterberg's 1913 book *The Psychology of Industrial Efficiency*, focused on personnel selection and placement (including the use of tests for these purposes), advertising, and occupational safety. Münsterberg was a German psychologist who was hired to teach at Harvard, later to become president of the American Psychological Association. He also became the first personnel consultant (for the Boston

Street Railroad Company), but his influence was curtailed when the United States declared war on Germany on April 6, 1917.

Another dominant force was Frederick Winslow **Taylor**. His "scientific management" approach surfaced early. As a young man, Taylor would compose lists of both the comely and unattractive women scheduled to attend a dance, so that he could apportion his time equally to both groups. He paid so much attention to his appraisal of the human resources at the dance that he missed most of the fun.

When he became an industrial engineer for a large American steel mill, in 1898, Taylor devised workplace strategies that are felt to this day. His 1911 book *The Principles of Scientific Management* would have been on the office shelves of Henry Ford's managers.

Taylor contended that each task should be maximally simplified, so that each worker would be doing the minimum as efficiently as possible, but doing it repetitively. The best worker at a given task was to be scientifically studied in terms of time taken and techniques used (**time and motion study**), and this exemplary performance would be the criterion against which other workers were measured and paid.

Management, on the other hand, would make all planning, pacing, maintenance, and related decisions. Taylor recommended that management further increase productivity by fitting the tool to the task (page 345). He felt that motivation and work productivity are determined by economic rewards, so he recommended **piece rate** pay. This was the origin of modern incentive plans and performance-based pay.

Critics of Taylorism saw it as a mechanistic approach to finding the one best way to perform a task. His supporters believed that workers were inherently lazy and needed to be continuously watched and measured, and this assumption sparked the rapid growth of unionism. Taylor, however, was actually very concerned with the human aspects of fitting the best employee to a given job. His theories and research on efficiency were designed to increase productivity for the company and to increase salaries while reducing fatigue for the employees, but from 1911 to this day, a debate continues. Is it fair for workers to increase their output by, as a contemporary critic of Taylor said, 362 percent for a 61 percent increase in wages? Is it good to make a few workers so efficient that many others are laid off? Should unions support scientific management and piece rate pay? And are the principles of Taylorism dehumanizing and demoralizing?

The **Gilbreths** were a particularly interesting couple. From 1911, Frank, an engineer, and Lillian, the first female psychologist, specialized in the reduction of unnecessary motion. We take kitchen design for granted, but the kitchen of 1900 bore little resemblance to that of 1950. Lillian Gilbreth introduced the concept of a narrow room with counter space along both main walls, and storage above and below the counter area, as a design for kitchen units on trains. (Your parents probably remember seeing apartments advertised as featuring Pullman kitchens.)

The Gilbreths were the original efficiency experts, and they practiced what they preached. For instance, Frank found that by buttoning his vest from the bottom up he saved 4 seconds; by lathering his face with two shaving brushes, one in each hand, he saved 17 seconds. The Gilbreths even charted the daily activities of their 12 children to reduce wasted time and effort. (You may have seen or heard of the film *Cheaper by the Dozen*. It was adapted from a book of the same title, a biography of the Gilbreths.) Even today, some time and motion consultants refer to the basic element of a motion as a **therblig**. Read it backwards and allow a little slack.

World War I

Despite the work of the pioneers, I/O psychology did not make a conspicuous mark—either as an academic discipline or as a profession—until after 1914, the beginning of World War I. For instance, the flagship journal of the field, the *Journal of Applied Psychology*, did not start until 1917. It remains the most important academic periodical in its area (Appendix C).

At the outset of World War I, the U.S. Army commissioned the development of a written test to screen unsuitable recruits from training programs. Here was industrial psychology at its best: applying the principles of psychology to solve critical, unique problems, in this case one that was monumental. When the most powerful industrial country in the world suddenly mobilized for war, millions of men were available, along with the communication and transportation systems to move tens of thousands of them where and when they were wanted. Which men (virtually all recruits were male) should be chosen, and how would they be best assigned?

Previous wars had been fought mainly with single-shot weapons. The early muzzle-loading firearm was less effective, in both rapidity of fire and penetration, than the medieval longbow or the Roman catapult. In fact, Dyer (1985) pointed out that Alexander the Great, who died 2,300 years ago, would have been quite at home with the strategy and equipment of any army up to the 1800s. With both sides using similar tactics and training, battles fought with these weapons depended mostly on numbers. If Side A with 1,200 men fought against Side B with 1,000, the result would likely be 2,000 dead and wounded, with the 200 survivors of Side A proclaiming themselves the victors.

World War I was fought entirely with the breech-loading weapon. Instead of cannons that shot an inert stone or metal ball inaccurately over short distances at the rate of one per minute, soldiers now had artillery pieces that could hurl explosive projectiles accurately from city to city, at a rate of five per minute. Some firearms automatically fed 100 rounds per minute into the breech and out the muzzle. These weapons meant that the projectiles, instead of being fabricated individually by the soldiers in the midst of battle,

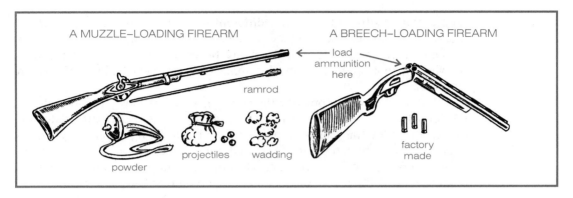

FIGURE 1.2 Firearm design changes

A small change in firearm design led to major changes in personnel psychology.

were *factory* produced by the millions. Survival now depended on mass production at home as much as on soldiers in the field. The old and the new firearm designs are sketched in Figure 1.2.

The power of the new weapons (for instance, a 10-man submarine could be an equal match for a 1,000-man battleship) plus a large, mobile population meant that for the first time in history, military recruiters had at their disposal millions of candidates more than were needed. How were they to be selected?

The groundwork had been laid by Wundt, who, as early as 1879, developed tests designed to predict learning ability. Then, a decade prior to the war, Alfred **Binet** had been commissioned by French educational authorities to devise a test to predict how certain children would fare at school. Although limited in purpose, Binet's innovative test-design strategy heralded modern **psychometry**, the science of psychological testing. A little later, just as the war against Germany was breaking out, Lewis Terman at Stanford University in California adapted Binet's concepts into the Americanized Stanford-Binet Intelligence Scale. Terman also coined the phrase "intelligence quotient" (IQ), (which he borrowed from a concept of a German psychologist).

Now a child's overall mental ability could be expressed by a single IQ number, thanks to Binet's testing innovation. Consequently, psychologists were in a position to adapt the new IQ test to a version that would suit the military's needs, and the American Psychological Association urged its members to lend professional assistance to the war effort.

Arthur **Otis** had devised intelligence tests for mass administration in industry (one of his tests is still being used occasionally to this day). Borrowing from Otis, the versatile psychologist Robert **Yerkes** designed an intelligence test for general military use.

Yerkes' version was administered not individually but to groups at a time. It was brief and simple to administer, easy to score in vast numbers, and the questions were suitable for a wide range of young adults. The scores ranged from 13 to 183, but on a different scale than that used for modern intelligence tests. Two such tests were developed, the **Army Alpha** for recruits who could read and write, and the **Army Beta** for those who could not read or who did not speak English. A sample of Army Beta items is shown in Figure 4.3.

Further test development followed. Job specifications were formalized, job knowledge (trade tests) were devised, predictors to select candidates for officer and pilot training were prepared, and counseling programs were instituted. The testing program was used for all recruits in all branches of military service, and in a 2-year period, some 1.75 million men were classified on the basis of their test results! Applied psychology had gone to war.

Between the world wars: The Hawthorne research

World War I brought not only political and economic changes, but sociological ones as well. Farm lads who had shown bravery and leadership and were promoted to positions of responsibility were not likely to go back to the farm when they took their uniforms off. A large group of psychologists had learned how to use tests efficiently to predict job performance. The world of work would never be quite the same.

For instance, the most influential early textbook for introductory psychology courses (Ruch, 1941) listed the civilian occupations of the army recruits of 1917, along with the ranges and averages of their Army Alpha scores. Examples were 132 for clergyman, 89 for auto mechanic, and 69 for day laborer (converting the Alpha scores to modern IQ scores). Ruch advised psychology students, "Naturally in attempting to choose your vocation you must know your own intelligence level [so you should] . . . take one of several standardized intelligence tests."

Not surprisingly, after the war, the testing techniques developed for the military were used to make selections for personnel needs in industry and education. At the same time, universities began to offer courses in applied psychology. Personnel psychology was now both an *academic discipline* and an *applied profession.*

In the mid-1920s, a Western Electric Company telephone assembly plant in Hawthorne, Illinois, taking leads from the work of Taylor, conducted routine scientific management research on variables such as the effect of plant lighting on productivity. The illumination in one room was left as it was; in another room it was varied, sometimes down to moonlight level. Astonishingly, every time the illumination was measured in either room, productivity increased, at least initially.

The puzzled management hired Harvard Business School professor Elton Mayo as a consultant. Following the ideas of Taylor, Mayo began what seemed at the time to be minor follow-up research on the effect of lighting and a dozen other variables on productivity. Again, Mayo soon concluded that no matter what changes were made, the workers' productivity immediately rose.

This finding began a series of four major studies over the next 12 years, which were documented in a classic monograph by Roethlisberger and Dickson (1939). Mayo had brought an atypical colleague, W. Lloyd Warner, into the project. Warner was a young anthropologist who had studied isolated natives in Australia (and not-so-isolated residents of Massachusetts). His background permitted the incorporation of anthropological field methods into the study.

One study by Mayo and Warner, on a group of assemblers whose working environment was not being altered, showed that they were all restricting their output to some unwritten standard. The researchers gradually switched their attention from the job situation (for example, illumination levels, the scheduling of work periods and rest breaks, and the style of supervision) to the attitudes, morale, and the social and status relations of the employees, that is, to *human relations*. The investigation of the human relations involved research on an unprecedented scale. Careful 90-minute interviews were conducted with over twenty thousand employees! These interviews disclosed the importance of the *informal social structure*, that is, the formation of work groups that established their own views of productivity norms, and pressured members not to produce either more or less than these norms.

Of course, by today's standards the research was poorly controlled. But one discovery, the energizing response to the simple act of paying attention, has become entrenched in history as the **Hawthorne effect**. The other discovery is the way social influence can limit output. These two major findings led to continued study of not just selection and placement, but also the *social* aspects of work that affect morale and motivation.

Just as **Freud** is frequently cited and discussed, but hardly ever read in the original except by a few academics, the name Hawthorne has become a cornerstone in social psychology, small-group processes, motivation, job satisfaction, and productivity. Yet, most of those who discuss, extol, or criticize the **Hawthorne studies** are unlikely to have read them.

To this day, the original reports are still being analyzed and interpreted by a few interested researchers. For instance, it's still not known for certain why the workers' productivity rose at each change, eventually to fall back toward the original level. Was it due to the novelty of the interventions, or to the prestige of being studied by a Harvard professor, or just to getting attention? Was there one worker in the group who had her own reasons for wanting to maximize her output, and who inadvertently motivated the others? Possibly the blue-collar worker of the 1920s was particularly responsive to all four of these influences.

The Hawthorne studies began a collaboration between social psychologists and industrial psychologists, but this partnership was not to be smooth. Social psychologists felt that they were the true academics, and that industrial psychologists, with their applied and profit-making orientation, probably belonged more in a school of business and economics than in a department of psychology. Industrial psychologists felt that their cut-and-dried approach to studying job analysis and time and motion was not applicable to investigating social dynamics. The two views gradually merged, and now most I/O psychologists have studied social psychology, and most social psychologists can apply social psychology theory to the workplace.

World War II

World War II brought a surging need for more of the personnel research that had been introduced in World War I. A generation had passed, and graduates of the industrial psychology doctoral programs that were started after World War I answered the call. Between the start and the end of the war, membership in the **American Psychological Association (APA)** rose from 2,600 to over 4,000. Over 2,000 of these psychologists had responded to the needs of the U.S. military, with 1,250 of them working full time on war issues (Gilgen, 1982).

The work of these pioneers was varied. Edwin Boring (who was to become the prime historian for psychology) edited a 1943 book called *Psychology for the Fighting Man* and wrote a textbook on military psychology. A postwar survey (Britt & Morgan, 1946) indicated that most American military psychologists were testing, interviewing, classifying, and counseling. Some analyzed data and developed training and counseling programs; a few worked on psychological warfare, military task performance, and equipment design.

The primary task, however, was to *classify* massive numbers of recruits, just as in the earlier war. The most important of the classification instruments was the new Army General Classification Test, which separated the recruits into general categories according to their soldiering aptitudes. In addition, several new tests, considerably more sophisticated, were developed and used. For instance, instead of measuring a single global attribute called "intelligence," psychologists assessed a number of specific aptitudes, which enabled them to make appropriate placements in programs such as officer or trade training. They also devised tests for new applications. What makes a good code-breaker, language translator, or instructions writer? The job skills were defined, and tests for them were created.

There was some spillover from military psychology to civilian applications even during the war. Factories were hard pressed to keep up with the production demands of the military. Psychologists in the United States and England helped in the areas of productivity, absenteeism, work schedules, and equipment design. Their Canadian colleagues studied the effects of fatigue and sensory deprivation on the performance of tasks requiring constant alertness. They also researched improvements to pilot training and morale. All these areas have been central to I/O psychology ever since.

So what What's the value of knowing the *history* of the topic you're about to dig into? You can't appreciate or evaluate something in a vacuum. You can't tell if a theory or argument is sensible without knowing where it came from. You can't decide if a career has a growing future without being aware of the relevant historical trends. You can't always tell if you're making a mistake without knowing something of the successes and failures of those who preceded you.

You might be hired because of equal employment legislation, and take it for granted, not knowing how recent it is. You might have to argue that you should be offered a position despite the legislation, based on your understanding of its history and purpose. In short, you can't tell where you're going unless you know where you are, and you can't know where you are unless you know where you've been!

In this war, no matter how well the military personnel were selected, trained, and motivated, some of the complex and powerful new equipment was beyond human ability to operate as designed. This led to the rapid rise of **ergonomics**, which redesigns equipment to suit the operator. Ergonomics, or human factors engineering, originally dealt only with improving industrial efficiency. During the war it was called upon to save lives and win battles. For instance, in research on equipment design, aircraft training devices were equipped to record every action of the crew. These recordings served both to select the most talented pilot recruits and to redesign the cockpit for operator efficiency. Other contributions of World War II to ergonomics will be described in chapter 11.

Gilgen (1982) describes 13 typical wartime projects, and Kronk (1979) documents the contributions of female psychologists to the war effort. Histories of the contribution of psychology to World War II have been documented for several countries: the United States (Napoli, 1981; Gilgen, 1982), Germany (Geuter, 1984), and South Africa (Louw, 1987).

Post–World War II

After World War I, the contributions of the first industrial psychologists were applied in modest measure to civilian life. After World War II, by contrast, it was as if the profession had learned from the earlier experience how to apply war-related advances to the postwar world.

In the 1950s, especially in the United States, industrial psychology achieved considerable stature and respectability. Academically, its research and statistical rigor earned it the reputation of being the most scientific of all the applied areas of psychology. In the field, industrial psychologists established private and consultancy practices, and many were hired as full-time members of large corporations. The discipline became a major force in shaping industrial efficiency, mainly by providing technical solutions to problems raised by clients.

The world's most influential governing body of psychology, the American Psychological Association, has continuously responded to the increasing impact of applied psychology and its reliance on tests. For instance, it first published its *Technical Recommendations for Psychological Tests and Diagnostic Techniques* in 1954. The American Psychological Association currently includes among its official divisions not only the Society of Industrial and Organizational Psychology, but also Applied Psychology, Military Psychology, Engineering Psychologists, and Consumer Behavior. Similarly, academic programs in I/O psychology (listed in Appendix D) have proliferated.

By 1970 the name of the discipline was gradually changing from *Industrial Psychology* to *Industrial and Organizational Psychology*, reflecting first the increasing integration of social psychology concepts, and then the development of a separate theory and literature in organizational behavior. These changes shifted the focus from the individual employee to the overall organization, from a micro to a macro or broad perspective.

Organizational psychology studies variables such as communication, group decision making, conflict management, organizational power, politics and social influence, team building, the impact of new technology on the organization, and organizational analysis and development. Some university courses are now called Organizational Psychology, and cover the micro topics under Human Resources Management.

Unfortunately, the name Industrial and Organizational Psychology is somewhat cumbersome, and the common abbreviation I/O Psychology is not immediately clear to the novice. In England, an alternative term, Occupational Psychology, is used.

Advances in I/O psychology have stemmed more from without than from within, as is often the case with applied disciplines. The major recent external influence has been massive sociolegal reform, which applied strong principles of human rights to all aspects of life, including the workplace. This change, first introduced in Scandinavia and the United States, prohibits workplace discrimination based on sex, race, origins, and beliefs.

The primary federal legislation in the United States is Title VII of the **1964 Civil Rights Act**; in Canada it is the 1979 Charter of Rights and Freedoms. In addition, most states and provinces have instituted further tightening of legislation that requires employers to treat their employees fairly and humanely. Legislation in many countries has prohibited practices of personnel discrimination that violate public policy, or that cannot be justified as job related.

Another influence that has gained acceptance in recent times is the general conviction that the greater the power, the more the responsibility. Thus, major employers are held accountable for the *quality of life* of both the employee and the community in general. Practices that were once seen as normal business conduct, for example, manufacturers loaning new cars with their odometers disconnected to automotive executives, or dealerships redesignating the model year of unsold new cars to make them appear a year newer, are now not just ethically questionable, but illegal.

The relationship between employer and employee, and between employer and society in general, has changed markedly in the past few decades. In the past, employers had total control over employees during work hours, and no responsibility after hours. For example, communities would tolerate local environmental damage by a major employer.

We now accept the notions of social responsibility, corporate ethics, and public accountability and reject any unfair, deceptive, and unsafe practices relating to the employee, the environment, and the end user. The new social conscience in the workplace has resulted in remedial and catch-up programs for the disadvantaged; comprehensive health, day-care, old-age security, and retirement programs; and attention to the quality of work life.

Present status

As a profession, I/O psychology is vibrant and valuable, especially in the United States. Most major American firms employ a staff I/O psychologist, although the job title (page 81) may read manager of employee relations, director of management development, senior staff specialist, or even director of advertising, business systems supervisor, or manager of consumer research. There are several hundred I/O psychologists practicing in Canada, and 15 times as many in the United States.

Most I/O psychologists have a doctorate (Ph.D.) degree; a minority work with a master's degree. (Appendix D outlines graduate programs and how to choose and apply to them.) Employment prospects are good. Of the doctoral graduates, one-third are working in colleges or universities, a quarter in industry, and another quarter in consulting work. Two-thirds of master's degree holders work in industry. Those with an undergraduate degree who have specialized in the I/O field may find employment working under supervision in a variety of settings.

How useful are these professionals? Many managers are concerned about the staggering cost of absenteeism and turnover, topics I/O psychologists have researched comprehensively. All matters of personnel handling, such as recruitment, selection, training and evaluation, are troubling to managers, and have been studied by I/O psychologists.

In a massive review of over 200 studies in which psychological theory was used to increase output, Katzell and Guzzo (1983) found that, in nine-tenths of the cases, higher productivity had been achieved on at least one concrete measure. Even allowing for the possibility that researchers may be less liable to submit negative results for publication, this overview strongly suggests that psychology can be usefully applied to the business world.

One Canadian bank reportedly saved $7 million in a year by following a psychologist's recommendations on dealing with absenteeism. The U.S. government reported an estimated $16 billion annual savings in the 1980s from the psychological assessment of its 4 million employees.

Another example stemmed from a strike by air traffic controllers in the United States. The government wanted to shorten the standard applicant screening program, which took three months. Psychologists showed that maintaining the lengthy procedures would actually save $8 million for every one thousand trainees. They pointed out other ways of reducing costs without sacrificing quality. These included raising the upper age limit to 35 without loss of efficiency, and shortening the training program for accepted applicants from four to two years.

The profession you are being introduced to can save not just money for the company, but the company itself. As corporations are harried by global competition, legislative restraints, a demanding **workforce**, critical customers, and employees and clients who are nontraditional, managers are hard pressed to satisfy everyone. Some organizations may have to change radically in order to survive, and many will benefit from consultations with organizational development specialists.

As an undergraduate course, I/O psychology has become increasingly popular since the 1970s, whether as part of a psychology major, a business program, or just as an elective. This is probably because students have become more aware of the occupational relevance of higher education. (Though aware that a course in I/O psychology no more makes them I/O psychologists than a course in history would turn them into historians, students correctly assume that some background in I/O psychology can only enhance their employability.) Graduate programs are also increasing, but more gradually.

As an academic discipline, I/O psychology makes solid contributions to our fund of knowledge in the social sciences and business. Research findings specific to the topics in this book are published in the **academic journals** shown in Appendix C. It is these journals that constitute what is known as the **literature**.

"THE LITERATURE"

Throughout most serious works of psychology, you will come across people's surnames followed by a date in parentheses, for example, Smedley (1988); sometimes both are parenthesized: (Smedley, 1988). This format is a code adopted in psychology to indicate, "I am citing (referring to) something published by the named person in the named year; you will find all the details you need to retrieve the source by looking at the list of references at the end of this article." Some knowledge of what is meant by *published* may be of interest and use to you.

Consider the difference between a professor and a teacher. Whereas a teacher is normally expected to relay what others have discovered or argued, a professor may be expected to profess the results of original research to colleagues and students. For the early professors, research meant little more than reading and thinking; the disciplines professed were primarily theology and philosophy. Now, the research of the I/O psychology professor, like that of all academic researchers, involves tying into the massive complex of "the literature."

Advances are unlikely to take place regularly and systematically without scientific research. Moreover, they serve little purpose unless those who are interested know about them. This exposure is effected by the literature, that is, the system of academic journals. Academic journals are magazines, but they differ from nonacademic periodicals in the following ways:

1. In nonacademic periodicals, articles are chosen for how they contribute to the sales and image of the magazine. Academic articles or "papers" go through a much tighter filtering process. The journal editor arranges for outside readers (experts in the area of the paper) to review the submission and recommend acceptance, rejection, or revision. They may be **blind reviews**, in that neither researchers nor reviewers know each others' names or institutions. A flawless paper might be rejected because it adds nothing to the existing literature.

2. Another difference is in the motivation of the participants. In nonacademic publishing, the editorial staff is salaried, and contributors are generally paid by the word. In academic journals, the editor and reviewers volunteer their work, and authors of accepted papers are not paid.

3. Nonacademic periodicals focus on eye-appeal factors such as design, graphics, illustrations, and layout; academic papers are simple and unadorned. Any illustrations are supplied by the author. Papers run on consecutive pages, without being interrupted by advertisements or the beginnings of other articles. (Most academic journals do carry advertisements, but they are generally confined to the back pages where they will not interfere with the papers.)

So what

- The 3,000-word essay required by your Introductory Psychology professor last year
- A research paper required in this course
- A master's thesis
- A doctoral dissertation
- Postdoctoral positions
- University faculty positions
- Publishing research papers or writing an academic book
- Finding the answer to a problem bothering your employer
- Getting answers to questions that bother you

What do all these have in common? They rely on being able to tap into the massive wealth of information contained in an academic library. Knowing where to find the reports and how to interpret them is likely to benefit you throughout your academic and your work career.

4. The language in nonacademic periodicals is based on readability and entertainment value. Academic papers are required to give as much clear information as possible in as few words as possible. For instance, the title of a magazine article is designed to be catchy and inviting; that of a journal paper is a minisummary of the entire article, so readers can know in advance if the paper will interest them.

5. Journals are costlier than magazines. Though cheaper to produce, their circulation is much lower, and the advertising revenue is minimal. The acquisitions budget for university libraries, which used to be mainly for books, is increasingly devoted to journals.

6. Academic journals tie into an elaborate system of information retrieval and sharing. The contents are systematically indexed in various indices and abstracting services so that any researcher can access all papers on a topic of interest.

Academic libraries share their holdings with each other, so if your library does not have a journal you need, the library will locate and borrow it from another. It typically works like this: You need a copy of a rare book or a paper in an obscure journal not held in your library. Your librarian sends a fax to the Library of Congress in Washington, D.C., or to the National Library in Ottawa. These libraries check their master catalog listing all the holdings in all the libraries in the country, and fax or e-mail back the names of libraries holding that item. Your librarian then contacts the nearest holding library for a faxed, mailed, or on-line copy of the item you want.

7. Academic journals demand detailed *documentation.* The papers must include enough information about the procedure and the data analysis techniques to permit **replication** (repetition of the study) by other researchers in the area. If a researcher exaggerates or falsifies, colleagues can uncover and disclose the errors. The publication of a paper in an academic journal invites criticism by other researchers, including yourself.

Appendix C illustrates the literature of I/O psychology. The journal most frequently cited in I/O textbooks, the *Journal of Applied Psychology,* is represented there by a table of contents of the latest issue available as this book went to press. When you scan some titles, note how efficiently each lets you know what the paper deals with. The best way to find out more about contemporary I/O psychology is to locate the latest of these journals, browse through some titles, and read the papers that attract your interest.

Material that is too extensive to be presented as a journal paper can be offered in book form. Typically, books organize and integrate the findings of many papers. In this case, the journals comprise the **primary literature;** the book, **secondary literature**.

Electronic retrieval

Academic communication is increasingly adding electronic methods to the printed page of old. The content is converted into electronic form, which permits instant access by academic libraries with on-line retrieval facilities. Instead of having to search their topics in card catalogs or printed abstracts, people engaged in library research can search electronic databases. For instance, most major academic libraries subscribe to Psychological Abstracts on CD-ROM, a system for instantly retrieving listings under the topic you select. These CD-ROMs are updated quarterly.

Another form of electronic searching and personal communication is offered by the **Internet**. This system was established around 1970 for researchers in the American defense industry and rapidly became a global network serving academics in all disciplines. It now serves the general public as well. The world's largest computer network, its gigantic size is impossible to define. It is known, for instance, that over a million computers are linked into it through some twenty thousand local networks, with more being added daily.

Virtually all major academic libraries have a local network that offers Internet access through computer terminals, which are open to students. Most large businesses also have a local computer network that is connected to the Internet. An alternative is to use your own computer and connect through your modem to a commercial Internet provider at your own cost.

The Internet can communicate throughout the world, wherever telephone services exist. You can access many library holdings, communicate with special-interest groups including those in different areas of psychology, and also with many of the academics whose papers have interested you.

THE ORGANIZATION OF THIS BOOK

Before delving into the contents of a book, it's useful to know how the book is organized and what design features are included to keep you on track. It's also fair for you to know what you'll get out of learning the contents (besides a grade in a course).

This book starts with two stage-setting chapters, of which this is the first. Chapter 2 reviews and explains methodology as it relates to I/O psychology.

In the ensuing chapters, the sequence of topics represents the typical progression encountered in a blank slate I/O situation. The starting place is various personnel hiring issues such as defining the job and recruiting and selecting candidates. Training and motivation of new employees are considered next. The organizational psychology topics start with the individual, progress to the small group, and culminate with the entire organization.

At this stage, our imaginary new corporation has a rationally selected, efficiently trained, professionally managed workforce. The next step is to improve the equipment and the physical work environment; this is dealt with in the three chapters on *ergonomics*.

Now, with ideal employees operating ideal equipment, we will soon have to deal with the resulting stock of finished goods! Can the psychologist help sell the product? The last main part, *Consumer Psychology*, addresses such topics as purchase decisions and advertising.

The format of the book

All introductory, or survey, courses emphasize the vocabulary of the discipline, which, it is assumed, students will learn. This can create a problem. The student wonders, "Exactly which terms am I expected to learn?" and the author wonders, "How can I put the same explanatory inflection and emphasis into my written material that I would give in a spoken lecture?"

When a word needs literary, as opposed to academic, emphasis, it is set in *italics*. Important terms and names that are to be learned are set in **boldface**, most often the first time they are used and are generally explained then and there. A word in boldface indicates that in a lecture it would be written on the board, signifying that it is to be well understood. A list of all such terms is provided at the end of each chapter. They are in the same order that they appear within the chapter, to make them easier to locate, and they are defined in the glossary. There are also brief biographical entries for the major historical figures in I/O psychology.

Many students make the mistake of reading nothing but the text of the chapter. Your learning will be more effective if you read everything in the chapter, including the figures and the beginning and end material.

Each chapter has a set of learning objectives, and a summary of the main topics. Reading both of these brief, introductory aids will help you to put the contents into perspective.

Each chapter ends with a Study Guide section, so that you don't have to buy a separate one. My experience indicates that students who do well in a course invariably follow the Study Guide carefully. It lists all of the terms and names that you should have learned from the chapter. If you're not sure of some of them, check them in the glossary at the back. Then comes the Issues to Consider section. If you can deal with each of them, that's a sign of effective reading.

The last part of the Study Guide is a set of multiple-choice questions. You should not look at them until you have studied the chapter and are ready to check how effective your learning is. Circle your answer choices, and check them against the correct answers at the end of the book.

The purpose of the book

Part 2 of this book deals with personnel psychology. This section makes up about half the contents of this book. Why is this area of study so prominent?

You will probably devote more of your waking hours to working at your job than to any other activity. Moreover, you will achieve more self-esteem and social prestige through occupational identification than through other variables such as inherited social position or wealth. If your work goes well, you have a good chance of being generally content. If you are unhappy on the job, this is likely to make you an unhappy person in general.

Virtually everything that clothes, houses, transports, cures, educates, or entertains you is the product of industry. And the means to acquire these goods and services will also come to you, indirectly or directly, from industry. What kind of a life would you be leading if there were no factories, communication and transportation systems, or machinery?

Every industrial organization relies on its personnel. No matter how successful a firm's products, reputation, or financing, without appropriate personnel it will ultimately succumb to competitors whose staff are more dedicated, innovative, or flexible. Industrial success and failure are usually attributed to personnel management practices.

Whether an entire nation rises or falls depends not so much on its natural resources, geography, or sociopolitical history as on its industrial personnel. As examples, countries such as Japan and Switzerland, hampered by many ill fortunes of geography and history, have achieved a level of success envied by most other nations. This can be attributed to the hands and the attitudes of the people—the personnel—of these countries.

So whether in terms of the individual, the corporation, or the nation, few topics are as central as personnel psychology. And few topics are as challenging and interesting.

The design of complex and dangerous equipment must take the operator's safety, convenience, and comfort into account. Without the discipline of human factors engineering, therefore, the applications of air transportation would be severely restricted. Poor ergonomics in a car may result in driver inconvenience, but in an aircraft cockpit its consequence would likely be disastrous. Space exploration and nuclear power generation would be virtually impossible. These systems are complex and unforgiving; the consequences of operator error could easily be fatal. Even simpler devices often benefit from this specialty of industrial psychology. Cars, furniture, appliances, surgical instruments, and books could be poorly designed, and therefore inefficient to use without the help of human engineering. After learning the material in the four chapters in Part 3 on the design and tools of the workplace, you will be able to evaluate the motorcycle, stove, or pencil that you buy not just on the basis of price or appearance, but according to meaningful product-design principles.

Consumer psychology touches your life daily. Just about everything you own came to you, indirectly or directly, through a purchase decision. No matter what your occupation is or becomes, some element of selling or marketing will probably be involved. The chapter on consumer psychology in Part IV will make you a more efficient seller, and perhaps a wiser buyer. The section on consumerism will help to protect you from the powerful influences of marketing forces.

I hope this introductory chapter has left you feeling impressed by the field of I/O psychology and optimistic about taking a course in it. Perhaps, however, we should end on a muted note of caution. The more impressive a science, the more it attracts **pseudoscience**. The word literally means "almost or near science," but it's used to refer to incorrect and often bizarre explanations or theories that gain a respectable appearance by borrowing concepts or terminology from real science. Pseudoscience appeals to many people who distrust science and yearn for simple or mystical explanations of complex issues.

There can be a hazy line between pseudoscience and "popular psychology," the translation of psychological concepts or theories into everyday language or situations. I/O psychology has its share of unfounded assertions and pseudoscience, and even quacks and fraud. For instance, every personnel office is bombarded by a stream of offers for recruitment services, seminars, tests, and other services. The recipients are rarely in a position to verify the credentials of the principals.

The last chapter will help to make you a more astute consumer. The rest of the book will give you the wherewithal to ask meaningful questions and to interpret the answers in accordance with fact and theory. You will have the ability, perhaps also the responsibility, to differentiate between science and pseudoscience. I hope you'll use it.

It was a pleasure, albeit some work, writing this book. May it be a much greater pleasure, and considerably less work, reading it.

Study guide for chapter 1

HAVE YOU LEARNED THESE NAMES AND TERMS?

organizations

industrial revolution

unions

kaizen

work

personnel psychology

W. Wundt

W. Scott

H. Münsterberg

F. W. Taylor

time and motion study

piece rate

Gilbreth

therblig

Binet

psychometry

Otis

Yerkes

Army Alpha

Army Beta

Hawthorne effect

Freud

Hawthorne studies

American Psychological Association (APA)

1964 Civil Rights Act

workforce

ergonomics

academic journal

blind review

replication

the literature: primary and secondary

Internet

pseudoscience

ISSUES TO CONSIDER

In what ways can knowing the historical background presented in this chapter make you a better employee or employer?

Most disciplines of study are hundreds of years old. Is this the case with I/O psychology? Why?

Why is such a common concept as work so difficult to define?

What was the state of I/O psychology at the beginning of the present century?

Who were the earliest contributors to I/O psychology, and what was the nature of their concerns?

What were the connections between the development of I/O psychology and military needs?

What were the purpose, procedure, and primary findings of the Hawthorne research?

If the Hawthorne studies were repeated today, what changes in results might you anticipate?

How have broad cultural changes influenced I/O psychology?

How have changes in legislation influenced I/O psychology?

What are some examples of ways in which I/O psychology has improved life?

What is meant by the literature of I/O psychology?

How are citations indicated?

What distinguishes an academic journal from other periodicals?

SAMPLE MULTIPLE-CHOICE QUESTIONS

1. The primary journal in I/O psychology is called
   a. *The Journal of Industrial Psychology.*
   b. *Industrial/Organizational Psychology Today.*
   c. *The World of Industrial/Organizational Psychology.*
   d. *Journal of Applied Psychology.*

2. The earliest test to predict performance was devised by
   a. Wundt, to predict learning ability.
   b. Binet, to predict school performance.
   c. Terman, to predict assembly-line skills.
   d. Otis, to predict sensory accuracy.

3. In World War I, American military recruits who could not write would complete the
   a. Army Alpha Test.
   b. Army Beta Test.
   c. Stanford-Binet Intelligence Scale.
   d. Otis Individual Test.

4. Which statement about the Hawthorne studies is correct?
   a. Duncan Hawthorne studied what workers liked and disliked about their jobs.
   b. Roethlisberger and Dickson wrote a book about Mayo's interviews conducted in the town of Hawthorne.
   c. Mayo interviewed two workers named Roethlisberger and Dickson.
   d. The results showed that productivity was affected by pay.

5. The title of an academic journal paper is worded so as to
   a. summarize the entire paper.
   b. interest the reader.
   c. describe the research methodology.
   d. state the main topic of the paper.

Answers: page 462

The experimental method . . . has been the great lever of all scientific work.

U.S. congressman William Welch (1850–1934)

Bird's-eye view of the chapter

Methodology may not sound like an exciting topic, but without it, this book—indeed the entire subject that it covers—would not exist. Methodology is a powerful tool that will let you evaluate, criticize, and appreciate the processes by which scientific theory is created. It lays the foundation for the contents of this and other scientific books.

Chapter 2

Methodology of industrial/ organizational psychology

The payoff from chapter 2   You will:

1. Differentiate between method and methodology
2. Clearly understand the importance of methodology
3. Categorize any study as empirical or nonempirical
4. Interpret any given correlation coefficient
5. Know what a correlation coefficient does *not* tell you
6. Understand the advantages and disadvantages of the field study
7. Thoroughly know the applications of both forms of survey
8. Know the cleverness and the advantages of archival research
9. Understand the rationale of factor analysis
10. See what an experiment offers, compared to correlational research
11. Learn and understand the vocabulary of the experiment
12. Appreciate the need for, and types of, experimental *control*
13. Differentiate between longitudinal research and case studies
14. Know research techniques appropriate to study large organizations
15. Understand the value of the review article or meta-analysis
16. Differentiate between population and sample
17. See the researcher's problems in adopting any population and sample
18. Differentiate among models, theories, and laws, and know their value
19. Know the meaning and importance of operational definitions
20. Appreciate the increasing application of ethical restrictions
21. Know how methodology relates to the academic literature

Methodology refers to a scientist's basic strategy of research. An essay is *nonempirical* in that it does not report quantitative results. Empirical (data-generating) research can be elementary, as where a hidden observer merely records behavior; this is termed a *field study* or *naturalistic observation*. It can be intricate, as in an *experiment*. Here all the participants are treated the same except for one specific treatment. That way the effects of the differing treatments can be measured. The most common methodology in industrial/organizational (I/O) psychology is of intermediate complexity; it is the *correlational* study, in which the relation between two variables is measured and then expressed mathematically. Though correlations show how two variables are related, they cannot show reasons behind the relationship.

WHAT IS METHODOLOGY?

How do we know what we know? Answers are only as good as the research, and research is only as good as the *researcher's method* and the *study's methodology*.

Method refers to the description of exactly how the researcher performed the study. The **methodology** is a more general sketch of the procedure and includes the category or type of research that the procedure represents. Whereas the *method* is detailed clearly in the published report, it is generally up to the reader to infer the *methodology*.

Why is methodology such an important topic? All sciences, including I/O psychology, advance primarily through conclusions derived from systematic research. Conclusions can be evaluated only in the light of the evidence that supports them, which, in turn, must be interpreted in terms of how it was obtained. It is not enough to know the findings or conclusions; one must also know how the findings or conclusions were derived.

If you have completed an introductory course in psychology you may feel confident with this topic. But since each specialty of psychology adopts its own approaches to research, we should examine the methodology of I/O psychology in particular.

The methodology of I/O psychology can be categorized into three main types: nonempirical, correlational, and experimental. Each of these will be discussed in turn, followed by two variants of the correlational approach: the case study and the longitudinal study. Also included are specialized techniques for research with large organizations and for studying consumer behavior.

NONEMPIRICAL APPROACHES

Empirical means research based, or supported by data (numbers). All of the sample papers presented at the ends of Parts 2, 3, and 4 are empirical. **Nonempirical** refers to any academic contribution to the discipline that is not based on data acquired by its author. Included in this category are articles reviewing past accumulations of empirical studies, essays presenting opinions or recommendations, and the material you are reading now.

The essay type of paper (article published in an academic journal; Appendix C) is more common in I/O than in other branches of psychology, perhaps because of the large number of business periodicals that skirt the division between academic and nonacademic. Such contributions should be interpreted as opinion, open to challenge and revision.

CORRELATIONAL RESEARCH

Correlation refers to the mathematical relationship between two **variables**. A variable is any attribute. Most attributes of interest to social scientists vary or change, hence the term "variable." Some common examples are age and weight, or gender or species, which vary not within an individual, but from one individual to another.

Virtually all correlations in psychology are calculated through the use of a mathematical procedure devised by Karl Pearson. The full name of such a correlation is *Pearson product-moment correlation,* abbreviated as **Pearson's r** or just **r**. A Pearson (or Pearsonian) correlation ranges from 0, indicating no correlation whatsoever, to 1, indicating a perfect correlation. These numbers between 0 and 1 are often termed **correlation coefficients**. The higher the fractional number, the stronger the relationship. A minus sign in front of the coefficient indicates an inverse relationship, meaning that as one variable goes up the other decreases.

The higher the correlation between two variables, the more accurately we can predict the amount of one from knowing the level of the other. For instance, if we knew a few people's height and weight, and if we knew that these variables had a correlation of 1 (a perfect or total correlation), then to know your height would be to know your weight too.

The correlation between height and weight is actually about .7, meaning that given a person's weight we would know the narrow range within which their height probably falls. If the correlation were zero, then knowing the level of one variable would be of no help in determining the level of the other. A correlation of −.7 shows the same strength of relationship (in the reverse direction) as one of +.7.

Correlational research allows us to state *how* two variables are related mathematically, but it does not permit us to conclude *why* they are related. For

Hidden sensors to detect and record traffic patterns show a good example of unobtrusive naturalistic observation.

instance, if we know that there is a high correlation between the amount of praise given to workers and their productivity—the most productive are the most praised, and the least praised are the least productive—then from knowing how much praise a worker receives, we can predict that person's productivity.

Why can we not conclude the reason for a given correlation? In the above example there is more than one possible explanation. Maybe the praise caused the high output, maybe the productivity induced the praise, or perhaps some third variable, such as the employee's attitude, was responsible for both the level of output and the level of praise. We are entitled to guess as to the reason but not to conclude.

A fourth possible explanation of a high correlation is simply *chance*. Maybe it was merely a coincidence that the most praised workers happened to be the most productive. But as increasing data support the connection, the likelihood of its being due to random or chance factors becomes remote. The exact likelihood of any obtained results having been due to chance is determined through using the statistical procedure termed data analysis.

The field study

The simplest type of scientific research is the **field study**, also known as **naturalistic observation**. These terms stem from the early history of animal psychology, where some psychologists contended that bringing animals into a laboratory for study would overly disrupt their normal behavior. To understand animals, the researchers argued, the scientists had to journey to the fields where the creatures lived. Then, completely hidden, they could observe the animals' natural behavior without interfering with them.

A scientifically conducted field study, especially if numbers or equivalent data were collected, would be considered empirical. The term *field study* is retained even where the researcher is observing behavior in a school, street, or factory. Field studies are regularly chosen for I/O psychology research, where the objective is to find the correlation between two variables, such as the quality of the cafeteria food and the employees' contentment. By definition, when a field study is performed, the individuals being observed must be unaware of the researcher. Where the individuals are human beings, this concealment presents serious ethical problems, hence field studies are decreasing in I/O psychology.

If the research objective were to correlate luncheon quality with contentment, why not simply go to the workers and ask? This question brings us to the next procedure for correlational research, the **survey**.

The survey

The survey is one of the oldest and most common procedures for collecting data directly from and about human beings. It's the most common procedure in I/O psychology research, where potential participants are invariably working-age adults, and therefore relatively verbal and literate, and where researchers are reluctant to impose laboratory manipulations upon them.

When the responses are given in *writing* the survey is called a **questionnaire**; when the answers are *spoken* it is an **interview**. (Sometimes the distinction between the two is blurred. For instance, the researcher could collect a completed questionnaire and then interview the participant about the answers. The respondent might answer on a computer terminal that simulates human interaction. Or a survey taker might help a respondent to fill out a questionnaire.)

Surveys in I/O psychology are employed for two main purposes: research data collection and personnel functions. Although the survey is a useful and practical starting point for data collection, the results are merely correlational and do not provide any conclusions regarding causality. As regards personnel functions, personnel officers characteristically use the survey for employee selection, ignoring the potential of this procedure for collecting personnel information after hiring, for instance, through the use of the problem-solving survey, the exit interview, or simply a routine "How's it going?" survey.

In the **exit interview**, an employee leaving the firm is invited to reflect on past experience. This is an opportunity for the employer to learn, in an atmosphere of reflective frankness, of areas that need improvement. Whether leaving because of retirement or due to unsatisfactory performance, such employees can typically provide a wealth of information on the strengths and weaknesses of the firm. In addition, the personnel officer has the opportunity of uncovering and dealing with any bitterness in the former employee. Feelings cannot be readily assessed from questionnaire responses, and, even if they are revealed, they cannot be immediately responded to.

The concept behind the "How's it going?" survey is that most employees have encountered ways to improve operations or systems, but have never been given a convenient and appropriate platform from which to voice these ideas. If every supervisor took every subordinate to breakfast or lunch once or twice a year for the purpose of inviting constructive feedback, the modest investment could be effective in improving both operational procedures and the organizational climate.

Both of these survey procedures, the interview and questionnaire, are widely used in I/O psychology research and practice, and both offer distinct advantages and disadvantages. Here is an inventory of the potential pros and cons of each:

Advantages of the questionnaire   There is only a short list of advantages for the procedure that is the most commonly used research technique. The first two, however, are of immense importance.

- The questionnaire is the most cost-efficient means of surveying a large group of individuals. It is inexpensive to draft and to type a page of questions, which can also be reproduced, distributed, and collected efficiently.

- The procedure is standardized. The same questions are presented in the same way to each respondent, and all of them answer in the same way on the same response form.

- A variable that can be tapped in this standardized fashion is writing ability. For instance, a question could say, "In the space provided, explain why we should offer you the position you are seeking."

Disadvantages of the questionnaire

- The questionnaire is inflexible. Some questions do not lend themselves to a "yes or no" answer, or relevant information that the respondent wants to or should include may not appear on the items of the questionnaire. Of course, skillful design of the instrument can reduce such problems.

- Questionnaires are subject to **demand characteristics**. That is, no matter how neutral or nonleading the questions were designed to be, the respondent is prone to interpret (from the wording, from the effect of previous questions, from the title of the document, and so on) what the "right" or "best" or "expected" answer is.

- Because of the ease with which questionnaires can be written, reproduced, administered, and collected, they invite carelessness in their design and administration. It is easy to collect more information than can be properly processed, interpreted, or used.

- Only a percentage—typically a small one—of those who receive a questionnaire complete and return it. The problem here is not one of numbers. If a researcher wants 100 completed questionnaires and the response rate is only 10 percent, it is still cost-effective to administer 1,000 forms to yield the required 100 answers. The problem is **nonresponder bias**, which is the systematic difference between responders and nonresponders. For instance, people opposed to an issue are more likely to return a questionnaire dealing with it than are those in favor of, or neutral toward, the issue. Thus, responders are not likely to be representative of the population surveyed.

One solution would be to raise the response rate in a portion of the research population. This can be accomplished by offering an inducement for responding, and/or by hiring an interviewer to convert nonresponders into responders. In the subset with the high response rate, the answers of the original nonresponders are compared with those of the people who had responded without extra inducements. Then the degree of nonresponder bias can be measured and taken into account as a correction factor in interpreting the answers of the entire group.

It is relatively easy to amass an impressively large array of data from questionnaires. Achieving a high response rate, however, does not eliminate problems. Respondents may answer carelessly, or even randomly; this is hard to detect and counteract. Some questionnaires contain repeated (reworded) questions throughout, so that internal consistency may be measured.

Researchers sometimes brag about their number of questionnaire respondents, as if a 500-response study were more valuable than a 50-response one. Five thousand respondents who are unrepresentative or indifferent will not necessarily provide useful data, whereas five accurate and representative responses could yield a clear picture.

- No matter how clearly and unambiguously the researcher tries to word the questions, there remains the chance—if not the likelihood—of misinterpretation. (When we instituted a research ethics procedure for students wanting access to lab rats, I designed a questionnaire on animal ethics for the applicants to complete. To elicit the students' plans for eventual disposal

A well-designed survey is one of the most widely used research tools. Personnel officers use them mainly for employment selection, but they may also be sources of personnel information after hiring.

of the rat, I included the following as the last item: State the disposition of rat at termination of project. One student's carefully penned reply was, "Should be fairly cheerful.")

Advantages of the interview

• In contrast with the questionnaire, an interview yields high response rates, as it is harder to ignore a survey taker than a piece of paper. Where potential respondents are not available, the interviewer can return, or make contact by telephone.

• In most face-to-face encounters considerable clinical data can be obtained. The interviewer can assess intangibles such as the respondent's confidence, comportment and carriage, and anxiety level. Similarly, the interviewer can note physical characteristics such as dress, grooming, and posture.

• The interviewer can also attempt to establish rapport with the respondent and assess its extent. Good rapport can elicit richer and more complete answers than can questions on the printed page.

• Unlike the questionnaire, the interview may fulfill expectations. Many people strongly anticipate being interviewed in some situations, such as during the hiring process. So even if hiring might be more accurate without a selection interview, to omit this process would be to violate the applicant's expectations (page 117).

• The interview can be highly flexible. For instance, the two participants can discuss the meaning of the questions. Flexibility is minimal, however, in the **structured** interview, where the questions are read to each respondent in the same way, making the procedure really a questionnaire that is read out loud. Flexibility enters with the **semistructured** format. Here the same list of questions is presented in the same way, but between the questions the interviewer can probe, that is, ask for clarification or expansion. In the **unstructured** version, the interviewer may ask anything in any order.

• An interviewer has the capability of administering a **stress interview**, which is not a strong option with the questionnaire. Many people who fail on the job have no trouble performing their assigned tasks. Their downfall is their reaction to job stresses such as criticism. The interviewer might criticize or even insult the applicant to expose any tendency to overreact to stress (however, see section on Ethics).

• An employee leaving a firm for virtually any reason can be administered an *exit interview* (discussed earlier in this section).

Disadvantages of the interview

• Even a structured interview lacks *standardization*. It's hard to remain unchanged in manner, voice, and appearance, over a period of time. An interviewer may start each interview in exactly the same way, but every response of the interviewee is likely to change the behavior of the former.

• A more serious criticism is *subjectivity*. For instance, when one person meets another, an impression, due, maybe, to nothing more than facial appearance, tends to be formed immediately, and it resists change. The effect of demand characteristics becomes more complicated by the interviewee's attempts to interpret the reactions of the interviewer. (Demand characteristics, introduced earlier in this section, here refer to the implied demands of the research intervention. When people are asked to serve as research participants or to answer questions, they try to guess what the "right" answers are. These guesses may affect their responses.)

• A selection interview is susceptible to the "first date" syndrome. In initial meetings where the relationship could ultimately become eventful, both parties behave with artificial care and skill.

• The interview is an *expensive* procedure for collecting data. To gather 1,000 hours of responses requires 1,000 hours of interviewing, yet 1,000 respondents could complete a questionnaire at a cost of a few hours of research time.

• Respondents tend to be more nervous in a face-to-face encounter than in a paper-and-pencil one, especially if the interview is seen as important. Thus, when used for selection, this method favors the applicant who is trained in being interviewed, or skilled in selling. When the interview is designed to gather research information, the respondent may feel intruded upon, embarrassed, concerned about making a good impression, or upset over the lack of anonymity. Any such emotion can distort the responses.

• Typically the researcher does not conduct the interviews in person, but hires others to ask the questions. These interviewers are usually paid by the number of completed interviews. Obviously, then, this system can invite dishonesty.

• The prime liability of the selection interview is its lack of validity (page 102). Unless the job position is that of answering interview questions, the attributes that are likely to impress the interviewer are probably not relevant to the job. At the same time, the interviewer, who probably does not possess clinical skills and training, is expected to serve as sender, receiver, recorder, and interpreter of complex interactions in an artificial and irrelevant situation.

It's almost certain that, already in your life, you have been asked to complete various surveys. And if you continue in I/O psychology, you are likely to be involved in designing, administering, and interpreting surveys. No other research technique is as useful in I/O psychology, and no other technique has as compelling a list of both advantages and weaknesses. You will meet the survey again, and Appendix B is a practical guide to survey design.

Increasingly, computers are used to administer questions and to receive answers and analyze the responses. Where the questions are nonchanging, this would be termed a *computer questionnaire*. Where the computer program varies or probes the questions as an interviewer might, it's termed a *computer interview*.

Archival research

Research on humans tends to be expensive and obtrusive, and it often raises ethical issues. Moreover, some human participants are not available when they are supposed to be, or are not cooperative when they do show up. Many are too eager to please and respond in ways that they tacitly assume are the proper ones.

These problems can be eliminated by examining not the present behavior, but *traces* of the earlier behavior of people. The term for this, **archival research**, is sometimes taken literally. For instance, to know the historical connection between turnover and climate, or between productivity and prosperity, the researcher could study factory archives showing turnover or productivity in conjunction with other old records that show the weather or some indication of prosperity.

More often, the term archival is used metaphorically. For instance, to determine if a new machinery layout causes less wasted motion, the researcher could paint the floor area of the old and the new layout with an inexpensive paint. The more the employees have to walk about the equipment, the more they'll wear off the coating. After a month or so, the paint scuffs around the two layouts can be compared.

As another example, suppose a car manufacturer starts a new quality control program in the midst of a production run. Surveying dealers about the benefits of the new program could be inefficient and could yield inaccurate results. An archival researcher could solve the problem simply, by comparing the incidence of recalls, dealer work-orders under warranty, and customer complaints before and after the change.

Archival research is often marked by innovation and cleverness in getting at and interpreting the wealth of traces that normal human activity leaves behind. An advertiser, wanting to know how popular a certain sports event on television is, would normally invest in a costly rating service. Alternatively, the advertiser could examine the records of a big city's water pressure. The clever assumption would be that a captivating event will keep viewers in their seats until it's over, whereupon large numbers will use the bathroom, causing a brief, sudden drop in water pressure.

Individuals can often perform their own archival research. To determine the most cost-effective car or tire, a researcher could compare the vehicle expenditure records of two municipalities, each of which uses a different brand.

Factor analysis

You have learned that correlation reveals the extent to which *two* variables are related. It is often important, however, to uncover the relationships in more than two variables. **Factor analysis** is a statistical procedure that shows the extent to which any number of variables are related. It also shows how much "clustering" there is in a group of variables, that is, which ones are linked into groups. Variables that are all strongly correlated with each other, and only weakly correlated with the others, presumably represent some common trait, ability, or factor.

For instance, suppose you obtain measurements on these five variables in a group of employees: performance, motivation, incentive, health, and age. Suppose that there's a strong connection among the first three, and that these three are not related to the last two on the list. Factor analysis would show the extent to which performance, motivation, and incentive form a single cluster, sometimes also called a "loading."

Factor analysis is widely used throughout many branches of science, although few researchers know that the procedure was developed by a psychologist, Charles Spearman, in England. The complex statistical procedure for analyzing data to uncover factor loadings (first described by Spearman in 1904) has been refined considerably, and is now performed by computers. When more than two variables are being examined, which is often the case, factor analysis is usually chosen to analyze the data. The procedure is still common in psychological studies and continues to be a favorite in I/O psychology. However, factor analysis can be misused. One review of over 150 factor analytic studies in applied psychology found poor statistical and interpretive applications of this technique, as well as inadequate reporting of the analysis (Ford, MacCallum & Tait, 1986).

The longitudinal study

Longitudinal means "along the longest direction or dimension." A longitudinal study takes place over an extended time period, although how long a study must be to merit the term is a matter of opinion. In child psychology, where this approach is common, a 6-month study would rarely be considered longitudinal, whereas an equally long I/O study may be considered longitudinal.

What largely defines a study as longitudinal is a focus on *development or change over time*. Any type of prolonged research could be termed longitudinal, but studies of development are typically *field* or *correlational* studies.

A classic example of longitudinal research is the 12-year-long Hawthorne study. Unfortunately, such examples are rare, especially in I/O research. For students performing research as part of their training, an artificial deadline requires a time-bound study. For academics, the faster a study is completed, the sooner it can be submitted for publication. Given today's accelerated pace, increased pressure to publish, and severe competition for research funds, we may never again see the results of a decade-long research program.

The case study

The terms **case method** or **case study** sometimes refer to a teaching or training procedure used by a group to solve an actual or hypothetical problem. They also apply to the studying and reporting on *one* client, a procedure that early clinical psychologists and psychoanalysts relied upon. When an I/O psychologist examines and reports on a single situation, especially after studying it in depth and applying some intervention or treatment to it, the report is also termed a case study.

The case study method is not a mutually exclusive category. Every researcher who reports on a firm's situation has performed a case study, and it may fall on either side of the empirical/nonempirical line, depending upon the emphasis placed on numbers or data. Alternately, a researcher could conduct a correlational case study, involving an intensive examination of one situation and the measurement of two associated variables. Finally, the researcher could perform an experiment in connection with a case study. Thus, just like a longitudinal study, a case study may fall under any of the other categories of research.

Research based on an individual case is appealing for the same reason that longitudinal research is unappealing. A case study tends to be limited in scope, and can often be completed in less time.

Overview of correlational research

We've touched on field studies, surveys, archival research, and factor analysis. There are so many variants of correlational research because correlational studies are the favorite of I/O researchers. Why is this?

Correlational research is attractive, especially for studies of people, because the researcher does not necessarily have to intrude upon the participants but only has to measure some aspects of their behavior. (Only the survey method requires interrupting a person's routine. Most people, however, don't object to answering a legitimate and well-presented survey, and because no treatment variable is administered, the ethical problems are unlikely to be a problem.) The weakness of correlational research is that no causal relationships can be assumed. For inferences of *causality*, the researcher must turn to the experiment.

The experiment

In casual speech, when we refer to experimenting with a new brand of coffee, we simply mean "Let's see what happens." In methodology, however, "experiment" has a specific, formal meaning.

The experiment is the only procedure that permits us to infer **causality**, that is, to assume the existence of a *cause and effect* relation. Only through performing an experiment may we conclude that variable *a* caused—influenced, affected, yielded, or changed—variable *b*.

An **experiment** is an artificial procedure dealing with two variables, in which the level of the *a* variable is systematically varied, so that its effect upon levels of the *b* variable can be measured. Consider again the example of our question regarding the relation between quality of lunch and contentment of worker. The question for the correlational researcher is, "Is there a relation between the two variables?" The experimenter asks, "Does one variable influence the other; does *a* cause *b*?"

To answer the question, the experimenter could *randomly* assign the diners into two groups. Each group would be so similar in formation and treatment that if they were provided with identical meals their ratings of contentment would average about the same. But if one group found its food to be better in quality, and the other received worse food, then any changes in the contentment scores could be attributed only to the changes in the food quality. That is, the level of the *b* variable (contentment) was made to *depend* on the level of the *a* variable (food quality).

The two variables in an experiment must be clearly distinguished. The *b* variable may be termed the *caused* or *influenced* variable, the *outcome* variable, or the **dependent** variable because its size depends on the *a* variable.

The *a* or *causal* variable is termed the **treatment** or **independent** variable. Another difference is that the *a* variable is *manipulated* (it must be administered in at least two intensities); the *b* variable is *measured*.

Here is another example of an experiment. A researcher locates 20 supervisors and separates their names into two matched groups of 10. (Matched means that the groups are so equivalent that if supervisory effectiveness were measured, all the groups would show similar averages. This will be further explained in the section on Matching Control.) One group is randomly chosen to be the **experimental** group; the other serves as the **control** group. (When one group gets some treatment and the other group gets a fake treatment or nothing at all, the terms *experimental* and *control* are used to distinguish between the groups.)

In our example, the members of the experimental group are assigned to experience sensitivity training. The others are also enrolled in a special program presented with the same degree of confidence or excitement, but involving physical training. A year later, measures are taken to show if, and to what extent, those given the sensitivity training outperform the equivalent group who was given a control treatment. The study thereby indicates whether or not sensitivity training improves managerial effectiveness.

Not all experiments would read like the above examples, since many experimental designs are possible. The above represents the most common, the **between-subjects design**, in which each participant (*subject*) is assigned to one treatment group, and the resulting data are analyzed *between* treatment groups. In the **within-subjects design**, each participant receives each treatment, and the data analysis is performed separately for (within) each subject.

What is common to every experiment is a *systematic administration of a treatment variable so that its influence on a resulting variable may be measured.* A final example will clarify this.

If you administer a survey during lunch to measure (a) whether workers eat meat or fish and (b) how often they smile over the next hour, you have performed a correlational study that can reveal only the extent of the connection between diet and facial expression. But if you randomly assign workers to either a meat table or a fish table, ensuring that both groups are treated the same except for the food variable, and then recorded their smiling, you have performed an experiment that entitles you to infer the *effect* of diet upon smiling.

In an experiment, the assumption is that in the *absence* of any treatment applied differently to two groups of subjects, the outcome variable, that is, the *b* variable, would be the same in both groups. But since a treatment *is* applied in an experiment, any difference in the outcome measure between the two groups must logically depend on the treatment, whose effect can then be measured.

The essence of experimental design is that any difference in the outcome measure cannot be attributed to anything except the treatment variable. This is accomplished by the proper application of **controls**, or procedures that eliminate alternate explanations. Four common controls, randomization, matching, E bias, and demand characteristics, are outlined next.

Randomization control

Suppose the researcher wants to divide 10 welders into two groups, apply a different treatment to each, and measure a performance variable. The researcher lists the welders' names alphabetically and assigns the first 5 to one group and the rest to the other. Would this create two groups whose performances would be about the same in the absence of any differential treatment? What if the 10 included 3 members of the Watson family, all famed for their welding ability? The use of the alphabet to assign subjects to groups could introduce various sources of bias that would make the two groups differ.

The most common solution is the **random** assignment of subjects to groups. In a random selection procedure, each individual has an equal chance of being chosen. For instance, if each name were written on a slip of paper, the slips were placed in a hat and mixed, and names were drawn "blind" for assignment to groups, then everybody's name would have an equal chance of being chosen.

Matching control

If you put the names of 100 welders in a hat and randomly divided them into two groups of 50, the performance of the two groups should be virtually identical. But if you did the same with only 4 welders, it is unlikely that one pair would perform the same as the other. The smaller the N (the number of participants studied), the less the likelihood that the group can be divided into subsets of similar performance.

To divide a small-N group into equivalent subsets, **matching** the subsets is generally necessary. In a matching procedure, the researcher needs to know what **organismic variables** (ones that are characteristic of the organism) are likely to influence performance. The researcher may determine, for instance, that the organismic variables that predict welding performance are age and years of welding experience. To match the welders on these two variables, the researcher might assign the oldest and/or most experienced welder to Group 1, and balance this person with the second-oldest and/or second-most-experienced in Group 2. Then the youngest and/or least experienced one is assigned to Group 1, and the closest match for this person goes into Group 2.

Matched groups provide a sensitive measure of the effect of a treatment variable, but the process of matching is not always simple. Knowing what variables to match may require a preliminary study. Whereas it is easy to match on one or two variables, it becomes increasingly difficult, if not impossible, to match on several variables. Imagine having to identify the oldest, most experienced, nonsmoking, locally trained, underweight welder, and then the second-oldest, and so on.

Control of experimenter bias

A researcher performing a study is likely to have some emotional investment in the outcome. Even the most dispassionate and objective scientist surely has expectations, assumptions, and hopes. It is possible that the researcher will, inadvertently and innocently, influence the outcome of the study, due to personal involvement. This influence is termed **experimenter bias**, often abbreviated **E bias**. Here, the term experimenter is used in the general sense of researcher, rather than in the sense of one who is performing a controlled experiment.

E bias could be totally controlled by hiring a technician to **run** the participants, that is, to conduct the trials. (The verb "run" stems from the time when most psychologists studied rats in mazes. Today, whether the individuals being studied are fish swimming, pigeons pecking switches, or factory employees answering questionnaires, the researcher still "runs" subjects.) A researcher who is blind to (uninformed about) the purpose and expectations underlying the study is unlikely to communicate **bias**; this is termed a *blind control*. Researchers always try to treat the participants neutrally, often by avoiding advance knowledge of which participants are receiving which treatment.

Control of demand characteristics

We have seen how the *researcher's* assumptions might influence the results. What about the *subjects'* assumptions? Unless the research is a *field study,* or unless the research subjects are a species other than human, research participants are likely to draw their own conclusions about the study. Regardless of what they are told (or not told), they are likely to make guesses about the purpose of the study and to conclude what the "right" or expected response is.

The participants' assumptions may influence their responses. Most people try to "cooperate"; others may try to sabotage the study. It is these alterations of response that constitute the *demand characteristics* of the study.

The phrase "demand characteristics" stems from the fact that every intervention carries implied expectations or demands. When you say "hello" to someone, a specific response is demanded by the social situation. When you ask people to serve as research participants, the typical response (given an appropriate context) is one of compliance and cooperation. In the Hawthorne studies (page 19), it was the demand characteristics of the intervention, not the changes in work environment, that so affected employee performance.

To control demand characteristics, the researcher can use a **double-blind control**. This metaphor means that neither the experimenter nor the participants know which is the treatment and which the control. Also, the instructions to participants are kept as neutral as possible. Finally, a posttrial interview can reveal how the participants interpreted the situation, so that adjustments in procedure or interpretation can be made.

Data analysis

The **data** (numbers) derived from a research study, whether correlational or experimental, must be analyzed so that the researcher can interpret what they mean. The dozens of available statistical procedures fall into one of two categories, *descriptive* or *inferential*. Descriptive statistics make sense of the data by describing, for instance, the range of data, or the various types of averages. Inferential statistics are more complex and much more useful. They are designed to explain what the numbers mean.

The procedure chosen for **data analysis** must be appropriate to the design chosen for the study and the types of measurements used. Here are simplified sketches of three imaginary examples, using (a) a correlational study with descriptive statistics, (b) an experiment, first with descriptive and then (c) with inferential analyses.

(a) Researcher Vera E. Smart wondered if a company program to teach sensitivity to the less fortunate would make employees more tolerant of a disabled colleague. Smart studied employees of two similar firms. One had recently sent all employees materials designed to increase their tolerance of nontraditional colleagues; the other had not. Smart asked employees to indicate their feelings by marking a point on a line labeled at one end, "−3: I'd quit if I had to work beside somebody with a disability," to the opposite end, "+3: I'd really welcome a coworker who had a disability." She found that the average score of the sensitized employees was +2; that of the non-sensitized employees was −1. She then reported a connection between a sensitization program and tolerance of nontraditional colleagues.

(b) Researcher Doug D. Purr predicted that training supervisors to listen would improve their effectiveness in dealing with subordinates. He located two equivalent plants. In one, the supervisors were required to attend a professional seminar program in effective listening. In the other, supervisors attended an equivalent program in accounting and record-keeping. In order to measure the effect of this independent variable, Purr asked employees to rate the effectiveness of their supervisors three months before the programs and three months afterward. This dependent variable was the score on a 7-point scale from −3, very ineffective, to +3, highly effective. The supervisors who experienced the control treatment received about the same average score of 1.6 both times. The supervisors who received the experimental treatment, the listening training, went from an average score of 1.7 to 2.5. Purr concluded that his hypothesis had been supported.

(c) Horace N. Carte hypothesized that members of an organization would file a lesser number of formal grievances if management kept them informed on the procedures to resolve problems. For his experiment, he chose a large plant whose employees received various company newsletters at their homes. A randomly chosen one-half of the employees of each section were sent a newsletter containing extra material on problem resolution. The other half, the control group, received an extra section on stress reduction. A year later, the experimental group had filed an average of .28 grievances per employee; the control group had put in an average of .34. How likely was it that this difference, in the predicted direction, was due to the treatment as opposed to chance? Carte analyzed the data using a statistical procedure called analysis of variance. It showed that such a difference could be expected by chance alone once out of 20 times. Thus, Carte inferred that there was a 95 percent likelihood that his treatment did reduce the number of grievances.

Overview of experimental research

The inherent logic behind the experiment is simple and obvious. Yet, it's a sophisticated research procedure, with many **designs** available. All the controls make it precise, but also somewhat artificial. The role of the researcher, that of a director of activities instead of a passive recorder of them, as well as the many systematic stages of the process, put more responsibility on the scientist than does correlational research.

The experiment does only one thing that correlational research can't do; it tells you not only how much two variables are related, but *why*. This little addition is of immense importance, and it makes the extra work of the experiment worthwhile. Suppose you were offered a job that you found out was associated with a high incidence of suicide. Would you not want to know whether suicidal people were attracted to, or just happened to be offered, that type of work—or whether something in that job drives the workers to suicide?

Frequently in I/O papers you will come across a research design that looks like an experiment but isn't one. A true experiment requires the independent or treatment variable to be systematically varied across groups. Suppose a researcher compares the productivity of two groups of employees, one that had been trained using printed manuals and another using videotaped demonstrations. The training appears to be the independent variable, the productivity, the dependent variable, and they may even be termed as such in the report. However, this is a **quasi-experimental** design that is really a correlational study. Unless the employees had been systematically (for example, randomly) assigned to either the manual-training or videotape-training groups, the study was not an experiment, and differences in productivity cannot be attributed to the training. For instance, possibly the older employees had received the manual and the younger ones the videotapes, and the productivity differences reflect the employees' ages or experience rather than their training.

RESEARCH TERMINOLOGY, TYPES, AND TOOLS

The basic strategy and vocabulary of research are easy to understand. Let's cover them now so they don't give you pause when they come up through the book.

Population and sample

Who gets researched, and do the findings apply to just those subjects or to anyone else? Suppose you wanted to measure the effect of a personal letter from a company executive thanking the employee for good service. You decide that the most appropriate methodology would be an experiment, in which a control letter, similar to the treatment but lacking the "thanks for the good service" line, would be sent to half of the participants.

You should next decide who will receive the letters. One possibility is to assign half of the firm's 10,000 employees to the experimental and half to the control group. Another is to assign five of the firm's ten security officers as experimental and five as control participants.

The first extreme would be expensive and unwieldy. The other would be limited in that the results would apply not to the entire firm but only to the security staff. How can you design a study that is neither unwieldy nor limited?

The solution is to differentiate between the **population** and the **sample**. If all the employees' names are placed in a hat and a small number are selected to serve as subjects, then whatever you discover about those tested applies to the entire pool of names from which you made a random drawing. The *population* is the group of individuals from which you draw a set of them, the sample. You perform the study on the *sample* only, and apply the findings to the population. In the case above, you might define the population as the 10,000 full-time salaried employees, and the sample as 100 of them.

In deciding what size to make the population and the sample, the researcher considers several factors. The larger the population, the more **generalizable** the results. If the population were the 100 employees in one division the results would apply or generalize to only that one division. But if the population were all 10,000 employees in the firm, the findings from the sample would apply or generalize to the entire plant.

The more generalizable the results, the better, so why not simply choose the population to be as large as possible? One problem with this is the difficulty of reaching all the members. The largest population conceivable, every living creature on the planet, would be impossible to study, without some means of identifying each individual and being able to call upon that individual to serve as a subject.

The other problem is that the larger the population, the more **heterogeneous** it's likely to be. High heterogeneity (variability) decreases the likelihood that the effect of a subtle treatment (like a letter from the boss) will be discernible. The researcher, therefore, wants as large a population and as small a sample as possible, so long as the effect of the independent variable will show through. In this way, maximum applicability is achieved for minimum effort. The smallest possible population would be the sample itself. For instance, if your professor performs a study on your class alone, the class would comprise both sample and population.

Hypotheses and operational definitions

Hypotheses are the predictions that are central to orderly research. A research hypothesis should be worded specifically enough to permit the prediction to be tested scientifically. For instance, a researcher may have noted that at several firms where all personnel wore uniforms, everyone seemed integrated and proud. The general research question would be, in the case of a correlational approach, "Is company loyalty related to the wearing of uniforms?"; with an experimental approach the question might be, "Does the wearing of uniforms increase loyalty in employees?"

These general questions would lead to a carefully worded prediction, such as, "There is a high positive correlation between employee loyalty and the wearing of uniforms" or "Wearing uniforms increases the loyalty of employees." Before proceeding further, the researcher would have to translate the variables into measurable indicators by specifying the meaning of "uniform wearing" and "loyalty." What are the operations required to apply the uniform versus nonstandard dress code treatment? What operations will be used to measure loyalty? By answering these questions the researcher has *operationally defined* the treatment (independent) and outcome (dependent) variables. Thus, an **operational definition** defines the variable in terms of the operations used to apply it.

As an example, the correlational hypothesis might be, "Employees' average scores on the Smedley Loyalty Index are higher in work situations in which the firm supplies standardized work garb to all members, than in similar firms in which there is no corporate uniform." An experimental hypothesis might be, "Employees provided with standardized work garb and instructed that all members of the firm are to wear it will, three months later, score higher on the Smedley Loyalty Index than their counterparts provided with an equal value of nonstandard clothes."

Operational definitions may be difficult to decide upon, and cumbersome to word, but they provide necessary precision to research. Unless the variables are operationally defined, the research cannot be performed properly or replicated by others.

Defining variables in operational terms has importance beyond research. In chapter 4 we will meet various *tests* used in industry, and we'll see that test scores are really operational definitions. For instance, if you apply for a job that requires honesty, you may find that your honesty level is operationally defined as your score on some standardized honesty test. Chapter 7 deals with employee *appraisal*. All the techniques presented are really attempts to define operationally the employee's performance level. At another level, the university I work for has a Mission Statement, and I include course objectives in my course outline for students. It would be preferable for these carefully worded objectives to be operationally defined, but like many such, they are not.

Models, theories, and laws

A **model** is a small, simplified representation. Just as a model car is much smaller and simpler than the one it represents, scientists often find it useful to create a mathematical, conceptual, or diagrammatic model of a complex entity. For instance, Figure 2.1 shows what you might look like as a simple flow model, in which this book is the input, and your performance on tests and exams is the output.

A **theory** is a proposed explanation. For instance, we can never know as a certainty how we came to be here on this planet, and there are diverse accounts. But the one that explains most of the relevant data is the theory of evolution, and it is therefore the most credible and the strongest.

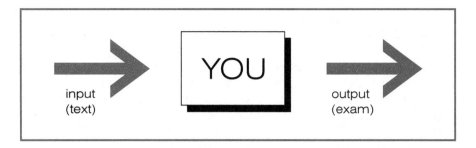

FIGURE 2.1 You: A simple model

This is a conceptual sketch of a complex unit. It depicts how you may process the information in this book.

Theories change as old data are reinterpreted and superseded by new. Where theories compete with each other, researchers try to test them. Ideally, the researcher will derive two competing hypotheses, one from each theory, and design a study that gives each hypothesis an equal chance of asserting itself. The one that is confirmed strengthens the theory from which it is derived.

How are theories derived? Theory construction is a matter of observing behavior, interpreting it, and forming hypotheses about it. Following these steps, the researcher formally consolidates a number of related hypotheses into a coherent, organized "super-hypothesis" or theory.

A theory, once formed, should be tested; here is a simple example. Workplace accidents may be painful, debilitating, and life threatening to the victim and disruptive, demoralizing, and expensive to the employer. What causes them?

An examination of personnel records shows that a few of the employees suffer most of the accidents, both at home and on the job. The resulting hypothesis is that these individuals have more accidents because they are *accident-prone*. Other related hypotheses show that various personality characteristics lead to work habits that predispose these workers to high accident rates.

Let's put these hypotheses to the test. We hire a "blind" observer to record the work habits of the workforce. This neutral judge rates the behavior patterns as to dangerousness, carelessness, and disregard of normal safety precautions. We also divide our workforce into one group who is presumably (according to our hypothesis) accident-prone, and another who is apparently safety conscious.

Keeping track of the two groups over the following year, we see if their accident rates differ significantly and in the way they were predicted. We will probably find minimal support for the hypothesis that the "accident-prone" employee is likely to have accidents in the future; we would need to look for another theory to explain job accidents. *Theory* validation is similar to *construct* validation, which you will meet in chapter 4 (page 105).

A **law** is simply an expression of a relationship that can be depended on to remain stable and invariable. For example, the connection between motivation and performance has been expressed as the **Yerkes-Dodson law** (Figure 2.2). Laws are similar to theories, except that laws are simpler, more concrete, and less global or comprehensive.

A statement becomes a law by general, prolonged agreement among the researchers in the area. Recent disciplines like I/O psychology are not associated with a long list of laws. This means that if you become a successful and innovative researcher in the area, a law might well be named after you some day!

Constructs and reductionism

Every discipline works with its own set of **constructs**, concepts that have been constructed and refined. I/O psychologists deal with constructs like productivity, employee appraisal, and job satisfaction.

Sciences can be listed in a hierarchy that indicates the extent to which a discipline's constructs can be easily and directly observed. At the bottom of this scale is physics, whose constructs such as mass or hardness can be shown with simple and direct-reading instruments. At the other extreme are disciplines like anthropology, sociology, and theology. Their constructs like peer pressure or goodness cannot be observed or measured directly. Psychology is just under these disciplines, near the top of the hierarchy. That's because psychological constructs like learning, disorders, and drive cannot be measured directly; rather, psychologists measure behavior (often on a test) and then infer from the behavior how much of the construct was present. The principal of **reductionism** states that a science may borrow the terminology from a discipline lower in the hierarchy, but may not use constructs from a higher discipline. So psychology cannot attribute job satisfaction to angels.

That also explains why the constructs of I/O psychology, such as motivation, job satisfaction, leadership, and organizational climate, are often defined as **inferred theoretical constructs** that deal with thus-and-such. The implication of inferred theoretical construct is that you can't open a person's head, locate where the job satisfaction is, remove it, and put it on a scale or other direct-measuring device. Rather, you have to examine the descriptive theories surrounding job satisfaction, measure it in ways that are consistent with the theories, and infer from the results how much job satisfaction was present.

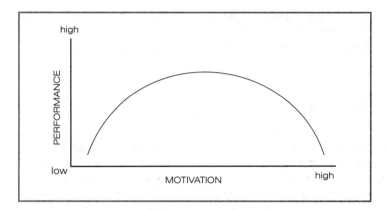

FIGURE 2.2 The Yerkes-Dodson Law

The Yerkes-Dodson law illustrates that your performance would likely be maximal when your motivation is at a middle level, rather than at the highest or
lowest level. Faced with extreme danger, for example, your motivation to act may be at the highest
level, but your performance would likely be maximal
in a less threatening setting.

Basic versus applied research

Psychological research is often thought of as belonging to one of two types,
basic and **applied**. Basic research is performed for its own sake. For instance,
a physiological psychologist might study thermoregulation in lizards for no
reason other than to learn how reptiles control their temperature. Conversely,
a psychologist who studies the effect of diet and exercise on people's weights
obviously hopes for findings that will be useful and practical for people.

Whether research is basic or applied is a matter of opinion and intent.
In some disciplines, research is invariably one or the other. Generally, as-
tronomers consider their work basic; medical researchers think of their work
as applied. Within the discipline of psychology, there is a wide range. At one
extreme, much physiological research would be categorized as basic. At the
opposite end, we find I/O studies, almost all of which are designed to be
applied. In fact, Appendix C shows that the most cited I/O journal is entitled
The Journal of Applied Psychology.

Intentions are not always fulfilled. A study could be performed with the
intent of being totally practical but end up being ignored. More important,
another piece of research could have been performed with no practical intent

in mind, and later provide immense practical benefits. (Picture Alessandro Volta's buddy telling him, 200 years ago, "Why are you trying to make frog legs twitch, Al? Do you think it will make your name famous?")

Review articles and meta-analysis

You can probably locate dozens, perhaps hundreds, of published studies on any topic that interests you. In trying to derive a simple answer to a simple question, you may encounter two problems. How can apparently contradictory results be reconciled? To what extent are the findings, even if not contradicted by other results, limited to the specific situation of that particular study?

For decades, psychologists have been relying on **review articles** to answer these questions. The journal *Psychological Bulletin* specializes in such papers. The author of a review article discusses the totality of the literature on a topic and attempts to derive general relationships through logic and intuition.

A **meta-analysis** takes a statistical rather than an intuitive approach to finding basic answers. This recent technique involves a re-analysis of the data from a number of studies, in an attempt to uncover overall trends. A good source of information on this topic is Hunter, Schmidt, and Jackson (1982). Throughout this book you will come across many references to both review and meta-analytic articles. We now turn to research procedures as they are used in the two most specialized areas of I/O psychology, the study of large organizations and of consumer behavior.

ORGANIZATIONAL PSYCHOLOGY RESEARCH PROCEDURES

Most psychologists who perform research on humans study individuals or small groups. Recently, organizations and their interactions with their members have attracted research interest; this topic will be covered in chapters 8 and 9. Because of their large and diffuse nature, organizations invite their own specialized procedures. The five main ones are outlined next.

Sociometry

In the technique known as **sociometry**, all group members are asked to indicate their relationship on a specified dimension with every member of the group. The sociometrist's queries may be: "List everybody you like," "Name the people you would approach to get something done," or "Next to each name, give the number of messages you sent last month." By combining the responses from all of the participants, the researcher can diagram the affectional relationships, competence ratings, and communicatory effectiveness. The researcher is particularly interested in discrepancies between the organization as it exists on paper and as it is perceived by its members.

To find out members' *perceived* social relationships, each participant might be asked, for instance, "Name the people who like you a little, moderately, a lot," or "List those who would like to have you as their immediate supervisor." Researchers, who may be either sociologists or psychologists, often contrast the actual sociometric relationships with the perceived ones.

Position analysis

The **position analysis** researcher compares the *job description* (covered in chapter 3), especially in terms of the job's demands, with the abilities of each job holder. The purpose is to effect an optimal match between abilities and requirements and to uncover any mismatches. Where a discrepancy is discovered, the tasks may be altered or employees may be reassigned. This technique is associated with large firms.

For instance, a sales manager is responsible for evaluating and responding to the performance of 30 sales representatives. They enter their orders into a new computer system, but the manager, who is not computer literate, cannot therefore respond to data at the end of each day, but only to data on the quarterly sales summaries. Because of this discrepancy, the manager is offered a choice: either turn the feedback function over to someone who can interpret the data, or learn how to operate the computer system.

Communications analysis

To perform **communications analysis**, the path of a message is traced to reveal at what step it is delayed or blocked, simply passed on, elaborated, or acted upon. Not only can the formal communication structures be contrasted with the *grapevine,* but the messages can be analyzed for content, for example, goal-oriented messages or irrelevant messages.

Suppose a firm is troubled by frequent rumors and by complaints of inadequate communication. All employees are asked to cooperate in a research project to determine the nature and extent of communication lapses. Each worker is furnished with a communications record form that lists each hour of the workday for a week. Whenever they receive any kind of message related to the company, they note on the form what the message was and the level of the person from whom it was received. The researcher analyzes the hand-ins and makes recommendations. The management evaluates the proposals and decides what changes to make. A copy of the report, along with any changes decided upon, is sent to all the participants.

Discretionary analysis

One way of evaluating the status of employees is to analyze their freedom to work unsupervised; this technique is termed **discretionary analysis** because it measures how much discretion they have. A typical query would be: "For what length of time do you perform your assigned tasks using your own judgment, without the direct review of your superiors?" Generally, the less direct control, the higher the worker's competence, responsibility, and salary expectations. Because people tend to answer questionnaires in the way they think they are supposed to, researchers may verify a sample of the responses.

Comparative analysis

To study one organization it may be helpful to perform a **comparative analysis** of other, comparable ones. People naturally compare, and they tend to focus more on the unfavorable aspects, that is, on what the other organization offers that their own does not. Any analysis procedure can be used.

Here is an example of a comparative analysis. At a university, students complain to their representatives that they have too little input into administrative decisions that affect them, and no clout to dispute professors' grades. The student leaders first ask the university administration for its response. The answer is that all committees include student representation, that students are free to contest marks with their teachers, and that more money is spent on student services such as **counseling** and job placement than at comparable institutions.

The leaders survey their counterparts at other universities. They find that their institution has the best record in student representation on committees and in student services. But in terms of dispute-resolution programs, other schools serve their students better. Armed with the comparative analysis survey results, the leaders (a) publicize the role of students on committees, (b) write an editorial in the student newspaper commending the administration for its generous student services offerings, and (c) prevail upon their administration to appoint an ombudsperson to mediate student complaints about grades.

CONSUMER PSYCHOLOGY METHODOLOGY

No matter how flawless a product's design and usefulness, without the right image, name, price, and buyer appeal, it is likely to fail. Product failures are common and expensive. Consequently, a great deal of research is directed at determining how to appeal to the purchaser. The main techniques for doing this are outlined below and will be covered in detail in chapter 14.

Surveys

Consumer psychologists want to know *why* you chose the brand of shoes, shirts, and skis that you did. The simplest way to get an answer to such a question is to ask it. Putting questions to consumers is the most common form of consumer research; it's the same survey procedure you read about earlier in this chapter.

You've likely been surveyed by mail or phone, or in a shopping mall, and you frequently hear media reports of the latest public opinion poll (survey). You've no doubt filled out cards to activate a product warranty, first answering questions on it that also constitute a survey.

Much research measures the effectiveness of advertisements, for instance, by asking a representative group of consumers about their recollections and opinions of ads. These survey results may influence the product's design, name, packaging, and advertising strategy. A coupon, a cut-out section of a print ad, which the consumer can mail for a small cash rebate or present at a store for a discount, also reflects reader response.

Clinical approaches

Survey respondents do not always know what the truthful answer to a given question is. Insofar as they do know the truth, they may not reveal it. You will learn in chapter 4 that in personnel selection, **clinical techniques** (procedures originally designed for use in clinical diagnosis or psychotherapy) can reveal thoughts, feelings, and perceptions that applicants would not be able or willing to reveal. The same techniques are applied to expose underlying consumer attitudes. Ever since Freud argued that behavior is driven by powerful internal forces and personality factors that may be uncovered through proper analysis, marketers have turned to clinical techniques. They have tried to disclose motives and traits that could be exploited for increased sales, and to find the unconscious triggers to buying decisions.

Other techniques

In various forms of **behavioral research**, scientists observe what people actually *do*. For instance, in a *focus group*, a group of consumers is asked to discuss some product issue, under the direction of a leader. In a similar strategy, a panel of consumers is asked to use the product, while being observed or questioned. And electronic data collection techniques allow marketing researchers to correlate purchases with promotional campaigns.

Other researchers combine the science of demographics with that of personality into the measurement of "lifestyle," and correlate this with buying patterns. Lifestyle research focuses on the activities, interests, and opinions of survey respondents. Queries may focus on the extent to which people influence, or are influenced by, others in shopping, what they do for leisure and entertainment, and how they evaluate prices.

To measure ad effectiveness, one technique uses the **eye camera**, in which participants wear a small camera on the head to record reflections off the cornea of their eyes (Figure 2.3). In this way, exactly what they've been looking at is documented. Most ads, especially print ads, are glanced at for only a second or two, unless this initial contact impels the viewer to look further. That's why advertisers try to include an attention grabber at the spot where most viewers fixate initially. In other cases it's important to know what portion of the ad is least conspicuous, for instance, to locate the required warning on a cigarette ad.

The eye camera permits an analysis of the *scanning pattern* that the advertisement induces. This is used to find the optimal location of the various components of the ad. The camera also measures gaze duration. The longer the gaze is held, and the more details the viewer takes in, the more successful the ad is considered.

Some researchers are interested in the *emotional impact* of an ad. They record various bodily changes that occur under emotional arousal. This is known as the **physiological approach**. Scientists take measurements of the pupil size, palm sweating, or the amount of squirming and shifting of volunteers who are watching a program or advertisement. To see if panelists like or don't like a television ad, they are provided with a red and a green button, and asked to indicate positive or negative feelings they experience during the screening by pressing one of the buttons.

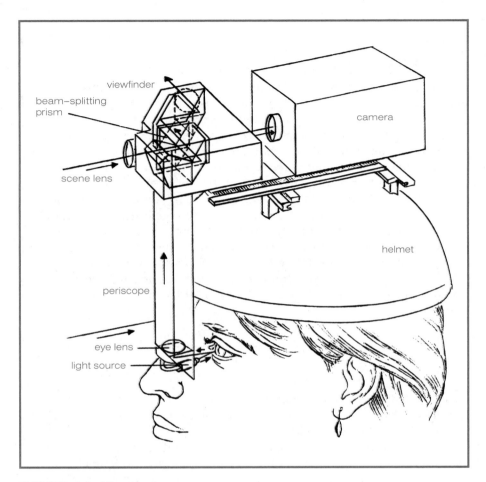

FIGURE 2.3 **The eye camera**

The eye camera is used to photograph the movement of the eye.
This allows researchers to determine the scanning pattern. They can
then position the elements of an ad in their optimal locations for maximum effectiveness.

RESEARCH ETHICS

Every profession has its ethical standards of practice, and none are more
rigorous than those of psychology. One historian (Gilgen, 1982) indicated
that until as recently as 1963, the only code of ethics that had been officially
adopted by a scientific organization was the American Psychological Association's code of 1953.

In I/O psychology, there are stringent ethical constraints on the use of
psychological techniques in testing and assessment. These are designed to

So what If only one chapter from this book stays with you permanently, it should be this one. Many questions will arise during your work life. What's the best way to respond to a challenge to your authority? How should you treat an absolutely outstanding subordinate? How can complex issues be communicated to semiliterate employees? How will unionization change former relationships? The best answers are likely to be found in recent pages in the academic literature. If you know how to access this trove of reason, data, and interpretation, you and your firm will be at an advantage. Conversely, others will often try to convince you that the answers are at hand, and that you should act accordingly. When someone tries to induce you to buy this assessment test, hire that proven expert, switch to this better brand of supplies or equipment, or impose a new theory of management, you will be in a position to ask to see the specific evidence upon which the claims are made. At that time, you can benefit from what you have learned about the principles of methodology and the value of having an open mind behind a skeptical eye.

ensure that the procedures used are fair, noncoercive, and never harmful. The ethical factors involved in employee or applicant assessment are described in detail by London and Bray (1980).

As for research, psychologists are required by their profession to follow specific ethical principles. It is not sufficient for research to be methodologically sound; it must be ethically sound as well. Research on humans requires more ethical considerations than do studies on animals, and I/O psychology research is invariably performed on people. There are three primary principles of ethical research:

• All participants must give their **informed consent.** This means that they serve voluntarily, without coercion, and with enough understanding of the project to make a rational decision about participating or not. (No participant should ever say, in hindsight, "If I had known *that*, I would not have agreed to participate.") Even after someone agrees to serve, it should be with the understanding that withdrawal is permitted at any time during the study.

• It often happens that a study cannot be meaningfully performed without some deception beforehand. Where this is the case, there should be a **debriefing** session immediately after the participant is run. To debrief is to explain what the deception was, and to allay any concerns.

- Some studies could involve a degree of risk or harm to the participants. For instance, you might want to study the effect of alternating one workweek schedule (Monday-to-Thursday, 9 hours a day) with another (Friday-to-Sunday, 12 hours a day). The ethical consideration might be, "Even among employees who agree to participate in the study, could any harm (short- or long-term, invisible or apparent) develop from working three straight shifts of 12 hours each?"

The factors involved in ethical considerations are by nature subjective. Accordingly, they should not be left to the researcher to decide. Some outside agency or individual, knowledgeable about research ethics, should evaluate the research proposal first. Many colleges and universities require any student or faculty member who wishes to perform behavioral research to obtain the prior approval of an "arm's length" ethics committee.

Students wishing to perform apparently innocuous I/O psychology research may feel confined by the ethical restrictions imposed upon them. They may feel that their proposed project is less disruptive or unethical than many of the classic studies they have read about. However, research ethics is a recent concern. In previous generations, anything that was legal was generally permissible.

A good source of further information on principles of ethical research is *Ethical Principles in the Conduct of Research with Human Participants.* It is available from American Psychological Association Order Department, P.O. Box 2710, Hyattsville, Maryland 20784. In Canada, both the Canadian Psychological Association and the main national funding agency for psychological research, the Social Sciences and Humanities Research Council (SSHRC), publish their own requirements for ethical research.

Most research in I/O psychology is performed by college and university faculty members, who generally spend more time in research activities than in teaching. Faculty often involve students in their research, undergraduates as participants, graduate students as coresearchers. A survey of 4,000 doctoral students and faculty members (Swazey, Anderson & Lewis, 1993) focused on exposure to or awareness of (a) serious research misconduct, for example, plagiarism and fabrication or falsification of data, (b) questionable practices such as keeping poor records or giving honorary authorship and (c) miscellaneous misconduct such as sexual harassment and ethnic discrimination.

The questionnaires and in-depth interviews indicated that approximately half of the student and faculty respondents had direct experience with at least two of the above types of research misconduct. No I/O psychologists were surveyed; however, allied disciplines including sociology and civil engineering were. The results of this study imply that research institutions should (a) clarify all aspects of ethical research, (b) establish independent bodies to hear and investigate reports of violations, (c) protect whistle-blowers from retaliation, and (d) foster a climate of ethics in which students and faculty share a feeling of collective responsibility to avoid research misconduct themselves, and to report it where perceived in their peers, subordinates, and supervisors.

METHODOLOGY AND THE LITERATURE

You were briefly introduced to what is known as the literature, the body of published academic research, in chapter 1 (page 25). Picture the existing body of knowledge as a road, with some parts older, straighter, and wider than others. The researcher's objective is to make this road longer, straighter, and stronger. The first step in research is to study the existing structure, both to define an area of weakness and to ensure that any discoveries will improve what's already there. To strike out in a totally novel direction would be like building a road that connects to nothing. That's why all studies begin with a review of the starting place. And by finding a recently published study, you can benefit from the author's review of the relevant literature.

The next step is to design the research so that the findings will improve a specific weak spot. The actual running of the study is often a relatively small part of the venture. The final obligation of the researcher is to add the improvement to the map, by publishing a report in an academic journal (page 24).

No methodology is inherently right or best. The choice is based upon the purpose of the study as well as upon practical and ethical considerations. Many studies in I/O psychology are correlational in design, because it is harder to perform experimental research. Many of the participants are university students, because they are accessible to researchers who are usually faculty members. Participation in research can be a valuable part of a student's educational experience.

Scientists rarely introduce a report with a statement such as, "This is a correlational study which will therefore show a mathematical but not a causal connection between the variables," or "This is an essay presenting my own opinion," or "We performed a controlled experiment in which the independent variable was three levels of incentive pay, and the dependent variable was the rate of absenteeism." Researchers assume that the reader will easily discern the methodology. Of course, the literature is aimed not at the undergraduate but at the professional psychologist.

Thus, as mentioned at the outset of this chapter, it is the reader's responsibility to recognize the methodology underlying each report, and to conclude independently how the material should be interpreted. You should guard against drawing *causal conclusions* from correlational data and be vigilant for researchers who themselves commit this error. Also note whether the participants are university students, especially if the researcher generalizes the findings to the work world.

And keep in mind that research is biased towards positive results. For instance, studies on the effectiveness of organizational development are likely to be conducted by organizational development practitioners who believe in what they're doing. Moreover, negative results are less likely to be submitted for publication and to be accepted if submitted.

As a newcomer to the literature of I/O psychology, one of your hardest jobs will be to maintain a balance between two opposing positions. One is a scientific, sharp-eyed, challenging skepticism. I/O psychology does not have a pope whose pronouncements are infallible. All we have are thoughtful, dedicated researchers, who make the best sense that they can out of human behavior, while studying it carefully and systematically, and who then expose their findings to the criticism of others who work in the same area. The other position in your balancing act is appropriate respect for the theories, interpretations, and recommendations of these scholars. Between these two extremes, you will apply your own experience, judgment, and common sense.

Study guide for chapter 2

HAVE YOU LEARNED THESE NAMES AND TERMS?

method and methodology
empirical and nonempirical
correlation, variable, Pearson's r, correlation coefficient
field study and naturalistic observation
survey, questionnaire, interview, exit interview
demand characteristics
nonresponder bias
interview: structured, semistructured, unstructured, stress
archival research
factor analysis
longitudinal
case method (case study)
causality
experiment
dependent, treatment, and independent variables
experimental and control groups
between-subjects and within-subjects design
controls
random
N
matching
organismic variable
experimenter bias (E bias)
run
bias
double-blind control

data and data analysis
designs
quasi-experimental design
population and sample
generalizable
heterogeneous
hypothesis
operational definition
model, theory, and law
Yerkes-Dodson law
constructs and reductionism
inferred theoretical construct
basic and applied research
review article and meta-analysis
sociometry
position analysis
communications analysis
discretionary analysis
comparative analysis
counseling
clinical technique
behavioral research
eye camera
physiological approach
informed consent
debriefing

ISSUES TO CONSIDER

How does choice of methodology influence outcome?

Which research methodology is most associated with I/O psychology?

What is the explanation for the answer to the previous question?

What is the purpose of data analysis?

Where did the terms field study and naturalistic observation originate?

How can demand characteristics be reduced?

Many people given a questionnaire do not return it. What's the harm?

The correlational researcher does not necessarily have to intrude upon subjects. What does this mean?

When should subjects be matched in treatment groups instead of being randomly assigned?

How are E bias and demand characteristics controlled?

Under what conditions might the population be the same as the sample?

Under what conditions could a researcher minimize the size of the sample?

Differentiate among models, laws, and theories.

What are the three main principles of research ethics?

Which research methodology, if any, is best?

What is the basic importance of this chapter?

SAMPLE MULTIPLE-CHOICE QUESTIONS

1. Regarding survey techniques, which list is short but powerful?
   a. advantages of the questionnaire
   b. disadvantages of the questionnaire
   c. advantages of the interview
   d. disadvantages of the interview

2. An experiment must have at least ___ treatment groups.
   a. zero
   b. one
   c. two
   d. more than two

3. The Hawthorne results were really due to
   a. demand characteristics.
   b. E bias.
   c. inadequate controls.
   d. effective interviewing techniques.

4. The most recent research technique is the
   a. field study.
   b. case study.
   c. longitudinal study.
   d. meta-analytical study.

5. The starting point for academic research is
   a. acquiring research funding.
   b. acquiring research subjects or participants.
   c. acquiring the necessary apparatus and facilities.
   d. reviewing the pertinent literature.
   e.

Answers: page 462

Part two

The people

Because I/O psychology is mainly about people, Part two on personnel and organizational psychology is the major part of the book; it's as big as the other parts combined. We start by looking at how you define the work, and then how you get the right people, keep them, and have them do the work correctly. We finish Part two with two chapters that examine the interactions between organizations and the people who make them up.

The people are the masters.

Edmund Burke (1729–1797)

Bird's-eye view of the chapter

This chapter begins the section on personnel psychology. This is the main section of the book, and the most important topic in industrial/organizational (I/O) psychology. The chapter covers the foremost topic within personnel psychology, that of personnel selection, and differentiates among various ways of describing the same job, from the job title to the job analysis.

Chapter 3
Introduction to personnel psychology

The payoff from chapter 3   You will:

1. Know why personnel psychology is "the most practical" course of study at the university
2. Know the derivation of the word "personnel"
3. Learn the major branches and offshoots of personnel psychology
4. Know how *individual differences* relate to personnel psychology
5. Understand the importance of individual differences
6. Know comparative *learning curves* for novices of various abilities
7. Know the meaning and importance of the concept of *stereotypes*
8. Appreciate the costs of hiring the wrong person
9. Learn the various ways of designating the same job
10. Understand the purposes and techniques of performing a *job analysis*
11. Know the meaning, importance, and approaches to the *job criterion*
12. Know the historical and current meaning of *job evaluation*
13. Understand the meaning of *compensable job factors*
14. Learn the concept of *job equity*
15. Be able to recognize *systemic discrimination*

W elcome to what may be the most practical topic you will study. After all, what would you be without people? Well, personnel is about people: people who transport you, feed you, instruct you, protect you, and sell you things. Not surprisingly, most of the literature of *applied* psychology deals with personnel, covering topics such as motivation, selection, assessment, leadership, training, communication, stress, human relations, and job enrichment. This rich and vibrant literature is still attracting energetic research effort.

WHAT IS "PERSONNEL"?

It's obvious that the word **personnel** refers to "persons." It has a peculiar spelling because the English adjective *personal* has acquired a meaning apart from "of persons." So the French spelling has been adopted; it derived from the Napoleonic military distinction between "matériel" (equipment) and "personnel" (people).

Personnel functions permeate every aspect of business and industry. Obvious aspects include recruiting, selecting, training, motivating, and promoting or firing the employee. Other topics are personnel related in a less apparent way. These include *organizational psychology,* which may be considered a branch of personnel psychology because organizations consist of and are designed to serve people.

Human factors engineering, which deals with fitting the equipment to the operator, is sometimes depicted as the opposite of personnel, but it should be deemed another branch of it. Similarly, *consumer psychology,* which deals with people selling to or serving other people, could be considered an offshoot of personnel psychology.

The early "personnel offices" were simple operations, involving little more than a folder of files for each employee. Today, the handling of the human resource calls for astute professionalism. Modern professionals have adopted the term human resources to describe their domain, and the personnel office of old has usually become the human resources department. Nonetheless, we will keep the term personnel psychology because it is the psychological aspects of human resources that we will be considering.

INDIVIDUAL DIFFERENCES

Without the concept of **individual differences** there would be no rationale for the scientific approach to personnel selection. We will see that the main

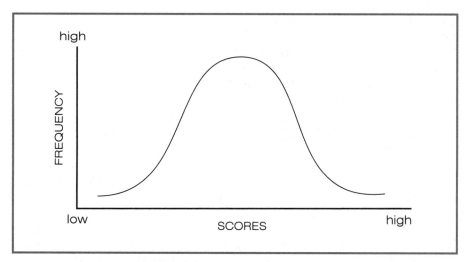

FIGURE 3.1 A normal distribution

A "normal" distribution curve demonstrates that if you measure a given quality or characteristic in a large group, you will find that the average or medium range occurs most frequently, drops off rapidly, and then levels on both sides. A normal distribution curve is therefore bell-shaped.

enemy of this approach is the *stereotype,* and we will see how part of the selection battle can be won through efficient recruitment procedures.

We would like to think that all people are equal, but they are not. Otherwise, there would be no need for the science of individual differences. Nor does anyone have the same advantages, circumstances, and luck. One hopes that each individual has the same opportunity for advancement, but even that is an unrealistic expectation. All we can hope for is a theory of individual differences that recognizes human diversity, singles out what aspects of the differences are relevant to job performance, and identifies these fairly and consistently.

When any attribute or characteristic is measured within a group, the scores will rarely be identical for everybody. Rather, the scores will be distributed from low to high. The larger the group, the closer to a **normal distribution** the scores will be. A graph of a normal distribution is shown in Figure 3.1.

Just as each of us has a unique appearance (identical twins excepted), we all exhibit unique *behavior.* If we consider any attribute or characteristic, we will find that some persons have a little of it, many have a moderate amount, and a few have a great deal. Figure 3.1 shows a graph of a typical distribution of any given trait across a large sample. The objective of personnel selection, put simply, is to identify those applicants who are at the right side of the graph in desirable characteristics, and at the left side in the undesirable ones.

The concept of individual differences is basic and important economically. Corporate survival depends upon the efficient use of all resources, including the human ones. It is obvious that one salaried employee who outperforms the others is more valuable. But even in the case of workers paid according to their production, high productivity is to be valued. The high performers are likely to have better morale, and they cost the employer less in overhead expenses per unit.

Moreover, the turnover rate is likely to be higher among the poor performers, and this is disruptive and costly in terms of recruitment and training expenses. Where the turnover involves dismissals (as opposed to retirements or voluntary resignations), there are likely to be contractual, legal, and morale problems.

Failures on the job are costly also to the employees themselves because such failures are unsettling to their lifestyle and damaging to their self-image. It can even be argued that these problems extend into society, in that poor performers contribute to national inefficiency.

One might argue that, rather than selecting for the most promising applicant, it is more democratic to choose at random from reasonable applicants, and rely on *training* to iron out the individual differences. In fact, the effect of training is to increase, rather than decrease, individual differences. Figure 3.2 shows a typical S-shaped **learning curve**. The performance level is low at the start of a new task. With repetition an employee improves rapidly until a plateau is reached and performance levels off.

STEREOTYPES

One of the most important jobs in motion picture production is that of casting director, because without the right actors and extras the film is unlikely to be convincing. The casting director requires acting ability in all participants, of course, but is primarily concerned with appearance. Each person on screen must look right for the given part. The hero must *look* heroic; the taxi driver should *look* like a taxi driver. Chambermaids should look like chambermaids; mobs must look like they are composed of mob members. The audience has clear expectations as to what a doctor, a lawyer, and an Indian chief are supposed to look like. In short, we all tend to base our opinions on **stereotype** impressions.

A stereotype is the expectation that certain categories of people, because of their appearance, background, genes, or profession, will behave in a known, predictable fashion. These associations are so ingrained by cultural

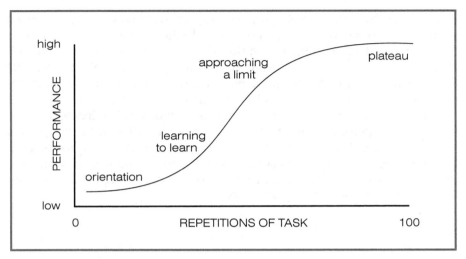

FIGURE 3.2 The learning curve

The learning curve is somewhat S-shaped. Your performance is slow when you are learning a new task, but improves quickly until you reach a plateau, a performance level that remains constant.

teaching that they are akin to proverbs. Redheads are tempestuous, women are emotional, Scots are thrifty, and fat people are jolly.

Stereotypes persist for two reasons:

1. People see what they expect to see, and they interpret behavior in conformity with their preconceptions. For instance, if you observed a crowd gathered at an accident and saw a scruffy teenage lad bending over a victim, you might easily infer that he was an attacker or robber. But you would be more likely to presume that a well-dressed white-haired person in a similar scenario was helping the victim.

2. People tend to behave in conformity with their *own* stereotypes. A woman is more likely to cry than a man because she has been taught that such behavior is expected of women. Von Baeyer, Sherk, and Zanna (1982) set up a job interview situation in which some female applicants were told that the male interviewer held *traditional* views of women, and others, that his views were *nontraditional.* When they arrived for their interview, the women dressed and behaved in precise conformity with the supposed attitude of their interviewer.

Stereotypes work in a circular fashion. Word, Zanna, and Cooper (1982) arranged a setting where white persons interviewed black people who were actually the researchers' colleagues. In contrast with how they interviewed whites, the interviewers' speech deteriorated when talking with the blacks, they spent less time with them, and they displayed less **immediacy** or friendliness. This behavior of the interviewers clearly placed the black applicants at a disadvantage. Faced with an interview handicap, they would acquit themselves less well, and thereby confirm the interviewer's stereotype.

In short, the application of the concept of individual differences is central to proper personnel selection, and a major impediment in this process is the ever-present stereotype. Yet, the job of the personnel selector is to be discriminating. The discrimination, however, must be limited to legitimate, job-related factors. Determining these factors and measuring them accurately is at the heart of personnel psychology.

PERSONNEL SELECTION

When you leave college and begin your first job, you'll be likely to quit during the first five years because you will not find the position adequately satisfying. If the selection process were more error free, you would stand a better chance of making the right choice the first time. Career-related failures are not to be taken lightly. Probably no decisions will have a greater impact on your life than those involving career moves.

Your ambition may well be to join the ranks of management and thus become an employer yourself. From the employer's viewpoint, no business decisions are more likely to lead to corporate success than making the right choices in the *personnel selection* process. At no other time is the slate as blank or the opportunity as great.

Personnel selection involves more than finding the "best fit" to *start* work. The right person is the one who is both *successful* at the work and who *stays* at it. Dumaine (1987) indicated that the cost to a firm of a new hire's leaving after a short time can range from $5,000 to $75,000. (The wrong person who does *not* leave can be even more expensive.)

SELECTION FOR WHAT?

This week Dale was asked four times, "What do you do for a living?" Each time, Dale gave a different reply. Yet Dale is a truthful person. How can this be?

The first "What kind of work do you do?" came from a bank official whom Dale approached for a loan. The next was from a vocational counselor who was hired to assess Dale's present and future career prospects. The third was from a job analyst whom Dale's company had hired to perform some personnel research. And the fourth was from someone with whom Dale started to chat at a party.

Obviously, there is more than one legitimate way to designate a job. In this section we will differentiate among four of them: job title, job requirements, job description, and the procedure known as the job analysis. We will also pursue the topics of realistic job preview, job evaluation, and the job criterion.

The job title

A **job title** is the equivalent of a person's name. It serves as an identifier, socially and often legally, without describing the person. A job title may have a specific professional, trade, or legal meaning, such as *registered nurse, stationary engineer,* or *certified public accountant.* Other titles such as *engineer, secretary, therapist,* or *financial adviser* have only connotations, not specific legal meaning.

Job titles often bear strong implied or emotional meaning, especially in Western culture, where one's status is linked to how a living is earned. (In Japan, by contrast, status is more a function of who one's *employer* is than of one's job title.)

Where the title is not locked into a legal definition, it should be treated flexibly. It is easy to change a designation from *secretary* to *executive assistant,* or *main janitor* to *maintenance supervisor* if the changes are appropriate and would please the incumbents. Hence, company policy should allow employees to have a job title reviewed.

The most comprehensive list of job titles is found in the *Dictionary of Occupational Titles* (DOT). This reference volume, which is published every five to ten years by the U.S. government, lists some thirty thousand job titles. The two-volume fourth edition was published in 1994. The DOT also classifies jobs based on the results of *job analyses.* The classification is based on (a) the type of work performed; (b) the level at which the worker operates in relation to data, equipment, and other people; and (c) the interests and abilities that are associated with successful performance. The *Canadian Classification and Dictionary of Occupations* (CCDO) is the equivalent in Canada.

Job requirements and recruitment

The **job requirements** are those worker attributes that, to put it simply, would be listed in a recruitment notice such as a newspaper classified advertisement.

MONTREAL

HEAD NURSE

Neurosurgery

**Challenging opportunity exist for the canidi-
date with the following experience:**

- **Bacheler of Science degree in Nursing.**
- **5 years nursing experience.**
- **Post graduate neuro course.**
- **Administrative experience.**
- **Demonstrated leadership & organizational abilities.**
- **Clinical expertise.**

**Qualified applicants are invited to send re-
sume to:**

Mrs. K.L. Johnson
PERONNEL DEPARTMENT
SUNNYRIVER MEDICAL CENTRE
1028 Valley Ave.
Montreal, Quebec H4A 2P7

The classified advertisement is an early step in the recruitment process. It should be worded concisely but still provide a clear definition of the job requirements.

The list of requirements should be clear, concise, and carefully worded to include only the most essential elements. **Cutoffs** should be avoided at this point; "adequate experience" is preferable to "one year's experience," "good typing skills" is better than "100 words per minute." The person who drafts the wording should be able to justify each phrase. The establishment of the job requirements is particularly important in planning the recruitment process. Care is called for, because this is the first step that extends outside of the firm.

One reason for dissatisfaction and turnover among new hires is the misleading depictions associated with much recruitment. The use of newspaper advertisements, recruitment agencies, and college recruitment visits can be flawed by inadequate communication and an overly favorable picture of the position and the employer. A useful technique is to enlist present employees to help in deciding how to recruit and in evaluating the applicants. They are likely to know others in their field and would present a realistic impression of the firm to the applicants. They would also have an investment in getting along with the new hire.

Another solution is the **realistic job preview** (RJP). Applicants may have developed unrealistic expectations about a position from many sources. For instance, the public relations efforts of firms and their industry, plus fictional depictions in the mass media, may lead to many illusions about the work.

The RJP consists of "telling it like it is" in interviews, publications, or even in audiovisual productions. Unfortunately, we cannot conclude that attempts at providing RJPs either are or are not effective. One comprehensive review of a hundred-odd studies on RJPs suggested that most corporate efforts at "eye opening" had little effect on variables such as turnover and commitment (Guzzo, Jette & Katzell, 1985). However, another review of 21 papers indicated that RJPs led to better self-selection, commitment, job satisfaction, and job tenure (Premack & Wanous, 1985). Perhaps the best practice, then, is to avoid inflating expectations during the recruitment process, rather than to emphasize the inevitable negative aspects.

Job description

The next level of complexity in the defining of a job is the **job description**. A typical job description is a narrative description, about one page long, which includes not only the job title, requirements, and duties, but also the remuneration and the chains of authority and communication. Included in the list of duties should be **performance standards** (minimum acceptable output) and the procedure for measuring the extent to which they are reached or exceeded.

The job description should also address the best-case and worst-case eventualities by listing promotion or transfer likelihoods, the nature of the probationary period, and reasons for, and policies involving, discipline or dismissal. It should include an overview of the working hours required, holidays provided, and policies regarding overtime. The employer may specify not only the day on which work is to start, but also, if applicable, the day on which it is to terminate, subject to extension by mutual agreement.

The job description should be presented to the first-choice applicant *before* the position is offered; the applicant will become an employee when both sides agree to all its terms. It should be treated as a formal document—in effect, a contract between employer and employee.

Despite the quasi-legal aspects, job descriptions should not be treated as inflexible documents. In fact, it is sensible company policy to invite incumbents to participate in a periodic review of the wording. After all, requirements and practices change, and the job descriptions should be kept up-to-date. The list of duties should be worded vaguely enough to permit flexible interpretation.

For instance, "The duties are (a) dust desks, (b) empty waste baskets, . . ." could be replaced with "Duties include maintenance, janitorial, and cleaning tasks such as dusting desks, emptying waste baskets, and similar work as assigned by the maintenance supervisor or requested by the office personnel." Otherwise, employees may view the specified duties as a complete list that is never to be exceeded. In influencing morale, actual duties may be less important than the perception or interpretation of the duties.

A **results-oriented description** (ROD) lists not only the tasks but also the results expected for each one. After they are hired, personnel generally never look at the job description. But an ROD is likely to be referred to often during the course of the work; it can be helpful in serving as a brief operating manual. An ROD also facilitates personnel evaluation. On the other hand, some tasks are hard to specify exactly, and many users of the ROD find themselves repeatedly amending it. The ROD is described by Klinger (1979).

Job analysis

The most detailed level of work definition is the **job analysis.** This is a listing of each component or element of a job, and it sometimes includes the training requirements as well. It is highly detailed, as well as long, tedious, and expensive. Unlike the other three levels, any of which may be drafted by most managers or by many employees, job analyses are performed by professional job analysts. Although complex, the job analysis is the ultimate answer to the question of what the work entails, and it is the starting point for basic decisions about recruitment, training, wage rates, and much industrial research.

Because job analyses are costly, time-consuming, and usually intrusive, the job analyst must decide whether an analysis is called for, and, if so, what the most appropriate procedure or procedures would be. The analyst should enlist the cooperation of the job incumbents before starting the analysis. In particular, they should be made aware of the difference between the work of the job analyst and that of an *efficiency expert* or *time and motion expert.* Being monitored by an efficiency expert is a threatening experience for most people.

The only book devoted to the topic of job analysis for the nonprofessional is a slim volume entitled *Everything You Always Wanted to Know about Job Analysis* Explained by Edward L. Levine, Ph.D. *and More . . . a Job Analysis Primer* (Levine, 1983). This is an excellent casual guide. Professionals would consult McCormick (1979).

McCormick's outstanding contribution is the Position Analysis Questionnaire (PAQ), which comprises a couple of hundred items, mostly dealing with job activities such as worker activity and mental processes, the job environment, and interpersonal relations (McCormick, Jeaneret & Mecham, 1972). McCormick's associates at Purdue University offer a computer-analysis service for completed PAQs. Some organizations that employ large numbers of people who have widely varying and highly demanding duties (for example, the U.S. Air Force) have their own internally standardized job analysis regimens.

The analyst chooses an analysis *procedure* that is appropriate to the job under examination. Variables that could affect the suitability of the method include the purpose of the analyses; the qualifications of the job analyst; the nature of the work organization; legal, contractual, and legislative issues; existing work or professional standards; and the overall character of the work and of the workers. There are many techniques (Levine claims "a number in the thousands"); the 11 most useful ones are outlined below.

Analyses of similar jobs   Analysts may consult a job analysis that was performed previously. Although this is a common starting point, the analyst often finds that the previously analyzed job is not quite identical to the one at hand.

Operations manuals   The job analyst will almost always consult appropriate *operations manuals* if they are available. The most useful ones contain not only the operating procedure but also performance records, which include common errors, learning problems, reasons for failure, and even the outcomes of *exit interviews*.

Individual interview   A number of job analysis procedures rely upon the *survey* approach (page 39). The most common of the survey techniques is the *individual interview*. Interviews should be extensive, targeting representative employees (successful and unsuccessful, experienced and inexperienced, and those at different stages of training) as well as supervisors and instructors. This procedure offers a complete picture, but there are drawbacks: Workers tend to offer incorrect or incomplete explanations of success or failure, they may not know what worker qualifications are necessary for good job performance, they have to rely on untrained memories and casual observation, and they typically offer subjective terminology such as "good judgment" or "dependable."

Survey   It is common to ask the employee, usually via a questionnaire, to describe the work. The survey may be a convenient starting point where the incumbents are literate and cooperative. But when an analyst relies solely upon this procedure, problems may arise in the interpretation and analysis of the responses.

Observation interview   When the analyst observes and interviews the employees as they work, the results are relatively accurate and complete, since all observations are made on the job. But the procedure is slow and costly, and of course it interferes with the work.

Group interview   In the *group interview,* a number of employees are interviewed simultaneously. This procedure saves the analyst's time, and the public nature of the responses usually encourages respondents to help each other with their recollections. It does, however, call for some degree of group skills in the analyst.

Technical conference   In the *technical conference,* the analyst interviews experts, usually supervisors or trainers. The weakness is that so-called experts may not know as much about the minute-by-minute job activities as the jobholders themselves.

Systematic activity log   Some methods rely entirely on the incumbent's co-operation. To add objectivity to the worker's reports, the analyst can ask the employee to maintain a running record of every task performed over a specified time period. In this *systematic activity log* (popularly known as the **diary method**) reports are entered at least hourly, and possibly as often as every quarter-hour. The diary method provides a complete and reliable inventory of the work elements; however, the recording can interfere with the work.

Check list   In this technique the employee is given a list of work elements and asked to check those encountered during specified time intervals. This procedure has several advantages: it is easy to administer to a large group, the workers can respond readily, and the analyst can tabulate the results easily. But it requires preliminary work to prepare the list of task statements, and it may not yield an integrated picture of the whole job. Finally, there are two procedures that make extra demands upon the skill of the job analyst.

Work participation   In this procedure, the analyst performs the actual job, usually while maintaining an activity log. There are many occupations for which this would be inappropriate.

Critical incident   Using this method, the analyst searches for only those work elements that the best and worst workers perform differently. This cost-effective but limited procedure is used by analysts primarily when looking for means of improving performance. It is designed to reveal all of the critical elements but does not offer an integrated picture of the entire task.

The analyst makes a "best-fit" decision to choose the procedure or procedures that will yield the most complete analysis to serve the purpose, at the minimum cost. Where these are expensive or intrusive (such as the systematic activity log or the work participation method), the analyst should first determine *when* most of the work elements occur. This procedure is called **time-sampling analysis.**

In *time sampling,* the analyst investigates the rhythms and variety of the work elements in order to derive a *minimum time period* (or set of time periods) during which every work element is likely to be exposed. It might be determined, for instance, that the work activities on a Tuesday morning and Friday afternoon include virtually every job element performed during the week. Samplings taken only during these times would therefore serve the purpose.

The job criterion

The term **job criterion** means *criterion of job success,* or *criteria that distinguish between successful and unsuccessful performances.* "How good a worker is Dana?" is a basic, fair, and common question. The same question, worded technically, is "What is Dana's *criterion* measure?"

A criterion measure can be calculated only after the employee has had enough time on the job to permit an accurate assessment of the job performance. The results establish whether or not the decision to hire was correct. Unless an *accurate* criterion measure is determined, it is almost impossible to evaluate basic personnel decisions such as modifying selection or training procedures, promoting or terminating the employee, or deciding on pay rates. The criterion is usually determined by management, although it may be beneficial to incorporate employee input. It is typically determined not in one session, but over a series of examinations.

The criterion may be *simple unidimensional,* such as "annual dollar volume of sales," or it could be *complex unidimensional,* for instance, "annual dollar volume of sales, minus the quota established for the respective territory, minus the sales expenses charged to that territory." Or, it could be *multidimensional*, such as productivity.

It is more sophisticated to devise a **criterion index** comprising elements to be individually scored, weighted, and combined into a single figure. For example, a criterion index for an insurance salesperson could incorporate many relevant performance measures such as progress during training, the number of new accounts opened in the first year, the quality of the accounts, the number of senior courses completed, and the closeness of communication with the sales manager—in addition to the dollar sales figures.

Some components for the criterion, like dollar volume, are *objective,* in that they can be read directly from the company records. Objective elements include most output or results measures, as well as attendance records, the fulfillment of record submission or reporting requirements, and the direct costs such as materials wastage or expense accounts.

The most direct cost of all, and one which is typically ignored in determining the criterion, is the *remuneration.* Whereas on an assembly line everyone may draw the same hourly pay, in many institutions one researcher, vice president, accountant, or professor may earn twice the income of a colleague. Another objective variable is **tenure**, in that a valued employee who stays for a decade represents a better hiring decision than one who leaves after a year. But few criterion studies extend over such long periods.

(The term *tenure* has three shades of meaning. As used in criterion determinations, tenure indicates how long an employee has remained with the same firm or at the same job. In academia, tenure is a privilege granted to faculty members who have proven themselves to the extent that they no longer have to apply for renewals of their teaching contracts every year or

So what Students want to do a good job in the courses they take. First, they need to have some understanding of how a good job is defined. What preparation will be required to do well on quizzes? On what basis are essays or term papers marked? At work, high ratings are equally important. On the job, it will also be necessary for you to know the criterion against which you will be measured. If you attain a supervisory position, it will be your responsibility to let your subordinates know what is expected and how this will be assessed. Without a clear job criterion, nobody knows where they stand.

two. In many jobs, especially unionized ones, tenure means security of employment once the probationary period is completed.)

Suppose you had to choose the best job candidate. If "best" meant the tallest or strongest applicant, or the fastest typist from the group, your job would be easy; these variables are easy to quantify. But imagine that you were asked to pick the person who's the most motivated, ambitious, and happy at work, someone who's trustworthy, loyal, and good with people. The applicant you choose should also be inwardly strong, a good follower but a potential leader, and generally pleasant to spend a work career with. Such personal characteristics are commonly sought, but their subjective aspect makes definition and measurement difficult.

A third group of possible components of the criterion are midway between the objective and the subjective. Examples include efficiency, indirect costs, relevant knowledge, quality of output, ability to work without direct supervision, trainability, flexibility, creativity, and safety habits.

Job evaluation

The concept of **job evaluation** originally referred simply to the remuneration associated with a given job. This is the "going" wage, which is determined mainly by supply and demand. If electricians earn twice as much as nurses, then an opening for a company electrician would be evaluated at double that of a company nurse.

The newer meaning of job evaluation stems from the human rights concept (which has become law in many jurisdictions) that all positions entailing *similar levels of training, qualifications, working conditions,* and *responsibility*—hence the same social value—should command the same compensation.

The trend in today's workplace is toward greater gender diversity in occupations and greater awareness of concepts such as comparable worth, or equal pay for work of equal value.

According to this argument, the company nurse should earn at least as much as the company electrician.

The concept of **comparable worth**, or *equal pay for work of equal value,* has been promoted mainly on behalf of female employees. This is because jobs that have historically been seen as "women's work" characteristically pay considerably less than those that are seen as "men's work."

Opposing arguments—of questionable validity—have been offered (invariably by men):

- The effect would be to increase personnel costs, since the higher-paid workers would not tolerate their wages being *lowered* to attain wage equity.

- If "women's work" begins to pay more, an increasing number of people (including men) will crowd into those fields, creating more competition and possibly greater unemployment among them.

- In a few cases, the wife's income is supplementary rather than essential for maintaining the family. Today many women work as the head of their household, but the "supplementary" stereotype persists.

- The working conditions for "men's" jobs are more arduous or dangerous.

- It is a difficult and subjective task to evaluate the worth and the demands of every position.

None of the above arguments justifies unfairness. Regarding the last two points, a number of consulting firms have devised sophisticated procedures for evaluating **compensable job factors**, or factors that are considered in determining what a given job is worth. These include variables such as the education, training, skill, abilities, and experience required to do the work; the mental and physical demands of the job; and the working conditions.

Another major factor is *responsibility*. For instance, how much freedom to make meaningful decisions does the jobholder have? How many subordinates does the worker supervise? What are the consequences if the employee makes an error? What size budget does the incumbent handle?

Other factors sometimes considered are the availability of applicants, the status and intrinsic satisfaction associated with the position, and the locale, for example, cost of living in the community, and the desirability of living in the area. The objective is to achieve two types of **equity** or fairness: **internal equity** (fairness within the firm) and **external equity** (fairness in terms of similar firms).

There are ways of measuring the acceptance of equity principles. King and Miles (1994) devised a very short (five-item) questionnaire called the Equity Sensitivity Instrument (ESI), and reported data on almost 5,500 participants, including managers, university students, and bank employees. It's certainly easy to administer, and its validity was verified by correlations with the results of other tests of related demographic and personality characteristics. This instrument is presented as Figure 3.3.

Three important concepts related to occupational equity are **affirmative action**, **equal opportunity**, and **accommodation**. *Affirmative action* refers to preferential hiring designed to correct a pervasive social wrong. For instance, if it were shown that the railway industry systematically discriminated against female applicants, an affirmative action program might require the industry to choose qualified female applicants over similarly qualified male applicants until a certain percentage of females had been hired.

At first glance, affirmative action might seem to be an unfair form of reverse discrimination. However, certain segments of the population (for example, women and visible minorities, especially those with economic, cultural, and language handicaps) have been grossly discriminated against in the past, including the recent past. This practice starts in the elementary and high school systems. Unless the pattern is broken, the status quo will be perpetuated,

WAISGLASS/COULTHART   12-9
© 1993 Farcus Cartoons/Distributed by Universal Press Syndicate

"Hey, wait a minute . . . only a man would wear green pumps with a blue chiffon dress!"

FARCUS. Copyright © 1993 FARCUS CARTOONS. Dist. by UNIVERSAL PRESS SYNDICATE. Reprinted with permission. All rights reserved.

Equity Sensitivity Instrument*

The questions below ask what you'd like for your relationship to be with *any* organization for which you might work. On each question, *divide* 10 points between the two choices (choice A and choice B) by giving the most points to the choice that is *most* like you and the *fewest* points to the choice that is *least* like you. You can, if you'd like, give the same number of points to both choices (for example, 5 points to choice A and 5 points to choice B). And you can use zeros if you'd like.

Just *be sure* to allocate *all 10* points per question between each pair of possible responses.

In any organization I might work for:

1. It would be more important for me to:
____ A. Get from the organization
____ B. Give to the organization

2. It would be more important for me to:
____ A. Help others
____ B. Watch out for my own good

3. I would be more concerned about:
____ A. What I received from the organization
____ B. What I contributed to the organization

4. The hard work I would do should:
____ A. Benefit the organization
____ B. Benefit me

5. My personal philosophy in dealing with the organization would be:
____ A. If I don't look out for myself, nobody else will
____ B. It's better for me to give than to receive

*To score the instrument, sum the points allocated to the benevolent response (i.e., items 1B, 2A, 3B, 4A, and 5B). Possible score range 0–50.

Source: Wesley C. King, Jr., Miami University, Oxford, Ohio.

FIGURE 3.3 **The equity sensitivity instrument**

This short questionnaire helps an employer to measure a potential employee's acceptance of equity principles.

The emphasis in today's workplace is on identifying and removing barriers. This may require modifications to accommodate employees with disabilities or special needs.

and the majority of qualified job applicants will continue to be white, middle-class males. It is largely up to universities and employers to use outreach and/or training programs that compensate for deficiencies to encourage nontraditional applicants to join the mainstream of success.

The concept of *equal opportunity* means that the hiring process cannot discriminate on any basis other than the ability to perform the work. This includes hidden or **systemic discrimination**, such as requiring that all applicants have a hefty minimum weight, which would have the *effect* of denying consideration to most women. The term *systemic* indicates that the discrimination is built into the system of requirements. Courts and other tribunals have consistently held in recent years that even if the *intention* of a hiring requirement is not discriminatory, if the *result* disadvantages any group, that requirement is unacceptable (unless clearly demonstrated to be essential for the job).

Accommodation refers to modifying the workplace so as to facilitate or accommodate employees with disabilities or special needs. An obvious example is the installation of ramps to replace stairs that would bar wheelchair-bound persons. The emphasis is on identifying and removing barriers. For instance, employees and applicants are asked whether the workplace presents any barriers that could be modified to accommodate their situation. A major task of I/O psychologists is to modify job analysis, recruitment, selection, training, and evaluation techniques to reflect the current trend toward making the workplace more acceptable and equitable. Two current challenges have been identified: (a) The increased emphasis on working as part of a *team*. Teamwork requires more interpersonal skills and integration with the organization's goals than does working independently. (b) The increasingly complex *cognitive* demands of the work require lower-level assistants to be replaced by fewer personnel who have greater responsibility.

In North America, much of the current (and likely future) growth in the labor force is made up of immigrants and members of minority groups, many of whom are women. This itself does not mean full fairness. Henderson (1994) points out that women and minorities make up half of the American workforce but only 5 percent of managers, and that the percentage of black executives rose from a minuscule 4.5 in 1983 to only 5.7 as late as 1991. Fairness will come when managers *value* diversity, recognizing that, as in a salad, variety is good. It will come when diversity is properly *managed*, for instance, presented as enhancing productivity and organizational morale, and encouraged by policies that permit the full development of every employee. And it will come when diversity is seen not as merely a personnel department issue, but as an *organizational goal*, enshrined (as it rarely is now) in the corporate mission statement.

At no time in the life of a job applicant or the employing firm are decisions more critical than during the selection process. In the following chapter, which discusses the topic of personnel selection further, we will examine the application of procedures designed to optimize the decisions for both sides.

Study guide for chapter 3

HAVE YOU LEARNED THESE NAMES AND TERMS?

personnel

individual differences

normal distribution

learning curve

stereotype

immediacy

job title

job requirements

cutoffs

realistic job preview

job description

performance standards

results-oriented description

job analysis

diary method

time sampling analysis

job criterion

criterion index

tenure

job evaluation

comparable worth

compensable job factors

equity: internal and external

affirmative action

equal opportunity

accommodation

systemic discrimination

ISSUES TO CONSIDER

Where does the word *personnel* come from?

What is the meaning of *individual differences,* and what is the importance of the concept?

What is the relationship between individual differences and training effect?

Why do stereotypes persist?

What does research conclude about the value of the *realistic job preview?*

Why are there so many procedural options in performing a job analysis?

What is the difference between a time-and-motion study and a job analysis?

Why is the concept of job evaluation receiving so much attention currently?

Can you think of examples of systemic discrimination in the workplace?

How does the law generally treat an employer whose policies disadvantage a vulnerable group—if there was no intent to do so?

When is affirmative action appropriate?

Why is the selection process so critical to both sides?

SAMPLE MULTIPLE-CHOICE QUESTIONS

1. The first decision a job analyst should arrive at is
   a. what procedure of job analysis would be most appropriate.
   b. whether a job analysis should be performed in this case.
   c. who should authorize a job analysis in this case.
   d. how the analysis would benefit the client.

2. The usual starting point in performing a job analysis is to
   a. consult analyses of similar jobs, if available.
   b. interview the employees involved.
   c. present a cost estimate to the client.
   d. schedule the most appropriate time for the work.

3. Women cry more easily than men because
   a. women exhibit immediacy better than men.
   b. crying women fit into a stereotype image.
   c. women are more sensitive than men.
   d. women's tear ducts are more easily activated.

4. Components of the job criterion such as output quality and creativity
   a. are considered objective.
   b. are categorized as subjective.
   c. would be considered partly both of the above.
   d. are usually determined by employees.

5. Which hiring requirement of a police department is showing systemic discrimination?
   a. Applicants must be almost six feet tall.
   b. Applicants must be able to lift twice their own weight.
   c. Applicants must be able to type 50 words per minute.
   d. Applicants must pass a law aptitude test.

Answers: page 462

Not everything that can be counted should be; not everything that can be counted counts.

Albert Einstein (1879–1955)

Bird's-eye view of the chapter

A basic responsibility of the industrial/organizational psychologist is to administer and interpret tests used for selection and placement. This chapter explains the basic characteristics upon which any such test can be evaluated, and gives some of the ways of categorizing them. After learning about tests (which will make you more of a test-wise student) you are introduced to both the strengths and weaknesses of these instruments.

Chapter 4
Psychometrics

The payoff from chapter 4   You will:

1. See the extent to which testing is a part of life
2. Know how personnel testing relates to psychometrics
3. Sense the history of psychometrics
4. Be able to define a test
5. Understand the characteristics by which tests themselves can be tested
6. Understand the several varieties of validity
7. Know how tests may be categorized
8. Understand the misconceptions regarding intelligence testing
9. Appreciate the value of situational tests
10. Know the meaning of stress test
11. Recognize the two basic approaches to scoring tests
12. Understand the need to be current on test theory, and how to do it
13. See how surveys can be tests
14. Recognize the limitations of, as well as the need for, selection interviews
15. Be able to use the questionnaire as a selection test
16. Appreciate the prevailing attitude toward being tested
17. Know the main weaknesses of tests
18. Appreciate ethical and public policy factors in personnel testing
19. See the rationale and the value of decision theory
20. Be able to hire a psychometrist and to understand the work performed

Testing is an inescapable part of modern life. Everything you eat, wear, live in, or use in any way has probably first been subjected to a variety of tests. And you know that nobody can attain professional status without confronting a series of tests.

The most important and most widely used tool of the applied psychologist is the *psychological test.* Such tests are relied upon in clinical diagnosis, counseling, education, placement, and evaluation. The science of selecting, administering, and interpreting these tests is called **psychometrics** (literally mind measure).

In industrial/organizational (I/O) psychology the primary use of tests is for personnel selection. Students know that they are unlikely to be offered a worthwhile job without passing a test. Managers know that the optimal use of tests may make the difference between successful and unsuccessful personnel selection. And corporate lawyers know that if their firm is charged with discriminatory selection, a strong defense would be records of test scores along with data supporting the appropriateness of the testing procedure.

As you recall from chapter 1, psychological testing began with Binet's procedure for predicting the school performance of one group of French children. It's a long way from that use of tests to predicting the work performance of a group of job applicants. Are tests valid for both purposes? This is a prime consideration in the discipline of psychometrics.

WHAT IS A TEST?

The word **test**, as most commonly used in psychology, refers to a *standardized procedure designed to predict some behavior.* For instance, a school psychologist might administer an intelligence test to a child, not for the purpose of measuring intelligence per se, but to predict the child's school performance.

"Test" may have other meanings as well. In order to be admitted into an institution of higher learning such as a dental school or to be offered employment, one typically first undergoes a selection procedure involving the administration of a test. Here the test is designed to predict the applicant's performance in dental school or on the job. More important, the tester hopes that the score on the test will foretell the applicant's level of success as a practicing dentist, or as the employee who some day will be promoted to head the corporation.

More specifically, the test is designed to predict those aspects of behavior that are deemed to be important. Those performance variables that distinguish between success and failure—between the person who, it is ultimately decided, was admitted in error or whose acceptance, it turns out, was a correct decision—constitute the *job criterion* (page 87). In short, a *test predicts the criterion.*

The term **standardized** indicates that the test is administered in a uniform, proper manner and scored according to previously established **norms**, or baseline scores. The term further implies that the testees can be *appropriately* evaluated against the standardization sample on which the norms were established.

CHARACTERISTICS OF TESTS

There are six basic characteristics on which every selection test can be evaluated. A few of them will require some effort to understand, but we'll start with the simple ones.

1. The **difficulty level** of a test should be such that not one of the scores collides with the **upper** or **lower ceiling**. (A ceiling is the highest or lowest score that is possible on a given test. The lower ceiling is sometimes termed the *floor.*) For instance, suppose on a test, where the range of possible scores is 1 to 10, that the lowest score is 6 and that several applicants score 10. Because everyone performed well, and especially because the upper ceiling was reached more than once, we conclude that the test was too easy. If one person reached the upper ceiling, we cannot tell exactly *how much* better that person was than the others (maybe the score would have been even higher if the ceiling permitted it); if two or more did so, we cannot differentiate among these top scorers.

2. The **dispersion** of scores is a simple concept. Consider two tests with maximum scores of 10. Test A yields scores ranging from 3 to 8; Test B shows a range of 1 to 9. Because Test B offers a wider range of scores it yields more dispersion in the results and hence is preferable. If the benefits of high dispersion are not clear to you, consider how useful you would find a test with zero dispersion (meaning that everyone tested achieved the same score).

Both dispersion and difficulty level are assessed in the same way, namely, empirically, by graphing the results and inspecting the graph. Figure 4.1 illustrates graphs of tests with different difficulty levels; Figure 4.2 shows tests with good and poor dispersions.

3. The common meaning of **reliability**, as you know, is the personality attribute of dependability. In psychometrics, however, it is a technical term that means *consistency.* Let's see what this means.

Suppose you administer a test to 10 applicants and Merle leads the group. A month later, you readminister the same test in the same way, and this time Merle scores near the bottom. Although that particular test may have been ideal regarding its dispersion of scores and difficulty level, it lacked *reliability.*

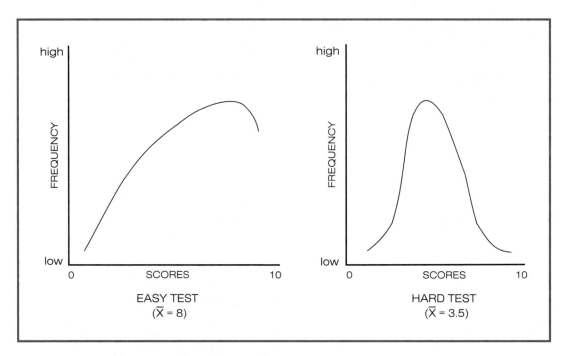

FIGURE 4.1 Graphed test results showing different difficulty levels

In an easy test few individuals score at the low end, whereas many reach the upper ceiling. In a hard test, scores are likely to be distributed normally with few reaching the upper ceiling.

Reliability is the most important attribute of a test. Regardless of its weaknesses in other dimensions, a *reliable* test may still be of use for some purpose. For instance, a test of employees' physical condition and attitudes to health that is designed to predict how long a person has to live, may prove to be inaccurate. But if the test scores show reliability, a different researcher may find that they predict something else, like heart problems. A test that lacks reasonable reliability, however, can serve no purpose whatsoever.

A perfectly reliable test would yield the same scores to the same testees, time after time. But of course it's impossible to readminister a test under identical conditions. If you do it the next day, testees will remember some of the items. If you wait a year, they will be a year older on the second administration. Hence, we never can tell the exact reliability of a test, but we can come close.

To measure **test-retest reliability** you administer the same test to the same group under similar conditions twice, with an intervening time gap.

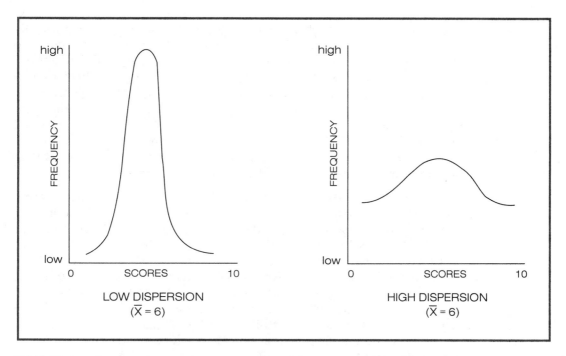

FIGURE 4.2 Graphed test results showing different dispersions

> The narrow, peaked shape of the low dispersion curve indicates that a high number of testees had similar scores. Conversely, when the dispersion is high, a greater range of scores is achieved, with a wide distribution among the students.

Each writer's score on the first administration is compared with the mark obtained on the second. The higher the correlation, the greater the test-retest reliability. The problems are the inconvenience of reassembling all the testees, and not knowing the effect of variables other than test reliability on the correlation. (These variables might include memory, practice, some kind of training or experience that took place between the two sittings, or just the passage of time.)

If a test is designed to measure a single attribute, all of its questions or items should measure the same characteristic. Hence, if there are a large number of items, your score on any half of them should be similar to your mark on the other half. One way to measure the **split half** or alternate form **reliability** is to compare your scores on the first half with those on the second (or your first and third quarters with the second and fourth). If your performance is likely to change as the test progresses—due to fatigue, practice, or a change in the difficulty of the items—the odd-numbered items could be compared with the even ones.

A third type of reliability is a statistic that measures how consistently the items are answered badly or well. Throughout all the test questions, do poor performers perform consistently badly, and do the high scorers do well? One statistic that measures this type of consistency is called **KR20** (for Kuder and Richardson). A KR20 of .7 and higher indicates good internal consistency.

Where scores are determined subjectively, researchers can determine **interscorer reliability** (the agreement between raters). No test can be expected to show perfect reliability on any of the four above measures. Rather, the test user expects a reliability coefficient much closer to 1 than to 0. Most standard selection tests offer coefficients between .6 and .9.

4. **Specificity** refers to the extent to which components of a test measure *nonoverlapping* attributes. Picture a test of muscle strength. Suppose its four subtests measured the strength of the left arm, right arm, left leg, and right leg. And let's assume that people's two arms are invariably the same in strength, as are their two legs.

You can see that in this case we could have assessed strength just as accurately by measuring only one arm and one leg. The two subtests for arm strength, the left arm and the right arm subtest, lacked specificity because they both measured the same attribute, arm strength.

Why is low specificity a problem? Testing is costly. It is usually expensive for the tester to choose, acquire, administer, score, and interpret tests, and it's psychologically costly for the testee to undergo them. Thus, any subtest that merely duplicates information offered by another, previously administered one, should be avoided.

Specificity is measured by correlating test scores across each other. If any two items, questions, or subtests are so highly correlated that knowing a person's score on one allows you accurately to predict the score on the other, then those two items lack specificity. The solution is to eliminate one, perhaps the one with the poorer showing on other characteristics.

5. **Validity** basically refers to whether a test does what it is supposed to. Managers want their tests to be valid just as when they pay for a raw ingredient with certain properties they expect it to possess those properties. Testees would have a great deal to complain about if they learned that a test on which their selection, promotion, or graduation were based, was invalid. And courts of law expect such tests to be valid in order to satisfy legislation regarding fairness.

Doubtless because of the complexity of validity, only about five percent of companies have any kind of validity data to support their testing procedures (according to Moon, 1987), and not all of these data would be convincing in court. There are five types, the most important of which are **predictive validity** and **concurrent validity**. These, together with content validity, construct validity, and face validity, should be thoroughly understood and clearly distinguished from each other.

The purest measure of whether or not a test performs as expected is its *predictive* validity. To assess the predictive validity of a test, you would administer it to *all* of the available applicants or to a group that fairly represents the applicant population. The second step consists of hiring *all* of those who took the test! These "new hires" are handled without regard for their test results, which should be sealed to prevent their scores from influencing any aspect of their early experience. When the work record has lasted long enough for a criterion score to be applied, this score is taken for each worker. Then the test results are unsealed and compared to the criterion scores. *The predictive validity is the correlation between test score and criterion score.*

The concept of predictive validation is appealing to employees, because it democratically gives every applicant a chance. It is also appealing to employers, because once a test is shown to have high predictive validity, the firm can use it for future selection with confidence and with reasonable immunity from charges of unfair discrimination in hiring.

Despite its appeal, predictive validation is so costly that it is rarely carried out. The problem, of course, is with the second step, in which all applicants who write the test are offered the job. It rarely benefits people to hire them for work they can't be successful at. Unsuitable applicants, once hired, may complain with justification that their hopes were falsely raised, and they may prove costly to the firm and hard to dislodge.

Yet, in practice, predictive validation does have some application. Imagine a pilot plant that needs 100 employees now, and in a few years the main plant will recruit 1,000 workers. The firm has three tests that might be useful in predicting how best to select those 1,000. So the first 100 applicants for the pilot plant (which is not expected to make a profit) are all hired. All of the 100 take all three tests. It would be of inestimable value to the firm to know which, if any, of the three tests shows a high correlation with job performance.

Should *every* selection test undergo predictive validation prior to each new application? That is, if one employer finds the predictive validity of some test to be .7 for hiring a maintenance crew, can another firm confidently use it to select *its* maintenance staffers? Contrary to earlier assumptions, it turns out that test users can rely on a substantial degree of **validity generalization**. This means that once the predictive validity is determined for one use of a given test, similar applications can be expected to yield similar results. (Details on what is meant by "similar" and on the type of test with the greatest validity generalization can best be found in the arguments of Schmidt, Pearlman, Hunter, and Hirsh, 1985, and in the rejoinder of Sackett, Tenopyr, Schmitt, Kehoe, and Zedeck, 1985.)

Unlike reliability, *predictive validity* is not an inherent characteristic of a given test; rather, it is linked to the test's *use*. It is meaningless to ask if a certain test is "valid." One may ask only if it is valid for a specified use. A test that is invalid for one purpose may be highly valid for another.

It is more common for a firm to be faced with the same question ("Which of these three tests best predicts the criterion?") without having the ability to perform a pilot plant or other costly study to answer it. If the question were slightly reworded to ask "Which of these three tests is most highly correlated with our *present* workers' performances?" it could be answered easily. The employer simply administers the tests to the *present* staff, and correlates *test* scores with *criterion* scores. The best test, presumably, is the one on which the top employee gets the highest score and the poorest performer the lowest. It is logical to assume that if this *concurrently validated* test is administered to applicants, it would accurately predict which applicant—if hired—would ultimately achieve the best work record. The administration of tests to *present* workers for this purpose is called *concurrent* validity because it measures the correlation of test score not with what the applicant will eventually do, but with the present or concurrent work record of the staff.

Concurrent validation is simple, easy, and inexpensive. The main cost is the interruption of production when the employees are taking the test. But there are weaknesses in this procedure. The major problem is that the present workers are a different group than the applicants. For instance, the poorest performers have probably been gradually removed from the present workforce, whereas those who are potentially the poorest still remain in the applicant pool. (That is, a test should identify hopeless cases as well as promising ones, but any present staff probably doesn't include dismal performers to be tested.) Similarly, predictive validation may reflect the *trainability* of workers. But the present staff has completed its training, and their experience is likely to influence their test scores in a way that is hard to detect or interpret.

The two types of validity we have just looked at, *predictive* and *concurrent,* are known as **criterion validities** because they are determined through an empirical correlation with some external criterion. (Although it would seem that *predictive* validity is to be preferred over *concurrent* validity, some data [Barrett, Phillips & Alexander, 1981] suggest that they are similar in value.) Because these determinations are based on logic, they are also known as **rational validities**. Other types of validity, the ones outlined next, are determined only through an internal examination.

Content validity is more applicable to tests of knowledge than tests of work potential. For instance, at the conclusion of a training program trainees may be tested on the material presented. If these questions did not fairly reflect the program's content, the test would lack content validity. Content validity is assessed by comparing the topics of the questions with those listed on the curriculum. The closer the connection, the greater the content validity. This assessment is subjective.

Content validity is related to *representativeness.* The essence of any test, you'll recall, is that it calls for a *sample* of behavior or asks questions on a *sample* of the material that was presumably learned. If you were given an examination on this entire book, and all of the questions were based only on this chapter, the content of the exam would not properly represent the material of the book.

Construct validity is complex because it has to do with how a test relates to the underlying *construct* (page 58). Here's an example. Suppose you want to devise a test for leadership. You would first have to ask questions like these: What hypotheses derived from leadership theory relate to your new leadership test? To what extent can these hypotheses be confirmed through the use of this test, that is, to what extent does your test follow logically from—and confirm—the prevailing theories of leadership? The greater the extent, the more construct validity your test possesses. Again, the evaluation is subjective.

On a simpler level, it is possible to assess construct validity empirically. If a leadership test that is considered valid already exists, you could compare scores on this test with scores on yours. Construct validation is a normal part of the scientific process. Even existing tests should be validated insofar as the theory related to the particular construct improves.

The simplest type of validity is **face validity**. Most people, whether job applicants or university students, don't enjoy being tested. So if the test *appears* to be irrelevant to its apparent purpose, anger or indifference would be a likely reaction. Therefore, a test should *look* like it will serve the purpose for which it is being administered, and to the extent it does this, it has face validity.

To measure face validity, you could simply ask those who are being tested to state what they think the test is designed to measure or accomplish. The more accurate the guesses, the higher the face validity. It can easily be manipulated by the wording of a title or label that is seen by the testees.

Validity is a more complex issue than the above treatment indicates. Some theorists propose more divisions; Messick (1980) lists 12 types of construct validity, and Guion and Crany (1982) differentiate among 8 varieties of criterion validity. By contrast, Landy (1986) argues that criterion, content, and construct validity are the same; the 3 names merely show the 3 types of *inferences* that can be drawn from the same test score. Binning and Barrett (1989) expand Landy's position, review the historical changes in the meaning of validity, and present thoughtful arguments for a single type of validity from various contexts: scientific, practical, technical, organizational, political, legal, and professional. The 5-way division of validity presented in this chapter emphasizes the differences for clarity, and is summarized in table form as Table 4.1.

6. The last characteristic of a test is its **discriminability**. Suppose a city hires you to test firefighter incumbents or applicants. Somebody suggests a rope-climbing test in which the score is the height climbed and descended in ten seconds. You devise, standardize, and administer this test to your standardization sample, and find the scores look good in terms of difficulty level

TABLE 4.1 Five types of validity: A summary chart

Type of Validity	Questions Asked	Procedure	Main Use	Example
Predictive	Do test scores predict a certain *future* performance?	Give test and use it to predict outcome. Later retest to determine outcome. Compare the two.	Selection and classification tests.	Ask dental school applicants to carve a specific design in a piece of chalk without breaking it.
		(EMPIRICAL TESTS)		
Con-current	Do test scores reflect *present* performance?	Give test. Obtain a direct measure of the other performance. Compare the two.	Substitute for above.	Ask practicing dentists to perform the same carving test.
Content	Does this test give a fair measure of performance on some important set of tasks?	Compare the test items logically to the content that the test is supposed to measure.	Tests of achievement or training programs, as an exam tests the effect of a course.	Student: "The topics on the exam weren't covered in the course." Prof: "That was to demonstrate low content validity."
Construct	How can scores on this test be explained psychologically?	Set up hypotheses. Test them experimentally.	Tests used for description, or in scientific research.	A new test for work motivation is compared with other measures (older tests of motivation, job behavior, and self-reports of motivation levels).
Face	Does this test *look* relevant to the job?	Ask students to guess what the test is for.	Tests should *look* meaningful. This will increase their acceptance in industry.	To predict an applicant's punch-press ability, use a simplified miniature press instead of the Stromberg Dexterity Test (fitting blocks into holes).

and dispersion. The testees like its face validity, and you are satisfied as to its construct validity. You repeat the test after a month and find high test-retest reliability. What else might you like to know about this test?

You already have other measures on the testees (various other scores on a set of applicants, and criterion measures on the incumbents). So what you'd like to know about the new test item is (a) does it discriminate between

So what You've just covered a lot of material on tests. Was it worthwhile? Consider that students sometimes feel that they were unfairly tested, but without understanding test theory they are not sure on what basis to complain. At work, not all assessment procedures are totally fair, and if you are disadvantaged by a test you'll now be in a position to propose improvements. And if you become a supervisor or manager, you may have to assess your own assessment procedures, and defend them.

the "good" performers and the "poor" performers? (b) do the best performers (as determined by your other measures) excel in rope-climbing, and (c) do the poor performers score low on it?

You can quantify discriminability of individual test items this way. Select a percentage of the testees to define the top and bottom group. (If the N is large, you might take the top and bottom **deciles** or 10 percent to compare; if small, you could choose the top and bottom **quartiles** or 25 percent.) The better the performance of the top testees compared to those in the lower group on a test item, the better the item's discriminability. The usual statistical procedure used for determining discriminability is called *point biserial correlation*.

CATEGORIES OF TESTS

Many tests are available; Sweetland and Keyser (1986) describe about a thousand of them in their section on tests for business and industry! With so many tests, it's useful to have ways to separate them, but when reading the divisions below keep in mind that some tests belong to more than one category. Also, tests are often administered not in isolation but in a **test battery** (an integrated group of tests). For instance, an employment test battery may include both ability and personality tests.

Of the many ways to categorize tests, the most obvious is the test's *purpose.* Tests are administered for medical diagnosis, psychiatric evaluation, admittance to Olympic competition, membership in **Mensa**, attainment of a journeyman's certificate, legal evidence such as lie-detection tests, and decisions on one's grade in a school course. We will concentrate on tests designed for applicant selection; however, the same or similar tests may be applied to decisions on employee transfer, promotion, or even termination.

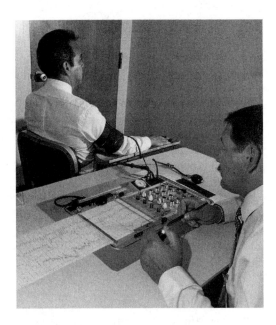

The polygraph or lie-detection test is based on the physiological approach.

Various schemes are used for categorizing tests for occupational selection. The following are the most useful divisions. Note that some of the upcoming categories, most of which are dichotomies, are not mutually exclusive.

Language versus nonlanguage tests

Most tests require fluency in the **language** of the tester or literacy on the part of the testee, although a few **nonlanguage tests** are available. It is difficult to design a test that is free of any requirement for verbal communication, but the instructions may be imparted via symbolic drawings, and the answers may be of the "performance" type, or chosen from a set of alternatives presented in symbol form. With the present emphasis on minority rights and on the desirability of employing disabled persons, nonlanguage or nonverbal tests are proving increasingly useful.

Speed versus power tests

In a **speed test**, the tasks are easy, and the score is the number of items completed in a limited time. In a **power test**, the items are more difficult, and the score is based on the *quality* of the responses emitted within a more generous time allowance. For instance, a test comprising the single task, "State why we should hire you; you may devote the entire afternoon to composing your answer," is clearly a power test; placing pegs into holes would be a speed test. Many tests are neither one nor the other, but combine some elements of both.

Individual versus group tests

Tests may be designed for administration to an **individual** or to a **group**. Individual tests, because of their much higher administration cost, are generally restricted to the evaluation of applicants to managerial positions. One of the major contributions of applied psychology was the conversion of the first major test, the Binet, from an individual test for children to a version designed for administration to a large group of adults, the Army Alpha and Beta.

By today's standards, the early group tests are quite deficient in several types of validity. Figure 4.3 shows some "complete the picture" items from the Army Beta. You can see how loaded these items were with cultural bias, and how they reflected the values and experiences of the test designers.

Verbal, performance, and paper-and-pencil tests

Verbal tests hinge on spoken responses; such tests are necessarily *individual*. In a **performance test**, the testees are required to *do* something, such as sort a given variety of objects into categories, track a target on a screen, or fit pegs into holes. In a **paper-and-pencil test** they *write* their responses. (Tracing a maze with a pencil would be considered a performance test because the skill is in solving the maze, not in choosing an answer.) Obviously, group tests, which are invariably paper and pencil, offer the most efficiency of administration.

Screening tests

A **screening test** is characteristically a simple, group-administered test of general ability designed for the initial rough screening of large numbers of applicants. Most of these tests measure general mental ability in 10 to 30 minutes and can be administered and scored by clerical level personnel. Tests such as the Otis Self-Administering Test of Mental Ability and the Wonderlic Personnel Test were widely used after World War II. Although generally perceived as intelligence tests, a more appropriate label for these general mea-

FIGURE 4.3 Army Beta "picture completion" test items

Among the earliest tests administered to large groups were the Army Alpha and Beta tests, based on Binet's individual test for children. The example above was administered to recruits who could not read. Note the cultural assumptions made by the test designers.

sures of verbal and numerical abilities would be scholastic aptitude tests (Anastasi, 1979).

Some tests are designed for screening lower level jobs. For instance, in the Personnel Tests for Industry both the instructions and the questions are presented on audio tape. The Basic Occupational Literacy Test (BOLT) assesses the written language level of marginally literate adults.

Attribute tests

Tests may be identified according to whatever *attribute* they're designed to measure. You might be assessed for your physical strength, musical ability, vocabulary, logical thought, or memory for digits, each via a different test. Characteristics commonly measured in occupational assessments are **interests**, **abilities**, **achievements**, and **aptitudes**. As an example, a candidate for the position of ambulance attendant may show a high *interest* in medicine, no current *ability* to drive a specialized vehicle, and a high *aptitude* for learning how to administer emergency treatment.

Within the category of *ability* tests, there are virtually as many types available as there are human abilities. Operators of sensitive and dangerous equipment, such as military aircraft, would be thoroughly assessed by **sensorimotor tests**. These typically measure vision and hearing, and possibly hand steadiness, hand-eye coordination, balance, and muscle coordination, strength, and endurance. A similar category is the **psychomotor test**, which demands less than the sensorimotor type. For instance, the Purdue series of tests require the testee to manipulate small objects such as pegs with the hand or simple tools.

Various widely used **clerical aptitude tests** measure lower level clerical ability. They primarily measure speed and also accuracy in perceiving details in, and handling, alphanumerical material.

Specific types of tests

Many tests are identified by the single attribute they are designed to measure. We will look at the two most widely measured characteristics, intelligence and personality. Then we'll turn to two more specialized and modern types of tests, the situational and the stress test.

Intelligence tests When most people think of psychological testing, the attribute that first comes to mind is **intelligence**. Psychologists administer more **intelligence tests** than any other kind. When managers are considering paying for applicant or employee testing, they often show the most interest in intelligence scores. These are the reasons why:

- Until recently, intelligence testing was routinely performed at many elementary or high schools, so most adults are familiar with it.

FRANK AND EARNEST. Reprinted by permission of Newspaper Enterprise Associates, Inc.

- The history of applied psychology is the history of intelligence testing, and practitioners are well trained in IQ measurement.

- There is a widely held assumption that intelligent people are generally superior, and that any person's intelligence can be accurately quantified.

- Managers may feel that they themselves have a high level of intelligence and prefer to associate with equally bright coworkers.

In fact, high scores on an intelligence test do not predict occupational success as accurately as high achievement on many other types of tests. However, intelligence scores are strongly correlated with school success, so the administration of an intelligence test might be appropriate when selecting for a position that involves lengthy, school-like training. Ghiselli (1966) found that intelligence tests reasonably predicted training success for skilled jobs that requires mental calculation, such as electrical work.

Many managers ask for an assessment of candidates' intelligence, when what they really want measured is creativity, learning ability, or even poise. The strongest claim that can be made for intelligence tests is that they're the best standardized and most sensitive instruments we have for predicting performance—at least in elementary school. Their major weakness is that there is no certainty as to precisely what intelligence is. They also suffer from the same shortcoming that weakens virtually all tests: they were standardized by white, urban, middle-class, male psychometrists largely on young, white, urban, middle-class males. Hence, the more the discrepancy between the testee and the original standardization sample, the less valid the testing process may be.

Personality tests **Personality** refers to relatively stable aspects of a person's behavior patterns and thoughts which differentiate that person from others. Because it includes variables such as motivation, honesty, and enthusiasm, personality is commonly assessed through testing in an employment context. Although not highly useful for predicting specific performance, **personality**

test scores can be used to gauge variables such as job satisfaction, interactional style, and commitment.

The usual approach involves a **personality inventory**. A typical inventory is the Guilford-Zimmerman Temperament Survey, which provides scales such as sociability, objectivity, and friendliness. Current theory identifies five basic dimensions of personality: extraversion, agreeableness, conscientiousness, emotional stability, and openness to experience. These are described by Digman (1990).

Personality may also be approached through the assessment of clinical measures such as paranoia, hypochondria, or depression. The assessment of such aspects is best left to a clinical psychologist or psychometrist who is aware of the limitations and strengths of the many tests for personality.

Personality is so complex, situational, and interactional that measuring it is problematic. Unlike intelligence or aptitude testing, where responses are right or wrong and the objective is to score as high as possible, there are no right or wrong answers on a personality test. If Jan goes to a clinician merely to seek better self-understanding, it would be to Jan's advantage to answer all questions candidly. But if Jan were applying for a position requiring total honesty or extreme toughness, we would expect the answers to be different. Although some tests try to measure lying or faking, there is no foolproof accuracy check.

A specialized type of personality test relies on the **projective** approach. According to the rationale of projective tests, each person, when required to interpret an ambiguous stimulus, will see it in accordance with personal wishes, fears, drives, expectations, and so on. The most widely used projective tests are the **Rorschach** (ink blot) and the **Thematic Apperception Test (TAT)**. Projective tests are relatively immune to faking, but they are highly dependent upon the interpretation of the responses by the clinician. The Rorschach is particularly questionable in this regard, but the TAT has shown itself to be useful in predicting personality attributes that are relevant to the workplace.

Employers can be extremely vulnerable to various forms of dishonesty in their own employees. Personality assessments can usefully predict honesty, according to a recent meta-analysis (Ones, Vishwesvaran & Schmidt, 1994), but honesty can change for many people as the situation changes. For that matter, even the definition of honesty may vary across time, place, and situation. And one of the characteristics of the **sociopathic personality** is not only deviousness but an ability to fool testers and tests.

Besides honesty, I/O personality assessors are interested in **locus of control (LOC)**. "Locus" means place or location. Some people seem internally driven; others are quite influenced (or feel they are) by external factors such as other people, fate, chance, or situations. These two types are termed **internal** *control* and **external** *control*.

"Internals" are more likely to become entrepreneurs, or to prefer work of a skilled, professional, or managerial type. They perform better at complex, information-processing work that requires motivation, initiative, and independence. Miller, Kets de Vries, and Toulouse (1982), studying executives of Canadian firms, reported that most were internals, and that the more the internalism of the leaders, the more the company's innovation and flexibility, and the status of the organization as an industry leader. On the other hand, "externals" who become frustrated with their job are prone to commit sabotage and vandalism (Storms & Spector, 1987).

Personality assessment for personnel selection has long been a controversial topic. Some literature reviews starting in the 1950s support it; others do not: "There is no generalizable evidence that personality measures can be recommended as . . . a practical tool for employee selection" (Guion & Gottier, 1965). Yet, personnel measures are routinely used in the selection of, for instance, law enforcement officers and flight attendants.

Many psychological attributes generalize across jobs. If you have good mathematical ability, you can likely put it to good use whether you work as a clerk, an engineer, or an actuary. Irving (1993) argues that personality does not generalize across jobs; for example, an extroverted personality may be suitable for one type of job but not for another. Accordingly, personality tests are useful in selection only if a job analysis (page 84) first indicates what personality aspects are relevant.

Situational tests   The above types of tests all seem artificial, or lacking in face validity. A managerial candidate could extract one of the intelligence test questions and ask, "What does my ability to answer this have to do with my potential as your vice president?" An alternative is the **situational test**, which measures how the candidate copes with a realistic sample of the work *situation*. For instance, to assess managerial response to an assortment of the typical problems that land in the IN half of the twin letter trays on the desk via memos, letters, notes, appeals, and records of telephone messages, the candidate could be administered an **in-basket test**. A trained observer evaluates how each candidate handles the same assortment of items in the basket. In the next search, the items may be somewhat different to ensure that the test closely reflects the job situation.

Similarly, a group of candidates for managerial positions that require leadership, interpersonal skills, and problem-solving ability could be assessed with a **leaderless group discussion test (LGD)**. Here a problem is assigned for the group to deal with in a given time period, and the quality of each candidate's participation is scored, preferably by a professional with training in objectively rating the contributions. The assigned format may be either cooperative or competitive.

The LGD test has shown value in assessing candidates for industry and also for occupations ranging from military officers to social workers. It has one weakness: An applicant might show outstanding performance when interacting in a group of fellow candidates, is hired, and fails to live up to that promise with colleagues and supervisors. The LGD is supposed to be a realistic

A stress test is designed specifically to measure a candidate's reaction to stress. Here, a marine is subjected to pressure as a part of the training regimen.

simulation exercise, but since the participants are all job candidates they do not properly simulate future coworkers. (The ultimate situational test, albeit a costly and limited one, would be to hire a candidate and rate the performance over a prolonged trial period.)

Stress tests   Many employees fail, not because of an inability to perform the required duties, but because of an inappropriate reaction to stress. Examples would be technicians who stay off work because a prankster defaced their lockers, a highly trained payroll clerk who quits after being sworn at by a shipper, a maintenance supervisor who lets important work slide because of family turmoil, or a second in command who is promoted to the top and succumbs to a stress-related disease. How can such reactions to stress be predicted?

Many candidates find that taking any test is stressful, but a **stress test** is *designed* to impose maximum pressure. For instance, the seven candidates for the job of the first American astronaut were subjected to a battery of physically and psychologically stressful tasks. Similarly, the initial training regimen for U.S. Marines at one time amounted to a 6-week stress test. The most frequent version applied in industry is the *stress interview,* in which one or more interviewers challenge, criticize, impose competing demands, and so on. (Stress test has a different meaning in medicine, where it refers to an examination of the cardiovascular system under exercise.)

TEST SCORING

Tests may be scored **objectively** or **subjectively**. An example of an objectively scored test is the **Minnesota Multiphasic Personality Inventory (MMPI)**. Because it's a long test that is commonly used in clinical psychology, it's invariably machine scored. The most widely used test in personnel functions is the assessment interview, an example of a subjectively scored test. In the latter case it is possible to impart a measure of objectivity, for instance, by having several interviewers rate the applicant on various scales and condensing the scaled numbers to a datum that *looks* objective. But if the final score stemmed from subjective judgments, the test still belongs in the subjective category.

Having you stand on a scale is a way of measuring your weight. If ten clinicians performed this test and all agreed on how much you weighed, we could assume the test was objective. On the other hand, having you interpret ink blots is a way of testing your personality structure; interviewing you is a way of assessing your employment suitability. You can see that these tests are hardly objective.

Recent decades have seen the introduction of computers for objectifying assessment. Computers are increasingly being used to present the test items and, of course, to quickly score, analyze, and report on their meaning. A good program, properly used, can offer objectivity and efficiency, but technology does not by itself mean validity. A comprehensive source of information on computer-based testing is Burke (1993).

THE TEST BATTERY

In the Great Depression of the 1930s, vast numbers of workers lost their jobs just as an influx of youngsters was trying to join the labor force. It was apparent that the only available work would be in a different line than the fired workers had been trained for and doing. The solution was the development of a major program to predict how successful an applicant would be in hundreds of different jobs.

The General Aptitude Test Battery or GATB was developed by the United States Employment Service in the early 1940s. From an examination of job analyses (page 84), the psychologists developed a $2\frac{1}{2}$ hour test battery or assortment of tests. Factor analysis (page 45) showed that the test collection measured nine basic aptitudes: general intelligence; verbal, numerical, and spatial ability; form and clerical perception; motor coordination; and manual and finger dexterity. Since then, a number of test batteries have been devised.

Brief case

"What makes my test *predictive*," asserts the psychometrist who uses it, "is its *standardization*." "And what makes your test *unfair*," replies the social critic, "is its *standardization*. If the testees are not similar to the people on whom the test norms were originally based, the testees may well be disadvantaged. It's like interviewing in English a person from Quebec who speaks only French, or like trying to measure pigeons' intelligence by giving them underwater tests designed to assess fish."

THE SURVEY AS A TEST

We have covered the survey in chapter 2 and dealt with personnel tests in this one. We have seen that the selection interview presents a number of problems for both sides. Now we will look at a procedure that combines the survey and the test to solve some of the problems relating to the selection interview.

The selection interview

Virtually nobody is hired without first being interviewed. In fact, the employment interview is the most common single selection filter. Schwind (1987) reported that 90 percent of personnel professionals have more confidence in this technique than in any other source of selection information, even though the predictive validity is between .1 and .2. (A validity coefficient of .2 indicates that about six percent of future performance is predicted by the test.)

The interview is commonly used *as though it were a test*. Now that we have examined test theory we can evaluate the use of the selection interview in this respect to determine how it violates principles of testing. One defect is *lack of standardization*. Interviewers may assume that they are behaving in a fair and neutral fashion, but all the while they might be emitting subtly different cues of interest, boredom, agreement, or disagreement with different interviewees.

Another liability is the influence of the *initial impression*. Interviewers tend to solidify their conclusion near the outset of the interview and to interpret subsequent observations in a way that confirms the initial judgment. A major source of any initial impression is likely to be the applicant's ap-

Brief case

Variants of the dispute regarding the use of separate norms are playing out throughout much of the world. In 1992, the fire department of Kitchener, Ontario (Canada), received over 2,000 applications for 21 openings. The department administered a screening test similar to the General Aptitude Test Battery, and selected the top 100 traditional applicants and the top 100 nontraditional applicants. (The province of Ontario designated these applicants as women, visible minorities, people with disabilities, and Aboriginal people. U.S. nontraditional groups comprise women, Hispanics, African Americans, Asians, people with disabilities, and Native American and other indigenous groups.) In the more rigorous, second-level testing, the top 21 scorers of the 200 were chosen, regardless of category. A white male who just missed the cutoff on the first test, but whose score exceeded the scores of some successful minority applicants, took action against the fire department, which then dropped its use of within-group norms. Subsequently, one neighboring fire department announced that all applicants would take the written test and the top scorers would be processed further; another fire department instituted a lottery to choose those who would be eligible for the physical tests.

pearance, and several studies have documented the undue influence of this variable. For instance, Beehr and Gilmore (1982) had undergraduates make hiring decisions for jobs, some of which required interaction with the public and some of which did not. The evaluators worked from résumés accompanied by photographs of the male applicants. These photographs were systematically varied, sometimes attractive, sometimes not. As expected, the more attractive the photograph, the more positive the recommendations.

Parsons and Liden (1984) showed that even when attractiveness per se is not a dominant factor, equally questionable variables affect personnel decisions. They found, in a factor analysis study of some 500 job applicants, that the applicants' speech mannerisms were much more influential than clothing and cleanliness. Their finding that male and female interviewers differed in their response to the sex and race of the applicant further emphasizes the subjective nature of interviews.

The final weakness is that the *skills* required for a candidate to be impressive in an interview are unlikely to be the ones required on the job. Few jobs would require you mainly to sit down and answer a large number of questions put by an interviewer.

Do the above weaknesses imply that the selection interview should be abandoned? Not necessarily. Applicants *expect* to be interviewed; to *not* interview could be interpreted as lack of interest. The interview also provides a means of evaluating variables that may be revealed only in a face-to-face encounter. And it offers an opportunity to answer the applicant's questions and to promote the job or the firm to the applicant. But the interview should be *structured* (Wiesner & Cronshaw, 1988), and should not comprise the only, or even the primary, selection procedure.

The questionnaire

The interview, like the questionnaire, is a survey (page 39), but the latter form avoids most of the interview's weaknesses. Most firms could easily devise a questionnaire to function as a custom selection test. An initial questionnaire would serve mainly as a "file opener" and first-level filter. Potential candidates could then be invited to complete a more detailed form; this instrument would constitute a written test. The questions would tap the candidates' intentions and opinions regarding those variables which the management has reason to consider the most salient.

Principles of proper test design and administration should be followed, and consultation with a professional is usually called for. For instance, scoring should be objective, the administration procedure should be standardized, and the instrument should be validated. In particular, the scoring should be blind, meaning that the scorer does not know the identity of the testee. Apart from serving as a test, such a questionnaire would also indicate to the candidate who will become the new employee what it is that the employer considers important.

ATTITUDES TOWARD TESTING

Whether they are university students hoping for a high grade or job applicants hoping for an offer of employment, people do not enjoy being subjected to a test. They typically feel nervous, disadvantaged, infantilized, or defensive. Applicants should be assured that no single test or item on it is critical, but that the pattern of test results will help determine personnel decisions that are in the applicant's interest. To improve a testing program, it may be helpful to seek feedback on the selection process from a sample of both successful and unsuccessful applicants.

It is convenient to use test scores as a means of reducing the number of applicants who are being considered for a job opening. Personnel officers may like the fact that the high scorers seem to fit their image of how a new associate should look and talk. However, the ethics of using selection tests to screen out nontraditional candidates are being increasingly questioned, and unethical practices are not merely frowned upon but prohibited.

Selection tests should be subjected to regular validity evaluations. The traditional use of tests is facing legal challenges on the basis that a given test is not perfectly fair, appropriate, or relevant. These problems are covered in the next section.

WEAKNESSES OF TESTS AND FURTHER INFORMATION

Tests and testers are widely available. Logically, then, if they always worked well no mistakes would be made by personnel departments. However, errors do occur; obviously, tests do not always work.

Tests can discriminate unfairly. Whenever the predictive validity of a test is less than a perfect 1 the test is probably discriminating on factors such as sophistication and experience in taking tests, or "test smarts." In fact, the fastest growing industry related to personnel assessment is the test coaching service.

Another problem is the conflict between *timeliness* and *standardization*. The older the test, the more the accumulation of data will presumably support its use, but the more likely some of its items will seem dated, irrelevant, and inappropriate. For instance, some of the items on some classic tests seem like invasions of privacy today. And the older a test, the less likely it is that today's testees will be the equivalent of the sample on which the norms were established.

Overreliance on tests invites **Type 1 errors**. This refers to **false rejections**, that is, the rejection of candidates who would have been successful if accepted, but who were not considered because they failed to achieve an adequate score on a test. It can also lead to **Type 2 errors**, or **false acceptances**, that is, acceptances of people who earned misleadingly high test scores.

Finally, as managers learn more and more about the applicants on the shortlist, they may have too much data to handle comfortably. At this point, the idea of condensing a complex human being into a few numbers that can be easily compared is appealing, and many managers are tempted to rely on test results more than they should.

Testing is undergoing rapid changes, as the instruments are introduced, revised, and discontinued. An informed consumer of tests needs to keep current. Classic texts on testing include Anastasi (1982) and Cronbach (1984), and a list of commonly used tests and suppliers is in Appendix D of McCormick and Ilgen (1985). The most comprehensive source of information (descriptive and evaluative data, source, and price) is *The Mental Measurements Yearbook*; the Library of Congress classification number is Z 5814 E 9T47. Besides the annual volumes, there is an overall revision about every five years. Another excellent reference is Sweetland and Keyser (1986).

ETHICAL AND LEGAL ISSUES

Personnel decisions generally have major impacts on lives. Insofar as these decisions are based on tests, the testing process must be fair. Moreover, ethical constraints are becoming tighter, as they become defined by law, by societal acceptance, in union contracts, in case law, and in professional guidelines. Whether as a testee or as someone who may be involved in establishing a testing program some day, you should be aware of these constraints.

Increasingly, applicants other than the once-traditional white male are applying for admissions, jobs, and promotions. Fairness requires that the selection procedures not disadvantage them. Three types of unfairness have been identified; all three are related to each other.

1. If you do badly on a test, not because you would perform poorly on the job but because people of your race, sex, social class, religion, or place of origin are disadvantaged by its requirements, the test is said to have **adverse impact**. This can be measured by comparing traditional and nontraditional applicants, in terms of the average test score, or the percentages who pass the test.

2. A test may have **single group validity**, meaning that the selection procedure was shown to be valid, but only for one group. For instance, it may have been established that a procedure for selecting accountants was valid for both whites and African Americans, but not necessarily for Asian Americans or French Canadians.

3. **Differential validity** means that the testing has been shown to possess different validity for members of different groups.

Apart from the test itself, there are requirements about how it is used. It should be chosen, administered, and interpreted only by someone with the proper *qualifications*. Most intelligence and personality tests are distributed only to licensed or certified psychologists, but some basic employment tests are available to responsible personnel officers. Nobody should have casual or accidental access to any test-related materials.

The privacy and sensitivity of the testee must be respected. For instance, testing should not explore factors such as marital status or lifestyle unless they are clearly and demonstrably job related, and the results should be used only for the purpose they were obtained. A simple safeguard for privacy is to adopt the ethical principle of *informed consent*: the testee should understand and agree to the test, how the scores will be used, who will see or have access to them, and the provisions for storing and/or destroying the records.

Testees have a *right to know* how psychological tests are used to affect their lives. If they request it, they are entitled to basic information on the design and purpose of the tests they took, how they performed and what those results mean, and how the outcome contributed to whatever decision was made in their case.

An excellent source of information on the ethical use of tests is the American Psychological Association, whose address is in the glossary. Its brochures on this topic include *Standards for Educational and Psychological Testing, Specialty Guidelines for the Delivery of Services by Industrial/Organizational Psychologists, Casebook on Ethics and Standards for the Practice of Psychology in Organizations,* and *Principles for the Validation and Use of Personnel Selection Procedures.*

For a half century, the U.S. government has been relying on its General Aptitude Test Battery to screen applicants for a wide variety of its job openings. It turns out that African Americans and Hispanics (originally Spanish-speaking people, usually of a Mexican or Central American background) score lower on average than white applicants. Generations of social, educational, and employment prejudice have left their mark.

To encourage the employment of African Americans and Hispanics, the government recently established two sets of norms specially for these groups. Their scores were compared only with those of other African Americans or Hispanics who took the test. Thus, a Hispanic who scored in the top decile of other Hispanics was rated as having performed similarly to whites who scored in the top decile, regardless of the Hispanic's absolute score.

This has caused a heated controversy. On one side, whites complain about unfair reverse discrimination, and suggest that hiring lower-scoring Hispanics will increase bigotry against them. The other side, which has so far prevailed, contends that the use of separate norms is an appropriate affirmative action tool needed to redress past inequities and give a chance to those who would otherwise continue to be rejected. A special panel of the National Academy of Sciences supported the within-group norms (standards applied only to a specified group), also pointing out that the General Aptitude Test Battery does not have demonstrated predictive validity.

CURRENT TRENDS

Testing is almost as old as civilization. In the Roman army, special privileges were given to the few whose vision was so keen that they could tell which star in a certain constellation was a double. The first modern test to predict performance was administered back in 1905; the first test to predict job performance was given only a few years later, and by 1917 personnel tests were being administered by the millions. After all this experience and refinement, what changes could still be taking place?

One problem with a standardized test is that it wastes time to make high performers start with the easy items and to force low scorers to try the harder ones. For tests administered by computer, a new program (Kyllonen, 1994) self-adjusts its difficulty level to the capabilities of the testee. Such a test offers **adaptiveness**, meaning that the questions are adapted to the testee's abilities. Adaptiveness yields a more precise measurement of high and low performers because the questions they work on are within their own range of ability.

The program also offers **generativeness**, which means that entirely new test items are automatically generated in response to the abilities shown by the testee. The items of ordinary tests are "hard coded," meaning that the questions never vary. The more such a test is used, the more data are available on performance norms, but the more likely it is that testees remember some of the questions and inform others. The feature of generativeness allows the questions to be "soft coded," which protects the test from compromise.

DECISION THEORY

It should be clear from the foregoing that the proper use of tests will reduce errors in personnel decisions. But can the error reduction be *quantified?* Is there a hidden cost to using tests, and can this cost be exposed? Answers to these problems are dealt with in a specialty of psychometrics called **decision theory**.

Decision theory is a procedure for quantifying the benefits of using a selection test, and for determining the pros and cons of raising or lowering the "pass" score on the test. Suppose you have 100 applicants (Figure 4.4) and that you are willing to hire all who will prove to be worth their salary. Suppose further that you have perfected a single test on which you have all 100 scores.

Should you accept only the top scorers? By so doing, you would probably be protected from hiring any workers who turn out to be failures at their work. But your workforce would be small and you would have rejected many applicants who would have proven successful. Should you accept all but the very lowest scorers? By doing this, you would benefit from a large number of good workers, but you would have hired many who turn out to be failures on the job. That is, whether you set the **test cutoff** (the division between applicant acceptance and rejection) high or low, you will experience both a benefit and a liability.

The steps that are followed in applying decision theory to test results, along with a numerical example, are shown below. The **criterion cutoff** represents management's decision as to the dividing line between a job success (an employee who would have been hired if the criterion score had been known in advance) and a job failure (an applicant who management would not have hired if the criterion score could have been known). This is a fixed decision which should not be changed during the application of decision theory. The test cutoff is the variable which may be moved higher or lower, to reveal the subsequent effect on the size of the four cells (false and valid rejections, false and valid acceptances).

1. Hire your first 100 applicants. Administer your best test to them. Six months later, establish a criterion score. In this example, both the test and criterion measures are 10-point scales.

2. Draw a 10 × 10 matrix showing the criterion scale vertically and the test scale horizontally. Within this matrix, draw one tally mark for each of the 100 workers. In the example, Joe scored 8/1, Sam 8/10, and Bob 1/9·on the criterion/test measures.

3. Decide what constitutes "job success" and draw in the criterion cutoff. In the example, under 4 is a "failure." Now play around with what you might have selected as your test cutoff. In the example, we have elected to hire only those scoring above 5 on the test.

4. You may now quantify the value of this test. If you hired without using the test, your success ratio was 60/100 = .6. But if you had used the test, you would have had 38 successes out of the 45 thus hired, or 38/45 = .8, by using a selection ratio of .45 (hiring the top 45 of the 100 applicants).

5. Now examine which of the two "good" (VALID) cells you need to increase, at the expense of also increasing two "bad" (FALSE) cells. Or, which of the two "bad" cells you need to decrease, at the expense of also decreasing a "good" cell. Adjust your cutoff either way, and you may again quantify the effect.

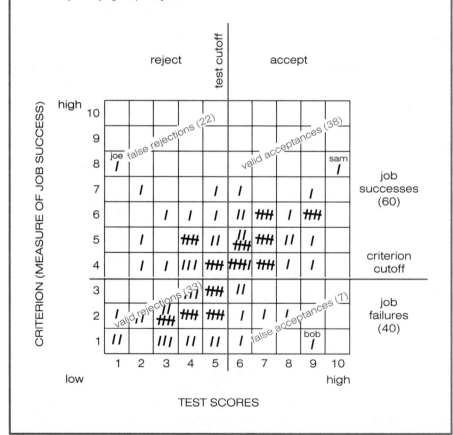

FIGURE 4.4 **An application of decision theory**

By evaluating the harm stemming from the size of the two "bad" (false) cells at various test cutoffs, management can determine which **selection ratio** will result in the most favorable **success ratio**. The *selection ratio* is the number of acceptances divided by the number of applicants; the *success ratio* is the number of workers defined as job successes divided by the total number hired.

The psychological test is to the I/O psychologist what the stethoscope is to the physician. Like the stethoscope, most tests are fairly simple instruments which don't tell the whole story about a person, and which need skill and judgment in their use. But when applied properly, tests and stethoscopes can help determine an appropriate diagnosis and treatment.

This chapter was not intended to make you a psychometrist. But either as a new employee or as a future personnel manager, you will surely encounter problems and questions related to personnel testing. You should now appreciate the many complex issues that attend this important subject.

Study guide for chapter 4

HAVE YOU LEARNED THESE NAMES AND TERMS?

psychometrics
test
standardized
norms
difficulty level
upper and lower ceiling
dispersion
reliability: test-retest, split half, KR20, interscorer
specificity
validity
predictive validity
concurrent validity
validity generalization
criterion and rational validity
content validity
construct validity
face validity
discriminability
decile, quartile
test battery
Mensa

language and nonlanguage tests
speed and power tests
individual and group tests
verbal, performance, and paper-and-pencil tests
screening tests
interest, abilities, achievements, and aptitudes
sensorimotor tests
psychomotor tests
clerical aptitude tests
intelligence
intelligence tests
personality
personality tests, personality inventory
projective tests
Rorschach
Thematic Apperception Test (TAT)
sociopathic personality
locus of control: internal and external
situational tests
in-basket test
leaderless group discussion test
stress tests
objective and subjective scoring
Minnesota Multiphasic Personality Inventory (MMPI)
Type 1 and Type 2 errors
false rejections and acceptances
adverse impact
single-group and differential validity
adaptiveness
generativeness
decision theory
test and criterion cutoff
selection ratio and success ratio

ISSUES TO CONSIDER

How would the world be different if there were no tests of any sort?

What is the importance of *standardization* in tests?

Which characteristics apply to all tests?

Which is the most important of these characteristics and why?

What are the two basic ways in which test characteristics are measured?

What is the benefit of high *specificity* in tests?

What are five types of test *validity*?

What is the problem in determining if a test does what it is supposed to?

Right now, are you engaged in a *speed* or a *power* test?

What is the distinction among *interest, ability,* and *aptitude*?

Why are intelligence tests often misused in employee selection?

What are the weaknesses of the *interview* as a selection procedure?

How can these weaknesses be reduced?

What are the weaknesses of tests in general?

In what ways can tests be unfair?

In what ways can testing be unethical?

What is the rationale of *decision theory*?

SAMPLE MULTIPLE-CHOICE QUESTIONS

1. The test characteristics that are determined in the same way are
   a. validity and dispersion.
   b. validity and difficulty.
   c. reliability and dispersion.
   d. dispersion and difficulty.

2. The only pure measure of whether a test does what it should is its
   a. reliability.
   b. concurrent validity.
   c. specificity.
   d. predictive validity.

3. It is meaningless to ask if a test has
   a. high predictive validity.
   b. reliability.
   c. concurrent validity.
   d. specificity.

4. The simplest type of validity to understand and to measure is
   a. face validity.
   b. construct validity.
   c. predictive validity.
   d. concurrent validity.

5. About how many different tests are available for business and industry?
   a. 50
   b. 100
   c. 500
   d. 1000

Answers: page 462

I attribute the little I know to my not having been ashamed to ask for information [from people] on those topics which form their own peculiar profession and pursuits.

John Locke (1632–1704)

Bird's-eye view of the chapter

This an intriguing chapter for students, because by discovering how to train or teach efficiently, they also find out how to learn efficiently. The chapter is based on the oldest and still dominant area of psychology, learning theory, and on one that is becoming dominant, educational psychology. Both areas provide a vast amount of information on how we learn and how we can best be taught. The chapter outlines the meaning, the importance, and some principles of training and learning, and contrasts training media.

Chapter 5

Personnel training

The payoff from chapter 5   You will:

1. Understand the concept of training
2. Know the difference between training and education
3. Know the consequences of providing no training at all
4. Understand the meaning and function of task analysis and job inventory
5. Differentiate between training and orientation
6. Appreciate the value of ongoing, comprehensive training
7. Understand factors related to who should perform the training
8. Understand basic principles of feedback and reinforcement
9. Learn the meaning and importance of serial factors in memory
10. Differentiate between short- and long-term memory

11. Appreciate the meaning and importance of consolidation
12. Understand the effect of timing on learning
13. Know the four types of transfer
14. Know the rationale, pros, and cons of each training medium
15. Know which training media seem tailored to the industrial/organizational (I/O) psychology context
16. See the need for training to ISO 9000 standards
17. Understand issues related to training the disadvantaged
18. Connect training programs to career development
19. Be skeptical of the value of any given training program
20. Be alert to the need for, and possibilities of, research on any training program

Think back to the last time you did something new, and then continuously repeated it. Maybe practice didn't make perfect and maybe sometimes you seemed to be doing it worse than the last time, but overall, the more you did it the better you performed. Training is an invariable consequence of starting new work and continuing it. The training or practice effect is demonstrated in a typical learning curve (Figure 3.2, page 79). No individual could be expected to show such orderly learning; the so-called S curve represents the *average* performance of a large number of learners.

If you plan to become a virtuoso violinist you would study for many years, under a sequence of teachers, in the expectation of a continuous training effect. If you are stranded on a desert island and survive by shucking oysters, you would find that each day's oyster-opening is faster. Whenever you encounter a new task and continue to perform it, training is what accounts for the improvement in performance. Whether you learn on your own through trial and error, or whether your progress is guided by systematic, formal, graduated instruction, training will inevitably occur.

TRAINING VERSUS EDUCATION

Learning about industrial/organizational (I/O) psychology is a new task for you. Does the *training effect* mean that the last 30 pages of this book will be easier for you to learn than the first 30 pages? You will find the answer later in this chapter. But learning material in a textbook is not the same as learning how to play golf or how to operate a punch press; one involves education and the others involve training.

Historically, **education** refers to a prolonged endeavor to reach some generalized objective, and **training** is associated with short-term efforts leading to clear-cut and concrete goals. For instance, you might take 12 years to acquire a broad set of knowledge and skills, and 12 hours to learn how to handle customer complaints.

Recently, the distinction between education and training has become blurred. The general education system is now emphasizing "life" or marketable skills, such as word processing, computer, or machine shop training. Conversely, some industrial organizations start new employees with as much as a year-long, formal classroom education program.

Informal education hardly requires a classroom setting; it occurs whenever a new experience is encountered. Similarly, *to train or not to train* is not an option. Lacking a formal training procedure, the worker will inevitably, perhaps without realizing it, *self-train*. Even after completing a specific training regimen, the employee will experience continuing on-the-job self-training over the following months or even years.

Objectives of training

"Psychology started with the Greeks." This not very illuminating sentence has been in my mind ever since I first heard it. It was the first sentence of the first lecture of my first course in graduate school, showing that the outset of a program offers an opportunity to make a first impression that lasts. One potential objective of training is *orientation,* which can include the establishment of appropriate attitudes, expectations, and allegiances. The use of a training program to instill attitudes and values that fit the organization's culture is described by Feldman (1989).

Another common and obvious objective is *skills* training. Employees are taught how to sell or service a new model, use a new communications system, or operate a machine. Other objectives deal with *verbal, intellectual,* or *cognitive* abilities, that is, facts, concepts, or strategies. Training can make staffers more flexible; for instance, one employee may sometimes be needed to perform the work of another due to vacations, illnesses, or temporary reassignments. And training can increase staffers' personal development and self-esteem.

Whatever the objectives are, they should be clear to and agreed upon by top management, trainers, and trainees. Supervisors in particular should participate. Research suggests that supervisors' opinions on the value of training vary widely in terms of whether they themselves and their subordinates need it (Ford & Noe, 1987).

Clear objectives are not common. One massive survey of a thousand U.S. corporations showed that only a quarter of them have an organized program for assessing training requirements (Saari, Johnson, McLaughlin & Zimmerle, 1988). Management may need to do some consultation and research in terms of organizational goals, assessment of needs, and perceptions of staffers when deciding upon training objectives. For instance, an obvious purpose of training is to remedy deficiencies. But deficiencies are not always apparent (and may be covered up) and may be due to something other than inadequate training. Useful starting places for establishing training objectives are job analyses, employee and supervisor surveys, and employee assessment reports.

WHAT SHOULD BE TRAINED?

You will recall that the *job analysis* (page 84) lists all of the job elements. A **task analysis** is similar, except that it lists only what the novice needs to be *taught* for efficient job performance. The starting point for the *task analysis* may be the *job analysis* if one is available, a *job description* (page 83), or simply an interview with an employee. The starting point, whichever one is chosen, is used to create a **job inventory**. This is a list of the job elements

- Gather data from professors regarding type and length of exam (and courses exempt from exams)
- Input data into computer program
- Obtain lists for class sizes
- Schedule for minimum overlapping, same-day, and consecutive-day exams
- Design, verify, print, reproduce, and post exam schedule for students
- Design, print, and circulate exam and proctoring schedule to faculty
- Book rooms with booking office; inform campus police
- Record arrival of exams from professors and verify conformity to standards
- Hire part-time staff as necessary
- Designate presiding officers for major exam locations
- Schedule proctors according to university policy
- Collect all exams; arrange for printing
- Report unsubmitted exams to professor's dean
- Package (with clear labels) and securely store printed exams
- Coordinate preparation of exam rooms with campus police and maintenance department
- Design seating plans for optimal communication and student flow
- Arrange layout of all exam supplies, including attendance and other record forms
- Arrange for special supplies, from computer forms to pianos
- Arrange to deliver exams and supplies to off-campus locations
- Pay for use of off-campus facilities and external proctors
- Arrange for accommodation of disabled and double-booked students
- Arrange for sick or no-show proctors, and unexpected student handicaps
- After exam: arrange for pick-up, storage, and delivery of answers and both used and unused question sets
- Restore exam rooms to normal configuration
- Arrange for deferred exams for students granted alternate sitting
- Maintain budgetary records for all examination expenses
- Field inquiries and complaints from faculty and students
- Report problems and suggestions to supervisor
- Prepare for next exam session

FIGURE 5.1 Job inventory, university examinations supervisor

that successful incumbents consider to be relevant. These elements are generally derived by surveying a group of employees. Figure 5.1 shows an inventory for a university examinations supervisor position.

WHO SHOULD BE TRAINED?

Industrial training is historically associated with the new employee. However, the modern approach differentiates between *orientation,* which is reserved for the newcomer, and *training,* which should take place whenever necessary on a career-long basis. This approach avoids the term "retraining," which implies that ordinarily a worker is trained once, but occasionally will have to be trained again for a different position.

In the past, a business could be passed down through generations, hardly changing from one lifetime to another. Currently, the rate of change is so much faster that, in order to survive, any business may have to undergo radical alterations from one decade to another. Moreover, in the past, if a major change required a new personnel mix, employee changes could be effected simply and deftly. Today, however, the longer a worker has been on the payroll, the more difficult it may be to dismiss that employee. It is no longer permissible to fire a typist because you would rather have a word-processor operator. The most common solution is to train an existing employee to perform the new task.

There are other benefits to promoting a climate that favors the learning of new skills; they all relate to flexibility. Employees who have mastered the greatest number of tasks are the most valuable to the employer, because they have the ability to *float,* that is, to lend a hand where needed. Flexible workers such as these may elect to interchange some of their tasks among themselves, thus decreasing monotony.

Finally, learning facilitates further learning. A worker who has already mastered a variety of tasks can be expected to acquire new skills in the future relatively easily. The ability to learn increasingly faster as a result of experience with learning is termed *learning set*, and this topic will be covered later in the chapter.

WHO SHOULD TRAIN?

Ideally, throughout their career, all employees should have a skilled and dedicated training specialist assigned to them. In practice, however, training is typically handled like this: "Welcome to the line; we're putting you next to Dana, our lead worker. You just watch Dana for a while, start when you're ready, ask if you have a question, and Dana will keep an eye on you."

Leaving the training up to good old Dana may invite problems. Primarily, the best *worker* may not be the best *trainer*. Also, whoever is chosen may resent having to dilute work-related efforts to spend time on the learner. Conversely, the mentor may be unwilling to share tips and secrets acquired over a lifetime of work experience. And other coworkers may resent not having been chosen themselves, inasmuch as the role of teacher or trainer implies a higher status.

A primary requirement of the trainer is to establish realistic *expectations* on the part of the learners. Tannenbaum, Mathieu, Salas, and Cannon-Bowers (1991) surveyed almost 700 U.S. Navy recruits on their expectations before and after a training program. There was a high correlation between the extent to which their expectations were met and their posttraining motivation to succeed in the navy, their feelings of self-efficacy or competence, and their commitment to the navy.

TRAINING PRINCIPLES
FROM LEARNING THEORY

How easily do you learn? This, of course, depends on many factors, such as how much you already know about the topic, how interested you are in it, how the material to be learned is presented to you, and on your state of mind at that moment. It also depends on what is meant by "learned." That term could mean *do you recognize having been exposed to the material?*, or it might mean *can you repeat everything word for word?* If learning can range from efficient to deficient and from partial to thorough just within yourself, imagine how much it varies from one person to another. In this section, we address the principles responsible for these differences.

The psychological variable that has the most impact on learning is *motivation*. Employees should preferably be selected for their interest in mastering the topic at hand, and the instructor should make it as interesting as possible. **Feedback** and **reinforcement** enhance motivation.

"I don't think we should say anything."

Feedback refers to the reporting of progress. *Positive reinforcement* refers to making the learner feel good about the process. Where progress is taking place, feedback itself is a reinforcer. Reinforcement could result from encouragement: a "pat on the back" or a progress report.

Most information is learned in a **serial** fashion. That is, Fact 1 is mastered, then Fact 2, then Fact 3, in a series. In such cases, the position of the material to be learned influences how easily it is absorbed. The items at the beginning and end of a list are most easily learned. Those positioned toward the center are the hardest to remember, so they should attract the most attention of learner and instructor.

Material that is *logical* or *meaningful* to the learner is absorbed much more quickly and easily than that which has to be rote memorized. Thus, merely presenting the material may be inadequate. For instance, if the instructor announced, "Never install a piston unless it's miked down a thou; did you get that?" the learners' affirmative nods may have meant that they heard the instruction, and from rereading their notes they will memorize it. It may not have meant that they understood it.

Learning must be *effortful.* During the initial presentation, the learners must attend and concentrate, even though the topics of their daydreams may be more captivating. During the learning, the material should be rehearsed slowly enough that the **short-term memory** is not loaded beyond its capacity of about seven items. Most of what we learn is needed only for the immediate moment. The location where you just put down your pencil, the position of your gaze at each moment of reading, the location of an itch—these need to be remembered for only a few seconds. A separate system, the *short-term memory,* handles these minutiae.

The process of what we generally refer to as *learning* is actually a conversion from short-term to **long-term memory**. This conversion is termed **consolidation**. *Effort* is needed to consolidate the material. This can be accomplished by rewording or repeating the material, not passively or mindlessly, but actively, by thinking about it.

The *blocks of time* that are scheduled for learning can influence its effectiveness. Generally, longer blocks of time should be scheduled for intelligent learners and global or problem-oriented material. Conversely, when the learners are intellectually limited, and when the tasks to be learned are more sensorimotor than problem oriented, shorter time blocks are more effective.

Which is more important, speed or accuracy? The *initial* emphasis should be on *accuracy.* It is not unusual for a trainer to have to ask newcomers to slow down. But whether the entire task should be presented at once, or as separate subunits to be mastered individually, depends on several factors. Some components do not make sense in isolation but only within a group, so they should not be separated. A compromise is to offer **progressive part training**, in which the instructor trains Task 1, then Tasks 1 and 2, next Tasks 1 to 3, and so on.

Transfer

It is sometimes easy to forget that, unlike education, work training is not an end in itself. Its purpose is to ensure that the job demands are met. This application of the training to the job is termed **transfer**. Not only should the training program run effectively, but there should be maximal transfer

So what Do you know classmates who get higher marks than you yet apparently put less time and effort into their work? Maybe they study smarter, not harder. Also, how you select your courses and how you study for them can make a difference in how much you learn for the effort you invest. For instance, if you intend to take several courses in languages, social sciences, and mathematics, it's better to spread them out one per year than to take several at the same time so that one doesn't interfere with the other. Learning is increasingly seen as a lifelong venture, so you are likely to be able to apply the above principles of learning theory throughout your education and career.

to the job itself. This is facilitated when the training resembles the work, and when ample practice takes place.

When skills learned in training are indeed carried over to the job itself, this is termed **positive transfer**. If the training *impedes* the job itself, this is termed **negative transfer**. Negative transfer usually stems from some life experience rather than from job training. Here's an example. As you know, vehicles steer with the front wheels. The exception is a lift truck, which may have to lift immense weights over the front wheels, so the less-stressed rear wheels have to do the steering. Because a rear-steer vehicle responds with subtle but critical differences compared to a front-steer one, a person with years of automobile driving experience may have more difficulty operating a lift truck than someone unfamiliar with cars.

More specifically, *transfer* takes place whenever one task affects the learning of another, either by **facilitation** or by **inhibition**. *Facilitation* and *inhibition* are the same as positive and negative transfer. Let's look at these important terms more closely.

Consider a person learning Task A followed by Task B. If A influences B, the effect is termed **proactive** because the influence is forward in time. If B affects A, the effect is **retroactive**, signifying backward in time. Thus, there are four possible transfer effects, namely, *proactive facilitation, proactive inhibition, retroactive facilitation,* and *retroactive inhibition.* The term learning set is more specifically termed proactive facilitation. The four transfer effects are illustrated in Figure 5.2.

The last term to introduce is **learning set**, which refers to the acquisition of generalized abilities or knowledge. Here's an example. Suppose you have to assign one of your managers to learn German quickly, prior to taking over the Berlin branch. Your candidates are Pat, who knows some French as a

TRANSFER	EFFECT	EXAMPLE		
Proactive Facilitation	A improves B	A Bike	B Tractor	
Proactive Inhibition	A impedes B	A Bike	B Forklift	
Retroactive Facilitation	B improves A	A Tractor	B Car	A Tractor
Retroactive Inhibition	B impedes A	A Car	B Forklift	A Car

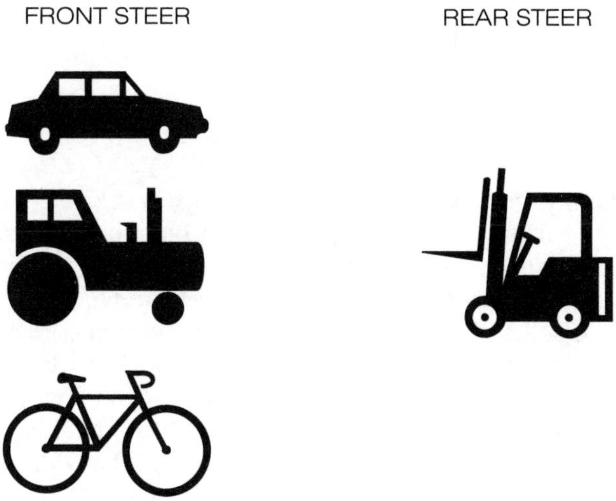

FRONT STEER   REAR STEER

FIGURE 5.2 The four kinds of transfer

The experience of driving a car would help you to learn how to drive
a bike or a tractor but would impede your training to operate a forklift.

second language; Jan, whose only language is English; and Val, who knows
five languages, but not German.

According to learning theory, Jan would be better than Pat, because
Pat's French vocabulary could interfere with the study of German due to
retroactive inhibition. But Val, who has mastered five languages, has formed
a proclivity for languages, known as a *learning set*, and would therefore be

the best choice to learn German efficiently. Learning set is another term for *positive transfer*. In this case it would be *proactive facilitation*, as the experience with five languages would facilitate the study of a sixth.

INDUSTRIAL TRAINING MEDIA

The menu of instructional media offers a richness and variety that few firms exploit in their training programs. There is no ideal technique for any situation; every procedure presents assets and defects. The choices can be based upon past experience, resources, trainee characteristics, and the nature of the task to be mastered. In our survey of the various media for industrial training, we'll start with the technique that is no doubt dearest to the heart of college and university students, the lecture.

The lecture

In a lecture, the information is presented "live" from the voice of one person to the ears of the listeners. The lecturer should be apparent visually as well as auditorily. Of course, a lecture can be combined with another format, as when it is presented through a recording, film, or typescript, but in the absence of a live speaker, the format should not be termed *lecture.*

If a lecture hall is so overcrowded that you have to listen to the talk over a public-address system in an adjoining hall, are you attending a lecture? No, you are listening to something similar to a radio broadcast, because you are deprived of both eye contact and feelings of intimacy and immediacy.

The lecture is the oldest of the formal instructional formats, because originally there was no alternative. It has remained the most common and traditional medium of instruction. Lectures offer powerful advantages:

• The human element provides the greatest potential for attracting audience attention.

• The lecture is the most traditional form of systematic communication; hence, newcomers *expect* to be talked at. Accordingly, training generally should *start* with the spoken word and aim not only to orient the newcomer, but also to instill pride and confidence in the industry, the firm, and the position.

• Another important advantage of the lecture is the opportunity for audience *feedback*. Feedback here refers to the smiles, frowns, and gestures of puzzlement, despair, boredom, or interest, which listeners may signal to an observant speaker.

• A lecture usually benefits from a staged social event quality, in that it incorporates an audience effect similar to a theatrical presentation or a religious service. The first words of the speaker constitute an event in a way that no opening of a book or pressing the START button of a teaching machine can duplicate. A charismatic or technically skilled lecturer can maintain interest more effectively than most alternatives.

• The range of speech dynamics exceeds the potential for differential emphasis afforded by the printed page. Furthermore, the speaker controls the flow of material, which can be an advantage in demonstrating a dynamic sequence.

Although lectures offer powerful benefits, they are subject to more problems than any other medium:

• The most serious drawback is that they are not efficient. It can be argued that a lecturer could, at a moment's notice and with no equipment or preparation, address an audience, and that therefore this is efficient. However, most lecturers invest considerable time in preparing their talks.

• Also, the more effective the lecturer, the higher the lecturer's fee and the larger the audience; the larger the audience, the more this format loses its advantages.

• Lecturers speak usually at 100 to 150 words per minute. One estimate puts the maximum speech rate that permits note taking at 135 words per minute. But listeners, unless they use shorthand, rarely write faster than 50 words per minute. Consequently, they have to devote so much attention to making their abbreviated record that they are often prevented from absorbing the flow of points.

• Consider the following sequence: The speaker starts with a written draft of the lecture material. The listeners, while under some tension, are obliged to "get" every point, and presumably convert all of them into their notes. If they are dedicated they will later try to convert their notes into an approximation of the speaker's original material. But listeners are not able to *consolidate* or reprocess the material while making notes, so they may find it hard to understand either the notes or the lecture points. And if these are put aside for a few days, the task may prove impossible. Clearly, it would be more efficient if the speaker had distributed copies of the original written draft of the lecture instead of essentially dictating it.

• Another weakness is that lectures are constrained by time schedules. It is the length of a symphony that determines how long the audience will listen to it, but the length of a lecture is usually determined by the time allocated for it. What if the lecturer finishes early or needs more time? Another timing problem is that most skilled speakers try to adopt a pace that is suitable for the slower members of the audience. This practice often frustrates and bores the others, who may not understand the reason for the slow pace.

• Because of its transitory nature, nobody generally hears a lecture except the students for whom it is designed. Such an audience is not in a strategic position to criticize the content or to point out errors. Accordingly, considerably more care can be expected in the preparation and delivery of a nonlecture presentation.

• Finally, the human aspects of the lecture can be distracting. Listeners may focus more on the speaker's clothing or delivery and speech mannerisms.

Print

Just as the words that you are presently reading could be read aloud to you by a lecturer, so can the content of a lecture be converted to the printed page. The main media of university instruction are the lecture and the page. The two formats show considerable contrast. The print medium offers attractive benefits:

• The lecture presents the material for a fleeting moment only; the printed page is permanent. Also, pages can contain considerable material in a small amount of physical space; the spoken word does not meaningfully exist in physical space. Thus, reference material—content that does not necessarily have to be memorized, but that does have to be accessible, such as company policy statements, trouble-shooting guides, telephone directories—must be printed.

• The main advantage of the written form is its *efficiency*. The production, multicopy reproduction, and distribution of printed materials are low-cost and fast. This medium is efficient also for the learner. People typically read at the rate of 100 to 500 words per minute, depending on their skill, the density of the material, and the purpose of the reading. (The term "speed reading" is usually reserved for rates above 500 words per minute.) This chapter will take about a half hour to read. The same content presented in lectures requires three hours.

• Words in written form are more accurate and specific. Most speakers encumber their presentations with repetitions, mannerisms such as interjections ("um"), and hesitations. Material that is well-written contains no waste.

• Written material can be manipulated physically by the learner. For instance, material that is peripheral or already known can be crossed out, and the more useful or difficult content can be underlined or highlighted. More importantly, the printed word can be manipulated mentally. Readers can choose their own pace, they can reread sections, and they can pause to think about what they have read. Most learning takes place in this "thinking about" or consolidation phase. *Consolidation* refers to the progression from short-term to long-term memory.

• Written material presents the clearest *organization*. Aids such as titles, headings, paragraphs, and punctuation are more convenient for the writer than for the speaker. Also, writing is often less ambiguous than speaking. (A student once asked me to check her lecture notes. I puzzled over "jockey top 2 poor eye-cue," until I reconstructed my words, which were, "Chalk it up to pure IQ".)

• Finally, text pages can be supplemented with professionally prepared *illustrations* that clarify the points. In clarity, then, the print medium may surpass the spoken word.

Unfortunately, print bears a number of disadvantages:

• People who make decisions about printed material are, virtually by definition, themselves highly literate. Accordingly, they may lose sight of the number of people who cannot effectively handle written material. The 1992 National Adult Literacy Survey of the U.S. Department of Education has some interesting implications for employers. If the workforce fairly represents the U.S. adult population, one-fifth of them may not be able to read simple safety instructions, and another quarter can barely cope with basic written information.

The situation is slightly worse in Canada. According to a 1987 study (the *Southam News survey* of some 2,400 Canadians), 2 million employed Canadians (one in six) have low literacy levels. Their deficiency does not seem to cause them much distress. Few of them think they need help with reading and writing on the job, and of these, fewer still would consider taking remedial instruction. And these individuals are twice as likely as those with higher literacy levels to feel that reading and writing on the job are not important.

The occupations held by individuals in the lowest literacy levels reflect the general pattern of the Canadian workforce. This means that they are *not* concentrated in occupations immune from on-the-job training. Clearly, then, the printed page should be offered only to those who can make use of it.

• Even for those who can read well, printed material can present problems. For instance, learning does not take place during moments of inattention. During a lecture, daydreaming is common, but it is usually sporadic, due to the dynamics of the presentation. But it is quite possible to force one's eyes to read every word on the page while one's attention is elsewhere.

- Moreover, there is usually more pressure to attend the lecture, because of its public and formal nature, than there is to open the book or training manual in private. The less motivated and the less professional the learner, the less the instructor can rely on the printed page being read.

- Most textual material is not formatted for optimal reading ease. For instance, newspaper columns are designed for compactness and flexibility; they are too short for ease of reading and the print is too small for most older readers. Textbooks and training manuals often adopt a format that is too crowded for comfortable reading.

- Finally, some learners regard written material as drier and less interesting than lectured content, and many are intimidated by the appearance of a large book.

Film and television

Training films were first used extensively by the U.S. military during World War II, and industry slowly adopted this medium thereafter. Since the 1970s, the television set has been gradually replacing the movie screen, especially for smaller audiences. Currently, the "how-to" *video* is becoming almost as common as the "how-to" *book*. (There are many associated formats, such as transparency slides, overhead projection transparencies, flip charts, and film strips, but these usually serve as ancillaries to another medium. Consequently, "screen" as used below will mean television or motion pictures only.)

When what is displayed on the screen consists of nothing more than a close-up of the lecturer, all the pros and cons of the lecture apply, except that this form of presentation lacks the human element. Because the latter was the strongest advantage of the lecture medium, we could conclude that a so-called talking head presented on a screen is a poor teaching device. Conversely, the best of all lecturers can prepare a flawless presentation and preserve it on film or tape for any number of showings. And if the alternative to watching a close-up of an expressive speaker on a large screen is sitting in the last row of a crowded auditorium, the screen presentation could be preferable.

The prime advantage of screen presentations is the potential for **special effects**, especially those involving motion. Sequences can be shown speeded up, slowed down, or can be intermittently stopped. Diagrams or animations can be included or superimposed, and the camera lens can **zoom** in or out. (A zoom lens permits the camera to apparently move toward and away from the object being photographed.) The editor can sequence the scenes with techniques known as laps, fades, dissolves, fast-cuts, and present multiple images with split screens.

Unlike a live demonstration, a screen can conveniently show the **subjective camera angle**. Consider how you would teach the tying of complex knots. Even if you repeatedly demonstrated tying the knots, the audience would be watching your demonstration from their view. But when they tried to replicate the knot, they would see their own rope from the opposite view, that is, they have to translate the *objective* view seen in the demonstration into the *subjective* view seen when they start tying. If the camera operator filmed the demonstration by aiming the lens over the instructor's shoulder, the screen would show the sequence the way it would appear to the learner.

The screen can portray events more *realistically* than other media. Whether for illustrating operational hazards, or for inducing emotional responses as in propaganda films, the screen can evoke a high level of identification and involvement.

On the other hand, acquiring the hardware to show filmic material is expensive. Commissioning the software (the films) can be even more costly. Modifying or updating the material is difficult with photographic film, but less so with videotape. Neither can compare to the ease of altering lectures or making occasional changes on the printed page. Thus, where training is infrequent, or where changes are routine, the screen is not the most practical medium.

Another weakness concerns *audience expectations*. When the screen lights up, there may be such a strong association with being entertained that the viewers have difficulty in switching to a learning mode. If all that is presented on the screen is a close-up of a speaker, reverie may replace note taking.

Motion picture equipment is not highly portable, and considerable electrical power is needed to operate it. Obviously, this medium is not always ideal for training in the field. Finally, people may not associate watching a screen with making notes, and if the cinematic techniques are distracting, the audience may be too captivated to record the points.

Trainers and simulators

Operators of complex machinery are often initially trained on a training replica instead of on the actual equipment. Picture the task of showing a trainee how to operate a highway truck tractor towing two trailers. Which way should the driver turn the steering wheel to back the three-unit assembly to the right? How much should the steering input either *lead* or *lag* the movement of the tractor as it reverses? Instead of reserving a $100,000 rig for training, a trucking firm could have the trainee acquire the "feel" by operating a toy truck hitched to tandem wagons.

FIGURE 5.3 A trainer: a low-cost vehicle hitched to tandem wagons

Or consider training a crew to dock a ship. A 10-foot long, battery-operated model boat would make a useful, low-cost, and safe training vehicle. Similarly, air traffic control trainees can practice with toy airplanes manipulated by rods over a model of an airport, to learn the relation between two-dimensional radar displays and the three-dimensional traffic it represents.

In short, **trainers** are practical low-cost substitutes for the real thing, designed to emphasize specific operational problems associated with complex equipment. A trainer is illustrated in Figure 5.3.

A **simulator** is an elaborate version of a trainer. When using a trainer, operators know they are in a toy-like device, but this is not so with a simulator. Because a simulator may cost more than the equipment it replicates, it is appropriate only for training operators in the use of expensive and dangerous machinery.

As examples, the flight crews of jet aircraft are routinely trained and checked on a simulator in which most components are identical to those actually used on the airplane. The simulated cockpit, which is supplemented with a three-axis motion carriage coordinated with audiovisual displays, makes the simulation hours closely equivalent to flight time. In fact, simulated flight is *more* useful for crew preparation than actual flight. Any combination of conditions—with emphasis on emergency sequences—can be programmed into the simulator by the training personnel, and the pilot's performance is recorded for later analysis.

A simulator for a 4-engine jet plane costs about $5 million, which is more than the price of the cockpit it represents. But the real aircraft costs ten times more, and it would be impractically dangerous and expensive to use one for the training of emergency procedures.

Simulators are mainly associated with aviation and aerospace applications. Apart from classroom training, the only way an astronaut can learn to handle a spacecraft is via simulator drills. In fact, without the availability of this equipment, the space program as we know it would have been impossible. Astronauts are trained in simulators that are so faithful to the operational equipment that the simulators themselves are capable of space flight.

Apart from aerospace applications, another use of simulators is for training nuclear power generating station personnel. The worst disaster associated with a nuclear power station, which took place at Chernobyl in Ukraine, has been attributed to the fact that none of the operators on duty had been exposed to computer simulations of mishap procedures. (Apparently, when they tried on their own to practice responses to emergencies, the reactor got out of hand.)

Simulators exploit the benefits of the film and videotape medium, especially in cockpit window displays that are computer-linked to the responses of the operator on the controls. The value of this combination of media is seen in the fact that all major airlines require periodic simulator checkouts for the flight crew. These experiences are so realistic that trainees have become airsick and even fainted in a simulated disaster.

The advantage that trainers and simulators have over the media discussed above is that they facilitate *active* rather than *passive* learning. In addition, they are *situational* rather than theoretical, and they are used to focus on the most *critical* aspects of operation.

The above indicates that simulators are ideal as an instructional medium. Their only disadvantages are that they are largely limited to sensori-motor tasks, and that they are very expensive to purchase, maintain, and operate. One type of simulator is drawn in Figure 5.4.

Virtual reality and tele-robotics An aviation simulator teaches the trainee what to do in response to signals from the instruments on the panel, the pictures on the windscreen, and instructions through earphones. All the while, of course, the trainee is strapped into a seat in the mock-up cockpit, looking straight ahead. But suppose the purpose of the training is to teach a firefighter how to navigate the corridors in a burning building. If one trainee makes left turns and another turns right, how can the simulated picture of the passageways keep up with all these movement variations? And when corridors intersect, how can the simulator show the view to the left, right, and straight ahead as the trainee looks in those directions?

In 1966, Ivan Sutherland put on a bulky helmet he had suspended from a ceiling in a laboratory at the Massachusetts Institute of Technology. Inside the headpiece was a device that showed an imaginary scene. When he turned

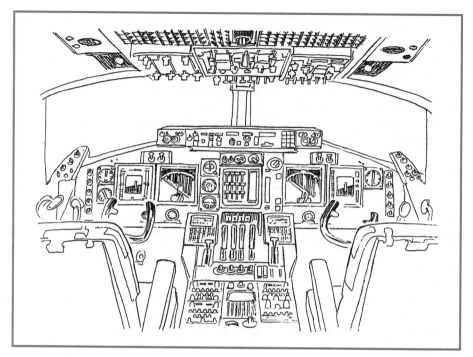

FIGURE 5.4 A simulator: a fully equipped cockpit

his head left and right, the scene in the helmet showed the view, although grainy and low resolution, to the left and right. That technology rapidly expanded and now displays computer-generated, three-dimensional scenes inside a lightweight, free-moving headpiece. Sensors can be attached to the operator's hands, which are then also shown in realistic motion in the headset. When the displayed scene is faithfully interactive with the motions of the person, it's termed **virtual reality** because of the realism experienced by the user.

Virtual reality is best known as an entertainment device, but it's being adapted for training. For instance, at the National Aeronautic and Space Administration's (NASA) Ames Research Center near San Francisco, you can don a helmet, gloves, and body suit, and reach down to the floor. Inside your wraparound three-dimensional-display goggles, what you see is the surface of Mars. You can seemingly pick up a rock, throw it, and walk over and pick it up again.

In another lab, researchers are working on the Telepresence Remotely Operated Vehicle (TROV), a versatile robotic device based on the new science of **tele-robotics**. This refers to a robot that interacts closely, naturally, and realistically with the operator. The TROV has three-dimensional cameras that move in response to the operator's head motions and show the resulting scene. It also has a robotic arm and hand that mimic the movements of the operator's arm and hand.

Students immerse themselves in a computer-generated world where they ride a virtual glass elevator over the open lobby of a high-rise hotel. They conquer their fear of heights without leaving the floor of the laboratory.

Tele-robots are used for exploration and manipulation as well as for training. They can locate, pick up, and dispose of a bomb; bring a water hose right up to a fire and aim it; and patrol premises for security purposes. One has explored an active volcano in Alaska, and the latest versions will likely explore planets long before people land on them. More details are in Reichhardt (1994).

Job performance

On-the-job training is the oldest and simplest training procedure. It remains the most common medium in the workplace, because in the absence of alternate provisions, the actual performance of the work constitutes the only training for it.

Job performance as a training procedure can be practical where (a) the worker is motivated and competent, (b) the job requirements are simple, self-evident, and noncritical, (c) suitable basic guidance is available, and (d) the principles of **active learning** (learning by doing) are important. This procedure, then, could be ideal for the training of a materials handler, a carton filler, or a chicken plucker, but not for a bus driver or a financial vice president.

The new employee typically looks forward to starting work and contributing to the organization. Having just completed or dropped out of school, this person is probably eager to work rather than return to a classroom. From the instructor's perspective, allowing the novice to start right in typically yields *positive transfer, active practice,* and *useful feedback* on performance. From the company's viewpoint, on-the-job training involves a minimum expense, integrates the new worker into the operations immediately, and may yield some payback on the first day.

On the other hand, a sink-or-swim introduction may induce apprehension or fear. The worker may develop improper techniques that become ingrained. And where the novice must function as part of a team, the others may resent having to "carry" the newcomer. Note that the advantages are attractive and visible; the disadvantages are more subtle and hidden.

A variant of job performance is **job rotation**. Here, the novice performs a variety of jobs in succession. Managerial trainees may spend a year in each of various divisions and assume full responsibility in each; lower-level ones may spend an hour learning different operations, merely getting the feel of the work. The objectives are to give trainees a broad perspective of the entire organization, to introduce them to a variety of colleagues, and to enhance their personal development.

It may not be realistic to throw a novice into a complex or responsible role. One useful modification is job shadowing, also known as understudy assignments. The trainee "shadows" another employee, watching and listening like an understudy for a theatrical role, and asking questions. Training may consist of a combination of job rotation and shadowing, with the trainee serving as a special assistant to the incumbent. The use of job rotation especially for managerial training is described in detail by Beatty, Schneier, and McEvoy (1987).

Vestibule school

Is there a way of combining some of the advantages of the above two training methods? One could establish a small training area within a plant, where distractions such as noise are reduced, where the equipment is a simpler version of the production units, where the instructor is chosen for teaching ability, and where the atmosphere is realistic but not intimidating for the trainee. This is a description of the **vestibule school** (vestibulum is Latin for entrance hall).

The vestibule school is highly effective for training workers in semi-skilled operations, as well as for evaluating their progress. Often, it provides a practical repository for simpler, outdated, or partly-worn versions of current equipment. The school can be used to train the new employee for a variety of tasks in order to determine which is the most suitable, and it serves to retrain or refresh the "old hands." When not in use for training, it can be used to build prototypes or perhaps to try new production procedures. The costs involved are "up front," not hidden.

However, it is expensive to maintain all the space, equipment, and people resources that support the school. Also, the vestibule school is typically designed to process only one or a few trainees at a time.

Apprenticeship

The oldest structured training system is an **apprenticeship** where a young trainee enters into a formal arrangement (often a legal contract) with an older, skilled worker, on a part-student, part-assistant basis. Contracts surviving from medieval times indicate that the apprentice could also be part servant and part adopted child, moving into the mentor's home for some years under a contract between the master and the apprentice's parents.

"The Sorcerer's Apprentice" is more than a colorful legend; sorcerers did exist, and they did take on apprentices. So did artists like Rembrandt, artisans like Stradivari, and common cobblers and stonemasons. Graduated apprentices are termed "journeymen," from the French *jour* (day), referring to the fact that such specialists would be paid by the day's work rather than by salary or contract.

What determines whether or not a trade will participate in the apprenticeship system? Modern apprenticeship programs are associated with trades that not only require substantial skill and knowledge, but are also concerned with public safety. Musicians may have undergone years of training, but because playing a wrong note is unlikely to cause injury, no apprenticeship program is available for them. As for professionals such as dentists, incompetence is rare, because of the prior training and the subsequent monitoring by their professional associations.

It is for tradespersons such as welders, steamfitters, vehicle mechanics, electricians, and plumbers that the state or province establishes and enforces elaborate apprenticeship regulations, often in conjunction with the respective industry and union representatives. The work of the apprentice-related trades tends to be more hidden from view than that of skilled trades that do not have an apprenticeship program.

The program typically lasts from two to four years, and combines classroom and hands-on experience. The latter is supervised by a journeyman, who must in turn answer to the regulatory authorities. The journeyman must pay the apprentice a stipulated amount, which increases from about half of the journeyman rate at the outset, to about three-quarters in the final year. The journeyman is obliged to provide the apprentice with a stipulated variety of experience and is limited in the number of apprentices he may contract with at a time.

The apprenticeship system offers a practical inducement to both apprentice and journeyman. The apprentice enjoys a comprehensive and real-life training program, which may offer contacts or partnership opportunities for the future, and receives some payment from the start. The journeyman benefits from low-cost help (it's increasingly common for the government to subsidize a portion of the apprentice's wages) and from an eager youngster dedicated to pursuing that trade.

However, a journeyman may perceive an apprentice as a bargain-wage laborer, who is assigned the least-desirable tasks. Thus, a mason's apprentice may spend all year carrying bricks, in violation of the regulation stipulating task variety. Or, in a tool-and-die shop the jobs in hand may require lathe operation only, even though the apprentice is supposed to be learning to operate a milling machine. The spirit of the rule limiting the journeyman/apprentice ratio can similarly be violated, when, for instance, a tradesperson teams with a retired silent partner to double the permitted number of apprentices.

A would-be apprentice must first apply to a journeyman, a requirement that may easily lead to discrimination. For instance, women and minority group members are grossly underrepresented in the skilled trades. Although one explanation is the scarcity of such applicants, another factor surely is the reluctance of journeymen to accept nontraditional individuals as apprentices.

Because the apprenticeship system typically involves various complex bureaucracies, there is the possibility of *inertia* and *inflexibility*. For instance, training curricula may fail to reflect advances in the trades. Many apprentices complain that much of the class material they are required to learn is irrelevant to the trade being taught. (It has been argued that housing costs are high partly because the building trades discourage changes such as freer access to apprenticeship positions, simplified apprentice training, and construction innovations like factory-produced modules.)

In a typical 4-year program, the apprentice spends the first half performing mostly background, maintenance, or set-up work. Could a fast learner with prior experience bypass some of this basic training? In some cases, no. In others, the reduction must be recommended by the journeyman, who would thereby lose some benefit. Another problem concerns apprentices who change residence; not all jurisdictions recognize credits earned elsewhere.

North American industrialists complain about a shortage of applicants for many skilled trades and blame it on the lack of apprenticeship programs compared with other nations. For instance, about 6 percent of the Austrian, German, and Swiss workforce is involved in apprenticeship. The rate for Canada is only 1 percent; for the United States it is 0.3 percent (Ruebens & Harrison, 1980).

Sensitivity training group

The **Training Group, T-Group**, or **Sensitivity Training Group** is a procedure for training people to interact smoothly with others. It grew out of the realization that people often demonstrated more skill in handling their machines, tools, flowcharts, and production projections than they showed in handling their managers, coworkers, and especially their subordinates.

The T-Group did not evolve from industry or education, but from psychotherapy. Psychiatrists and clinical psychologists found that many of their clients were suffering not from mental illness but from an inability to interact constructively with other people. To help these patients by converting the one-on-one therapy session into a course on interpersonal skills would have been expensive, ineffectual, and perhaps a violation of psychotherapy principles.

Rather, a few clients were assembled to experience the small-group dynamics that would eventuate, and to interpret interactional styles under the guidance of a professional. In particular, the group members would learn how to increase their sensitivity to the feelings and unspoken wishes of the others. The T-Group has become an interpersonal skills training procedure in its own right, no longer confined to the psychotherapist's office.

The procedure is simple. A group of about six persons sits in a circle with the leader. The conversation may flow without guidance, or it may be somewhat focused by the leader. Eventually, the members learn how to express their feelings effectively, how to object constructively, and how to recognize emotional reactions in themselves and in the others. They may find out, perhaps for the first time, exactly how their social behavior is *perceived* by others.

This is only a generalization; there are a dozen variants, such as Transactional Analysis, Gestalt Therapy, and Marathon Encounter. Many group programs have been designed for business managers and executives. Some programs use techniques of group simulation, such as **role-playing** or **role reversal.** For instance, individuals who annoy each other may each be asked to take on the role of the other person and thereby gain empathy for the other's thoughts and emotions.

T-Groups are useful because they address the most pervasive problem in many organizations, that of inept interactions. When the group comprises industrialists, the topic designated for the group conversation might be some specific, ongoing problem. In this way, not only should the members acquire social skills, but the task orientation may itself serve a practical outcome.

T-Groups should be effective because they rely on *active participation.* Attending a lecture or reading a book may suffice for learning to design a transportation schedule. But in order to learn to fly an aircraft, a novice requires supervised hands-on training because of the complexity of the process and the need for machine-operator feedback. People are more complex than aircraft, so it is unlikely that handling skills can be derived from a book. The T-Group provides a *situational drill,* offering both firsthand experiential and secondhand or observational exposure to the problems and solutions of personal interactions. Many participants report that the experience was not only illuminating but also stimulating, and that the skills learned in the group carried over into relations with family and community.

The downside is that T-Groups are surrounded by potential pitfalls. The success depends largely on the trust and goodwill of the participants. But groups are typically established in order to solve interactional problems— hence in an atmosphere of mistrust and ill will. Success is also a function of the leader's skill. However, there are no apprenticeship or university credentials in group leadership, and there are no restrictions on who can be a group leader. As the principles of group sessions became generally known, unqualified people representing themselves as T-Group experts have offered their services to the public and to corporations. This is unfortunate because the responsibility of the leader is extraordinary.

Comments and conversations within a group session are supposed to be spontaneous expression of feelings that expose interactional shortcomings. Rules are established at the outset to facilitate this freedom and to protect members from its effects. One such rule is that members should not allow any residues from the meetings to contaminate their outside feelings or behavior. But inside the protected confines of the group, one can tell associates or bosses what one thinks of them. This is liable to shatter goodwill, egos, and relationships.

In a group the members gradually learn and adopt the terminology of sensitivity training. "I understand your point" becomes "I hear you," and "I want to say this" becomes "I'd like to share this with you." Although the specialized language may help smooth interactions within the group, it could impede communication when applied outside the group. In role-playing exercises, participants may place more emphasis on their acting performance than on trying to experience the feelings, or they may perceive the activity as demeaning or silly.

Participants often find it easy to adjust to the conventions of a training group. But the objective is to *transfer* the interactional skills to the real world outside the group, and this is not always successful.

Training conference, case, and games methods

In a **training conference**, a group the same size as for a T-Group is assembled with an instructor. The objective of this group meeting is not to explore feelings, emotions, and relationships, but to solve a specific, real-life problem through discussion among the members under the guidance of the instructor.

In the **training case** an actual or a made-up but realistic case is presented to group members, who are usually at the managerial level. They are asked to analyze and propose solutions for the case problems. In the original procedure developed at the Harvard University School of Business, the learners ponder and research the case individually, then discuss it in a group under the guidance of a trainer. The rationale is that in the group sessions the learners see that there's often no single ideal solution, and that compromises have to be resolved through consensus.

A variant of the training case is the **incident process**, the presentation of a single incident rather than an integrated case. Here the trainer typically has formulated a specific solution to the given incident, and guides the learners toward discovering it.

A **business game** is actually a simulation. It's called a game because the trainees are typically separated into two imaginary business situations that are described in detail, and the two teams compete and interact in a realistic way. In a simulated office setting but under the eye of the instructor (sometimes a group of instructors), the teams have to apportion responsibility, set priorities, solve problems, and carry out decisions. But each decision might be countered by a response from the competing team. As in a chess game, time is limited and pressure is high.

The rationale of the business game is that if management trainees make mistakes in a simulation, these will not be repeated in real situations. Another objective is to let potential managers experience the type of complex and frustrating stresses that go with the job.

A number of well-designed games are available, and they are widely used. Thornton and Cleveland (1990) mention that these simulations are used for management training in most of the major U.S. corporations.

Courses in academic settings

Most major corporations are located in urban areas that have not only secondary or high schools but postsecondary educational institutions as well. Remedial training in basic school subjects is generally offered by high schools at no charge, and most postsecondary institutions have courses that may be relevant to the job situation.

The person in charge of corporate training should be aware of these offerings, and should form liaisons with local educational institutions. Most colleges and universities offer programs such as continuing education, lifelong learning, or part-time studies. Courses in these programs are often scheduled for evenings or Saturdays. Many forward-looking companies encourage their employees to upgrade their academic qualifications, offering time off work where necessary. Often, the tuition for approved university courses is rebated after a suitable grade is earned, or, where necessary, the fee is paid in advance.

Programmed instruction

The last of the training media used in industry is termed variously automated trainer, teaching machine, computer-aided (or assisted) instruction, autoinstructional device, or programmed learning procedures. We will refer to it as **programmed instruction**.

A book or manual can be read passively and thus not absorbed at all. It can be read actively but entirely misunderstood. Unlike a book, a private instructor can assess understanding, pace the presentation of new material accordingly, and thereby ensure maximal learning progress. But private instructors are expensive.

Programmed instruction, usually via a computer, combines the economy of the book with the efficacy of the private tutor. It presents the learner with carefully organized sequences of material, calls for responses, and provides instantaneous *feedback* on the answers. In the simplest format, the learner receives material that presents facts and questions. The correct answer is hidden until the trainee responds. If the response is correct, the learner advances to the next section; if not, the factual material is repeated until it is clear.

In a more elaborate version, the learner sits before a television screen that starts by giving factual information. Then a question based upon this information is asked on the screen, and the learner answers by operating a keyboard. A correct response might result in a display of "Nice going!" followed by further factual information. If the response is wrong, the screen might show, "Sorry, let's back up and then we'll try a similar question," and it does.

The material to be learned may be presented in either a **linear** or a **branched format** (Figure 5.5). In the former, the same material is presented identically to all learners, although individuals control the pace and may back up as far and as often as they wish. In the more sophisticated *branched* presentation, the program may skip intermediate steps when it receives successful answers.

Automated trainers serve as individual tutors that never proceed too slowly or quickly, and that never lose their patience, composure, or concentration. These "tutors," moreover, adhere to many important principles of effective learning: *feedback* of results is immediate and frequent, *reinforcement* is regularly provided, the learner benefits from *active* participation, and there are timely opportunities for *consolidation*. Learners should experience less *boredom* because of the interaction, and less *frustration* because of the individual pacing.

Industry favors this approach because once the hardware is in place the "tutor" is always available for instant use at no cost. At one time, job applicants would be summarily rejected if they did not show "normal trainability." Thus, instructors would have a homogenous group of trainees. With today's increased flexibility in applicant qualifications, slower learners can use the programmed instructor to catch up at their own pace.

The more sophisticated versions record the students' progress and error patterns, so that extra help can be targeted, and/or the program can be im-

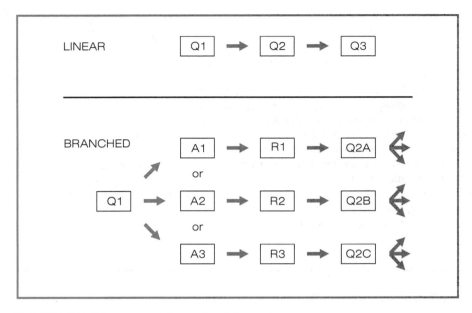

FIGURE 5.5 Linear and branched formats

Traditional training programs follow a linear format, but sophisticated software programs can assess trainees' responses and advance the training by deleting intermediate steps when appropriate.

proved. Although automated trainers do not consistently result in higher test scores, they do shorten the time that most learners require to achieve a satisfactory level.

An important advantage for areas such as aviation or the military, where training must be complete and consistent, is the *standardized* aspect of automated training. It is also useful for the teaching of *progressive sequences,* as in mathematics or vocabulary.

On the other hand, although it may be economical to use the trainer once in place, it is expensive to acquire the hardware and software. Hence, automated trainers may not be cost-effective for small organizations.

Also, it is inconvenient to modify an established program, and it is hard to program attributes such as judgment or social skills, which could be subtly dealt with in face-to-face teaching. Global concepts are harder to teach, and sensorimotor skills are not readily adaptable to this technique.

Learners experience some drawbacks as well. After the initial enthusiasm because of the novelty, they may dislike the robotlike impersonality. They may become frustrated at not being able to seek clarification (except on the program's terms), at the lack of flexibility in all aspects except rate of progress, and at the "jumps" in the frames (if the program is branched). And as with any training program that uses technology new to the learner, the teacher should be sensitive to the fear of the unfamiliar.

Brief case

Boeing Aircraft established an elaborate training program for disadvantaged applicants back in the 1960s. The program has become a model for other major manufacturers. It includes these five components:

1. Applicants are assessed on their deficiencies, and *remedial* training is provided in subjects like English and mathematics.

2. *Prevocational* training deals with basic work habits such as punctuality and appearance.

3. *Preassignment* training covers job skills in a vestibule school setting.

4. *On-the-job* training is provided by a trainer sensitive to the problems faced by these learners.

5. *Postjob* support is offered in the form of counseling, as well as assistance with medical, transportation, and financial needs.

TRAINING FOR ISO 9000 STANDARDS

In the days of cottage industries prior to the industrial revolution, standardization was of little concern. As long as the fletcher (arrow maker) made sure that the slots in the arrows fit the bowstrings made by the bowyer (bowmaker) in the next cottage, there was no problem. But in the last 200 years, assembly-line production and worldwide transportation and communication brought the need for increasing standardization. An industry might buy materials from dozens of others, each of which in turn has its own suppliers. How to ensure that everything matches and fits?

The first focus on standardization was in weights and measures. The current emphasis adds standards of *quality*. One set of standards has so dominated manufacturing that awareness of it is becoming as important a qualification for being hired as computer literacy. A decade ago most industries offered computer training, and employees or applicants not interested were likely to be left behind. Today, industries are requiring their staffers to learn a new set of standards.

In 1987, the Geneva-based International Organization for Standardization published what is known as the **ISO 9000** series of standards. (The abbreviation is ISO instead of IOS because "iso" is the Greek word for "equal," which symbolizes the consensual process used in developing the standards. The standards have series names like ISO 9001 and ISO 9002.) This organization comprises the 90 countries that represent 95 percent of the world's industrial output. The standards focus on manufacturing, but include software and service industries.

Some 2,000 major U.S. corporations, about 600 Canadian ones (largely in Ontario), and 30,000 companies in the United Kingdom have been registered to ISO standards. Almost all firms in the European Economic Community subscribe, and they are no longer dealing with nonconforming suppliers. In the North American automobile industry, all major manufacturers have agreed on ISO standards, which are, in turn, being imposed on their 30,000 suppliers.

ISO-registered companies are bound not only to quality standards but also to processes and administrative mechanisms. It can cost as much as $100,000 for staff training time, ISO documentation, hiring an external consultant, and registration fees. This new set of standards is a relentless trend sweeping across industries throughout the world, and points up the need, even for mature corporations with well-trained employees, to maintain training facilities and resources. If you apply for a job, especially in manufacturing, you can expect the topic of ISO 9000 to come up. Knowing its history, nature, and importance could give you an edge.

TRAINING DISADVANTAGED PERSONS

Increasingly, corporations are helping with a serious social problem, that of people who are chronically unemployed or relegated to menial tasks because of social and economic, and language and cultural barriers. Merely "giving them a chance" is not adequate; many of these people could benefit companies that develop recruitment, counseling, and especially training programs for them. And the benefits extend to the community.

RECOMMENDATIONS FOR TRAINING PROGRAMS

It's tempting for management to assume that an existing training program is a good one. In fact, training takes training; it doesn't come naturally. For instance, when selecting an appropriate training medium, decision makers should analyze its pros and cons in relation to available human and physical resources. The best option usually is a combination of media if only because changing the instructional medium increases alertness and attention. Nonetheless, the techniques of instruction should not command more concern than the content of the material.

Training opportunities should be featured as a fringe benefit and should not be restricted to newcomers. Completion of successive levels should be treated as landmarks in the employee's career, representing a prudent investment by the firm in its human resources. (It's possible that staffers will expect increased responsibilities and therefore higher pay following extra training. If this is not possible, the matter should be clarified beforehand.)

Brief case

Bell Telephone established these four steps for the career planning and development of its employees in Pennsylvania:

1. Interested employees complete a detailed self-assessment exercise. It includes values, experience, potential, goals, and a possible schedule for attaining these goals.

2. Resources are provided to help the employees clarify their goals in terms of realistic opportunities available at Bell.

3. Employees prepare a Personal Development Plan listing their objectives, related experiences, and requests for future job assignments, and review this document in a meeting with their supervisor.

4. With the supervisor, the employees prepare a five-year development plan focusing on their future job path at Bell. This document is relayed to the human resources department for consideration whenever a job opening occurs.

Training should be linked to **career planning** and **career development**. Career *planning* is designed to show you how your interests, strengths, limitations, and opportunities can best match your goals and expectations, and how your objectives can be attained. Some corporations and most higher educational institutions offer career planning facilities. Career *development* is the lifelong process of actualizing your occupational objectives. Many major corporations provide career development resources; one example follows in the above Brief Case.

An effective training program serves the interests of both employer and employee. Today all industries are vulnerable to global forces that threaten their existence. The better trained the employees, the more likely the corporation is to survive, prosper, and retain all of its employees. But today's employees are more vulnerable to job termination than in the recent past. The more extensive and varied the training, the more likely are any victims of downsizing to land on their feet.

A recommended source of further information on personnel training in industry is Goldstein (1993). Career planning is addressed by Hall (1986); career development is covered in detail by Storey (1979).

The need for research

Even if a training program seems to be "working," it should be periodically reviewed. Similarly, a flawed program should be challenged even if it was designed by an expert; all training should be subjected to systematic evaluation through the use of an appropriate methodology.

So what You can expect that some day your new job, or a promotion for your present job, will include a training program. On the basis of what you've just read, you understand the need for an evaluation of such a program, and you'll be in a position to offer a constructive response. Even if asked for comments immediately afterward, you can ask for time to experience how the program matched its purposes. When the time for feedback is opportune, you can make your recommendations, and thereby benefit your employer and your career.

Typically, both instructors and learners are enthusiastic and confident about the value and relevance of a complex training program. The trainees who most value the program perform best in it and become the best workers. These results are fed back into the program, its reputation is enhanced, and the next group of trainees works even harder and more confidently. Of course, the high correlation between the training and the job criterion could have been the result of everyone's expectations. Rising stars given management training are likely to be the ones promoted to management positions. But the promotions could have been due only to the same attributes that led to their being selected for the training.

The academic literature on employee training represents a major gap. There's a scarcity of well-controlled, long-term field experiments examining the overall effect of various training and development approaches. One problem is deciding what the overall end result should be, and how it can be quantified. Another is the perception that research projects could interfere with the profit-related objectives of the organization.

At least some criterion measure of performance could be assessed before and after training. But in a review article, Tannenbaum and Yukl (1992) cited research indicating that of 10 companies surveyed only 1 actually measured behavioral changes following training. The impetus for examining the value of any training program should come from top management. A survey of trainers revealed that nine-tenths of them neglected to evaluate their training programs because it was not required from the top (Bell & Kerr, 1987).

Work is becoming more complex, employees are increasingly diverse, global technological and social changes are requiring the learning of new skills, and training is becoming more common and elaborate. All these forces point up the need to study what kind of training is preferable and why.

Study guide for chapter 5

HAVE YOU LEARNED THESE NAMES AND TERMS?

education training
task analysis
job inventory
feedback
reinforcement
serial
short-term and long-term memory
consolidation
progressive part training
transfer: positive and negative
facilitation and inhibition
proactive facilitation and inhibition
retroactive facilitation and inhibition
learning set
special effects: zoom, subjective camera angle
trainer and simulator
virtual reality and tele-robotics
active learning
job rotation
vestibule school
apprenticeship
Training Group, T-Group, Sensitivity Training Group
role-playing, role reversal
training conference, training case
incident process
business game
programmed instruction, linear and branched format
ISO 9000
career planning and development

ISSUES TO CONSIDER

What are the component sections of an averaged learning curve?
What's the historical difference among orientation, training, and education?
What is the difference between a job analysis and a task analysis?
Which of the training principles can you apply to this course?
Why is the topic of transfer so critical in industrial training?
Why can it be said that there is no one ideal instructional medium?

When should the subjective camera angle be used?

What is the distinction among trainers, simulators, and vestibule schools?

What are the drawbacks to the simulator as an instructional medium?

What is the oldest structured training system?

How should the problems associated with apprenticeships be addressed?

Which training procedure originated in the field of psychotherapy?

How would you handle weaknesses you perceive in your future training?

In what ways might a training program accommodate your individual problems?

What are your plans for career development?

How might knowing the contents of this chapter make you more employable?

SAMPLE MULTIPLE-CHOICE QUESTIONS

1. The starting point for a task analysis is a
   a. job analysis or a job description.
   b. survey.
   c. list of training objectives.
   d. personnel report.

2. The vast majority of what you learn goes into your
   a. short-term memory only.
   b. long-term memory only.
   c. consolidated system.
   d. central nervous system.

3. The main problem with printed training materials in industry is the
   a. possibility of the learner's not concentrating on the page.
   b. intimidating appearance of printed instructions.
   c. likelihood that the assigned material will not be read.
   d. illiteracy rate.

4. By law, a T-Group leader
   a. must have completed an apprenticeship.
   b. must have an appropriate university degree.
   c. must have participated in some T-Groups.
   d. needs no qualifications whatsoever.

5. Training programs may receive unjustified approval due to
   a. active participation.
   b. E bias and demand characteristics.
   c. techniques of group simulation.
   d. stringent roles regarding confidentiality.

Answers: page 462

*Our best conjectures, as to the true spring of
actions, are very uncertain.*
Phillip Stanhope, Earl of Chesterfield (1694–1773)

Bird's-eye view of the chapter

This is the first of four chapters that deal with the employee, now finally at work. The topics in chapters 6 and 7 relate mainly to the individual (as opposed to small or large groups). In this chapter we deal with two primary topics, motivation and job satisfaction. Without motivation, effort and productivity are apt to be low; in the absence of job satisfaction, high motivation is unlikely.

Chapter 6

Motivation and job satisfaction

The payoff from chapter 6   You will:

1. Understand at what point the employee first *benefits* the employer
2. Understand the *importance* of motivation
3. Know why motivation is considered a core area of psychology
4. Know the historical *roots* of industrial motivation theory
5. Know the three *meanings* of motivation
6. Appreciate the strengths and weaknesses of *Maslow's* theory
7. See the similarity between *Maslow and Freud*
8. See the continuity from *Maslow to Herzberg*
9. Understand the meaning of the *two-factor* theory
10. Appreciate the benefits of the *job characteristics* theory over the two-factor theory
11. Understand *achievement motivation* theory and its benefits
12. Know the weaknesses of the *need* theory
13. See the value of *expectancy* theory
14. Know why *balance* theories came from social psychology
15. Understand why balance theory is of particular interest today

16. Understand *goal setting* theory
17. Know why it is considered both a cognitive and a behavioral theory
18. See its relevance to the *management by objectives (MBO)* approach
19. Understand the behaviorism approach
20. Know the complex terminology of behaviorism
21. Appreciate the pitfalls of using aversive stimuli
22. Understand *intrinsic* motivation and its conceptual problems
23. Understand various aspects of money as a motivator
24. Appreciate the meaning and importance of job satisfaction
25. Understand the flow of research on job satisfaction
26. Know employee characteristics related to high or low job satisfaction
27. Know *organizational* variables related to job satisfaction
28. Appreciate why motivation/satisfaction theory is still in the making

U p to now, we have been considering the processes involved in getting the employee ready to work. That is, we have dealt primarily with recruitment, selection, and training. At last, this investment is on the point of paying off; the employee is now *making* money for the employer instead of *costing* money.

Most occupational problems involve not *things,* but *people,* and many such problems can be traced back to inept interactions, that is, to poor "handling." The handling of people-problems can be examined in terms of the *individual,* the *small group,* and the *large group.* Chapters 6 and 7 cover the individual; chapters 8 and 9 deal with the small and large group respectively. These separations are necessarily arbitrary. All of the topics covered in the four chapters affect people both as individuals and as members of various groups. But the topics covered in this and the next chapter are those that *usually* are directed at, or of concern to, the individual.

We'll start with the crucial and complex topic of work motivation, continue with what job satisfaction means and how it is measured, and turn in the next chapter to how employee performance is evaluated.

THE MEANING OF MOTIVATION, AND CURRENT THEORIES

Consider your own motivation at this moment. Is there not something that you would prefer to be doing right now rather than reading this? If so, why are you reading it? Could you explain your behavior without using the construct of *motivation?*

Think back to your first year of school, and to all your classmates. How many of them, do you suppose, are as successful as you are? What accounts for the difference? *Could you explain it without including motivational concepts in your explanation?*

Consider two business organizations, one successful and the other constantly on the brink of failure, mired by labor strife. What primarily differentiates the two? Or contrast two countries. One is disadvantaged in terms of location, natural resources, and **industrial history**, and yet it outproduces others that are blessed with every advantage. Could you account for these differences without considering the aspect of motivation?

Your behavior, that of industrial workers, and even the behavior of nations can be explained through many constructs, such as training, talent, opportunity, and luck. But much of this behavior is best understood in terms of *motivational* theory. When we see two brothers, raised together, one becoming president of his country and the other a ne'er-do-well, it's hard to explain the difference without considering the construct of *motivation.* Perhaps this is why students, when choosing a topic for term paper research in an industrial organizational (I/O) psychology course, pick motivation more frequently than any other topic.

Students are not alone in showing interest in the topic. The question of what impels human behavior has attracted the steady interest of philosophers from the time of the early Greeks. Today, *motivation,* along with *learning theory* and *perception,* is a "core" area of psychology and the oldest of the topics psychologists have been actively studying for a century. Motivation still attracts a large number of entries in textbook indices and in the topics listed in *Psychological Abstracts.* The word *motivation* appears with equal prominence in the literature of *personality.* Clearly, academic psychologists feel that they cannot understand behavior without considering what factors *drive* it.

One of the first industrial psychologists, Frederick W. Taylor (page 15), wrote in the early part of this century that the prime motivator for workers was money. According to Taylorism, if the physical environment is designed to *permit* hard work, and the pay rate is designed to *reward* hard work, high productivity would be ensured by the workers' own self-interest. The Hawthorne studies (page 19) led to the opposite conclusion, which is that workers are not motivated so much by money but by what we would now call organizational climate. They work to be recognized, respected, and valued.

In the 1950s many academic psychologists interested more in humans than in animals lost some of their keen interest in motivation as a critical explanation of behavior, turning instead to cognitive and then to affective constructs. That is, drives and needs (which seemed to explain animal behavior) didn't account for human action as sensitively as did people's feelings, thoughts, and the ways they interpreted events.

Nonetheless, the construct of motivation has recently become popular among I/O psychologists in particular. In the first half of this century, it was assumed that people worked so that they could eat; occupational motivation seemed unworthy of consideration by either employers or scientists. By the 1970s, however, a major review (Mitchell, 1979) reported that a quarter of all papers in organizational psychology dealt with motivation!

Motivation is of particular interest to employers. If bosses could, just by waving a wand, replace any of their staff with alternates, probably half the workers in North America would be instantly switched. Why? Is it because these employees are not *able* to perform the work required? Is it because they are too weak or too stupid? Surely in almost every case, the answer would be that they are simply not sufficiently *motivated* to perform to their highest ability. IBM was once estimated to spend over $4 billion yearly to motivate its employees (Hellriegel, Slocum & Woodman, 1986).

The inferred theoretical construct (page 58) **motivation** is used in three ways in psychology. The first relates to *drives,* and explains behavior directed at satisfying biological or instinct-driven needs, such as acquiring water, food, or air. The second meaning relates to the personality dimension of *ambition,*

What motivates people? There has been much research devoted to motivation, and researchers consider it both a trait and a response to environmental (situational) factors.

and explains why some people strive to accomplish far more than others. The third relates to the *immediate situation,* and would, for instance, explain whether or not right now you will continue to concentrate on reading this, or take a break.

Prior to 1950 it was generally assumed that happy workers were more productive. When psychologists in the 1950s began concerted research into industrial motivation, they sought more specific formulations. They needed *theories* that gave rise to *specific predictions,* which in turn could be tested by research. In response, a number of theories have been proposed in the past 30 years.

The fact that many theories of motivation are under active consideration suggests that we have no single theory that is universally useful. This is to be expected; whatever does motivate us is exceedingly complex. We can show that a rat's performance in a maze is a function of its hunger for the food in the goal box. But your performance in learning this material is a function of what? The running speed of an Olympic athlete is a function of what? The productivity of a factory employee is a function of what? What motivates mothers to care for their children? Whatever it may be, it is more elusive than the number of hours since the last piece of cheese.

At the moment, industrial motivation researchers are not sure whether motivation should be considered a **trait**, that is, a stable characteristic of one's *personality,* or a response to *environmental,* that is, situational, factors. It is both. Picture a row of 10 homes, in each of which a youngster is being asked to put out the garbage. That each youngster moves at a different speed shows that the *trait* of motivation is distributed differently among people. But when an ice-cream vendor rings the come-and-get-it bell, the activity level of the 10 youngsters is considerably different, showing the effect of *environmental* variables on behavior.

Many of the approaches to understanding motivation assume that people have certain basic *needs.* There is a seemingly unlimited number of needs that can be proposed to explain motivation, so the literature on this is rich and varied. We begin by looking at the four most dominant of the **need theories** (theories that assume the existence of and focus on basic human needs), those of Maslow, Herzberg, Hackman and Oldham, and Murray.

Maslow: Hierarchy of needs

One of the earliest, and the most cited of the motivational theorists, is Abraham Maslow. Maslow (1943) proposed that you are motivated to satisfy all your "needs" in a specific order, from "lower" needs to "higher" ones (Figure 6.1).

Physiological needs refers to your primary drives for food, water, air, and sleep. If you are hungry and thirsty, any job that provides food and drink will be welcome. But if you are not hungry and thirsty, you would be motivated by your *safety needs,* for instance, for a safe, secure environment. Working as a bomb disposal technician in a minefield would not have much appeal unless you were starving.

After the above two levels of needs are met, a job would have to meet your *social needs* in order to be satisfactory. Maslow recognized that almost certainly your work will closely involve other people besides yourself. "Belongingness" includes your need to have a friendly work environment, to exchange affection, and to be a contributing member of a group. When your social needs are fulfilled, Maslow feels that you would want your *ego needs* fulfilled. "Esteem" is the need to feel confident, independent, and strong, and to feel that others recognize your value.

Next in the hierarchy of needs are *cognitive needs.* These include knowledge and understanding, and the need for meaning and predictability. When these are met, according to Maslow, you look for the fulfillment of *aesthetic needs*—beauty, symmetry, balance, order, and form.

With *self-actualization* you reach a state of self-fulfillment in which you realize your fullest potential. No matter how friendly your coworkers, and regardless of how valued a contributor you are, it's unlikely you would feel fully motivated if you perceived your job as unfulfilling. Maslow felt that this is the only need that may show up differently among individuals. In a

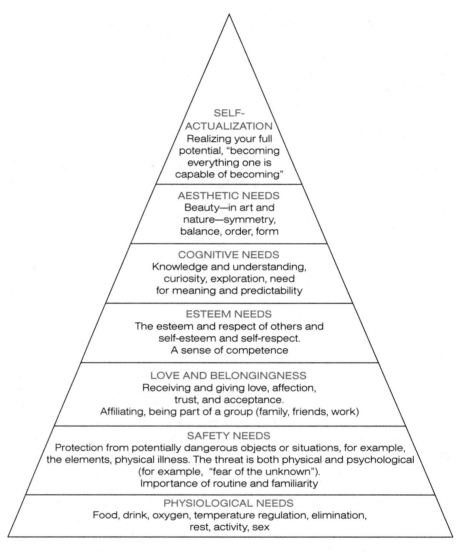

FIGURE 6.1 Maslow's needs hierarchy

Maslow proposed that needs are satisfied in a specific order. Only when the lowest needs are met, there is motivation to seek fulfillment of the next level.

later formulation, he added "transcendence," a state of relatively permanent indifference to the lower levels.

Maslow's needs hierarchy theory is appealing because of its logical simplicity. It is common sense that *physiological* needs must be satisfied before a person will work to satisfy the *belongingness* needs, which, in turn, are more basic than the need for *self-actualization*. It is logical that once a need is

So what A theorist doesn't have to be right to be important. It's worth knowing about Maslow because his concepts like a "hierarchy of needs" and "self-actualization" have become part of our language and culture. His theory is presented in management seminars, taught in business and management courses, and you can expect to hear about it during your work career. His other useful contribution is the point that motives sometimes conflict, and when they do, one may dominate the other. Think of Maslow when you have tickets to a rock concert on the same night that you have a date with a very attractive person who dotes on classical music.

satisfied, it no longer motivates. It is easy to accept the premise that the highest-order needs are unlikely to be satisfied so fully that they cease to motivate.

It is reasonable to think that upon starting your first job, you would be most concerned with your pay and job security. Only when these are satisfactory would you be concerned with psychological issues like your reputation or image. With these no longer of concern, you would be ready to address your ultimate and unique potential, such as writing a book on the philosophy of work.

Although Maslow was not an industrial psychologist, his *needs hierarchy* theory has attracted and continues to attract much attention in the literature. Like most simple theories, it seemed to be easily applicable. For instance, when lower-order needs are unmet, employees presumably should respond mainly to expectations of physical and financial security. When these needs are satisfied, workers will be more responsive to the *social* interactions of the job, and executives (who presumably are not troubled by abrasive socialization) must have their need for self-actualization fed.

How much support has Maslow's theory had throughout more than a half century? Unfortunately, every person who engages in a suicide mission shows that the *esteem* needs can in fact overpower the *safety* needs, in contradiction to Maslow. Some people—perhaps circus performers or movie stunt performers—seem best able to satisfy their egos by disregarding their safety. And researchers' attempts at confirming the existence of a *hierarchy of needs,* that is, a list of needs that are satisfied in order, have not been successful.

Wahba and Bridewell (1976) conducted the most comprehensive review of research on Maslow's theory, and they failed to find solid support for it. The researchers observed that the concept of *need* is not clear. For instance, are Maslow's *needs* psychological or physiological? Are they in force only when unsatisfied, or are they there permanently? Nor was Maslow very clear about his meaning of the "highest" needs. Inglehart and Hildebrandt (1990) also pointed out the failure of research to support Maslow.

How should Maslow be regarded today? Maslow's contribution is analogous to Freud's (although much simpler). Like Freud, his value is mostly historical; it does not show how motivation functions in the workplace. His position is more of a philosophy than it is a theory that yields hypotheses, which can be tested empirically.

Unfortunately, both Maslow and Freud:

- devised intuitive arguments, based not on empirical but on psychiatric, clinical, and case-study data;

- presented some arguments that presently are seen as weak or even incorrect;

- incorrectly assumed that all people are driven by the same innate pressures;

- relied on sometimes ambiguous and philosophical definitions;

- attracted much attention in the general public, who adopted some of the terminology into everyday language. But most importantly,

- both opened doors through which many researchers have traveled.

Motivator-hygiene theory

Even if Maslow's theory were supported by both logic and empirical research, it would still present problems in *application*. For instance, how can managers inspire employees whose motivational needs keep *changing*? How can every employee's need for self-actualization be defined and responded to? To deal with these questions, Herzberg (1966, 1974) proposed a theory of both *motivation* and *job satisfaction*. Like Maslow's hierarchy, Herzberg's *motivator-hygiene* theory is simple yet **heuristic**. (*Heuristic* in this sense means that it leads to further research and theory.)

When Herzberg questioned white-collar workers about what made them *happy,* the answers related to their achievements, responsibilities, recognitions, and advancements. They attributed *unhappiness,* or poor attitudes, to inadequate salary, troubling policies, and unsatisfactory interpersonal relations. He concluded that *dissatisfactions* are not caused by the lack of sources of *satisfaction*. Herzberg agreed with Maslow's contention that people have basic inborn needs. But he modified Maslow by postulating just *two* types of needs, "which, moreover, do *not* operate hierarchically."

One type produces *job satisfaction*. These are **motivator needs**, in that they impel the employee to excel. They are a variant of Maslow's *self-*

So what Suppose you're offered two long-term positions. They're similar, except that in one, the duties are repetitious and the pay is higher, but the other has various features of job enrichment. Wouldn't you choose the latter? Herzberg's most important contribution to I/O psychology is that it was he, more than any other theorist, who sparked the current movement toward job enrichment.

actualization needs and comprise the employee's level of responsibility, personal growth and advancement, and, especially, the sense of achievement. These "human" needs for challenge and autonomy might be satisfied by responsibility and recognition for important accomplishments, in short, by "job enrichment."

The second type comprises **hygiene needs**. These "maintenance" needs or extrinsic factors are satisfied by, for instance, pay, security, and working conditions. Because of the two types of postulated motivators, Herzberg's position is also known as the **two-factor theory**.

Herzberg argued that workers should be encouraged to try to fulfill their *motivator* needs, not their *hygiene* needs, because working to satisfy the former leads to productive activity. This is accomplished when there is *job enrichment,* in that interesting work provides the opportunity to satisfy motivator needs.

Herzberg felt that some motivators simply keep you from being *unhappy,* just as a meal keeps you from being hungry—for a time. A pay raise keeps you from being unhappy—until you feel hungry for another. Herzberg termed such incentives *negative motivators* or *hygiene maintenance factors,* because their absence causes unhappiness, but their presence does not guarantee long-term contentment. These factors are differentiated in Figure 6.2.

Herzberg is a widely cited name in motivation and job satisfaction, though his influence is weaker now than it was in the 1970s. Current researchers are concerned about the small amount of empirical support his theory has received. For instance, in a review paper on the two-factor theory, King (1970) reported little research support for it.

This has not stopped managers from trying to apply it. Like Maslow's theory, it has the ring of validity, it is complex enough to require some attention but simple enough to be understood by nonacademics, and it is fairly easy to apply.

The main reason for its weakness is now becoming apparent. Herzberg differentiated between the two factors on the basis of employee *interviews.* Asking workers what motivates them assumes that people have insight as to what impels their behavior. In fact, psychologists themselves are unsure about

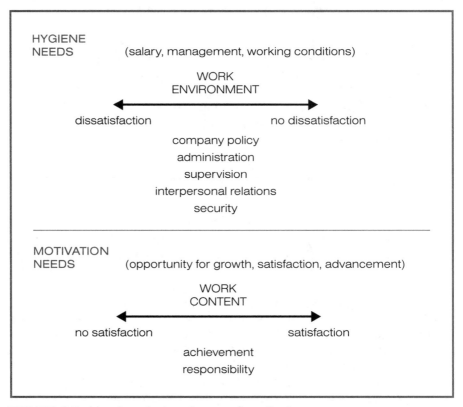

FIGURE 6.2 Herzberg's two types of motivators

Herzberg's two-factor theory distinguishes between hygiene needs, which at best keep you from being dissatisfied, and motivation needs that promote satisfaction.

what motivates people in general. How can we expect laypeople to understand their own individual motivation? Maybe Herzberg detected two types of motivators simply because people tend to ascribe the *rewarding* aspects of work to their own efforts, and the *unrewarding* aspects to job-related factors.

Job characteristics theory

Herzberg had changed the emphasis from the worker to the work. Ten years after his book on the two-factor theory, the impact of the work on the worker was refined by another theory. The **job characteristics theory** of motivation was proposed by Hackman and Oldham (1976), who studied characteristics

So what Don't you expect that early in your work career, your employment will offer you a reasonable amount of the five, rather basic, characteristics listed below? If you attain a managerial level, would you not feel some responsibility for ensuring as much job enrichment as possible for your employees? That a job, perhaps yours, should be designed so as to satisfy the worker is now taken for granted. That's due more to Hackman and Oldham than to any other theorist. Their 1976 paper was titled, in part, "Motivation through the Design of Work." That an organization should *design* the tasks it pays people to perform and that the success of these designs could be quantified were innovative concepts. Although some jobs, by their very nature, are not easy to enrich, these ideas are widely embraced today, to your benefit.

of jobs (such as whether the work was varied or repetitious) that most related to employee satisfaction.

They felt that *positive job characteristics* cause a *positive emotional state,* which serves as a motivator. That is, an employee with the right kind of work will be motivated to do it well. This theory is considered a needs theory because it assumes that employees have a need for growth.

Hackman and Oldham felt that to motivate the worker, it's necessary to *redesign the job* so that it provides certain characteristics. The work should be meaningful, the worker should have a feeling of responsibility, and know exactly how well the job is being performed. Specifically, the job should

- Provide an opportunity to complete some entire, recognizable unit, so that the employee perceives **task identity**.

- The work should have some impact on other people, in order to provide a feeling of **task significance**.

- The work should also provide **autonomy**, that is, the authority to make decisions oneself.

- It should offer *variety*.

- Finally, the job should offer **feedback**, or some form of reporting to apprise the employee about the result or effect of the individual work effort.

Hackman and Oldham (1975) also devised a test for quantifying these five aspects; it is an employee questionnaire called the **job diagnostic survey**.

A sophisticated instrument for its time, its basic validity and also its limitations are documented by Spector and Jex (1991).

Like the two need theories that came before, this one also has commonsense appeal. Unfortunately, researchers seeking evidence for the existence of the postulated characteristics have not been successful, even using factor analysis (page 46). Several studies have shown that where the five characteristics are present, employees rate their jobs as satisfying. But these have been correlational studies, which do not permit the conclusion that the one caused the other.

Of course there are many jobs that could and should be enriched for the self-respect of the worker. Yet, we should not ignore the effects of demand characteristics on the *interpretation* of "enrichment." Suppose we were constantly warned that our diets were unhealthy, and that the solution lay in "enriched" meals. Would it not be easy to find that people fed from a menu labeled "enriched" would report feeling healthier and happier? As with the diet warning, we have persistently been informed that much work is demeaning, degrading, simplistic, and frustrating!

It's not surprising that before-and-after studies show more job satisfaction or productivity after the institution of a job enrichment program based on the Hackman and Oldham set of five characteristics. In a commendably long-term study, Griffin (1991) examined some 500 bank tellers following job enrichment changes. After a half year, attitudes had improved. But at the two-year mark, there was a significant performance improvement, and this was still present at the four-year mark.

Maybe the effect of *job enrichment* is partly due to the feeling that one is *supposed* to prefer it. An interesting study by Cherrington and England (1980) showed that the best way to predict which employees would respond favorably to job enrichment was to ask them if they would like their job enriched; that is, workers who *wanted* their jobs enriched valued the changes.

Murray: Need theory

Henry Murray's influential book on *personality* (1938) contained enough material on *motivation* to constitute a theory of people's needs that has attracted psychologists interested in work motivation. Murray and his successors (for example, McClelland, 1961; Atkinson & Feather, 1966) named over 20 needs, which—contrary to Maslow's concept—do not operate in any particular order or hierarchy, are learned rather than instinctive, and can operate in any combination. Murray's approach, also known as *achievement theory* or *need theory*, is sometimes attributed to McClelland or to Atkinson.

The need that has the most relevance for the work situation is *ambition*, which Murray termed **need for achievement**, abbreviated **nAch.** How is nAch measured? The most common procedure is for the psychologist to have the

According to Murray's need theory, the most relevant personality attribute in the workplace is the need for achievement (nAch). This attribute is measured using the Thematic Apperception Test (TAT), which consists of having the test candidate create a story from a picture.

test candidate create a story from a picture. The results are evaluated by quantifying the *achievement imagery* in the picture (TAT is discussed on page 113). To overcome the limitations of the TAT, which must be individually administered by a qualified psychometrist, Stahl (1983) designed a paper-and-pencil alternative test that is easier to administer and more objective to score.

TAT need-achievement scores have shown remarkably high correlations with success. Not only do successful businesspeople show a higher nAch than unsuccessful ones, but the nAch scores of children measured and followed over their lives predict their success as adults. Even the level of a nation's success correlates well with the nAch scores of its people.

Most important, the nAch scores of executives correlate with the success of their firms. In addition, research has shown that managers with high nAch respect their subordinates more, are more open to new ideas, and are more accepting of participatory democracy. In short, such managers are better suited to lead and motivate the contemporary employee of the kind who values such attributes (Schultz & Schultz, 1986).

Another need relevant to I/O psychology, postulated by Atkinson and Feather (1966), is the **need to avoid failure**. People high in this need will avoid undertaking certain tasks because of their concern with performing poorly. These two needs have an interesting relationship with the kind of

So what Are you going to take a break now, or will you continue studying? Vroom would explain your decision by applying a formula that basically has you asking yourself, "What will I *get* if I do struggle on?" (or "What will I *lose* if I quit now?"), and "How do I *rate* either outcome?" Won't the grade you get on your first test influence your *expectations* of your next grade, and therefore affect your *motivation* to study? That is, you rationally assess what actions are most likely to get you what you want. Before we engage in a task, we consider exactly what's in it for us. This is something we all do constantly, not just in the workplace.

task that people of different personality types either undertake or avoid. People with high nAch prefer tasks with a *moderate* difficulty level.

Such people are not at their best when dealing with a "sure thing" on the one hand, or "shooting for the moon" on the other; their motivation is highest on tasks where there is a 50–50 chance of succeeding. People high in *need to avoid failure,* by contrast, avoid tasks with moderate difficulty, preferring either sure things (where there is no fear of failure) or "long shots," where a failure can be blamed on the odds.

The implication of the nAch literature is that a personnel department's mandate is not so much to *manipulate* motivation as it is to *select* for people already high in this predictive, dominant, and stable personality characteristic.

Because of the direct applicability of this theory to personnel selection, more research has been conducted on it than on any of the other *need* theories. For instance, one study (Steers, 1975) indicated that the higher your need for achievement, the more satisfactory you will find your work. Another conclusion (Stahl, 1983) was that the most successful managers have a high need for achievement, and the least successful managers are those with a high need for affiliation.

Social psychology has identified similar needs that relate to the workplace. A basic need for human beings is *competence* in handling their environment (this has been described in detail by Sternberg & Kolligian, 1990.) Bandura (1990) contends that competence comes from **self-efficacy**, the belief that you are able to do what you intend to do. Self-efficacy can result from your past successes, from seeing someone else succeed at the same task, from encouragement, and by remaining calm and relaxed rather than agitated. And Ozer and Bandura (1990) report that the more their self-efficacy, the harder people will work.

The last of these needs is the **need for power**, or domination over others. Since most corporations operate in a hierarchical fashion in which the higher the rank the greater the power, attaining promotions can satisfy this need. McClelland's (1975) book on this need, which he interpreted from TAT responses, suggests that people attain power through aggression, persuasion, helping others, or manipulating feelings by arousing guilt, devotion, or anger. (This need will come up again when we deal with leadership in the next chapter.)

The limitation of need theories is that whereas they accurately describe *present* correlates of motivated and unmotivated personnel, they do not address how to *increase* motivation. (And most people wish that others' and their own motivation were higher.) Another weakness is that all of the original and early research was performed on males. Females' needs may be different and more complex than those of males. In addition, findings that may be applicable to one type of work situation may be irrelevant to others. What makes the best employee and the best manager may differ in, say, a police force, a symphony orchestra, and a think tank.

Expectancy theory

Animals, of course, respond to their needs, and do so without much cognition or rationality; that is, they do not have the ability to weigh, think about, or evaluate these needs. Theories like Maslow's portray the human as a creature responding to needs without really thinking about them. Obviously, how much effort you expend is influenced by what you expect to get from the effort. If you really value the end result and you're pretty sure your efforts will be successful, you're likely to work harder.

In an attempt to add a **cognitive** (or thought) component, Vroom (1964) applied **expectancy theory** to industrial motivation. Victor Vroom argued that your behavior is influenced by both your *degree of certainty that some outcome will follow the behavior,* and by *how much you value that outcome.*

Because of the emphasis on both your *expectancy* of an outcome and the *attractiveness* of this outcome to you, Vroom's expectancy theory and its several variants are also termed *expectancy, valence-expectancy,* or *valence-instrumentality-expectancy (VIE)* theory. (*Valence* is borrowed from the chemistry concept of the power and direction of a chemical attraction; *instrumentality* indicates that you would evaluate how "instrumental" a certain action will be in bringing about a certain outcome.)

Of course, your relevant experience will greatly affect your expectations. As an example, Feather (1966) gave female undergraduates anagram puzzles (making up words from lists of letters) to solve. Half started with simple anagrams; the other half began with impossible ones. The first group expected to do well on the rest; the second expected to fail to solve any of the rest. And on the last 10 anagrams, which were the same for both groups, the first group did much better than the second.

Vroom pointed out that the employee must be *able* to do the assigned work, or there'd be too much frustration to expect high job motivation. But Schmidt and Hunter (1992) showed that the employee's *overall abilities* and *conscientiousness* are even more important than the specific skills needed to do the job, thereby somewhat weakening Vroom's theory.

Lawler and Porter (1967) supported Vroom's theory, adding that another variable affecting performance is **role perception**, or how workers think about themselves and their jobs. Ragins and Sundstrom (1989) expanded it further to include the need for employees to know exactly what's expected of them, and (especially for women) to know how to achieve a reasonable feeling of control or power within their organization.

As you might assume from the above examples, expectancy theory has attracted considerable research, much of which supports its general propositions. (Some negative results were attributed to people not being motivated by rational thought processes; others were blamed on inadequate definitions of the variables.)

There are a number of problems attending research in, and application of, expectancy theory. The mathematical formulae involving the valences and instrumentalities are quite complex, and difficult to use for the precise prediction of motivated behavior. At the same time, its comprehensiveness helps it fit in with many other theories.

Most of the research on expectancy theory has used a *between-subjects* design (page 49). The problem here is that "valence" and "expectancy" are defined as individual variables. As Mitchell (1974) pointed out in his theoretical paper, such research should use a *within-subjects* design, because one person's levels of these variables are not necessarily comparable to those of others.

Although the theory can be applied to situations apart from personnel motivation (for example, to product purchasing decisions), within personnel it is cumbersome to calculate the exact values of the expectancies and valences. A more serious weakness is that employees may be swayed by misunderstandings or emotion or may not have at hand all the information they need to make a rational decision.

Nonetheless, managers can adopt three steps to make use of Vroom's concepts. They can (a) maximize *expectancy* through appropriate assignments and adequate training; (b) maximize *valence* by ensuring that the rewards for good performance are meaningful to the employees; and (c) heighten *instrumentality* if employees clearly know that the rewards will directly follow from the defined performance (Pinder, 1991).

Balance theories

For a half century, social psychologists have been trying to explain and predict behavior on the basis of our need for consistency or harmony in our thoughts. Because this need is a product of our mind rather than a biological need, such theories, termed **balance** or **equity theories**, like *expectancy theory*, belong to the cognitive category.

Balance theories are based on the premise that the individual strives to maintain a state of mental harmony or balance. In an early statement of the theory, Adams (1965) argued that employees weigh in their minds how much they contribute to their employer, versus how much the employer contributes to them. Adams, like many other psychologists, added the notion that employees compare themselves to others. "Let me see," each employee asks, "what is *my* ratio of input to outcome, compared to the ratios of my colleagues?" Where there seems to be an *inequity*, the employee experiences a feeling of imbalance or tension, which is relieved by adjusting one of the variables. The usual way is to reduce the output, that is, to work less.

Of all the theories of motivation, *balance* seems to have the most interest for employers, especially when called by its alternate name, equity theory. Employers are vitally concerned with compensation issues, and *equity* is a prime aspect of compensation. Their goal is to provide both external equity (compensation consistent with that of the competition) and internal equity (fair compensation within the organization) (page 90).

Unfortunately, a number of problems may arise in trying to set salaries equitably:

- The salary necessary to attract a recent college graduate may cause resentment in some of the old-timers.

- Employees have a high threshold for overpayment, that is, it takes a large raise before they feel overpaid, but a minuscule threshold for underpayment (a tiny discrepancy in this direction causes a feeling of resentment).

- Feelings of underpayment tend to fester and grow, whereas a feeling of overpayment is short-lived.

- Although balance theory holds that some perceptions of inequity can heighten motivation, *equity* is required out of fairness, under normal compensation practice, and, in some cases, by law.

Balance theory readily predicts the effects of under- or overpayment on productivity. Consequently, most tests of this theory have involved university students performing a "temporary job" in a laboratory setting, where motivation is manipulated through the payment system. In a review paper, Mowday (1983) concluded that whereas the results of *underpayment* were consistent with the predictions, the results of *overpayment* conditions caused uncertainties in interpretation. (The overpayment manipulation typically consisted of telling participants that they were unqualified for the work at hand. Their increased output may have been in response to the damage to their self-image. It has also been suggested that in real life no employee would feel overpaid; a more realistic assumption is that no firm would pay more than an employee is really worth.)

In the face of dissonance, people do not have to restore balance by changing their behavior, such as by asking for a raise, adjusting the output, or even by quitting. They may restore their state of internal balance by changing their *attitudes,* as by convincing themselves that they are not being underpaid, or that their coworkers are *not* "getting away with murder."

Many studies have generally supported the basic concepts of balance theories, and new concepts formulated in the future will probably incorporate some aspects of balance or equity. Managers mindful of balance theory should clarify to employees how they are to be evaluated and how the performance will relate to their pay. Furthermore, employees should know what their colleagues do and have an idea of what they are paid for doing it, so that the inevitable comparisons of inputs and outcomes will be based on fact.

Goal setting theory

The **goal setting** approach is another motivational theory in the cognitive class, which can also be listed in the behavioral category. Work motivation, according to this position, can be understood only in terms of the individual's conscious, purposeful intentions to work toward a goal. Before starting work, people *plan* it. If the work—and the pay for it—goes according to plans, motivation and satisfaction are maintained.

The theorist associated with this contention, Locke (1968), pointed out that the employee's behavior is directed largely by *intentions,* which the employer measures by *performance goals.* Goals, Locke argued, provide both *direction* and *mobilization.* The more difficult the goal (as long as it remains within reach), the greater the motivation, given appropriate *feedback* by management, and *acceptance* by the employee.

This is an appealing theory, both logical and relevant, and few motivational theories are as well supported by research as Locke's. "Recent reviews of work motivation state that in practice, goal setting is one of the most valid and reliable theories of human action. . . . [It] is cost effective, requiring limited staffing and financial resources" (Ballentine, Nunns & Brown, 1992).

It has been repeatedly demonstrated that (a) workers with goals outperform those lacking goals, (b) the more *specific* the goal, the more motivating it is, and (c) difficult goals are more motivating than easy ones. Moreover, the value of goal setting has been demonstrated in both unionized and nonunion settings (Locke & Latham, 1984).

The most famous early study (Latham & Blades, 1975) supporting Locke's concepts dealt with truckers who neglected to pile the optimum num-

TABLE 6.1 Effect of task difficulty on performance

	Theory	*Task difficulty*	*Performance prediction*
E X P E C T A N C Y	• easy tasks raise expectations and motivation • hard tasks lower expectations of success so motivation decreases	EASY MODERATE HARD	↑ ~ ↓
N E E D	• those with high need for achievement are most motivated when the probability of success is .5	EASY MODERATE HARD	↓ ↑ ↓
G O A L S	• hard goals raise performance standards, and therefore the performance itself	EASY MODERATE HARD	↓ ~ ↑

Three theories predict performance as a function of task difficulty.

ber of tree logs on their vehicles. When each driver was assigned a specific weight goal (although there were no rewards or punishments attached to meeting or missing the goal), the load weights increased significantly.

The notion that behavior can be predicted on the basis of what a person *intends* to do seems so basic—if not trivial—that, prior to Locke, little research had been performed on it. It turned out that the implications of the theory have been anything but trivial. For instance, people striving to reach specific goals outperform those with general ones. Also, the more challenging the goal, the better is the performance—provided the goal remains within one's capabilities. And the reason *feedback* is effective is that it raises one's goals.

This theory supports the popular management technique of **management by objectives (MBO)**, which developed independently around the same time. In MBO employer and employee agree on specific, measurable goals, followed by regular feedback on their attainment. It is generally accepted that both goal setting and MBO are successful.

Of all the theories that deal with the complex topic of what motivates people, goal setting is the easiest to apply in industry, at least for jobs that have clear-cut goals. And goal setting has remained an active and vibrant topic for motivational research. But it does not seem comprehensive enough to provide a unified and global explanation of motivation, and the following questions and problems remain:

- Many jobs cannot be divided into bite-size components.

- We do not know how to measure employees' intentions with accuracy, or how to influence them effectively.

- We are not sure whether differences in behavior are a function of goals being set internally, or imposed from outside (Erez, Earley & Hulin, 1985).

- We have few clear answers on the relation of individual differences to goal setting. Are one's intentions determined by nAch, self-esteem, or something else?

- What aspects of the MBO approach account for its apparent success?

- Other questions that have to be dealt with include who should set the goal, and how high it should be.

If we chart the performance predictions as a function of task difficulty as in Table 6.1, we see disturbing lack of consistency; there is no type of task on which all three theories agree.

Behaviorism

Experimental psychologists are sometimes referred to as *rat runners.* Why? Because they have conducted thousands of studies on the performance of laboratory rats running through mazes. This extensive research literature, which started in the last century, has been directed at finding out what motivates an animal to *learn* a task or to *perform* it.

A vast amount is now known about performance as a function of *reinforcement* (the consequences of the performance). Much of this information has been successfully applied to humans. For instance, children with severe learning disabilities have been effectively taught through the use of the same motivational variables originally defined in the rat maze.

The application of *learning theory* to behavior goes by many names. It is termed **Skinnerian** from the influence of B. F. Skinner, who devoted his professional life to defining the influence of reinforcements on behavior. It is called **operant conditioning**, or operant behavior, because the subject *operates* or behaves in some way to bring about the reinforcement. It is termed **instrumental** for the same reason; the subject is instrumental in receiving the reinforcer. One application of learning theory is **behavior modification**.

This term originated in psychotherapy, where the therapist used **reinforcers** to change the client's *behavior.*

Reinforcement (page 134) strengthens (or increases the probability of) the behavior that it follows. A manager who sends you a note of thanks with a gift certificate for filing a report early is using reinforcement in the expectation that you'll be more likely to file your next report early too. **Punishment** has the opposite effect; it is the event that follows a behavior, which weakens that behavior. If your boss scowls at you every time you interrupt a speaker at a meeting, the scowl is an aversive (unpleasant) stimulus that weakens or decreases the probability of the event it just followed. It doesn't matter whether you actually receive the aversive stimulus or you expect to; the preceding behavior is likely to diminish.

The example of receiving thanks for completing the project early is known as **positive reinforcement**, the giving of a reward. But reinforcement can also consist of *removing an unpleasant stimulus,* in which case it's termed **negative reinforcement**. Suppose your employer provides a counselor for you to see when you are under stress. If you find that talking to the counselor relieves your stress, your talking serves as a negative reinforcer, and you'll likely make another appointment the next time you feel stressed. Or if the noise from the shop floor is annoying you, and you find relief by shutting your door, you're more likely to shut it the next time.

Students are often confused by the positive-negative distinction, especially by the difference between negative reinforcement and positive punishment. To keep them straight, remember that *punishment decreases* the response, whereas positive or negative *reinforcement increases* it. These distinctions are shown in Table 6.2.

Another distinction to keep in mind about reinforcement is that it can be primary or secondary. **Primary reinforcement** is the satisfaction of a *biological* need for food, water, and so on. **Secondary reinforcement** is *learned,* not biological, and accounts for virtually all reinforcement in the workplace. For instance, Makin, Cooper, and Cox (1989) described a company whose tanker trucks transported hazardous liquids. With this type of operation, the motto is "Better safe than sorry; if you're not absolutely sure, ask!" The company introduced a reinforcement plan that gave the drivers a small pay bonus every time they phoned for advice on the handling of the particular load.

In former times, reinforcement was presumably primary: workers worked hard or starved (the giving of food would be a primary reward), or perhaps they were whipped (in which case the cessation of the hitting would be negative primary reinforcement). It's hard to find a pure example of primary reinforcement in the modern workplace. However, the distinction between primary and secondary is often blurred; a special rest break for having a productive work shift is a primary reinforcer in that it lets you relax when tired, and a secondary reinforcer in that it has symbolic meaning too. A gift certificate to a fancy restaurant is a secondary reward even though technically it consists of food. Money is a typical secondary reinforcer, and it brings

TABLE 6.2 Types of reinforcement and punishment

		STIMULUS	
		PRESENTED	REMOVED
RESPONSE	INCREASES	**POSITIVE REINFORCEMENT** You keep your workspace neater when your tidying up is followed by praise.	**NEGATIVE REINFORCEMENT** You follow the rules so as not to be penalized.
	DECREASES	**POSITIVE PUNISHMENT** Your machine makes an unpleasant noise when started incorrectly, so your rate of faulty startups decreases.	**NEGATIVE PUNISHMENT** You stop parking in prohibited areas after receiving fines for doing so.

Examples of the differences between reinforcement and punishment.

with it other secondary reinforcers such as prestige and respect, but it can be exchanged for primary reinforcers such as food and shelter.

Punishment can be an effective motivator, but we should be aware of some of the problems associated with it (Maier & Verser, 1982):

- Punishment causes frustration and hostility, particularly in the unco-operative and the emotionally unstable—the most likely recipients of the punishment!

- Punishment produces associations other than those intended. For instance, it focuses attention on avoiding being caught, rather than on improving the performance.

- Punishment highlights what *not* to do. The listing of the penalty for each possible infraction, for instance, can give otherwise constructive people a lot of destructive ideas.

- Punishment tends merely to stop or inhibit some action, rather than to replace it with the correct one.

- Punishment creates negative associations. When a major objective is to instill a favorable, constructive attitude, the use of punishment will be counterproductive.

- Punishment induces fear. Fear, in turn, deters flexibility and the acceptance of new concepts.

If punishment is associated with so many problems, one would assume that it is rarely used, but this is not the case. Why is punishment still a commonly applied reinforcer?

(a) Punishment is *traditional,* both historically and in the childhood experience of many of today's adults. (b) It also appears, at first glance, to be highly *effective.* (c) It typically gives some satisfaction to the punisher. (d) Probably the main reason for its continued use is its ease of *administration.* A shout, an insult, a demerit, a demotion, docking a day's pay—these are all simple, direct, and immediate reinforcers. Relying on rewards can be much more difficult. (e) The use of rewards may require that they be identified first. It's much harder to know what will *please* somebody than what will displease. An action designed by a supervisor to be rewarding may be interpreted by the subordinate as manipulative. (f) Also, the worse the performance, the more the need for some kind of reinforcer, but the less the opportunity for administering a *reward* reinforcer.

Another principle of instrumental learning is the *timing* and the *schedule* of the reinforcers, whatever their type. Reinforcers that occur close in time to the behavior are more effective than those separated by weeks or months. Shamir (1983) wondered if *immediate reward* (in the form of receiving tips) was correlated with job satisfaction or motivation. He simply administered a questionnaire to some 300 hotel employees, half of whom received tips. Job satisfaction was rated higher by the tip-receivers, and the researcher attributed this to the greater autonomy associated with the relation of pay to skill.

The effects of the *schedule* of reinforcers are more complex. **Partial reinforcement**, where the reinforcer follows the behavior sometimes but not always, is more effective in the long run than **continuous reinforcement**, in which the correct act is always reinforced. Within partial reinforcement, **variable ratio reinforcement**, where the individual never knows which occurrence of the correct behavior will be reinforced, is more effective than **fixed ratio reinforcement**, in which a reinforcement regularly follows every so many acts of correct behavior.

Suppose, for instance, employees are being encouraged to pick up litter. The most effective reinforcement schedule would be to reward their pick-up action about every third time it is performed, but on a random basis. (The term "effective" in this paragraph would be measured in terms of how many times the employees would continue to pick up if the reward program were discontinued.) These are illustrated, in both an industrial and a classroom context, in Table 6.3.

Operant conditioning was defined in terms of the actions of lab animals. It was refined and applied to humans in the case of infants, the learning disabled, and the mentally ill. It is in some use in prisons, reformatories, and the military.

TABLE 6.3 Examples of reinforcement schedules

Schedule	Example
Fixed Ratio	You deliver pizzas @ $3/delivery.
Variable Ratio	You work as a door-to-door salesperson.
reinforcement administered	↑ after certain *number* of responses ↓ based on time since last reinforcement
Fixed Interval	Few exams mean few opportunities for reward (A's) so you don't study much.
Variable Interval	An announcement "There will be lots of surprise tests" makes you study more!

Reinforcement is most effective when it is administered variably on a random basis.

What about industry? In a broad sense, life itself is a gigantic Skinnerian chamber. We are all subject to rewards and punishments, and industry is no exception. Nonetheless, behaviorism has been applied to occupational motivation only since the 1970s, whereupon it has attracted considerable attention. The vast literature on the applications of behaviorism has been reviewed by O'Hara, Johnson, and Beehr (1985). *Feedback* has long been related to high morale in studies on humans. Haynes (1986) differentiated among three types: (a) the informative feedback of straightforward, judgment-free *information,* such as production figures; (b) *reinforcing* feedback, involving praise and reward, (c) the *corrective* feedback of guidance and direction.

Intrinsic motivation

An **intrinsically motivated** person does the work for its own sake; **extrinsic** (external) **motivation** is, by contrast, some outside benefit or reward. If you are studying this book out of interest (grades and course credit being irrelevant to you), your motivation is *internal.* But if your sole justification for studying is your score on the next test or exam, the score is an external motivator. Most people are largely motivated *externally* to work; in fact, one way of differentiating between "work" and "play" is to determine whether the activity is motivated internally or externally. Contrast, for instance, the person who is paid to mount a horse and get to work, with the person who pays for horseback riding.

Which is better, internal or external motivation? Every professor wishes that the students were there only to *learn,* totally indifferent to grades. University administrators yearn for faculty who volunteer to teach extra courses for the enjoyment. National politicians fantasize about corporate directors who set examples by drawing subsistence pay, rather than demanding what amounts to 30 to 50 times that of their entry-level employees; citizens wish their elected representatives were indifferent to power, prestige, or pay. Most of all, every employer dreams of a workforce that has to be *forced* to take its paid holidays.

The unfortunate reality is that work is often seen by the incumbents as routine, onerous, and unrewarding. This work is justified only by the external rewards; to try to increase the intrinsic motivation would be difficult. Is it worth the effort? Deci (1975) felt that those who work under the "carrot and stick" feel a loss of control over their actions, so it is important to provide an atmosphere of competence, pleasure, and autonomy on the job. He argued, accordingly, that tying rewards to performance reduces internal motivation, and supported this with laboratory studies that used puzzles and games as the task. However, other research (for example, Phillips & Lord, 1980), using more employment-related tasks, did not support Deci's argument. So perhaps the development of *intrinsic* motivation should *not* be the primary goal of managers.

What is the relative influence of internal versus external rewards? It may depend upon the job characteristics. For instance, with low-level work, extrinsic rewards increase the employee's *intrinsic* motivation. But providing the same extrinsic rewards for intrinsically motivating work will *reduce* the intrinsic motivation (Mossholder, 1980).

Research in internal versus external motivation presents a number of conceptual difficulties. It is not always simple to differentiate between intrinsic and extrinsic motivation. People who, in our terms at least, "sacrifice" their lives for a cause are responding to some sort of captivating motivation, but whether this is internal or external is a philosophical question. Consider the assembly-line employees in the People's Republic of China, who work as long and hard as physically able, not for the pay (in a country where until recently there was little to buy), but as a means of supporting the political ideology of the country. There is no doubt that they are strongly motivated, but by what? If you find your work motivating because you feel that you and your work are important, is that internal or external motivation? If propaganda makes you believe you and your work are important, after which you feel motivated, is that internal or external?

Consider a typist in the former Soviet Union who had no interest in the job itself. The typist was transferred from a button factory to a chemical company. Because the government valued chemicals over buttons, employees in a chemical company were accorded privileges that enhanced the lifestyles of the workers. They were allowed to shop at special stores, get medical treatment at special clinics, and vacation at special resorts. After the transfer, the typist became more motivated and even enjoyed the work. Is that intrinsic or extrinsic motivation? In the case of countries like Japan, where an ethic of hard work and loyalty to one's seniors is a basic part of cultural tradition, it's also hard to know if work motivation should be considered internal or external.

Another problem is distinguishing between the motivation inherent in the *worker* (some are more internally motivated than others) and in the *task* (some are more internally motivating than others). In every case there's a complex and ill-defined interaction among the worker, the task, and the worker's own perceptions of the task at hand. Another difficulty is defining a *motivator* as internal or external, as in the case of the employee who is highly internally motivated—to earn money. A third involves *time*. Work tends to become more routine and boring over the months and years; research participants are often tested over periods of mere hours. Lastly, there's the social climate both within and outside the organization.

The motivation of money

Occupational motivation was not a major problem in the days when most people either worked or starved. Managers knew that to increase productivity, it was necessary only to raise the pay (or, if they could get away with it, they could threaten to lower it). Money is still a tempting motivational tool for managers, because it is *easy to manipulate* and *traditional*.

Despite its apparent simplicity, money is a complex motivator. When employees are administered a questionnaire listing all possible benefits that they might derive from their work, and asked to rank order them in importance, "money" or "pay" is listed high, but not at the top. For instance, Herzberg, Mausner, and Snyderman (1959) found that achievement, recognition, the work itself, responsibility, and advancement were rated as more important than the pay. However, questionnaires carry strong *demand characteristics* (page 41), which may have induced respondents to rate these job benefits as more motivating than they really are.

Also, people regularly state that once they reach a certain income level, they will stop working for money (Maier & Verser, 1982). Yet, as it turns out, once the specified income level is reached, people develop further needs that had not been anticipated originally. We may conclude, then, that *money is a more important motivator than employees say it is.*

When we turn from the lower-level workers to the executive level, we find another complication. People typically achieve top management status partly because of their high *need for achievement*. For such people, continued salary increases become important not for any advancement to their lifestyle, but as a symbol of progress.

Through **projection** (the attribution of one's own feelings to others) such managers may assume that others have the same motivational responses as they do. What may happen, then, is that the top managers attempt to transfer or promote a middle management person in exchange for a salary increase, and find, to their astonishment and disappointment, that the middle manager is not willing to assume the extra responsibility or to disrupt the family by moving. So we may conclude that *money is less important to middle management than upper management assumes it is.*

Much research attention has been paid to the *manner* in which payment rates are calculated. *Piece rate* (production-based pay) seems fair in that the hardest worker earns the most. Historically, it is the oldest and most commonly used method of determining pay. But it brings the following problems:

- There is an increasing tendency to perceive piece rate pay as demeaning, as if it implies "The only measure of your worth is your output."

- Productivity may fluctuate through variables beyond the employee's control, such as equipment breakdown or a shortage of supplies.

- Many jobs are hard to measure in terms of "productivity." If professors, doctors, or police officers were paid on a piece rate basis, exactly how would their remuneration be calculated?

- Finally, there is considerable evidence in the early literature that social pressures may make it uncomfortable for one employee to exceed the output norm established by the group.

Time based pay is the simplest system. If all employees show the same number of hours or months on their time records, they all receive the same remuneration. The weakness, of course, is the lack of incentive for greater effort.

Seniority based pay assumes that the experienced employee is worth more than the novice. This seems fair to the old-timer who argues, "I have given the best years of my life to the job." But effectively, the motivating factor here is nothing more than the employee's remaining long enough on the job to command a high rate. Also, eager young workers may feel resentful over their lower rates.

The final approach is the *bonus* or *merit* pay system, in which the security of a fixed salary serves as a base rate, but extra talent and effort are rewarded with additional money. When the bonus intervals are short enough for the association between effort and bonus to become apparent, this system is increasingly favored.

Most of the research on how much pay is enough, or on the connection between pay and job satisfaction, is based on equity theory. As you might expect from common sense (if not from equity theory), research consistently shows that perceptions of being underpaid are associated with dissatisfaction.

The ways in which organizations can improve job satisfaction through effective leadership, "job involvement," and so on, are presented in the next two chapters.

TABLE 6.4 Nine motivational theories: A summary chart

Theory	Main construct
1. Maslow	hierarchy of needs
2. Herzberg	motivation may lead to job satisfaction hygiene may lead to job dissatisfaction
3. Job Characteristics	individual differences in needs and perception
4. Manifest Needs	needs based on personality and nAch
5. Expectancy	behavior influenced by expectancy of outcome or result
6. Balance and Equity	cognitions and interpretation of balance between input and outcome
7. Goal Setting (MBO)	intentions to fulfill goals
8. Behaviorism	stimulus or reinforcer response
9. Intrinsic	work = "play"

Motivation: An overview

At this stage you have read an outline of nine theories of industrial motivation, and probably feel confused. Table 6.4 simplifies the similarities and differences among the nine, and the following paragraphs may put the problem into perspective.

In one of the first comprehensive books on industrial psychology, Blum and Naylor (1968) ended the section on motivation with, "This chapter may be somewhat disappointing to those who believe that the psychologist should know all about motivation and hence should be able to explain motives and predict behavior. In many respects one of the great differences between the psychologist and the layman is that the psychologist is much more reluctant to make predictions about behavior."

Some decades later, we have more theories to consider, more questions to ask, and more sophisticated research techniques with which to ask them. Yet, we still do not have all the answers.

Motivation isn't enough. Otherwise (with rare exceptions) no student would get a grade lower than "A," no heart attack or stroke survivor would continue to chain-smoke cigarettes, and there'd be no middle-age obesity.

Even if it were adequate to explain behavior, motivation is not clearly understood. S)metimes a lab chimp, stuffed with bananas, will work hard to

FRANK AND EARNEST. Reprinted by permission of Newspaper Enterprise Associates, Inc.

earn a small banana pellet. Other times the same ape, even though food-deprived and obviously hungry, will apparently not feel like "working." These changes cannot be predicted or explained. If we hardly understand motivation in nonhuman primates, how can we expect to understand it fully in the human?

If someone were to descend from the Mountain bearing the secrets of human motivation, calling out, "Come and get it," industrial motivation would have to wait at the end of the line. We would first want to solve life-and-death problems relating to the motivation of criminals, tyrants, and disturbed children. Despite our searching, we do not have all the answers to human motivation. The human mind and spirit are too complex.

JOB SATISFACTION

The pursuit of happiness has such historical, philosophical, and social force that helping people to be happy has become a major industry: books, seminars, various cults, and psychotherapists all claim to show you the way to inner contentment. Given the impact of your daily work upon your life, the topic of happiness on the *job* should certainly interest you. And from the employer's standpoint, we have seen in the first half of this chapter that you work better when you *want* to. Accordingly, job satisfaction is of interest to managers as well.

The meaning of job satisfaction

Suppose your instructor asked you to measure your classmates' *motivation* for this course. Because motivation can generally be inferred from behavior, you could measure attendance, lateness, participation, and consultation with the instructor after class. Outside of class, you could measure how often

Think of the work you do at present. How well does each of the following words or phrases describe your work? **In the blank beside each word below, write**

Y for "Yes" if it describes your work

N for "No" if it does NOT describe it

? if you cannot decide

WORK ON PRESENT JOB

____ Routine
____ Satisfying
____ Good

Think of the pay you get now. How well does each of the following words or phrases describe your present pay? **In the blank beside each word below, write**

Y for "Yes" if it describes your pay

N for "No" if it does NOT describe it

? if you cannot decide

PRESENT PAY

____ Income adequate for normal expenses
____ Insecure
____ Less than I deserve

Think of the opportunities for promotion that you have now. How well does each of the following words or phrases describe these? **In the blank beside each word below, write**

Y for "Yes" if it describes your opportunities for promotion

N for "No" if it does NOT describe them

? if you cannot decide

OPPORTUNITIES FOR PROMOTION

____ Dead-end job
____ Unfair promotion policy
____ Regular promotions

Think of the kind of supervision that you get on your job. How well does each of the following words or phrases describe this? **In the blank beside each word below, write**

Y for "Yes" if it describes the supervision you get on your job

N for "No" if it does NOT describe it

? if you cannot decide

SUPERVISION

____ Impolite
____ Praises good work
____ Doesn't supervise enough

Think of the majority of the people that you work with now or the people you meet in connection with your work. How well does each of the following words or phrases describe these People? **In the blank beside each word below, write**

Y for "Yes" if it describes the people you work with

N for "if it does NOT describe them

? if you cannot decide

CO-WORKERS (PEOPLE)

____ Boring
____ Responsible
____ Intelligent

Think of your job in general. All in all, what is it like most of the time? **In the blank beside each word or phrase below, write**

Y for "Yes" if it describes your job

N for "No" if it does NOT describe it

? if you cannot decide

JOB IN GENERAL

____ Undesirable
____ Better than most
____ Rotten

Note: Each scale is presented on a separate page.
The Job Descriptive Index is copyrighted by Bowling Green State University. The complete forms, scoring key, instructions, and norms can be obtained from Dr. Patricia C. Smith, Department of Psychology, Bowling Green State University, Bowling Green, OH 43403.

Source: Patricia C. Smith. Copyright Bowling Green State University, Department of Psychology.

FIGURE 6.3 Sample items from the Job Descriptive Index, revised, 1985

The Job Descriptive Index is the most widely used measure of job satisfaction.

recommended or assigned readings are checked out of the library, and you could count what percentage of the class checks the posting of quiz marks in the first four hours. All these measures could be compared with those obtained from other courses.

Now suppose the assignment were to assess your classmates' *satisfaction* with the course. The problem here is that satisfaction is not always represented by behavior. Surely you have taken courses that left you bored, frustrated, angry, and discouraged, but you somehow worked even harder in these than in other courses that you loved. Your motivation to work hard may have stemmed from a sense of obligation, from a need to get a decent grade, or from wanting to prove to yourself that you could do it; maybe it was rewarding to earn a high grade from a disliked instructor. How, then, would you measure your classmates' satisfaction?

Like all constructs in psychology, job satisfaction is defined in terms of the techniques used to measure it. Sometimes work *behavior* is measured, under the assumption that production, turnover, absenteeism, and tardiness reflect satisfaction. Most commonly, employees are simply *asked* about their satisfaction level.

That's partly because in the 1930s, a student named Robert Hoppock devised the first job satisfaction rating scale, and administered it to virtually every working person, from unskilled laborers to professionals, in a Pennsylvania town. (The ratings were rather high, more so in the higher occupational levels.) Ever since then, the most common way of measuring job satisfaction has been the individual's *self*-rating, generally on a questionnaire.

A widely used measure of job satisfaction is Smith, Kendall, and Hulin's (1969) **Job Descriptive Index**. It consists of a short set of questions on the degree of satisfaction with the work itself, supervision, pay, promotions, and coworkers. A sample of this questionnaire is shown as Figure 6.3.

Self-ratings, though commonly used, invite a number of problems:

• People are rarely asked the global question, "How satisfied are you with your job?" Rather, they are asked to rate their satisfaction with specific aspects of their work, such as pay, fringe benefits, and relations with supervisors. The aspects chosen for the survey will certainly reflect the researcher's definition of job satisfaction, but will they represent the employees'? Consider workers who don't like their colleagues but don't care about this: their work attitudes aren't affected.

• When all the responses to the various aspects are to be condensed into a single number representing overall job satisfaction, how are the components to be weighted or combined?

• Questionnaire responses are always susceptible to *demand characteristics;* the wording, design, or title of the questionnaire can influence the outcome. There is a general *climate of dissatisfaction* in much of the North

So what Are *you* satisfied with your present "work"? Do you ever think about it? You should. Your job satisfaction has to do with how you get along with family, neighbors, or roommates, and how well you sleep at night. It relates even to how long you will live; several researchers (for example, Brill, 1978) have shown that work satisfaction predicts longevity. In fact, Palmore (1969) examined a large number of variables in hundreds of people over a 13-year period, and concluded that work satisfaction was the best single predictor of longevity, especially in older males. He ultimately concluded that environmental factors were more predictive of longevity than even genetic influences (Palmore, 1971).

American workforce. It's increasingly held by employees, for instance, that assembly-line work is demeaning, and incidents of labor strife are widely reported. Labor harmony is not "news," so it is ignored in the mass media. Thus, the public generally assumes that many people are unhappy at work. How can we separate the employee's independent, subjective appraisal of the job from the demand characteristics of the question?

- There is no doubt a powerful **recency effect**. Life, on or off the job, visits a variety of pleasures and rough patches upon us all. Questionnaire responses may be influenced by the season's weather, or which side of bed the employee got out of that day.

- Survey answers are responsive also to the prevailing social climate. In every community, it is generally known that so-and-so company is a good place to work, whereas at such-and-such the workers are invariably embroiled in strikes, work-to-rule, and legal actions against the employer. If a new employee feels, "This job gives me everything I ever hoped for, but I must be unhappy at it, because everybody else seems to be," how can we fairly and accurately appraise that person's job satisfaction?

- The survey technique brings with it pressures to lower the satisfaction ratings. One such pressure is the respondents' assumption that a low rating might bring about improvements or more appreciation of their efforts, whereas a high rating could make improvements harder to get. Another is that when respondents think back over the past year's experiences, they may recall problems and frustrations more sharply than the day-to-day sources of job satisfaction.

Because self-reports involve so many problems, researchers turn to *be-havioral* measures of job satisfaction. Measurements of turnover, absenteeism, and productivity, for instance, are more objective than self-reports. Are these measures accurate reflections of job satisfaction? Older employees are more satisfied than younger ones (Howell & Dipboye, 1982); youngsters tend to be less satisfied with life in general. But if the oldest employees are off work for medical reasons more than the younger ones, will absenteeism rates accurately reflect job satisfaction?

Job satisfaction research

Some time ago, Locke (1976) counted over three thousand published studies on job satisfaction! This huge body of research was not concerned with the value of job satisfaction to the individual employee; the context of the studies was that a satisfied worker is better for the employer in terms of absenteeism, turnover, and possibly productivity. Let's look at a few of these studies.

Taylor's simplistic views of "scientific management" (page 15) dominated concepts of job satisfaction throughout the first half of this century. Convinced that money is the prime motivator, Taylor argued that *scientific management* meant increasing worker efficiency and instituting an incentive system for compensation, so that earnings would be maximized for both employee and employer.

Much of the early research in what was then called industrial psychology examined the variables on which Taylorism focused. These studies, mostly in the United States, England, and Germany, examined how the work environment could be changed to reduce fatigue. The research focused on variables such as illumination, noise, and music.

Meanwhile, the Hawthorne studies (page 19) were strongly suggesting that scientific management was not simply a matter of incentive systems and job efficiency. Workers evidently respond just as much to the *social* demands of the immediate work situation.

Most of life's activities are repetitive and, for many people, boring. Logically, work activities should be repetitive and boring too. But in a climate of **job entitlement** (the feeling that one is *entitled* to this or that), work is *supposed* to be challenging, rewarding, varied, and enjoyable. In fact, Staw (1986) suggested that job satisfaction is less determined by external factors (such as tasks and environment) than by the worker's own disposition.

Staw analyzed data from three longitudinal studies by Berkeley's Institute of Human Development that followed a group of California males from the 1920s throughout their lives. The researchers had measured the correlation between affective characteristics (for example, being sympathetic, hostile, cheerful) in younger years with subsequent job satisfaction. Staw concluded that those who started life with positive personality characteristics (being likable, giving, and so on) were more content with their jobs.

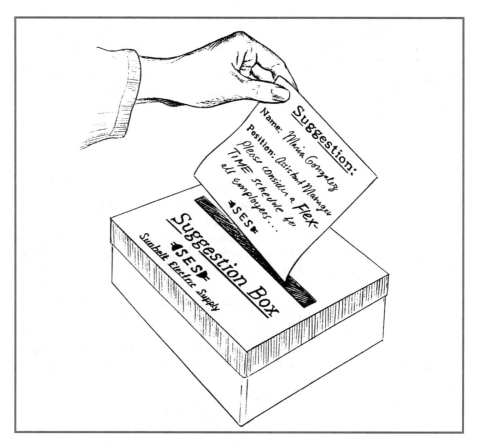

Researchers have found a high correlation between job satisfaction and participative decision making.

Herzberg's position on motivation continues to relate to job satisfaction. For instance, Abdel-Halim (1983), through an analysis of questionnaire responses, found the correlation between job satisfaction and *participative decision making* to be quite strong (+.5). Between job satisfaction and *task repetitiveness* it was, as you might expect, inversely related (−.4).

Many studies have examined *employee characteristics* to see if, for instance, women are more satisfied than men, or older workers more than younger. A number of generalities can be drawn, but the correlations are weak. In any case, the connection may well be the result of the type of *work* rather than the type of *worker*. For instance, older workers are more satisfied with their work than younger employees, according to a review by Rhodes (1983). But older employees may enjoy their work more, not because of their age, but because they have managed to find more enjoyable positions. As an example, the higher the job status the higher the average job satisfaction, and high-status positions are generally held by older people.

Of course, satisfied *people* are likely to be satisfied *workers*. Some people have a temperament that makes them easy to satisfy. Indeed, one study measured job satisfaction five years apart, and found it to be quite stable (Staw & Ross, 1985). And Levin and Stokes (1989), in a combined laboratory and field study, found that some people are generally negative, both on and off the job. Maybe there's even some genetic component to one's disposition to be, or not to be, generally satisfied. One study in Minnesota suggested that identical twins reared apart have somewhat similar ratings of satisfaction with their work (Arvey, Bouchard, Segal & Abraham, 1989).

In any case, one meta-analysis (Tait, Padgett & Baldwin, 1989) of studies encompassing twenty thousand individuals found that there is a strong connection between job satisfaction and general life satisfaction. The only exception was that studies published prior to 1974 did not find this connection for women. One explanation is that work is so central to men's lives that it's always been hard for them to separate their work and nonwork feelings. In past generations, women could make this separation, but the modern working woman is demographically similar to her male counterpart, and she attributes the same importance to work as do men.

Education is probably related in a complex way to employee satisfaction. On one hand, as the average educational level increases, some people can use their qualifications to achieve more desirable and satisfying jobs. On the other hand, individuals who stayed in school to get a good job may find themselves educationally overqualified for whatever openings exist, and may therefore be more dissatisfied with the job they get.

It's equally difficult to say whether women are less or more satisfied than men. Any differences must be minor; a major literature review by Brush, Moch, and Pooyan (1987) reported no meaningful sex difference in job satisfaction. Witt and Nye (1992) found that both men and women, in various work settings, reported the same high job satisfaction as long as they felt they were dealt with fairly in terms of pay and promotion.

The variables are complex. Women have traditionally suffered from sex discrimination barriers that kept them in low-level positions. But women used to have lower expectations than men, and so were more easily satisfied. As women's expectations rise, their satisfaction levels may decrease. Mottaz (1986) indicated that (at least in low-level jobs) women place more importance on good relationships at work, and men are more satisfied by pay, titles, and power. Also, women in traditional positions are less satisfied than those who have managed to break into what has traditionally been considered as men's work.

Current research is looking less at characteristics of the person and more at the nature of the *organization* in which the person works. In a book on the relation between the employee and the organization, Mowday, Porter, and Steers (1982) defined **attitudinal commitment** as the employee's iden-

Brief case

Have you ever gone into a bank and said to yourself, "I bet this teller is just filling in time here and won't remain very long; I wouldn't be surprised if the one who served me last week will end up as manager some day"? Wright's (1990) survey of hundreds of California bank tellers found that those re-porting career opportunity as the prime mo-tive for working at the bank were more achievement-oriented, competitive, and likely to volunteer for extra work, and they social-ized with colleagues less during working hours. Wright termed this "organizational commitment."

tification with and involvement in the organization. A worker with high at-titudinal commitment believes in the organizations's goals and values, is will-ing to work hard for the benefit of the company, wants to remain associated with it, and feels highly loyal to it.

The Mowday et al. book suggests that a firm can enhance attitudinal commitment by ensuring that new employees are encouraged to contribute meaningfully to the organization. The firm should also ensure that its ex-ecutives are perceived as trustworthy, confidence-inspiring, and dedicated to reaching the organization's goals, rather than to using their positions to fur-ther their own objectives. Firms with high attitudinal commitment show a much lower rate of *turnover*. Absenteeism and productivity are also linked to commitment, but not as strongly (Mobley, 1982).

Another line of research is examining the connection between *attitudi-nal commitment* and *behavioral commitment*. Is it possible that you might feel loyalty, respect, and affection for your employer, but be indifferent about extending yourself at work? Such research examines, for instance, the per-formance of employees who are determined to do the best job possible for an organization to which they felt no allegiance.

An example of the current trend toward *integration* is evident in research on how job satisfaction is related to a group of variables. For instance, Shep-perd (1993) looked at the incentives offered, how important employees think their contributions are, the effort needed to do the job, and the quality of the work.

WHAT DIFFERENCE DOES HIGH JOB SATISFACTION MAKE?

Chapter 1 introduced you to the meaning of "work." After the comment that many people view their work negatively came the observation that a major objective of I/O psychology is to move the perception of work in a more positive direction. One reason to maximize job satisfaction is that it's a professional responsibility to improve the human condition.

A more practical reason is the logical assumption that a contented worker is a better employee. We expect, for instance, high job satisfaction to be related to measurable improvements in *productivity* and declines in **withdrawal behaviors** (absenteeism and turnover rates). Researchers tend to look for what they expect to find. If you were an expert in job satisfaction (maybe you had come up with a theory to explain it, a test to measure it, or a procedure to increase it), wouldn't you be interested in research designed to show how much *better* it was to have satisfied employees?

Unfortunately, the correlates of job satisfaction are exceedingly complex. Consider, as an example, three factors involving **turnover**:

1. Turnover isn't necessarily good or bad. Low turnover should reduce costs for recruitment, selection, and training, but might it not also increase stagnation and "deadwood" employees? I/O psychologists distinguish between two types of turnover: **functional turnover**, which improves the workforce, and **dysfunctional turnover**, or the loss of valued workers.

2. Alternative job opportunities can influence turnover rates. One corporation may have employees who have no other place to find work; another may experience a large competitor opening a plant across the street. The two businesses may have different turnover rates that have nothing to do with the satisfaction of their employees. Or turnover rates in the same plant measured in 1970 and again in 1990 may reflect periods of economic expansion and contraction, rather than changes in job satisfaction.

3. The relation between satisfaction and turnover may differ for good and marginal workers. For instance, there's some evidence that poor employees are more likely to quit because of job dissatisfaction than superior ones (Spencer & Steers, 1981).

What about **absenteeism**? Even this is hard to measure. Some workers routinely miss Fridays and Mondays due to hangovers; others are single parents caring for sick children. Some employers have liberal absence policies with convenient opportunities to make up missed shifts; others have strict limits and automatic penalties for absences. Some organizations have an unwritten policy that employees are expected to book two days a month off in the slack season; in others it's generally understood that nobody takes off work unless it's absolutely unavoidable.

Moreover, some workers have considerable workplace power and independence; others know they can easily be fired. Some jobs are not greatly affected by absences; others are. (For instance, an assembler or electrician who misses a week is easily replaced; a surgeon or professor who takes a week off could cause substantial disruption.) And possibly, absenteeism is related not to job satisfaction in general, but to some specific aspect of it. It's not entirely surprising that, in general, research has not supported a close link between job satisfaction and absenteeism.

So we'll leave turnover and absenteeism, and ask if happy employees are not measurably *better* workers. Not really, according to massive reviews of the literature (Brayfield & Crockett, 1985; Iaffaldana & Muchinsky, 1985). And even if they are, would it be because high job satisfaction improves performance, because good performance increases satisfaction, or because some people are good performers and easily satisfied?

In short, then, despite energetic efforts to show high correlations between common measures of job satisfaction and three basic measures of job behavior, it comes down to this: it's better to be happy than unhappy, but pretty much the same work gets accomplished in either case.

WHICH MOTIVATION/SATISFACTION THEORY IS RIGHT?

Having employees who are highly motivated to do a good job, and who are perfectly satisfied with their work world: these are universal objectives of managers. Enjoying what you do and wanting to do it well: these are surely your objectives too. You have just finished a chapter that tells just about everything psychology has to offer on occupational motivation and satisfaction. Does this mean that now you can fulfill the objectives?

The most frustrating aspect of taking a first course in I/O psychology is having to learn so many theories of motivation and satisfaction and of knowing that the large number of theories means that no one of them really works. "I wish we could have fewer theories and more facts," students often complain.

Human beings and their interactions are exceedingly complex. Facts are easy to acquire, but it's much more challenging to come up with theories that explain all the facts. None of the theories that you have read can prescribe how to explain and control motivation and satisfaction for all people in all circumstances. But each theory that you have read goes some of the distance, and each can be valid and useful in some circumstances.

If you feel somewhat frustrated, consider that some day when you are thinking about a master's thesis or a doctoral dissertation on the topics of employee motivation or satisfaction, you'll be glad to have so many theories to integrate, to derive testable predictions from, and to improve. Indeed, if you take advantage of the present proliferation of theories, the next generation of students may have yours to add to the list!

Study guide for chapter 6

HAVE YOU LEARNED THESE NAMES AND TERMS?

industrial history

motivation

trait

need theories

heuristic

motivator and hygiene needs

two-factor theory

job characteristics theory

task identity

task significance

autonomy

feedback

job diagnostic survey

nAch; need for achievement

need to avoid failure

self-efficacy

need for power

cognitive

expectancy theory

role perception

balance or equity theory

goal setting theory

management by objectives (MBO)

Skinnerian, operant, instrumental conditioning

behavior modification

punishment

reinforcement: positive and negative

reinforcement: primary and secondary

reinforcement: partial and continuous

reinforcement: fixed and variable ratio

intrinsic and extrinsic motivation

projection

Job Descriptive Index

recency effect

job entitlement

attitudinal commitment

withdrawal behavior

turnover: functional and dysfunctional

absenteeism

ISSUES TO CONSIDER

Why is motivation considered one of the core areas in psychology?

Why is motivation termed an inferred theoretical construct?

Why is Maslow's needs hierarchy such a popular concept?

How did Herzberg's theory improve on Maslow's?

How did Herzberg's choice of research participants contribute to the development of his theory?

Why are Hackman and Oldham the first modern motivational theorists?

How else might Griffin's study (page 174) be explained?

What are the strengths and weaknesses of expectancy theory?

Why is partial reinforcement preferable to continuous reinforcement?

Why are motivation and work satisfaction covered in the same chapter?

Why are the results of using money as a motivator inconsistent?

What are some problems with measuring satisfaction by using self-reports?

Why has research on satisfaction switched to organizational factors?

What are the advantages and disadvantages of attitudinal commitment?

What problem is associated with behavioral commitment?

Why is there no definitive theory explaining motivation and satisfaction?

SAMPLE MULTIPLE-CHOICE QUESTIONS

1. An extension of Henry Murray's theory is that managers should
   a. select personnel who are intrinsically high in motivation.
   b. focus on raising the motivation of employees.
   c. select applicants with moderate motivation
   d. ignore the topic of motivation.

2. The motivation theory/theories that are well supported by research are
   a. balance theories and goal setting theory.
   b. Maslow's needs hierarchy theory.
   c. job characteristics theory.
   d. intrinsic motivation.

3. The motivation theory that most relates also to job satisfaction is that of
   a. Hackman and Oldham.
   b. Murray.
   c. Skinner.
   d. Herzberg.

4. If you score high in nAch, you would probably prefer a task of ___ difficulty.
   a. great
   b. moderate
   c. minimal
   d. no

5. High attitudinal commitment is strongly associated with
   a. high turnover.
   b. low turnover.
   c. high productivity.
   d. low productivity.

Answers: page 462

The progress of human society consists . . . in . . . the better and better apportioning of wages to work.

Thomas Carlyle (1795–1881)

Bird's-eye view of the chapter

Applied psychology specializes in tests and measurement or "psychometrics." You met this topic in chapter 4, but that was in the context of applicant *assessment*. Now we apply psychometric techniques to the employee, as we enter the realm of work *appraisal*.

Chapter 7

Employee appraisal

The payoff from chapter 7   You will:

1. Appreciate the importance and inevitability of routine appraisals
2. Understand the difficulties on both sides of the appraiser's desk
3. Know the many functions that appraisal can serve
4. Appreciate the role of establishing the *job criterion* prior to appraisal
5. Know basic principles regarding the appraisal *process*
6. See the need to communicate the process throughout the organization
7. Know something of the changing emphasis in the appraisal literature
8. Differentiate between *subjective* and *objective* techniques
9. Know problems attending *objective* methods
10. Learn suitable procedures for both very large and very small groups
11. Appreciate the role of the personnel file in rating
12. Understand the types and designs of *rating scales*
13. Know the problems associated with *subjective* rating techniques
14. Comprehend the prevailing attitude toward evaluations
15. Know the types of self-appraisals and the pros and cons of using these
16. Understand *upward* and *downward* rating
17. Know principles of *improving* employee evaluation
18. Appreciate the *legal* implications of any appraisal method
19. See the role of appraisal *feedback*
20. Recognize the contributions that I/O psychology can make to appraisals

How many tests and examinations have you taken during your years of schooling? How many papers, reports, presentations, and other projects have you completed? When you think of the total number, you'll have a picture of how regularly you have been *assessed*. These assessments are important to you. They determine pass or failure, low marks or high, graduation or not, and maybe the type of job and economic future you can anticipate.

When you enter the work world, you may have seen your last final exam, but you won't be free from assessments. Nor will these be any less important to you than your school exams were. Work assessments may determine whether you are promoted or fired, retrained or transferred, offered more responsibility, or switched to less important work, and, ultimately, whether your job gives you the lifestyle you want.

From the employer's perspective, employee assessments have enormously important implications. Undetected shortcomings on the part of employees have obvious costs. Less apparent costs might appear when the employee is finally fired, and sues for wrongful dismissal on the basis that the absence of early warnings constituted a tacit acceptance of the job performance. And superior performance, if undetected, bears the often-hidden costs of dissatisfaction and underutilization.

Just as testing and grading students is a problematic task for professors, employee appraisal is often the hardest part of supervision. In the workplace this task has not only performance and efficiency implications, but emotional, organizational, remunerative, and legal overtones as well.

INTRODUCING APPRAISAL: PURPOSE, PROCESS, AND PRINCIPLES

Employee appraisal serves global functions that permeate the entire organization. The organization should be clear on what these are, because some methods of appraisal work better for some purposes than for others. Obvious functions include the making of rational and fair decisions regarding *promotions, placement, transfers or dismissals,* and *remuneration* (salary increases and merit pay), as well as determining and increasing the *efficiency* of the workforce.

There are a number of less obvious functions as well. Accurate appraisals are crucial for the *evaluation of recruitment, selection, and training* procedures. Appraisal can determine further *training* needs, and occasionally *counseling* needs. It can increase employee *motivation* through the feedback process (page 173) and may provide an evaluation of *working conditions*. And it can improve employee *productivity* by encouraging the strong areas and modifying the weak ones. Further, employee evaluation can improve *managerial effec-*

MESSAGE
From: Marks@sun.daycare
To: Ppena@eco.diaper
Subject: Shipment

Received the 2 dozen re-usable
diapers. When I re-order please
make the size adjustment strip
longer. Thanks!

Move Delete Save Reply Close

Appraisal is indirect for persons who run their own business. They receive feedback from their customers, suppliers, and others in their business network. These assessments may be helpful to keep the business competitive.

tiveness by making supervisors more interested in and observant of individual employees. If required to *justify* making an unfavorable personnel decision, the employer may need to turn to the performance evaluation records.

Appraisal is important for *research,* both corporate and academic. Often, changes are made to improve employee performance. Is there actually an improvement? The answer often lies in the appraisal records. Rassenfoss and Kraut (1988) reported that half of all personnel-related research is on performance appraisal.

What if you run your own business, or if you work in a commune or cooperative? Even if there's no supervisor looking over your shoulder, you are still subject to ratings from customers, suppliers, competitors, and colleagues. Besides, most of us like to have an idea of how we're doing, and because people often identify themselves in terms of their occupation, appraisal can help with our *self-definitions.*

You'll recall that the best selection test is one that accurately predicts the *criterion* (page 87), and that predictive validation consists of correlating test scores with criterion scores. The test scores are easy to obtain. Now is the time to address the other correlate, the *criterion* scores, that is, the accurate assessment of employee performance.

Brief case

To be motivating, performance standards should be high enough to constitute a goal, but low enough to be attainable and lead to positive feedback. Industrial/organizational psychologist Philip Bobko reported consulting for an organization that had established a performance standard of 80 percent customer satisfaction. A middle manager in- creased this to 85 percent to ensure that the standard was met. Other managers down the chain of command made similar alterations. Finally, the employees who had to deal with clients were faced with an unrealistically high performance standard, and naturally suffered from low work satisfaction.

Proper appraisal, as implied above, begins with *defining the criterion* (such as absenteeism, productivity, or safety) for the individual employee, and by establishing the *organization's* overall and appraisal *goals*. For instance, one appropriate goal for an organization could be the fair and comprehensive evaluation of all of its members. This could be accomplished by defining and quantifying "fair and comprehensive evaluation," rating supervisors on their performance in evaluating subordinates, and rewarding those who do well. The organization must decide whether the purpose of employee assessment is to evaluate or improve worker training, to decide on promotions or transfers, to settle disputes, to conduct research, or to provide feedback.

More specifically, performance standards (page 83) that define good or exemplary performance should be established. The standards should be explicit; broken into small, attainable but meaningful parts; agreed to by the employee; and communicated clearly. A book by Eden (1990) and a major paper by Bobko and Colella (1994) review the literature documenting the effect of the organization's expectations upon motivation, satisfaction, and performance, especially for new employees.

Another preliminary step is the assessment or *training of the evaluators* themselves. Unlike most managerial functions, having to make a formal appraisal of an associate is often seen as an unpleasant task (McGregor, 1957), partly because of inadequate training. The training of evaluators will be covered on page 226.

The procedures and the schedule of appraisal should be systematic and formal, even though there is no perfect system. Most major firms adopt an annual schedule of appraisal (Sims, Veres & Heninger, 1987), but employees in a new job or undertaking new responsibilities probably should be evaluated more often than that.

Finally, the appraisal goals and procedure should be *communicated* clearly to all tiers of the organization. Like an exam, an evaluation process can be perceived as threatening, demeaning, unfair, and intrusive. Hence, the communication should be designed to present the evaluation in a positive light to new employees, veteran workers, supervisors, and top management.

METHODS OF APPRAISAL

Most of this chapter is devoted to the wide variety of techniques that has been developed for measuring performance. The extent of this variety is due partly to the diversity of the work itself; a system that works well for evaluating an insurance seller might be inappropriate for a car assembler, an aircraft pilot, or a college professor. It's also due to changing currents in assessment theory. During and shortly after the 1960s, researchers were concentrating on the development of better rating scales. A number of these were developed, all proving to be equally accurate. In the 1980s, the focus turned from the type of rating scale to the characteristics of the rater, and the recent emphasis has been on the dynamics of both the entire organization and the appraisal process.

As mentioned, the issue of employee appraisal is closely linked with that of defining the job criterion. Just as in determining the job criterion, there are two basic approaches to appraising employees, the objective and the subjective. It is unlikely that any method is entirely the one or the other, but the basic difference is that **objective measurements** would be the same regardless of who made them, whereas **subjective measurements** refer to evaluations based on personal opinions. For instance, the instruction: "Rate the happiness level of each employee on a five-point scale from 'Miserable' to 'Ecstatic'" would be quite subjective, whereas "Observe each employee over a typical one-hour period and record the number of smiles and frowns you see" would be relatively objective. We will start with traditional objective methods, followed by subjective ones; then we'll turn to specialty procedures.

Objective appraisal methods

In appraising performance, managers presumably seek measures that are clear, unambiguous, independent of personal opinion, and therefore fair. It's easy to record how productive or how fast an employee is. Such quantifiable information, discussed by Landy and Farr (1983), could even be performed by a machine or computer. Objective measures, as implied by the word *objective,* are relatively immune from the effects of partiality. Ford, Kraiger, and Schechtman (1986) performed a meta-analysis of some 50 samples of performance data, and concluded that the objective ones were virtually free of

So what Did your last boss or teacher let you know how and when you'd be given regular, timely evaluations? Was the process fair and sensitive; for instance, did your overall good efforts overshadow the occasional slip-up? Did you feel that your evaluator used accurate measurement tools, followed written procedures, and was comfortable in doing this? Was your assessment so general that it could have applied to many of your colleagues, or was it specific, for instance, taking into account your background and providing guidance relating to your future? Were the results communicated to you promptly and constructively, and were you invited to think about them and respond? Not all workers can answer yes to all the above questions. If and when you have your own employees, what will their answers be about you?

racial bias. Here are a few light-hearted examples of possibilities for objective performance measurement:

- seer   number of fortunes predicted per week

- sayer   number of sooths said

- sewer   number of shirts sewn

- sewer worker   number of sewers shoveled out

- suer   number of defendants sued

- sawyer   number of cords of wood cut

However, there is a long list of errors that can, if care is not applied, weaken objective measures:

1. **Deficiency** refers to the tendency of objective measures to yield only a partial picture of the job. Most employees are expected to accomplish more than simply write up orders, assemble computers, or wash so many windows. Suppose, for instance, a university administrator decides that students' evaluations of courses are too subjective, so faculty are to be rated according to the number of pages they publish, or the number of lecture words they speak in a year. Or picture a police department that has an overall goal of "improved community relations and positive client service interactions." These objectives are hard to define, quantify, and assess, so the officers are rated on number of charges laid for law infractions, percentage of reports filled in properly and on time, and so forth.

2. **Opportunity bias** refers to differences in the work situation that create unfairness in the application of an objective measure. Typical measures are the number of products assembled, repaired, or sold. But one assembler might suffer from a shortage of components, one mechanic might encounter an impossible repair job, and one seller might be assigned a poor sales territory. Moreover, many organizations have a few members within the same job level whose duties are unique: one firefighter may be assigned to fire prevention work, one police officer to breathalyzer operation, one professor to distance education. Even the timing of the appraisal can result in unfairness. Suppose hospital nurses are rated on the average time they take to respond to a call for service during a specific week. Maternity nurses may have consistent demands on them throughout the year, whereas emergency room nurses might be understaffed during summer holidays, and overworked at year-end.

3. There is inconsistency in the managerial position that "I want to assess behavior objectively, so *I'll* decide which objective measures to record." To evaluate research contributions, one university administration may weigh the writing of a book as the strongest academic contribution a professor can make; another may regard this as a commercial venture that should be ignored. Or to weigh the amount of teaching, one administrator may count the total number of students taught; another may consider only graduate or seminar courses as worthy of counting.

4. Another problem with objective measures is that the behaviors they purport to document are rarely as simple and unified as would seem at first glance. Determining "absenteeism," for instance, seems straightforward. However, if one employee skips 100 days in a year, always on Fridays and Mondays, while another takes 100 days to recover from heart surgery, should both have the same absenteeism rating?

5. In the early days of research on appraisal, it seemed appropriate to evaluate on the basis of productivity. Back then most jobs were in factories that employed large numbers of people who had identical, unchanging tasks and similar equipment. Today there are fewer instances where productivity serves as a useful and independent primary measure of employee worth. Can you judge firefighters by how many blazes they extinguish, pilots by the distance flown, or books by the word count? Many current jobs require long-term planning, careful judgment, and people-handling skills—attributes that lack a countable output measure. Also, employers are now expected to hire the nontraditional worker partly for the benefits to the larger community, benefits that also defy quantification.

6. **Sampling error** results from selecting examples of behavior that do not accurately represent its totality. Of course we all have successful periods and difficult ones. The more the data fluctuate, the more extended the time period of data gathering should be.

Brief case

The contract for a typical Canadian police service includes the following provisions for personnel files: Officers may see their file at any time by appointment, and must be informed when anything is added to it or when a supervisor pulls the file. Objective performance data (for instance, records of specialized training, and scores on the annual shooting-range test) and any commendations stay filed permanently; adverse data such as reports of citizen complaints or the required self-reports of drawing their weapon in public, are automatically removed after two years. The annual supervisory rating is filed permanently, and officers may append their comments to the rating. They may file grievances if these policies are violated.

Here are some common approaches to objective appraisal:

The personnel file   The oldest and most traditional source of "hard" data is the personnel file. Properly kept files will contain copies of commendations, awards, warnings, or reprimands; records of absenteeism and lateness; records of accidents, grievances, and "incidents"; information on complaints by or about the employee; and the employee's remuneration and career path.

One problem with relying on personnel folders is that the inferences as to the meaning of the variables may be quite unjustified. For instance, work is increasingly focusing on creative as opposed to routine tasks. If you just count the number of grievances filed by the worker, you can't tell if a record of numerous grievances indicates a troublemaking obstructionist or someone with a strong social conscience. A record of accidents may indicate carelessness or a willingness to extend oneself.

Another problem is that many types of notations never appear in most employees' personnel files. The typical employee does not have accidents, does not file grievances, and does not steal company property. All this points up the need for businesses to review their policies and procedures in connection with the personnel file.

Computerized performance monitoring   The newest wrinkle in employee evaluation includes **computerized performance monitoring (CPM)**. Businesses that include intensive computer use, such as insurance, telephone, and banking, can easily document worker input, thereby showing attendance, errors, task speed and completion, and the like. As a second example, an **active badge** worn by employees can track their whereabouts and movements and chart this at a central location. Thirdly, a new generation of security cameras, which are inexpensive, unobtrusive, and high-resolution, can monitor workstations around the clock.

To the employer or rater, these techniques have the advantage of being objective and detailed, but to employees, they raise the specter of "Big Brother" looking over their shoulder every second of the workday. Another problem is that not all data are easy for a machine to monitor. This invites the inappropriate use of data that happen to be easily collected. Suppose you were assigned to learn the contents of some publications, and you learned that your grade was based on computerized library records showing when you took out and when you returned these documents.

To compare how evaluators rate visual versus computerized data, Kulik and Abrose (1993) had undergraduates perform a 2-hour computer exercise on a variety of tasks. One of the tasks included a simulated employee evaluation, in this case, of a typist's performance. A videotape showed the typists performing a variety of work, some performing well, others poorly, and the CPM apparatus gave data on the typists' speed, again either showing above or below average performance that was sometimes consistent with, other times contradictory to, the visual information. Which had the greater impact on the evaluations, the visual or the CPM information?

The visual data were more influential in determining the ratings, suggesting that raters pay relatively little attention to CPM data when they have observational data too. This is not surprising, in that CPM data are relatively "dry" and unfamiliar. It shows that the latest technology is not necessarily preferable to what it replaces. (Ironically, in this test of CPM, the students' own data input was being monitored! The students took the least amount of time to evaluate the work when they saw good performance.)

Subjective techniques

Subjective measures are those that are the personal opinions of the rater. A rater could, for instance, simply write a report evaluating the employee. This is sometimes termed an *essay evaluation*. It is often considered too subjective and free-flowing to be satisfactory to either party.

If the rater were to compare the best and worst employee performing the same task, most of the behavior may be similar. Only a few aspects of the work may be performed differently by the two. When the evaluation focuses on only those components that differentiate the two, it is termed the *critical incident* method (page 86).

Rating scales, checklists, and comparisons   Three other techniques have been devised to make the subjective process as fair as possible. They are **rating scales**, **checklists**, and *comparisons*, which we'll cover in turn.

Rating scales are shown in Figure 7.1. They are termed **graphic rating scales** because the rater makes a mark along a horizontal line or set of alter-

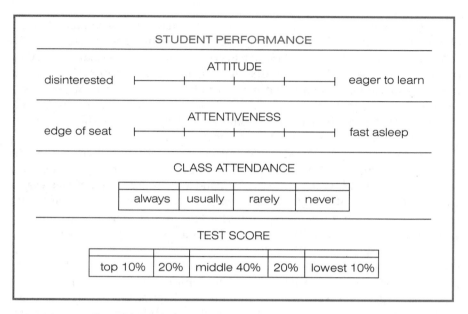

FIGURE 7.1 Graphic rating scales

Here are four examples of graphic rating scales. The top two, in which
the rater puts a mark anywhere on the line, are continuous; the lower
two, in which the rater checks one box, are discrete.

natives, as if on a graph. As you see in the figure, scales may be **continuous**
or **discrete**.

Although such rating scales are simple, appealing, and popular, they
invite unfairness. (Common rater errors are outlined at the end of this section.) Different raters may assign different arbitrary numbers to the same
behavior, and it may be hard for each of them to explain the judgments,
and hard for the ratee to understand or benefit from them. An alternate type
of rating scale, designed to reduce these problems, is the **Behavioral Observation Scale (BOS)**. A typical BOS is shown in Figure 7.2.

As you see in Figure 7.2, the focus here is on the specific *behaviors* of
the student (or employee). The behaviors that are rated have to be chosen
carefully. They are not there simply to constitute an inventory of employee
attributes and tasks, but to provide measurable indicators by which the top-
performing employees can be differentiated from the worst ones. This is an
application of the *critical incident* technique (page 86). Details on the BOS
are described in Latham and Wexley (1981). A recent literature review indicated that the BOS is an excellent evaluation procedure that is appropriate
across various cultures (Latham, Skarlicki, Irvine & Siegel, 1993).

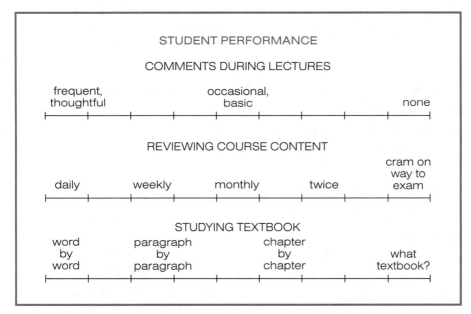

FIGURE 7.2 Behavioral observation scales

Behavioral observation scales rate specific behaviors. It is more accurate to use these to distinguish high performers, provided the anchor words of the scale are chosen carefully.

The BOS procedure is simple and straightforward, but it depends upon the rater's ability to recall behaviors that represent typical employee activity. The BOS was derived from a more sophisticated procedure that had been developed by Smith and Kendall (1963), and is being used increasingly now. (This reference is still the most comprehensive source of basic information on the BOS.) This is the **Behaviorally Anchored Rating Scale (BARS)**. Here, relevant examples of performance are listed as "anchors" that allow easy conversion to numbers on a scale; the example shown in Figure 7.3 will make this clear. The rater chooses the one phrase that best typifies the employee's behavior; the phrase gives the score on that dimension or area of performance.

The construction of a BARS includes a number of steps. Typically, 5 to 10 task dimensions—generated from a meeting with a group of employees or supervisors, or from a job analysis (page 84)—are listed. Then employees are asked to come up with real-life examples of exemplary, average, and unsatisfactory behaviors for each of the listed dimensions. The next step is to get consensus by supervisors that these examples are appropriate to the dimension, and that the number of points assigned to each example is fair.

	PROFESSORS' RAPPORT WITH STUDENT
RATING POINTS	BEHAVIOR
5	Senses when someone's lost, corrects problem patiently and clearly
4	If asked question after class, stays behind to answer
3	If asked question, replies "See me during office hours"
2	In office, seems distant and indifferent
1	Doesn't keep office hours
0	When approached, humiliates and dismisses student

FIGURE 7.3 A behaviorally anchored rating scale

This scale is created by first determining what qualities are being measured and then choosing behavior examples that assess those qualities. In this example, specific behaviors shown by professors are rated.

Developing a BARS takes time, thought, and work, but once constructed, it has three strong advantages:

1. It is usually easy for the rater to *apply* the descriptions to each employee.
2. The ratings can provide useful feedback to the employee in terms of strengths and weaknesses.
3. The descriptions can be designed for any type of work.

To use a checklist, the rater is given a list of descriptors (for example, "punctual," safety-conscious," "unfriendly") and asked to put a check mark next to each one that applies to the ratee. These descriptors may be positive, negative, or mixed. In a **weighted checklist**, safety might be weighted as worth three points, for instance, punctuality as two, and friendliness as worth only one point.

In a more elaborate type of checklist, the rater is given not a "yes" or "no" decision on each descriptor, but a scale. Most scales have five points, labeled, for example, "never," "rarely," "average," "often," "always." In this type, the rater is required to answer each item for each subordinate, although there may be provisions for a "not applicable" response.

Where there is a small group of employees engaged in similar work, it may be appropriate to use the **employee comparison method**. The simplest of these procedures is the **ranking** method. Suppose there are 10 department store clerks. The rater decides on a criterion, for instance, enthusiasm, and ranks the employees. It is usually easy to decide upon the first one or two and the last few, but it is often difficult to differentiate among those in the average range. Of course, more than one rater, and more than one criterion, can be used. Ten employees could be reasonably rated among each other, but it would be hopeless to try this on a group of 100 individuals.

An alternative is the use of **paired comparisons**. Each pair of employees is studied to determine which of the two is the better or worse of the pair on a given dimension. As an illustration, suppose you're in charge of choosing a snack for the cafeteria, and there are three different snacks for you to evaluate. You take any two, say, Yummo and Chocko, take alternate bites out of each, and decide you prefer Chocko. Later, you compare the winner with another brand, Snacko. Chocko wins again, so you know that Chocko surpasses Yummo and Snacko. Then you make a side-by-side comparison between Yummo and Snacko, and rate Snacko higher. Now you have a hierarchy: Chocko over Snacko over Yummo.

This is a simple and accurate procedure to use on a small number of individuals. However, the required number of paired comparisons is $n(n - 1)/2$ where n is the number of individuals. If the number of dimensions on which you were doing the rating were five instead of just one, you would have to multiply the number of comparisons to be made by five. This means that to rate 100 employees on five variables, you would have to make some 25,000 comparisons!

The above methods of comparing employees are not suitable for large numbers. To rate, say, 100 individuals, the **forced distribution** method is practical. Each person is rated as belonging to one of about five categories. These might be bottom 10 percent, low 20 percent, middle 40 percent, high 20 percent, and top 10 percent. Of course, the divisions can range from rough, such as 20–60–20, to fine, for instance 5–10–10–15–20–15–10–10–5.

This assumes that the dimension being evaluated is distributed reasonably normally, that is, in a "bell-shaped" distribution. It may not be the case, however, that some fixed percentage of workers happen to be excellent, good, average, below average, and poor. Logically, one would expect most seasoned employees to be at the upper end of a distribution of performance. Where all employees are performing satisfactorily, as is often the case, both the workers and the raters may object to a system that arbitrarily defines half of the employees as below average.

Distributional rating scale   Most rating scales require the rater to come up with a number that represents the totality of the ratee's performance. The rater does not consider how the performance being rated is distributed, that is, whether the ratee performs in a certain way all the time, half the time, or rarely. In **distributional ratings**, the rater estimates the frequency of various levels of performance, and can later examine the descriptive statistics of the distribution.

So what Suppose that in your course, marks are "bell curved," that is, determined by a forced distribution method. The top fifth of your class will receive an A; the bottom fifth will fail. Would you not feel that your mark was determined not only by your own efforts and skill, but by whatever fate determined the abilities of the classmates in your year? What if your school has very high admission requirements and attracts the best students in the world? Would you not feel that classmates who "failed" may have deserved a decent pass mark? Would this rating system not turn colleagues into competitors?

To test this recent variant of the BOS, Steiner, Rain, and Smalley (1993) had over 400 undergraduates each view four short videotaped lectures, delivered by an actor in either a good, average, or poor style. The control participants viewed all average lectures; other students saw highly variable or slightly variable lectures. The students rated the lectures on both the BOS and a distributional rating scale.

Using the BOS, the participants rated 10 items of instructor performance on a 7-point scale from "never" to "always." In the distributional rating scale, they rated the same 10 performance items, but estimated the percentage of the time applicable. What was the effect of extending the reporting range from a scale of 7 to a scale of 100? The researchers reported that the distributional ratings were more sensitive to highly varied performance, and were lower than those obtained with the BOS. They suggested that the distributional ratings provided richer and more accurate information.

Problems with subjective rating procedures There are a number of problems and weaknesses with subjective ratings. Let's look at the main difficulties, starting with three common and related ones.

1. (a) **Leniency** is, of course, the tendency to avoid rating anyone as poor or unsatisfactory. Where the rater wants the goodwill and cooperation of the workforce or wants to avoid hurting anybody's feelings, the leniency error can be expected. (b) In contrast, the tendency to overuse the low end of the scale is termed the **strictness error**. (c) Grading everybody "Average" even in the face of a wide range of performances is the **central tendency error**. It is common for two reasons: (i) most people are by definition "average." This is more the case with employees, because the best performers are most likely to get promoted (within the firm or elsewhere), and the worst

ones are most likely to leave the job. Hence, most ratings can be expected to bunch up in the middle—becoming an error when the rater minimizes whatever performance variations there are. (ii) It seems safest, and perhaps more democratic or fair, to rate everyone as "satisfactory." High ratings can lead to expectations of costly rewards; low ones are upsetting. And the rater knows that employees who work together are likely to compare their ratings, which can lead to conflict.

2. Another error is the so-called **halo effect**. This originally was a metaphor referring to someone with a favorable reputation who enters a new group, and is seen as being incapable of doing wrong. A similar situation is the person who achieves a conspicuous success in one endeavor, and is consequently overvalued in other contexts. But the term has become much more generalized. It now refers to the rater's being influenced—either favorably or unfavorably—by any factors that should not be considered. It is a form of stereotyping, and can result in a rating that is too high or low.

Suppose you're a rater, and that you happen to value friendliness. You might overrate an employee who always smiles. Or if you know that a certain employee received a low evaluation last year, you might lower your rating this year. The saying "Nothing succeeds like success" also plays a part. Any of your subordinates who performed really well would thereby make you look better, and they would be easier for you to give feedback to—so you would therefore presumably like them better. And is it not easier to give higher ratings to those you like?

Raters may have to differentiate between what might be termed a legitimate halo—an employee who always performs extremely well or poorly—and bias caused by the undue influence of one observation. A good source of information on this and other issues regarding the halo effect is Cooper (1981a, 1981b).

3. All ratings may lack reliability (page 99). A supervisor may rate Sandy higher than Lyn one year, and Lyn above Sandy the next, even though both employees maintain the same levels of performance. (Reliability problems may also be associated with objective measures of work performance.)

4. **Contamination** is rating that is based on the spillover from irrelevant behaviors. For example, salespersons who contribute suggestions at sales meetings may receive superior ratings in comparison to those who say nothing. These behaviors, which have no connection with demonstrated selling skills, may still influence the ratings.

5. Ratings can be influenced by the **primacy** (first impression) and especially the recency effect (page 194), in which one early or recent positive or negative incident weighs heavily in the rating. Steiner and Rain (1989) exposed almost fifteen hundred psychology students to a series of lectures. The videotaped presentations were of average quality, except for one very good or very poor one, which was shown either at the outset or at the end

One of the weaknesses of subjective ratings is that raters may, perhaps inadvertently, be influenced by "similar-to-me" considerations.
Researchers have documented the existence of bias based on race
or gender as well as on less visible characteristics such as religion
and lifestyle.

of the series. Some students viewed the presentations in a single sitting, others
over a 4-day period. There were recency effects in both series, suggesting that
one discrepant episode that occurs just before the evaluation can influence
it unduly.

6. Finally, we must acknowledge the fact that many people harbor deep-
rooted personal prejudices, and that personnel evaluators are not immune.
For instance, raters may not have the same attitudes toward males and females. Many researchers, including Swim, Borgida, Maruyama, and Myers
(1989), have documented how gender stereotypes can bias evaluations.

Few of us are totally unaffected by visible racial characteristics, and we
rarely ignore a foreign accent or even a dialect of our own language. Much
research has documented the influence of prejudice on evaluations. For instance, Schmitt and Lappin (1980) showed that white and black appraisers
gave higher ratings to those of the same skin color as their own. Lack of
minority status "visibility" will not necessarily protect the employee. If someone's religion or lifestyle is felt to be less acceptable than others, it is likely

Brief case

In 1994, the documentary television program *60 Minutes* exposed questionable performance appraisals in the U.S. Marine Corps. The program suggested that the subjective ratings by white officers kept black marines from promotions, and even subjected them to demotions and discharge. Without providing evidence or relevance, a Marine spokesperson explained that the blacks weren't smart enough. One of the rejects was immediately accepted into Harvard Law School. Another explanation was that blacks don't have the necessary technical abilities. A black officer was rejected for Marine Corps flight school, and then became a navy pilot. He commented, "Fitness report means Do you fit in with your commanding officer's idea of what a Marine should look like?" The Marine Corps is now converting subjective to objective measures where it can.

known within a work group, and may invite some level of (possibly inadvertent) victimization.

Many of us are quick to decide that we like or dislike someone else. It is easy to find a person who somehow reminds us (by the clothes, the voice, or even the individual's name) of characteristics that we did or did not like in someone else. Similarly, the ratee's *attractiveness* or similarity to the rater (**similar-to-me error**) can influence the rater's judgments. No matter how objective an evaluator tries to be, complete fairness will inevitably remain more of a target than a reality.

Recently, I/O psychologists have been extensively studying the role of **affect** or feelings on evaluations. A typical research strategy is to have participants in a lab setting rate imaginary "employees." To bring more realism into an experiment, Robbins and DeNisi (1994) had a group of management students—who thought they were helping improve course evaluations—rate their feelings of admiration, respect, and liking for three of their professors. Would their affect predict the course evaluations? If so, did this happen in the cognitive or in the evaluation stage?

A month later, the students evaluated the professors using the BARS technique. (Examples of rating criteria were professor behaviors such as showing outdated films in class and testing for trivial details.) The affect for the professors seemed to influence not only the outcome of the performance evaluation, but also the cognitive process used to arrive at the evaluation. This was especially the case where the cognitive process included making judgments, as in deciding how to weight various aspects of the professors.

Peer rating

Now that you have learned a variety of techniques for performance evaluation, we have to raise other possibilities, because assessments are not necessarily made only by supervisors. Whether at school or on the job site, is it possible that your *colleagues* can assess your performance more accurately than the person assigned to rate you? If your answer is yes, would you like your classmates to determine your course grade?

Suppose you are assigned to overhaul the appraisal system for a business, and the employees' representative announced that the workers wanted to evaluate each other. What concerns would you have about such peer assessments?

In peer rating, which came into use in the United States during the 1940s, employees, whether welders, shippers, clerks, or deans, rate each other. After reviewing the research literature on peer assessments, Kane and Lawler (1978) concluded that one's colleagues can indeed provide valid appraisals. Subsequent research has verified this, especially in higher job levels. As for lower job levels, a study of American army enlisted personnel that compared peer ratings with supervisor ratings found supervisor ones more accurate (Oppler, Campbell, Pulakos & Borman, 1992).

There are several varieties of peer rating. In **peer assessment**, colleagues rate each other just as a supervisor would. An alternative is **peer ratings**, in which colleagues rate each other on specified dimensions. In **peer rankings**, colleagues rank each other's performance (best, second best, and so on) on various dimensions. But the most accurate form seems to be **peer nomination**, in which the group selects the best or most outstanding member (sometimes the worst one, too) on given dimensions. The dimensions might be group generated or supplied by the employer.

It is becoming increasingly common for employees to work in self-managed teams. Because the members work in close proximity, and because each individual's performance can influence the success of the team, peer assessment might be particularly applicable here. A number of field and laboratory studies have verified its accuracy.

For instance, Saavedra and Kwun (1993) performed three experiments on almost 200 undergraduate and graduate business students. They worked in small groups for 10 weeks on case analyses and presentations; their course marks were computed as follows: 40 percent on the group projects, 10 percent on peer ratings, and the rest on exams.

The researchers determined that the most outstanding contributors were the most discriminating evaluators. The explanation was that work colleagues compare others with themselves in making the assessments. The best workers are aware of the upper performance limits, and can use their work level as a benchmark in comparing the contributions of the others. Another possibility is that the same qualities that lead to outstanding performance may also contribute to accurate evaluation.

Self-managed teams have proved effective in the workplace. Each individual's performance contributes to team success, and peer assessment can be particularly accurate.

Is peer evaluation the way of the future? One possible problem is that there are often differences between intentions and interpretations. Management may intend to increase employees' **empowerment** (autonomy) by permitting peer evaluation. But employees may see colleague rating as an extra and inappropriate imposition that forces them into an unpleasantly competitive popularity contest, especially when the ratings are used to determine who receives a limited number of rewards. For instance, Cederblom and Lounsbury (1980) reported that professors who relied upon peer assessments for pay raises and promotions assumed that friendships would influence the evaluations and this, of course, was unacceptable to them. A final problem is that the disclosure of negative peer ratings can breed disharmony and alienation within the group.

Self-assessments   If you were assigned to teach a course whose students announced they wanted to assign their own grades (arguing that individuals know themselves better than anyone else does), would you permit it? What if peer ratings were impractical, and you found grading students an unpleasant task?

Some jobs may be just about impossible for others to assess. Picture a spy sent behind enemy lines, single-seat space capsules where the astronauts are out of touch with ground controllers, a professor who teaches behind closed doors in an institution that doesn't seek student course evaluations, a clinical psychologist whose sessions must be held in private, or an executive whose duties are ambiguous. How could you possibly design an evaluation plan for a situation such as one of these, in which nobody is able to evaluate the employee's performance?

There is a way. With **self-assessment**, the employees rate themselves according to set (and preferably agreed-upon) criteria, using any of the methods outlined in this section. Consider, however, that in a job application résumé, the statements represent a type of self-rating. If they were invariably accepted as accurate and complete, why do employers also require letters of reference?

If you were concerned about the *leniency error* influencing self-assessments, you'd have support from several studies; people rate their own work higher than others do. For instance, Meyer (1980) had almost 100 engineers compare their own performance to that of their colleagues. They all rated themselves as better than three-quarters of the others, an obvious statistical impossibility. Thornton (1980) compared self-ratings with those provided by supervisors, subordinates, and peers. The most conspicuous error, as you might expect, was leniency. Leniency in self-assessment was also reported by Martin and Klimoski (1990).

The leniency error is not inevitable. Farh and Werbel (1986) showed that this error is reduced if the ratees are told that their self-assessments will be checked for accuracy. And there seem to be interesting cultural differences regarding leniency. Farh, Dobbins, and Cheng's (1991) study of almost one thousand Taiwanese employees in a variety of firms found that these Chinese workers rated themselves lower than did their supervisors!

Research suggests that self-ratings focus more on interpersonal skills, whereas supervisory ratings look more at job skills and initiative (Hoffman, Nathan & Holden, 1991). Incidentally, it's not unknown for supervisors, reluctant to rate their subordinates, to invite them to appraise themselves. These would then be self-assessments masquerading as supervisor ratings.

Latham, Skarlicki, Irvine, and Siegel (1993) report various advantages attributed to self-appraisals. The employee's dignity is respected, and the supervisor can function as a counselor rather than as a judge. Also, self-appraisals can enhance workers' self-motivation and decrease their defensiveness.

Although often opposed by management, self-appraisals should be accurate. After all, who knows about all of your own work better than you yourself? But because employees are rarely trained in performance appraisal, and because the self-appraiser is hardly a neutral judge, it's important to ensure that the self-raters know exactly what is to be evaluated, on what basis, and what errors to watch for, especially leniency. Shore and Bleicken

(1991) reported that self-appraisals are quite consistent with supervisory appraisals, at least in older employees.

Subordinate and client assessments   **Downward appraisal**, in which supervisors evaluate subordinates, is the norm. Recently, however, employees are being invited to assess their boss; this is termed **upward appraisal**. An example of this is the use of students' evaluations of their courses, which has become standard procedure in many colleges and universities.

Meyer (1980) had a group of blue-collar employees rate themselves, their supervisors, and their estimate of the supervisors' ratings of them. Self-ratings were unrealistically high. After an interview with the supervisor, in which the job performance was rated and discussed, the employees were again invited to rate the supervisors. Now that the employee saw that the supervisor's rating was not as favorable as the self-rating, nor as favorable as expected, the employee's rating of the supervisor was downgraded. It seems that people do not like those who apparently underrate them, and that it is hard to be objective about someone who is not liked.

In course evaluations, the students performing the upward appraisal are invariably anonymous; in downward evaluations, the raters are invariably known to the ratees. Antonioni (1994) wondered if accountability (requiring raters to identify themselves) would make the process more palatable to a group of insurance company managers being evaluated by their subordinates. He had one group of subordinates evaluate their managers anonymously, and another group identify themselves on the ratings. The managers receiving the accountability ratings preferred this approach, and they received higher ratings. The raters, however, preferred the anonymity condition.

How does this upward appraisal compare with the traditional downward type? Schneider, Hanges, Goldstein, and Braverman (1994) acquired students' ratings of almost 150 professors on seven variables such as organization, availability, and personal style. Then the researchers had the professors' chairpersons rate them on another seven measures such as publications, professional activities, and colleagueship. On the variables that related to interpersonal skills and cooperativeness, there were high correlations between the students' and the chairs' ratings of the professors. Schneider et al. suggested that at least in jobs where service is provided to customers, the clients' evaluations are consistent with those of supervisors.

The context or purpose of subordinate ratings should be made clear to all involved. As mentioned earlier, people do not like being evaluated. It's especially troubling to be rated by subordinates. Managers may feel that such a process undermines their authority, and subjects them to unfair, retaliatory downgradings. Raters are likely to be more candid and negative if they see the purpose as constructive feedback, and more generous if the ratings determine pay or promotion.

This ends our coverage of a variety of techniques, both subjective and objective, to evaluate employees. Neither objective nor subjective measures

So what Schooling is driven by ratings. Students earn marks, diplomas, and degrees; professors earn tenure, promotions, and awards. If your school has students evaluate courses and professors, are the evaluations anonymous? If so, would you rate more objectively and responsibly if you had to identify yourself? Are you aware of who gets to read the course evaluations, and the uses to which your ratings are put? Does it make a difference? Do you feel you need the protection of anonymity, or do you think your instructors are entitled to know who said what? If your professors had to give you your course grade in a face-to-face discussion, do you think that the marks would be higher?

are themselves inherently good or bad. What's important is that all the potential weaknesses of any method used be understood and compensated for.

Improving evaluation

In today's corporate climate, fair, accurate, and humane performance evaluation has considerable impact on efficiency, morale, and courtroom judgments. Unfortunately, employee evaluation is not always easy. The rater has to be at once critic and praiser, adviser and judge, colleague and adversary. One solution is to *separate* these incompatible roles, using more than one appraisal procedure or rater. For instance, every January there could be a rating by one office to determine raises and promotions; every June another faction performs a counseling rating.

Cleveland, Murphy, and Williams (1989) point out problems caused when performance appraisal has different and conflicting goals. When the purpose is to assess promotion suitability, the rater has to compare *between* individuals; when the purpose is to determine training and development needs, the rater must perform *within* individual comparisons. A third possible purpose is to serve organizational needs such as deciding future staffing and training programs. Cleveland et al. cite many studies showing that the purpose of the ratings influences both the outcomes and the processes of the evaluations. Again, the solution is to identify the objective of the appraisal, and to tailor the procedure to the specific purpose.

Another way of improving assessment is to *train* the raters, something that probably less than half of corporations practice. Sims, Veres, and Heninger (1987), in suggesting how training can improve evaluations, covered areas not traditionally considered, such as employee motivation and aptitude. They even provide a workshop plan to address these variables. In particular, they concentrated on the social relationship between evaluator and evaluatee, and offered the following suggestions:

- Raters should be trained to focus on the *behavior* of the employees, not on the employees themselves or on their personalities.

- Raters should be made to understand that evaluation should be *constructive,* not disciplinary, focusing on any weaknesses and how they can be improved.

- The evaluation process, which may take place once a year, should not be isolated from other aspects of supervision during the rest of the year, such as good communication and the setting of clear and measurable goals. These goals may take the form of a "contract" that defines specific goals, which then will be the core of the evaluation session.

- Raters should be trained so that they are comfortable with the evaluation process, and should know how to increase the comfort level of the subordinates by letting them know the process, purpose, and the behaviors that will be covered.

- Appraisers should be trained in how to record the work behavior that will be reviewed during appraisal and how to document the proceedings of the appraisal itself. These objectives can be attained through a workshop, simulations, role reversals, and feedback to the appraisers.

- And of course appraisers should be reminded of the common rating errors as outlined earlier in this chapter.

Attitudes toward evaluation

People dread an appraisal process that they perceive as an unfair procedure, which focuses on their weaknesses. Students rarely like their courses' testing and grading procedures, and many teachers hardly relish student evaluations of the course. Managers dislike having to rate subordinates, or having to be rated by their supervisors. Unions argue that the fairest way to assign promotions and tenure is seniority, not performance evaluations. Yet, the principle of accountability requires that performance gets rated. The result is that increasingly in the work world, performance review is being conducted on at least an annual basis, but with little enthusiasm, and with considerable apprehension, on both sides.

The notable exception to the negative impact of evaluation is seen where performance appraisal is properly integrated into an effective MBO program (page 181). Here, appraisal serves as a diagnostic and recognition device, rather than as a punitive or threatening procedure.

Every aspect of the employee appraisal system—its introduction, its conduct, its consequences—should be handled with utmost care. Recommendations for this can be found in texts on personnel management. What is appropriate for coverage here is research on popular assumptions regarding the effect of the ratings upon employees' *attitudes*.

Pierce and Porter (1986) administered attitudinal questionnaires to American governmental workers both before and after the introduction of a mandatory performance appraisal system. Would the attitudes toward the appraisal system be a function of the ratings received? Basically, no. How about the attitudes toward the employer? Here there was an effect, in that the lower-rated workers thought less of the employer. (Is that why student evaluations of courses generally occur *before* the students receive their marks?)

Public attitude is reflected in the law of the land. Latham et al. (1993) point out that as employees become more aware of their civil and contractual rights, they are finding that courts are increasingly taking their side, not the employers'. These researchers also cite data indicating that employees are three times more likely to sue their employers than they were a decade ago. The phone book's Yellow Pages listings under "Lawyers" are increasingly showing ads for specialists in wrongful dismissal and employer discrimination cases.

Federal law has recently become quite specific on employment as related to employee assessment. In the United States, the Civil Rights Act of 1964 prohibits employment decisions that are influenced (without job-related justification) by race, religion, color, national origin, age, marital status, and disability. It also requires that employment selection procedures be demonstrably valid. Furthermore, the Supreme Court has ruled that where promotion criteria are subjective, those criteria must be subjected to the same type of analysis for appropriateness and fairness as any objective or standardized test (Latham et al., 1993).

Throughout North America, courts are prohibiting the use of appraisal that is unfair and discriminatory. This means that if you give a rating based on factors that are not entirely job relevant, and if this results in the employee's not getting a raise or a promotion, you could find yourself being sued for your actions. Courts are increasingly dealing with performance appraisals and seem to be saying, The more your power, the greater is your accountability.

In Canada the federal Human Rights Act prohibits any discrimination based on race, national or ethnic origin, color, religion, sex, marital status, disability, or any past criminal conviction that was later pardoned. It also requires that job performance assessments must be relevant to the task, and prohibits any internal agreement or contract that includes discrimination as defined above.

DILBERT. Reprinted by permission of UNITED FEATURES SYNDICATE, INC.

A likely reason for so much discord and litigation around ratings is that the expectations are unrealistic. The employer may assume that appraisal will show employee weaknesses that will be corrected through better training or improved motivation; the employees may expect the appraisals to show how hard and well they work, resulting in a raise or a promotion. The employer may worry that a positive appraisal will make it hard to discharge a marginal or redundant employee; employees may worry that a negative appraisal will jeopardize their chances for advancement and even their job security.

In spite of theoretical and legal pitfalls, and despite the general distaste and misplaced expectations surrounding them, formal performance evaluations occur in most organizations in North America. Many firms engage outside consultants or assessment centers for this purpose. Employee appraisal will long remain a major area in which the discipline of I/O psychology can aid the corporate world and the individual worker.

Feedback

Suppose your course instructor announced that you would eventually learn your final course grade, but there'd be no information on how you performed on your midterm tests and term assignments. Would that bother you? Suppose you wanted to learn how to shoot accurately, and could choose either a target range (where you can see where each bullet hit) or a skeet range (where all you can tell is that you hit the clay bird or you missed it). These are issues of *feedback,* or informing people how they performed.

In the ideal situation, the purpose of appraisal includes motivating the ratee to improve and showing clearly and specifically how to do so. Ideally, the ratees had participated in designing the assessment procedure so that it would serve these purposes. The rater, skilled and trained, knowing there will be a postappraisal interview for feedback, has performed the ratings carefully,

Brief case

The competition in the telephone market came to Canada later than to the United States. In the early 1990s Northern Telecom Canada came up with a list of 12 *core competencies* for its product management wing at its Norstar plant in Calgary. (These included skills such as business leadership, analytical skills, initiative, planning, and organizing.) Then the managers' competencies were assessed, and gaps were filled though training and hiring. Now all of the employees, even those on the shop floor, are being made aware of what their competencies are, which ones are deficient, and how to improve them. Performance appraisals, merit pay, and promotions are based on the attainment or development of the core competencies. The concept of core competencies is driving hiring decisions, team composition, and training budget allocations. Training ensures that the skills are taught and that the information about the concept of core competencies is given. Competency analysis finds out the extent to which the skills and information are *applied*. And performance appraisals focus on the development of competencies identified by the organization as critical to its success.

accurately, and according to a logical rationale, accepting full accountability and inviting comments on the appraisal.

Moreover, the feedback is smooth, comfortable, supportive and constructive, and highly goal-oriented. It extends into issues of career planning and development. In addition to the formal feedback sessions, casual feedback takes place whenever helpful, even weekly. The employee understands the feedback, considers it fair and accurate, and responds appropriately with specific solutions to the problems that were exposed. Receiving supervisory feedback is like listening to your personal fitness trainer or your figure skating coach.

In the less than ideal, there is no feedback, or what there is makes the ratee defensive and resentful. It's an annual torment for both sides, because the worst workers need the most encouragement and counseling, but are subject to the most criticism; the best workers invite the most pleasant feedback, but need it least. The feedback is distorted by raters who see their job either as correcting poor performance or as making the process easier for both sides by giving positive comments only.

No other area of I/O research has come up with as consistently uniform conclusions as the many studies on feedback. Feedback to employees on the results of their appraisals is critical to the improvement, possibly the survival of the organization, as well as to the morale of the individual and of the entire organization.

Competence and the organization

Are you a competent student? How could you measure this? If at your own employment interview you were asked for your views on employee competence, how would you answer? Could you market yourself in terms of your competencies? If you were good at a certain job, how would you determine the competencies you'd need to move to a higher level?

Traditionally, being competent meant being able to do the work as well as the average worker in that position. Now, with organizations starting to examine what skills they need in their employees to meet their goals and to be successful, the term implies *excelling at tasks that the organization needs performed.*

The coverage of competence ends our treatment of the appraisal of individuals. Since we'll next be turning to two chapters on the organization, the Brief Case (page 230) shows how competency appraisal can be applied to the organization as well as to the individual. Increasingly, organizations, especially major service ones such as police departments and governmental bureaucracies, are examining what their mandates are and how these are being fulfilled.

In the next chapter we will be examining leadership. Any organization needs effective leadership, but organizations of different types or at different stages of growth may need different kinds of leadership. A core competency analysis may help decide.

Study guide for chapter 7

HAVE YOU LEARNED THESE NAMES AND TERMS?

objective and subjective measurements

deficiency

opportunity bias

sampling error

computerized performance monitoring (CPM)

active badge

rating scale, checklist

graphic rating scale

continuous, discrete

Behavioral Observation Scales (BOS)

Behaviorally Anchored Rating Scales (BARS)

weighted checklist

employee comparison method

ranking

paired comparisons

forced distribution

distributional ratings

leniency, strictness, and central tendency errors

halo effect

contamination

primacy

similar-to-me error

affect

peer assessment, peer rating, peer ranking, and peer nomination
empowerment

self-assessment

downward and upward appraisal

ISSUES TO CONSIDER

What is the role of formal assessments in your life?

What is the role of performance appraisal in industry?

What is the connection between *test characteristics* and *appraisals*?

What type of rating scale is appropriate for what type of performance?

What are the pros and cons of the *paired comparisons* method?

What are possible problems with *subjective* ratings?

Which problems are more serious, those associated with *objective* or *subjective* ratings?

Which rating error is akin to *stereotyping*?

How should the personnel files on students and professors at your institution be handled?

If your grades were self-determined, how would you go about doing assessing yourself?

How could appraisal that affects you be improved?

What accounts for the prevailing *attitude* toward the evaluation process?

Will courts of the future increasingly rule in favor of employers or employees?

Why do many firms hire outside consultants for employee evaluation?

Was the Robbins and DeNisi study an example of field or laboratory research?

SAMPLE MULTIPLE-CHOICE QUESTIONS

1. The usual reaction to the appraisal process is
   a. positive.
   b. negative.
   c. neutral.
   d. unknown.

2. A paired comparison of 10 employees on one variable would require how many matchups?
   a. 1
   b. 10
   c. 45
   d. 100

3. A professor who bell-curves the course marks is using which method?
   a. paired comparisons
   b. forced distribution
   c. BARS
   d. BOS

4. The error of deficiency is associated with which technique?
   a. BOS
   b. BARS
   c. objective measures
   d. paired comparisons

5. The simplest procedure to rate many individuals is the _____ method.
   a. forced-choice distribution
   b. paired comparisons
   c. BARS
   d. objective

Answers: page 462

Take This Job and Shove It (song title).

Johnny Paycheck

Bird's-eye view of the chapter

People rarely work alone or in small groups isolated from the larger organization. Organizations are dynamic, and they can have a marked influence on our behavior, work-related and otherwise. This, the third of four chapters on dealing with people at work, includes *leadership, communication, human relations,* and the *quality of work life.*

Chapter 8
Introduction to organizational psychology

The payoff from chapter 8   You will:

1. Understand what is meant by *small group*
2. Understand the meaning and attraction of the topic of *leadership*
3. Appreciate the size of the academic literature on leadership
4. Understand the place of Freud in leadership theory
5. Realize the difficulty of objectively validating Freudian constructs
6. Understand the *trait* approach to leadership
7. Know the difference between the *trait* and the *behavior* approach
8. Understand how *consideration* and *initiating structure* were uncovered
9. Know the main survey instruments in leadership research
10. Appreciate the importance of Fiedler in leadership research
11. Be aware of the implications of Fiedler's arguments
12. Appreciate the advances brought by *path-goal* theory

13. Know the further advantages of the Vroom and Yetton *decision-making* argument
14. Know the origin and value of *attribution* theory
15. Understand the statement, "Maybe there's no such thing as leadership"
16. Appreciate the importance of human communication
17. Differentiate between formal and informal communication
18. Understand the meaning and importance of grapevine communication
19. Know some principles of effective communication
20. Know the history and meaning of the human relations movement
21. Know the origin and meaning of Theories X, Y, and Z
22. Understand what is generally meant by *quality of work life*
23. Appreciate the origin and importance of *employee assistance programs*

Organizational psychology focuses on the well-being of the employee and the organization and includes the study of organizational structure, processes and procedures, communication channels, reputation and climate, ways of introducing and measuring change, and productivity. **Organizational psychology** separated from industrial psychology in the 1950s, when the focus of study shifted from the individual to larger units. By the 1980s it became prominent as a specialized discipline (especially in business and management schools), covering the social psychology of work groups and the whole organization. The division between industrial and organizational is becoming blurred, with some theorists seeing organizational as a branch of industrial, some viewing it the other way around, and others arguing that there's no distinction at all anymore.

The topic known as organizational psychology in psychology courses—often termed **organizational behavior (OB)** in business courses—deals with behavior of people in large, organized groups. It studies the behavior that affects and is affected by an organization, and deals with organizational theory, organizational development, and relationships within the organization. Most of its constructs come from psychology, especially social psychology, but it also draws from the other branches of social science, such as sociology and anthropology, as well as from political science and economics. For this reason, organizational psychology relies on many theories that attempt to integrate the relevant findings from these diverse disciplines.

Industrial/organizational (I/O) psychology combines a micro and a macro approach. The micro perspective covers most of the topics that focus on the individual, such as training, motivation, and satisfaction, which we dealt with in the Personnel (or "Industrial") section of Part 2. In the macro approach (represented by the chapter following this one), the main unit of study is the organization itself. The present chapter deals with issues that primarily involve the organization in the context of the small group. The next chapter, which ends our coverage of personnel-related topics, deals with the macro organizational topics such as unions, working women, and organizational change.

THE IMPORTANCE OF ORGANIZATIONAL PSYCHOLOGY

The hospital you were born in is an organization. So, of course, is every school, club, service group, and house of worship in which you may participate. Every item of your clothing, food, and recreation is, directly or indirectly, the product of huge organizations—without which you would not be able to get lunch today, watch television tonight, or go for a drive this weekend.

Clearly, human culture is based on organizations. We humans make up our organizations, which in turn help to define our culture and determine many of our attitudes and convictions. Ethnic and national factors have been related to patterns of work habits, management styles, quality of products, and consumer behavior. As the world seemingly shrinks and speeds up due to advances in communication and transportation, an awareness of these large-scale factors becomes a major part of understanding I/O psychology.

These topics are complex. As no two people are alike, so no two organizations can be alike, except in one respect. Organizations are under more stress today, economically, politically, and socially, than ever before. As North American industry reels from competitors in other countries, its survival may hinge on our understanding of the human dimension in the large group.

A BRIEF HISTORY OF ORGANIZATIONAL PSYCHOLOGY

Organizational psychology is a recent and rapidly growing topic, reflecting the importance that organizations have on our lives. Although not the subject of formal study until recently, organizations themselves are older than recorded history.

The importance of functioning within a group has long been apparent. What changed cave-dwelling hominids into the first humans might have been the discovery that group cooperation resulted in greater success than the sum of all individual efforts. It was probably the formation of these primitive groups that led to the use of language, which, in turn, helped hominids to evolve into humans. The first organizations were local. The first groups of hunters, healers, weavers, or fighters grew up together and knew each other.

The conquests of the Roman Empire obviously depended upon the application of organizational principles. So did the establishment of all civilizations. Not surprisingly, classical political philosophers, from Plato to Machiavelli, stressed the importance of organizational principles.

As civilization progressed, the fate of the worker fell to conditions that would be considered deplorable by today's standards. For most people, work filled their days and their lives. Their toil started in childhood, and ended only at their death, which likely occurred on (or because of) their job. There were probably fewer complaints than there are now, because until recently, everyone's social role and occupational duty were usually inflexible and limited.

The industrial revolution was marked by mechanized factories in which labor was divided into simple, repetitive components. Prevailing philosophies of the time explained and justified what was going on in these work settings. Adam Smith's 1776 book *An Inquiry into the Nature and the Causes of the Wealth of Nations* explained how what he was the first to call "division of labor" led to efficiency. Charles Babbage is known mainly for his invention of a mechanical computer, but his 1832 book *On the Economy of Machinery and Manufacturing* explained in further detail the economic advantages of division of labor.

Following the publication of Charles Darwin's *On the Origin of Species* in 1859, other contemporaries argued that the theory of the survival of the fittest extended in the social context too. Just as the most fit animals flourished, so did the most fit managers. According to this **social Darwinism** philosophy, those who attained power and wealth were designed and destined to succeed. The so-called **Protestant work ethic** was a social doctrine, which held that hard work is valuable for its own sake, and success is the result of God's rewarding ambition and diligence. (Both philosophies handily ignored the influence of poverty and prejudice, and clearly separated the roles of employee and superior.)

An early writer who focused on the most efficient organizational structure was Max Weber. This German social theorist argued that the most efficient organization was a fair but rule-bound bureaucracy with a strict chain of command, selection by merit, and high specialization. Promotions were to be based on merit and technical qualifications rather than on personal factors.

The role of the early industrial psychologists in contributing to an understanding of the human side of work, as well as the influence of the two world wars, is outlined in chapter 1 (page 16). The early theorists such as Münsterberg considered only the *individual,* and the influential Frederick W. Taylor focused on getting the greatest output from the individual worker. The Hawthorne-inspired *human relations* approach of the 1930s and 1940s dealt primarily with the *small group*. The entire organization was addressed by Douglas McGregor, who in the late 1950s coined the terms Theory X (a social Darwinism approach to management) and Theory Y (a management style that accepts that workers are people too). You'll meet McGregor again in this chapter.

The first university degree in *organizational behavior* was granted by the Harvard Business School in 1941; the first textbook was *Human Relations in Industry,* which appeared in 1945. By 1960 the field was established and growing.

The name of the American Psychological Association's Division of Industrial Psychology was changed to Division of Industrial *and Organizational* Psychology in 1973. In 1976, Dunnette published the *Handbook of Industrial and Organizational Psychology,* which included 37 topics (with an apology in the preface for omitting another 4) and ran to 1,740 pages.

Consider the present size and complexity of businesses. Some corporations employ more people than were alive on the globe at the start of the Christian era, and they reach into more countries than the Church did 300 years ago. Largeness is typically associated with slow and gradual change. But businesses are facing on the one hand global competition, a rapid change in the composition of the workforce, and rapid technological developments, and on the other hand a social climate demanding *equity* and *entitlements*.

For instance, in Western nations, the assembly line, for all its mechanical efficiency, is faulted in the human dimension. Assemblers object to the repetitiveness and simplicity of the work, the lack of social interaction, and the lack of control over pacing, tools, and techniques. Meanwhile, Japanese workers strain to make their assembly lines even more efficient. The present challenge of organizational psychology is to develop an organizational structure and process that is at once efficient, humanistic, and consistent with the prevailing culture.

As social barriers melt, and as new relationships are defined, the present situation is captured in the last speech scheduled for delivery by U.S. president Franklin D. Roosevelt. He would have commented, if he had lived one day longer, "If civilization is to survive, we must cultivate the science of human relationships—the ability of all people, of all kinds, to live together and work together" (Bass & Ryterband, 1972).

What is a small group?

To see the difference between a **small group** and a **large group**, picture an organization with 500 employees, clearly itself a large group. The firm includes, among others, 5 maintenance people, 12 secretaries, 8 warehouse/shipping staffers, 10 salespersons, 10 managers, and 20 production people. Each of these sets of persons has its own concerns and problems, and each comprises a small group.

The secretaries, for instance, may include fresh high school graduates, young married persons with families, and live-alone singles on the verge of retirement. In terms of who joins whom for lunch, and of who socializes together after work, the 12 secretaries comprise three subgroups, each with its own leader and its own communication conventions.

Human beings are social animals, and people rarely work alone. Nor do they interact closely with large numbers of coworkers. Rather, the *immediate social surround* of the workplace becomes the employee's job-time family. Like one's family at home, this small group is typically the most important determinant of one's attitude and disposition.

The immediate social surround is usually an informal group in that it is not defined and structured. Yet, these small groups establish communal norms that define proper dress, behavior, and production. Leadership develops within these groups, sometimes conflicting with the leadership structure imposed by management. Communication within these groups can be far more meaningful to the individual than communication transmitted through formal channels. The art of industrial human relations can be seen as an attempt to make the values and objectives of the small group those of the large group.

Management should handle people adeptly by accommodating not only the individuals themselves, but also the various groups with which people form strong social or psychological attachments. Problems are often raised not on behalf of individuals or by the entire organization, but by these *small groups.* Because of their varied and amorphous nature, they can be hard to identify and to deal with.

We start with two fascinating topics borrowed from social psychology: leadership and communication. Then we look at what are generally called human relations and the "quality of work life."

LEADERSHIP

Leadership is a core topic not just within industrial psychology but also within organizational psychology, social psychology, sociology, anthropology, and business. It helps to link all of social science. The pervasiveness of this topic is not surprising if we consider the following reasons:

- Leaders, by definition, are *conspicuous.* Every day, newspapers, magazines, and television bring us many images of leaders in politics, business, athletics, and fashion.

- Most of us value the attribute of *power,* and associate it with leadership.

- We are aware that the *success* of all institutions—the family, the army, the university, the corporation, or the entire country—is often attributed to the quality of the leadership.

- We know that whenever people gather, especially in a work context, one of them will invariably assume a leadership role.

- Those who become researchers probably perceived their professor as their leader in courses.

- Most students probably look forward to following various leaders in their occupational future.

- It's hard to imagine enjoying your work or achieving your potential under an inept leader.

By the time you read this, the number of published studies on leadership may have exceeded ten thousand! Leadership is a construct with, as you saw above, many faces. This complexity accounts for the lack of a single unified theory in this area. (There is not even agreement among theorists as to how the various positions should be categorized and organized.) Here is a sampler of the basic currents in leadership research, representing about half of the existing theories.

Person-related theories

Historical figures like Alexander the Great, Caesar, Michelangelo, Lincoln, and Churchill were all "great." Many people fantasize about being great themselves, and probably harbor such wishes for their children. It is not surprising, then, that the earliest theories of leadership started with the position that there is something special about certain *people* that makes them "great" people, and therefore leaders.

Psychoanalysis Sigmund Freud wove a complex, interlocking explanation of human behavior that was based on his experience with patients undergoing the "talking treatment" that he devised, *psychoanalysis*. Freud is to psychology what Hippocrates and Galen are to medicine. His theories have immense importance, but not because of their utility or their validity. They are important because Freudian constructs have become a part of everyday language, and because many people still accept most of them. So it is appropriate to have an outline of Freud's position on leadership.

Freud felt that some people become leaders as a *defense mechanism* to protect them from weaknesses experienced in early life. For instance, a lack of attention in childhood could impel you to seek fame. A sense of impoverishment from the family's shortage of money could drive you into profitable business ventures. Severe toilet training could motivate someone to strive toward a position that permits the application of obsessive control over subordinates.

Psychoanalysts regularly examine the backgrounds of recent world leaders to find events that support the Freudian interpretation of compensatory behavior. It's hard to conduct concrete research to validate Freud's explanations of behavior, because most of his constructs defy objective quantification. (How would you test the argument that defense mechanisms are designed as a *subconscious* process to protect the *ego*?) Researchers who believe in psychoanalysis tend to find what they search for.

Trait approach The **trait theories** logically propose that *leaders* have personality characteristics or *traits* that differentiate them from *followers*. This position is rooted in the historical picture of the "great man" as someone who has the "right stuff." In fact, it was long accepted that greatness must be genetic. This would explain (only to those unaware of the immense influence of social and environmental factors) why so many sons of leaders themselves became leaders.

Much early research was aimed at identifying leadership *traits*. This literature was subjected to one of the earliest meta-analyses (page 60) by Stogdill (1948). He concluded that a handful of characteristics are found primarily in leaders, but that mere possession of these traits does not guarantee leadership. Rather, leadership is a matter of the appropriate combination of these *traits* (such as intelligence, dependability, and activity) with the *environment* (for example, the nature of the followers and of the organization).

Stogdill could not isolate any one trait that was a prerequisite for leadership in all situations. However, more recent meta-analyses uncovered what seem to be leadership personality traits (Stogdill, 1974; Lord, DeVader & Alliger, 1986). These include *self-confidence* and *dominance.*

Is it the trait of *charisma* that accounts for leadership? House (1977) argued that sometimes followers are not influenced by the usual immediate concerns, but by their religious-like devotion to a leader who sets a "transcendent" or moral goal. This situation is seldom seen in Western business organizations, so *charismatic leadership* has rarely been studied in industrial psychology. Yet it could explain the fierce devotion of some Far Eastern employees, and the influence of some leadership in voluntary organizations.

An interesting research project would be to analyze political leaders' appeal. A start was made by House, Spangler, and Woycke (1991), who used various means to measure the relative charisma (and other traits) of all U.S. presidents up to Ronald Reagan. House et al. found that presidents with a power-seeking personality had high charisma, especially when their administration had to cope with major crises. Conversely, those seen as having a high need for achievement were rated low in charisma.

Behavior-related theories

Another early approach looked at what leaders *did* differently than nonleaders. The implications are obvious. If leadership is a matter of personality *traits,* the correct corporate response is to search for people possessing them. On the other hand, if *anybody* can be an effective leader as long as appropriate leadership *behavior* is displayed, then the *behavior* should be addressed.

An extensive and influential series of studies on leadership behavior was started in 1950 by the Personnel Research Board of Ohio State University. For instance, Halpin and Winer (1957) analyzed thousands of observations of leader *behavior* to uncover common factors. They concluded that there were two distinct aspects to leadership, **consideration** and **initiating structure**.

Consideration refers to the nature and extent of the leader's response to subordinates' need for warmth, trust, and respect. *Initiating structure* refers to getting the job done. This includes planning, organizing, assigning, communicating, monitoring progress, and encouraging high standards. Once it became apparent that leaders generally possess these attributes, it became important to be able to measure them. The primary measurement tools have been two questionnaires.

Subordinates fill out the **Leader Behavior Description Questionnaire** (LBDQ). This was originated by Hemphill and Coons (1957) and expanded by Stogdill (1974). Employees are shown pairs of brief descriptive statements and asked to check which of each pair applies to their leader.

Leaders themselves fill out the other questionnaire, the **Leadership Opinion Questionnaire** (LOQ), devised by Fleishman (1957). Here the respondents select which of each pair of behaviors they feel they *should* choose in their work. The most widely used of the leader evaluation questionnaires is the expanded version of Stogdill (1963); it is known as the LBDQ-XII.

Fiedler's contingency theory

Is good leadership *authoritarian* or *democratic?* Surely this depends on the immediate *situation,* and on the nature of the particular *leader.* Fiedler (1964, 1965, 1967) has inspired more research (both by academics and by students) than any leadership theorist; his theories dominated leadership studies in many countries for two decades.

Fiedler contended that leadership involves an interplay between *leadership style* and the immediate *situation.* Assuming that a good way to study leaders is to ask them what kind of associates they *dis*liked, Fiedler studied leadership style with the **Least Preferred Co-worker (LPC) Scale.** The design of this questionnaire is shown as Figure 8.1.

"What kind of person have you found you worked *least* well with?" the questionnaire asks. A leader rated as having a *high LPC* score is one who thinks well of even the least preferred associate; a *low LPC* leader has a negative opinion of that associate. The higher the LPC score, Fiedler reasoned, the more the leader's concern with interpersonal relations, as opposed to just getting the job done. This is the presumed difference between the leader who can still *like* an unsatisfactory subordinate and one who cannot.

What is meant by *situation?* This, according to Fiedler, depends on the *relationship* between leaders and followers, the amount of *task structure,* and the leader's *power* or authority. The ideal leadership position, Fiedler proposed, is one in which a popular leader with high power is directing a structured and routine task. (Contrast this with a disliked director of a volunteer group where goals are unclear.) Studying a wide variety of groups, Fiedler (1967) correlated leaders' LPC scores with their groups' success.

NAME _____

People differ in the ways they think about those with whom they work. This may be important in working with others. Please give your immediate, first reaction to the items on these two pages.

Below are pairs of words which are opposite in meaning, such as "Very neat" and "Not neat." You are asked to describe someone with whom you have worked by placing an "X" in one of the eight spaces on the line between the two words.

Each space represents how well the adjective fits the person you are describing as if it were written:

very neat	8	7	6	5	4	3	2	1	not neat
	very neat	quite neat	some-what neat	slightly neat	slightly untidy	some-what untidy	quite untidy	very untidy	

FOR EXAMPLE: If you were to describe the person with whom you are able to work least well, and you ordinarily think of him or her as being <u>quite neat,</u> you would put an "X" in the second space from the words Very Neat, like this:

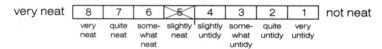

very neat	8	7	6	5	4	3	2	1	not neat
	very neat	quite neat	some-what neat	slightly neat	slightly untidy	some-what untidy	quite untidy	very untidy	

If you ordinarily think of the person with whom you can work least well as being only <u>sightly neat,</u> you would put your "X" as follows:

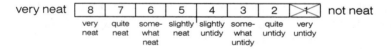

very neat	8	7	6	5	4	3	2	1	not neat
	very neat	quite neat	some-what neat	slightly neat	slightly untidy	some-what untidy	quite untidy	very untidy	

If you think of the person as being <u>very untidy,</u> you would use the space nearest the words Not Neat.

very neat	8	7	6	5	4	3	2	1	not neat
	very neat	quite neat	some-what neat	slightly neat	slightly untidy	some-what untidy	quite untidy	very untidy	

Look at the words at both ends of the line before you put in your "X." Please remember that there are no right or wrong answers. Work rapidly: your first answer is likely to be your best. Please do not omit any items, and mark each item only once.

Source: F. E. Fiedler, A Theory of Leadership (New York: McGraw-Hill, 1967)

FIGURE 8.1 Design of the Least Preferred Co-worker Scale

Fiedler's contingency theory states that leader effectiveness is contingent upon two factors: leadership style and the favorableness of the situation. This questionnaire measures the leader's nature to determine style.

LPC

Think of the person <u>with whom you can work least well.</u> He or she may be someone you work with now or someone you knew in the past.

He or she does not have to be the person you like least well, but should be the person with whom you had the most difficulty in getting the job done. Describe this person as he or she appears to you.

	8	7	6	5	4	3	2	1	
pleasant	8	7	6	5	4	3	2	1	unpleasant
friendly	8	7	6	5	4	3	2	1	unfriendly
rejecting	1	2	3	4	5	6	7	8	accepting
helpful	8	7	6	5	4	3	2	1	frustrating
unenthusiastic	1	2	3	4	5	6	7	8	enthusiastic
tense	1	2	3	4	5	6	7	8	relaxed
distant	1	2	3	4	5	6	7	8	close
cold	1	2	3	4	5	6	7	8	warm
cooperative	8	7	6	5	4	3	2	1	uncooperative
supportive	8	7	6	5	4	3	2	1	hostile
boring	1	2	3	4	5	6	7	8	interesting
quarrelsome	1	2	3	4	5	6	7	8	harmonious
self-assured	8	7	6	5	4	3	2	1	hesitant
efficient	8	7	6	5	4	3	2	1	inefficient
gloomy	1	2	3	4	5	6	7	8	cheerful
open	8	7	6	5	4	3	2	1	guarded

His interpretation of a large mass of apparently inconsistent data led to his famous **contingency theory** of leadership: *Leader effectiveness is contingent on* (depends on) *the leader's nature* (as measured by the LPC score) *and the favorableness of the situation.* (The more *structured* the task, the more *favorable* it would be to the leader.) The main specific predictions arising from his analysis are (a) *low LPC leaders are more effective in either favorable or unfavorable situations,* and (b) *high LPC leaders are more effective in moderately favorable situations.*

Was Fiedler right? A vast amount of research has examined contingency theory. Peters, Hartke, and Pohlmann (1985), for instance, reviewed over 100 published studies on it. Schriesheim, Tepper, and Tetrault (1994) discuss how to improve the methodology of research based on the LPC scale, and they cautiously support Fiedler's position. Generally, the research has supported Fiedler, although the support has been stronger in laboratory, as opposed to field, research.

One of the appealing aspects in this area is the availability of a ready-made questionnaire, the LPC, with considerable *face validity* (page 105). The main weakness is that the LPC is simply a score on a paper-and-pencil test, whose construct validity and reliability are still uncertain.

Insofar as Fiedler is right, contingency theory has interesting implications. To choose the best leader, a company would measure the favorableness of the task and the LPC scores of leader applicants. In working with an existing leader, the company would measure the same variables, and attempt to match them by changing the task characteristics. The leader's style could be changed instead, but with more difficulty, according to Fiedler, Chemers, and Mahar (1976).

Path-goal theory

Picture three memorable leaders: a sports coach, the head of a country that is threatened with wartime destruction, and the president of an industrial corporation. What they all have in common is that in each case the good *leader* is a good *motivator*. Specifically, according to House and Mitchell (1974), a good leader determines the best *path*, in a particular case, to induce subordinates to attain the desired *goal*. House and Mitchell termed this the **path-goal theory**.

Path-goal theory can be considered (a) a *situational* theory in that it holds that good leadership behavior varies according to the situation at hand, (b) a *cognitive* theory in that it says that a good leader makes subordinates understand how they can attain their goals, and (c) a *contingency* theory in that it indicates that the leader should make followers see how best to achieve their goals.

House and Mitchell argued that an ideal leader assesses the nature of both the subordinate and the task at hand and adjusts the leadership style accordingly. Path-goal theory presents the following four possible styles of leadership:

1. The **directive** leader specifies exactly what all subordinates are to do.
2. The **supportive** leader emphasizes concern and consideration for all of the subordinates.
3. The **participative** leader consults with the group on all matters relating to the task.
4. The **achievement-oriented** leader is primarily task or goal oriented.

Path-goal theory has been tested in research (for example, Schriesheim & Denisi, 1981), which generally supports it only partially, if at all. Keller (1989) showed that an important variable in the acceptance of a leader can be the extent to which the followers want their task to be clarified or structured. This still-evolving theory shows both problems and promise. The problems are definitional. Constructs such as paths, goals, and leadership styles are complex and hard to define operationally.

The promise of this theory is that it is flexible, appealing, and integrative. Leaders and situations often change; path-goal theory is flexible enough to ride with these changes. Moreover, its basic premises are intuitively logical. Path-goal theory integrates aspects of several other theories, such as expectancy theory and Fiedler's contingency theory.

Cognitive theories

The above theories have all focused on the leader in terms of the leader's behavior or personality. The leader's thought processes or cognitions must also be considered. And recently, the role of the *follower,* particularly in terms of interpretation or cognition, has been considered. Approaches based on these factors are termed cognitive.

Decision-making model of Vroom and Yetton A prime responsibility of a leader is astute *decision making.* Vroom and Yetton (1973) examined the *norm* for behavior in terms of who makes *decisions,* the leader or the subordinates; hence their formulation is known as a **normative model** of leadership, or *normative decision theory.*

They examined the *followers' acceptance of the leaders* and described the possibilities, from autocracy through consultative, to group consensus. They also classified the ways in which a leader could induce the group to *participate* in reaching a decision as well as to participate in different types of situations. Finally, they developed a comprehensive model that a leader can use to decide which strategy in any given case will yield a decision that is effective, reached quickly and efficiently, and accepted by the group.

The Vroom-Yetton model can be considered a *cognitive* theory, because of its emphasis on the leader's understanding the decision-making process. Since Vroom and Yetton pointed out that different problem situations call for different types of decision making, their theory is also described as *situational.* This model was designed for managers to use in solving their real-life problems, by providing them with a detailed, rational prescription for action. In this context, it seems practical and useful; however, the only aspect of leadership that it deals with is decision making.

TABLE 8.1 Leadership theories and models

Theory construct	Theory name	Individual's qualities	Influencing factors
Person-related	Psychoanalysis, Trait	Special individual	Heredity, Environment
Behavioral		Any individual	Environment
Cognitive	Decision making Attribution	Any individual	Cognitions
Situational, cognitive, and contingency	Path-goal	Individual traits	Environment, follower's perceptions, expectations, and motivation
Contingency	Fiedler	Individual traits	Situations

This table compares and contrasts the main approaches to leadership outlined in the text.

Attribution theory   The concept of **attribution**, borrowed from social psychology, is attracting considerable research interest, although the evidence for it so far is unconvincing. This concept looks at how events are *interpreted,* that is, to what they are *attributed,* by both leaders and followers. For instance, Green and Mitchell (1979) contended that leaders attribute various reasons to their subordinates' behavior, and that these attributions determine how the leaders will treat their subordinates.

The sex of the leader and followers has been examined in terms of attribution theory. For instance, Dobbins, Pence, Orban, and Sgro (1983) found that leaders were more tolerant of the infractions of subordinates who were of the same sex as themselves. And Goktepe and Schneier (1989) found that **emergent leaders** (those who assume guiding roles in leaderless groups such as work teams) are equally likely to be men or women, but they are apt to have masculine gender role characteristics whether they are male or female. Such findings have troubling implications for women, who are (at least until gender equality prevails throughout the workplace) more likely than men to be in subordinate roles.

Is it really possible that leadership per se is not as important as peoples' expectations or attributions regarding the leadership role? Smither (1988) cites research suggesting that (a) leaders are so *similar* (privileged white males) that they all "lead" in the same way, (b) few leaders have very much real control over the organization, and (c) they have even less control over outside, global factors that spell the difference between failure and success.

So what Without communication, what's left? What would you be like if you had been raised in a family where no communication took place? How would you make friends or arrange a date if there were no means of sending and receiving information? What would a college be like if there were no communication within it, or between it and the outside world? What would a factory or industry be like if the communication in it were faulty or absent? Without effective communication skills, how would you be able to assert your rights? Would you be offered an employment interview, a challenging position, or managerial responsibilities? Could you ever play a leadership role if you are a poor communicator? Like the success of business and industry, your own future depends largely on your communication skills.

The question of the *followers'* attributions and behavior is more interesting. Obviously, some groups are easier to handle than others. As for their attributions, perhaps "leadership" is simply an inference that the followers use to account for events. For instance, suppose a researcher measures both the attributes of a leader and the performance of the group. Say that the best performance takes place under the leader who scores highest in "friendliness." The researcher might conclude that a friendly leader makes for productive followers. However, an alternate interpretation is that high-performing followers tend to *perceive* their leader as friendlier.

That is, maybe there's no such thing as leadership. When people are asked how they lived to the age of 100, they usually ascribe it to some practice. When leaders are asked what made them leaders, they generally do the same. Just as the centenarian was probably confusing correlation with causation, so, likely, were the leaders who ascribed their leadership to various traits. Is it not possible that what we call leadership is merely *social influence*? Maybe it's simply that people *attribute* outcomes, especially positive ones, to "leadership."

Table 8.1 compares and contrasts some of the approaches to leadership outlined above.

COMMUNICATION

Most animals communicate, and so do many machines. But nothing on Earth communicates with as much sophistication and elaboration as the human being. This page is a communication device, as, in a sense, is a university. People spend about three-quarters of their waking hours communicating (lis-

Effective communication has a major role in the global business scene and within the individual organization. Voice mail systems, fax machines, and E-mail are among the devices that link businesses across the continent and the globe. They have also made it possible for many people to work out of their homes.

tening, speaking, reading, or writing). Much of the electronic equipment in your home (telephone, television, computer) is devoted to communication. At work, communication takes up much of lower-level workers' time—and the higher the level, the greater the percentage of work hours devoted to communicating, according to studies in the 1970s.

Formal versus informal communication

Formal communication usually follows established channels or routes that respect the structure of the organization. It tends to be permanent, in the form of memos, postings on bulletin boards, newsletters, and meetings where minutes are taken. In a firm with only 100 individuals, if each person could communicate to any other, there would be a total of 4,955 possible directions of communication. To make this less unwieldy, three communication channels are used: *downward, upward,* and *horizontal.*

Brief case

Anybody who's studied a computer manual or tried to operate a programmable telephone knows that people in the communications business aren't necessarily very good communicators. When American Telephone and Telegraph (AT&T) merged two business units into Global Business Communications Systems (GBCS) in 1992, the new leadership decided that a program was needed to improve communication among the 26,000 employees. Table 8.2 shows a chart of their comprehensive new communications program.

Downward communication, often as directives or news-type information, flows from the top. **Upward communication**, typically in the form of requests, reports, or suggestions, is passed from lower to higher levels, and is more vulnerable to being stopped in its tracks (or "filtered") than is downward communication. **Horizontal communication** flows between similar status departments or units. It may be formal or informal.

Informal communication rarely leaves a physical trace, and it varies considerably among groups and individuals. Hence, it is harder to document than is formal communication. It is exemplified by the **grapevine**. Grapevine communication travels sporadically, sometimes in widening chains, sometimes slowly, with few of those hearing it passing it on. It may travel via several interlocking units. For instance, a secretary who is part of an office grapevine may pass the news to an assembler who spreads it throughout the production grapevine.

Grapevine news may include personal gossip, corporate data, or the latest joke. Its transmission is influenced by the personality characteristics of the participants, the nature of the information, and the physical location of the members.

One massive study (Foltz, 1985) asked 32,000 North American employees where they got their information and where they wished they received it from. Happily, the immediate supervisor turned out to be both the most frequent and the most preferred source of information. The grapevine was ranked as fifteenth and last in preference, but it averaged second in actual sources of information.

The grapevine can easily become a conduit for rumors, that is, unverified assumptions. As they pass from one person to another, two forms of distortion are possible. Some rumors become longer and more elaborate, as each participant adds an embellishment; others become simplified and easier to continue. They become most vigorous when the content is ambiguous and salient to the participants, and when the latter are emotionally aroused.

"They wanted to improve top-down communication."

TABLE 8.2 Communication provisions at Global Business Communications Systems

Practice	Descriptions	Participa-tion*	Feedback mechanism	Human Relations critical focus area**
Ask the President	Associates write, phone, or AT&T-mail questions or concerns to president of GBCS.	I/G	Acknowledgment of receipt within 24 hours. Written response from Pat Russo within 48 hours.	CC
Answer Line	Associates call an 800 number with questions, issues, or requests for business-related information.	I/G	Call acknowledged within 72 hours. Written or telephone response to associate from subject expert.	CC
Chats	Small, face-to-face group meetings with business unit president and GBCS associates.	I	Associates receive immediate feedback at meeting on issues raised or questions asked. Associates provide feedback to Pat via survey following the meeting.	CC
Bureaucracy Busters	All associates can submit ideas to recommend changes to existing policies or processes that will reduce or eliminate bureaucracy.	I/G	Acknowledgment of receipt within 48 hours. Written acceptance decision; share of stock award/recognition.	CC
All Associates Broadcasts	Video: Quarterly broadcast to all associates. Associates can view live at 60+ sites, dial-in and listen via 800 number, or view via tape after initial broadcast.	I/G	Associates can call in during broadcast and ask questions. Questions are answered live if time allows. All questions and answers are published electronically after the broadcast. Associates can provide feedback via survey after the broadcast.	

Practice	Descriptions	Participa-tion*	Feedback mechanism	Human Relations critical focus area**
	Audio: As needed audio broadcasts on specific subjects. Associates dial in live via 800 number or can listen to recording for several days after initial broadcast.	I/G	Live Q & A during call. Associates can provide feedback via survey after broadcast. Trends show an increase in Ask the President calls after each All Associates Broadcast.	CC
Performance Excellence Partnership (PEP)	Performance and developmental initiative that ensures all associates have measurable objectives linked to GBCS business results.	I	Coach/associate review and revise objectives 3 times (minimum) per year. Objecties/accomplishments discussed in total at annual salary review. Associates provide upward feedback to coach twice a year.	O
Progress Sharing Plan	Compensation plan for all GBCS associates.	I	Monthly results published in *Goalposts.* Quarterly results published in *Bigger Bucks Bulletin.*	R
Recognition Programs	Various programs that allow coaches and/or associates to nominate each other for performance recognition.	I/G	Peer/coach recognition; awards.	O
Associate Opinion Survey (AOS)	Semiannual survey to all associates that assesses their feelings about the work climate. This is our key measure of associate value.	I	Business unit results shared through various communication vehicles. Group results shared down to lowest level possible while still maintaining anonymity and integrity of data.	O

*I = Individual; G = Group
**CC = Cultural Change; R = Rewards and Recognition; O = Ownership

Source: Organizational Dynamics, Winter 1994. © 1994 American Management Association, New York. Reprinted by permission of the publisher. All rights reserved.

This comprehensive program was designed to improve communications among the 26,000 employees of Global Business Communications Systems.

Brief case

Why was the space shuttle *Challenger* launched on January 28, 1986, only to explode a minute later, killing the crew of seven? After all, by that year the space program was mature and successful, and this mission was the most routine and unchallenging of the series to date. The potentially fatal problem of vital fuel seals leaking under the prevailing temperature conditions was known to the engineers, who warned about it. So how did this worst disaster of the space program happen? One explanation (Weick, 1987) is that the electronic communication channels used by NASA did not allow the engineers to show by voice and facial expression how seriously concerned, how worried, and how frightened they felt about the danger.

Effective communication

Effective communication is a prerequisite for success in almost every endeavor. Here are some ways of improving communication:

- The sender tries to confirm that the message was received and understood. This attempt may range from watching the expression of a listener to requesting a formal written reply to a memo.

- The sender duplicates the communication. For instance, an important message may be imparted both orally and in writing.

- The language should be appropriate to the situation, user-friendly, and clear. One executive memo said, "This is to inform you that we had the entire area tested for dangerous contaminants such as PCBs and lead, and that the results were negative." The readers may well wonder if a "negative" result is good or bad.

- Communications should be as simple and minimal as is reasonable. Many people are overloaded with communication input.

- In face-to-face talking, body language (postural and expressional cues) should be consistent with the words spoken.

- In communicating with people from a different culture, it may be important first to learn which communication conventions differ between the cultures. (Most facial expressions translate easily across cultures, but body gestures often do not. There are also variances in some cultures regarding the appropriate distance between conversing people, the directness of the gaze, and the use of touching.)

- Politeness is the lubricant of discourse. Unfortunately, the conventions of etiquette are subtly dependent on time, place, situation, and culture. How punctual you are for a meeting, how quickly you raise the matter at hand, how loudly you speak, how directly you say "No," how diplomatically you phrase an alternate suggestion—these all vary according to each case, and considerable sensitivity is necessary. Perhaps the increasing numbers of women managers will lead the way. Research has shown that women are considerably more sensitive to such nuances than men (for example, Kipnis & Schmidt, 1985).

Communicating through computers

Increasingly, communication is being transmitted electronically, within the firm and beyond, through E-mail (electronic mail), computer conferences, computer "bulletin boards," and electronic "blackboards." These procedures have a number of appeals:

- The transmission is instantaneous and inexpensive, regardless of the distances involved.

- Set-up times for meetings are reduced; participants can remain at their desks.

- Of course, travel expenses are eliminated.

- Electronic communication can't be monopolized by one dominant, talkative individual.

- Contributions can be spontaneous, unhampered by the need to wait for "dead air time" to get a word in, or by status differences that inhibit low-ranking contributors.

- Finally, to increase spontaneity, as in brainstorming, the identities of the message senders can be concealed.

Gallupe, Dennis, Cooper, Valacich, Bastianutti, and Nunamaker (1992) found that the brainstorming of American and Canadian undergraduates was more productive and satisfying by computer linkage than in person. On the other hand, most people communicate more effectively by voice than via a keyboard. Many individuals, especially older ones, may be uncomfortable with computers. And electronic communication (like the printed page) lacks the voice dynamics and inflection, as well as the nonverbal behavior, which make the human voice the most subtle and sensitive of communication devices.

HUMAN RELATIONS

Prior to the 1900s employees were regarded as expendable commodities. Any equipment that failed to pay its way was to be discarded; employees were considered to be part of the equipment.

What changed this perception was the merging of four forces:

1. The **scientific management technique** included the notion that management should "remove the causes for antagonism between the boss and the men who work under him" (Taylor, 1947).
2. Industrial *technology* reached new heights. These advances increased productivity but dehumanized the nature of work.
3. The power of *trade unions* took an immense upswing at the turn of the century.
4. Social psychologists began to study social forces in the workplace.

These four forces developed into the **human relations movement**. The term broadly refers to *interactions,* and implies an emphasis on relational styles in teamwork, such as communication, conflict resolution, and leadership. The goal of the human relations approach is to enhance the workplace through improving the social interactions, not only among employees but especially between workers and managers.

The human relations movement had started by the 1940s, but it became a mainstream topic since the 1960s, when prominent social psychologists started analyzing how organizations affect their members. For instance, Chris Argryis proposed that an organization can go through developmental stages very much like people do, and Rensis Likert described four types of organizational structures and managerial behaviors. The most influential of these organizational theorists was Douglas McGregor. Partly because he became the best known by managers, McGregor changed the way we view organizations.

Borrowing from Maslow's hierarchy of needs (page 167) and from humanistic theories of personality, McGregor (1960) differentiated between two quite different types of organizational management. Although his views were models rather than theories, McGregor distinguished between what he termed **Theory X**, traditional management, and **Theory Y**, an opposite approach to management called **humanistic** in that it deals with the personal concerns of individual employees, rather than the production concerns of the firm.

Here's a picture of a Theory X firm. Management holds the common view that nobody enjoys working, so all of the naturally lazy employees must be induced or forced to be productive. This should be accomplished through the application of rewards and punishments that cater to employees' physiological and safety needs. However, because people avoid autonomy, the employees will not object to the state of regimented control.

The Type Y management approach emphasizes human relations rather than productivity. Employees are perceived as responsible, trustworthy, and internally motivated.

Now picture a Theory Y organization. Here, employees are perceived as responsible, trustworthy, and *internally* motivated to perform well. Thus, the best way to handle them is to provide autonomy, self-actualization, and challenge. One might expect production to be much higher in this type of organization, because oppressive organizational structures alienate workers, which decreases productivity, which makes managers even more authoritarian and oppressive, in a vicious circle.

The preceding two paragraphs probably convince you that a Y organization is better than an X one. McGregor did not say so, but his readers made this judgment because Y sounds more humanitarian, pleasant, and consistent with North America's value of individualism.

One weakness of the human relations approach is its emphasis on social interaction at the expense of productivity. With inadequate productivity, the firm will fail, regardless of how good the employees feel about themselves, their management, and their jobs. Research has shown that employees do like organizational changes toward the Y model, but has not shown that the changes necessarily improve productivity.

Another difficulty is Maslow's assumption that every employee wants to be autonomous in the first place, and the notion that organizations function appropriately when their members value and achieve autonomy. The final problem is the difficulty in performing meaningful research on what are really a generalized set of value statements about a generalized theory of behavior. Theory X reminds us of *Freudian personality theory,* and Theory Y reflects *humanistic personality theory,* the two theories that most resist empirical verification.

Nonetheless, McGregor's writings led to widespread programs to make organizations as "Y-like" as possible. Theory Y became a buzzword for caring about employees.

Around 1980, the global economy changed, and with it the emphasis on organizational theory. The United States, long the world-respected and envied industrial leader, was being overtaken by a small country that the United States had defeated in war, a country with a vastly different culture and corporate style. While American corporations were staggered by industrial strife, losses instead of profits, and massive layoffs, Japanese competitors were seen to be working in blissful harmony, filling American roads with their cars and American homes and offices with their electronic goods.

Suddenly the major Japanese industrial organizations were being scrutinized, and differences became apparent. Japanese corporate culture is based on conventions such as lifetime employment, mutual respect between employer and employee, the use of broad-based consensus to reach decisions, and a fierce loyalty and devotion to the company by all employees. The workers put in much longer hours than their Western counterparts accept, women are restricted to lower-level positions, and promotion is slow.

William Ouchi wrote a book for managers, which proposed combining American and Japanese organizational approaches into what he called, tongue-in-cheek, **Theory Z** (Ouchi, 1981). The solution to the American downtrend, according to Ouchi, is to change the corporate culture. He advocated long-term employment, individual responsibility but consensual decision making, and moderate specialization.

We are still a long way from applying Theory Z. Halloran (1983) observed that the average American worker is productive only 55 percent of the time, and stays with the same company for about $3\frac{1}{2}$ years. A young Canadian entering the workforce is likely to change jobs five times before retirement. Ouchi implies that the Japanese worker is responding to the Japanese organizational style. It's more likely, however, that the Japanese manager is responding to workers who are acculturated to respect elders and authority and to bring honor to family and employer.

QUALITY OF WORK LIFE

Expectations on the quality of life keep increasing. For instance, young people once just wanted to be married. Now they generally expect that the marriage will be blissful, and if the reality is less than ideal, separation or divorce will

In keeping with their cultural values, Japanese workers bring to their jobs a respect for authority and a fierce loyalty to their company. Here, employees in a quality circle consider themselves part of a large team and focus on kaizen, ways to improve quality and productivity.

likely ensue. Many young people once just wanted a job, which they expected would be generally unpleasant. Now very often the job is expected to be fulfilling, rewarding, and challenging (but not too much); otherwise, the employee may feel hard done by, and morale drops.

A recent extension of the human relations approach, **quality of work life (QWL)** is the state of well-being on the job felt by employees. It involves humanizing the work by responding to the social variables that make the job fulfilling. This approach is not based on a specific theory, nor is it attached to a particular technique. Rather, the goal is to make every employee feel like a dignified and valued member of an integrated team that includes everyone on the payroll. It's an attempt to reconcile the need for managers to manage and control, and the employees' need for humanitarian considerations.

The subjective aspect makes it difficult to define and improve the QWL. Not only are there individual differences, but there are also cultural ones. For instance, Hofstede's work (page 273) suggests that North Americans strive for material success and value assertiveness, whereas Swedish workers value cooperation, interpersonal relationships, and protection of the weak.

Nonetheless, since the 1970s, QWL issues have been of growing concern to employers aware of their responsibilities and concerned about the costs of disgruntled employees. Klein (1986) surveyed 125 major American firms about QWL programs. Half indicated that such a program was in place or impending, and only a dozen had no such program or plans for one. These are typical components of QWL efforts:

1. *Communication* is facilitated, not only downward (from management) and laterally (between equivalents), but also upward. For instance, suggestion boxes are provided, or employees are invited to communicate with executives via electronic mail. Contributions are acknowledged and/or rewarded. The downward communicating is frequent and collegial, rather than authoritative.

2. Emphasis is placed upon *job security*. Although few firms can offer the lifetime employment expectations associated with major Japanese corporations, employees are shown that management accepts as much responsibility as reasonably possible for their continued income.

3. A concerted effort is mounted toward identifying and reducing occupational *stressors*. Work may not always be fun, but it should not impair the employee's health or state of mind.

4. Care is taken to ensure equity in all matters, whether pay, privileges, or prestige. Perceptions of unfairness are bound to occur, but they are invited to be expressed, and they are taken seriously.

5. As much *job enrichment* as possible is encouraged. Employees are invited to develop additional skills and responsibilities and rewarded for their attainment.

6. Employee input is sought regarding *job design*. Nobody knows how a given task can be made more efficient, safer, or more pleasant than the person who carries it out.

7. A *teamwork* approach is encouraged. Every employee is made to feel that subordinates, colleagues, and management are close associates on the job. This may take the form of collegial labor-management negotiating procedures, the replacement of assembly lines by self-managed workteams, the reduction of status barriers, and the establishment of **quality circles**.

Quality circles, which originated in Japan, are regular voluntary meetings (typically weekly) among different factions of part of the organization to discuss improvements. Although the main benefit is to the employer, employees' suggestions may improve their work life. A meta-analysis of 33 studies (Barrick & Alexander, 1987) found that half of them attributed benefits to the use of quality circles. Another benefit, suggested by Buch and Spangler (1990), is that the meetings allow members from different levels of the work unit to get to know each other, which possibly explains why participants are more likely to be promoted.

8. Employees are invited to *participate in decision making,* especially when the decisions affect their job. A meta-analysis of some 50 studies (Miller & Monge, 1986) found that the main result of participative management was higher job satisfaction. Of course, employees should be expected to participate only insofar as they feel competent to make managerial-level decisions and to express them comfortably. Training is sometimes required. A survey of the heads of almost 200 U.S. companies (Harper, 1992) indicated that the greatest challenge they presently perceive is the increased participation by employees in management issues, in the service of QWL.

9. Many jobs like law enforcement, nursing, and teaching bring extremely positive and negative work experiences. What would be the effect of trying to raise the highs and lower the lows? One would assume that reducing negative job experiences will enhance morale, and focusing on positive work experiences will reduce psychological distress. Do workers evaluate the overall quality of their work life by weighing or combining the positives and negatives, or do the two operate differently? To find out, Hart (1994) studied questionnaire responses from some fifteen hundred Australian teachers.

Hart concluded that morale and psychological distress operate on different dimensions. Positive experiences strongly determined morale, and negative ones only affected general psychological distress, not work morale. Hence, QWL cannot be enhanced only by reducing negative job experiences, but it can be improved by increasing the opportunities for positive work experiences.

As you may have guessed from reading the above inventory, most QWL programs bear some cost, and not all are successful. Not all employees would agree on how their work life could and should be improved. But as technology increasingly removes the workers from the end product of the work, and as employees become intolerant of any dehumanizing aspects of the workplace, QWL issues will remain at the forefront of the solution.

EMPLOYEE ASSISTANCE PROGRAMS

QWL programs are general, in that they serve all the employees about the same amount. But some members of an organization may need services far more specific and powerful than those offered by QWL. What's the employer's responsibility to members whose personal problems or practices impair their work and possibly imperil colleagues and clients? Firing such employees, especially long-term ones, may be difficult, both legally and morally. Many people have problems, and in spite of their disabling potential, society wants them to be gainfully employed. If the employer does nothing, these problems can be costly in terms of productivity and absenteeism, accidents, theft, insurance rates, and general morale. Surely the employer should play some role in assisting them.

Employee assistance programs (EAPs), with which an organization seeks to identify and help its members with their problems, are recent, but have become common among major employers. Members may be referred for help by a supervisor, but self-referrals, as with any form of psychotherapy or counseling, are better because of their voluntary nature. Programs are generally contracted to external practitioners in various disciplines, although some major firms sponsor in-house facilities. (External facilities offer more confidentiality to the employee and less cost to the employer; in-house operations are more convenient for the users.)

The original target of EAPs was alcoholism and drug addiction, but the areas covered are much wider today. They typically include not only substance cessation programs (for alcohol, prescription and illegal drugs, and cigarettes), but also stress reduction training and various forms of counseling, including financial, family, and psychological. Apart from identification and treatment of problems, there's also an increasing emphasis on their prevention.

As with any form of **psychotherapy**, it's hard to evaluate the effectiveness of EAPs, but obviously, EAPs that are offered but not used serve no purpose. To determine what induces workers to self-refer, Milne, Blum, and Roman (1994) administered a questionnaire (on attitudes toward EAPs and motivation to use them) to over three thousand employees of a large communications firm across four American states. As one would expect, those who indicated they would use the program had attitudes of trust and confidence in the program's confidentiality and credibility.

The results turned up another factor required for use of an EAP, that of "organizational neutrality," meaning that nothing in the program could be used against employees. Across the states, all managers had similar attitudes toward the program; the lower-level employees did not. This indicates the importance of not only offering an EAP, but of trying to present it in a positive light, and of determining the employees' attitudes to the programs.

One value in the EAP approach is that, like QWL programs, it combines the need for managerial control with the need for a humanitarian workplace. Another value is the recognition that poor performance is not necessarily the fault of the management or the organizational philosophy; it can and often does originate outside the workplace. Insofar as helping employees helps the employer, everyone benefits.

MEASURING PROGRAM EFFECTIVENESS

As mentioned before in the context of training, it's important to determine the *attitudes toward* and the *value of* a program. If a program is instituted unilaterally by management or employees, it can easily be perceived as a method of the one side to gain an advantage over the other. And the program should be reviewed periodically to see if all its long- and short-term components are being tried and do serve their purpose.

An effective way to gauge a program's success is to survey personnel at intervals. One short instrument (Warr, Cook & Wall, 1979) asks workers to indicate on a 7-point response scale how satisfied they are with the following aspects of their job:

1. Freedom to choose their own method of working

2. Recognition they get for good work

3. The amount of responsibility they are given

4. The opportunity to use their abilities

5. Their chance of promotion

6. The attention given to suggestions they make

7. The amount of variety in their work.

A short measure of job stress is offered by Corbett (1994); the questions ask for evaluations of the following:

- Are you under constant pressure at work?

- Do you find work piles up faster than you would like?

- Do you find yourself working faster than you would like in order to complete your work?

- Can you do your own job automatically without thinking?

- Do you feel controlled by the machinery/equipment you use?

- Does your work involve repeating the same tasks over and over again?

Organizations need to be lean, productive, and practical in order to compete. But their members are people, people with feelings, aspirations, and fears. Unless the human side of the organization is responded to appropriately, the success of the organization is in doubt.

Study guide for chapter 8

HAVE YOU LEARNED THESE NAMES AND TERMS?

organizational psychology; organizational behavior (OB)
social Darwinism
Protestant work ethic
small group; large group
trait approaches or theories
consideration and initiating structure
Leader Behavior Description Questionnaire
Leadership Opinion Questionnaire
Least Preferred Co-worker (LPC) Scale
contingency theory
path-goal theory
leader: directive, supportive, participative, achievement-oriented
normative model
attribution
emergent leaders
communication: formal, upward, downward, horizontal, informal, grapevine
scientific management technique
human relations movement
Theories X, Y, and Z
humanistic management
quality of work life (QWL)
quality circles
employee assistance programs (EAPs)

ISSUES TO CONSIDER

Why does the topic of leadership so interest academics and nonacademics?

Why is there no single accepted theory of leadership?

Why do we always seem to start theoretical discussions with Freud?

What is the basic argument of the trait approach to leadership?

What is the most widely used instrument for measuring leadership?

Who is the dominant leadership theorist?

What is meant by *situation* in leadership theory?

Why is path-goal considered a situational theory?

What are the logical pros and cons of path-goal theory?

What is the force of the word *normative* in normative decision theory?

Why is the normative theory considered a *cognitive* theory?

What is the argument that there may be no such thing as leadership?

Why is downward communication more reliable than upward?

Do employees typically receive their information from their preferred source?

How might this chapter improve *your* communication skills?

What forces combined to initiate the human relations movement in industry?

What determines the "quality of school life" for you?

Is this class closest to Theory X, Y, or Z for you?

If you'd like the previous answer to change, how could this be brought about?

Do you/should you have the student equivalent of a QWL program and an EAP?

SAMPLE MULTIPLE-CHOICE QUESTIONS

1. Which leadership traits were identified in recent meta-analytic studies?
   a. self-confidence and dominance
   b. consideration
   c. efficiency
   d. high nAch

2. The American Psychological Association added "Organizational" to the name of its Industrial Psychology division around
   a. 1930.
   b. 1950.
   c. 1970.
   d. 1990.

3. About how many studies have been published on leadership?
   a. 100
   b. 1,000
   c. 5,000
   d. 10,000

4. A massive study on "who employees preferred to get information from" found the answer to be, From
   a. colleagues.
   b. the grapevine.
   c. the middle or senior management.
   d. the immediate supervisor.

5. In the history of human relations, the decade of the 1960s introduced
   a. quality circles.
   b. Theory X and Theory Y.
   c. Theory Z.
   d. Hawthorne's human relations approach to the small group.

Answers: page 462

If the ability to produce goods to meet human wants has multiplied so that each man accomplishes almost thirty to forty times what he did before, then the world at large ought to be about thirty to forty times better off. But it is not. Or . . . the working hours of the world might be cut down to one in thirty of what they were before. But they are not.

Stephen Leacock, 1869–1944

Bird's-eye view of the chapter

In this, the last of the four people-related chapters, we cover large-group issues, the macro issues of organizational psychology. We start with the meaning and nature of organizational *structure,* and then look at samples of research comparing organizations across *cultures,* which leads into the topic of organizational *development.* In the second half of the chapter we examine *unions, women* in the workforce, and *ethics,* and end with a consideration of *organizational culture,* and likely *future trends* in the nature of the corporate organization.

Chapter 9
Organizational psychology

The payoff from chapter 9   You will:

1. Appreciate the importance of *organizational psychology*
2. See the meaning of organizational psychology in terms of its origins
3. Understand the role of the original and the present *industrial revolution*
4. Appreciate the varied approaches to organizational psychology *research*
5. Know the concept of *organizational development*
6. Know something of the techniques of organizational development
7. See the contributions of *industrial sociology*
8. Appreciate some large-group differences among various countries
9. Understand the contributions of Hofstede
10. Perceive what we can learn from the Japanese work experience
11. Better understand various perspectives related to *trade unions*
12. Understand modern approaches to *dispute resolution*
13. See how dispute resolution can be built into the organization
14. Understand the special work-related problems faced by *women*
15. Be aware of current legislation affecting sex bias
16. Be sensitive to the climate and culture of an organization
17. Appreciate ethical aspects of corporate life
18. Predict what changes can be expected in organizations of the future

Company A tried everything, from raising wages to improving working conditions. Yet the incidence of grievances and strikes, and even of theft and sabotage, kept increasing steadily, and the turnover rate soared. Meanwhile, Company B was similar, but productivity and morale were high, jobs were sought after and cherished, and management was respected. Yet, wages were lower than at Company A, and by most measures, working conditions were inferior. Company A was afflicted by a "climate of dissatisfaction," and Company B enjoyed a "climate of satisfaction." What accounts for the differences in the two firms? Such issues are at the heart of organizational psychology.

ORGANIZATIONAL STRUCTURE

Organizational structure is the relationship among groups, as well as between individuals and the organization, in terms of responsibilities and authority. The design of organizations and its influence on behavior has long interested industrial/organizational (I/O) psychologists.

Formal structure

A simple way to examine organizational structure is to view an **organizational chart**. The chart shows the tasks that are performed, and the formal lines of authority. It may be *flat* or *tall;* an example of each, both with 25 members, is shown in Figure 9.1. Each box represents a specific job, and the lines between boxes show the reporting structure. The **span of control** (the relative number of subordinate boxes) may also be flat or tall.

In the flat structure, represented by Platypus, there are few hierarchical levels, with many supervisors reporting to each manager. You can see that the tall structure has more reporting levels and presumably better supervision of the smaller number of subordinates.

There's a current move to "flatten" organizational structure, on the assumption that fewer levels will put decision makers closer to the front line, reduce the bureaucracy, and make communication simpler and more direct. In the car industry, one examination (Treece, 1990) put the number of management layers between shop floor assemblers and top management at 17 for Ford, and 22 for General Motors. Similar-sized Toyota, whose productivity surpasses either, had 7 layers!

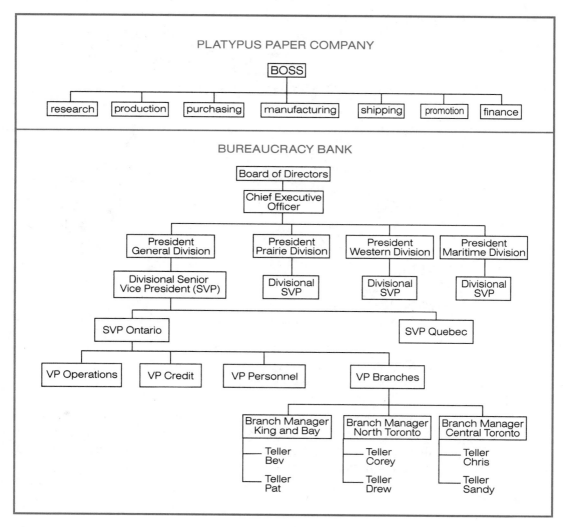

FIGURE 9.1 Organization charts for flat and tall organizations

Informal structure

Outsiders know an organization mostly by its formal structure; the members know it more by its informal structure. The formal organization is the structure as shown on a firm's organizational chart; the informal organization is the set of relationships that has developed over time. Consider, for instance, an apartment building or student residence. The structure is apparent at the outset; the *relationships* become clear only after considerable time and exposure.

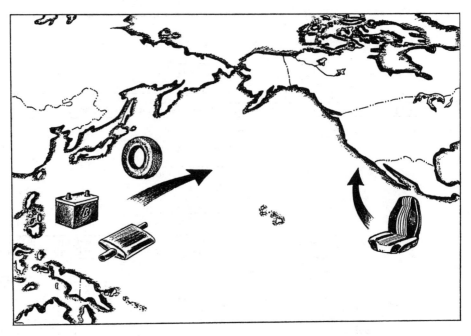

FIGURE 9.2 Sourcing in the auto industry

North American auto manufacturers may order parts and components from countries around the globe.

You are probably halfway through this course now. You surely perceive your instructor, many of your classmates, and your university somewhat differently than you did on the first day. A newly hired employee knows what the organization chart or the signs on doors indicate about who has what power and who gets what things done, but only with time do these relationships become clear.

ORGANIZATIONS ACROSS CULTURES

It's important to understand cross-cultural aspects of organizations for two reasons. (a) Today it's easier to communicate with someone across the globe than it was to talk with someone across town just a century ago. With advances in global transportation and increasing specialization, it may be easier to **source** (obtain components or materials) from another country than from next door (Figure 9.2). And in terms of marketing, businesses are increasingly thinking globally. (b) Maybe countries can teach each other something. Consider the case of Japan.

So what You participate in a variety of organizations. The better you know their structure, the more effectively you can interact within them. For instance, you must be somewhat aware of the organizational structure of your college or university. You know that the basic functional levels are *administration, faculty,* and *staff.* If you think about it, you know that administrators have different responsibilities such as managing the financial and legal aspects of the organization, and overseeing the academic wing. Some staff maintain and clean the property, others provide secretarial services. But do you know who has the power or responsibility to do what for you? Do all secretaries or department heads have equal power? Do you know the chains of command so that if your request is rejected you know the next level to take it to? Do you know who can give you this information?

Japan: A special case

How do we measure the industrial success of a country? In terms of production, Japan leads the world in the manufacture of automobiles, many consumer products such as video cassette recorders or cameras, and manufacturing tools such as robotics. For instance, in 1980, for every industrial robot working in Canada, there was one manufacturer of industrial robots in Japan!

In terms of industrial relations, Japan is a leader in implementing group consensus and employee participation, lifetime employment for men, and devoted loyalty to the employer by all workers. Whereas the North American worker stays with an employer an average of three to four years, a Japanese who signs on with a large firm expects to devote an entire working life to that company. In North America, absenteeism is a major and chronic problem; in Japan, it is virtually unknown, and managers have the problem of employees who refuse to take their paid holidays, because they feel that taking a vacation indicates a lack of loyalty to the firm!

In terms of industrial efficiency, the ratio of production output per person-hour of work ranks the Japanese worker as one of the world's most productive. For instance, in the 1970s, Japanese steel workers were about three times more productive than their North American counterparts (Halloran, 1983). The gap was reduced substantially during the economic downturn of the 1980s.

As for product quality, Japanese manufacturers of components and subassemblies are so dependable that major assemblers (notably automobile companies) order their parts to be delivered precisely when and where needed. In this **just-in-time (JIT)** procedure, wheel rims are delivered to the tire manufacturers at the precise stage of tire production; the tires, newly mounted on the rims, are brought to the chassis assembly area where they go from the tire delivery truck directly to the waiting, half-completed cars. It's as if the whole country were a single, integrated manufacturer.

In terms of quality, **frequency of repair records** maintained by the researchers of consumers' organizations invariably show Japanese products to surpass competing brands from other countries. For instance, whereas the American automobile is shipped to the dealer "for final assembly," as one consumer critic derisively termed it, the car buyer in Japan rarely visits the showroom, and purchases the chosen model sight unseen, confident of its quality directly off the assembly line. When one dealer attempted to sell American cars in Japan, more person-hours had to be invested in bringing the cars up to Japanese standards than were invested in the car's original manufacture!

The industrial success of Japan cannot be attributed to geographical good fortune; it is not located close to many of its customers, or supplied with abundant raw resources. Further, this country, unlike North America, experienced wartime destruction that decimated its industrial infrastructure. The explanation lies in the nature of the Japanese personality, social structure, and attitude toward work, and in a willingness to accept ideas from other countries. For instance, the automated assembly line was learned from Western industry.

Japanese management is associated with a team approach and decisions by consensus. Managers are sincerely and deeply respected, yet lack the status symbols and high wages standard elsewhere. North American culture, with its emphasis on individuality and independence and its distrust of authority figures (both governmental and corporate), does not lend itself to the Japanese model. The challenge for Western industry will be to learn from the best of other cultures, as Japan did, and to apply those aspects that can be adapted.

Cross-cultural I/O research

The subtle differences in the way people of different nations think, communicate, work, and do business are of current research interest. The researchers may be cross-cultural social psychologists, or they may be industrial sociologists. (What is **industrial sociology?** There often is no distinct division between the concerns of the industrial *psychologist* and the industrial *sociologist*, as both social scientists deal with similar variables. Generally, the larger the group under study, the more the field belongs to sociology.) And, of course, the researchers may be organizational psychologists.

Even among nations of English-speaking people, interesting differences have been detected—for instance, the contrast between a society that is "open" (in which prestige and success are available to anyone), and one that is "closed," in which status is determined by heredity. Bass and Ryterband (1979) concluded that the British worker feels a sharp class distinction from management, as well as a loyalty to fellow workers, and even a wish to destroy the upper classes.

By contrast, the American worker strives to join the upper class, and meanwhile supports the existing system. Such findings are important because, as noted by Biesheuvel (1987), societal forces compel many people to change their jobs, expectations, and lifestyles through the course of their careers. He points out that many people fear that the future will bring economic, ecological, political, and military turmoil. This can result in stress-related illness, family instability, escapes into drug use and suicide, and even violence, terrorism, and local wars.

We're now going to sample several research approaches to comparing and contrasting organizations in different cultures.

Attitudes toward work Dutch organizational psychologist Geert Hofstede designed an extensive Likert-type questionnaire that the giant multinational firm IBM sent to all 160,000 of its employees. Hofstede carefully analyzed the 100,000-plus replies. The reason for his ambitious study—the largest psychology survey ever conducted—was that these employees worked in 67 countries or districts. The analysis indicated that the *country* of the employees, rather than their age, sex, or occupational level, was the determining factor in their attitudes toward work.

Hofstede identified four areas that separated cultures around the world. These variables are described next and summarized in Table 9.1.

1. **Individualism** versus **collectivism** refers to whether the members of a culture focus on their own personal concerns, or on the concerns of their entire people. When you examine the figure, note how individualism is more valued in the wealthier countries.

2. Of course people differ in their resources and abilities, which means that they wield more or less "clout." This unequal distribution of influence may be glorified by one culture and suppressed in another; Hofstede used the term **power distance** to reflect these two extremes. In a high-power-distance culture, authority is emphasized, and there are many discrete ranks, clearly demarcated by titles, power, and status symbols. In low-power-distance countries, low-ranking employees are less intimidated by their superiors, and the differences between them are minimized. The table can show you in which countries it would be critical for you to determine the rank of the person you would contact, especially for negotiations.

3. How well are you going to do in this course? Which company is going to report record profits this year, and which one will declare bankruptcy? Which new product will surpass sales projections, and which will be

TABLE 9.1 Hofstede's conclusions about cultural differences

HIGH INDIVIDUALISM	HIGH COLLECTIVISM
United States	Colombia
Australia	Venezuela
Great Britain	Pakistan
Canada	Peru
HIGH POWER DISTANCE	LOW POWER DISTANCE
Philippines	Austria
Mexico	Israel
Venezuela	Denmark
(former) Yugoslavia	New Zealand
HIGH UNCERTAINTY AVOIDANCE	LOW UNCERTAINTY AVOIDANCE
Greece	Singapore
Portugal	Denmark
Belgium	Sweden
Japan	Hong Kong
HIGH MASCULINITY	HIGH FEMININITY
Japan	Sweden
Austria	Norway
Venezuela	(former) Yugoslavia
Italy	Denmark

Hofstede's extensive cross-cultural research identified four variables that distinguished attitudes toward work in cultures around the world.

the next Edsel? The future is, virtually by definition, uncertain. How you (or how companies) respond to uncertainty turns out to be another culturally determined variable, according to Hofstede. He termed this **uncertainty avoidance**.

In countries with low uncertainty avoidance, people are tolerant toward risk-taking and unconventional behaviors and opinions. In a high-uncertainty-avoidance country, people dislike uncertainty, and are generally more nervous, stressed, and aggressive. They prefer more formal regulations, reject nonconformists, and "seek absolute truths" and "correct" decisions. Such employees do not expect much in the way of job mobility, and put considerable value upon lifetime employment. The table shows those countries that scored at the extremes on this variable.

4. The last of the main dimensions that Hofstede identified was termed **masculinity** versus **femininity**. The difference hinges on the extent to which a society permits both men and women to adopt a variety of roles and positions. A culture that restricts some positions to men and others to women is "masculine," according to Hofstede, in that the men play dominant, assertive roles (and value materialism and profit), whereas women are relegated

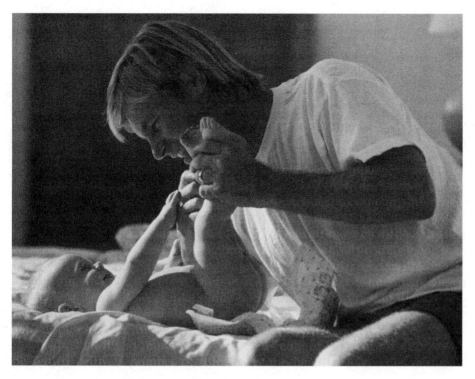

This scene typifies the flexibility of gender roles that are found in countries with high femininity, according to Hofstede's study.

to service-oriented and caring roles. Men go out to work while women keep house. In a "feminine" culture, emphasis is placed upon caring relationships and the quality of life. Women are free to work as they will, and men may be given paternity leave to stay home and help with a new baby. Preserving the environment may be valued more than making a big profit.

If you're interested in pursuing this area, the original study was reported by Hofstede (1980), and was updated by Hofstede (1983). Then, both Jaeger (1986) and Black and Mendenhall (1990) extended the findings into a consideration of what kind of organizational development interventions (page 277) would be appropriate for the various cultures identified by Hofstede. The question of what kind of managerial style would best match these cultures was examined by Jackofsky, Slocum, and McQuaid (1986), and a detailed and updated analysis of Hofstede's approach is found in Adler (1991). For a less academic exploration of these issues, see Tully (1990).

Handling conflict As a follow-up to Hofstede's work, Ting-Toomey et al. (1991) hypothesized that in handling conflict and "saving face," people from collectivist cultures would show more concern than those from individualistic cultures. Collectivists would, for instance, avoid humiliating opponents, and offer excuses for their errors. She also predicted that individualists would show more domination, as opposed to accommodation or avoidance, in resolving conflicts.

As part of a series of studies, Ting-Toomey administered questionnaires to almost one thousand students in the United States, Japan, Korea, Taiwan, and the People's Republic of China. The instruments measured participants' concern with saving their own face and that of opponents, and their preferred techniques for conflict resolution. The Japanese were most adept at "maintaining their own face" in a conflictual situation, and the Koreans were at the opposite end of the scale. For conflictual resolution strategies, American students showed the strongest tendency toward domination; their least preferred approaches were obliging their opponent and avoiding the conflictual situation.

Work goals   Harpaz (1990) surveyed over eight thousand randomly selected workers in seven industrialized countries on their most important *work goals*. He found that the most common goals, from a list of eleven, were *interesting work* and *pay,* and that *opportunity for promotion* consistently ranked lowest. The top three per country were as follows:

- United States: Interesting work, Pay, Job security

- Great Britain: Interesting work, Pay, Job security

- West Germany: Pay, Job security, Interesting work

- Japan: Person-job match, Interesting work, Autonomy

- Belgium: Interesting work, Pay, Job security

- Israel: Interesting work, Interpersonal relations, Pay

- Netherlands: Autonomy, Interesting work, Interpersonal relations

Notice that the one discrepant report is from Japan, where "person-job match" was rated highest.

Management   Can managerial and organizational practices that are successful in one culture be translated effectively into another? Ever since 1978, the People's Republic of China has been trying to change to a free market system by encouraging entrepreneurial and creative management. Do Western organizational values work in Eastern cultures?

To find out, Okechuka (1994) had senior managers rate over 300 subordinate managers on a questionnaire that measured characteristics related to managerial success. The participants were from similar financial and manufacturing organizations in Canada, Hong Kong, and China. The most important predictors of managerial effectiveness were not the same across cultures.

Supervisory ability was an important one in all three countries, but the number-one predictor varied. In Canada it was self-actualization, in Hong Kong it was self-assurance, and in China it was intellectual ability. This suggests that Western organizational values are not easily adopted in non-Western cultures.

The above studies show that organizations operate differently and sometimes apparently better in different countries. Sparked partly by this realization, I/O psychologists have been studying ways of helping organizations to change, grow, and develop. This aspect, organizational development, is our next topic.

ORGANIZATIONAL DEVELOPMENT

The practice of **organizational development (OD)** seeks to encourage all group members to further both their individual objectives and the organization's goals, with emphasis on harmonious relations. The specialist in accomplishing this task is often referred to as the **change agent**.

OD started after World War II, when the social psychologist Kurt Lewin established a facility in Maine called the National Training Laboratories (NTL) to spread his new T-group technique (page 151). Lewin championed the use of the survey to uncover attitudes and problems in the workplace, which could be dealt with in T-group and other meetings. Since then, Lewin's use of direct experience to bring about change has proliferated into a number of variants, the main ones of which are outlined next.

All of the following may be directed by either an **internal change agent** or an **external** one. An internal agent is a member of the organization; an external one is an outside consultant. Browne and Cotton (1973) reported that their survey of OD practitioners indicated that only the largest firms—those with over ten thousand employees—maintained an internal agent. Since the time of that survey, smaller firms, especially in the United States, have been adopting this practice, especially where the organization is sensitive to interpersonal relations and involves the public, such as hospitals. These agents are typically termed *personnel development officers*.

Process consultation

Unlike the T-group leader, who faces an artificial, laboratory-like situation, the *process consultant* teaches a real group how to solve its actual problems. Gradually, the consultant intervenes with questions and comments about the *processes* taking place at the meeting. The procedure is analogous to modern psycho-therapy, except that the client is an organization rather than an individual.

A book by Schein (1969) described six steps in the process. (a) The *initial contact* with the consultant is generally made by an executive who realizes that a problem exists. (b) In exploratory meetings with the executive, a *contract* specifying the objectives is formulated. (c) The *setting and methods* for the consultations are established. (d) *Data gathering and diagnosis* are performed by observing and surveying employees. (e) *Intervention,* which can be simple or elaborate, according to the problems and objectives, takes place. (f) Finally, there is an *evaluation and disengagement.*

Planned negotiation

In **planned negotiation**, the role of process consultant shifts from the outside expert to each member of the host group. Once the techniques of *process consultation* have been demonstrated, the members continue on their own. The objective is to gradually reduce the time from data-gathering to feedback to finding solutions. Finally, work colleagues learn how to continuously exchange information, review experiences, maintain harmony and productivity, and negotiate new commitments.

Intergroup problem solving

It is not uncommon for members of different groups within the same organization to compete with each other. Sometimes this competition is designed into the system, or at least encouraged, to increase effort. If and when it becomes counterproductive, the change agent may bring the competing groups together. The objectives of this **intergroup problem solving** is to resolve the source of the conflicts, which may be problems such as conflicting responsibilities or uncertain lines of authority.

Confrontation meeting

Sometimes a problem is so apparent that there is no need to work on the diagnosis. The change agent assembles those involved at a **confrontation meeting**. The objective is to articulate the problem, expose the attitudes to it, and facilitate the solution. The latter usually includes establishing priorities, setting targets, and drawing commitments to action.

Goal setting

The change agent arranges for many pairs and teams within the organization to specify their goals and to review their past performance. This procedure operates more smoothly where the principle of goal setting has been extended into the management by objectives (MBO) model (page 181).

MBO is a popular approach for clarifying most employees' chief concerns: exactly what am I to do, and how is my performance to be measured? Ideally, the manager and employee arrive at these decisions mutually, and they encompass a wider range of goals than the immediate task. The goal-setting procedure can (and should) be applied to the whole organization, to groups within it, as well as to the individual, and the goals should be as quantitative as possible.

Third party facilitation

In **third party facilitation**, problems that are severe and intimate (such as interpersonal friction) may be assigned to someone who has skills in diagnosing and resolving them. It is convenient to select a trusted member of the organization, because this third party will be aware of its nuances, and will be available for follow-up consultation as needed.

Buddy system

Most of life's problems, in an organization or out of it, are so minor and transient that they do not call for any of the above formal procedures. Rather, they require a momentary outside opinion. To seek such an opinion from a friend may not be satisfactory because the friend, by definition, lacks objectivity.

In the **buddy system**, each member is linked with one other (the buddy), who then is available to serve as a sounding board—casually, conveniently, and as soon as even a minor question or problem arises. Sometimes all novices are automatically buddied with an experienced mentor of a similar status or occupational level.

Joining up process

The introduction of a new member into an established organization can be smooth and uneventful, but in some cases it can create disruption, unrealistic expectations, "first date" behavior, suspicions, and uncertainty. Besides or instead of assigning a buddy to the newcomer, it may be helpful to establish a **joining up process**. Typically, this comprises a workshop involving new hires, management, recruiters, and coworkers, which is designed to establish connections and integrate the novice.

Survey guided feedback

There are many advantages to using **survey guided feedback** as a starting point for organizational change. As explained in chapter 1, the survey is an efficient means of collecting data and it is comprehensive. In addition, this form of upward communication lets all members of the organization know that the management is concerned about the employees' attitudes and opinions. It also alerts employees to the existence of problems and permits them to "ventilate" any anger they may harbor.

The survey taps employees' opinions about variables such as organizational structure and processes, leadership, and the coordination and communication among various factions. It can be distributed to all employees, or to a representative sample.

The following principles should be adopted when a survey is the starting point in organizational intervention. The introduction to the survey is as important as the questions themselves, so the preamble should explain the rationale. This usually includes citing some problem, preferably phrased in a positive and constructive manner. Respondents should be given the option of forwarding the completed survey form to the survey taker, or, to ensure anonymity, to an intermediary such as a trusted colleague, or to an outside consultant.

Also, provision for *feedback* should be specified. For instance, there may be an undertaking to circulate a summary of the responses (in writing or orally at a meeting) within a couple of weeks, along with proposals for change. Finally, although some questions may be particular to the situation, other items should be standardized so that they can be repeated in subsequent administrations of the survey. In this way, changes over time can be tracked and assessed.

Studies (such as Bowers & Hauser, 1977) have shown that the use of survey results, if followed by appropriate responses, is an effective and efficient technique of organizational development. Standardized questions can be adopted from the *Survey of Organizations* (Taylor & Bowers, 1972).

In addition to knowing the above nine specific approaches, it may be useful to conclude with several principles for effective intervention recommended by OD specialists: (a) The "entry point" should be the part of the organization where success seems most probable. (b) Changes should be rapid enough to permit an ongoing momentum, but slow enough to allow consolidation. (c) The interventions should be consistent with the members' capabilities. (d) Finally, there must be a pervasive aura of consideration and democracy in the organization, which may require some redistribution of power.

How useful does research show OD to be? It's difficult to tell, because the changes expected from OD are long-term and diffuse. Also, employers often resort to OD as a response to basic problems in the organization, problems that can distort the outcome measures. And employees may interpret the OD efforts as a way of getting them to work harder or complain less.

The good news is from Nicholas (1982), who reviewed studies that included nine different types of OD. At least half of them attributed concrete, solidly measurable improvements to the intervention. The bad news is from Terpstra's (1981) examination of over 50 studies of organizational intervention (half of which involved OD). The more scientific the study, the less impressive were the results. Those studies that used small, casually selected samples, poor controls, and questionable outcome criteria were the ones that reported the most brilliant success of the intervention.

TRADE UNIONS

Unions are part of our culture today, yet it hasn't always been considered permissible for workers to negotiate issues like wages and work conditions with their employer. A century ago, in response to working conditions that were seen as unsatisfactory then and would be considered deplorable, if not illegal, now, British unionists who tried to organize strikes were charged with "conspiracy in restraint of trade." It was these workers who were the first to receive legal recognition in 1868.

Shortly after the initial British unions, legal recognition was won by a number of European ones in the late 1800s. Legally sanctioned unions sprang up in the United States in the mid-1800s, and their Canadian counterparts caught up in 1881 with the formation of the Federation of Organized Trades and Labor Unions of the United States and Canada. This group later split into the American Federation of Labor (AFL) and the Trades and Labour Congress of Canada (TLC) in 1886.

Occupational expectations rose dramatically in the early 1900s, especially in terms of working conditions and job security. Pay, security, benefits, safety, and comfort were *minimal*; hours of work were often limited only by the extent of human endurance. At this time, the spread of literacy, combined with mass communication via pamphlet, telephone, microphone, and newspaper, helped employees to organize for their benefit. Unions provided employees with what they desperately needed: the power of numbers and a sense of identity and pride. Alderfer and Smith (1982) found that unions comprised the strongest *identity group*.

The rise of trade unions in the early 1900s helped to alleviate miserable working conditions. This scene in a garment factory in Chinatown, New York City, is a reminder that such conditions do still exist.

Unions in North America

In much of the world, the union movement is gradually increasing in strength. In the United States, however, the proportion of (nonagricultural) workers who belonged to a union rose sharply around 1940, then fell from 30 percent in the 1950s to 20 percent in the 1980s, probably due to labor legislation that decreased the need for unions, and partly because of the prevalence of a somewhat negative attitude toward them. Total membership is currently about 17 million; between a fifth and a quarter of the total labor force has been a union member. These unions are occupation-specific. Few professionals or professors belong; almost all nonmanagerial workers in automobile plants, mines, and the steel industry do. A current trend is for unions to cooperate with management to save the company from closure. For instance, of the 570,000 members of the United Steelworkers of America, over 44,000 work in firms that they partially own.

The 4 million Canadian union members make up over one-third of the working population. Canadian unions, like those in Germany and England, are historically linked with one particular political party and are politically active, whereas American unions are relatively apolitical. In Canada, there are almost one thousand unions. A quarter of these, accounting for about 95 percent of the membership, are affiliated with national or international umbrella groups; the remainder are local independents.

Canadian unions are more numerous per capita than American ones, no doubt because public policy and laws in Canada are more supportive of unions, but the Canadian ones are typically smaller in membership. They range from the International Association of Siderographers (with some four members) to the giants, such as the Canadian Union of Public Employees (CUPE), the National Union of Provincial Government Employees, the United Steelworkers of Canada, the Public Service Alliance of Canada, and the United Food and Chemical Workers, which together have a six-figure membership (Chen & Regan, 1985). As of 1992, the membership in CUPE was over 400,000, equally divided between women and men.

One in five Canadian workers is a government employee (municipal, provincial, or federal), and 90 percent of these workers are unionized. Almost half of all union members in the country, including professors, are employed in governmental work (Christensen, 1980). These unions are particularly powerful because of their large membership, their sophistication in dealing with politicians, and the fact that their remuneration is funded by the taxpayer rather than by a profit-making employer.

Trade unionism seems to be widely misunderstood in North America, for several likely reasons:

1. Considering the impact of unions on individuals, organizations, and nations, research on the topic is scant. Few research papers on unionism are published, and hardly any unions engage organizational psychologists to work with them. Because of Frederick Taylor's emphasis on "scientific management" early on, unionists associated industrial psychology with worker exploitation. Researchers are seen as managerial types, unsympathetic to the lowly worker, and sharing few values with union leaders who worked their way up from the bottom. Moreover, psychologists are seen as the "hired guns" of management. What makes this worse is that unionists emphasize *equality* (except in terms of seniority); psychologists assess workers to measure skill *differences*. Unionists prefer to link each member to specific, limited duties, whereas psychologists promote job enrichment, resulting in a blurred integration of duties.

2. No doubt because of the lack of research, little is taught about unions, even in I/O psychology. A recent survey of 75 current I/O textbooks revealed that of the 42,092 issues covered in them, only 572 dealt in any way with unions (Barling, Fullagar & Kelloway, 1992). Many business schools address unionism mainly in the context of how to counteract it.

3. Another reason for the confusion is that the public may have a vague feeling that unions may have been necessary once, but are not required now, yet most people know someone in a union who feels otherwise.

4. Unions are not consistent, making generalizations difficult. There's a wide variety of unions in North America, and even in the same union, each

local may have unique procedures and objectives. Moreover, some unions change these procedures and objectives from time to time.

5. The general public hears about unions mainly in the context of strikes, and these are often seen as unreasonable, disruptive, or threatening. (Picture a single mother who has to miss work in order to tend to her children because their teachers—who make much more money than she does—are on strike.) So let's next review the pros and cons of unions from all sides.

Advantages of unions to the employee

• The employer inherently has more power than the employee. The basic purpose of a union is to reduce the size of this difference. History has seen a variety of power differentials between work associates. In extreme cases, one member of the team owns the other. The farmer has command over the horse; the master controls the slave. In terms of employer/employee relationships, the early employers had almost complete control over the employee. The latter, if beaten or unpaid, could sue, but the most likely alternative would be to quit (and to starve).

Recent laws have better protected the weak, but power is still weighted heavily against them. For instance, if the employee wants to negotiate working conditions, the boss can say, "If you don't like them, you can quit"; at the same time, employers can unilaterally make changes in their own favor. In the work world, one side offers its capital and the other tenders its labor. But the right to work is not protected by laws, police, or the military, whereas management does call upon them to protect the capital assets. With a union, the employees have a more equitable share of the power. Although regulations differ in various countries, the following paragraphs describe some typical provisions:

• Once a legal union has been formed, the employer is required to negotiate the terms of the basic or first contract or *collective agreement*. Each time the agreement expires, either side may renegotiate any of the terms. The employer is required to negotiate with the elected representative(s) of the union. If an agreement is not reached, or if the employer ever violates any of its terms, the employees have the option to withdraw their services as a group.

Much of the scanty research on unions has addressed their effect on compensation, and the conclusions are clear. Union members are paid up to one-fifth more than their nonorganized counterparts, as well as receiving more generous fringe benefits, especially deferred compensation such as pensions, medical entitlements, and vacation pay (Freeman & Medhoff, 1984). Other studies have indicated that union wages are less susceptible to local conditions of supply and demand or to changes in the economy.

Job security is a primary concern of unions, and most collective agreements protect jobs in various ways, especially for the most senior members. (Surely many high-level managers—who are currently being released due to corporate downsizing or merging—wish that they had the benefits of union membership!) Overall, union members are more likely to be laid off than nonunionized employees (Freeman & Medhoff, 1984), but this is largely because unionized firms are more likely to experience wide business cycles and to rely on temporary layoffs in the downturns.

Practically, a union provides employees with a mechanism for addressing concerns; psychologically, it gives members a feeling of power, especially concerning the ability to retaliate against managerial wrongs. The latter are no doubt sometimes only imagined, but they can be real; workers have been punished, even dismissed, quite arbitrarily. The formal grievance system that is almost always included in the collective agreement protects employees from unjust, harmful personnel practices. Just as the ability of the employer to dismiss an employee at will was a powerful tool, both psychological and real, the union's ability to threaten to strike goes a long way to equalize the power relationship.

- With experience comes knowledge about how to beat the system. Terms like "shirking" and "fiddling" are commonly applied to employees; it's easy to make up a list of ways in which employees can cheat their firm. Ways that employers can manipulate their workforce are not so well known or entrenched in our vocabulary, but it happens: management can simply downclass a job, that is, reclassify it as lower-ranking, while at the same time adding more responsibilities to it. It can replace permanent workers with part-time or contract ones who have no entitlements with the firm, or it can get workers to compete with each other. It's hard for an individual employee to understand what's happening throughout the entire organization and to counteract it. Union membership means that employees have a representative who also has an overall perspective and won't let the boss get away with this type of corporate fiddling.

Disadvantages of unions to the employee

- Only a minority of employees belong to a union, for a number of reasons. Invariably they decide to unionize with the expectation that beneficial change will soon follow, but negotiating the first contract can take years. Because this is a give-and-take bargaining procedure, the benefits are seldom as one-sided as anticipated. Hence, members of newly formed unions may feel disappointed.

- Union membership is expensive. The cost is up to the members themselves and could conceivably be negligible, but union leaders typically argue that without a strike fund in reserve, the union has little effective power. Dues, strike funds, and special levies and donations usually add up to hundreds of dollars per year. Most of this money goes to operate the union itself; Francis (1991) calculated that only 4 percent of Canadian dues are spent on strike pay. And if the union calls a strike, the members lose income that may not be replaced by the settlement for years, if at all.

• Employees may feel a barrier between them and management, insofar as communication to management has to pass through the union bureaucracy. Moreover, the employer-employee relationship tends to become increasingly adversarial, focusing on rights, contract interpretations, and benefits won by counterparts in other unions.

• The highest-skilled employees, those who least need the protection of union membership, tend to become "downclassed." Invoking the concept of pay equity, unions tend to minimize differences among the "brothers and sisters," giving the same attention to the custodian as to the master welder, and showing more concern with raising the former's pay than the latter's. There's less incentive for a unionized employee to attempt upgrading through continued education and improved performance, as unions tend to reduce variations in compensation based on such achievements, and emphasize seniority instead. A merit-based pay system benefits both sides, but union members who don't receive a merit increase can enter a grievance over it. Thus, a merit plan in a nonunionized firm tends to become a system of automatic pay raises for everybody in a union one.

• Although some prestigious occupations such as airline pilots are widely unionized, unions are generally associated with blue-collar work, which deters many professionals from wanting to join them.

• Legislation now gives many nonunion employees certain rights that formerly only union members enjoyed. Nonunionized part-time and contract workers, for instance, also benefit from a safe working environment—but not from job security or automatic pay raises.

• Employees who identify with management and aspire to high-level promotion may oppose unions, which are seen as contrary to the management's interests. Moreover, dedication and superior performance are less likely to be rewarded in a union environment; for instance, bonuses and profit-sharing plans are rarer, and pay is more likely to be uniform within each job class.

• Large unions can become bureaucratic, and the leaders can ignore the wishes of the members and even exploit them. Where the union belongs to an umbrella group, members may feel that it is not serving their interests. Such feelings can lead to decertification (disbanding the local union).

• Unions suffer from "bad press." They are more likely to make the news in the context of problems or controversy than from benefiting their members, the employer, or others.

• Unions often oppose management's attempts at job enrichment (unless the changes also enrich the pay).

• One current trend is for management and unions to seek a mutually improved outcome. The results may mean some losses to the unionists, who might interpret this as double-crossing by their leaders. For instance, at contract renewal time, management may give two alternatives: Accept a 4-day workweek (with a cut in pay) or a workforce reduction of one-fifth. The union leaders recommend to their members the 4-day option, in order to maintain the workforce. Unionists, especially those with the most seniority (who would have the greatest immunity from workforce cutbacks) oppose the shortened workweek.

• A major rationale for union membership is that in negotiating terms of employment with the employers, workers are at a disadvantage and would be better served by experienced union representatives than by bargaining individually. But not always. Suppose you're a talented senior secretary who sometimes runs the whole company. If you feel entitled to a large raise in salary, there's nothing to stop you from asking for it. But if you belonged to a union, your elected representatives would negotiate your terms of employment, and these would be the same for all senior secretaries.

• Many modern organizations are fostering a "family" feeling by blurring the distinction between the managers and the managed. Insofar as this teamwork approach is beneficial to both sides, unionization, which draws sharp distinctions between the two, would be counterproductive.

• Finally, some employees feel that it is management's prerogative to set the terms of employment, and that their bosses will do so fairly and properly. To form a union would be seen as an unnecessary affront to the employer.

Advantages of unions to the employer

• The formation of a union tends to follow long periods of increasing strife and animosity between employer and employee. Both sides suffer from the tension and distraction—until a detailed contract is agreed upon. Most labor agreements work smoothly; thus, the employer benefits from the peace and harmony that stem from a clear, detailed, and mutually accepted contract.

• The communication between the two sides in a nonunion environment may be uncertain, strained, and flawed. The collective agreement will typically specify formal lines of communication that management often finds preferable, and which therefore could be more inviting for the employee to use.

- Many senior supervisors or middle managers are uncertain as to the limit of their responsibilities. For instance, a supervisor may routinely train and evaluate workers, but not be sure if the authority extends to replacing one of them. Collective agreements typically specify duties. In the example given, the authority to hire and fire would be defined as a managerial prerogative, and managers cannot join unions. Supervisors would have to clarify their authority before knowing whether they would be a member of the union. This reduces role ambiguity within the organization.

- Unionized firms are more stable, especially in terms of their senior employees. This invites more care in selection and training. For instance, Jackson, Schuler, and Rivero (1989) compared personnel practices in over 250 organizations. They found that unionized employees were more likely to experience objective, formal appraisals, and to be given appropriate training based on the results. Such practices are obviously in the employer's interest.

- Because questionable personnel practices can be challenged through the grievance procedure, management in unionized firms is likely to review these procedures. Such a review is likely to render them not only more fair but clearer and more efficient too.

- Union contracts generally penalize management for exposing employees to hazardous conditions; for instance, such workers may command higher pay, and all accidents are more likely to be reported. This can increase awareness of occupational health and safety issues by both sides, leading to a healthier workplace in terms of accidents, training, and work scheduling. The end result is likely to be lower insurance costs for the firm.

Disadvantages of unions to the employer

- Management loses some of its accustomed control and authority. Apart from the psychological discomfort this may cause, unions strive for permanence and consistency that can reduce management's flexibility to meet changing situations.

- Forming a union is a bureaucratic, unwieldy, and wasteful method of achieving the objectives that all employees feel entitled to.

- The existence of a union can create a confrontational atmosphere. It's difficult for a firm to counter its business competitors when it has to dilute its efforts due to an in-house adversary.

- The ultimate union tactic, the strike, is counterproductive, inasmuch as the resulting disruption, animosity, and loss of productivity damages the very firm the employees depend on for their living.

- The specification of duties reduces role ambiguity, but it also can cause inflexibility and inefficiency. Imagine a custodian who is not allowed to perform any electrical work—including the replacement of burned-out light bulbs. As another example, picture the maintenance of windows in a skyscraper. The trickiest step is the installation of hanging scaffolds to hold the workers and move them to the next window. After the calking operation, the whole expensive setup has to be repeated just for cleaning. The contractor is unionized, and the calkers are not allowed to clean the glass too.

- In a nonunionized firm, management can recruit promising personnel by offering whatever compensation it takes. In a unionized one, compensation is rigidly fixed for each job class, reducing the hiring flexibility.

Advantages of unions to the nation

- It is the democratic societies that are the most productive and efficient, and every one of them has a viable labor movement. At the least this indicates that unions are compatible with industrial success; at the most it suggests that unions are responsible for it.

- Some countries benefit from unions in that the less advantaged are helped the most, making the populace more homogeneous.

- Social benefits such as safety, security, and equality may be addressed initially by unions and may then filter down to society in general.

Disadvantages of unions to the nation

- Unions could harm nations insofar as those at the lower end of the social scale—the transient, the illiterate, the disabled, the immigrant, the isolate, the social outcast—are largely bypassed by the union movement. And when essential public service employees (such as police or firefighters) mount a protracted strike, the nation is essentially held at ransom.

- The early philosophical appeal of unions lay in their valid complaint that too much power was concentrated in the hands of a few industrialists and politicians—who made the rules and passed the laws that suited them. Now, ironically, unions themselves in North America have amassed inordinate, concentrated, economic power. Like the governments they once complained of, they "tax" people by forcing them to pay substantial dues. Like the industrialists they once criticized, they use some of their funds to finance lobbyists and pro-union government officials and political parties.

Union membership is substantial, especially in Canada, where 4 million members (out of 11 million employees) pay about $750 million in annual dues. This amount is even more powerful than the numbers imply, because union members generally work together to further the aims of unionism more than industrialists or politicians do to advance their own objectives. Unions can exert undue influence on politicians to enact legislation to serve unionists' interest at the expense of the country as a whole.

As you know, employers had unrestricted power in the early days of industrialization. With the rise of unions, control was gradually shared by the employee, but unreasonable demands that could force an employer into bankruptcy would hardly benefit the employee. Recently, the balance of power has tilted toward unionists, many of whom work for the government or for monopoly utilities, and are therefore unconcerned about the financial health of their employer. Thus, the direct and indirect power of modern unions may not bode well for the financial health of the country.

• Wages are characteristically higher for union members than for their nonunionized counterparts. Some businesses counteract this cost by transferring their unionized jobs to countries where wages are lower—to the detriment of their own nation.

Issues for unions

A collective agreement may contain hundreds of clauses within a thousand pages. Each one of the tens of thousands of such agreements is unique. Yet, a few central issues permeate virtually all of them.

• How much is paid for how much work? *Remuneration* and *work hours* dominate collective agreements. In the earliest factory contracts of the mid-1800s, assemblers worked 60 to 72 hours a week for one-tenth the pay of middle-level managers. Modern contracts give assemblers about one-third the salary of managers, for half the hours worked in 1850.

• Unions focus on the worker's right to some *control* over the workplace. The central provision of the first major automotive contract was the limitation of the speed of the assembly line. Some modern contracts permit the line to stop entirely if an assembler is concerned about safety or quality. (This provision, which started in large Japanese automobile assembly plants, is still rare in smaller organizations and in some industries such as building construction.)

• Collective agreements emphasize *job security, social benefits* (such as health care), and *equity,* that is, the fair treatment of all members and the fair resolution of all disputes.

Dispute resolution

Most unions came into being because employer and employee could not solve a problem on their own. Employees found their only alternative, courts of law, to be unsatisfactory for financial reasons, but the company often had a legal firm at the ready, and courts and lawmakers tended to favor big business over the individual. Also, the long delays in most civil trials usually worked more to the benefit of the employer. It's not surprising, then, that collective agreements invariably contain procedures for resolving disputes.

In the military, dispute resolution is simple. The higher-ranking member gives an order; the lower-ranking one salutes and obeys. Prior to unions, the industrial model followed the military one. Even with the advent of unionism, disputes could lead to prolonged legal and strike actions.

Now that it's so important to the well-being of the firm for disputes to be settled deftly, a number of third party mechanisms have been adopted. In a **conciliation** or **mediation** procedure, an outside party (a conciliator or mediator) is hired to listen to both sides, and try to bring them together by encouraging an open discussion by both sides. If unsuccessful, the third party simply walks away. An **arbitration** procedure, however, imposes an obligation on the disputing parties. The arbitrator listens to both sides, but then, in most cases, like a court of law, makes a decision that is binding on both sides. The arbitrator may be an individual, or a tribunal of three, where each side chooses one arbitrator, and the two choose a third to chair the tribunal. Arbitrators ensure that both parties are treated equally and fairly, with all evidence heard by the other side, which has an opportunity to respond.

A mediator's involvement can be terminated at the whim of either of the disputants, but an arbitrator is required to decide the outcome. Both are outsiders brought in to help resolve a dispute. An **intravenor** is a member of the organization, most likely an executive, who can elect to assume an arbitrator's role or decide not to. These third party procedures are charted in Figure 9.3.

Brett, Goldberg, and Ury (1990) cite a number of studies that report that in disputes of various types, the participants prefer mediation to arbitration. This, they say, is because mediation exposes information that increases mutual understanding, and ends up reconciling both sides' interests. Arbitration, which focuses on disputant's rights rather than on their interests, is quicker and more efficient, but the solution is more likely to bring about recurrences of the dispute.

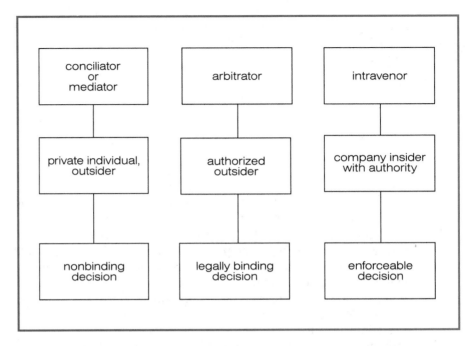

FIGURE 9.3 Three dispute resolution models involving a third party

To study intravenor variables, Conlon and Carnevale (1994) had over 200 business students pretend to settle a business dispute presented on a computer. Among the four independent variables were their roles, defined as either *mediator* or *intravenor,* and the disputants, depicted as being cooperative or otherwise.

The intravenors imposed settlements in two-thirds of the cases, more so when the disputants were portrayed as uncooperative. Compared with the mediators, the intravenors tended to use forceful pressure tactics. The more progress the disputants were making, the less the third parties intervened, whereas the longer the dispute lasted, the more the intervention. The study indicates that the role of intravenor can be effective in dispute resolution, even though the intravenor may have personal interests at stake.

If all else fails, the employees can elect to strike. Stagner and Effal (1982) assessed worker attitudes as a function of their involvement with a strike. In comparison with attitudes displayed on questionnaires months before and after a strike, *during* it the workers valued the union and its leaders more, felt more militant toward the employer, and were more willing to participate in union activities. Brett et al. point out that struggles over power, whether in the form of a strike, an election, or a war, "often create new injuries and disputes and leave a residue of anger, distrust, and a desire for revenge."

Brief case

The multinational, nonunionized courier firm FedEx has devised a dispute-resolution procedure called the Guaranteed Fair Treatment Procedure; employees call it "GFT." It's an expensive, time-consuming program to maintain, but given the need for over 100,000 employees to work productively, co-operatively, and accurately, FedEx has found it to be a good investment. The procedure varies slightly from one country to another, but here are its four steps in general terms:

• The complainant discusses the problem with the immediate manager.

• If the latter fails to satisfy the employee, the issue is relayed up the managerial chain for further review.

• Ultimately, the senior vice president of the division can uphold the decision, overturn it, or initiate a board of review.

• A board of review comprises members selected by both sides as well as representation from the personnel department; decisions of the board, which are to be rendered within two weeks, are binding on both sides.

Dispute Resolution Systems Design   The newest application of dispute resolution is the specialist who designs a dispute resolution system. This aims at reducing the costs and maximizing the benefits of conflict. The following principles from Brett et al. have been adopted by the system designer, and can apply to disputes both between and within organizations.

• *Consult first; give feedback after*   The systems designer expects organizational conflict to be inevitable. As soon as disputes originate, there should be a structure and process for airing them, so that they can be resolved at the outset. Following this stage, whoever is in a position to prevent a recurrence should be provided with feedback of the problem and its resolution.

• *Focus on interests*   Negotiations should be framed as a cooperative process to reconcile interests. For instance, the starting point may be an exchange of information about each side's interests.

• *Build in "loop-backs" to negotiations*   Negotiations may become a power struggle, or the perceived differences may be so large that the disputants cannot establish a range within which to negotiate. **Loop-backs** refer to a form of "reality testing," for instance, by determining what solutions in similar cases have been achieved in other negotiations or in the courts. After this, the procedure loops back into the negotiations.

• *Arrange procedures in order of cost*   Depending on the nature of the organization and its characteristic disputes, and on the resources available, some resolution procedures are more economical than others. A hierarchy should be established, in which the least costly alternatives are exhausted first.

• *Provide disputants with the required negotiation skills, resources, and motivation* Negotiators should be taught **integrative bargaining** (maximizing joint gains), rather than **distributive bargaining** (maximizing their own gains). Integrative bargaining seeks a multi-issue solution that gives each side more than it would receive simply by compromising on each issue; distributive bargaining assumes that there is a "fixed pie," which is apportioned through negotiation. Examples of resources that should be provided are consultants and information. As for motivation, participants may need to receive incentives to use the procedure that's best for all, rather than the one they perceive to be to their individual benefit.

Increasingly, firms are installing dispute-resolution procedures designed to impart fairness to employees and to forestall unionization. An example is shown in the Brief Case of FedEx.

WOMEN'S ISSUES

Few sociological changes have been more dramatic than that of the role of women throughout the 1900s. In previous times, men comprised virtually all artisans, tradespeople, salaried employees, members of the military, and community and political leaders; employment for women was pretty well limited to low-level domestic duties. What's recently happened was termed, in an essay on organizations of the future, "the feminization of the workforce" (Offerman & Gowing, 1990). As an example, women accounted for some 60 percent of the total growth of the U.S. workforce from 1970 and presumably through to the year 2000. Moreover, about three-quarters of working-age women in North America are either employed or looking for a job. As with many cultural changes, there are likely to be misunderstandings about what women expect and are entitled to, and communication difficulties over this.

The origin of gender roles at work

What is "women's work," and how did it get to be that way? Why is it that in all societies known to anthropologists, males and females are expected to behave, especially in work roles, appropriately to their sex? We start our search a long time back. In almost all nonhuman primates (monkeys and apes), the males, being the robust and expendable sex, do most of the attacking, defending, and exploring. In the human as well, males are taller, heavier, and stronger, so for thousands (perhaps millions) of years, this primate role separation has led to or encouraged a differentiation between men's tasks and what was taken as women's work.

All cultures define roles for men and women—as well as for children, the elderly, and the disabled—and there are various ways of explaining and understanding these roles. Generally, early human males went hunting while the females maintained the cave and the children. Men designed, built, and used the machinery of warfare; women wove cloth. Men dominated; women served. These primary roles formed the basis for occupational differences between men and women that can be seen to the present. Progressive educators try to reduce the impact of these long-held assumptions, and to raise the self-image and occupational expectations of young women.

This may explain why "outside" and "traveling" work is associated with men, whereas women traditionally work indoors. High-profit, high-tech, and high-prestige work is typically male; greeting and serving jobs, typically female. Thus most locomotive engineers, aircraft pilots, and boat captains are male; most company receptionists and restaurant greeters are traditionally women. In the corporate world, women are likely to be in purchasing, personnel, or public relations; high-paying and high-prestige areas such as finance or marketing are usually associated with men. Male lawyers have traditionally practiced lucrative business law; women lawyers were more likely to run community-service clinics or to practice matrimonial or advocacy law. North American physicians, the higher earners among professionals, have traditionally been men, whereas in countries such as Russia, where medicine was seen as a low-paying service operation, it's not unusual to find that three-quarters of doctors are women.

Historically, jobs that lost their prestige quickly changed from men's work to women's work. When bank tellers were seen as custodians of the all-important money, they were men. As the position changed to that of "mere" service, it was taken over by women. The first operators of the new typewriters were men, but when the work lost its allure, women took over. When books were rare and expensive, librarians were men, but as books became common and inexpensive, women took over. (Now that libraries are regaining importance, we may see the proportion of men increasing.)

Women's work has been seen as temporary and not needing much training; men are expected to work steadily until retirement. Men have been expected to become principals or professors, women to teach kindergarten. Men have aimed at becoming executives, women to work as secretaries. Low-level jobs are associated with high turnover, and women are typically given low-level positions, but even in the case of male and female graduates of prestigious business schools, the females are more likely to be self-employed or unemployed a decade after graduation, presumably because they may be discouraged from reaching their potential by the major employers.

Brief case

Power once meant immunity from ethical accountability. Police, armies, and political and corporate leaders acted with relative impunity. But in the 1970s an American president (Richard Nixon) was forced to resign because he was held in some measure responsible for the unethical acts of his staff involving a break-in. A decade later, President Reagan's staff evidently had to take pains to not let him know about their arms sales to Nicaragua. More recently President Clinton has had to defend himself against ethical charges involving financial and sex-ual matters, and a Japanese head of state had to resign because of accusations of financial improprieties. In this climate of accountability, a major American bank has tried to institute a corporate culture of scrupulous ethics for its ninety thousand employees. The training device is a game called "The Work Ethic" that presents players with ethical dilemmas related to banking. The ensuing dialogues demonstrate that top management takes ethics seriously, and encourages reports of improper behavior.

Prejudice against women has been ingrained and pervasive, even at the university level. Goldberg (1968) asked female undergraduates to rate the quality and importance of professional articles written either by John MacKay or Joan MacKay. The same papers were rated higher when attributed to a male author, even when the topic dealt with traditionally female areas such as dietetics. Not surprisingly, male students made similar ratings (Paludi & Strayer, 1985; Lott, 1985). This form of bigotry is seen even in professionals who should know better. When psychology department chairpersons were asked to evaluate résumés either with a male name or a female one, the males were rated higher and judged suitable for a higher-level position than females with the same résumés (Fidell, 1970). All of this is obviously unfair and discriminatory; in a democratic society that values justice, these facts are upsetting to both women and fair-minded men. As lawmakers, many of whom are now women, have become aware of prevailing sex-related inequity, "women's work" has increasingly been the object of legislation throughout most of the Western world.

Industry must play a major role in correcting sexism. In Canada, where one-fifth of families are now single-parent ones, over half of all women work outside the home. But these working women make only about two-thirds of men's earnings. Many are offered only part-time jobs, which do not include benefits such as pension plans and unemployment and medical insurance. According to figures from the U.S. Census Bureau, throughout the 1970s American women also earned 62 percent as much as men. By 1986, women's wages were 70 percent of men's. This increase may simply mean that more female college graduates are filling senior positions.

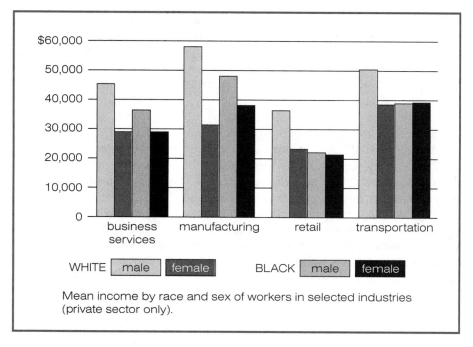

Mean income by race and sex of workers in selected industries (private sector only).

Source: The Glass Ceiling Commission figures as represented in the New York Times, March 16, 1995. Reprinted with permission of the New York Times.

FIGURE 9.4 Race, sex, and paychecks

A 1995 report by the Glass Ceiling Commission found that white men constituting 43 percent of the workforce hold 95 percent of the senior management positions. White women hold about 40 percent of all jobs nationwide and less than 5 percent of the senior management positions. The report was based on 1990 census data.

Women are increasingly assuming management roles, but rarely at the top. A ceaseless stream of figures documents the "glass ceiling"; here are two examples. Stroh, Brett, and Reilly (1992) compared over a thousand managers at 20 major American corporations and found that women earn substantially less than men with the same background and ambition. Solomon (1990) showed that female corporate vice presidents earn 42 percent less than males who were their close counterparts. Figure 9.4 compares paychecks of white and black men and women.

One way for ambitious women to adjust to these organizational barriers is to start their own business. Here, women seem to be holding their own. In Canada, of the 75,000 new businesses started in 1984, two-thirds were started by women. Moreover, the survival rate after the first three years of new businesses is about 50 percent for those run by women, compared with 25 percent of those run by men.

In the United States, a woman was burned alive in the 1800s for being a witch. According to Canadian law, women were not actually "persons" until 1929. Surely there were fairminded and logical thinkers back then. How could such situations prevail? The last aspect to understand about sexism is that it's been marked by **rationalization**, the making up of seemingly logical reasons or explanations.

When women were denied entrance to medical schools (a common practice as recently as 60 years ago), it was supposedly because they were too frail to undergo the training. Some schools that started to admit women barred them from performing surgery on the pretext that they lacked the requisite manual dexterity; however, women were meanwhile accepted as seamstresses—because of their manual dexterity. Part of this rationalization is the assumption that every individual conforms to the prevailing stereotype that surrounds their group. Thus, a male who is nurturing is seen as abnormal, whereas a nurturant woman is seen as proof of the biological nature of the female. It's difficult but important for us all to realize that such traits are the result of long-held cultural expectations and pervasive social learning, not of biology.

LEGISLATION

The important concepts of equal opportunity, comparable worth, and affirmative action (page 90) have been related to various disadvantaged groups, but especially to women. We will use women as the example, but ethnic or other minority groups could be substituted.

Equal opportunity means that gender is disregarded in all personnel decisions, starting with recruitment. *Comparable worth, or equal pay for work of equal value,* means that each job must be evaluated for its value according to criteria such as qualifications and responsibility. If welders and nurses are thereby judged to be equally valuable, and if welders are paid twice as much as nurses, the latter's pay should be raised to that of the welders. Jobs must pay the same if they involve equivalent training, responsibilities, and importance.

Affirmative action policies would mean that women are accorded preferential personnel-decision treatment until their representation in positions of authority matches that of their representation in the population. That is, firms must actively recruit women for their plum jobs, and offer those positions to female applicants even if a male contender is equally or perhaps slightly more qualified.

For readers of this book, surely social justice is an objective to be cherished and striven toward. Social justice often starts with one group militantly demanding fair treatment. Then the principles of equity filter down to benefit other victims of bigotry. Just as many of the employment benefits won by unions soon become common in nonunion organizations, the equal rights being demanded by women will eventually apply to others. When women attain full equality, so will the other groups, who at present may not be fully aware of their disadvantaged position in society.

ETHICS

Would you like your friends and acquaintances to regard you as an ethical person? Think of the various organizations with which you are affiliated, such as your school, religious organization, or sports group. Would it be important to you that these establishments have a reputation of being ethical? Now suppose you become the head of one of them. Imagine how important it would be to you that your group is known as one of integrity, and that you are seen as contributing to this reputation.

Most people in public life want to behave ethically, and to be seen as such. Political leaders, members of the clergy, and professionals like physicians and professors have long cherished a reputation for having high principles. The question was never whether or not to be ethical, but what was the ethical thing to do. The ethics of commerce, however, traditionally fell into a somewhat different category, because business is business. (As characters from the film series *The Godfather* would say before pulling the trigger, "This isn't personal. It's business.") Every business decision has ethical implications, often in conflict with one another.

In recent decades, business has joined the move toward scrupulous conduct. Today, business executives strive for a personal and corporate reputation for conscientious behavior, often underscoring it with the development of a corporate code of conduct. As with world leaders, they do not always find it easy to determine what constitutes proper behavior.

Psychology and other professions have long-established, carefully worked out principles of conduct, but business ethics are more complex and less codified. One solution is to institute a program of *training* in ethics; another is to engage an *ethicist* as a consultant. If all else fails, a suggested criterion for evaluating business conduct is this: decisions or actions made behind closed doors should not change if they took place in public.

Whistle-blowing

Suppose you are working at a splendid new job for an organization you like. Your task is to handle the disposal of waste, including some that's toxic. You

So what   Congratulations on your new job! What you weren't told at your interviews were the answers to questions like these:

Should you wear formal or informal clothing?

Do you park anywhere, or in an area assigned according to your rank?

Do you address your supervisor and executives by first name, and should you ask your assistant to use your first name?

Do colleagues have titles you're expected to use?

Are there key people you should meet?

Are there workplace rituals you should observe, like always or never using flipcharts at meetings?

Will you have a separate, closed-door office or workspace that you keep to, or do people mix?

Should you decorate your workspace with plants and personal mementos or keep it businesslike?

Can you replace your office furnishings with better quality items you have at home?

Do you talk to anybody about your work, or are there expected lines of communication?

When do you communicate in person, by phone, by memo, or by electronic mail?

Should the language you use in conversation and reports be formal or casual?

discover that your boss is taking bribes from a disposal firm that dumps your refuse by the side of a road. What would you do?

A book by Hirschman (1970) suggests that you would have two options. One is to "exit"; that is, to consider leaving the firm because your philosophy is "love it or leave it." The other is to "voice"; that is, to speak up within the organization, or to **whistle-blow**, disclosing the wrongdoing externally. Of course, speaking out could imperil your reputation for loyalty, and perhaps your job security too.

In a massive study, Graham (1986) surveyed almost ten thousand American federal government employees across the country about their experiences with observing wrongdoing at work. She found that dissent within a group does not come easily. Nearly half claimed to have observed serious malfeasance; three-quarters of this group had done nothing about it. But of those who "voiced," one-third reported the incidents only to their immediate su-

Do you refer to your employer with reverence, pride, or casualness, and how should you refer to the competition? Should you smile a lot or look serious, and are joking and bantering welcome or discouraged? Does water-cooler chatting focus on work, news events, sports, company gossip, or the latest joke? If a colleague tells you a story or legend about the company, should you read between the lines?

Will you be working with your predecessor's secretary, or do assistants move up when their boss does? Will your presence be resented, perhaps by someone who hoped to get your position? Are novices in your job expected to be eagerly assertive or politely reserved? Are suggestions for change welcome?

Should you bring lunch, should it last two minutes or two hours, and with whom should you eat? Are alliances based on status level, functional area, gender, or seniority? Do you join others for coffee, or keep working while drinking it? Should you stay after hours or leave right on time? Is after-work socialization expected? Are partners included? What's the view on emotional liaisons with coworkers? If a male remarks on the color coordination of a woman colleague's outfit, will it be considered expected politeness or incipient sex harassment? Is the company committed to a charity project you'll be expected to participate in?

Your first week on the job will establish you as the likely future CEO, or as the next person to be terminated. Knowing the answers to questions like the above, none of which are in the company Mission Statement or employee manual, means *reading the organizational culture.*

pervisor, while the other two-thirds persisted in eventually taking the matter higher up. How can this be explained?

Graham discovered four stages of dissent: (a) As an obvious first step, the dissenters had to observe the wrongdoing and view it as serious. (b) Then some of them took personal responsibility for acting on their observation. (c) They then had to conclude that, with disclosure, the problem would be rectified, and that true loyalty is served by correcting mistakes, not ignoring them. (d) Once the problem had been exposed to a supervisor, the reporting employee felt an increased commitment to see the issue through to rectification.

One must suspect that although many of Graham's respondents were acting in good conscience in the public interest, some were disgruntled workers retaliating. Regardless of motives, employees who whistle-blow are increasingly being protected from retribution by contract or by law.

ORGANIZATIONAL CLIMATE AND CULTURE

Concepts such a "group norms" have been studied since the 1930s, and "climate" has been the topic of essay and research since the 1950s. Climate is the psychological environment, usually measured by attitude-type surveys just as job satisfaction (page 191) is. But **organizational culture**, the *shared pattern of thought and action,* has only recently been investigated. Culture is harder to study and measure, because it underlies or accounts for climate.

A review article on the concept of organizational culture (Schein, 1990) points out that any group with a shared history will have its own culture, involving identification with leaders, group identity, policies, and rituals. A comprehensive book by Trice and Beyer (1993) lists myths, symbols, rites, and stories as components of organizational culture.

ORGANIZATIONS OF THE FUTURE

The workplace changes presently occurring are massive and disruptive, but they afford us a window into what the future holds. You have already been introduced to the concept of the new industrial revolution (page 7). Now we'll look at what will be the organizational challenges and solutions of the next generation.

Global *competition* is becoming fiercer. Some long-established companies are failing, and many are shrinking or merging to survive. Competition for job openings is increasing, and companies may have to justify the rejections. Skills will need to be higher as routine tasks are automated, yet there are fewer applicants with skilled trades. In the face of these difficulties, it will be increasingly important for human resources departments to function with skill and professionalism.

The *workforce* is changing. Women, especially those with children, are becoming the majority of hires, and dual career couples as well as employees from nontraditional groups are becoming common. In addition, the workforce is aging. Some employees will bring devastating psychological, social, drug, and attitudinal problems to their workplace. Others will be underskilled, hired partly due to societal or legislative pressure. Organizations, whether industry, government, educational, or nonprofit, will need help to steer through the problems occasioned by change, social tensions, and human concerns.

The nature of *work* is also changing. The most common form of employment has shifted three times, from hand-to-mouth to agricultural to manufacturing to service. Currently, the service sector (economic activities in which the outcome is relatively intangible) comprises over two-thirds of both the employment and the gross national product of the United States

(Offerman & Gowing, 1990). Work-related communication is increasingly electronic and cognitively demanding. Organizations will have to understand and master these changes.

The nature of the implied or formal *employment contract* is changing. In the 1970s, doing well at a good job meant an assured career. Now the concept of job security is fast fading; employers are reducing costs by replacing full-time with part-time workers, and using shortened or lengthened workweeks to staff their operations according to need. Career paths used to be vertical; the bright stars steadily ascended the corporate hierarchy. With fewer layers of management now, there are fewer opportunities to rise. Career paths are becoming increasingly horizontal, as employees undertake additional responsibilities, but not necessarily higher status or pay. Organizations will have to design a system that will fairly reward employees of the future who have career expectations of the past.

The *work environment* is changing to increase safety, physical and psychological comfort, and the control of the physical workplace environment. More employees will work outside the office, for instance, at home. Organizations will have to rewrite job descriptions, communication procedures, and performance standards.

The *marketplace* is changing as well. For instance, the North American Free Trade Agreement of 1994 encompasses a population of 360 million, and the major European industrialized countries have banded into their own common market. Formerly totalitarian regimes that disdained the processes and products of a free market society are dissolving, and the new order is struggling toward joining the free enterprise system. Organizations must accommodate to different and fast-changing cultures by fostering an atmosphere supporting innovation, quality, and acceptance of different values.

The consequences of *errors* are increasing. For instance, the questionable organizational personnel practices of a major oil company led to the payment of a billion dollars in damages when one of its tankers ran aground. Equipment, pharmaceuticals, procedures, and chemicals are ever more potent. Every action, every product invites catastrophe, litigation, and irrevocable loss of prestige. Organizations are going to have to be at once open-minded yet cautious, forward thinking yet mindful of past disasters.

Managers are faced with severe constraints stemming from employment *legislation* and from a new set of *attitudes and values* on the part of employees. Yet, the survival of the organization requires that managers make optimal use of the human and machinery resources, sometimes adapting successes associated with other countries and cultures. The heart of this challenge is organizational change, communication, and training.

Organizations are subject to more *accountability* than ever before. There is steady pressure for the observance of ethical practices, both directly (for example, treating employees and clients fairly) and indirectly (such as possible impacts of their sourcing or selling practices on the environment of

Management at the Zebco Novelty Co. continued to be puzzled by the company's declining productivity.

far-off countries). Many firms are drafting a mission statement designed to define a favorable organizational climate.

The cost of *conflict* is increasing. A strike at one location can cause far-reaching and long-lasting disruption; a disgruntled employee can cause untold damage. Organizations will have to focus on team-building, intergroup problem solving, and deft mechanisms for conflict resolution.

Sociological variables are subtle and slow moving, and we are the end product of a thousand generations of increasingly solidified values and opinions. As organizational psychologists, social psychologists, and sociologists refine ways of examining broad social trends and movements, we will be better able to understand and control the relationship between the individual and society, instead of the one being swept along under the total control of the other.

Applied psychology seems to be one of those disciplines that excels in a crisis. It was born, honed, and strengthened in the two global conflicts of this century. Before the century is over, we can confidently anticipate that it will offer humane, practical, and proven solutions to the problems of the organizations of the future.

Study guide for chapter 9

HAVE YOU LEARNED THESE NAMES AND TERMS?

organizational structure

organizational chart

span of control

source (sourcing)

just in time (JIT)

frequency of repair record

industrial sociology

individualism versus collectivism

power distance

uncertainty avoidance

masculinity versus femininity

organizational development (OD)

change agent, internal and external

planned negotiation

intergroup problem solving

confrontation meeting

third party facilitation

buddy system

joining up process

survey guided feedback

conciliation

mediation

arbitration

intravenor

loop-backs

integrative versus distributive bargaining

rationalization

whistle-blowing

organizational culture

ISSUES TO CONSIDER

Why is organizational psychology such a recent topic?

How did the early philosophers contribute to past views of the workplace?

When would you use each of the described OD techniques in a company?

What are the prerequisites for the hiring of a change agent?

What is the difference between a buddy and a third party facilitator?

Does OD assume a Theory X or a Theory Y approach?

What are some implications of Hofstede's study on work attitudes and culture?

Why was Theory Z given that name?

Why could Theory Z be applied, or not be applied, in North America?

What is your attitude toward unions, and why?

What are the emotional dynamics during a strike?

How could dispute resolution techniques have helped you in your own personal or school-related conflicts?

Which dispute resolution technique would you prefer, and why?

What's your attitude toward affirmative action?

What should the qualifications be for a company ethicist?

Is whistle-blowing disloyal?

How can you determine the climate and the culture of an organization?

How are you preparing yourself for joining the organization of the future?

What might an organizational chart reveal about an organization?

What aspects of other cultures might be relevant when working or trading with them?

SAMPLE MULTIPLE-CHOICE QUESTIONS

1. An organizational chart contains
   a. the communication lines among different organizations.
   b. communication lines within an organization.
   c. generalized job titles and formal lines of control.
   d. informal and formal lines of communication and authority.

2. How many questionnaire responses did Hofstede process in his study of national differences in attitudes toward work?
   a. 100
   b. 1,000
   c. 10,000
   d. 100,000

3. Hofstede found that Canada is high in
   a. individualism.
   b. power distance.
   c. uncertainty avoidance.
   d. masculinity.

4. If women are underrepresented in a certain job, they may receive preferential hiring treatment, in accordance with
   a. equal opportunity.
   b. comparable worth.
   c. affirmative action.
   d. union regulations.

5. In general, women earn what fraction or percentage of men's earnings?
   a. 100 percent
   b. 90 percent
   c. 80 percent
   d. two-thirds

Answers: page 462

Part three

The workplace

So far, we've mainly been examining various ways to ensure that the person fits the job. Now we turn to how the job can be altered to fit the person. How can the workplace be made more employee-friendly? How might your work schedules be made to work with your internal clock rather than against it? How might you tell if you are provided with the right equipment to work with? And how do we respond to design problems in the most basic work tool of all, the English language?

The night cometh, when no man can work.

John 9:4.

Bird's-eye view of the chapter

Today's employers are expected to protect the employee from any job-related mishap, and employees expect to work in safety, comfort, and psychological contentment. This chapter examines the issue of occupational health and safety.

Chapter 10
Occupational health and safety

The payoff from chapter 10   You will:

1. Know the meaning and importance of *occupational health and safety*
2. Understand the pressures on industry of *accountability* and *responsibility*
3. Know the factors leading to concern about workplace safety
4. Know which occupations are—and aren't—the most hazardous
5. Understand the myths and realities of the "accident-prone" employee
6. See why some workplaces are inherently hazardous
7. Realize the responsibility of the organization for health and safety
8. Know how to conduct a safety audit of your own home
9. Know the meaning and nature of *substance abuse* in the workplace
10. Know the meaning and management of *stress*
11. Understand the origin, meaning, and treatment of various aspects of *chronobiology*
12. Know the implications of sudden time zone changes
13. Know the consequences of studying all night

14. Understand the myths and realities of *PMS*
15. Understand the nature and prevention of *repetitive strain injury*
16. Know the meaning of *job design*
17. Know various approaches to improving job design
18. Learn the various possibilities for alternate *work schedules*
19. Become acquainted with *job sharing* and *homework*
20. Know the meanings and uses of *job rotation, job enlargement,* and *job enrichment*
21. Understand the meaning of *work teams* and *quality circles*
22. Be aware of the consequences of introducing *new technology* into the workplace
23. Know some techniques for increasing the *acceptance* of new technology
24. Consider principles of *workspace design* in improving your own workspace
25. Know the pros and cons of designing a *landscaped* office

Nobody knows how many workers were killed in the construction of the Pyramids, the Great Wall of China, or the temples of the Mayans. How many ships dropped on the shipwrights or sank with all hands at the launching? There are hardly any records of fires, building collapses, or other disasters in workplaces. Probably nobody cared much at the time.

The same indifference applies to occupation-caused illnesses of the past, which were surely as numerous as the deaths caused by falls, burns, and explosions. We don't know how many lungs were diseased due to various underground operations even prior to King Solomon's copper mines, or from exposure to cotton dust or grain dust. Nor are there records of eyes damaged by candle-lit workrooms. We do know that the cute phrase "mad as a hatter" derives from nervous system damage caused by chemicals used in making felt hats.

We also know that job-related dangers were hardly eliminated with the advent of contemporary workplaces and modern medical treatment. In fact, in the United States alone there were over a quarter of a million new cases of occupational illness in 1990, and over nine thousand workplace deaths in 1994 (National Safety Council, 1991 & 1995). Today's worker is at risk from not only accidents but also from chemicals, various kinds of airborne pollutants, and physical strain. These, then, are some of the life-and-death concerns that come under the topic of occupational health and safety.

THE IMPORTANCE OF OCCUPATIONAL HEALTH AND SAFETY

Did you ever hear stories from your grandparents about being hurt at school, on a trip, or on the job? If so, you probably learned that the mishap was blamed on fate, or what the law called an "act of God." Today, courts are ruling that if someone drinks at a bar or even at your home, and suffers a mishap on the way out, whoever provided the liquor is responsible. If a child bruises a knee at recess, the school may be held to account.

The concept of *accountability* is consequential in the workplace. People are increasingly aware of and concerned about health matters, and vigilant about environmental toxins, and physicians are becoming specialists in **sick building syndrome**, or the "twentieth-century disease." In the 1970s, many office buildings were designed to be airtight to reduce the costs of temperature control. This can result in everything from chemicals to viruses being circulated by the ventilation system. Some buildings were designed to have a slight negative air pressure to keep the heated or cooled air from escaping, thus pulling industrial or traffic fumes into the building. Sometimes the building design, such as a defective air circulation system that spreads pathogens, has caused illness, but public fear has led to apparent cases of mass hysteria, especially in users of school buildings.

Apart from the legal liability, there are moral and ethical issues as well. Many workplaces are potentially hazardous, and individual employees are less likely than the employer to be aware of the potential dangers. And employees are much less likely than the employer to have the wherewithal or the authority to improve workplace safety.

Everyday consumer machinery such as cars or power tools can injure. Again, it's largely industry's responsibility to foresee dangers, and to protect the user by adequate warnings and especially by foolproof product design. Household accidents are often related to poor design of buildings, tools, and labels, so again some legal and moral responsibility lies with industry.

Workplace accidents and illnesses are costly, disruptive, and unpleasant, and some jobs are inherently hazardous. Law enforcement work has a reputation for being dangerous, but a worker is much more likely to be injured in forestry or in mining. Exposure to risks that are hidden and that may gradually accumulate must also be considered. Until recently, for instance, it would have been dangerous for a young person to work pumping gasoline, because gasoline fumes contained lead vapor, which damages the growing nervous system. And firefighters and soldiers can be exposed to subtle toxins whose effects may show up years after the exposure.

Few settings are entirely free from some level of hazard. But unlike the home, we have little control over the workplace. Accordingly, laws protecting the worker are common, and their violation could result in the closing of the offending operation. Employers are expected or required to protect the employee's body and mind on the job, and to some extent after work as well.

The researchers and consultants who help achieve these objectives work in the field known as occupational health and safety. They help to establish a "climate" of health and safety, applicable to employees and customers alike, and responsive to the issues and findings presented in this chapter.

ACCIDENTS

The topic of accidents is complex. Imagine that in the first year's operation of one plant, an employee rushing to work killed a parking attendant, resulting in an inquest, extensive investigations by safety officials, an increase in workers' compensation costs, lawsuits, and the institution of an expensive safety program. Across the street in a small family-operated business, there may be frequent cases of back strain, stumbles on poorly lit stairs, tripping over extension cords, and chemical spills, none of which was reported or resulted in time off work. Which plant was safer?

Every day, hundreds of boats collide or run aground; maybe once a year the results are catastrophic and make worldwide headlines. So what's the boating accident rate? A fatal workplace accident occurs in the United States about every hour. Does this mean the workplace is dangerous? Consider that in the same hour, about 10 deaths will occur in the home and on the road.

Research on accidents focuses on the *worker* or on the *work.* Let's look at some highlights.

The "accident-prone" employee

Are there *people* who are likely to have accidents of greater severity and frequency than expected by chance? The identification of such persons—if they exist—would be an important element of employee selection, job assignment, and training.

Accident repeaters have been recognized and studied since 1940, but it is still not conclusive that the person who had five accidents in the first decade on the job will have another five in the next 10 years. Accidents are influenced by unpredictable chance factors, and these are not distributed evenly. Also, researchers have only recently differentiated between accident repeaters who *cause* accidents involving themselves or others, and repeaters who lack the training, experience, or skill to *avoid* accidents.

In looking for characteristics associated with **accident proneness**, researchers (for example, Cooke & Blumenstock, 1979) have implicated physical *weaknesses* such as poor vision, hearing, and reaction time, as well as *youthfulness* and *inexperience* on the job (the two often go together), and *old age.* (The often-absent employee may consequently be relatively inexperienced.) Unsafe *work practices,* such as showing off and disregarding safety rules, are an obvious and established accident factor. Other research (for example, Hansen, 1989) has blamed *social adjustment* and *personality characteristics* leading to negative attitudes toward people in general and to the work situation in particular. (We should keep in mind that accident research such as cited above is necessarily correlational, even though the researchers draw causal implications.)

The accident-prone job

Accidents are largely *situational,* and some jobs are inherently more hazardous than others, as are some job environments. For instance, a sudden increase in noise can impair communication and attention. Or, the nature of the work may cause employees to have periods of fatigue, stress, or distraction that make an accident more likely.

Most jobs can become hazardous if workers feel that safety is not important to the organization—for instance, if there's no *training* in safe work practices, no *reminders* of the need for safety (for example, safety posters) and no appropriate safety *equipment* such as hard hats, **eyewash stations**, and fire extinguishers.

But jobs can be examined for specific ways to make them safer. For instance, Sanders and McCormick (1993) identified three types of workplace improvements: **Exclusion** designs *prevent* accidents, such as a punch press that can be operated only by both hands so the presser can't leave a hand under the die when it springs down. **Prevention** designs make accidents *less likely;* for example, handrails may prevent persons from falling down stairs. And **fail-safe** designs reduce the *consequences* of accidents; for example, padding placed on obstacles that someone could bump into reduces the likelihood of injury.

The accident-prone organization

In the home, a loose rug might present a hazard to a handful of people, none of whom are likely to consult a lawyer after a fall. At the workplace or in a hospital or nursing home, the same rug could skid under or trip any of a thousand people. The homeowner who buys a floor maintenance machine shops carefully, perhaps watches demonstrations, and brings home a light duty machine, reads the instruction manual, and tries it out at leisure. If the operator loses control, hardly any damage ensues. At work, the purchase agent orders a powerful device to maintain the factory floor. When it arrives, a supervisor tells the maintenance employee to unpack it, start it up, and get to work with it—starting in the chemical storage area.

In your daily home chores, you do the dishes, mow the lawn, climb a short ladder to hang a picture; if you have to move a heavy box, you think nothing of waiting for help to handle it. The work is varied, brief, and totally under your control. At work, you could spend seven hours just packing cartons, operating a computer terminal, or running a lathe. If your duties include moving heavy objects, you'll try to do it yourself; if you have to climb a ladder it may be a tall one.

Probably all homes and workplaces would benefit from a **safety audit**, a careful walk-through by an outsider with training in *occupational health and safety*. For reasons implied above, safety audits are hardly ever performed in homes, but should be a routine procedure in most workplaces. Besides the visible aspects, the audit will confirm that the organization ensures two things in its employees: a safe work *attitude,* and safety *knowledge and skills.*

At the workplace, someone should be in charge of safety issues specifically. The safety officer can:

- ensure that safety issues are part of the corporation's general company policy.
- review safety content in orientation and training programs.
- publicize past accidents and present hazards.
- encourage the reporting of, and investigate, accidents, near accidents, and potential hazards.
- reward employees who show exemplary or helpful safety concerns.
- provide reports to management and feedback to employees about safety issues.
- ensure the proper installation of appropriate safety equipment.
- see that the equipment is clearly and conspicuously labeled, and that employees are trained in its proper use.
- enlist the support of all levels of management in creating a safety-conscious work climate.

What if the workplace poses certain risks that are generally acceptable to most people as the price of modern industrial society, but are somewhat more ominous for certain types of employees? The concern about the possible connection between high-voltage electrical transmission lines and some forms of cancer may influence the location of a company day-care facility for the children of working mothers. Pregnant women might be susceptible to low levels of chemicals associated with the manufacture of, for instance, storage batteries or computer chips.

Some organizations try to protect the particularly vulnerable employee with a policy of **protective exclusion**. This policy might, for example, bar pregnant women from an environment that is a potential risk to their condition. A logical extension of this well-intentioned policy would require the testing of applicants or present employees for pregnancy, a possible invasion of their privacy. In fact, the U.S. Supreme Court ruled in 1991 that such a policy constitutes a form of sex discrimination and is therefore illegal.

A somewhat related issue is the disease of **AIDS (Acquired Immune Deficiency Syndrome)**. Because it's lethal, incurable, and contagious, and because it was originally associated with gay men and intravenous drug users, many people refuse to work with infected persons, even though many victims contracted it from a spouse or a blood transfusion. Because AIDS cannot be transmitted though casual contact, U.S. law prohibits any form of AIDS-based employment discrimination. The recommended procedure for handling concerns is the use of educational programs to reduce fears, misconceptions, and the likelihood of contagion through unsafe personal practices.

Concern to provide a hazard-free workplace now extends from the factory or construction site to within the office walls.

MALADAPTIVE HABITS AND SUBSTANCE ABUSE

When a person's ability to do the job is impaired through the consumption or usage of any substance, it falls under the general term of **substance abuse**. The substance may be controlled and legal, such as tobacco, alcohol, or certain prescription drugs; it may be an illegal product such as marijuana or cocaine.

The extent of the problem has been well documented. One-third of North Americans use tobacco regularly. Two-thirds report that they consumed alcohol in the past month, and about 15 percent say they used illicit drugs during the past year (U.S. National Institute on Drug Abuse, 1991). Half the instances of absenteeism and accidents are thought to be related to the above substances, and many of the problems affect the family as well as the job. The organizational culture may encourage alcohol use; for instance, drinking may be a part of the social custom at executive lunches, or a particular trade or industry may be associated with after-hours social drinking.

What is less clear is the solution. Research is difficult because of the privacy issues involved, as well as the complex and interactive nature of substance abuse. Self-reports are always suspect, correlational data can be misleading, and the administration of drugs in a laboratory setting poses ethical and interpretive problems.

Requiring people to submit to chemical testing for drug use is a controversial issue. On one side is the ethical principle of the right to privacy and the issue of self-incrimination that oppose these "urinary witch-hunts" and indirect measures of a person's "lifestyle" that may be irrelevant to work performance. On the other side is the right of the employer to set standards that are reasonable and consistent with the law, to protect its workplace, its reputation, and its clients.

Compulsory drug testing started in the U.S. military, spread to athletes, and is making its way into the workplace. It's most common in work venues affecting public safety, such as utilities or transportation, and was instituted in 1990 by the Toronto Dominion Bank, which has drug tested ten thousand new employees. (A 1994 decision by Ontario's Human Rights Commission ruled that the bank's compulsory drug testing is intrusive but permissible, as it does not constitute an undue violation of the employees' privacy. The Canadian Civil Liberties Association is appealing the ruling.)

Many people strongly oppose this testing. One caller to an open line radio program said that when she had to provide a urine sample, "I felt that my whole body was being violated." Not surprisingly, a survey of American college students (Murphy, Thornton & Reynolds, 1990) found that they disapproved of employment-related drug testing—in proportion to the amount of illegal drugs they used themselves.

Where a screening program is instituted, it might be announced well in advance, and presented in a safety and medical context (to protect employee health and safety on the job site), rather than as an expression of a company "no drugs will be tolerated" policy. Some employers make drug screening a precondition for new employment, but an option for present employees. If drug use is detected in an employee, the consequence can be referral to an *employee assistance program* (page 262), rather than disciplinary action.

Gambling is a pastime that dates at least to the ancient Egyptians. With the widespread availability of venues for legal gambling, the problem of addiction is likely to affect the workplace, where it can lead to white-collar crime (because eventually, gamblers will lose). Many communities offer gambling-cessation programs such as Gamblers Anonymous.

Smoking

Compared with illicit drug use, smoking seems trivial. It's a worldwide habit, one that's enjoyed by about one-third of North Americans. But cigarette use can cost the employer as much as $5,000 per year per smoking employee, according to data cited by Greenberg (1994). (The cost relates to illness, accidents, and even computer failures.) He also pointed out problems with simply banning smoking at the workplace. There's the violation of smokers' rights (making smokers something of an "oppressed minority"), and the risk of lowering morale by segregating smokers from nonsmokers. So the organization must adopt a policy that is acceptable to all employees, smokers and nonsmokers alike. How to do this?

Greenberg divided over 700 clerical workers into four groups, each given a different videotaped presentation of their company's new smoking ban. In the presentation, one group received detailed information about the *harmful effects* of smoking; another received scanty information on this. Each group then received either a high *social sensitivity* message expressing concern and sympathy about smokers' having to quit, or a low social sensitivity message that focused on the business reasons. The third variable was "outcome severity," defined as whether the employees were nonsmokers, light smokers, or heavy smokers.

After the presentation, the employees were surveyed on their reactions to the ban. The best acceptance was found in the group that received the detailed information on the dangers of smoking, plus the high sensitivity message. The heavy smokers were least accepting, but they showed the most benefit from the high sensitivity communication. It's too bad the research was based only on an immediate questionnaire instead of a long-term behavioral measure. However, nobody likes new restrictions, and Greenberg's research shows that communicating the fairness of a restriction makes it easier to accept.

STRESS

Work, almost by definition, is something you have to do though you'd rather not (page 12), so there's an element of stress merely in the word "work." Moreover, life itself visits problems on all of us, and the rough patches of daily living necessarily spill over into the workplace. Jobs are rarely glassy smooth; few people enjoy just one week of work that does not include difficulties and frustrations. For instance, change is unsettling, and consistency can cause the stress of boredom. Presumably, most people, if asked whether their job is stressful, would answer yes. And stress is increasingly being cited by medical researchers as a contributor to illness and even to death. Not surprisingly, occupational stress has steadily attracted research since the mid-1970s.

What, exactly, is stress?

You surely don't need this book to tell you what stress is, but that doesn't mean it's a simple concept. The term originated in physics and engineering; a bridge designer must know how much stress the structure will accept before deforming or breaking. The word has been adopted by social science, to refer to *psychological pressure and unease, usually associated with some threat.*

Like many transplanted terms, stress has not proven to be easily quantified. Nor is it well conceptualized. Is stress always harmful? Is it sometimes desirable? Do some people, such as race-car drivers, thrive on it? Are some individuals (and industries) successful because of it? Does stress reside in the personality, or is it caused by the situation? What's the difference among the stress of daily hassles, the stress of a sudden change or loss, and the stress of a jolting event like a car crash?

Here are more problems that face stress researchers:

- There's a considerable variation in how people *respond* to the same stressor, and little is known about stress tolerance.

- Moderate stress *improves* performance in most people.

- There are well-understood physiological responses to stress, but they do not always match subjective feelings and the behavioral responses.

- Further, there is no doubt an interaction between the bodily responses, the feelings, and the interpretations.

Generally, stress is unhealthy because it causes the secretion of stress hormones that strain the body, for instance, by raising blood pressure, interfering with digestion, and possibly weakening the immune system. Stress has been implicated in a variety of disorders from insomnia to cancer. One survey of 500 Canadian police officers (Vulcano, Barnes & Breen, 1983) found a much higher than expected incidence of digestive problems; similar results have been reported for other high-stress occupations.

Causes and consequences of job stress

In all jurisdictions where this book is likely to be read, a worker incapacitated by a falling object on the job site would receive compensation, all or most of the normal wages until recovery is complete, free medical and rehabilitative treatment, and maybe even a cash award for pain and suffering. What about the worker who claims incapacitation due to job-related stress? One problem is determining if the stress is truly disabling, and determining if it is job related.

The "falling object" here may be the *pace* of the work, the social or physical *environment* of the workplace, faulty *feedback*, or *harassment* by associates. Another possible cause is **role ambiguity**, or uncertainty about what to do. If you weren't sure exactly what was expected of you, or if you knew the objectives but weren't sure how to go about attaining them, you would

So what You're doing sort of OK at school, and generally like it. But you often feel overwhelmed by the amount of work. You don't meet deadlines, and don't know whether to ask for an extension, hand the work in late, or give up and take whatever happens. Your classmates call you a "grind," and you wish you could work less. The quality and effort you invest in your work doesn't seem to pay off in higher grades. You don't know whether it's because you worked improperly (and whose fault that was), or because the quizzes or marking were unfair; and you don't know what to do about it. Better feedback about your work would help in finding out how you should go about improving for the next time. But the professor appears to be oblivious to you as a person, or, perhaps, seems to dislike you. These problems are interfering with your friendships, appetite, and sleep. Your motivation is slipping, and sometimes you look for an "out" like getting treatment (and maybe a note) from a doctor, or even quitting.

Substitute the words "job performance" for "schoolwork," "pay" or "promotion" for "grades," and "supervisor" for "teacher," and you have a typical picture of job-related stress.

be bothered by role ambiguity. Your instructor may be unsure whether psychology faculty are expected to provide counseling to students, or just teach the courses assigned. Business faculty may be uncertain of their role—should they guide the administration in managerial policies or serve only the interests of colleagues? Maybe a faculty member feels that the objective is to please the class, but doesn't know exactly how to accomplish this.

Another source of stress is **role conflict**. Students suffer from this constantly. If you attend the party, you won't finish your essay on time. You accept the position of residence manager, and experience conflict between the role of classmate and that of rules-enforcer. Imagine the conflicting demands arising out of family and professional roles that some of your professors—perhaps more so the females than the males—experience. A common role conflict at school and on the job is the need to perform work quickly and well. Where jobs are complex and poorly defined, role conflict is frequent.

Many employees feel that their job is stressful, and I/O psychologists warn about the consequences. For instance, Beehr (1990) associates occupational stress with more absenteeism and higher turnover, decreased performance quality, and negative attitudes to the job and the organization.

When occupational stress is severe and unremitting, it can lead to **burnout**. This term, which became popular in the 1970s, refers to work-related emotional and physical exhaustion leading to apathy, insensitivity to others, reduced performance levels, feelings of despair, futility, or helplessness, and finally withdrawal or quitting. It is particularly associated with front line service occupations like nursing, social welfare case work, and law enforcement. A common instrument for quantifying burnout is the Maslach Burnout Inventory devised by Christina Maslach (Maslach & Jackson, 1981).

Yet, some workers thrive in these demanding and presumably stressful environments. Watson and Clark (1984) suggest that the *personalities* of some people are *predisposed* to a burnout reaction to stressors; these people, who are introspective, generally dissatisfied, and concerned with their own shortcomings and failures, are described as having **negative affectivity**.

Stress management

Some of the responsibility for handling stress lies with the *individual*. The two most effective approaches to managing stress are *social support* and *coping strategies*. A number of researchers (for example, Vulcano, Barnes & Breen, 1983) have indicated that a person who feels able to count on emotional or practical support from friends or colleagues will experience less stress from the same problem than someone lacking this support. If the stress is work related and the support comes from work associates, so much the better.

Coping strategies can be *learned,* whether through exercise, meditation, biofeedback, discussion, cognitive reappraisal, or supportive counseling. The perception of having some *control* over your own life and especially your work environment seems beneficial.

If you discover that the reason your feet hurt is that your shoes are too small, that can be a useful finding. Similarly, analyzing the *source* of stress may be helpful. If it's that your personal standards are unrealistically high, it's a simple matter to strive for a B– rather than an A+. Maybe the problem is simply not knowing exactly what's expected of you and the steps you should follow to meet the expectations. If so, why not make an appointment with the professor, boss, human resources officer, or school counselor to get some answers?

Tight shoes are easily apparent. But many stress victims *attribute* their problems to the wrong sources. Do you blame the standards or indifferent measurements of your performance when the real reason is something else, like your not knowing or doing what's required? And do you let your work stress interfere with your family relationships?

Are your *defense mechanisms* impairing your finding the solution? For instance, are you using *avoidance* to protect yourself from facing the realities of the requirements? Do you allow *denial* to convince yourself that the work is easy and you can handle it later? Do you let *projection* turn your attention

Stress management techniques are important features of employee "wellness" programs and employee assistance programs.

toward the motivations and attitudes of your instructor or classmates rather than toward your own?

If there is a real problem affecting you and your colleagues (such as a quiz announced with inadequate time for preparation or an exam schedule that puts all your exams on the first two days of the exam window), do the social pressures of *conformity* deter you from speaking out because your classmates aren't willing to complain? Do you use inappropriate, self-defeating coping mechanisms such as taking drugs like stimulants or alcohol? If you decide to cope by working through the night, the section on "Shift Work versus Chronobiology" may particularly interest you.

Some of the responsibility is the *organization's*. Stress management help is often offered at school through student services facilities, and at work through employee assistance programs. In addition, organizations can help improve the match between the employee's *interests and duties,* the **person-job fit**. Organizations can also try to improve the worker's sense of *control* through delegation and participative decision making and better communication and feedback processes. Many corporations offer employee "wellness" programs involving health counseling, fitness facilities, and time management techniques. A good source of information on stress prevention and intervention programs is the February 1990 issue of the journal *American Psychologist,* which ends with four excellent papers on this topic.

SHIFT WORK VERSUS CHRONOBIOLOGY

Chronobiology (from *chronos,* or time) refers to the science of *natural bodily rhythms* or internal clocks in a world of 24-hour operations, or 6-month tours of duty in a submarine or at an arctic weather station. Our brains are influenced by various "biological clocks" that influence our hormone levels, kidney function, body temperature, and blood pressure.

Circadian dysrhythmias

About 50 million years ago, a new type of creature evolved. A lackluster little mammal with hands instead of paws and claws, it had a new kind of eye that could focus sharply and see color and detail. (It possibly lost its facial fur because its sharp eye allowed individuals to recognize each other by appearance instead of smell.)

The new "primate eye," in exchange for better bright-light vision, lost the ability to see in dim light. How could this scrawny night-blind critter compete in the African jungle with the big cats that slept in the heat of the day and hunted in the evening? At dusk, the early primates used their grasping limbs to climb high up a tree and stay motionless and out of harm's way until daylight.

For millions of generations, primates survived because their body "turned off" during the 12-hour equatorial night. To show how this has affected you, calculate how many times a *day* you have to empty your bladder. Now imagine what your sleep would be like if you had to urinate that many times at *night.* Clearly, kidney function follows a day-on, night-off schedule.

It's not just the kidneys. Your primary organ, your brain, is also programmed with a **circadian rhythm**. (Circadian is from the Latin *circa,* about, and *diem,* a day.) Dozens of circadian rhythms in the human body have been documented. Prior to the use of oil lamps five thousand years ago, and candles one thousand years back, everybody relaxed or slept during the hours of darkness, and the circadian rhythms kept us alert during the day and sleepy at night. The invention of electricity transmission and the light bulb in the late 1800s permitted people to work at night, but few did so until recently.

Only in the last few generations have the work habits of humans seriously and dangerously clashed with their evolutionary past, especially in **circadian dysrhythmia**, the disruption of the normal daily cycle. The present problem is threefold: (a) the extent of work shift rotation (alternate weeks on day shifts and night shifts), (b) the critical nature of night work, and (c) the effects of sleep deprivation.

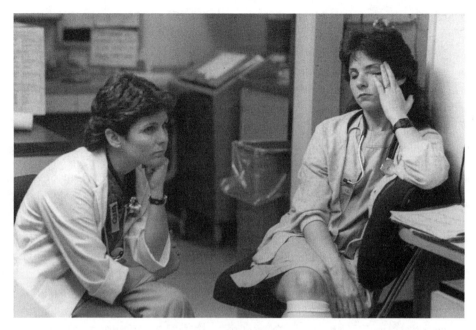

Nurses on the night shift show signs of fatigue and stress associated with circadian dysrhythmia, the disruption of the normal daily cycle.

The extent of shift work   The number of these jobs is higher than you might think. Consider how many people today work either in industry or in health care, realms that were virtually nonexistent until the last 150 years. Astoundingly, *one-third* of all such employees are subjected to variable shift schedules in Canada (Hahn, 1991). Among *all* U.S. workers, one in four works nights or evenings. American night shift workers are found primarily in health care, then in data processing, utilities, and manufacturing, and lastly in transportation (Charland, 1992).

The critical nature of night work   It is these people on night shifts who monitor seriously ill patients, military and law-enforcement surveillance, and the operation of nuclear power generating facilities. In factories where production goes on around the clock, these people operate powerful and sometimes dangerous machines. In hundreds of 24-hour data processing centers, they punch in how much money you owe, or what funds were transferred from one country to another.

   Microsleep refers to short periods of dozing, which leaves the person disoriented upon waking. People have surely been dozing on the job ever since there have been jobs to doze on. But when a shepherd, rug weaver, milkmaid, or sailboat pilot nodded off, the consequences were trivial. That cannot be said about a data entry clerk, jet plane crew member, or hospital intern.

Five brief cases

• In 1979, a nuclear power plant in Pennsylvania almost reached "meltdown" (a self-perpetuating nuclear implosion), following a fairly routine problem that began around 4:00 A.M.

• In 1984, a leak in a chemical plant in India left thousands of dead and hundreds of thousands injured. This worst industrial disaster in history took place just after midnight.

• In the same year, the two worst train accidents in the United States occurred at 3:58 A.M. in Colorado, and at 4:56 A.M. in Wyoming.

• In 1986, an accident at a nuclear power station at Chernobyl in the Ukraine caused hundreds of deaths; thousands of people were evacuated, and the plant was permanently closed. It took place at exactly 1:23 A.M.

• In 1989, an oil-laden supertanker ran aground in Alaska, rupturing its hull—at 12:04 A.M. A moment's carelessness in conducting a routine task eventually cost the shipowner billions of dollars.

Sleep deprivation   How well could you thread a needle, monitor a radar screen, or make a critical business decision—after working through the night? The body is at its lowest level of performance between 2:00 and 4:00 in the morning. A succession of recent disasters involving the operator's failure to remain vigilant have one thing in common—sleep deprivation (see Brief Cases above).

Of course, researchers can find what they look for, and if there were a suspicion that, say, high noon were a dangerous time, we could probably list cases of noontime disasters. But when the time of day of mishaps is corrected for exposure rate, the wee hours of the morning do look ominous. In a major review of Japanese near-collision train incidents, 82 percent took place between midnight and morning (Charland, 1992).

How can tolerance to shift work be measured? The Standard Shiftwork Index measures psychological well-being, anxiety levels, and any disruptions to health, sleep, and social life. This questionnaire also measures job satisfaction and personality. It was devised by Folkard et al. (1993), and fully described in an article by Barton et al. (1993).

Is working nights on a permanent basis necessarily stressful or harmful? Barton (1994) administered the Standard Shiftwork Index to some 600 nurses and midwives in Great Britain, half of whom had opted for a permanent night shift, instead of a rotating night shift.

Those who had chosen night work reported fewer problems in just about all of the many variables tested (for instance, sleep disturbances and fatigue). One explanation could be that their attitude was, "I'm doing this because it pays more, and it frees my days to spend with my children," rather than, "Drat! Next week they're putting me back on nights." Another explanation is that the body adjusts in time to a reverse sleep-wake cycle.

Besides the daily circadian rhythms, **ultradian rhythms** occur *more* than once a day. Examples are stomach contractions associated with hunger. A number of studies in the 1960s and 1970s (for example, Klein & Armitage, 1979) showed that various capabilities that may relate to work performance can follow 90-minute schedules. These include alertness, verbal and spatial ability, and susceptibility to visual illusions.

Infradian rhythms occur *less* often than daily. An obvious example is menstruation. A less apparent, recently publicized infradian rhythm is the **seasonal affective disorder (SAD)**. A few researchers (for example, Lewy, Sacks, Miller & Hoban, 1987) have suggested that the shorter periods of daylight associated with winter induce depression and have demonstrated that exposure to artificial light may be a preventative or cure. Of course, the winter blues, if they really do exist, could be caused by things other than reduced daylight. Wehr, Sack, and Rosenthal (1987) reported on cases of *summer* depression! Maybe some people simply are intolerant to the cold; others can't take the heat.

The menstrual cycle and its effects

The question of how the menstrual (from *mensis,* or month) cycle affects performance is of recent research interest, both because of the upsurge in research on women's issues and because about half of new hires in North America are female. In women of child-bearing age, about every 28 days the ovaries release extra estrogen, which thickens the lining of the uterus (to prepare for a possible pregnancy). Halfway through the cycle, an ovum is released. If conception doesn't occur, the lining dissipates, resulting in menstruation. These hormonal events are well understood biologically, but psychologically and behaviorally the events are far less clear.

Much recent public attention has been paid to **premenstrual syndrome (PMS)**. This refers to a cluster of symptoms that occur in the few days preceding menstruation. They include fatigue, irritability, backache, headache, tension, depression, and mood swings. Probably those same symptoms can be associated with many activities, from raising children to performing many types of work (including writing a textbook). There is no agreement in the medical literature about which of the many physiological changes are responsible for PMS, and sufferers have not been found to be any different hormonally from nonsuffering women.

Wade and Tavris (1993) blame the popular misconceptions about PMS on the failure to differentiate between *physical* symptoms (such as abdominal cramps and fluid retention, which have a medical basis and generally respond to medical treatment) and *emotional* ones. They point out that people detect in themselves what they are led to expect, and the more the publicity about PMS, the more the women who count themselves as victims. (When filling

Brief case

The following has been adapted from Hahn (1991): The other day, a senior air traffic controller told me that many controllers work 200 hours a month *overtime*. I was incredulous. This was subsequent to March 1991, when, in a well-publicized case, an exhausted controller closed the tower at Halifax International Airport after falling asleep at his post. He was near the end of his second 16-hour shift in less than two days. "He was essentially falling asleep in his chair, waking up and not knowing if he had been asleep for 30 seconds or 10 minutes," the regional director of the Canadian Air Traffic Controllers Association told me. "That's when he decided he couldn't provide a safe service to anybody." At 4:30 A.M. the controller went to sleep on the tower floor.

out daily mood diaries, men and women don't differ in emotional symptoms or mood swings. But when the diary is titled "Menstrual Distress Questionnaire," men magically lose their irritability, depression, and fatigue!)

For the majority of women, there's no convincing evidence that moods or work performance are cycle-dependent, or that women are any more emotionally variable than men. As Carole Wade and Carol Tavris put it, "The impact of any bodily change, whether it is circadian, ultradian, or infradian, depends on how we *interpret* it and how we choose to *respond* to it" (emphasis added).

Time zone changes

If you fly from Vancouver to London, you (and your pilots) step off the plane after 10 hours into a day that's 8 hours ahead of your biological clock. What is the effect of changing time zones? How would your body react if you were in an environment that provided no clues as to time or day? These questions have become important only in the present generation of workers, the first who may be required to shift time zones or (usually in military or aerospace applications) to work in an environment lacking the normal time cues.

After westward flights, during which your biological clock loses time, your circadian rhythm must **phase-delay** to adjust; after an eastbound trip, you must **phase-advance**. The delay adjustment is easier. Monday morning blues may be a form of so-called jet lag, resulting from retiring and rising progressively later from Friday to Sunday.

REPETITIVE STRAIN INJURY

Your body is designed to be moved with variety and frequency, not to overload some structures and immobilize others. But much work is repetitious. If you observed a drummer, dentist, or ditch digger at work, you'd see them holding their limbs, even their entire body, in the same position (generally a somewhat unnatural one) for much of their work period. When you continuously hold your body (particularly the hands, wrists, and arms) in a fixed position, the muscles, tendons, nerves, and ligaments are likely to complain. It's worse if you continuously repeat a motion, particularly one that's at the extreme range of limb movement, as when stretching to paint a ceiling.

The resulting condition is termed **cumulative trauma disorder** in the United States, and cervicobrachial disorder in Japan. In Canada the condition is called either musculoskeletal injury or **repetitive strain injury (RSI)**. Let's use the simplest of these terms, RSI.

"For her years of service as a data processor and for keypunching in 3,789 records in one eight-hour shift, please welcome our employee of the year, Peggy Neal!"

RSIs have long been workplace related. There are reports of scribes in the early 1700s who were unable to work because of the pain, and medical journals of the 1800s described telegrapher's cramp, packer's wrist, process worker's arm, and postman's shoulder. Operators of vibrating equipment like jackhammers suffered from "white finger disease," a blanching and numbness in the fingers. Back then, the employee would try to ignore it, or would be replaced by a younger worker.

Symptoms of RSIs range from tingling or numbness, and weakness in the fingers, hands, wrists and arms, to severe neck or back pain. The wrist is susceptible to an inflammation known as **carpal tunnel syndrome**. Most sufferers are female, only because it's work typically performed by women that induces RSIs. Supermarket cashiers, data processors, and keyboard operators are likely victims at work; pianists and knitters are vulnerable too.

As the condition becomes more publicized and common, and as people become less tolerant of work-induced maladies, RSIs are attracting considerable attention. Ontario's Workplace Health and Safety Agency reports that RSIs, which constitute half of all claims to the Workers' Compensation Board, cost Ontario businesses millions of dollars per year just in lost time.

Most sufferers improve on their own; if not, there are various medical treatments. In a few cases, the condition can be permanent and disabling. It is preventable, though, through workstation modifications such as properly designed seating or wrist supports, attention to proper posture, rotating varying duties among employees, and providing adequate rest periods. Why don't you put the book down and have a stretch?

JOB DESIGN

Designing the job to increase productivity began with the first industrial revolution, but concepts were first studied and codified primarily by, as you will recall, Frederick Taylor in the early 1900s. He recommended breaking the job into simple components, each to be repeated by the same worker, who would become efficient in this limited piece of work with a minimum of qualifications and training. Taylor bragged about the resulting efficiency in production, and his concepts fit with the times of high unemployment and low worker education.

Within a few decades, however, the pressure on the workers clashed with changing concepts of worker entitlements and the laws and unions that quickly developed. Workers felt bored, infantilized, alienated, pressured, and resentful; in a word, dehumanized. The recent emphasis, then, has been on the humanization of work. Work should be physically and psychologically as agreeable as possible to those who perform it. One major avenue to achieving this objective is **job design**. Here, management or consultants examine changes to the work *equipment* and *processes* and even the *relationships* among employees.

Work schedule variations

Work, which invariably needs light, used to take place from sunrise to sundown. With the advent of artificial light and the need for around-the-clock services, the hours were increased to the endurance level of the workers. By 1850, there was a debate on whether it was socially responsible to reduce the workday to only ten hours, which would leave the workers with idle time! The prevailing schedule established a century later in the Western world was eight hours a day, Monday through Friday.

With the increased time needed to prepare for work (dressing and grooming, commuting, and workstation setup), and the increased leisure time options, the most recent trend is to reschedule the 35- to 40-hour workweek into fewer sessions. The use of four 10-hour days or three 12-hour ones is termed the **compressed workweek**.

To determine the effect of instituting a compressed workweek, Moores (1990) performed a meta-analysis on 15 empirical studies (out of some 200 papers he reviewed). He concluded that the main result is increased job satisfaction. Minor effects are reduced absenteeism and increased productivity; the only negative outcome is slightly increased fatigue.

Another variant on the standard work schedule is **flextime** (sometimes spelled flexitime). Giving employees some flexibility in the hours they work may be convenient for them; staggering the start and stop times spreads out the travel rush hour. This practical plan originated in Germany in the 1960s, spread from there to Canada, and then to the United States.

The range of hours within which the employees may elect to work is the **bandwidth**. Within the bandwidth, a company usually requires that all employees are on duty for a specified period known as **core hours**. When employees may come and go as they please, as long as the week's total (or more commonly the day's total) is the agreed number, this is called **gliding time**. Usually, however, the hours must be scheduled in advance, which is known as **flexitour**.

Is flextime beneficial? In another meta-analytic review of 60 papers, Estes (1990) concluded that flextime mainly improves job satisfaction (as was found for compressed workweeks). Also, absenteeism is reduced and productivity is enhanced. The employer also benefits from more efficient use of company resources such as machinery or employee parking.

Sometimes an extreme form of flextime is essential for the employer. Consider a restaurant that needs 10 employees for a few peak hours, and only 2 workers for the rest of the business day. A useful option here is **peak time pay**. Employees who work only during the peak hours are offered up to double earnings. This makes it worthwhile for them to come in, and saves the employer the cost of regular wages during the off-hours when the extra help is not needed.

Various factors have combined to promote the use of **job sharing**, in which two employees share a single job:

- Women, who are increasingly working, frequently share occupational areas with their husbands and often want or have to maintain off-the-job commitments as well. The strictures against **nepotism** (showing favoritism to relatives) used to be interpreted as meaning that relatives could not work under the same roof, but now it's common for spouses to be allowed to work together.

- As harsh economic conditions require some companies to downsize and to increase their efficiency to survive, part-time employees offer more flexibility than a full-time one putting in the same total hours.

When two employees share the same job title and duties, they may agree between them how the work and hours are to be apportioned. Ideally, the employees benefit from the flexibility, and the employer gets the variety and energy of part-time workers with the integration and commitment of full-timers. In practice, however, part-timers and work sharers may feel less commitment to their job and may provide less integration for the firm.

Prior to the first industrial revolution, much of what we now consider to be "work" was performed at home. With the advent of mechanized factories, most employees had to travel to the work site. Now, with much work involving long-range planning, telecommunications, and computers, there is a new opportunity for an additional variant of the work schedule, **homework**, or assigned duties performed at home. It is estimated that some 3 million Canadians, for instance, perform some paid work at home.

Homework saves the employer from having to provide the work facilities, as well as amenities such as food services, washrooms, and parking. Theoretically, homework offers the employee the maximum in convenience and comfort, as well as savings in clothing, child care, and travel. Some workers-rights advocates, however, contend that homework changes an 8-hour slave into a 24-hour one.

The availability of jobs is changing. One current trend is toward a longer workweek; another is toward the increased use of casual employees. That's because if more person-hours are required at the plant, inducing present employees to work overtime saves the costs of recruiting, selecting, and training, and it does so without incurring the responsibility of having unneeded employees on the payroll should the work slacken off. Where overtime is not a solution, part-time or contract workers are often hired, sometimes from firms that supply temporary help to a variety of employers as needed. Thus, work is becoming at once longer and shorter.

Job rotation, enlargement, and enrichment

The design of jobs is also changing. Consider an assembly line in which each employee performs one simple, repetitive task. If the employees periodically rotated to a different workstation, all would learn each component. This provides some variety and a feeling of cohesiveness. In the event of an absence, any employee could fill in the missing station effectively. This is known as job rotation (page 148). Some firms encourage this by paying a bonus for each new skill mastered. Job rotation contributes to **job enlargement**, which refers to increasing the number and variety of tasks performed. Insofar as the added tasks represent the same level of skill requirements as the original duties, this can be termed **horizontal loading** of tasks.

In **job enrichment** the emphasis is on increased autonomy. The employee has more control over how the work is to be performed and how it fits in with the rest of the operation. Insofar as the employee is given some level of management responsibility (such as how the work is to be planned and scheduled), it is termed **vertical loading**. Job enrichment stems from the *job characteristics model* of Hackman and Oldham (page 172), which strives to match the characteristics of the job with the psychological needs of the worker. Research has generally supported the use of job enrichment in improving both performance and job satisfaction (Fried & Ferris, 1987).

Work teams and quality circles

How can the inherent efficiency of, say, a car assembly line be reconciled with the desire to humanize the individual tasks? One compromise, introduced by Swedish automobile manufacturers Volvo and Saab for their assembly operations, was to replace the assembly *line* with assembly *bays*. In each bay, a team is responsible for a major operation, such as the assembly and testing on an engine or transmission. The members of the team jointly decide on tasks and schedules, generally share or rotate the tasks, and take collective responsibility for the finished component. Plant costs are higher and productivity is slightly lower, but morale and teamwork are improved. Insofar as an entire logical unit is the team's responsibility, the group is termed a **natural work team**.

Sometimes an employee is assigned an integrative job to do. When an entire product or subunit is up to an individual, it's termed a **natural work module**. This practice harkens back to the centuries of the artisan or craftsman, who would cobble a pair of boots or build a shed from start to finish.

You were briefly introduced to work teams and quality circles on page 260. The concept of the quality circle originated in Japanese car assembly plants (which all still rely on the assembly *line*). After each workday or at week's end, some of the workers from each line meet with their supervisor or manager in a circle (implying that everyone's contribution is equally welcomed) to discuss ways of improving quality and efficiency.

Quality circles have not always proven beneficial outside of Japan, where *kaizen* (page 11) is a way of life on the job. In North America it's likely that the first few meetings will serve to demonstrate how the procedure is supposed to work. After a number of meetings, all the obvious suggestions will have been made, so switching to a monthly schedule may be appropriate. By this time, employees may resent being asked to work for management, which is how they may see it.

Imagine that you are part of a crew of 10, hired to spend the summer painting houses. After a week of agreeable work, you're asked to have regular meetings with the boss to discuss how to paint more efficiently. You realize that making good suggestions will benefit not you, but the boss, who would then need only eight of you. But quality circles can focus on *improving work life* by reducing stressors and increasing comfort and safety. And managers should reward useful contributions so employees don't feel that the meetings are a way of taking advantage.

New technology in the workplace

People generally resist change, especially when it is imposed from above, and when it is not accompanied by adequate explanation and training. Automation is not new; various forms of it have been introduced steadily for over two centuries. Nor is opposition to it new. All types of technological changes have generally been met with fear and resistance.

As an example, three-quarters of the workforce now needs computer skills at work (Jewell & Siegall, 1990). With the introduction of computers into firms where some employees are unfamiliar with them, the term *computer phobia* has entered the language. As robots are designed to replace much manual work, people may feel that their livelihood is threatened. And when the robots are controlled by computers, the discomfort may be extreme. Machines such as computers and robots can increase the worker's speed, strength, and reach, and therefore the responsibility of—and the possible danger to—the operator. (Should the driver be inattentive, a hand cart or horse-drawn carriage is unlikely to go off a bridge; a car on cruise control may.)

If new technology is offered as an opportunity for the operator to gain higher-level skills and advancement, it may be viewed positively. Training should be comprehensive and paced by the individual learner. And the equipment should be proven in terms of increased efficiency and ease of use by the operator. More details on computers will be covered in chapter 13.

Brief case

Despite advances in robotics, telephones are still most efficiently assembled by hand. In a Swedish modern-day version of the Hawthorne telephone assembly plant, the assembly workstations were standard and fixed in height. As employees of atypical statures were hired, many of them had to adopt awkward postures to perform their repetitive work. After consulting with I/O psychologists, the employer simply replaced the work platforms with easily adjustable ones that could be used from a sitting or standing position, and slightly improved the ventilation and lighting systems. This entailed discarding perfectly serviceable workstations and buying a set of quite expensive ones. Thereupon, the employer asked for a cost/benefit analysis. In the first two years, the savings (from substantially lower sick-leave time and turnover) exceeded the total cost of all the improvements—by nine times! *Adapted from Spilling, Eitrheim, and Aaras, 1986*

Workspace design

Consider the place where you do your work for this course. Does it require you to stand, sit, or lie down while working? How are the furniture and equipment arranged? Are the items of equipment you use most close at hand? How is the rest of the material filed and labeled? What changes in the arrangement have you imposed? What further alterations would you like in illumination, furniture, storage? These questions come under the topic of **workspace design**, the arrangement of individual workstations, of workstation divisions, or of an entire organization.

A workplace should be safe and efficient for both the incumbent and for any temporary replacement workers. It should be (a) designed for logical and fluid communication with other related units within and outside of the company; (b) environmentally suited for long-term exposure, for instance, as regards ventilation and illumination; (c) psychologically acceptable in terms of, for example, privacy, space, and decor.

Workspace design should be not only physically suitable but psychologically appealing as well. One current trend is the **landscaped office**, which was originally an attempt by European manufacturers to reflect the design of the "town square" into their buildings. The work areas are as open and free of walls as possible, with individual work areas marked by decorations such as planters. Communal or conversational areas, such as snack facilities or lounges, are located at intervals. The rationale is to make colleagues feel part of a team and communicate more freely than would be the case with private offices. This "open" office design also saves the firm money. However, the research literature (for example, Davis, 1984) indicates that although socialization is indeed increased, employees miss their privacy, and often report decreased satisfaction, concentration, and productivity.

The design of private offices has interested several researchers. One consistent finding is that the *open desk* arrangement, in which the visitor and office occupant are not located on opposite sides of the desk, creates the impression of a more comfortable office, and a more friendly occupant (for example, McElroy, Morrow & Wall, 1983). Also, McElroy, Morrow, and Ackerman (1983) found that professors with open desk arrangements were more extroverted and friendly, that more traditional, high-status faculty preferred closed desk arrangements, and those who did so were evaluated lower by students (Zweigenhaft, 1976).

Office design has physical as well as psychological implications. As nontraditional employees join the workforce, increased attention will be given to those with special office design needs. For instance, people with disabilities or different statures particularly need properly designed work spaces. This is the province of the human factors engineer or ergonomist, whom we'll meet in the next chapter.

Study guide for chapter 10

HAVE YOU LEARNED THESE NAMES AND TERMS?

sick building syndrome

eyewash stations

exclusion, prevention, and fail-safe designs

safety audit

protective exclusion

AIDS (acquired immunodeficiency syndrome)

substance abuse

role ambiguity

role conflict

burnout

negative affectivity

person-job fit

chronobiology

circadian rhythm

circadian dysrhythmia

microsleep

ultradian and

infradian rhythms

seasonal affective disorder (SAD)

premenstrual syndrome (PMS)

phase-delay; phase-advance

cumulative trauma disorder

repetitive strain injury (RSI)

carpal tunnel syndrome

job design

compressed workweek

flextime

bandwidth

core hours; gliding time; flexitour

peak time pay

job sharing

nepotism

homework

job enlargement

horizontal loading

job enrichment

vertical loading

natural work team

natural work module

workspace design

landscaped office

ISSUES TO CONSIDER

How do you account for the fact that as workplaces become safer, employees *complain* more about working conditions?

How would you study whether or not accident-prone employees really exist?

What's the difference between the concerns for safety at home and at work?

What's the role of the *organization* in worker safety?

What are some of the current issues around *protective exclusion* and AIDS?

Why do substance-abuse researchers not fully rely on self-reports and correlational data?

What issues relate to workplace drug testing?

Why is it difficult to quantify stress?

How can *you* benefit from the findings on stress management?

Why were the effects of shift work considered unimportant until just recently?

How real is PMS?

Who benefits from a compressed workweek?

What are the causes and benefits of job sharing?

How could the design of *your* workplace be improved?

How would you modify the work *schedules* in a factory that you were in charge of?

Would you like to see all assembly lines replaced with *work teams*?

How is new technology affecting *your* work life?

How could the workplace design of your school be improved?

SAMPLE MULTIPLE-CHOICE QUESTIONS

1. Carpal tunnel syndrome
   a. affects operators of vibrating equipment.
   b. is a form of RSI that is more likely to afflict women.
   c. is the most common RSI, according to Ontario's Workplace Health and Safety Agency.
   d. is a hereditary disorder.

2. Coming to lectures (for full-time students) represents what type of rhythm?
   a. circadian
   b. ultradian
   c. infradian
   d. circadian dysrhythmia

3. Al's Aviation allows employees to put in their workday anytime from 6:00 A.M. to 10:00 P.M. These hours are the
   a. bandwidth.
   b. core hours.
   c. gliding time.
   d. flexitour hours.

4. The *least* desirable option for most employees would be
   a. horizontal loading of tasks.
   b. vertical loading of tasks.
   c. job enlargement.
   d. homework.

5. Which could be termed the "least modern"?
   a. natural work team
   b. natural work module
   c. quality circle
   d. peak time pay

Answers: page 462

Man is a tool-using animal . . . without tools he is nothing, with tools he is all.

Thomas Carlyle (1795–1881)

Bird's-eye view of the chapter

Without tools and machinery, we would have to live in a pretty primitive state. But inept design in modern, high-performance equipment can cause not just inefficiency but immense tragedies. The most conspicuous examples of the benefits of ergonomics are seen in military and aerospace applications, but ordinary consumer goods are also subject to ergonomic improvements. Ergonomics looks at the strengths and the limitations of the human operator, and at the basic concepts of systems, controls, and displays.

Chapter 11
Introductory ergonomics

The payoff from chapter 11   You will:

1. Know why behavioral scientists also study *machines*
2. Appreciate the extent of the danger from poorly designed equipment
3. Know what ergonomics is, and how it originated
4. Understand why the best examples of human factors engineering (HFE) are from aerospace
5. See the historical connection between HFE and warfare
6. Know the meaning of *person-machine system*
7. See the role of both cognition and physiology in HFE considerations
8. Know what types of tasks are best for machines, and what types best for people
9. Know principles of *controls* and *displays*
10. Recognize examples of good and poor displays, especially visual ones
11. Learn the best uses for and types of auditory displays
12. Understand *frequency analysis*

Surely you'd want your workplace to be free of hazards, and job requirements to match your strengths and weaknesses. Your equipment and task demands should highlight your best performance without overloading your cognitive and physical abilities. This is where the work of the human factors engineer makes a difference in your daily life.

THE IMPORTANCE OF THIS TOPIC

If psychology is the study of behavior and engineering is the study of machines, why would the *psychologist* be interested in *machines?* The answer is that just as the most sophisticated computer would be useless without the human programmer, people would be reduced to a primitive level without machines. Person and machine are now intertwined; to study the one is to consider the other.

Every tool or machine is potentially useful and potentially dangerous. When the cave dweller's stone club broke due to defects in design or assembly, the only harm would be that the rabbit escaped or that the stone hit someone. By contrast, on the day you read this, someone will be scalded while reaching over a boiling pot to adjust a poorly located kitchen range control. An automobile will crash when someone inadvertently turns off the headlights while trying to operate the windshield wipers. Such domestic accidents are often related to poor design. When we look at some examples of poor design in *high performance* machinery we find awesome consequences. Following are six reports that point to the immense cost in lives and materiel that can—and sometimes do—result from flawed designs in twentieth-century versions of the stone club.

DEFINITIONS

So far, we have emphasized only *personnel* psychology. It essentially assumes that there is a given physical plant, comprising production machinery, materials-handling equipment, typing and clerical devices, furniture, and maintenance apparatus, ranging in complexity from a pencil to an earth mover. As you recall, the objective of personnel psychology is to optimize the selection, training, and treatment of the employees so that they in turn operate the given equipment efficiently, happily, and safely.

In contrast to personnel psychology, the **human factors engineering (HFE)** approach takes the person, not the plant, as the "given" or fixed factor. Workers have limitations, both mental (attentional and perceptual) and physi-

Six brief cases

• Two British pilots, one in a Phantom jet and the other in a Jaguar, were practicing dogfights. The Phantom pilot forgot that on this exercise his fighter jet had been fitted with operational Sidewinder missiles. Nothing in the cockpit warned him that these deadly, heat-seeking missiles were on board and live. With a touch of a finger he destroyed an $11 million Jaguar aircraft and nearly killed its pilot.

• At an American underground complex, a technician was working on a Titan intercontinental missile. When he reached for his socket wrench, the socket head detached from the handle because of the way it was designed. The tool fell several hundred feet to the base of the silo and bounced up from the concrete pad, gashing a hole in the fuel tank and igniting the contents. People were grateful that the damage was limited to $10 million. The Titan rocket is designed to carry nuclear warheads.

• A corporate pilot left his aircraft at the fuel ramp, saying, "Fill it, please." The fuel attendant (a young lad) saw the word "Turbo" on the side of the engine (indicating that the motors were fitted with turbochargers for high altitude operation). He assumed that turbo was the same as turbine and that turbine meant "prop jet" engines, so he filled the fuel tanks with jet engine kerosene instead of gasoline. There was nothing in the design of the aircraft's fuel filler opening to prevent a jet fuel nozzle from entering it. The plane managed to lift off before the engines quit. There were no survivors.

• A transport ship capsized off England in 1987 when seawater flooded in through an improperly closed ramp. There was no dis-

play in the control room that showed the ramp's position. Over 300 passengers drowned. Just to the east, a similar mishap drowned almost one thousand people in 1994.

• A Prowler naval jet was approaching the USS *Nimitz*, the world's largest warship, for a night landing. The landing signal officer saw a problem and radioed the pilot to abort the touchdown. The pilot, straining to control a 25-ton machine approaching a bobbing, darkened, 600-foot runway at 150 miles per hour apparently missed the message. He died, along with 13 others, in a $150 million crash that prevented 12 other jets, fuel tanks almost dry, from landing. If the ship had not been near the Florida coast, many others would have died. Only a succession of lucky breaks prevented this accident from destroying the entire $2 billion nuclear-powered ship.

• At the nuclear power generating station located at Three Mile Island in Pennsylvania, a simple pressure relief valve failed. Despite alarm signals immediately sounding and flashing, despite the presence of experienced senior engineers supported by top nuclear power experts who were rushed in from across the country, the display panels (showing some 1,600 dials, gauges, charts, and windows) did not allow operators to see the whole picture accurately enough to realize the simple solution. The plant was finally shut down just short of a catastrophic meltdown. The billion-dollar facility will never resume operation, and the worldwide nuclear power industry lost badly needed public confidence.

cal (reaction-time and strength). The maximum operating speed of a machine is a limiting factor; the same applies to a person. It's easy to replace a machine with one that works five times faster, but not so easy to similarly replace an employee. Rather than trying to modify the person, the HFE scientist designs, engineers, or changes the equipment to fit the human operator.

Equipment has always been "engineered," to some extent. But the focus has been on the *mechanical* aspects of engineering, which ensure that nothing breaks, quits, or overheats. Long before mechanical engineering was a formal profession, its principles were applied. When a stagecoach driver pulled back on the brake handle, there was a reliable mechanical linkage that forced the brake shoe against the wheel rim. It did not matter that an immense amount of pressure was required on the brake handle to slow the heavy coach. The coach was given equipment; drivers with merely average arm strength were not hired.

In the days of horse-drawn coaches, nobody conducted the systematic tests that would have revealed that a person's leg can push four times harder than the arm can pull. So the fact that a coach with a foot pedal brake could be safely slowed by an average driver, not just by a strong-armed one, was not known. Thus, some early automobiles relied upon hand levers for braking and former coach drivers to operate them.

Because machines were considered expensive and the operators expendable, the employee was expected to adapt to the equipment. Today, by contrast, both operator and machine represent valued resources that must work together efficiently and safely.

Virtually all accidents are related to human error. Machines rarely break; more often the operator makes a mistake. And when machines do break, the fault can usually be traced to someone's mistake in assembly, maintenance, or operation. Human engineering reduces these human errors by modifying the machinery in accordance with psychological principles. This science is alternately called human engineering, human factors engineering, biomechanical engineering, ergonomics, engineering psychology, and man-machine engineering, which is giving way to **person-machine engineering**. As with much of industrial/organizational (I/O) psychology, its history is brief and vibrant.

THE HISTORY OF ERGONOMICS

Wickens (1992) cites three factors in the history of ergonomics:

1. World War II experience showed that training the operators of various equipment was not enough to ensure success; some machinery had to be modified.

2. Later, technological advances in machinery's speed, size, complexity, and even temperature meant that the limits of the human being had to be understood and compensated for.

3. The terminology of behavioral psychology started to be replaced by the language of information theory and cybernetics. Terms such as feedback and channel capacity, when they are applied to describe people, allowed the operator to be treated as an integral extension of the high-tech equipment. The computer's capacity, memory, or speed demands would not be over-loaded; exactly the same considerations would be applied to the operator.

Prior to 1915

Machinery has existed for almost as long as the human species. Prehistoric people devised snares and tiger traps, and ancient civilizations designed and built exceedingly complex machinery. During the industrial revolution of the 1700s, many machines were grouped under one roof and driven by a central power source in the first modern factories.

After 1760, factories became increasingly central to political and military power and, in turn, increasingly relied upon other machinery of production, transportation, and communication. Entire countries gradually became dependent upon their factories; conversely, the factories became dependent upon their countries for the required infrastructure and personnel.

In these early factories the emphasis was on *mechanical* engineering, in that the machines were expensive, but the humans required to operate them were easy to acquire, train, and replace. If a worker lost a hand in a machine, his final wage payment might be withheld because the machine had to be shut down and cleaned. If the work did not require physical strength, children were hired; if muscles were needed, only the strongest men were hired, and only for as long as their health lasted. In short, machines were valued over people, and, wherever possible, the operator had to fit the machine.

Notable exceptions were instruments that people fashioned for their own use. Some of the tools and kitchen and grooming utensils of ancient Egypt are so similar to modern equivalents that HFE principles must have been applied, simply by trial and error. Musical instruments, artists' brushes and palettes, and hand weapons were all designed for optimal efficiency. But the design was a matter of art, not science.

One innovator who applied scientific principles to the design of equipment deserves another mention. Taylor (page 15) applied his training in mechanical engineering to the study of steelworkers as early as 1881. They mainly moved various materials by muscle power and shovel. The workers were required to supply their own shovels, and Taylor noted that they all brought similar, standard-design tools.

The materials ranged from lightweight ashes to dense slugs of iron. After controlled trials, Taylor concluded that the average worker could move the most material over the course of a day when the weight of each shovelful was about 22 pounds. Accordingly, he designed a series of shovels for each type of material, such that each loaded shovel would weigh the optimal amount. The practice of employees' providing their own tools was changed from that time forward, and the employer provided the workers with shovels that were appropriate to each work area. Taylor's equipment improvement resulted in the workforce changing from 500 to 140 shovelers.

Other countries soon took note; for instance the Experimental Psychology Laboratory was established in 1912 in England and focused on the relationship between workers and the design of their equipment. In 1913 Hugo Münsterberg (page 14) published *Psychology and Industrial Efficiency* in the United States, a book that argued not only for scientific personnel selection but also for the systematic evaluation of working conditions. Meanwhile, Frank Gilbreth (page 15) applied his time and motion study to bricklayers. From his simple modifications to equipment and procedures, the number of bricks laid per hour almost tripled.

Between 1915 and 1940

World War I was the first multination war based as much on machine-to-machine combat as on man-to-man fighting. It was a conflict that depended on ships, trucks, tanks, long-distance artillery, and automatic-firing small arms. As before, the machines were valued, and the soldiers were "cannon fodder," instead of "factory fodder." Although parachutes had been demonstrated back in 1797 and were available from the war's outset, pilots were not provided with them, for to "go down with the ship" was considered manly, and more important than saving the lives of military personnel.

Although this war showed that battles could be won as much by machinery as by bravery, there was little in the way of scientific design of the equipment to suit the soldier. Horses still played an important part, and one would no more think of modifying a tank to make it more acceptable to its driver or gunner than one would imagine trying to redesign the horse.

Even in the design of the airplane, engineering was confined to the mechanical aspects, to ensure that the engine would not quit and the wings would not break off. Human factors did not have to be considered as long as factories were turning out these wood-and-fabric, one-man craft faster than the military could put them to good use, and as long as there were lines of lads eager to take the place of comrades who had died in a training accident or in combat.

Most airplane accidents take place during landing. How much of a problem would a landing accident be for other flyers? Since these aircraft operated from grass fields, surviving pilots were simply trained to avoid holes left by previous crash landings. From the squadron perspective, there was no need to improve the aircraft in an attempt to reduce the accident rate.

Nor was there a need to improve the ergonomics for the pilots themselves. These aircraft flew only in fair weather, during daylight, on two-hour missions, and at low altitudes. The cruise speed was the same as that of today's cars, and the controls were so simple that trainees were expected to "solo" after five hours of flight training. The displays were equally simple, comprising only a few instruments.

After all, there was little information that needed to be displayed. From their open cockpits, pilots could tell most of what they needed to know by direct observation. (Some of them were instructed always to rescue the plane's clock after a forced landing, because that was the one high-precision instrument in the panel!)

In short, hunters were taught how to fire machine guns, truck drivers to operate tanks, and motorcycle operators proved particularly adept at learning how to fly aircraft. There was no need for the human factors engineer.

Subsequent to 1940

World War II could not have been fought as it was without HFE. Consider the battle tank. No longer a one-seat contraption, part farm tractor, part truck, part bulldozer, and part field artillery piece, the tank had become a complex, powerful, long-range fighting unit with a crew of three to five.

Its main cannon was so powerful that training the gunners presented a problem; the rounds were too expensive for gunnery-range potshots. The HFE specialist had to determine what types of low-cost training versions would yield a training effect that would transfer to the real thing.

Aircraft now flew twice as high, four times as fast, five times as long, and twenty times as far as their World War I counterparts, each with more firepower than an entire World War I squadron of planes! But the pilots had the same types of body and brain as their fathers who flew what were essentially motorcycles with wings just a generation earlier.

Trainees could not learn to fly World War II aircraft in the limited time available unless the planes were designed to accommodate the limitations of the learner. Even experienced pilots couldn't operate in combat without proper cockpit design. When one of these aircraft crashed it meant a large loss. Since they needed special runways, a landing crash could mean that the airfield was out of action until the runway was repaired. As the cost of losses mounted, the value of HFE principles increased.

For instance, in a two-year period, the U.S. Air Force attributed over 400 accidents to the crew's confusion between controls that raised the wing flaps and those that retracted the landing gear (McFarland, 1946). Another cause of accidents was the control that switched the source of fuel supply,

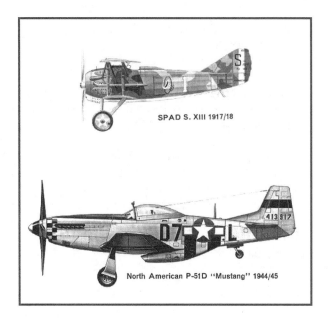

SPAD S. XIII 1917/18

North American P-51D "Mustang" 1944/45

The equipment of World War I was primitive in comparison to weaponry and machinery developed during World War II. It became apparent that, apart from training the operator, it was necessary to make modifications to the equipment, and from this developed the science of ergonomics.

when a tank was depleted, to a full one. It took so long to operate this control that crews were losing engine power, and sometimes the aircraft, during the changeover.

After the war, HFE experts moved to private industry, applying the same principles that determined control placement in a submarine to the placement of knobs on a domestic range. Manned space exploration grew from planning to reality during the 1960s, and from the earliest stages, space vehicle design was based on HFE principles. Aerospace operations would be impossible without the careful application of ergonomic concepts.

BASIC CONCEPTS OF ERGONOMICS

So far, we have covered why the principles of ergonomics are important, what the most frequently used technical terms mean, and how this topic has evolved. Now we turn to what these basic principles are.

Person-machine system

A **system** is any set of components that functions as an entity. You read this with a visual system that, in turn, is fueled by another system, the cardio-vascular. Both systems comprise dozens of organs and billions of cells. Ex-

The bicycle and rider form a person-machine system, in which the machine connects and functions with the person.

amples of simple systems are a pencil, pen, or piece of chalk. A system that connects to one or more humans is termed a **person-machine system.** The nearest telephone or light switch are typical components. Other examples are a hammer, a bicycle, a punch press, a television set, an automobile, a steel mill, and a jetliner.

What are the distinguishing features of a person-machine system? A tree, certainly a system, is neither mechanical nor designed to link with humans, so it does not qualify. The concept of motion or moving parts is inherent in the usual image of person-machine systems. Hence, a painting hanging on a wall, although designed to interact visually with humans, would not be considered a person-machine system. (A human factors engineer could, however, study the effect of the painting on the work or recreational environment.)

Sometimes it is difficult to tell whether the term person-machine system applies, but more examples may help. A surgeon's scalpel, even if constructed from a single piece of stainless steel, would be a person-machine system because HFE principles are applied to its design. A robotic welder on an assembly line is a person-machine system, not because the robot takes the place of or resembles a human, but because a human controls and therefore interacts with the robot.

Controls and displays

When the machine is simple, such as a bow and arrow, the user operates it quite directly, and by direct vision and touch can easily tell how the device is responding. But when the machine is large and complex, like a railway locomotive, the connection between operator and machine cannot be so direct. Instead, controls and displays are the devices through which operator and machine communicate with each other.

A **control** is used to instruct the machine. Common controls are a light switch, steering wheel, typewriter key, water faucet, and piano key. Through a **display**, the machine communicates with the operator. A fuel gauge and speedometer are common displays in an automobile; household examples are a room thermometer or radio dial. A device can serve as both a control and a display, as in a tiller on a sailboat, a toggle switch labeled "Off" and "On," and the dial that operates a range burner and lets you see the heat setting.

Physiological and cognitive factors

Just as the *mechanical* engineer must be conversant with the physical characteristics and limitations of *materials,* the *human* engineer must take into account the equivalent properties of the *operator.* A machine may "concentrate on" or monitor 100 activities simultaneously, but what about a human? How many controls can be operated at once, how many displays can be read simultaneously, and how many decisions can be considered at the same moment? How long can an operator monitor a radar screen before there is a chance that a blip will be missed or misinterpreted because of fatigue? How long could the operator listen to a sonar (auditory) display without the loss of accuracy?

An aircraft engine can be designed to "breathe" at high altitude, but what about the pilot? Space vehicles are routinely sent into orbit, but half of their occupants are incapacitated, usually transitorily, by motion sickness. A word processor offering limitless memory and lightning speed will serve little purpose if it strains the operator's hands, eyes, or neck. A fire extinguisher could be a marvel of design, manufacture, and fire fighting ability, but could totally fail because its instructions are hard to read in a smoky environment, or because the safety pin resists removal by hands that are shaking with exertion or fear.

The human engineer studies both the *cognitive* (mental) and the *physiological* (body) aspects of human performance. Often the two are related, as in job performance under conditions combining danger, noise, and vibration, or involving *circadian dysrhythmias* (page 324).

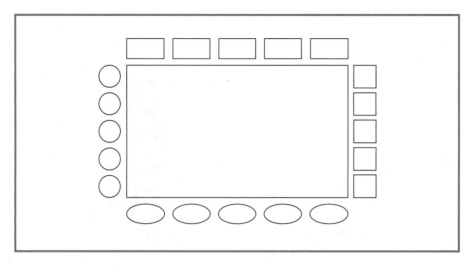

FIGURE 11.1 Arrays of five controls

The rectangle represents a cathode ray display. What would be shown on it depends on which perimeter buttons are pressed.

In some ways human cognition operates with brilliant speed and efficiency; in other ways it is severely limited. For instance, the mind is often required to identify a single item in a group, such as the 3rd switch in a line of 4. This would present no problem. But suppose the operator had to operate the 9th in a row of 15 switches, or check the 12th in an array of 20 dials. A counting machine could perform this in milliseconds, but could a human do so at a glance?

The maximum array from which each component can be singled out without difficulty seems to be *five*. That is, the eye and brain are able to see five objects both as a set and as individual components. That's why pharmacists, when filling a prescription, count pills by fives, and why a group of 20 controls in an aircraft is arranged in four sets of five each (Figure 11.1).

In reading music, a player is required to perform the same task of identifying each note by its location. Musical notation is generally written within a 17-line range, but no musician could identify the location of every note over that many lines. By arranging the notes into 5-line "staffs," any and every note can be identified at a glance (Figure 11.2).

Now we are ready to look at person-machine systems, controls, displays, and physiological factors. First we examine when a task is given to a machine and when to its operator. We then differentiate among control function logic, control location logic, and control stereotype and discriminability. Next we consider how displays are received by the operator, and investigate principles of display design. The section on physiological factors gives more detail on the sense organs and examines other aspects of the limitations of the human operator.

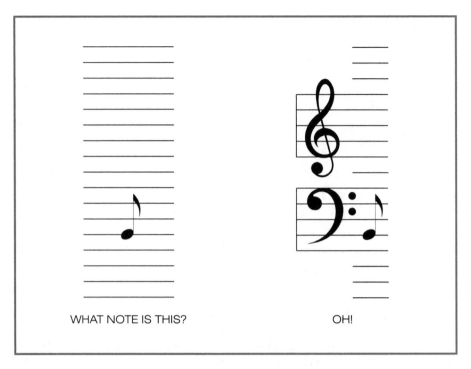

FIGURE 11.2 Using arrays of five to identify musical notes

ALLOCATION OF FUNCTION

The human engineer must decide when to allocate a task to a machine and when to leave it to the operator. Since the days of cave dwellers, machines have gradually increased our strength, reach, and speed. The modern world still relies upon machinery to overcome the physical limitations of the human, but many additional machine attributes are also exploited.

Humans are essentially one-channel processors, meaning that we can focus on only one operation at a time. We cannot concentrate on two activities such as walking and chewing gum simultaneously. People *seem* capable of performing many activities at once because they rapidly switch the focus of concentration, and much of the activity is habitual. But a machine *can* "concentrate on" any number of tasks at once, devoting full "attention" to each.

On one hand, machines perform *counting* work superbly; people do not. Machines show flawless *memories;* human memories are selective. Machines excel in *standby* functions, never getting tired or bored, or losing concentration or memory. They react or respond more quickly and are vastly more immune to *hostile environments.* On the other hand, the more *judgment* and *interpretation* are called for, the more the task should be assigned to a human. Humans are better at a number of visual tasks such as both *reading* and differentiating between **figure and ground**, as in identifying structures in an aerial photograph. (The words you are reading make up the *figures;* the paper is the background or *ground.*)

In addition, humans easily differentiate between *familiar and novel,* between *expected and unexpected,* and between *pattern and nonpattern.* They are also remarkably adept at *threshold sensing,* or detecting *small intensities* of various sensory stimuli. Finally, machines can monitor and respond to variables not detectable by the human receptors. There are many of these; examples are barometric pressure and electromagnetism.

CONTROLS

Have you ever driven a car that was new to you, and had difficulty operating it? Controls do more than simply allow the operator to communicate with the equipment. And they do more than ensure that the machinery is operated efficiently and safely. They can also make the user feel competent, comfortable, and assured in handling the machine, even if it's an unfamiliar one. Let's see how controls can be designed to serve all of these purposes.

Control function logic

Often a control effects some motion in the machine, and it is possible to mimic this motion in the control itself. When the motion of the control parallels that of the outcome, the control movement shows **control function logic** because the movement of the control demonstrates the consequent motion of the machinery.

An example is an automobile window that moves either up or down. If the control operates an electric motor, which in turn moves the glass, the switch should move in the up/down plane, and DOWN should lower the window and UP raise it. (If the window is operated *manually* the input is restricted to a rotary crank for mechanical reasons. Regardless of which way the crank turns to open the window, this handle cannot apply control function logic.) Another example is a control that operates electric motors to adjust the seat position in a car. The ideal control is shaped like the seat; moving it adjusts the seat correspondingly.

FIGURE 11.3 A standard range design

Can you figure out which knob you would turn to switch the right front element on?

Control location logic

Controls have traditionally been located according to the *mechanical design engineer's* preference. Thus in an aircraft, the designer wants all electrically connected controls on one panel, and all those connecting mechanically (through wires or levers) on another. Similarly, the designer would like to place controls that operate left and right wing units in the center of the panel, and those that operate a roof light on the top of the control area.

But the *human factors* engineer wants the controls located wherever the operator would *expect* to find them. The control that opens or shuts the left fuel tank should be located adjacent to the left tank fuel gauge; the landing gear control should be at the bottom of the control panel next to the landing gear display, and the heater, air conditioner, and ventilation switches should all be together, regardless of how they operate or to what area of the aircraft they relay their effect.

Few consumer items show particular attention to good ergonomic design, but some can be found. An excellent example of human engineering is the *push bar* commonly found as a latching device on institutional doors. It is positioned at hand height, and pushing it is a natural motion that mimics the operation of the door itself, so it illustrates both function and location logic.

In automobiles, it's easier to find lapses in ergonomic principles than good demonstrations of them. For instance, a single control (or adjacent ones) should operate front wipers, rear wiper, front washer, and rear washer. Another control should operate headlights, parking lights, and instrument lights. The control for the interior light could be incorporated in this light control or located on the light itself. New car customers are impressed by image and paint and unaware of ergonomics, so designers apportion their resources accordingly.

A prime example of poor ergonomics in a common domestic item is the kitchen range. Figure 11.3 illustrates a standard range design; try to conclude what control operation will turn the right front element to a low heat.

Control stereotype

The control you probably operate most frequently is the on/off switch. It is usually designed to move vertically because the hand can flick a lever up and down slightly more easily than side to side. But the up/down switch rarely causes something to move up or down; it usually turns power on or off, eliminating the possibility of control function logic.

An arbitrary convention that becomes established is termed a **control stereotype**. For instance, North Americans are accustomed to switches that move *up* for ON, *down* for OFF. In Europe, switches move *up* for OFF, showing the culture-bound nature of control stereotypes.

The most universal example of a control stereotype is the rotary dial that effects "more" or "less," as in a radio or television sound-intensity knob. There is no inherent logical reason why clockwise means louder; it has simply become standardized. Other common examples are the placement and operation of hot and cold water faucets. Cold is right; hot is left. And they do not operate like radio dials. Can you tell from memory which way the cold and hot faucets turn for "more"?

A useful stereotype, and one that became universal throughout the world around 1975 is the **PRNDL** convention for the automatic transmission control in passenger vehicles. (If you didn't recognize it, the letters stand for PARK, REVERSE, NEUTRAL, DRIVE, and LOW.) Before this standard was adopted, drivers accustomed to one automobile would, in another, shift into the wrong gear. Some earlier automatic transmissions placed REVERSE to the right of LOW, and drivers needing Low for an emergency suddenly found their automobile in REVERSE.

Control discriminability

Most cars' dashboards look fashionable, tidy, and consistent, with many controls lined up as similar-looking knobs or levers. If each control were a different *shape* and required a different *motion* to operate, the appearance may seem messy, but there would be less chance of a driver's operating the heater when wanting the radio. The more the controls are distinguishable, whether by appearance, touch, location, or mode of operation, the more they provide **control discriminability**. An example of this is seen in the controls of the "D" series Citröen, designed in 1957.

Affordance

You want to exit through a door that has no knob, but a horizontal bar across it at hand height. How do you open it? Without thinking, you push against the bar, and are not surprised when, in response, the door unlatches and moves away. This is because the bar *affords* no other interpretation. A package can be easy or hard to open, a telephone obvious or impossible to operate at first encounter, a digital watch or video cassette recorder easy or hard to reset in spite of much experience with it, all because of its *affordance*. **Affordance**, or the extent to which a control affords only the correct inter-pretation of how to operate it, is a function of both the intrinsic *properties* of a control and of the way the control is *perceived*.

DISPLAYS

Displays, you will recall, permit the equipment to communicate with the operator. The more sophisticated the equipment, the more ergonomic the display should be.

Sensory medium

Since a display is a message from the machine to the human, the message must be directed to one of our senses. The senses that respond to external stimuli comprise *sight, hearing, touch, olfaction* (smell), and *taste*. Taste is not used by human engineers, nor is smell much used as a purposeful signal. There are wide individual differences in olfactory sensitivity, and any smell, once detected, soon adapts out. On the other hand, minute quantities of olfactory signals will quickly permeate vast areas, so smell does have limited application as a signal. Where people are at risk of exposure to dangerous but odorless gases, a distinctive-smelling "tracer" gas may be mixed with the harmful material. If any of the latter escapes, the tracer serves as an olfactory warning display.

Just as we rely primarily upon our **distance senses**, vision and hearing, the human engineer aims virtually all displays at either the eyes or the ears of the operator. There are distinct differences between the functioning of the eyes and the ears, differences that are exploited in ergonomic design.

The eye is our most important sense organ; more information can be conveyed visually than through all the other senses combined. Consequently, the convention is to choose a visual display unless there's some reason to use an auditory one.

The common reason to switch from sight to hearing is that the eyes are occupied to capacity and cannot accept additional input. A second reason involves the variables of *urgency* and *attending*. A visual display requires the operator to attend to, or concentrate on, the display panel; an auditory signal does not. An auditory display can get through to a dozing operator who is oblivious to a flashing red warning light. The more urgent the message, and the less the guarantee that the operator will attend to a visual display, the more the engineer needs to choose sound. Hence, routine displays in an aircraft are visual; urgent messages (low altitude, impending stall, loss of cabin pressure) are auditory.

"Attending" is not simply a matter of staying awake. Alert, vigilant nuclear power plant operators might happen to be walking from one panel to another when a warning signal is emitted, so again the signal should be auditory. It's for the same reason that your telephone rings at you; you don't watch your phone to see if you should answer it. Everyone who's been awoken by a call knows that the eyes can be closed, but not the ears. (Some pessimistic futurists predict that the last thing most of us will hear is a signal announcing an emergency. It may be a small consolation to remember at that time, as we hear a specific pattern of what is known as the "yeow" or the "beep," that the sound was judged effective and distinctive by human engineers.)

Environments unsuitable for any visual display include those that subject the operator to darkness or severe vibration. Even a high-tech visual display on a face protector might not appear sharp if the operator were subjected to extreme motion. Another problem with vision is that the display must be designed according to appropriate *size* and *distance* parameters; a far-off display might be too small to read. That's why "clear the way" signals on emergency vehicles are both auditory and visual. Drivers are inaccurate about localizing or estimating the distance of an ambulance siren (Caelli & Porter, 1980), so the siren alone would not suffice.

A third sense modality, the **tactile** (touch) sense, has limited but interesting application. If you have ever pulled your car to the side of the road because your steering wheel started to vibrate, you were responding to your tactile sense. Since the automotive engineers did not purposefully design this behavior into the car, it would not ordinarily be considered a tactile display. But three examples can be found.

- One danger in flying is that the pilot might stall at low altitude while concentrating on taking off or landing; large aircraft require thousands of feet of altitude to recover. ("Stalling" doesn't mean that the engine quits as in an automobile; when an aircraft stalls there's a sudden transition from flying to falling.) Human engineers have incorporated into the pilot's *control yoke* (the control column, originally called the "stick") a **stick shaker** that vibrates when an onboard computer determines that a stall is impending. Pilots are trained to take instantaneous antistall action when the yoke vibrates. Since the primary correction is to push the yoke forward, this tactile display includes *display location logic.*

- The moment of landing is particularly hazardous. Landing demands precise control activities, there's minimal margin for pilot error, and the pilot is likely tired. Among other critical activities at this moment, the pilot must apply wheel braking to slow a 300,000 pound aircraft touching down at 100 knots. A trifle too much brake pressure will lock a wheel, resulting in a blown tire, a skid, or a fire in the wheel assembly.

The HFE problem is how to ensure that the pilot responds instantly to wheel locking at the moment when there is already a state of *sensory overload.* The solution was a computer that detects a main wheel starting to turn slower than the nose wheel (which doesn't have brakes). A **toe shaker** then vibrates whichever brake pedal the pilot should reduce the pressure on.

- The final example of tactile displays is in devices that help blind people to communicate. For instance, books in **Braille** substitute tactile symbols for visual letters. Some research has been conducted with the **tactile typewriter**, where vibratory pads are attached to the person's back. With nine pads and three levels of vibration, there is an alphabet of 27 "letters" that might some day be used to communicate with someone who is blind and deaf. Many devices for visually impaired people, such as watches and clocks, typewriter and telephone keys, and thermometers have transferred the display medium from sight to touch.

We have seen that human engineers usually choose visual displays, switching to auditory when necessary. Next we will examine the HFE principles of common visual and auditory displays. (Before we do, however, see if you can find two visual metaphors in this paragraph, metaphors that demonstrate our reliance on vision.)

Visual displays

The most frequently monitored display is the automobile speedometer. Except for some racing cars, where the professional driver is more concerned with engine speed than road speed, every car accords the largest and most central display to the device that was originally called the "speed-o-meter."

Practically nobody purchases an automobile without sitting in it first and looking at the dashboard. Consequently, these displays are determined more by *design* engineers than by human factors or mechanical engineers. Customers cannot assess the accuracy or longevity of the components, and they are generally oblivious to the human engineering variables. Since buyers are invariably influenced by appearance, speedometer design has shown a persistent violation of HFE principles.

The earliest popular speedometer design was the "open window" fitted to the Model T Ford. The speeds were labeled on a turning drum rotating behind a window that exposed slightly more than one speed at a time. The driver always located the speed display in the same spot, and by observing the speed and direction of the turning drum, could estimate the rate of acceleration or deceleration.

The next popular design was a moving pointer on a full circle around which were speed labels. This was a regressive step because now the eye had two tasks. First it had to locate the pointer, then it had to determine at which number the pointer was aimed. But the round dial looked more stylish.

As car design increasingly emphasized horizontality, the dash display area became lower, and the round dial was replaced with a semicircle. The problem here was that only half the display space was available, so the numbers were more crowded. Moreover, as performance was increasing, more numbers had to be accommodated in the reduced space. For instance, the top speed shown on some of these displays was twice the maximum speed of the Model T.

As styling increasingly determined sales, the speedometer was relegated to a rectangular opening about six inches wide by two inches high. Now drivers had two problems: crowded numbers, and uneven placement. (The numbers at the sides of the display were spread out more than those at the top center.)

Another "advance" was the *thermometer* design, where a moving central rod indicated the speed as a column thermometer shows temperature. The flaw here is that it takes more time to locate the top of the column than it does to locate the position of a pointer.

The "advance" of the 1980s was the digital display, where the speed was shown in numbers just as a digital watch shows the time. The advantage is that a single eye flick to a stable location suffices, just as in the Model T speedometer. The problem is that rapidly changing digits don't let the driver see the rate of speed change. (The optimal solution is a combination digital/dial display, but the cost has confined this design largely to a few aircraft altimeters.) Figure 11.4 illustrates various speedometer designs.

If the most common display of all, the speedometer, violates the basic principles of visual displays, some understanding of these principles should encourage better designed, safer machinery. There is no design for the perfect visual display, but the following principles can be used to evaluate the merits of any display.

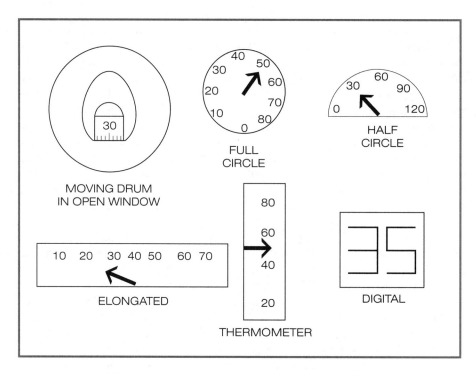

FIGURE 11.4 Changing styles in speedometer designs

The seven principles of visual displays Principle 1 is **clustering**. Displays representing similar functions should be located adjacent to each other (Figure 11.5). If there are three *engine* displays in an automobile (for example, coolant temperature, motor speed, and oil pressure), they should be located in the *engine cluster*. The more complex the machine, the more clustering is called for. An aircraft may require 10 displays for each of 4 engines. Obviously, the 40 engine displays should not be located wherever the *design* engineer or *production* engineer finds most convenient.

Principle 2 is **status: normal/abnormal**. Operators are rarely expected to monitor all displays constantly. Rather, they should *scan* or review the displays in a specific sequence at specified intervals. The main purpose of the scan is to differentiate between normal and abnormal readings. Consequently, the displays should facilitate this determination. Each display should clearly show normal, warning, and danger levels.

Patterns of clustering can be exploited, as where four dials show the exhaust gas temperature of each of four engines, with the pointers aimed at the center of the four to indicate "normal." Then, if one engine's temperature is abnormal, its pointer will alert the pilot clearly, in the course of the next scan. Normal/abnormal can be aided by standard color codes, with green indicating normal, yellow showing some departure from standard, and red

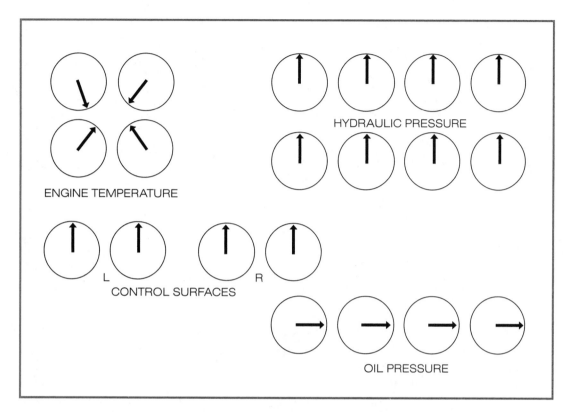

FIGURE 11.5 Clustered displays

Displays representing similar functions should be clustered together.

indicating an abnormality. Flashing red is a universal signal that always means "Do something immediately."

Automobile tachometers (engine speed displays) should show more than the "red line" or maximum rate, which few drivers reach. Every engine has a normal operating range; this should be shown in green. In the same way, the engine temperature display should indicate more than "cold" and "hot"; it should differentiate among *normal* operating temperature, too *cold,* too *hot,* and *danger.* Figure 11.6 illustrates this principle.

Principle 3 is to use an **annunciator** wherever appropriate. This is a visual signal that is not displayed during normal operation, but that illuminates to indicate abnormal status. Consider the oil pressure of an automobile engine. The pressure may suddenly drop to zero once in the 10-year lifetime of a car, whereupon the driver has mere seconds to stop the engine before ruining it. To expect the driver to monitor an oil pressure gauge every half minute is unrealistic. An annunciator that can display a flashing red "Stop: Check Oil" shows better human engineering than an oil pressure gauge; driv-

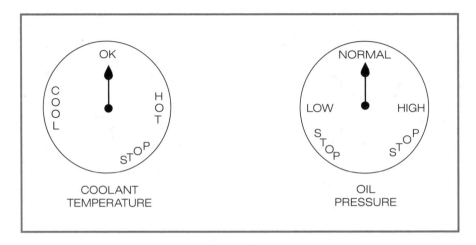

FIGURE 11.6 Displays showing status normal/abnormal

Ergonomic displays indicate abnormal status clearly, often with color codes.

ers who consider annunciators "idiot lights" show they do not understand HFE principles. Annunciators are illustrated in Figure 11.7.

Principle 4 is **display function logic**. A fuel quantity display should move vertically, symbolizing the position of the top of the fuel. A temperature display should also be oriented vertically since most thermometers are vertical; moreover, it should convey the image of a thermometer. Where displays can be equally logical moving sideways or up/down, they should be given side motion to more easily distinguish them from the others. The *design* engineers prefer to impose the same format on all displays, but the *human* engineers should ensure that the sales staff understand and can explain the advantages of an HFE-based design. Figure 11.8 illustrates some examples of display logic.

Principle 5 is **display location logic**. Displays should be located in proximity to their associated controls. For instance, the display indicating the position of the landing gear on an aircraft should be located close to the control that raises and lowers the gear. A good example of *display location logic* is the common household thermostat, in which you can read the temperature and adjust it in the same place.

Principle 6 is **eye movement control**. We see sharply enough to read an instrument only within a narrow field; that is why *saccadic* eye movements are necessary (page 394). An eye movement camera takes motion pictures of the reflections from the **cornea** (the outside front of the eye), thereby showing what the operator was looking at (page 64). The human factors engineer can mount an eye movement camera on the operator, which would remain in place throughout the handling of the machinery and record eye move-

yellow	ENGINE COLD	ENGINE HOT	red
red	FUEL LOW	OIL PRESSURE LOW	flashing red
yellow	SEAT BELTS	BRAKES WORN	orange
orange	BATTERY DISCHARGE	SLIPPERY OUT	yellow

FIGURE 11.7 Annunciators

Annunciators are visual warning signals that light up only to indicate an abnormal status.

ments, including the scanning of visual displays. The displays are then positioned in the location and pattern that permit the most efficient eye motion.

The equipment that places the most severe visual demands upon the operator is the single-seat, high-performance combat aircraft. The pilot must perform most of the duties of a three-person crew of a jetliner, in addition to managing more firepower than a World War II battle cruiser, all the while evading enemy fire. And it is not possible to take a break, order a coffee, or even stretch. This overloaded operator may be furnished with the ultimate in visual display human engineering, the **head up display (HUD)**.

The most advanced HUD shows a combined graphic, numeric, and symbolic representation of the most critical information regarding navigation and aiming, all on a single transparent panel directly in the line of vision through the windscreen. The pilot can monitor the display and forward view simultaneously, instead of having to lower the line of vision to scan the instruments. Automotive engineers are searching for a cost-effective means of incorporating a speedometer HUD on the windshield so that drivers can monitor their speed without lowering their gaze. This feature became available in a few models in 1989.

The less eye movement in a scan, the better. Automobile displays located at the sides of the instrument cluster are invariably smaller than the primary displays at the center. But because the acuity of *peripheral* vision is lower than that of *central* vision, the lateral displays should be relatively large. Peripheral vision excels at detecting *motion,* so moving displays can be located to the side.

Principle 7 is **standard placement**. All aircraft provide six basic displays: altitude, air speed, compass heading, banking, and the rate of altitude change and pitch change. All aircraft manufacturers have agreed upon a standard

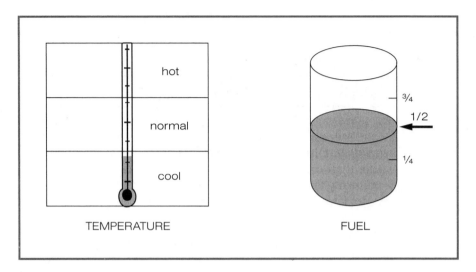

FIGURE 11.8 Display function logic

It is logical for temperature and fuel displays to move vertically; the first corresponds to a thermometer and the second to the level of fuel in the tank.

placement of these six displays in all their models. Thus a pilot can perform the same scan regardless of the aircraft model.

The two dominant displays in many cars give the car speed and the engine speed. These displays, the speedometer and the tachometer, are invariably located side by side. In some automobiles the speedometer is on the left, in others it is on the right. Like aircraft manufacturers, car makers should agree upon a standard layout for common displays. A driver of any automobile wanting to check the fuel level or the engine temperature display should be able to count on finding it in a given segment of the instrument array. (General Motors, by recording drivers' eye movements, found that displays located left of center were checked first and most often. This implies that the speedometer should be on the left.)

The standardization of automotive displays will probably not come about until it is required by legislation, which, in turn, follows public demand. When the public objected to cars' bumpers locking together in minor collisions, regulations on a standard bumper height were enacted to solve the problem. There is not, as yet, much public demand for sound ergonomics in car displays.

Controls, of course, should be standardized too. Here, more from custom than from any concerted agreement, auto manufacturers have made slightly better progress. The steering wheel is always in the same location, even if the horn control is not. The ignition and the headlight control are well standardized; the wiper and defroster controls are not.

AUDITORY DISPLAYS

It was noted on page 357 that auditory channels are used primarily when the visual ones are loaded to capacity (which happens easily). But there are applications in which sounds work *better* than sights for communication from machine to operator. The prime example of this is in *warning* signals, because the operator does not have to *attend* to an auditory display for the message to be received.

Warnings

Most auditory or aural displays function in the same way as the visual annunciator; that is, they are "Off" during normal operation, and they emit a signal to indicate an abnormal status. Since sound signals are used largely for *emergency* warnings, particular care must be applied to their design. For instance, operational problems in aircraft tend to arrive in groups, so each warning sound must be *compatible with* and *distinguishable from* all other warning sounds. Also, the sound intensity must be adequate to pierce whatever other noises are in effect, while remaining tolerable.

"I've got to go to the bathroom."

In one needless tragedy, the flight crew on a passenger jet heard the loud "ground proximity" warning horn. (This routine warning signal is activated whenever the altitude is less than one thousand feet; it self-extinguishes as soon as the display shows that the landing gear is down.) While preparing the aircraft for descent, the crew noticed that one of the landing gear lights failed to show that the wheels were ready for landing. As they attempted to see the effect of installing a replacement light bulb in the gear display, the crew canceled the annoying warning horn with an override switch. With the low-altitude emergency signal deactivated, they failed to notice a slight nose-down pitch, and they flew into a swamp at cruising speed.

Many HFE questions arose. Was the display unnecessarily loud? Should the override control have been temporary instead of permanent? Should the cockpit have been designed *without* an override control? Should there have been a backup warning device? As you see, controls and displays relate to more than operating efficiency; they may involve life and death.

A recent advance in auditory displays is the use of a recorded human voice, either real or artificial, which announces emergency messages such as FIRE IN ENGINE THREE or ALTITUDE UNDER ONE THOUSAND. The newest wrinkle, stemming from HFE research in England, involves an audio tape containing a wide assortment of tone sequences rather than voices, which might be too intrusive and distracting. Each tone sequence mimics the **prosody** of the human voice. Prosody refers to the cadence (the rhythm and inflection) of normal speech.

For instance, the rhythm of the phrase "Cabin pressure dropping" would be, if you use your imagination, dot-dot dot-dot dot-dot. For "Landing gear down" it would be dot-dot-dot dash. Moreover, the **timbre** (sound quality) of each tone set is distinctive, and the tones have a gradual onset instead of a sudden one, so that the stress on the pilots is not compounded by a startle reflex. Finally, the more serious the emergency implications of the message and the longer the message is needed, the louder, the higher pitched, and the more rapidly the tones are presented.

The other common application for emergency auditory signals is in the intensive care unit of a hospital. Many patients are connected to a monitor that signals when some physiological parameter exceeds a preset limit. Like pilots, nurses tend to face their serious problems in bunches. An incubator suddenly emits three warning alarms, one because the infant's temperature is too low, another because the heart rate is too high, and a third simply because some other detecting device became detached.

A new device emits signals that not only call attention to a problem, but also identify its nature and severity. A dot-dot-dot falling in pitch mimics the prosody of "temperature," and changes in the pitch indicate the direction. A single, repeated beep represents the word "heart," and the pitch indicates whether the rate is above or below the limits allowed; the more a limit is being exceeded, the louder the signal. The signal for "Detached Electrode" is quieter and distinctive.

A basic voice display has recently been added to some cars, but here it seems more a novelty than an advance in display engineering. For instance, few of these signals are designed to be activated once the car starts to move, when they would be of more use. This is probably because automotive executives must consider the legal implications of designs. Unlike the case with aircraft, anyone with a driver's license, regardless of competence or training, can drive any new car model without instruction. Suppose, the company lawyers might warn, that a driver rounding a snowy curve is startled by an unseen person announcing, "The outside temperature indicates the possibility of slippery roads," and loses control, and sues the manufacturer. Or suppose the driver sued because the warning was *not* heard. Unfortunately, good human engineering is not always good legal engineering.

Students sometimes ask if a *live* human voice is an "auditory display." Technically it is, although in practice the term "display" implies an artificial or machine-generated message. Increasingly, synthesized voice displays *are* being used in high-tech environments. Since much signaling takes place from live voice to ear, the spoken word message is addressed in chapter 13.

Frequency analysis

The ears are good at detecting a signal that is buried in background noise; this is termed **frequency analysis**. In fact, it is not unusual for the *noise* to be louder than the *signal*. (The *quantification* of signal and noise, the **signal to noise (S/N) ratio**, is explained in chapter 13, page 406.) You may already know that any signal can be transformed into any medium. For instance, the sound of a drumbeat could be converted to a visual signal; a flash of light could be transformed into a beep. Is there a difference between the eye and the ear in the ability to detect a signal that's buried in background noise?

Picture this. During rehearsal, an orchestra conductor stops the playing and reprimands the second oboist for playing an F-sharp instead of F-natural. The conductor easily detected one note while 80 other musicians were playing. Now suppose the sounds of the orchestra were transformed into a *visual* display, in the form of lines on an oscilloscope. Could the conductor detect a wrong note in the visual depiction of the musical sounds? No; the conductor would barely be able to differentiate between loud and soft passages, and between generally high and generally low notes.

The human brain is supremely adept at identifying a "buried" signal sent to the ears, but it does a poor job at separating signal from noise when the eyes process the data. Consider the task of identifying the signal of an approaching aircraft. In **radar**, electrical energy is beamed at the sky, and any reflections back from an aircraft are transformed into a visual signal or blip on a screen, which is monitored by an operator. The "background noise" for a flying aircraft is just empty sky, so the reflected signal is conspicuous, and the radar operator's eye can detect it without difficulty.

Now consider the problem of detecting submarines. Unlike an aircraft, which has nothing but air around and above it, a submarine has water (which is much denser than air) around it, and a solid seabed beneath. Thus, the noise level is relatively high, especially if the submarine is distant from the observer. If the reflected signals or echoes from the submarine were displayed visually, the operator would be unable to separate signal from noise. So the signals are displayed auditorily; the system is termed **sonar**. Like the conductor detecting one note in a sea of sounds, the sonar operator can detect the echo from a submarine in a sea of echoes.

At this stage, you know the *meaning, background, importance,* and *basic principles* of ergonomics. In the next chapter we turn to interesting ways in which the principles are *applied* to make our interactions with machines more effective and safe.

Study guide for chapter 11

HAVE YOU LEARNED THESE NAMES AND TERMS?

human factors engineering (HFE)
person-machine engineering
system
person-machine systems
control and display
figure and ground
control function logic
control stereotype
PRNDL
control discriminability
affordance
distance senses
tactile
stick shaker, toe shaker
Braille and tactile typewriter
clustering
status: normal/abnormal
annunciator
display function logic and display location logic
eye movement control
cornea
head up display (HUD)
standard placement
prosody and timbre
frequency analysis
signal to noise (S/N) ratio
radar and sonar

ISSUES TO CONSIDER

What was the common factor in the six Brief Cases that started the chapter?

In what way is the *ergonomics* approach the opposite of the *personnel* one?

What is ironic about the word "factory"?

Why was HFE not needed prior to World War I?

What *person-machine systems* are within your view at this moment?

Compared to a machine, what is the human mind best at and worst at?

What is the significance of a group of *five* for human perception?

In what way are you a one-channel system?

If you own or use a car, what lapses in ergonomics can you identify in it?

What is the first principle of visual displays; why is it so important?

Why is the term *idiot light* idiotic?

Can you think up an original example of *control stereotype?*

When is *control discriminability* important; when is it irrelevant?

Why do virtually all telephones ring rather than blink?

What is the benefit of the head up display (HUD)?

What is the present status of display/control *standardization* in cars?

How does your ability in *frequency analysis* benefit you?

SAMPLE MULTIPLE-CHOICE QUESTIONS

1. How would a human engineer apply *control function logic* to a window crank?
   a. by making the window go in the same direction as the crank handle
   b. she wouldn't
   c. by applying large and clear labels
   d. by using color codes

2. Which of these is a person-machine system?
   a. the brain
   b. the heart, lungs, and blood
   c. a knife
   d. a sealed window

3. Which type of display is watched most?
   a. thermometers
   b. altimeters
   c. barometers
   d. speedometers

4. The clearest indication of "status normal/abnormal" is the
   a. gauge.
   b. dial.
   c. window.
   d. annunciator.

5. Sonar would likely replace radar
   a. in bad weather.
   b. in a poor S/N environment.
   c. with younger operators.
   d. with older operators.

Answers: page 462

La carrière ouverte aux talents (Give the tools to those who can handle them).

Napoleon Bonaparte (1769–1821)

Bird's-eye view of the chapter

This chapter shows ways in which human engineers work with *measurements* (both of and by humans) and the *environment* (of the workplace, the home, and the university). It covers the influence of atmospheric conditions on behavior, including variables such as air pollution and noise. It deals with how people are affected when they are in *motion* and the effects of *aging*. The chapter particularly considers our most important sense, vision.

Chapter 12
Applications
of ergonomics

The payoff from chapter 12 You will:

1. See how ergonomic shortcomings can lead to serious consequences
2. Learn basic principles of *anthropometry*
3. Know some HFE-related principles of *metrology*
4. Appreciate the contributions of *environmental psychology*
5. Understand the effect of the ambient *atmosphere* on job performance
6. Know how *temperature* in particular influences job behavior
7. Have an inkling of the effect of *air pressure*
8. Understand something of *air pollution*
9. Be familiar with the meaning, measurement, and effects of *noise*
10. Understand how the effects of *motion* can influence performance
11. Relate the effects of motion to high-performance equipment
12. Know about research on and effects of *weightlessness*
13. Be aware of how motion can induce visual illusions
14. Know how *aging* affects performance and the senses
15. Know the importance of protecting yourself from high-intensity sounds
16. Understand something of how light and lighting work
17. Thoroughly understand the process and consequences of *dark adaption*
18. Know the meaning of *light adaption*
19. Know the basic structure and physiology of the *eye*
20. Understand why principles of ergonomics are often not followed

W hat has ergonomics done for you lately? If you've worked at a desk, it just might have saved your back. At a computer terminal, it might have protected your wrists, neck, and eyes. And if you've flown a plane, it just might have saved your life.

A REAL-LIFE PROBLEM

Here is one of the earliest problems that faced the human engineer in applying ergonomic theory to the real world of aviation, a world that many people depend on for their vacation and business trips and for their national security.

When the pilot lowers one wing (raising the other) the movement is called a **bank**. To know the degree of bank, pilots compare the horizon (from which we get the word "horizontal") with the bottom of the windshield.

The degree of bank had to be displayed in the cockpit, and this seemed simple. For flying at night or in clouds, pilots were provided with a *bank indicator,* which showed a horizontal line that itself banked automatically, functioning as an artificial horizon. If the pilot banked left (left wing down) the horizon indicator on the bank display rotated clockwise (or in effect banked right), simulating the apparent horizon seen through the windshield.

In the same way, the display of **pitch** (the up-down tilt of the aircraft's nose) showed an artificial horizon that rose when the plane pitched downward, and lowered to show that the nose was raised. Many crashes were attributed to pilots' misreading these simple, basic indicators of bank and pitch. Could the displays be improved?

Some novice pilots were provided with displays that registered in the opposite way. They were told, "Think of the bank and pitch indicators as miniature airplanes that you are viewing from behind." With the new displays there were no mishaps associated with misreading the pitch and bank indicators! In both the original and the modified design, *display function logic* (Figure 11.8, page 364) prevailed.

The *original* logical connection was between the movement of the aircraft and the view of the horizon. The *modified* logical connection was between the motion of the plane and the motion of the display. The human engineers had not predicted that one logical connection would turn out to be much more intuitively natural than the other.

The aircraft industry modified the display convention, even though the modification meant rendering the original instruments obsolete and retraining existing pilots. Now, before a new display is introduced, the *principle* of display logic is tested against the *practice,* in both simulated and real flight. Figure 12.1 shows this display in both versions. (Both displays are showing a climbing left turn; that is, the aircraft's nose is up, and the left wing is lower than the right.)

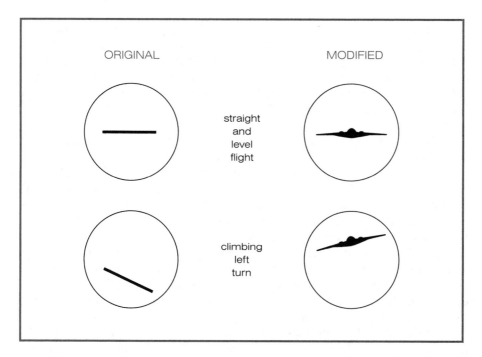

FIGURE 12.1 Pitch and bank indicator: Original and modified

In the original design, the indicator moved in the opposite direction to the plane to show the apparent horizons. Though this was a logical function display, it was misread by pilots. The design was modified so that indicators moved in the same direction as the plane.

In this chapter we will touch on some of the most interesting applications of HFE to our efficiency, safety, and comfort. Few areas of research enjoy such wide-ranging diversity.

MEASUREMENTS OF PEOPLE

A car designer had better make sure that the seats in the new model will fit all potential occupants and drivers, from the tallest to the most obese. An aircraft seat designer must ensure that all flight crew members—old or young, male or female—will find all aspects of the cockpit suitable. And the aircraft's passageways, washrooms, and emergency equipment must accommodate all sizes and shapes of potential passengers, whether they're dressed for the tropics or for the arctic.

These needs involve the science of **anthropometry**, literally meaning "man measure." The word refers to the recording of human body measurements (**static anthropometry**), or the range of body movements (**dynamic anthropometry**). Source tables show the measurements of the 5th, 50th, and 95th percentiles of the sample studied. (The 50th percentile is the average measure; the range between the 5th and the 95th represents the middle 90 percent.)

The practice of disregarding the requirements of people outside of the 5 to 95 percentile range is based on the principle of diminishing returns. For instance, the height of a 95th percentile male is just over 6 feet; that of a 5th percentile female is just under 5 feet. A driver's seat designed to accommodate people between 5 and 6 feet will suit only 90 per cent of drivers, but to make it fit the midgets and giants representing the outside 10 percent would raise the cost disproportionately to the benefit.

That's why lawn chairs are not designed to hold a 250-pound person, and doorways do not suit seven-foot-tall individuals. However, an escape hatch on a cruise ship or passenger aircraft would have to allow the passage of someone in the 100th percentile, who may be wearing winter clothing or may be confined to a wheelchair.

Dynamic anthropometry is more complex. For a seated operator, the most convenient locations for the overhead and lateral controls would depend on whether the user were an arthritic older person or an amateur boxer, on whether the operator preferred an upright or a reclined seat back, and even on the clothing worn. The range of operator movement within which all the controls must be located is the **workspace envelope**. Human engineers differentiate between the *normal area* (the area of the envelope that can be reached with ease) and the *maximum area* (that which could be attained briefly, with effort).

Since work is generally performed in a seated position, it's not surprising that more research has been conducted on seat design than on other items of operator equipment. On one hand, chairs have long been the most common form of furniture, and one would assume that by now the design has been perfected. On the other, when you think of the range of seats—bus seats, secretarial chairs, theater seats, sports bleachers, barber chairs, dining chairs, lounge chairs, bicycle seats, car seats, horseback saddles—and of the wide range of people who will occupy these seats, you might guess that improvement is possible.

A few terms of anatomy will help. The back edge of the thigh just above the knee joint, the *popliteal* area, is referred to as the "knee-back," and let's call the rounded part of the buttocks the "rear."

An examination of seating studies led McCormick (1970) to conclude that people prefer most of their weight to be borne by a small portion of the rear. It is important that the front of the seat be no higher than the distance between floor and knee-back, lest too much weight be borne by the thighs.

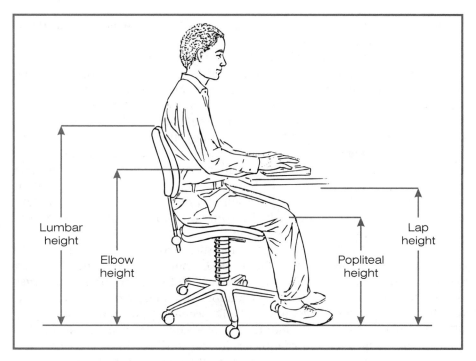

FIGURE 12.2 Some chair design parameters

The starting points in chair design are the height of the seat and the rake (angle) of the seat back. Seat height should be adjustable from 15 to 19 inches, or 17 inches if fixed. Of course, other factors, such as the nature of the job and the height of the work, can modify these figures. The rake should be at an angle of about 4 degrees back from the vertical for a work position, and about 8 degrees for relaxation. These principles are shown in Figure 12.2.

MEASUREMENTS BY PEOPLE

The world would be more convenient if everything were standardized, but it's not. For instance, in the television industry there are at least three broadcast systems, five electrical standards, eight videotape systems, and three stereo conventions, all mutually incompatible.

Just as there's no global uniformity in politics, religion, or language, the world has more than one measurement system. If the world's languages were subjected to an HFE analysis, English would show a number of weaknesses (outlined in the following chapter). It is futile to expect the world to adopt any one language as a universal standard, yet there are attempts at limiting measurement systems to a single standard one.

Measurement systems can be contrasted in terms of HFE variables. Of the two prevailing systems, one is the *metric,* named after one of its units, the meter. The other is variously termed *standard, British imperial,* and *American;* let's call it the *inch* system. These two systems, the metric and the inch, illustrate how human engineering can be applied to **metrology**, the science of measurement.

Attempts to standardize a system of weights and measures can be traced to earliest civilizations. The need for standardization—and precision—became more apparent with the growth of international commerce and the development of equipment with interchangeable parts. This attracted the military mind of Napoleon, who established a committee to solve the problem; the committee formulated the metric system.

The metric system of weights and measures was uniform, simple, easy to understand, and comprehensive. But it lacked human engineering. The inch system, like the violin, was "human engineered" by trial and error over centuries of use and refinement. For instance, commonly used linear measures are based on 12s rather than on 10s, because units like feet and yards must frequently be divided into equal divisions, and 12 has more divisors than 10. As another example, the millimeter and centimeter are too small for most household use and the meter is too long, in comparison to the inch, foot, and yard.

Most of the inch-based countries are trying to convert to the metric system. Insofar as this means that people will be familiarized with the metric system, there is no objection. Where the conversion implies the ultimate demise of the inch system, there are several grounds for concern.

One is that the inch system is more ergonomically sound. Another is that it is entrenched into permanent physical structures. In every room of every building, most components are sized according to round-numbered, inch-based units. The third objection is that the inch system is not confined to a few die-hard countries; it's in worldwide use. The world over, aircraft altitude is measured in feet, typewriters and printers are calibrated in characters per inch, plugs, jacks, and other connectors are standardized in inch fractions, and most videotape is inch-based.

The solution is to accept **bimetrology**, in which both systems are accepted. This would not be new. For decades, cars from throughout the world have specified metrics for spark plugs and inches for wheel rims. For a century, hunters have carried inch-based shells in one pocket and millimeter-based rounds in the other. There's nothing inconsistent in a photographer's ordering a 4 × 5 inch print from a 35 mm negative, or a doctor hoping to lower a patient's blood pressure by 10 mm and weight by 10 pounds.

People should not have to serve measurement systems; measurement systems should serve people. Although the metric system seems at first glance to be a candidate for a universal language of measurement, the HFE benefits and the entrenchment of the inch system cannot be dismissed.

ENVIRONMENTAL PSYCHOLOGY

Environmental psychology refers to the effect of the "surround" on behavior. This topic encompasses *work space* (whether a restaurant kitchen, a nuclear generating station control center, or a children's playground), *work environment* (from the color of classroom walls to the arrangement of the space shuttle's cockpit), and *living environment* (from the layout of a college residence to the spacing of city parks).

Environmental variables are more general or amorphous than the other influences we have been examining. In research, the environmental psychologist examines the effect of an independent variable on a dependent one. (Such studies are often correlational, but the variables are still termed independent and dependent, albeit incorrectly.) Typical *independent* or causal variables include:

- *building design* such as architectural style, and room and passageway layout;

- *physical environment* such as furnishings and decor;

- *ambient environment* (local and surrounding) such as illumination, noise, and temperature control;

- *community environment*, for example, layout and facilities; and *transportation facilities* such as roads, parking, and public transportation.

The *dependent* or caused variables that environmental researchers can measure are:

- *performance of activities* such as work and sports;

- *physical welfare* such as health and safety;

- *physical comfort* such as noise or temperature; and

- *personal space* and *social interaction* (McCormick, 1969).

Such research is not easily generalized. An ideal residence layout at one university might be unpalatable to students at another one; suitable furnishings in one office might be rejected by workers in another.

The concept of personal space refers to the area around a person within which nobody else may enter without causing a feeling of intrusion. Our response to our personal space is influenced by situation (we accept a stranger right next to us in a crowded elevator, but not on a deserted street); status (we accept more proximity from persons of the same status than from those of a different status); context (spacing is quite different during a date than a music lesson); culture (for instance, normal business or social conversations between two people are held close together in some parts of the world, and far apart in others).

Whereas personal space is portable, *territoriality* refers to the fixed locations that a person regards as one's own. One's residence, locker, and accustomed seat in a classroom all reflect the concept of territoriality. The concepts of "my area" should be considered in the design of buildings, for instance. When common areas of apartment buildings and college residences are totally separated from personal territory, these areas tend to be littered, defaced, and treated with indifference. But when the building design implies that a hallway or corridor is part of one's own "property," the areas are treated more similarly to the private quarters.

Within one's own territory, another variable is the layout and furnishings of the room itself, which was addressed in the section on Workspace Design (page 335). Research on this topic has been based on studies conducted on university students. They have been asked to interpret the personalities of imaginary office occupants, from drawings of the latter's offices. Usually the participants choose from **bipolar** adjectives (opposites, such as warm and cool). Despite the research weaknesses, it is clear that room design does affect the "psychological climate."

ATMOSPHERIC CONDITIONS

In the old days, our grandmothers solved ventilation problems quite simply: they would tell us to keep the bedroom window open lest we sleep in stale air. Now the concerns are pervasive, subtle, and not so simply rectified. We worry about secondhand cigarette smoke in the lunchroom, toxic fumes in the factory, and the unseen effects of cathode ray tubes or formaldehyde fumes in offices with sealed windows. Even though workplace atmospherics present few of the problems associated with grandma's times, many employees now are vigilant about certain atmospheric conditions under which they work, and some modern workplaces are potentially hazardous. The same person who is indifferent to a poorly designed workstation can be affronted by a moderately cool office—in the winter.

Temperature

The environmental variable that people seem most concerned about is temperature (if people were limited to one piece of weather forecast information, they would usually choose to know the next day's temperature). Not surprisingly, employees are sensitive to the temperature of the work environment.

In fact, the most common environmental constraint in union contracts is the upper and lower limit of the workplace temperature.

The human being is a supremely adaptive creature, and people do become acclimatized to temperature extremes. Indeed, the word **acclimatization**, which is applied to getting used to anything, originally meant adjusting to temperature changes. In hot or cold working environments, partial acclimatization occurs within a week. Complete acclimatization to heat takes place in two weeks; to cold, it takes months or even years.

Ensuring that employees are temperature comfortable is complicated by the fact that people give off heat themselves. A resting adult male generates 1 kcal/min (kilocalorie per minute), which is about the heat given off by a 60-watt lightbulb. The body heat generated by a person under exertion can reach 20 times that amount! In designing protective clothing for astronauts to wear in space outside their vehicles, it was less of a problem to provide air than to regulate the body temperature.

Heat is transferred by **convection** (heat transfer to the air), either through **radiation** or through *evaporation*. Factors that affect the efficiency of heat transfer through these methods are *temperature differential* between the skin and the surround, *temperature of the environment* (objects such as room walls), *air circulation,* and *air humidity.*

At ordinary temperatures, *humidity* has negligible effect on comfort, but it plays a major role under hot or cold conditions. The hotter the air, the more the body depends on the evaporation of sweat for skin cooling, but the higher the humidity, the less the evaporation. Very cold air is also harder to tolerate under high humidity.

Regardless of humidity or circulation, however, the hotter the air the greater the physical stress during the performance of vigorous work. Performance of mentally demanding tasks also decreases under hot conditions, especially above 90°F, and after fatigue sets in.

Cold-related problems are presented by various work environments: the arctic, most bodies of water, artificial refrigeration, high altitudes, and, of course, outer space. Since the convection effect of cooling depends on the circulation of air around the skin, the concept of **windchill** incorporates both temperature and wind speed. The original **windchill index** (Siple & Passel, 1945) provided a scale of subjective sensations, ranging from hot at 80, pleasant at 200, cool at 400, cold at 800, and so on. This index allowed one to see, for instance, that air temperature of 0°F (−18°C) with a wind gusting at 40 mph (64 km/h) would have the same effect as a temperature of −54°F (−47°C) with no wind.

Most precision work is manual, literally meaning "performed by the hands." The hands are the most difficult part of the body to keep warm, because hands have the greatest amount of surface area to volume. Victims of exposure to cold weather are more likely to suffer damage to toes, which are harder to protect. Once the skin temperature of the hand drops below 60°F, manual performance decreases. One of the hardest challenges in aero-

space clothing is to design a glove that gives mechanical and thermal protection while allowing finger movement.

Air pressure

Atmospheric pressure (also known as barometric pressure, since the measuring instrument is a barometer) is of professional interest to weather forecast-
ers and to people who dive under water or travel to high altitudes. Humans
can tolerate wide extremes of ambient air or water pressure. The problem
with low air pressure is not the pressure itself but the lack of oxygen. Military
crews are expected to operate at altitudes as high as 30,000 feet at **ambient**
(local) air pressure. However, above 10,000 feet they must be protected from
hypoxia, insufficient oxygen. (Slight effects of hypoxia occur during prolonged exposure to an altitude as low as 5,000 feet in sensitive or unaccli-
matized individuals; at 25,000 feet, they'd soon pass out.)

Extreme *pressures* can be tolerated, but rapid *changes,* especially to a
lower pressure, are dangerous. The most serious aspect of *decompression sickness* is the formation of nitrogen bubbles in the bloodstream, a response to
the same laws of physics that cause bubbling in a soda bottle when you take
the top off. It is to avoid this condition that divers must ascend to the surface
slowly, and combat pilots are outfitted with pressure suits for high altitudes.

Air pollution

Pollution is a vague and affect-laden term. Chemicals such as chlorine, fluo-
rides, or minerals may be considered as pollutants or as treatments, depending
on origins and attitudes. The same bacterial count could be considered evidence of purity in one case and of pollution in another.

Atmospheric pollution has always existed, but it used to derive from
sources that people could generally detect by smell. Currently, the most lethal
contaminants (like asbestos fibers or nuclear radiation) are undetectable to
human senses. Moreover, much industrial pollution exposes not only the
employees but also the surrounding community to toxicity.

Pollution is a widespread problem. Carbon monoxide can build up in
poorly ventilated areas where there are high levels of engine exhaust and
cigarette smoking. Farmers and groundskeepers may be exposed to dangerous
chemicals from pesticides. Workers in industries involving lead (such as battery manufacturing), asbestos, nuclear energy, and older, large electrical trans-
formers containing PCBs are vulnerable to the long-term effects of low-level
exposure. In terms of demonstrated harmful effects, atmospheric and water
pollution attracts public alarm, but noise pollution is underrated as a health

FRANK AND EARNEST. Reprinted by permission of Newspaper Enterprise Assoc., Inc.

hazard. This is no doubt related to the fact that noise is apparent, whereas other pollutants are, with few exceptions, hidden.

Radiation

An *ion* is an atom that has lost or gained an electron and, trying to restore its rightful balance, is chemically reactive. Ionizing radiation has the ability to penetrate most substances, including your body, and then to form ions. The effects of ionizing radiation—various illnesses or even death—would be of concern if you work in a hospital or laboratory that uses X rays or radioactive isotopes in diagnostics, treatment, or research.

Radiation is complex to measure because there are various types. Gamma radiation, a common form, is calibrated in **roentgens**. The amount of radiation absorbed by the body is measured in **rads**, and the biological effect of the radiation absorbed is defined as **rems** (**r**oentgen **e**quivalent, **m**an).

Another form of ion, quite different from ionizing radiation, is negatively ionized *air*. Air ionizers, widely available for use in homes, are touted as having a wide assortment of beneficial properties. The rationale behind the claim is that the clean, fresh smell associated with the outdoors right after a severe thunderstorm results from the passage of lightning bolts that increase the proportion of negative ions. The next link in the chain of logic, which is somewhat weaker, is that people feel better in the ionized air.

In the 1950s a number of studies attempted to show favorable biological and behavioral effects of negative ions in animals and humans (for example, Kornblueh, Piersol & Speicher, 1958). The beneficial claims were not substantiated by any satisfactory theoretical basis, nor were they replicated by subsequent research. (Ions purportedly healed injuries, improved moods, helped respiration, and facilitated vigilance, for instance.) One review (Frey, 1961) concluded that the total research did not support a conclusion that the relative concentration of ions (positive or negative) had any meaningful bearing on human health or performance. No subsequent body of evidence has yet supported the installation of negative ion generators where people work, sleep, perform critical tasks, or recover from illness. Nonetheless, these devices are widely promoted.

NOISE

A useful definition of **noise**, suggested by McCormick (1970), is "unwanted sound that has no informational relationship to the task or activity at hand." Industrial noise involves two concerns, the noise to which workers are exposed on the job (and its effect on both job performance and worker health) and the noise that the overall operation imparts to the larger community.

How does noise affect performance? This was a popular undergraduate research question a few years ago. The hundred-odd published academic studies that have addressed this issue led to the conclusion that performance may be increased, decreased, or unchanged by noise. The inconsistent results are due less to the noise itself than to the interpretations associated with it.

Consider this example. Suppose that as a research participant you reported to a laboratory where a person in a white lab coat asks you to start counting the beans in a jar. As you get started, the room starts to rumble and vibrate. Knowing that the lab has vibratory capacity, you dismiss thoughts of earthquakes or explosions, grit your teeth, and continue your assigned task with minimal decrement. Now switch the scene to your kitchen. Again, you're measuring or counting something. Suddenly your kitchen starts to rumble and vibrate. Presumably, your performance would undergo an interpretation-related decrement.

Or consider airport noise. In one city (which we may call Obee City), residents around an airport have been complaining about being disturbed by hobby pilots flying at night. Meanwhile, a second city (which we may call Skare City) is blockaded; all supplies must be airlifted in after dark. Objective measurements show more noise at the airport of Skare City, but the noise induces a comfortable sleep, whereas the noise in Obee City causes insomnia and anger. Besides how we interpret it, another variable that affects the response to noise is habituation. A common experience, such as visiting someone who lives close to a subway, and research (for example, Culbert & Posner, 1960) show that people do habituate to noise.

There are established procedures for predicting public reaction to any type of environmental noise. The professionals who can draft such predictions, *acoustical engineers,* also specialize in reducing noise through adjustment of machinery, isolation measures, and the installation of sound baffles. They can also prescribe appropriate hearing protectors, such as ear plugs or earmuffs, which can reduce sound by 40 dB.

MOTION

We have seen the trouble that people can get into, just by staying put. In motion, there are additional problems. The physics of motion is complex, because it involves many parameters, such as direction, acceleration, and velocity. Vibration-like motion includes other variables such as its *frequency* and *amplitude*. The *biomechanics* of the human in motion is even more complex, because it involves posture, seating or stabilizing fixtures, and the body part measurement. Finally, the human engineer has to consider the *psychological* aspects of motion, which involve physiological, interpretive, and training variables, and motion's effect on different types of *tasks*.

A common problem in moving vehicles is *vibration*. In land vehicles, where vibration is primarily vertical, what mainly determines whether the vibrations are increased or decreased is the operator's *posture*. For instance, head motion is substantially reduced through a standing posture, in which the legs act as shock absorbers. Since most operators are seated, seat design has attracted considerable investigation.

In a typical study, Simons, Radke, and Oswald (1956) compared belt-level vibrations at typical heavy truck vibration frequencies of 1 to 6 Hz (**Hz** stands for **hertz**, or cycles per second) with three types of seats: a standard military truck seat, a contoured chair, and a seat with a built-in suspension system. They found that the first two seats amplified the vibrations, whereas the suspension seat reduced them effectively. Suspension seats have become a common option on transport trucks, and they are available on a few sports utility (jeep-type) vehicles.

The effects of *acceleration* and *deceleration* (sometimes termed *positive* and *negative acceleration*) are important in the operation of many types of moving machinery. For instance, drag racers may attain a velocity of 280 mph within 6 seconds. The occupants of space vehicles re-entering the atmosphere experience a velocity change from 25,000 mph down to 3,000 mph within a minute. An aircraft flying through turbulence, a car undergoing heavy braking, people on a roller coaster—all are subjected to the effects of acceleration.

G refers to the pull of gravity; right now you are being pulled toward the ground with a force of 1G. Typical modern combat aircraft are designed to withstand G forces between +15 and −7. That is, the aircraft can pull out of a dive so sharply that it "weighs" or pushes *down* on the wings with 15 times its normal weight. Conversely, the pilot could be flying straight and level at high speed, and then lower the nose so sharply that the aircraft pulls *up* on its wings with 7 times its weight. The aircraft designer guarantees that the wings will not fall off from these stresses. The question is, can the pilot withstand them?

What happens to a seated person under acceleration forces? With +G forces, before 3G is reached the person cannot rise from a sitting position, and **grayout** (the dimming of peripheral vision) begins. At 5G, **blackout**

A fun way to experience the effects of acceleration and deceleration

(blindness) ensues, soon followed by unconsciousness. With −G forces, −3G causes **redout** (the visual field looks red), followed again by unconsciousness. In other words, a seated operator cannot withstand nearly the range of up-down G forces that an aircraft can. However, human tolerance can be increased to over +6Gs through the use of a G suit, which has cuffs that automatically inflate at various body points to counteract G-induced blood flow.

We can withstand considerably higher G forces when they are not perpendicular to the main axis (the up-down line when standing) of the body. Under favorable conditions of training and motivation, seated operators can tolerate 10G and even momentary extremes of +29G and −22G. Since the acceleration needed to attain escape velocity (18,000 mph) is either 2G for 7 min, 5G for 3 min, or 15G for 1 min, it is easy to understand why astronauts lie on their backs during blastoff.

Eiband (1959) estimated that well-designed rear-facing seats could permit injury-free collisions involving 40G, even in aircraft. Another simple and low-cost method to increase survivability would be to instruct people in how to prepare for a collision at the last second. (They should lean forward, especially trying to brace the head against a barrier, preferably cushioned in the hands, arms, or in their coat.)

We have been exploring the effects of *high* G loads, but should also touch on the effects of *zero* G (weightlessness). Initially, the problem in conducting studies of this state was finding a means to demonstrate it here on Earth. Working in a weightless environment was approximated by underwater training. Locomotion was simulated through the use of a buoying harness, and long-term health effects were based on paying volunteers to endure total bed rest. True weightlessness could be induced by putting an aircraft into a **Keplerian trajectory** (an increasingly downward pitch), but this experience is limited to less than one minute.

Now that data are available on the effects of long-term weightlessness in outer space, some conclusions have been reached: (a) Many astronauts subjected to prolonged weightlessness are temporarily incapacitated by motion sickness; this susceptibility cannot be predicted or "trained out" beforehand. (b) The main physiological results are deterioration of the circulatory system and bone density. (c) Under zero G trained people can communicate, operate sophisticated controls, and use a variety of tools. The Russian cosmonaut Valerie Polyakov had lived and worked for 437 consecutive days aboard the space station *Mir* when he touched down in March 1995. (d) Tasks generally take longer to perform under the effects of weightlessness and require specially designed procedures and tools.

Motion-induced illusions

Operators of moving machinery, especially high-performance versions, are subject to many influences that can interfere with normal perception. Pilots are often deprived of clues for visual orientation when flying *blind.* (This refers to flying by instruments rather than by visual reference to the outside.) Divers and astronauts are deprived of most gravitational cues as to which way is up and down. Acceleration gives a false impression of pitching up, deceleration of pitching down. That's one reason why pilots are advised to maintain a constant velocity during final approach, lest they overshoot (land too far down the runway). Another common illusion is that of reverse motion. If a steady motion, such as a turn to the left, is maintained for a prolonged period, as soon as the turn is stopped and the vehicle is moving straight, the operator has the feeling of turning the opposite way.

When a person fixates on a stationary point that appears against a featureless background, after a few minutes the point seems to move around; this is called the **autokinetic effect**. Thus, if you watched a stationary point of light in an otherwise black background, the light will give the illusion of motion. A pilot might be fixating on a bright star to maintain a course and, due to the autokinetic effect, suddenly conclude that the light must be a marker light on another craft and become disoriented when the light later resembles a star again.

Brief case

The hardest single task in the modern world may be that of landing a fighter jet on a carrier at night. Here's why: Landing planes safely requires adhering to standardized procedures, but every landing at sea is different. Moreover, on land it doesn't matter if the plane touches down ahead of or beyond the usual landing point; on a carrier it has to be exact. Land runways don't move, whereas carriers move randomly on all three axes (roll, pitch, and yaw). The carrier itself is moving forward at full speed, but the narrow runway is angled away from the direction of the ship's movement. The pilot, exhausted after a long mission, feels psychological pressure from the low fuel status of the aircraft and the deadly consequences of making the slightest error. Add to all this the perceptual illusions caused by severe deceleration and the lack of visual references other than points of light, and you understand what is meant by task difficulty.

AGING

The more sophisticated the machinery, the more judgment, experience, training, and maturity are called for in its operation. An operator who is entrusted with such equipment should have demonstrated a track record of competence and stability. Logically, then, the most sophisticated machinery should be assigned to the oldest operators. But some of this machinery imposes severe environmental and sensory demands on the operator.

Older people have less muscular strength, less tolerance to temperature extremes, and poorer sensory ability. Hence, an important consideration in the physiological aspects of human engineering is the effects of aging. Aging is a complex topic because various parts of the body "age" differently. Also, some components deteriorate due to age alone, others decline as a function of both age and lifestyle, and a few improve with age.

Vision

When the muscles of the lens are relaxed, the normal eye is focused for long-distance vision. To see close objects, muscles around the lens make its shape more spherical. As people age, almost all become **farsighted**, unable to focus on close-up objects. This condition, in which near objects are focused behind the retina, is called **presbyopia** (from the Greek *presbys,* an old man, and *opos,* eye).

Presbyopia increases gradually at a constant rate from childhood until the fifth decade of life. Thereafter, presbyopia remains constant. One-half of 40-year-olds and three-quarters of 50-year-olds need glasses for reading. This means that most older operators either wear glasses for close work, or that visual displays should not be positioned close to them. It also means that professional eye examinations are called for as a function of the age of the operator and the viewing distance of the work. For instance, a pilot should be able, without moving the head, to focus on a fine-print airport map clipped to the control column two feet from the eyes, primary displays two to three feet ahead, the long-distance view out of the window, and overhead displays one foot away. A pilot with poor accommodation may have to be furnished with multifocal eyeglasses.

Hearing

There are differences between the two "distance senses," vision and hearing, in their susceptibility to both aging and heavy use. Unlike vision, hearing hardly diminishes at all through aging alone. It is true that hearing ability, especially for tones in the higher ranges above 2,000 Hz, diminishes with age in typical groups tested, but these groups are made up of people who have lived among the usual noises of civilization. Audiological examinations of Australian aboriginals, who live in a noise-free environment, show much less decline as a function of old age.

A moderately high level of sensory stimulation, on the other hand, damages hearing but not vision. Someone who reads all day under bright lights will not suffer vision impairment (although extremely bright light will damage the retina). Exposure to moderately intense *sound* causes two types of damage, temporary and permanent. Right after exposure to loud sounds, hearing ability is diminished. By the next day, most, but not all, of the original hearing ability is restored.

How loud is "loud"? Being a musician, a profession that demands acute hearing, induces gradual deafness, especially when the music is amplified. Several studies (for example, Rice et al., 1968) found that rock musicians are deafer than their nonmusical peers, and Axelsson and Lindgren (1982) reported that almost one-half of orchestral players had subnormal hearing.

Sound volume is measured in **decibels (dB)**, a unit of relative sound intensity. It was named after Alexander Graham Bell (a victim of deafness), who invented the telephone merely as a byproduct of his research into audiology. The original unit, the **bel**, turned out to be too large for practical use because the average person can detect differences of a tenth of a bel; hence, the decibel, $\frac{1}{10}$ bel, was adopted. Decibels are calibrated in a logarithmic scale, which means that 60 dB is 10 times as loud as 50 dB. With normal hearing, the loudest sound you can tolerate is almost a billion times louder

TABLE 12.1 Representative sounds in two units of measurement

Decibels	Source	Sones
140	siren at 100 ft	250
130	rock concert at 30 ft	200
120	jet plane at 200 ft	150
110	small aircraft at 100 ft	75
100	riveter (operator)	50
90	heavy industry (worker)	25
80	fast sports car (driver)	15
70	party (guests)	8
60	typical lecture	4
50	office (business)	2
40	office (professor's)	1
20	rustling leaves	0.2

This is a comparison chart of different sound intensities of common sounds, in decibels and sones.

than your *threshold acuity* (the least intense stimulus you can detect). A logarithm scale compresses the numbers by a factor of 10 times for each interval so they aren't unwieldy.

Decibels are *objective* measures of sound pressure, but the *perception* of *loudness* is more important than the reading on a decibel meter. Legislation planned for New York City would have restricted car horns to a specified decibel limit. When it turned out that the traffic noise so masked the perception of the new horns that people ignored them, the legislation was dropped (Garfield, 1983). However, under a 1990 New York law, it is illegal to play a car radio loud enough to register 80 dB from 50 feet away; the penalty can reach $500.

To provide a measure of the *subjective* perception of loudness, a new measurement unit, the **sone**, was devised for easier understanding by the layperson. A quiet ventilating fan might register three sones; a fan that *sounds* twice as loud would show six sones. Sones follow a ratio scale, so if you required an appliance half as loud as one rated at two sones, you would look for one rated at one sone. Table 12.1 contrasts the scales.

In terms of daylong exposure to common frequencies, the sound intensity above which hearing is damaged is 85 dB; at high frequencies (around 10,000 Hz) the danger level is 75 dB. The damage is mainly a function of *volume* and *duration;* a 10-second exposure to 91 dB causes the same damage as a 1-second exposure to 100 dB.

Noise-induced hearing loss is influenced mainly by the noise *"peaks"* and the *pitch* (sound wave frequency) of the sounds. Most jurisdictions require employees to be provided with ear protectors (and warning signs) when the work environment exceeds 85 dB continuously, or 95 dB at any moment. In 1991 Canada set a maximum sound level of 87 dB for federally regulated workplaces. People attending a rock concert or listening to loud music through earphones are probably subjecting themselves to stimulation that would be illegal in the workplace.

LIGHT

Virtually all tasks require some vision, and, therefore, some form of light. Most industrial activity, at least in technologically advanced countries, takes place under *artificial* light. It is to be expected, then, that artificial lighting is of prime concern to the human factors engineer and the environmental psychologist. The following is a simplified outline of this topic.

How light is measured

There are three basic terms to differentiate in *photometry,* the measurement of light.

1. **Light intensity** is the light that comes from a source in a given direction, such as light from the lamp above you now. A standard candle emits one **candela** of light.

2. **Illuminance** is the amount of light falling on a given object. The measurement units are the **lux** or, in the older system, the **foot-candle**. A foot-candle is the amount of light from one candle falling on an object one foot from it; a lux is the light from a candle at a distance of one meter.

3. **Luminance** is the light that is *reflected* by an object (or emitted by an extended source, such as diffusers). Examples are indirect room lighting and lighting from long fluorescent tubes covered with translucent baffles. The unit of measurement, the **footlambert**, is the same as a foot-candle, except that the light meter is aimed at the *work* instead of at the *light source.* (Readings of

footlamberts would be lower than that of foot-candles, unless the work is a perfect reflecting surface.) The metric equivalent is *candela per square meter.*

How the effects of light are measured

One approach for determining the effects of light is to measure *vision* under different illumination. How well we see is defined in terms of **acuity**, of which there are several types. For instance, **minimum distinguishable acuity** measures the smallest detail that the person reports seeing, and **dynamic visual acuity** is the ability to make such detections when the viewer and/or the target is moving. In either case, the subject is usually asked to recognize increasingly smaller stimuli, which may include *letters, gratings* (a series of parallel black and white lines), and *Landholt rings.* The latter are circles with a part missing (like the letter C), and the subject reports where the openings appear.

Many studies measure the *performance* of various tasks under different light levels. Alternatively, researchers may determine the **critical illumination level,** the amount of illumination above which no improvement in performance takes place. And some researchers measure *physiological* responses under varying illumination conditions.

Illumination requirements

Illumination requirements typify the misperceptions that permeate our attitudes to human behavior, especially work-related behavior. The misperceptions derive partly from myths surrounding the variables involved, and partly from the efforts of hucksters wanting to increase sales. Consequently, most industrial, commercial, and educational buildings are slightly overilluminated.

It was an attempt to determine the optimal illumination levels for assembly work that led to the discovery of the Hawthorne effect (page 19). After that false start, research on illumination requirements continued, and it is now known that several variables affect just how much illumination is needed.

   • **Reflectance** refers to the proportion or ratio between the light falling on an object and that bouncing off it. The higher the reflectance, the less the illumination is needed. If the walls, ceiling, and floor are all painted the same, reflectance is increased due to **interflections**, but high reflectance may increase glare. The usual compromise is to reserve the highest reflectance surfaces for the ceiling and upper walls.

   • **Glare** is high-intensity light that reduces your comfort or ability to see clearly. The most common source is a surface that reflects the source light back into the eyes of the operator. It is usually controlled by the number and placement of the **luminaires** relative to the work and the operator, as well as by glare shields and low-glare surfaces. (Luminaire is the technical term for a complete lighting fixture.) Usually several low-power luminaires will cause less glare than one brighter one, but will cost more to buy and operate. One 500-watt luminaire gives off slightly more illumination than five 100-watt ones.

- It's easy to understand **contrast**. Picture two sewing machine operators, both sewing on white cloth, one using white thread and the other working with black thread. Or, look at the period ending this sentence, and imagine trying to find it on black velvet instead of on white paper. What is the effect of *contrast* and *illumination* on *performance?* Performance follows an inverted-U function; it improves with higher illumination up to a point, but then too much intensity causes discomfort and hence lowers performance. The lower the contrast, the lower the performance, especially under dim lighting conditions (Figure 12.3).

- **Luminance ratio** refers to the proportionate difference between the light illuminating *work,* which is usually well lit, and that of the *surround,* which is generally dimmer. Picture the workplace of a dentist or surgeon. The entire room is lit moderately, while a tiny work site is intensely illuminated. For comfort, the luminance ratio should be limited; for instance, the illumination intensity of this page should be no more than three times that of the adjacent surroundings, and no more than 10 times that of the most remote and dark surface in your room. If it is essential to focus attention on detailed work, the ratio can be higher, which is why surgical and dental lights are so intense.

- Is the *type of luminaire* of much consequence? Light sources may be incandescent (the common or tungsten lightbulb), fluorescent, mercury, or sodium, in a number of variants. There is modest evidence that fluorescent lighting leads to fewer errors than incandescent in factory tasks. This may be because fluorescents are more diffuse and therefore prone to less glare.

- The **spectral quality** of the luminaire refers to its color. Just as daylight is faintly blue, incandescent luminaires are yellowish. Fluorescents are inherently more blue-green, but they can be designed to emit various tints. Where the work involves color discrimination, it is important that the luminaires have the appropriate **hue** (color). Colored items are almost invisible under lighting of the same color.

However, research on the spectral qualities of luminaires usually emphasizes the psychological aspects, that is, hues that are supposedly warm, receding, cheering, and so on. The effect of color on behavior and appearance has attracted not only the cosmetic and home decoration industry but also "popular psychology" pseudoscientists who will confidently rec-

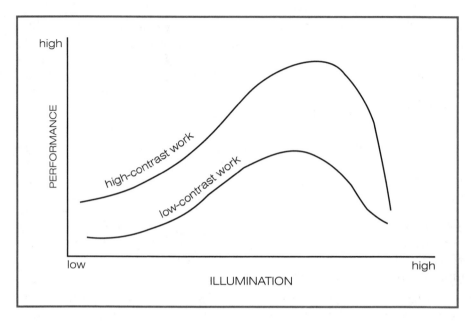

FIGURE 12.3 The effects of lighting on performance

When there is high contrast between figure and ground, performance
is at a higher level than when contrast is low. In both cases, however,
performance declines when illumination becomes too intense.

ommend appropriate colors for specific personalities, stores, and prison cells.
They will even purport to "diagnose" your personality on the basis of your
color preference. So far, the claims seem stronger than the scientific evidence.

DARK ADAPTION

Because of our dependence on sight, HFE sensory research has concentrated
on the visual system. An understanding of even the relatively simple aspect
of dark adaption requires some knowledge of how the eye works.

We "see" the world because light reflected from what we look at stimu-
lates **photoreceptors**, light-sensitive cells on the retina, at the back of the
inside of the eye. There are two types of these photoreceptors. Named after
their shapes, the **rods** and the **cones** have the same basic function, but they
work slightly differently.

So what   Have you wondered why high-tech consumer equipment seems to be associated with certain colors? Audio components are mostly black; computers and printers all seem to be the same nondescript tan. If a store offered an attractive pink stereo or red computer, should you be different and buy them? The answer is yes and no, and it all has to do with glare. Years ago, professional cameras were finished in matte (dull or nonreflective) black, so that in extreme close-up photography the lighted object wouldn't reflect off the camera surface and back to the object, causing a slight overexposure. Black became associated with quality high-tech goods, and makers of audio equipment started copying the camera look, which is why you can't tell the amplifier from the CD player in dim light. If a pink stereo appeals to you, buy it! Around your computer screen, you don't want glare off the frame. A black frame would cause uncomfortable contrast; a very rough white surface would be hard to keep clean. The color known as "putty" turned out to be the best compromise. Other components such as printers are standardized on putty for consistency.

Cones permit the perception of color, form, and motion, but require high levels of illumination to do so. Rods are blind to color and to fine form. They merely detect motion of fairly large objects, but they do so even in minimal light.

The rods are located around the periphery of the retina, which is why you might see a moving object out of the corner of your eye without being able to tell what it is. Cones are located throughout the retina, and are most densely packed in a small depression on the retina, the **fovea**. Since there are many more rods and cones (in the peripheral or nonfoveal retina) than there are axons (pathways) connecting with the optic nerve, dozens or even hundreds of receptors share each axon. But in the fovea, each cone has its own "private line," allowing maximal acuity from the fovea.

Whereas peripheral vision covers a field of about 180 degrees, the foveal cones subtend an angle of about 2 degrees. This means that there are two visual systems, a narrow one for **high-resolution** work such as reading, and a broad one for peripheral motion detection, especially in dim light. (Resolution is a measure of visual acuity, the ability to resolve, that is, differentiate, fine lines.) These structural and functional aspects of the eye are shown in Figure 12.4.

When the eye is dark adapted (adjusted to darkness), it can just detect the amount of light represented by one candle at a distance of 30 miles.

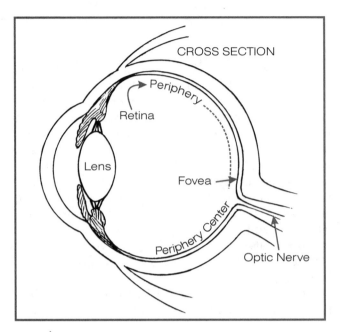

FIGURE 12.4 Cross section of the eye

When the eye is light adapted (adjusted to bright light), you could raise them to the noonday sun, flick them open for an instant, and see the sun (though a prolonged look would be painful and damaging). The range of intensities between these two extremes is a billion to one!

It is possible for a sensory organ to function over such an extreme range because it has a sophisticated system for adjusting the intensity-range. The change from day to night vision is due partly to the *iris,* the opaque, pigmented circle with an opening (the *pupil*) in the center. The size of the pupillary opening changes, causing the amount of light admitted to the retina to vary, but only by a factor of 16 to 1. That is, the pupil admits 16 times more light when dilated than when constricted. Obviously, some other mechanism accounts for the difference between the dark- and light-adapted state.

This mechanism is the switch between *rod vision* and *cone vision.* Under bright light the cones, particularly those located in the fovea, permit high-resolution, narrow-field perception. Thus, to read these words, the eye jumps its gaze point in rapid, controlled, but jerky changes called **saccades**, each encompassing about eight characters. The normal duration of these fixations is about $\frac{1}{4}$ second, but can be less when the eye is rushing. In dim light the cones are not functional, so the rods are active. The intensity of the ambient light determines which photoreceptors are active, the rods or the cones, for they are not designed to both be "on" together. The eye's switch

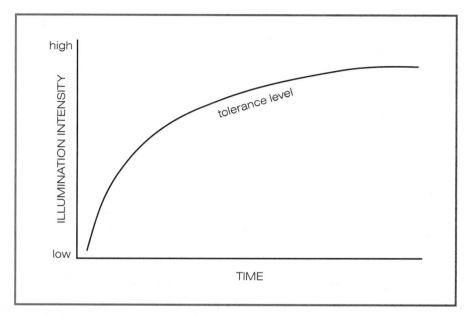

FIGURE 12.5 The light adaption curve

Adaption from darkness to light takes a few minutes, as the eye's photoreceptors that respond to bright light—the cones—become active.

from rods to cones is **light adaption**; changing from cones to rods is **dark adaption**.

Light adaption takes place in only a few minutes. For instance, after you attend an afternoon motion picture, you are dazzled when you first step into daylight, but become light adapted in a few minutes. When you go from daylight into a dark room, you become halfway dark-adapted in five minutes, and almost completely dark-adapted in a half hour, a slower process than light adaption. A graph that plots the stimulus threshold on the vertical axis and time on the horizontal axis makes up an *adaption curve*.

Figure 12.5 shows a *light-adaption curve*, which is constructed as follows: A person, kept in a totally dark environment for an hour, then is asked to adjust a variable light to be as bright as tolerable, as quickly as possible. The increasing intensity of the light plotted against time makes up the light-adaption curve.

A **dark-adaption curve**, shown in Figure 12.6, is constructed as follows: A light-adapted person is suddenly placed in total darkness. A light is gradually brightened until the person just detects it. The minimum amount of a stimulus that can be perceived is the **stimulus threshold**. These, plotted over time, make up the dark-adaption curve.

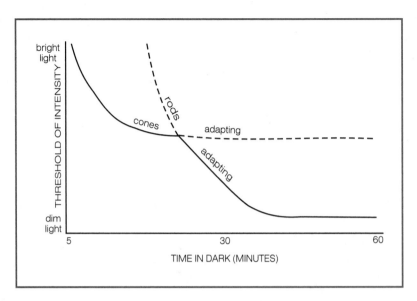

FIGURE 12.6 The dark adaption curve

This curve is two curves. It is constructed by bringing a light-adapted person into total darkness, and then gradually brightening a light to the stimulus threshold. This level, the threshold of vision, plotted over time makes up the dark adaption curve.

The dark-adaption curve is really two curves. The curve showing the rapid change over the first 5 or 7 minutes is the result of the cones *increasing in sensitivity*. By the time their maximum sensitivity is reached, cone activity is replaced by rod activity. Like the cones, the rods show a rapid increase in sensitivity for about 5 minutes, and a further, more gradual increase over another 25 minutes.

Cones and rods differ slightly in the color they are most sensitive to. Cones respond best to yellow-green; rods are most sensitive to blue-green. To understand this statement, picture a row of variable-intensity lights, each with a different colored filter, with intensities adjusted so that each light has the *same objective brightness* shining through the filter. (The darker the filter, the more intense the light would have to be.) If all the lights started at a subthreshold (invisible) intensity and were gradually increased, the first that would be detected by the light-adapted eye would be yellow-green. The first seen by the dark-adapted eye would be blue-green (but since rods do not see color, the blue-green light would be perceived as gray). The sensitivities to different colors are shown in Figure 12.7.

The difference between rods and cones is complex, and not all current applications are based on a full understanding of this factor. For instance, some automobiles use red as the color of their "ergonomic" dashboard dis-

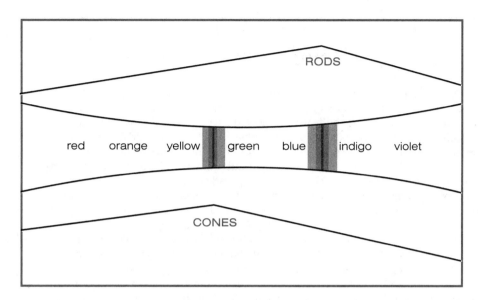

FIGURE 12.7 The sensitivity of rods and cones across the color spectrum

Rods are most sensitive to the blue range and cones to the yellow range. The differences within each of the two lines are exaggerated.

plays. This gives only a minor benefit because a car driver cannot attain full dark adaption as long as headlights are illuminating the road.

Some traffic safety engineers assume that marker lights on night vehicles should be blue, as that is the color best seen by the dark-adapted eye. They are wrong. Blue is the best color for threshold dark adaption only in that if the dark-adapted eye is shown a red and a blue light that are equally intense, the blue will be seen first. But a blue-green light would be seen before the blue one. Moreover, a blue filter greatly reduces a light's intensity. Thus, an unfiltered light will be detected at night long before the same light covered with a blue filter. Also, night drivers are unlikely to be fully dark adapted. (In the 1950s it became popular to install a transparent blue disc on the stoplights of one's car. Some drivers used to put dim blue lights around the windshield. A little thought will show that these were not useful steps.)

Does all this mean that blue should no longer be used as marker signals on vehicles such as highway snowplows? Consider that the worst choice for stop-and-go traffic signals is red and green because of the prevalence of red-green color blindness. Still, these colors should be kept because they now constitute a display stereotype in that they have become universally recognized signals for STOP and GO. Drivers are now used to a flashing blue light indicating a fire vehicle or slow-moving truck. Many jurisdictions reserve the color *chrome yellow* for school buses only.

Brief case

During the night bombing of British cities in the early 1940s, the German crews operated under blackout conditions, both to avoid detection and to maintain dark adaption. By the time the bombers were detected by the British, the bomber crews were in a state of dark adaption that the British pilots would need over 30 minutes in pitch blackness to match. The British could have maintained all crews in darkness every night, while the pilots waited for a signal indicating that the bombers were approaching their particular sector. Knowing that the rods are least sensitive to the *red* end of the spectrum, human engineers arranged for the RAF pilots to be supplied with dark red goggles to wear while waiting.

How did this work? Since rods are least sensitive to red, in a dark red environment they saw nothing but darkness. In this state, rods underwent the chemical changes constituting dark adaption, that is, the eyes became dark adapted. Since cones do respond well to red, they remained partly light adapted under the goggles, thereby allowing the pilots to read, play billiards, or chat naturally. That is, the eye was designed to be either dark or light adapted. But under dim red illumination, the eye is both dark adapted *and* partly light adapted.

There is little equipment that cannot benefit from the application of the ergonomic principles that have been outlined in this chapter.

The main determinant of further application is *public acceptance*. For instance, the Citröen, the most ergonomically advanced car sold in North America in the 1960s, was a sales disaster. Public acceptance requires public education. It is hoped that long after you have finished the course for which you are reading this, you will look for proper human engineering in your purchases and let the manufacturers know when you find deficiencies.

Study guide for chapter 12

HAVE YOU LEARNED THESE NAMES AND TERMS?

bank and pitch

anthropometry: dynamic and static

work space envelope

metrology, bimetrology

environmental psychology

bipolar

acclimatization

convection, radiation

windchill, windchill index

ambient; hypoxia

roentgens, rads, rems

noise

hertz (Hz)

G units, positive (+G) and negative (−G)

grayout, blackout, redout

Keplerian trajectory

autokinetic effect

farsightedness, presbyopia

decibel (dB), bel, sone

light intensity

candela

illuminance

lux

foot-candle

footlambert

acuity

minimum distinguishable acuity and dynamic visual acuity

critical illumination level

reflectance, interflection

glare

luminaire

contrast

luminance ratio

hue; spectral quality

photoreceptors: rods and cones

fovea

high-resolution

saccade

adaption: dark and light

dark-adaption curve

stimulus threshold

ISSUES TO CONSIDER

What are the implications of marketplace globalization for anthropometrists?

Why is *dynamic* anthropometry more complex than static anthropometry?

Why is it inadvisable to try to discard the inch system of measurement?

What's the difference between personal space and territoriality?

Why is it difficult to generalize results of environmental psychology research?

What is "noise"?

What is the distinction among *blackout, redout,* and *grayout?*

What is the difference between aging effects in the eyes and the ears?

Why are many buildings overilluminated?

What would be the worst color to use on maps for pilots who fly at night?

What would be the effect of not having any foveas?

What indicates that dark adaption is not due solely to changes in the iris?

What color should the instruments of a car be at night?

Should color-choice for safety be based solely on physiological factors?

SAMPLE MULTIPLE-CHOICE QUESTIONS

1. The environmental variable that attracts most *attention* is
   a. precipitation.
   b. wind.
   c. humidity.
   d. temperature.

2. Compared to acclimatization to *heat,* acclimatization to *cold*
   a. takes more time.
   b. takes less time.
   c. takes the same amount of time.
   d. this issue has not been studied

3. At what elevation is the beginning of *hypoxia* possible?
   a. 1,000 feet
   b. 5,000 feet
   c. 10,000 feet
   d. 25,000 feet

4. The *critical level of illumination* is
   a. lighting appropriate for critical tasks.
   b. the lighting level that initiates criticisms.
   c. the lighting level above which performance does not improve.
   d. the lighting provided to inspectors and critics.

5. Which takes place faster, dark adaption or light adaption?
   a. dark adaption
   b. light adaption
   c. neither; they are both the same
   d. this is not yet known

Answers: page 462

Speech is civilization.

Henry Brooks Adams (1838–1918)

Bird's-eye view of the chapter

This chapter deals with a new topic in I/O psychology: communication ergonomics. It will give you interesting and sometimes surprising information on common items. These include books, typewriters, video display terminals, and the English language. Finally, the chapter covers ways in which word choice affects behavior.

Chapter 13
Communication ergonomics

The payoff from chapter 13   You will:

1. Know the importance of words
2. Know what is meant by *intelligibility* and how it is measured
3. Understand how the English language presents ergonomic problems
4. Understand *solutions* to the above problems
5. Realize that there are various levels of "technical" English
6. Know the meaning and importance of *text*
7. Appreciate the principles of *text layout and design*
8. Understand various *keyboard* designs
9. Understand the special problems associated with *video display terminals*
10. Understand the application of communication principles for *traffic* regulation
11. Know the meaning and implications of *color blindness*
12. Appreciate the meaning and principles of effective *documentation*
13. Know that clarity and affective factors are influenced by *word choice*

O ur ancestors initially communicated nonverbally. It was when the spoken word was added to the gestures and grunts that our forebears became human. It is primarily this use of *language* that sets the human apart from the millions of other species.

The history of the human species—and especially of civilization—is also the history of **communication**. In fact, our species probably owes its survival to its communicative abilities. The first humans were unlikely contenders in the competition for survival. Without fangs, claws, armor, agility, or speed, they relied upon cooperation among themselves and on their ability to impart their knowledge to their children. This cooperation and education, in turn, relied on speech. Our ancient communication system, the voice, still accounts for most human communication.

SPEECH

In view of the considerable time you have spent reading, the next statement may surprise you. Most of the world's communication is *voice-to-ear,* not paper-to-eye. Consider the height of technological sophistication, the space program. During each second of every mission, thousands of bits of information are sent between spaceship and ground. But when a malfunction almost doomed the Apollo 13 mission, this information was not conveyed by telemetry, but by command module pilot Jack Swigert announcing, "Houston, we've got a problem."

Measuring intelligibility

Speech is understood by the listener not simply from the words themselves, but from the context or expectation, and from the speaker's nonverbal signals. One study documented how much more easily speech was understood when the listener not only heard but also *saw* the speaker (Sumby & Pollack, 1954). Yet, in telephone, aircraft, battlefield, and other areas of technical communication, the listener does not see the speaker. Artificially produced simulated voices, or *synthetic speech,* are becoming commonplace. In the simpler version, prerecorded messages such as "Fasten your seat belt" are played as required; in the modern version, the machines are loaded with **phonemes**, the basic sound elements of speech, and a computer combines the phonemes into words and phrases. Machines regularly announce emergency messages to operators and will soon be routinely used to convert the printed page into language for sightless listeners.

Given the prevalence of situations where the speaker and listener cannot see one another, it's easy to appreciate the necessity to quantify speech *in-*

Brief case

Throughout most of warfare's history, the commander on a hill could survey the entire battlefield and send simple instructions by sound signals or flag displays or via messengers on fast horses. High-tech communication meant signal mirrors or carrier pigeons! Today, the command structures and processes are more complex, and the speed and range of offensive capabilities are staggering. Clear, detailed, and unambiguous communication is essential.

Yet, Orlov (1993) points out that military researchers focus on hardware, not on communication. "Few authors address what army operators say after pressing the push-to-talk button on their radios. Commanders must say what they mean and subordinates must understand what they hear. An army can have the most technologically advanced communications systems available, but if the soldiers do not understand what they say or hear, then they are unlikely to succeed in battle." He also observes that in the U.S. Army's *Operational Terms and Symbols* field manual, there are no definitions for "defeat" or "destroy," terms that are important to the commander who is trying to communicate what is to be done to the enemy. Proper communication can result in life or death on the battlefield; it can also determine the survival or failure of a modern business for the same reason.

telligibility. There are, according to Adams (1989), four types of test material that are used to assess intelligibility:

1. The listener can be asked to write *nonsense syllables,* such as faz or zaf, that are presented by a standardized voice.
2. An alternative is to use *phonetically balanced words,* whose sounds are proportional to those used in ordinary talking.
3. In the *modified rhyme list* technique, the listener hears a target word and has to identify it from a list that includes both the target and other words that rhyme with it.
4. Finally, in the *sentence test,* standard sentences are spoken and written down by the listener.

More of such research is performed on English than on any other language. It's a good thing, as will be shown in this chapter.

Ergonomic problems of English

The *technical* versions of voice-ear communication, such as those used in aviation, are mostly in English. Unfortunately, the English language presents many communication problems.

There are dozens of **homonyms** (also termed homophones), words with different spelling and meaning but identical pronunciations, such as threw and through and faun and fawn. Homonyms can appear even in threes: to, too, two; wails, whales, Wales; Gail, gale, Gael; their, they're, there; by, bye, buy; Don, don, dawn; we, wee, whee; your, you're, yore; yew, you, ewe; Gay's, gays, gaze; pale, pail, Pale; rain, reign, rein; and peek, peak, pique. There are words that are even spelled and pronounced the same, but which can be used as either a noun or a verb, and not always in the same way. Examples are bear, tie, effect, and wake.

The meaning of such words is clear only when they are used in context and in writing. Consider the sentence *We took the lead in environmental protection, led by our research on lead contamination.* As another example, I once announced in class—so the students thought—"You'll have to use eunuchs"; the computer system I was referring to was Unix.

Consequently, English is a poor language for verbal transmission through background static, that is, where the signal-to-noise (S/N) ratio (page 367) is poor. The S/N ratio is the strength of the signal divided by the strength of the background noise. The dB units (page 387) of sound pressure use a logarithm scale, in which the denominator of a fraction is subtracted from, not divided into, the numerator. Hence, if the signal were 50 dB in a background noise of 30 dB, the S/N ratio would be 20 dB. An S/N ratio of zero means that the background noise is as loud as the signal; a negative ratio indicates that the noise is louder than the signal.

The main problem in talking and listening in high-noise situations is that English contains many rhyming, monosyllabic words. All the following, for instance, might be used in aerospace: You, drew, flew, true, blue, knew, view, skew, grew, blew, slew, new, chew, due, dew, and do. Whew! This is particularly a problem because the electrical transmission of words often "clips" the beginning of a sound. (Sometimes the transmission system needs a moment of energization before it transmits a sound and thus loses the initial sound.)

Some systems are designed for "peak clipping" to eliminate sounds that are too loud. In short words, the first sound is often the loudest. Under clipping conditions, rhyming monosyllables cannot be distinguished from one another. Nor is it possible to differentiate among the letters A, J, K, or among B, C, D, E, G, P, T, V. Picture this conversation over a static-filled radio:

"This is crew 'B.'"

"Did you say crew 'B' or crew 'G'?"

"'B' for 'Bertie.'"

"Thank you, crew 'G' for 'Gertie.'"

Apart from the problem of rhyming, many letter names are *homonyms,* as in B (bee), C (sea), I (eye), J (jay), P (pea), R (are), T (tea), U (you), Y (why). Many digits are also homonyms, as seen in the words *won, too, for,*

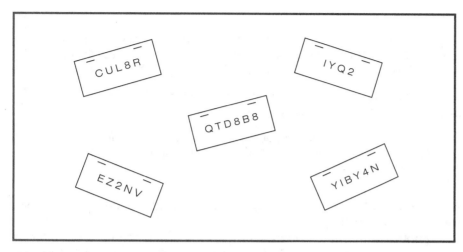

FIGURE 13.1 Homonyms on license plates

ate, and *oh.* (To stretch a point, we could add *sicks,* as in "He sicks his dog on strangers.")

A small American brewery ran this print advertisement for some time with no problem: PFEIFFER'S: THE BEER WITH THE SILENT "P" but ran into a homonym problem when the ad was spoken over the radio! As a final example, many personalized license plates are based on homonyms (Figure 13.1).

Solutions to English's ergonomic shortcomings

Problems of clarity in English are reduced by spelling the words with the **phonetic alphabet**, in which each letter is replaced by a standardized word. For instance, instead of spelling "ergonomics" ee, are, gee, oh, en, oh, em, eye, sea, ess (the foregoing is *phonetic spelling,* not to be confused with the *phonetic alphabet*), it would be spelled Echo Romeo Golf Ocean November Ocean Mike India Charlie Sierra in the phonetic alphabet (Figure 13.2).

After a number of variants, the phonetic alphabet has been standardized and is now in worldwide use. Although its components, Alfa, Bravo, Charlie, Delta, and so forth sound simple, they have special characteristics. The words are *distinctive* (none sounds like any other), *immune to clipping interference* (they do not rhyme with each other), have *high penetrance* (they "push through" static), and are *multilingual* (they can be pronounced by people of various non-English languages). Most of the words in the phonetic alphabet (all but two) have at least two syllables. The two-syllable ones are **spondees,**

ALFA BRAVO CHARLIE DELTA ECHO FOXTROT GOLF HOTEL INDIA
JULIETT KILO LIMA MIKE NOVEMBER OSCAR PAPA QUEBEC ROMEO
SIERRA TANGO UNIFORM VICTOR WHISKEY XRAY YANKEE ZULU

FIGURE 13.2 The phonetic alphabet

The words of the phonetic alphabet were selected for their distinct-
iveness; they do not rhyme, and they can push through static.

words in which both syllables are equally and strongly accented, like railroad, staircase, or baseball.

Another solution to communication problems is the use of a *restricted, specialized vocabulary.* In the 1965 motion picture *The Bedford Incident,* an American destroyer had flushed a Russian submarine to the surface after a long, harrowing chase. Each had the capability of destroying the other; tension was high. After many hours of nonstop concentration, the radar and weapons control officer on the *Bedford* collapsed and was replaced by a junior officer. The "Fire" button on the new antisubmarine weapon was exposed, and the safety cover removed.

Not long after the gung ho captain of the *Bedford* rammed the sub, he assured his officers, "The *Bedford* will never fire first. But if *they* fire one, *we'll* fire one." The inexperienced missile officer, a finger on the FIRE button, heard the captain say the words "Fire one," and his finger jabbed the button. With this reflex, a sub-seeking torpedo was launched into a ballistic trajectory, to float down by parachute. A minute later, when the Russian captain heard it hit the water, he knew that all on the sub had but a moment to live. At the last moment, he launched four nuclear-warhead torpedoes at the *Bedford.*

Fiction became reality 23 years later (at least in terms of the fatigue factor and the failure to obtain confirmation). During the Iran-Iraq War, sleepless American seamen were patrolling the Persian Gulf escorting oil tankers through the Strait of Hormuz. They mistook the confusing radar signal from an off-course Iranian passenger jet for an Iraqi fighter jet starting an attack run. Almost 300 innocent lives were destroyed by one push of a finger.

Similarly, loss of life due to the misuse of restricted, specialized vocabulary is not confined to film fiction. Air traffic controllers routinely instruct pilots, "Clear the intersection" or "Clear the active [runway]," meaning "Scram—now!" At a Canadian west coast airport, the controller radioed the operator of a runway snowplow to "CLEAR THE RUNWAY." The plow operator assumed that the instruction meant to stay on the runway—clearing the snow. The plane, just on the point of touchdown, crashed into the plow. The problem was that "insider" language was used on an "outsider" who had not been instructed in it.

Even among insiders, specialized language can be misused. A passenger jet pilot, realizing that the impending landing had to be aborted because the speed was too high, suddenly needed maximum thrust, an extreme power setting used only at takeoff. Pulling back on the control yoke to gain altitude, he barked the nonstandard phrase "TAKEOFF POWER" to the copilot. The latter, assuming that the pilot wanted the power off, killed the engines. Once again nobody survived.

In technical, critical communication, the specialized, restricted *vocabulary* is used according to a standardized **syntax**, that is, rules for the *use* of these words. These conventions are applied differently by (a) casual air users such as citizens band (CB) operators, notably truck drivers, and service operations such as delivery, repair, and taxi drivers and dispatchers; (b) police, fire, ambulance, and civil defense operations; and (c) air traffic and military users. The more serious the *consequences* of misunderstanding, the more strictly the rules are applied.

Consider the common situation in which one person wants to communicate to the other, "Repeat your last recent transmission; I did not fully understand it." Such a message is often interrupted under poor transmitting conditions.

Without standardization, the wording could be, "Wait a moment; what was that you just said?" "Pardon?" "Would you mind repeating your very last message?" "Excuse me, I didn't get that last bit." "I beg your pardon; would you mind repeating the last sentence?" "Hold on; I didn't quite understand about the last stuff." "What was that?" "Just a sec, there, I missed the very last part of what you said." All such variants are replaced by the standardized phrase SAY AGAIN.

Or consider a police dispatcher who needs to communicate, "Would all of you officers on duty out there get a pen and pad ready right away. If you're driving I'll give you a moment to slow down first. I'll be giving you a description of a car we want you to be on the lookout for. And after you write down what I give you, keep your pen poised because I'm going to follow this with a description of a suspect to keep your eye out for. Okay, ready?" The same message, using standardized, restricted vocabulary and standardized syntax, would be HEADQUARTERS: ALL UNITS, TWO ITEMS.

Other common messages in communication where the S/N ratio is close to zero involve whether or not a message is understood and the answers of "yes" and "no." "Did you get that?" or "Did you hear me?" are signified with the verb **copy**, as in "Copy?" "Copy." "Yes" and "no" are replaced by "affirmative" and "negative" (though under extreme clipping conditions affirmative and negative can be confused).

A specialized vocabulary reduces misunderstandings mainly because of its reduced repertoire of terms. The effect of vocabulary size on intelligibility was shown in a classic study by Miller, Heise, and Lichten (1951). Each participant was given a list of words to review. Then the words from the list were presented under various unfavorable S/N ratios, down to −18 dB. Under

Truck drivers communicate via citizens band radio.

all noise conditions, the fewer the words in the list, the higher the intelligibility. That is, there were more correct word recognitions when the words originated from a 2-word list than from a 4-, 8-, 16-, 32- or 256-word list.

Now that you have the theory behind the ergonomics of radio communication, you may find the application interesting. Below are three examples of the specialized, restricted vocabulary and the standardized syntax, in typical two-way conversations. Note the increased difficulty that you have in understanding the messages as the vocabulary and syntax become more specialized in the progression from citizens band radio to police to air traffic communications. (Keep in mind that as a *reader*, rather than a *listener*, you have the benefit of punctuation.)

Citizens band   "Breaker, breaker; Big Daddy calling on nineteen. Any you goodbuddies gotcher ears on?"

"Hey, Big Daddy, this is Purple Pickup. Uh, what's your twenty, where ya headed?"

"We're a twelve-wheeler tooling along the 401 over by the Fina. What's yours and how ya reading?"

"Real good, Big Daddy. Whatcha haulin'?"

Police   "Three-three-eight, HQ."

"Standby, three-three-eight. [Pause.] Go, three-three-eight."

"I'll be ten-seven for five, and then I'll be taking an early lunch. Would you have S-three ten-nine me on two?"

"Ten-four, three-three-eight."

"Do you want me to head up to the PI for backup?"

"Negative for now, three-three-eight."

"Ten-four. Did my twenty-nine come back yet?"

"You're breaking up, three-three-eight."

"Do you have my ten twenty-nine?"

"Negative."

"Ten four."

Aviation   "Toronto Approach, Charlie Tango Mike Romeo Bravo."

"Charlie Tango Mike Romeo Bravo."

"Cessna one-seven-seven RG, flight level one-zero, squawking one-two-zero-zero, ten miles southeast, with ATIS Echo, landing."

"Tango Mike Romeo Bravo squawk-ident."

"Tango Mike Romeo Bravo."

"Romeo Bravo, descend to three thousand on two-eight-zero; southbound traffic one mile ten o'clock, altitude unknown; winds nine at two-three-zero, runway two-two left; right circuit; third behind seven-four-seven heavy turning final, call at five miles on one-two-six-point-three; check gear down."

"Romeo Bravo out of ten for three on two-eight-zero, call at five on one-two-six-three, traffic and runway in sight, three green."

TEXT

The written word is referred to as **text**; the letters, digits, and other symbols of text are called **characters**. The benefits of this medium of communication have been outlined previously (page 140). We can only guess when text was first used, but we know that writing was well established six thousand years ago.

Dozens of allusions to what we now refer to as text appear in the Old Testament, which, of course, is itself a written document. In fact, biblical references to the written word have become common metaphors, for example, "writ in stone" and the "handwriting on the wall." Indeed, it is hard to imagine the success of the world's major religious or political ideologies without the use of the inscribed word.

With the invention of the printing press around 1450, the importance of written communication rose rapidly. The typewriter, widely used since

1900, essentially put a miniature printing press in most offices and later in many homes. This machine offers an interesting and vivid study of human factors engineering (HFE).

The typewriter

The typewriter played a prominent part in the history of industrial sociology, but we will consider only its HFE aspects. Although originally patented in the early 1700s, the first practical commercial version was sold by Remington and Sons, New York, in the late 1800s. (Electric models first appeared in 1920.)

A standard keyboard arrangement, established in the earliest models, is in universal use today. In this layout, there are four rows of characters, each row containing about 12 keys. Because of the first six letters in the second row from the top, this arrangement is referred to as the "QWERTY" design; it is shown in Figure 13.3.

When Christopher Latham Sholes designed the QWERTY keyboard in the 1870s, his only concern was to reduce the jamming of keys that resulted from typists' fingers outpacing the clumsy key responses. To prevent the operators from exceeding the machine response speed, Sholes distributed the most common letters (E, T, O, A, N, I) throughout the keyboard, and located common letter combinations, for example, as ED, in such a way that all have to be operated by the same finger. Characters that rarely occur together were placed next to each other at the far right and left of the keyboard, since it was the outside keys that had farthest to travel and were most likely to jam.

Sholes's purposefully inefficient QWERTY keyboard actually followed a few HFE principles. For instance, the number and width of the rows reasonably match the capability of human hands. There was a small attempt at assigning the weakest fingers to the rarer characters and the stronger fingers to the more frequently used ones, and the clumsy thumbs were used only for one large space bar. In short, the main design consideration was the minimization of jamming by *slowing the operator.*

When, in the 1930s, the key linkages had been refined to the extent that jamming was no longer a problem, the American psychologist August Dvorak studied character frequency and finger control more carefully. An early human factors engineer, Dvorak designed an ergonomic keyboard.

Dvorak arranged the keys so that the best-controlled fingers, the index and middle ones, operated the most frequently used characters, while the rarely used characters were assigned to the third and fourth fingers. Both hands operated an equal number of characters, whereas the QWERTY keyboard gives 60 percent of the work to the left hand. The ten characters of the "home" (center) row, AOEUIDHTNS, comprise the five vowels and the five most frequently used consonants, with which 3,000 English words can

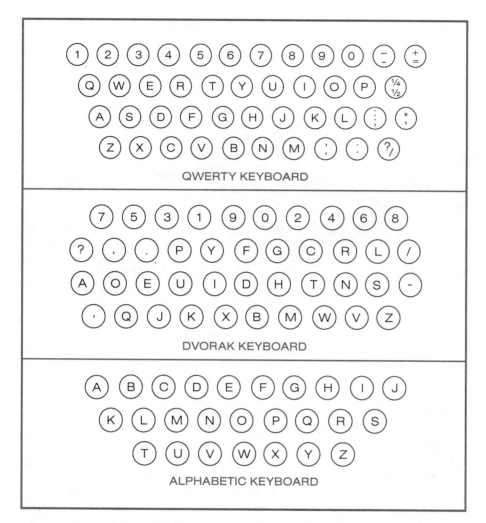

FIGURE 13.3 Three keyboard designs

Even though the Dvorak keyboard increased typing speed, the
QWERTY design held firm and still prevails.

be spelled. (The home row of the QWERTY design, ASDFGHJKL, can make
only 100 words.)

The strongest support for Dvorak's design came from a U.S. Navy study,
which concluded that this keyboard increased typing speed by at least 25
percent. Some typewriter companies offered it, but sales were poor. The several millions of QWERTY models in use created a standard that became impossible to dislodge. (We-have seen, in earlier chapters, that good ergonomics
frequently fails to translate into good sales.)

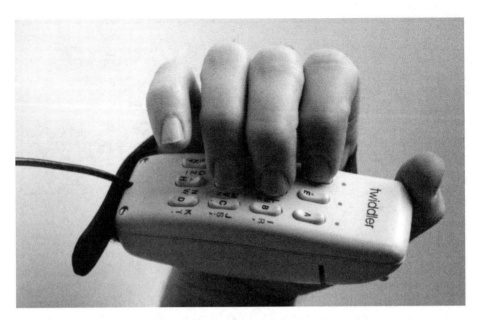

An input device that is both keyboard and mouse, the "Twiddler" frees the entire upper body and arm from having to accommodate to a fixed keyboard.

Although there is some evidence that novices learn to type more easily on the Dvorak keyboard and that experienced operators substantially increase their speed on it, other research weakens the argument that the QWERTY design is an ergonomic disaster. Salthouse (1984) studied typists experienced with the standard keyboard. He knew that key-pressing **latency** (delay between the stimulus onset and the response) is about 250 milliseconds (msec), or a quarter of a second. How, then, did skilled typists routinely perform at double the expected maximum rate? The explanation is that typists do not operate one key at a time, but *groups* of keys, in which motion to more than one key is started simultaneously. It's doubtful, then, that an improved keyboard layout could result in much greater typing speed.

With the modern, touch-sensitive keypads, the third and fourth fingers are not much disadvantaged over the first and second. In fact, an examination of Salthouse's data indicates that the weak fingers average 218 msec per keystroke, while the strong fingers take 212 msec. Since these two figures are virtually identical, there is no longer a strong argument for changing the standard keyboard arrangement, even if it were a practical possibility. Although the standard keyboard violates some principles of HFE, the problem obviously is not serious. Some modern keyboards can be user-programmed to operate under either system, but Salthouse's research reduces the value of the more ergonomic alternative.

For completely inexperienced operators, would not a keyboard that arranged the characters *alphabetically* be best? Each letter would be located approximately where the typist expected it. Norman and Fisher (1982) compared typing speed on an *alphabetic* keyboard, on a *standard* keyboard, and on one in which the keys were arrayed *randomly*. They found that the standard keyboard was best, even though none of the participants had ever operated one. Moreover, the typists did not clearly prefer the orderly, alphabetic arrangement. (The explanation was that since we don't type characters in alphabetical sequence, the standard arrangement makes as much sense as the alphabetic one.)

Text design and layout

A traditional typist has few decisions to make about layout; there are standard formats to follow for the business letter, the personal letter, the legal document, and so on. A book designer, by contrast, has a myriad of choices to make.

There are numerous typefaces with different **fonts**, each in a variety of sizes. Number of columns, margin size, page dimensions, and color are a few of the other variables at hand for the book designer. Increasingly, word processing equipment is offering this flexibility to writers.

Book designers also consider **legibility** or *eye* response (picture a clear, sharp photocopy), and especially **readability** or *brain* response (think of a well-designed block of type). Readability is influenced by the *physiology* of reading. The eye rarely moves smoothly, whether looking around the room or reading. Rather, it moves in saccades (page 394). It is only in the brief (100–400 msec) *resting* state between each saccade that the eye can see. In reading, the eye makes *reading saccades* of rightward movements that take in a **reading field** of about eight characters, *correction saccades,* which are small leftward movements, and *line saccades* in which the eye makes a large leftward sweep to the beginning of the next line.

In normal reading, the eye averages about four saccades per second, each jump fixating on *overlapping* words. (Most words, then, are seen more than once, but the reader has no impression of this.) Each reader adopts a slightly different pattern of these three types, and individual patterns differ according to the difficulty of the material, the concentration of the reader, and the layout of the text. The effect of page design on readability and memory has received little research attention, considering the number of pages that are being studied at any given time.

McKinstry (1988) reported that at normal reading distance (about 40 cm), the maximum span of vision is about 13 cm. Bouma (1983) argued that a **justified** (straight) *left* margin was necessary for moving the eye from line to line efficiently, but not so a justified right one. He also concluded that

THE VISUAL MECHANICS OF READING HAVE BEEN STUDIED TO
DETERMINE THE OPTIMAL FORMAT FOR TEXTUAL MATERIAL OF THIS
GENERAL NATURE. LEGIBILITY REFERS TO WHETHER IT IS POSSIBLE
TO READ A GIVEN CHARACTER OR WORD. THE PRESENT SPECIMEN
MATERIAL IS HIGHLY LEGIBLE, AND CERTAINLY THE TYPE FONT AND
PUNCTUATION ARE CLEAR AND UNAMBIGUOUS. BUT IT MAY NOT BE
AS COMFORTABLE TO READ AS THE REST OF THE MATERIAL.
IMAGINE THE ENTIRE BOOK APPEARING LIKE THIS SAMPLE OF TEX-
TUAL MATERIAL. READABILITY REFERS TO HOW COMFORTABLE A
WORD, PARAGRAPH, OR SCREEN DISPLAY IS. THIS SAMPLE DEM-
ONSTRATESHOWMATERIALCANBEPERFERFECTLYLEGIBLEWITHOUTNE-
CESSARILY BEING VERY READABLE.

THIS IS A SAMPLE OF MATERIAL THAT IS TYPED IN A
FONT THAT HAS NO SERIES TO HELP YOU RECOGNIZE

THE CHARACTERS WHEN YOU ARE ABLE TO SEE ONLY
THE TOP OR BOTTOM HALF OF THEM

HERE, BY CONTRAST, THE SAME THING BUT PRE-
SENTED IN A FONT WITH SERIES YOU MIGHT BE ABLE

TO DETECT THE DIFFERENCE IN READIBILITY, EVEN IN
A FAINTER FONT

FIGURE 13.4 The value of text design and serifs in letter recognition

the minimum ratio between *line length* and *interline space* should be 30:1.
Hence, the longer the lines, the farther apart they should be, lest the eye
skip a line. An example of this is seen in newspaper layout, where maximum
print density is achieved by the use of a two-inch column width.

McLean (1980) recommended that words should be set close to each
other (about the width of the letter "i" apart), and that there should be more
space between lines than between words. If the space between lines is excessive, however, the eye has trouble finding the beginning of each successive
line, which is lower than expected (Lee, 1979).

Type fonts are classified as **serif** or **sans serif**. Serifs are the decorative
little finishing marks at the tops and bottoms of most letters. For large quantities of text, serif fonts are more *readable,* because reading is not as much
a matter of the eye detecting letters as it is the *brain recognizing words.* To
illustrate the value of serifs in word recognition, try to decipher the same
two lines of letters in Figure 13.4. Similarly, lower case (noncapital) letters
are easier to read than upper-case (capital) letters.

THE VIDEO DISPLAY TERMINAL

The latest development in text is a product of the current generation. This is the use of communication equipment that includes a television-like screen for displaying text. We'll call it a **video display terminal (VDT)**; a common alternate name is video display unit.

As electronics and computers made their way into offices, the operator had to communicate with the equipment through punch cards, and the machines replied via a printer. (In VDT terminology, text on paper is a **hard copy**; VDT printers were once called *hard copy terminals*.) It was simply to make this two-way communication more direct that the printer became a television-like cathode ray tube (CRT) display instead of a hard copy, and the punch card step was eliminated. The marriage of computer, keyboard, and CRT was so successful that the VDT suddenly became a common office fixture in industrialized countries. Almost all industries are now dependent upon the VDT.

The VDT makes considerable demands upon the operator. For instance, it's not unusual to enter ten thousand keystrokes per hour. Usually, the only consequence of a reading or typing error is that a magazine is sent to the wrong address or a customer is billed for $300 instead of $30. But a slip in data entry can amount to problems that are not easily rectified. For instance, the Prudential Insurance Company of America held a $93 million mortgage on a shipping company that went bankrupt in 1987. A clerk in the outside law firm hired by Prudential's law firm had recorded the amount as $93,000. The omission of three keystrokes potentially cost Prudential $92,907,000!

Errors in data entry can cost more than money. Pilots, air traffic controllers, and astronauts also watch VDT-like displays for long periods and enter data on keyboards. Here a small mistake could result in an aircraft flying over the wrong country or an astronaut heading for the wrong planet!

Early aircraft were modest performers, operated by pilots who were so enthusiastic that HFE improvements were not sought by manufacturer or operator. In the same way, the early VDTs were not subject to careful HFE analysis. It's not surprising that modern HFE analysis has revealed human design shortcomings in early VDTs, just as was the case in early aircraft.

Visual responses

The VDT operator is required to make three main visual responses: convergence, accommodation, and adaption. These responses occur in all normal vision but are critical in watching a screen.

Convergence refers to the direction of the gaze when the eyes fixate upon a near object. When looking at work that is only arm's length away,

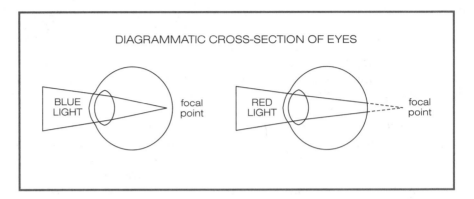

FIGURE 13.5 Focal points of red and blue

Only one color can be in perfect focus at any given time because the eye refracts each color slightly differently. The focal points of red and blue are the farthest apart, and so these colors should not be used together where accurate vision is necessary.

the eyes do not aim straight ahead as they do when looking at a distant object (or when not looking at anything). They converge toward the center, that is, the right eye turns slightly to the left of straight ahead, and the left eye turns to the right, so that they both fixate on the same point. **Accommodation** refers to the focusing of the lens of the eye, so that the image projected on the retina is sharp. **Adaption** refers to the response of the eye to the level of illumination. This response is partly carried out by the iris, which changes the size of the pupillary opening, and mainly performed by the retina itself.

Accommodation is hindered when the characters are fuzzy or when the contrast between character and background is insufficient. VDT characters are inherently less sharp and usually less contrasting with the background than characters printed on paper. The VDT operator typically interchanges the gaze between the screen and printed text or various off-screen elements, and there is generally a distinct brightness contrast between the two. This contrast strains the adaption processes of the eye. Grandjean (1983) reported that 10 percent of VDT operators suffer almost daily eye discomfort, and 50 percent of all operators experience occasional impairments. (However, these prevalence rates are not different in non-VDT users working in similar environments.)

Following television broadcast conventions, early VDTs presented light characters on a dark background. However, both Bauer and Cavonius (1983) and Radl (1983) demonstrated that dark characters on a light VDT background make for substantially better readability and enhanced user comfort. This "printed page" mode is preferable, according to Radl, because contrast between figure and ground is increased, contrast between screen brightness and the papers to which operators often refer is reduced, screen glare and reflections are reduced, and the eye works more efficiently in terms of acuity and depth of focus.

North Americans call the use of dark symbols on a light background **negative contrast**. In Europe, where this mode is more popular, it is called **positive presentation**. (Refer to the section on "The Affect of Word Choice" later in this chapter.) In North America, where VDTs use a slower raster rate—akin to lower resolution—flicker is more of a problem, because it's more noticeable and annoying with light backgrounds. But modern VDTs use a slower "decay" to compensate for the slower raster rate, so a modern North American VDT will still be more pleasing to the user in the negative contrast mode.

Colors have been studied thoroughly. Various hues differ considerably in luminance or brightness. If white is given a luminance of 100 percent, yellow's luminance is 89, green's 59, red's 30, and blue's 13.

Because of the differences in brightness (and for other reasons) colors also vary in *visual acuity,* which is high for white and green, lower for red and blue. That is, you could more easily differentiate the letters e, c, o, or S versus 5, if they are presented in the high acuity colors. Reynolds (1982) also points out that since green is produced by a single electron gun, green characters are likely to be sharp for technical reasons.

Each color is refracted differently through the eye, so only one can be in perfect focus at any given time. If yellow-green or white are in perfect focus, blue will be focused in front of the retina and red behind it (Figure 13.5). Hence, red and blue should never be used in combination where accurate vision is needed. (Blue, the hardest color to focus on, is an unsuitable color for work that requires precise visualization.)

Although some colors are better than others, particularly in terms of individual preference, the color of the display is not as important as adequate contrast between *figure* and *ground.* Different hues with similar luminance ratings do not provide adequate contrast.

Two important attributes of a VDT screen are **resolution** and **acutance**. *Resolution* refers to the finest detail that the screen can display; *acutance* is the sharpness of the border between character and background. As for how long each line of characters on the screen should be, Bassani (1983) proposed that lines should have 40 to 80 characters; this is consistent with recommendations for printed text.

Aspect ratio is the height to width ratio. The early round television screens soon evolved into a more esthetically pleasing 3:4 (three units height, four width) conformation. VDTs perpetuate this horizontal, 3:4 format, although a vertical orientation such as a 4:3 aspect ratio would make high density text easier to read, according to the research of Bouma. Most VDT screens have an aspect ratio of 3:4.4, which is more horizontal than optimal (Figure 13.6).

FIGURE 13.6 Aspect ratios of video display terminals

The most common aspect ratio is 3:4.4.

With the increased popularity of desktop publishing, the newest advances are a literal full-page screen with an 11:8.5 ratio, or a 4:3 screen that can be rotated to make the longer dimension vertical or horizontal.

User complaints

The introduction of *any* new technology typically invites user complaints. It's easy to understand why. The experienced employee suddenly becomes a novice, the innovation is generally perceived as benefiting the employer more than the employee, first generation equipment usually has some ergonomic shortcomings, and change itself is inherently stressful for most people.

Virtually all tasks impose some visual demands on the employee. It is to be expected that some eye complaints are associated with many types of work, and that most VDT-related complaints relate to eye discomfort. But these problems are considered reversible and functional rather than permanent. Indeed, Läubli, Hünting, and Grandjean (1983) found eye impairments in all categories of office employees.

VDT operators have to maintain their heads, arms, and hands in a constrained posture for prolonged periods, so considerable attention has been paid to the optimal positioning of the chair, screen, and keyboard. Observing that most posture-related complaints are due to improper equipment, Grandjean (1983) recommended that keyboards, source documents, and screens be movable rather than fixed, that chairs have high, adjustable backrests, and that a footrest be provided. Most keyboards can be adjusted to have either no incline at all or a slight *positive incline,* in which the back is higher than

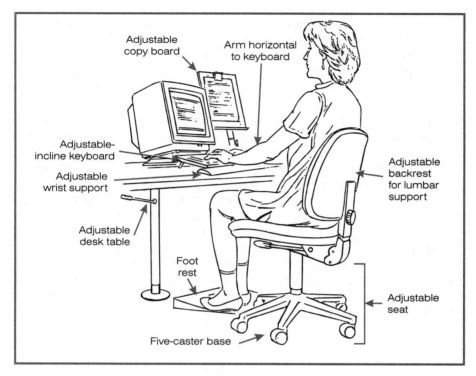

FIGURE 13.7 Optimal video display terminal location

the front. Current research is finding considerable individual differences in incline preference. A few operators who rest their wrists on a support prefer a *negative incline,* apparently because the raised front reduces the chance of hitting keys accidentally. It seems that keyboards should offer much more incline adjustability than almost all of them presently have.

An *optimum location* can be determined for every item of equipment that the user needs to watch or handle. Variables that need to be considered are the importance of the component, the frequency and sequence of use, and the consequences of misuse. Primary displays (those that are most important to monitor) should be located in the *natural sight direction.* This important cone of sharp vision covers 30 degrees, from 15 degrees below horizontal to 45 degrees below horizontal. Secondary displays that are looked at only occasionally should be within 15 degrees of the natural sight direction, because comfortable vision is confined to this arc (Figure 13.7).

The location of *controls* is more complex. It depends, for instance, on the range and type of movement required in their operation, on the strength needed to move them, on their tactile or visual discriminability, and on whether the controls are found visually or "blind" (most—but not all—VDT operators *touch type,* that is, operate the keyboard without looking at it).

Most jobs involve three physical segments, the work, the **surround** (for example, the workbench, or in the case of the CRT the frame of the screen), and the *background* (the room itself, or in the case of the CRT the documents being copied or read). An established principle of ergonomics is that each segment should be no more than three times as bright or dim as the adjacent one. Doran (1983) also recommended that the terminal be furnished with separate controls for brightness and contrast, red or blue not be used in colored characters, flicker be absent even at maximum screen brightness, and that the surround or frame of the screen be free from glare.

Many operators feel uneasy about the long-term effects of radiation such as X rays, radiant energy, and radio-frequency energy emanating from the CRT. This is easy to understand, as radiation is undetectable and harmful, and all of these types can be measured in front of a CRT. However, the levels of radiation from modern units are no higher than that of natural background radiation, which is itself about 1 percent of the safety limits.

The problems revealed by research on VDTs are not as serious as the more extreme user complaints have suggested. Many of these complaints may be due to improper use or training, or to the discomfort commonly associated with the introduction of a new technology.

COMMUNICATING FOR VEHICLE DRIVING

"Oh, *LASER*. Well, I'm sorry, but that still looks like an 'O' on your application to me."

Questions about driving are like questions on how people hold their spoons while stirring their coffee. The behavior may be common, but it does not excite much research interest. Most studies on this topic examine, indirectly or directly, the communication aspects.

What is it that drivers look at? You might assume that the fixation point is the middle of the road ahead, but studies with eye cameras (page 64) indicate that (when a driver is not following another car) the main fixation point is the right edge of the lane, about 200 feet ahead (Gordon, 1966). This finding suggests that road engineers should ensure that the right-hand road edge is clearly demarcated rather than blending into the shoulder.

Road signs are vital to safe and efficient traffic flow. They have to be clear, unambiguous, and nondistracting, and appropriate for both natives and strangers. The messages include permissions, prohibitions, limits, and many types of information. These must be legible day and night from moving vehicles and fully intelligible from the briefest glance possible.

Some of the principles for efficient radioed speech communication apply to the design of road signs. These include the use

FIGURE 13.8 Pictograms in road signs

of a restricted, standardized vocabulary and a standardized syntax. Thus, we see SLOW instead of SLOWLY and CLEARANCE 15′ instead of IF YOU'RE TALLER THAN 15 FEET, YOU WON'T FIT! In addition, road signs make use of *graphic symbols,* which are designs that connote meaning through standardized, self-evident **pictograms**. Some are shown in Figure 13.8.

   Pictograms are stylized figures, many of which have been standardized internationally, such as a knife, spoon, and fork to indicate food availability, or an adult leading a child to indicate a school crossing. Examples of the standardization of otherwise meaningless symbols are the shape of the signs. For instance, an octagon (eight-sided figure) is reserved for STOP messages, and triangular signs always bear cautionary messages.

Color blindness

The most important colors that drivers should be able to distinguish, especially in cities, are red and green. Unfortunately, many drivers are deficient in their ability to distinguish colors, particularly red, green, orange, and yellow. Some degree of color blindness affects about eight percent of males and almost one percent of females. Of the over 10 million Americans and 1 million Canadians who were born color blind, many remain unaware of their vision deficiency.

Fortunately, in addition to being *color* coded, traffic lights are *position* coded with the STOP light located on top and the GO light below. Some are *size* coded as well, with a larger STOP light. And some lights have the word STOP printed on them, but this is identifiable only from close up. In addition, the red is slightly purple and the green slightly blue; some color-deficient drivers can differentiate between them with these alterations of hue.

Since the continued universal use of red and green as the primary color signals now constitutes a *display convention,* it would be impractical to change these colors. A feasible solution would be to add *shape* coding. For instance, an octagon could signify STOP, a circle GO. Such a shape convention could be extended to stoplights on the rear of cars. In parts of Europe, stoplights are square and larger than the round go lights.

The two "most opposite" colors, red and green, reflect early maritime history, when red and green were presumably considered the two most distinguishable colors, particularly in fog. Ships were required to show marker lights, red to denote the left side and green the right. When the first traffic signals were installed in the 1800s, green was arbitrarily chosen for "go" and red for "stop."

As a result, green became associated with safety and red with danger. Emergency vehicles such as fire trucks were painted red, which is unfortunately the color that first becomes invisible under low illumination. Fire departments now have to decide whether to keep the red (the worst color for rod vision, page 394) as a **display stereotype** or repaint the vehicles yellow-green. At night, white or yellow-green would be seen best, but in daylight they would not convey a message of emergency to most people (and they would be less conspicuous against a snow-covered background).

DOCUMENTATION

In casual parlance, **documentation** refers to verification or proof, as in "Let me see your documents." In the specialty of technical communication, documentation refers to the operations manuals or instruction booklets that accompany a complex product.

Prior to the industrial revolution, virtually all products were made in the home or on the farm, for use by that household only. After the mid-1800s, factory-produced, complex equipment for domestic use became widespread. When the first sewing machines were offered to women and the first mower-threshers to farmers, they were accompanied by the first instruction manuals.

Today, even commonplace items are technologically advanced and highly complex. How to set a digital watch, how to operate a videocassette recorder, or how to use a telephone with all sorts of extra buttons is far from intuitively obvious. With a modern computer, the documentation is likely to outweigh the hardware and software combined. With current aerospace, military, and nuclear power plant equipment, the documentation for each unit could fill a library.

Increasingly, users depend on the documentation in order to use the product or system effectively and safely. A recent topic within communication deals with how documentation can be improved.

Principles of effective documentation

Documentation should follow a number of principles for maximal effectiveness:

- The engineers who design the product are generally given the responsibility of writing the instructions for users. It is a mistake to ask people who are thoroughly familiar with the equipment, well-steeped in the terminology and jargon surrounding it, and not experienced in teaching to play this role. Instead, the engineers should explain the procedures to someone skilled in translating them into language that is appropriate to the user.

- To know what language is user appropriate, it becomes necessary to determine the users' background and their approach to the equipment. Consider, for instance, a computerized word processor: One may be installed in an office where the secretaries are happy with their old typewriters and reluctant to become involved with computers, screens, and edit commands. In another office, the secretaries may be computer literate and relieved to have their obsolete equipment replaced by the modern version. In a third case, the equipment may be bought by an independent entrepreneur who wants to play with the latest toy.

Further complicating the definition of the user, one purchaser of the equipment may just want to know, "What keys do I press to make it do the following specific job?" and another may ask, "What can this equipment do for me?" In one case, the commands might be presented as a quick-reference key; in the other, considerable theory and background may be appropriate.

- An important step is **field verification**. Here, suitable users are monitored while they follow the instructions. Their timings for completing given tasks as well as their errors are recorded. They are also interviewed about problems they have with the instructions.

- Similarly, when the documentation is first introduced, users should be invited to phone the firm to ask questions and to report problems. This

Brief case

No matter how user-friendly the equipment and how complete the accompanying documentation, users are likely to need help. Corporate resources allocated to providing this assistance can be immense. For example, 55 million people use the computer network and software products of Novell, Inc. (a number that the firm predicts will grow to 1 billion worldwide by the year 2000). Every weekday, almost 20,000 phone calls for help are answered by Novell's 1,750 technical services personnel in Utah. (When callers have to wait, a "hold jockey" announces how many are ahead and the estimated delay.) In addition, there's a massive online help facility; at the rate of 2 million per month, users electronically access assistance programs on CD-ROMs that are continuously revised and updated. To make the communication with users two-way, Novell field tests new products by sending them to a stratified sample of users who have agreed to report on their experiences. The firm also invites users to tell the support staff what changes they'd like. Suggestions are relayed to the technical staff, who maintain an "enhancement database"; the latter is reviewed by the development staff for ideas to put into practice.

provision is generally termed **user support**. A toll-free number should be provided. This is cost-free to the person who phones, but each call is paid by the recipient. Hence, the more the problems and questions, the more the cost to the firm.

  • The final draft of the documentation should be edited by a specialist, who will review variables such as clarity of language, suitability of illustrations, ease of finding specific topics, organization, and layout. In most major cities, there are documentation verification specialists or professional writing centers that perform such tasks.

WORD CHOICE

We have already seen that within the same language, there can be several variants relating to syntax and word choice. We have touched on conversational English, CB English, police radio English, road sign English, and air traffic control English. In addition, there is legal English, academic journal English, university calendar English, dictionary English, medical report English, classified advertisement English, office memo English, government news release English, religious service English, political campaign English,

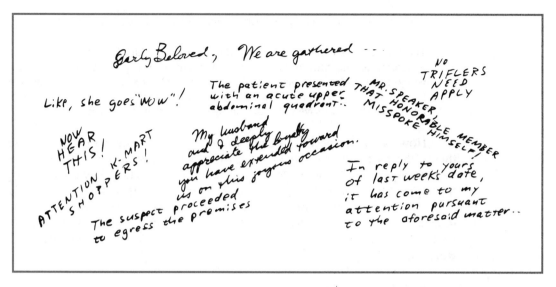

FIGURE 13.9 Specialized word choice and syntax

motion picture and stage play English, parliamentary English, and so forth (Figure 13.9).

Each field of endeavor has its own specialized vocabulary, and sometimes a specialized syntax as well. Communication is enhanced when such groups use the common vocabulary of ordinary English.

Word choice for clarity

Rarely has something been written or said that could not have been reworded to improve the clarity and efficiency of the message. Some vegetarians, to indicate that they eat eggs and drink milk, call themselves *ovo-lacto*. (Why replace two syllables that people understand with four syllables that they do not?) As another example, to inform students that their tuition covers three to five courses per semester unless otherwise authorized by a dean, a university published this notice:

> Tuition regulations currently in effect provide that payment of the annual tuition entitles an undergraduate degree candidate to full-time enrollment, which is defined as registration for 3, 4, or 5 courses per semester. This means that at no time may an undergraduate student's official registration for courses drop below 3 without a dean's permission for part-time status and that at no time may the official course registration exceed 5.

A charge card company recently enclosed this notice to its subscribers:

The Minimum Payment due each month shall be reduced by the amount paid in excess of the Minimum Payment Due during the previous three months which have not already been so applied in determining the Minimum Payment Due in such earlier months, unless you have exceeded your line of credit or have paid the entire New Balance shown on your monthly statement.

How can we expect road signs to be clear when the people who make them refer to them as *ground-mounted confirmation route markers?* How can we expect personnel workers to be clear to employees when they refer, among themselves, to *dismissals* as *placing on nonduty, nonwork status?* How should signs inform members of a university community that smoking is no longer permitted in the institution? Depending on whether the prime objective was clarity, brevity, compliance, or psychological acceptance, the wording could be

- THANK YOU FOR NOT SMOKING

- NO SMOKING ALLOWED

- SMOKING PROHIBITED

- STUDENTS, FACULTY, STAFF, AND ADMINISTRATION HAVE AGREED THAT THIS IS A NONSMOKING INSTITUTION

How would you reword this notice, which appeared in a public building? NOTICE TO ALL OCCUPANTS AND VISITORS—IN THE EVENT OF FIRE ALL ELECTRICAL POWER MAY BE TERMINATED—IT IS ESSENTIAL THAT IN THIS EVENTUALITY EGRESS FROM THE BUILDING OCCURS VIA THE STAIRS ONLY.

Reading used to be considerably more demanding than it is today. Here are some thoughts on education by John Locke, who also wrote, in the late 1600s, "To write and speak correctly gives a grace and gains a favorable attention to what one has to say."

The globes therefore must be studied, and that diligently; and I think may be begun betimes, if the tutor will be but careful to distinguish what the child is capable of knowing, and what not; for which this may be a rule that perhaps will go a pretty way, *viz.* that children may be taught anything that falls under their senses, especially their sight, as far as their memories only are exercised: and thus a child very young may learn, which is the Aequator, which the Meridian, &c. which Europe, and which England, upon the globes, as soon almost as he knows the rooms of the house he lives in, if care be taken not to teach him too much at once, nor to set him upon a new part, till that which he is upon be perfectly learned and fixed in his memory.

Gunning (1952) devised a **fog index** to rate readability. The criteria included the average number of syllables per word and number of words per sentence. For instance, newspaper copy (text) averages an easy 14 words per sentence, standard writing averages 17 words per sentence, and 25 is considered difficult. Locke's passage above contained 144 words in one sentence.

The affect of word choice

Words can induce *affect* or emotion as a response. Even people's given names go in and out of fashion and can variously convey strength or weakness, conservatism or modernity, as well as the individual's personality.

A number of studies have shown that people's names induce images and expectations. The same findings relate to company or product names. Car marketers know that the color of a car has a major influence on sales, and that the *name* of the color is as important an attribute of the color as the hue, saturation, and brightness of the color. One car company, Subaru, found that their poorest selling color was Twinkle Silver. When the same gray was renamed Fine Silver, it became Subaru's most popular color.

One of the most important Canadian crops is canola; canola oil is widely used in the food and chemical industries. The sudden success of this crop did not follow some agricultural equipment invention. It did not follow the development of a new seed. Nor was it the result of discovering new uses for the crop. Canola became important only after its name was changed from rapeseed.

The Brief Case on page 430, which depicts fictitious events, is not about museum security. It merely demonstrates the ways in which, just as language itself changes over the generations, reactions to words can reverse in the space of a few years. Until recently, "man" was legitimately used in the context of "mankind," masculine pronouns routinely doubled as masculine and feminine without offense, and the above Brief Case could have passed without comment. Even the titles of mainstream books of a generation ago, such as *How to Motivate Men* (McQuaig, 1973) and *How to Motivate Salesmen Without Increasing Sales Costs* (Zabriskie, 1973), reflect the way in which "personnel" used to mean "male personnel."

Now it is increasingly felt that such terminology is *sexist* in the same way that derogatory words attached to racial groups are *racist*. Just as terming a man "boy" is usually derogatory, calling a woman a "girl" is demeaning. (That Ottawa museum—which was slated to have been called the National Museum of Man—has been named the National Museum of Civilization.)

It is not enough to communicate clearly and effectively; one should also communicate without offending. A **euphemism** is a replacement term that reduces the harshness or negativity of the original. Substitute words that make unpalatable concepts sound acceptable are common in the funeral in-

Brief case

At the world-famous National Museum of Man in Ottawa, one exhibit demonstrates how manmade materials, combined with careful workmanship, have improved our safety and comfort. Another display imaginatively documents the milestones of manned space flight. Because of the popularity of these exhibits, the new museum was faced with a manpower problem pertaining to security. Since there are no apprenticeship programs in security, there is no such thing as a security journeyman. Every director wonders if he should install automated equipment to solve the problem without increasing the number of "nonproductive" man-hours. The first suggestion, that of installing mantraps, was rejected by the museum's lawyers, who warned that if the traps proved too effective the director could be charged with manslaughter. In this case, however, the board chairman (a skilled statesman, nominated for *Time*'s Man of the Year Award) decided to man the security stations around the clock with specially trained policemen, all under the direct supervision of the newly appointed security foreman. Now *every* workman in *every* division is required to report any security incident to a designated girl in the policeman's office.

dustry, where death is referred to as *slumber, rest,* or *repose.* Of course, any word choice that reduces the burden on mourners seems appropriate. In the same way, people once called crippled retards were later termed physically and mentally handicapped, then multihandicapped, more recently people with special needs, and finally multiply challenged people.

The less pleasant aspects of personnel management are often expressed with euphemisms such as dehiring, outplacement, or asking for a resignation instead of firing. Is this a misuse of the euphemism? Remember that murder is murder, even when called terminating with extreme prejudice, offing, or taking out. On the one hand, words should not give offense through careless use; on the other, the seriousness of an action should not be artificially cleansed through the use of a clever euphemism.

Conversely, a **dysphemism** is a word designed to make an innocuous or neutral concept sound negative. In a strike, for instance, it is hard for unionists to demonstrate against replacement employees termed colleagues. When such employees are termed scabs, picket line violence against them is more likely. Table 13.1 gives some examples, with extra boxes for you to add some of your own.

The "emotional engineering" of words has been polished to a fine art throughout the world. Like all tools, words can build or destroy, they can uplift or disparage, they can activate or freeze. Like all tools, they should be used with respect and care.

TABLE 13.10 Euphemisms and dysphemisms

EUPHEMISM	CONCEPT	DYSPHEMISM
junior associate	striker replacement	scab
maintenance engineer	janitor	garbage collector
dehired, outplaced	fired	kicked out, canned
exceptional person	slow learner	retardate
social disease	gonorrhea	the clap
restroom	toilet	the can
emerging nation	third world	backward country
passed away	died	kicked the bucket
previously owned	used car	junker, rust-bucket
nervous breakdown	mental problem	batty, nuts
senior citizen	elderly person	geezer

A few thousand years ago, Plato offered a superb *structural* definition of the human. Humans, he wrote, are "featherless bipeds." If Plato had been asked for an equally trenchant *functional* definition of the species, he may well have come up with "the creature that speaks."

Humans have made words; words have made us human. It is not surprising, then, that human factors engineers can play a role in improving the use of this most basic of human tools—the spoken, written, and displayed symbol.

Study guide for chapter 13

HAVE YOU LEARNED THESE NAMES AND TERMS?

phonemes
homonym
phonetic alphabet
spondee
syntax
copy
text
characters
latency
font
legibility, readability
reading field
justified type
serif, sans serif
video display terminal (VDT)
hard copy
convergence, accommodation, adaption
negative contrast, positive presentation
resolution and acutance
aspect ratio
surround
pictogram
display stereotype
documentation
field verification
user support
fog index
euphemism
dysphemism

ISSUES TO CONSIDER

What are the problems in measuring intelligibility?

Why is "clipping" a particular problem in the English language?

What are the characteristics of words in the *phonetic alphabet*?

In what circumstances have *you* ever used a restricted, specialized vocabulary?

What are the advantages of the *Dvorak* and the *alphabetic* keyboards?

What is the best letter and/or character design for optimal *readability*?

What are the psychological and physiological demands on a VDT operator?

Why is the combination of *red and blue* text inadvisable?

What accounts for the prevalence of VDT-user complaints?

What are advantages and disadvantages of *pictograms*?

How should the incidence of *color blindness* be addressed in traffic signals?

What cases of inadequate *documentation* have you experienced?

What *euphemisms* and *dysphemisms* can you add to the blank spaces in Figure 13.13?

SAMPLE MULTIPLE-CHOICE QUESTIONS

1. Characters are
   a. interesting or unusual people.
   b. interesting or unusual personalities.
   c. interesting or unusual letters.
   d. letters or graphic symbols.

2. The research of Salthouse on keyboards indicated that keyboards should
   a. be switched to the Dvorak design.
   b. be switched to the alphabetic design.
   c. stay with the QWERTY design.
   d. be further researched.

3. Research indicates that in order to be readable, text needs
   a. left justification.
   b. right justification.
   c. both left and right justification.
   d. no justification.

4. Which color has the lowest luminance?
   a. red
   b. orange
   c. green
   d. blue

5. The earliest known documentation accompanied
   a. early aircraft.
   b. the original typewriter.
   c. both sewing machines and mower-threshers.
   d. the Model T Ford.

Answers: page 462

Part four

CHAPTER 14 Consumer Psychology

The
product

Many business failures are due to inadequate sales. Part four has
a chapter on marketing that shows how consumer psychology is
used for marketing.

Everyone lives by selling something.
Robert Louis Stevenson (1850–1894)

Bird's-eye view of the chapter

The previous chapters ensure that there's a properly chosen, trained, and motivated workforce, operating with optimal equipment and good communication. This idyllic combination should yield a warehouse brimming with the finished goods; now it's time to study how the goods can be sold. Without consumer acceptance of the end product, it doesn't matter how well the organization has operated. Many psychologists specialize in predicting and influencing human behavior. When the same theories of prediction and tools of influence are adapted to the marketplace, we enter the lively world of consumer psychology.

Chapter 14

Consumer psychology

The payoff from chapter 14   You will:

1. Understand the meaning and importance of consumer psychology
2. Know the history and present status of consumer psychology
3. Recognize the role of consumer psychology research
4. Appreciate the cost of incorrectly forecasting product success
5. Recognize the value of surveys as research tools
6. Know the common survey techniques
7. Understand the application of clinical psychology to consumer research
8. Appreciate the rationale of focus groups and client labs
9. Contrast above techniques with behavioral research
10. See and evaluate Freud's influence on consumer research
11. Know the meaning of lifestyle and psychographic research

12. Understand the meaning and importance of demographic data
13. See how the VALS approach integrates the above techniques
14. Understand the need to evaluate advertising effectiveness
15. Know the use of the eye camera and physiological techniques
16. See the research value of using split runs
17. Understand the use of the consumer jury in evaluating television ads
18. Understand the use of direct responses for research
19. Appreciate the weaknesses of consumer research
20. Evaluate advertising effectiveness in the light of its goals
21. Understand the relation between advertising and consumer demand
22. Consider conflicts between the goals of public policy advocates and promoters

I magine a world without advertising or promotion of any kind. How would it differ from the present one? What products, familiar to you, would probably remain unknown in such a world? How would business and industry be different than they are? And how would your thoughts, your values, your life differ from the way it is?

WHAT IS CONSUMER PSYCHOLOGY?

No matter how expertly a company solves its personnel and equipment-design problems, the effort is to no avail if the results are not sold or used. In this chapter we will explore some of the strategies of marketing, especially the most conspicuous aspect, advertising.

Consumer psychology includes the behaviors of buying and selling. (The selling aspect is covered here; the buying aspect is covered immediately following this chapter.) These two are among the most frequent and important of human behaviors. For many people, more daily decisions have to be made about "buying" than about any other activity. In industrially developed countries, individual consumer spending accounts for two-thirds of the gross national product.

Although the exchange of goods is as old as civilization itself, and while the behavioral science aspects of marketing were addressed early in this century, the concept of consumer psychology as a formal academic discipline started only recently. The American Psychological Association established its Division of Consumer Psychology in 1960. Since then, however, the specialty has grown steadily and now includes marketing and promotion, as well as how people perceive marketplace offerings and what motivates their behavior as consumers.

Most of the 350-odd members of the division deal with marketing. Hardly any of them address the opposite side, consumer protection. This is not surprising: psychologists are trained to study and predict behavior; they are at the forefront in the use of tests and data analysis; and they study perception, emotion, and motivation.

The number of academic journals in consumer psychology has expanded rapidly since the *Journal of Advertising* was started in 1960. The most prominent title is the *Journal of Consumer Research,* which was founded in 1974. Other important ones are the *Journal of Consumer Psychology,* the *Journal of Consumer Marketing, Psychology and Marketing,* and the *Journal of the Academy of Marketing Science.* Another basic source is the *Association for Consumer Research Annual Conference Proceedings,* which runs to some 600 pages.

MARKETING RESEARCH

The topic of research in general is addressed in chapter 2 and Appendix C. Here we will look at the research of the consumer psychologist.

The need for marketing research

In past times, the peddler would buy some pots and pans from the maker, and sell them door-to-door. If the buyers said they preferred longer handles, the peddler would pass that on to the maker, and the next week would have the improved model to sell. Today, the marketing manager works in an executive office suite deciding on promotional campaigns for New England and New Zealand. Isolated from the end user, the manager hires a market research firm for guidance in making the decisions. The market research firm, in turn, could be owned by, or might employ, consumer psychologists.

Market research is of immense importance because of money—a vast amount of resources is devoted to making us buy. For instance, a billion dollars has been spent promoting carbonated soft drinks alone (Cleary, 1981). Some 40,000 television ads are produced annually, at an average cost of $200,000. The average American can be exposed to 1,500 advertising messages every day, from all sources. There are some 300,000 brand-name products for sale, including as many as 9,000 in a supermarket. Some five million businesses compete just in the United States. This all means intense competition, which, in turn, requires sophisticated marketing. About $300 is spent yearly on advertising for every individual in Canada; in the United States the per-person figure exceeds $400.

The cost of failure can be immense. A century ago, if a cobbler tried a new design that failed, the only consequence would be a pair of unsold shoes. Today, if a footwear manufacturer designs shoes with round toes when consumers prefer square ones, there will be a warehouse full of obsolete shoes, and possibly a bankruptcy and lost jobs. Not surprisingly, most research by consumer psychologists relates to effective selling.

Every year some 5,000 new products are packaged and promoted in North America, and new services and systems are added to the mix daily. Some firms, like Coca Cola, rarely add new items. Others make product innovation the corporate goal; the 3M Company has originated some 50,000 new products.

Most new products will fail; some 80 percent will be withdrawn from the market within two years, and few of the remaining 20 percent will achieve the original expectations set for them. These failures are inordinately expensive. Research and development budgets of $10 million per product are not

Brief case

Prior to developing a new car model for the late 1950s, the Ford Motor Company conducted market research at an unheard-of level. Marketing experts advised Ford to design a medium-priced car to fill the gap between the entry-level Ford/Mercury models and the luxury Lincoln. When Ford agreed, the market research was stepped up. To determine just the *name* for the new car, a year was spent examining eighteen thousand possibilities! The result was the Edsel. It accounted for less than one percent of cars sold in its first (and best) year, 1957. When the Edsel Division (and dealer network) was scrapped in 1959, Ford's and Ford dealers' losses totaled almost a half billion dollars. (Misreading public acceptance of the Edsel was not the only forecasting error at this time. Ford's marketing experts also assessed a new type of car, the small European import. This trend was dismissed with the derisive observation, "We make more cars in a day than they do in a year." Soon after, more Volkswagens were being sold in a week than Edsels in a year, some of them in former Edsel dealerships.)

unusual; nor are marketing costs of $50 million in the first two years considered excessive. RCA spent 15 years developing its VideoDisc before launching it in 1981. When the general buying public didn't respond, it became a several-hundred-million-dollar flop. These examples show how the results of market research are unpredictable.

Early results don't always predict ultimate success. The first new Edsels were in short supply, whereas Volkswagen's original sales campaign in the United States sold two Beetles. (If you're interested in trivia, the designers of the board game Trivial Pursuit attracted hardly any orders from retailers when the game was first introduced at major trade shows. It later generated over a billion dollars in sales.)

Until recently, new ideas spread slowly. Now, there is emphasis upon the rapid transfer from one country to another. Until recently, marketing meant the firm's communicating to the consumer. Now, the firm needs to hear *from* the consumer as well. In the past, successful products could be sold for decades; today the **product cycle** time can be measured in months before it's considered obsolete. (Many consumer electronic items sold in Japan have a product cycle time of a mere 90 days.)

As we saw, marketing research is not always successful. Worse, it's hard to determine just how successful a given research project is. With all that in mind, we can review techniques of *marketing research*.

Corporations spend millions of dollars on product and consumer research. The survey is the most common form of consumer research. Here it is conducted in person; surveys are also conducted by mail and by phone.

The survey

Consumer psychologists want to know if you prefer this brand to that, why you decided to take the last vacation where you did, what car you would most like to own, and on what types of products you would choose costlier brand-name items over generic ones. The simplest way to get an answer to a question is to ask it. Putting questions to consumers—the *survey* (page 39)—is the most common form of consumer research.

You've likely been surveyed by mail or phone, or in a shopping mall. You frequently see media reports of the latest public opinion poll or survey. When filling out a card to activate a product warranty, you've likely answered questions on it that constitute a survey.

An effective ad presumably embeds the name of the product into the mind of the viewer. To measure the memorability of an ad, two survey methods are widely used. In the **aided recall** approach, an appropriate sample of consumers is surveyed after exposure. (In a laboratory setting, consumers may be asked to leaf through a magazine or to watch a television program including ads, or they may be surveyed at home after the ads have been run.) They are asked if they *recall* an ad for the product in question. If the answer is yes, they are asked to describe what they remember, and then to answer specific questions about the ad.

In the **recognition** approach, the respondents are *shown the ad* and asked about it. (Do you recall seeing it? Did you notice the name of the product or the advertiser? Did you read more than half of the words in the ads?) To correct for *false positives* (untrue "yes" answers) respondents are also shown nonexistent ads. Recognition taps a lower level of learning than recall and is an easier task because you don't have to reconstruct the stimulus. Advertisers who want the consumer to recognize the product (such as a soft drink) when they pass it on the *shelf* would be more interested in recognition; those who want people to think of the brand (such as a car) *before* they shop would be concerned with recall. As would be expected, one study (Singh, Rothschild & Churchill, 1988) found more accuracy in the recognition technique, at least for television commercials.

Survey results may provide input for the design, name, packaging, and advertising of products. For instance, a product may have ten features—too many to promote effectively in most media. Which features would consumers be most responsive to? How can they be communicated clearly?

The weaknesses of the survey technique are the assumptions that people understand the questions and answer them accurately without regard for what they consider the desired or socially acceptable answer should be, and that behavior shown in a research project will translate into sales in the store. As an example, a long-term field study of survey responses and garbage dump contents (Rathje & Murphy, 1992) found that survey responses overstated the amount of healthy food consumed and understated the amount of junk food and alcoholic beverages that the garbage analysis showed.

The clinical approach

Clinical psychologists are trained to explore clients' hidden feelings, emotions, motivations, and hopes. The same probing techniques of interviews and tests that are used to help people with their conflicts and compulsions, and their fears and frustrations, can be adapted to determine why people buy or don't buy.

Survey respondents do not always know what the truthful answer is. Insofar as they do know the truth, they may not reveal it. (If you had to explain why you chose the last pair of shoes that you bought, would you be able to untangle the complex underlying motivations that led you to that selection in that store at that moment?) You recall that in personnel selection, *clinical* methods, especially *projective* techniques, can reveal thoughts, feelings, and perceptions that applicants would not be able or willing to reveal. The same techniques are applied to exposing the underlying consumer attitudes.

When Nescafé, an early brand of instant coffee, was launched, a sales figure was predicted on the basis of the product's qualities, survey responses, and the advertising budget. The failure of Nescafé sales to reach the expected level caused consternation in the coffee industry.

In a study to find the explanation, each of two groups of women was shown a shopping list and asked to describe the personality of the lady who had prepared it. The two lists were the same, except that the coffee was a traditional brand in one, and Nescafé instant coffee in the other. The "personality evaluations" allowed the respondents to *project* their *own* feelings and attitudes onto the imaginary homemakers who had drawn up the list. These projections showed that instant coffee buyers were seen as lazy and wasteful, and thus explained why the sales were low.

This study has become a classic that is traditionally cited (for example, by Haire, 1950) to illustrate how the techniques of clinical psychology can be usefully applied to marketing. Unfortunately, clinical assessments in the practitioner's office are of dubious accuracy, and here we are applying projective instruments for purposes other than were originally intended. And, as with many human endeavors, we are more likely to hear of the successes of this approach than the failures.

Focus groups and client labs

The **focus group** has the same relation to clinical methods of consumer research as group therapy has to individual therapy. Like group therapy, it benefits from economy of numbers, in that one leader deals with a group of people at a time, and members of the group can react to each others' contributions.

A group of six to eight people is assembled, often over a meal. The people invited may represent the industry, consumer groups, or ordinary people who can articulate their opinions. A problem is set by the leader for the group to discuss, and specific follow-up questions are asked at intervals. The leader keeps the group focused on the topic, hence the name of the technique. The proceedings may be videotaped (from a hidden camera, but with the knowledge and awareness of the participants).

The focus group (originally called the interactional workshop) is intermediary between the survey and the clinical approaches. It's like a survey in that the agenda is predetermined and the questions are guided; it's clinical in that feelings and reactions are sought and probed.

In the **client lab**, representative users of the product or service are asked to *use* the product (or discuss the service), generally in a small group. They are monitored for how they feel about, or problems they have with, the product or service. In a focus group, you might be asked about your experiences with barbecue grills; in a client lab you might be asked to try to take one out of the box and assemble it.

Behavioral research

The *survey* strategy asks people to *say* what they do. The *clinical* approach asks *why*—in terms of the often-hidden, deeply underlying reasons—they do it. In behavioral research, scientists observe what people actually *do,* generally in a real-life setting. This technique can pay off despite problems of sampling, control, and ethics. (The ethical dilemma is that the researcher cannot obtain informed consent without asking for permission to observe, and people generally change their behavior when they know it's being recorded.)

For instance, Atkin (1978) reported direct observations of how women accompanied by children chose a breakfast cereal in supermarkets. In two-thirds of the cases, the children made a selection, which was then usually accepted by the shopper. Would either of the other techniques outlined above have so clearly directed the cereal firms to aim their promotional campaigns at children? (We'll talk about ads aimed at children later.)

Now that many large grocery stores are equipped with electronic scanners that read the product code and relay each purchase to a computer, marketing researchers can tap into these data. For instance, a panel of shoppers is paid to provide **demographic** information (age, income, education, and so on), and to permit their purchases to be electronically monitored during the scanning. Some panelists receive special coupons in the mail or test ads on cable television. Promotional campaigns are often tested in different locations.

Personalities, lifestyles, and psychographics

In the early 1900s, Freud argued that we are driven by powerful internal forces and personality factors that could be uncovered through proper analysis. In short order, clinical psychologists devised many tests to describe and quantify motivation and personality. Naturally, market researchers have been searching for the analysis or testing technique to disclose motives and traits that could be exploited for increased sales. "After all," they thought, "if the science of psychology can uncover the unconscious reasons behind dreams, feelings, or habits, surely we professionals can find the unconscious triggers to buying decisions." In the 1950s consumer psychologists conducted extensive research on motivation to uncover symbols that would appeal to the unconscious motivations of buyers.

For example, Evans (1959) compared the personalities of Chevrolet and Ford buyers because, although the cars were similar, the advertising appealed to different buying motives. He administered the Edwards Personal Preference Schedule, a personality test based on the Thematic Apperception Test (page 113) to recent buyers of either brand. But after analyzing the scores of 1,600

Brief case

• Expensive perfume is traditionally packaged in heavy, elegant bottles designed for the dresser-top. One manufacturer offered its perfume in a portable container so that users could bring it with them on trips. It turned out that women who travel a lot rarely use expensive perfume except at home; the new packaging was a flop.

• A brewery sponsored an equestrian event but gained no increase in sales. It seems that the "horse crowd" drinks, but not usually beer.

• A maker of a speaker featuring innovative technology advertised its superior performance in audio magazines. Sales were disappointing. The marketing division suspected that the type of person this product would appeal to enjoys innovation per se, and so the next ad campaign—in mountain-climbing and underwater exploration magazines—featured only the advanced technology. This appeal to the personality type of the "innovator" led to satisfactory sales.

recent buyers, Evans found negligible personality differences between the Chevrolet and Ford owners.

Although disappointing to motivational psychologists who assumed a predictable relationship between scores on a personality test and brand choice, Evans's research began a flurry of hundreds of other studies on questions such as whether brand-loyal buyers differ from non-brand-loyal consumers, if specific television programs attract certain personalities, and the connection between personality and being persuasible.

Subsequent research has not proved much more useful than Evans's original study, for the following possible reasons:

• Personality theory was designed to differentiate clinical populations, not consumer types.

• Your score on a personality test is not greatly influenced by your disposable income, your age, your cultural background, and your sex, but your purchasing decisions are strongly related to demographic variables.

• Many purchase decisions are determined by situational factors, such as what your boss or your neighbor just bought, or whom the salesperson reminds you of.

• Personality variables are usually determined by an intensive evaluation of hundreds of individuals, who may not accurately represent the hundreds of millions of consumers who form the buying public.

- Knowing your unconscious processes does not necessarily translate into influencing how you spend your money.

- Many of Freud's notions are of questionable validity in the first place. For instance, there may be no such thing as the subconscious or unconscious mind.

As some researchers kept searching for personality correlates of consumption, others combined the science of demographics with that of personality (especially motivational) groups, into what was termed **psychographics**. This term combines "psycho," referring to lifestyles, and "graphics" from demographics.

Of course, marketers have long targeted specific types of people, such as young bachelors, housewives, or elderly women. Lifestyle research simply narrows the focus by looking at the **activities**, **interests**, and **opinions (AIOs)** of survey respondents. For instance, people are asked to what extent they influence or are influenced by others in shopping, what they do for leisure and entertainment, and how they evaluate prices. This provides a specific target market on which to base advertising, packaging, and the naming and pricing of products.

Few psychological studies use research samples of more than 100 individuals, but psychographic measurements often include thousands of participants. One reason is that these studies attempt to measure complex and subtle variables in a heterogeneous population; another is that they are invariably sponsored by major corporations or their marketing agencies.

Most of the research on psychographics has been applied to promotion. Using psychographic data, advertisers first zero in on a specific type of prospective buyer, tailor the ad to attract the attention of the target person, and design the ad to appeal to the motives that will induce that person to buy. There's little evidence of marked success.

One weakness of the psychographic approach is that it's driven by applied concerns, not theoretical ones. The impetus typically comes from an advertising agency, not from a scientist or professor, and the agency personnel may be stronger in persuasion than in academic rigor. Academics tend to systematically build upon what has been accomplished; marketers value originality. Scientists emphasize cooperation; marketers keenly feel the competition with each other. Consequently, each major psychographic study, for all its impressive numbers, tends to use all new material, making comparisons and continuity difficult. Then, when the project is over, there is unlikely to be follow-up and further analysis.

An exception to the lack of standardization is VALS 2, a psychographic system for segmenting American consumers and predicting consumer behavior. It is illustrated in Figure 14.1.

VALS 2 is built on a concept—self-orientation—and a new definition of resources. Resources in the VALS 2 system refers to the full range of psycho-

Brief case

Isuzu Motors *Rodeo* sport-utility vehicle was languishing at the bottom of the category. Isuzu was trying to compete with Ford, Chevy, Nissan, and Toyota to reach the macho, pickup-driving segment of the population. The famous "Joe Isuzu" Clio award-winning commercials were not working.

Isuzu surveyed the few buyers it had for the *Rodeo* and found them to be VALS Experiencers, a young, risk-taking, energetic group. This group did not care about the ma-cho aspects of the *Rodeo:* Experiencers thought it was "fun."

Isuzu used the VALS™ 2 words and concepts that best target Experiencers with its advertising agency. The agency developed several spots, including "Stay Between the Lines" and "Mud Puddle" to emphasize the breaking-the-rules theme that is so attractive to Experiencers.

Sales increased 60 percent within six months, leaving the *Rodeo* the best-selling sport-utility vehicle in the market.

logical, physical, demographic, and material means and capacities consumers have to draw upon. Consumers pursue and require products, services, and experiences that provide satisfaction and give shape, substance, and character to their identities. They are motivated by one of three powerful self-orientations: principle, status, and action.

Actualizers are successful, active, sophisticated, "take charge" people with high self-esteem and abundant resources. Principle-oriented customers seek to make their behavior consistent with their views of how the world is or should be. They include Fulfilleds and Believers. Status-oriented consumers have or seek a secure place in a valued social setting. Strivers look to others to indicate what they should be and do, whereas Achievers seek recognition and self-definition through achievements at work and in their families. Action-oriented customers like to affect their environment in tangible ways. Makers do so primarily at home and at work, Experiencers act in the wider world. Both types tend to become intensely involved in their activities. Strugglers' lives are constricted. With limited economic, social, and emotional resources, and often in poor health, Strugglers experience the world as pressing and difficult.

In Canada, a system called Canada Lifestyles describes a wide variety of consumers categorized by gender as well as by language, such as French-speaking residents of Quebec, and English-speaking people from the other nine provinces. It needs to respond to current demographic changes. People are marrying later and having children later. Many aren't marrying, and those that are may well get divorced. One-fifth of households are single-adult ones. There are more professional women and more ethnic diversity. People move; almost half change addresses every five years and have to find new sources

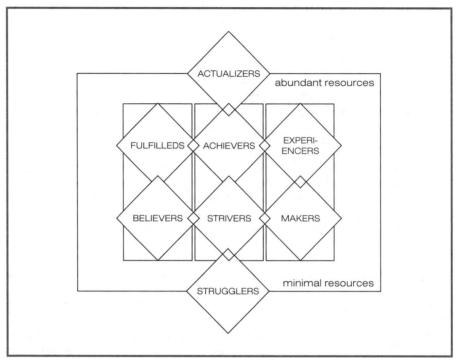

FIGURE 14.1 VALS™ Segmentation System

of services. And teenagers and seniors have more **disposable income** (money left after deductions and necessities) than in the early 1980s.

Measuring ad effectiveness

Think fast here. The car fairy has just tapped your shoulder and announced that you will receive the new car of your choice if you can think of the brand that you want before coming to the end of this sentence. If you managed to express your thought in time, what brand was it? Mercedes-Benz spends almost $1,000 in North America each year for every new car sold here. Do you think there's a connection between the ad expense and your brand choice?

In some cases (for example, perfumes, cosmetics, and soaps) the advertising can cost more than the ingredients. The expense of advertising has led major agencies to employ psychologists to evaluate the effectiveness of ads. These researchers have devised a number of techniques:

The eye camera   The eye camera detects and records how your gaze responds to a picture, such as an ad. This device was introduced on page 64 and illustrated in Figure 2.3. Eye camera studies are useful for comparing the eye's response to various ad layouts. They are less accurate in predicting the success of any ad, because of the difference between what you look at now and what you do later as a result, and the difference between research participants in a lab and the large population of ad viewers.

Physiological measures   The researcher may want to assess the *emotional impact* of an ad. Under emotional arousal, the **autonomic nervous system** (the part of our nervous system that controls automatic life functions such as heart rate and digestion) shifts from the **parasympathetic** (relaxation) mode to the **sympathetic** (emergency reaction) mode. Under sympathetic arousal, many body parts are mobilized for what is often termed fight or flight. For instance, the palms sweat and the pupils enlarge.

Pupil size can be measured by photographing the eyes with a calibrating camera; this is termed **pupillometry**. Pupillometric evaluations of various ads show which are more arousing, and when used with the eye camera, pupillometry can show which *part* of the ad is most arousing. However, "arousal" as measured by pupil dilation is hard to interpret. When men are shown photographs of nude women, their pupils enlarge; when women are shown photos of naked men, theirs do not. When shown pictures of babies, women's pupils enlarge; men's do not. And when men *or* women view unpleasant scenes, their pupils dilate.

The split run   Magazines are effective as an advertising medium because people read them when they are relaxed and therefore receptive. Consequently, considerable research has been conducted on the effectiveness of magazine ads. As with much research, there's the problem of applying laboratory findings to the outside world. One solution is to publish various ads on a **split run** basis. For an extra fee, a magazine will publish one version of an ad in copies delivered to one area and a different version in the copies sold elsewhere. (Some magazines publish different regional versions.) This enables the ad agency to compare some criterion of effectiveness, such as sales, in the various areas.

There are problems here as well. It is hard to control the *equivalence* of the different geographical areas. Also, an ad may have a *residual* effect that does not become apparent during the period of the test. Even if the effect is immediate, the consumer response may be masked by the **pipeline effect**; early orders are filled from stock already in the system.

Research on television ads   Television is an expensive medium for advertising. But with the prevalence of television and the potential of televised ads to arouse emotions and present a story, massive research is directed to this medium that brings sales pitches into your home.

In one research technique, a consumer jury, a panel of representative people, is seated in a studio and shown television programs including ads. Each panelist is provided with a red button and a green one, and asked to indicate any positive or negative feelings they experience during the screening by pressing one of the buttons. One objective is to test commercials for viewer acceptability, so they won't be switched off at home.

When watching television at home, many viewers **zip** (use their remote control to switch to other channels) or **zap** (use of the control to silence the sound during a commercial). Some people **time shift**, or program their video-cassette recorders to record programs of interest for viewing later and, during playback, fast-forward through the commercials. The research assumption is that only the commercials that are "red-buttoned" in the studio would be zapped at home.

Direct responses

A **coupon** is usually a dollar-bill-size cutout section of a print ad that the consumer can mail (generally for a small cash rebate) or present at a store (usually for a product discount). At first glance this seems a cumbersome means of offering a price reduction to the consumer. However, only a tiny proportion of coupons, typically two percent, is redeemed. Advertisers use coupons primarily to measure *reader response*. When coupons are used, their main influence is to induce consumers to *change* brands.

Despite their popularity, coupons present problems. If the offer is particularly attractive, the return rate may not indicate an interest in, or loyalty to, the product. Some consumers may return coupons for idiosyncratic reasons, such as just to receive mail. The promoter wants to put coupons in the hands of potential buyers, but there's no way of excluding steady customers. And many consumer advocates oppose coupons because of the wasteful handling costs.

Direct mail marketing has been widely used for 50 years. Consumers originally ordered goods, usually from catalogs, by mail. They are now more likely to use the telephone to order items advertised in home-delivered flyers, on television, or in specialty catalogs. In larger firms, the orders are keyed to various ads, so that their effectiveness can be assessed.

The experiment

Given the critical impact of marketing research, consumer psychologists are increasingly turning to the experiment to find answers. Here is one example.

Labels are recent. In the past, there were few products to consider, their identity was obvious, and name brands or manufacturers were virtually unknown, even among the few buyers who could read. Since the 1930s, advertisers have been emphasizing brand names, implying that they ensured quality, value, or prestige. Soon, the label, featuring a name, became the most conspicuous aspect of most products. A half century later saw the inception of what are known as generic labels, no-name brands, off-brands, private labels, or bargain brands, which generally have a less favorable public image compared to the brand-name version.

How does the name influence the buyer? Bushman (1993) reasoned that insofar as a product was purchased and consumed in public, self-conscious people would be very influenced by a brand name, especially when in a group. He studied over 300 people (half of them college students) in a field experiment on their ratings of two peanut butters, a name brand and a bargain brand.

Participants were assigned to one of four independent variable conditions: brand product with the brand label, brand product with the bargain label, and bargain peanut butter with the one label or the other. The participants performed the trial either alone or with their companion(s) and the experimenter. They also completed a standardized paper-and-pencil scale that measures public self-consciousness.

The higher the score on the test, the higher the participants rated both products that were identified as brand-name ones (and there was a small audience effect in the predicted direction). This might explain the popularity of products such as jeans and footwear that bear a famous name for all to see.

Researchers have given considerable attention to the effect of *pricing*. If you decided to buy a $20,000 car, how much effort would you expend in negotiating a lower price? If you picked out a $200,000 house, how much price negotiation effort would you invest there? Would you exert more effort to save $15 on a $150 item or to save $5 on a $50 purchase; is the more compelling variable the dollars saved or the percentage saved?

Darke and Freedman (1993) asked adult visitors to the Ontario Science Centre in Toronto if they would take an extra 20-minute walk to save money on a plane ticket. The 160 participants were told that the savings would be one of these: 1 percent, 5 percent, $5, or $25. In this correlational study, the $25 savings produced the most "yes" replies; the percentage savings seemed irrelevant to these people.

A follow-up study tested psychology students at the University of Toronto for the effort they would make to get either a large discount and a large saving, a large discount and a small saving, a small discount and large saving, or a small discount and small saving. Participants responded positively only to the *large percentage* or the *large amount* saved. This research suggests that sales should focus on the percentage saved where the dollar amount is small, on the dollars saved where the percentage is small, and on both where both are meaningful.

Why research is not foolproof

Despite immense expenditures of time, talent, and funds on marketing research, it is hard to predict which products will succeed or fail, and why. New items do not always start in the laboratory. Sometimes the innovation is a new way of using an existing item, and the innovators are the users, not the makers.

For instance, in the days when everyone carried a handkerchief for blowing their nose, Kleenex tissues were marketed for women to wipe cold cream off their faces. It was only when the manufacturer discovered that both men and women were buying the product as a substitute for the handkerchief that the marketing approach caught up with consumer practice.

Similarly, prior to 1958, American Express merely sold traveler's checks. At that time it introduced the first general purpose credit card, the American Express card. The appeal was to high status, with the promotional theme "You've earned it." Later the theme became insurance, with the slogan "Don't leave home without it." Today, credit cards have changed the way people shop and handle their money.

Other products catch on in a context entirely different from their origin. For instance, around the beginning of this century, there was widespread fear and concern over sexuality, especially masturbation. Some physicians proposed dietary modification, especially vegetarianism, as a means of reducing "animal impulses." A sanatorium with religious affiliations at Battle Creek, Michigan, wanted to furnish its clients with a cold, grain-based breakfast, which was thought to be physically and morally healthier. To this end, an inventive employee with an interest in food processing devised a process to convert kernels of corn into small flakes. Young Dr. W. K. Kellogg single-handedly initiated a new industry and changed much of the world's eating habits. He hardly expected the application of his invention to take this direction.

Yesterday's research does not necessarily provide today's answers because of rapid changes. New products are introduced much more suddenly than in the past, products have shorter life cycles, the buying public is changing in many ways, and public policy, new legislation, and the consumer movement have their impact. Marketing research now offers good opportunities for psychologists to help firms and their advertising agencies promote goods and services in an effective, affordable, and nonoffensive way.

Advertisers argue that the objective of promoting products that are considered harmful is to influence consumers who are already using the product to switch brands.

ADVERTISING TYPES, GOALS, AND EFFECTIVENESS

Advertising is a necessary ingredient of marketing. In the early 1900s, the scholar J. T. Dorrance aptly observed, "Advertising is the principle of mass production applied to selling." Whether it's a handwritten flyer on street posts announcing your garage sale or lost dog, or a multimillion-dollar campaign for a new car, advertising is communication that can serve many purposes.

The goal to sell

Of course the main objective of advertising is to *sell*, but the technique can be **hard sell** or **soft sell**. The hard sell approach extols the product's attributes, such as an ad that shows the three ways a painkiller fights headaches fast. Soft sell ads use techniques like humor or an image; an example is featuring nothing more than the image of the rugged Marlboro Man to promote Marlboro cigarettes.

To compare the two approaches, DeBono and Packer (1991) compared people who were high and low in **self-monitoring**. *Self-monitoring* refers to the tendency to "look good." High self-monitors do whatever they have to in order to present themselves well; low self-monitors follow their own values, hence they behave consistently regardless of social influences. This personality construct is similar to the better-known *locus of control,* which was covered on page 113.

People of these two personality types were presented with either a hard sell (quality-oriented) or a soft sell (image-oriented) ad for a cola, then asked to try the cola, which was really a **generic** or non-brand-name product. As expected, the high self-monitors rated the cola higher following the soft sell ad; the low self-monitors were more influenced by the hard sell version.

Other goals

Ads may have other goals. The objective may be to increase *awareness,* or to develop **primary demand** (demand for a product category rather than a specific brand) through **pioneering advertising**. California fruit growers have successfully promoted the consumption of raisins and olives, and the same has been done for butter and milk by the Ontario dairy industry.

Or, the purpose may be to change peoples' *attitudes.* For instance, electricity providers have alternately promoted the consumption and the conservation of electricity. Another goal is to create or maintain an *image* for a product, as a diamond cartel campaign has done. Some promotions are termed *institutional* advertising, as when a gasoline company offers tips to improve fuel economy. For well-known brands, "reminder" advertising simply keeps the product's name before the public, for example, print ads that show nothing but a Chanel perfume bottle.

Often these goals are vaguely combined, and attainment is hard to measure. Could you define exactly what made you purchase the pen that you are using? Do you know exactly why you'd prefer a certain brand of car? What did you last use to wash your hair? Why did you choose that brand?

It's hard to measure the impact of advertising because the influence may be indirect and long term. Ad agencies would have the sponsors believe that product success follows from a skillful campaign. But when the product is considered to be harmful, the advertisers argue that the objectives and results are not increased total sales, but "brand differentiation." That is, advertisements don't induce nonsmokers to smoke and nondrinkers to drink, but the ads merely protect the *market share* of the client, by inducing users to switch to the client's brand.

Back when cigarette smokers were invariably male, there seemed to be few prospects for conversion to smoking. Thus, the target in the 1920s was women. Print ads featured females smoking, and the **copy** (text) had the

6.0, 6.0, 6.0, 6.0, 6.0! If I had to rate milk as an after-sports drink, it would definitely get the gold. Besides being a better source of potassium than the leading sports drink, it has more vitamins and minerals per ounce. And how do I like it? On ice, of course.

MILK

What a surprise!"

This is an example of pioneering advertising, where the objective is to promote a product category rather than a specific brand.

models asking the men smokers to "Blow some my way." Other female models said in the ad, "Light a Lucky and you'll never miss sweets that make you fat." These techniques have been analyzed and documented by Taylor (1984).

One could argue that advertising has limited effectiveness. For instance, it's estimated that 65 percent of supermarket buying decisions are made not in advance, but in the store. Advertising may make customers more susceptible, but price, packaging, and display are probably more salient. There are many examples of products that did not sell well despite massive advertising (from Edsels to Pillsbury's Space Food Sticks) and others that sell well in the absence of it (from marijuana to university courses).

Why is there such a gap between advertising research and investment and consumer behavior? Human motivation is complex and is understood only dimly. If you asked a psychiatrist who was trained in introspection and self-understanding, "Why did you just buy that particular comb?" the answer would likely be hesitant at best. We cannot expect even a consumer expert to understand all the variables that account for the myriad purchasing decisions of huge populations of consumers.

Academic research is public and therefore self-correcting. If a scientist reports to the entire academic community that a new form of therapy cured half the schizophrenics tested, other researchers will replicate the procedures and publish *their* results if contradictory. But marketing research is typically covert. Only the sponsor is given the test results and predictions, and failures are not likely to be openly attributed to the weakness of the marketing researchers. Insofar as advertising research becomes more academic and less proprietary, its goals will more likely be attained.

Does advertising lead or follow demand?

It's a widely held conviction that advertisements *induce* consumer demand. If this were so, it would place substantial responsibility on the advertising industry in general, and the specific sponsor of each ad in particular. During the earliest years of mass media advertisements, some campaigns exerted an enormous influence on the buying behavior of millions of gullible and compliant consumers. However, a generation ago, advertisers began to survey customer wishes that originated *outside* the ads themselves and to cater to those preexisting pressures.

For example, in the early 1970s, North American automobile manufacturers saw that they were losing their market share to Japanese makers who achieved almost half of the total sales. This threat was dampened only by the institution of import quotas levied by the governments of the United States and Canada against the Japanese cars.

Surveys indicated that many North Americans felt that the local manufacturers deserved to suffer some sales loss, because they were guilty of promoting inappropriate standards such as high power and large size, rather than economy of purchase and operation, and quality of design and finish. That the Japanese offered the latter virtues, which turned out to appeal to customers despite the American ads, was seen as a failure of the advertisers and manufacturers to address the "right" variables.

The relation between ads, sales, consumer demands, and world affairs requires some explanation. For every species that presently populates this planet, hundreds of others have evolved, failed to achieve competitive success, and vanished into extinction. The same has applied to the automobile industry. In

"Hey! Not this new stuff... Me want Jurassic Coke."

both cases, the struggle for success included a wide variety of approaches, mutations, and variations. Car manufacturers have tried every conceivable size, shape, configuration, and market slot.

What sold most successfully from the 1950s were the typical American cars, with seating for six, soft suspension, powerful but unrefined engines, aggressive styling, rear-wheel drive, and annual styling changes. Small cars such as the Hudson Jet, the Nash Metropolitan, and the Willy's Henry J consistently failed to achieve success. High-quality cars designed to last for 30 years similarly failed; the Rolls Royce assembly facility in Springfield, Massachusetts, had to close because of inadequate sales. It was because of these experiences that the advertisements stressed appearance, power, largeness, and "all new" models every year. That is, ads *followed* consumer demand more than they *caused* it.

Advertisers try to impose their ideas at their peril. In 1985 Coca Cola's blind taste testing indicated a general preference for New Coke over the original Coke, so the formula was changed. Consumers protested and even sued the company! Within six weeks the complaints forced Coca Cola to reintroduce the original formula. The company had overlooked consumers' dislike of feeling manipulated.

PROMOTION AND THE PUBLIC INTEREST

If advertising can daily induce people to drink millions of bottles of soft drinks—high-profit substitutes for water—can it induce them to engage in activities that are healthy and prosocial? Advertising was partly responsible for spreading the practice of smoking from men to women. If advertising can change attitudes toward women's smoking, can it change attitudes toward spouse and child abuse? If advertisers are permitted to use public channels of communication, are they obliged to use these media in a socially responsible fashion? Increasingly, the answers to such questions are held to be "yes."

Television has the ability to project powerful images that can shape public opinion. A televised commercial generally presents a story that tries to involve the audience empathetically and emotionally, and this can influence public perceptions of the groups depicted. For instance, Goulet (1986) analyzed a small sample (100) of commercials shown during prime time in Canada, and found that the elderly are underrepresented in all commercials except those for health products, in which they are overrepresented. Commercials generally exaggerate to make their point. Where the depiction is deemed to violate the public interest, complaints are likely to follow. Hence, advertisers are now trying to present ethnic groups, women, and elderly persons in favorable contexts to avoid portraying stereotype images.

Advertising directed at children

As recently as two generations ago, advertising was rarely directed at children. Today, the situation is different: (a) many children watch more television than most adults, (b) children often have a major influence on the purchase of products such as breakfast cereal, snack foods, beverages, and toys, (c) children are highly susceptible to televised messages, especially those featuring their favorite characters, and (d) the average child sees 20,000 television commercials per year, 1,000 of them on Saturday mornings (Action for Children's Television, 1977). More recent data suggest that a child may see 60 ads for toys, totaling about 3,000 per year, while watching Saturday morning television. This has led to debate on whether advertising to children over public airwaves should be permitted at all.

Serious concerns have been raised over the trusting nature of children and the way ads can hamper their decision-making skills by focusing on product attributes that should not be considered important or that will lead to disappointment. Robertson and Rossiter's survey (1977) found that children who viewed television for long hours were more likely to be disappointed with their Christmas presents than those who were short-time viewers. Social theorists are alarmed by aspects such as the emphasis on materialism, the need to be liked or to follow what the group is doing, and the use of attractive child models that are inherent in these ads.

The impact of such ads is obvious; if they weren't effective, they wouldn't be used. The impact is also verified by research. For instance, Goldberg and Gorn (1978) showed one group of children a televised toy commercial, another group a control program. The kids were then invited to play with either a "nice" boy who didn't have the toy, or a "not so nice" boy who had it. Most of the control group chose the "nice" playmate; two-thirds of the experimental group chose the toy owner.

In the United States, codes or guidelines adopted by advertisers and broadcasters (under the threat of regulation) have curbed the most flagrant abuses. One of these is that commercial content should be clearly separated from program content, and program hosts or cartoon characters should not deliver sales messages. In Canada, the province of Quebec has prohibited all television ads directed to children, and the U.S. Congress recently passed a bill limiting the number of minutes of commercials during programs directed at children.

Future trends

There are many questions for which we have no clear-cut answers. Can an advertisement induce a *need* in you that was not there before? What is the relation between the *enjoyability* of a commercial and its long-range *influence?*

What determines decisions about major issues such as the city to live in or whether to attend college?

Academics tend to make their goal the attainment of knowledge, not profits. But marketing research is expensive; charges for preliminary projects like surveys or test marketing can run into six-figure amounts. How can the cost-benefit ratio be accurately determined?

If cigarettes or alcohol were introduced as new products now, they would be prohibited as addictive and deadly drugs. Yet, they are legal, although controlled. What restrictions should be placed on their promotion? What restrictions should be placed on the televised advertising of personal hygiene or contraception products?

What is the obligation of the advertising industry to use its influence for the public good? When does high-technology monitoring constitute an invasion of privacy? When does a promotion cross the line between salesmanship and deception? These questions engage the philosopher as much as the psychologist.

As we have seen in the first 13 chapters of this book, without industry, there would be less to life. We end with the observation that without marketing, there would be less to industry.

Study guide for chapter 14

HAVE YOU LEARNED THESE NAMES AND TERMS?

consumer psychology

product cycle time

aided recall

recognition

focus group; client lab

demographic

psychographics

activities, interests, and opinions (AIOs)

values and lifestyles (VALS)

disposable income

autonomic nervous system

parasympathetic and sympathetic nervous systems

pupillometry

split run

pipeline effect

consumer jury

zip, zap, and time shift

coupon

hard and soft sell

self-monitoring

generic

primary demand, pioneering advertising

copy

ISSUES TO CONSIDER

What academic background would prepare you to be a consumer psychologist?

Why is consumer protection not a typical interest of consumer psychologists?

Why is marketing research now such an integral part of promotion?

Which survey approach would be simplest to administer?

What are the weaknesses of the clinical approach to marketing research?

How might the results of a focus group be misleading?

What is the weakness of the VALS approach?

How useful are physiological techniques?

What are the pros and cons of the split run research technique?

How direct are direct responses?

What are the advantages of coupons to the marketer?

What are the disadvantages of coupons to the buyer?

Which ads have you encountered that combine various advertising goals?

Can you think of another example of an advertisement that leads and one that follows?

What role should psychology play in determining restrictions on advertising?

SAMPLE MULTIPLE-CHOICE QUESTIONS

1. When did the APA originate its Division of Consumer Psychology?
    a. 1900
    b. 1920
    c. 1940
    d. 1960

2. Representative users are asked to try the item, and to discuss it together, in the
    a. clinical interview.
    b. focus group.
    c. client lab.
    d. aided recall approach.

3. To tell which part of an ad is emotionally arousing, researchers would use
    a. the eye camera.
    b. pupillometry.
    c. the split run.
    d. both the eye camera and pupillometry.

4. Conspicuous examples of the power of advertising are
    a. soft drinks and cigarettes.
    b. the Ford Edsel.
    c. coupons.
    d. space food sticks.

5. In behavioral research, scientists might observe
    a. animal behavior in a laboratory setting.
    b. people making shopping choices in the supermarket.
    c. physiological changes using an eye camera.
    d. a focus group discussing a product.

Answers: page 462

Answers for sample multiple-choice questions

Chapter 1	Chapter 5	Chapter 9	Chapter 13
1. d	1. a	1. c	1. d
2. b	2. a	2. d	2. c
3. b	3. c	3. a	3. a
4. b	4. d	4. c	4. d
5. a	5. b	5. d	5. c

Chapter 2	Chapter 6	Chapter 10	Chapter 14
1. a	1. a	1. b	1. d
2. c	2. a	2. b	2. c
3. a	3. b	3. a	3. d
4. d	4. b	4. a	4. a
5. d	5. b	5. b	5. b

Chapter 3	Chapter 7	Chapter 11
1. b	1. b	1. b
2. a	2. c	2. c
3. b	3. b	3. a
4. c	4. c	4. d
5. a	5. a	5. b

Chapter 4	Chapter 8	Chapter 12
1. d	1. a	1. d
2. d	2. c	2. a
3. a	3. d	3. b
4. a	4. d	4. c
5. d	5. b	5. b

Epilogue

The goals of psychology are to describe, understand, and influence the behavior of people and animals. The objectives of *industrial* psychology are to describe, predict, and understand the behavior of people at work. Can a textbook adequately predict and explain occupational behavior? Unfortunately, no, for a number of reasons:

- It is the nature of a textbook to compartmentalize. People, however, are not arranged into chapters; they function as integrated wholes, which are much harder to deal with, both academically and conceptually.

- Textbooks imply that human behavior is predictable and regulated by rules. But people are immensely complex, and if they do follow rules, we are far from having the full script.

- We do not know all the outside variables, or combinations of them, that affect behavior. For instance, one personality type, under a certain weather condition, when confronted with a specific stimulus, may act in a novel and unexpected way. All we can do is make generalizations and hope that they are not too broad.

- Most of what we know (or think we know) is based on *research*. Research, however, tends to be artificial, time limited, and not easily generalized beyond the test parameters. For instance, an estimated four-fifths of the world's academic literature on industrial psychology is based on studies conducted solely in the United States.

- Researchers and textbook authors tend to assume idealized and simplified situations, which are rarely matched in real life.

One can but try. I hope this book has been a useful attempt.

If you are a student or colleague who just finished reading this book, you are in the best position to evaluate it. Did it meet your expectations? Is there any way it could have been improved for you? Drop me a note with your comments. I would enjoy hearing from you.

Alan Auerbach,
Wilfrid Laurier University
Waterloo, Ontario
Canada N2L 3C5
E-mail: Internet aauerbac@mach1.wlu.ca

Appendix A
How to
be a wise
consumer

The last chapter in the text covered the many ways in which psychology is used to sell goods to you. This appendix shows how to avoid being sold. It outlines the history of the consumer movement, and specifies procedures for consumer product testing. It also lets you know where you can find the information to become a discerning consumer and, in the process, to improve the quality of what is offered you.

We have become a nation of consumers. Our consumption is not restricted to manufactured products like toothpaste or cars. We consume (in the sense of pay for and perhaps attend, willingly or otherwise) institutions such as schools, hospitals, and prisons.

We consume, in a similar sense, postal, police and fire-fighting services. And we consume (by choosing from alternatives, and again, paying for) our politicians and elected officials, some of whom attract our "purchase" decisions with the same techniques as the toothpaste or car promoter. Increasingly, political, religious, and corporate ideologies are being promoted with techniques similar to those adopted by sophisticated advertisers of household products.

Each of us, it has been estimated, is importuned to "consume" something over a hundred times each day. Philosopher Ivan Illich has seriously argued that the unwritten curriculum of the North American school system is aimed at teaching all of us to participate in the producer/consumer matrix. Any societal direction so pervasive as the imperative to *consume* deserves a counterforce. This opposite pressure, the consumer movement, protects us from becoming victims of marketing forces. This appendix, then, will protect you from the techniques of the consumer psychologist.

THE CONSUMER MOVEMENT

Consumers, as we know them today, are a recent species, still limited to the more affluent parts of the planet. The norm for most people throughout history has been that little was needed, wanted, or expected, and that people were self-sufficient, making by themselves virtually everything they consumed, from their food to their clothing and furniture.

Historically, laws and customs governing the rights apportioned to employer/employee, landlord/tenant, doctor/patient and husband/wife were weighted heavily on one side of each pair. But social movements involving trade unions, tenants' rights associations, patients' rights groups, and women's rights coalitions have gradually equalized the balance of power between the two sides.

Similarly, in the early relations between buyer and seller, all questions of rights used to be defined by the phrase *caveat emptor*. This was more than the warning "Let the buyer beware"; it was a principle of law that stripped the purchaser of most power. The social movement that has swung the power toward the buyer's side may be termed the consumer movement.

The consumer movement started later than the other shifts of power. Laws protecting purchasers were not effective much before the 1930s, and they originally protected buyers only from dangers that were both hidden and life threatening. Gradually this protection was extended to *promotional accuracy* and *product efficacy*. That is, it became impermissible to advertise leaky shoes as waterproof or to sell to unsuspecting mail order customers a "timepiece" that turns out to be a nonfunctioning fake.

Consumers' associations have been formed in many countries. The umbrella organization to which they belong is the International Organization of Consumers Unions (IOCU). The major American group, Consumers Union, has published *Consumer Reports* since 1936. The Canadian counterpart is the Consumers' Association of Canada.

The Consumers' Association of Canada grew out of the Wartime Prices and Review Board (WPRB), a federal agency set up near the start of World War II to control undue rises in the prices of consumer goods that were becoming scarce. Since women controlled 80 percent of the retail market, the WPRB enlisted the cooperation of 56 presidents of national women's organizations in combating price inflation. In response, the presidents worked with the government to establish a consumer branch of the WPRB. In 1947 the women's groups established a peacetime consumers' association, and called it the Consumers' Association of Canada (CAC). Men were allowed to join in 1961.

CAC now operates on three levels. Nationally, it published *Canadian Consumer,* which was first offered in French and English in 1963, and became a monthly periodical in 1981. Before discontinuation in 1993, it reported on some five thousand comparative product-testing projects. In addition, the national group monitors federal policies affecting consumers, such as housing policies and pharmaceutical pricing. It represents consumers at hearings before agencies that regulate systems such as broadcasting, telephones, and transportation.

At the next level, there are eight provincial and two territorial groups that monitor consumer activities within their jurisdiction. In the United States, most consumer-related legislation is handled at the state level; in Canada consumer protection and regulation is provincial. The third level is the local; there are some 60 of these branches throughout Canada.

CAC's operating funds come mainly from its approximately one hundred thousand members. The balance is supplied by the federal and some provincial governments. All CAC workers are unpaid volunteers.

In 1970 consumer advocate Ralph Nader founded the first Public Interest Research Group (PIRG). PIRGs are statewide or province-wide organizations funded and operated by college or university students. In the United States, the state groups support a national one; in Canada, local PIRGs typically support a provincial one.

The purpose of a PIRG is to investigate social, environmental, and consumer issues, and to mobilize the resources of the university and the community toward their resolution. PIRGs thus act as a bridge between students and the rest of society and provide them with an opportunity for the practical application of academic knowledge.

Financing comes from students' fees when the formation of a chapter is accepted in a student referendum. The largest single PIRG is that of Massachusetts, which has a budget of over $3 million per year. A typical group is WPIRG—the Waterloo Public Interest Research Group—based at the University of Waterloo in Ontario.

At the governmental level in Canada, a federal agency dedicated to consumers' interests, Consumer and Corporate Affairs, was established in 1966. Provincial governments have gradually followed suit by establishing agencies that protect those consumers' interests that fall within provincial jurisdiction, such as environmental protection, credit information, and bankruptcy legislation.

Recently, the consumer movement has extended the purchaser's rights into the principle of implied warranty. This concept holds that any marketed item must meet normal and reasonable expectations of performance. For instance, if an overcoat disintegrates after 18 months of ordinary use the supplier cannot point to a label reading One Year Guarantee and thereby disclaim responsibility; courts would hold that overcoats are expected to survive for several years.

The newest extension of purchasers' rights is the lemon law, which was a response to complaints about automobile defects that dealers seemed unwilling or unable to rectify during the guarantee period. Lemon laws have been passed in a number of states and provide that if a product suffers from a serious and recurring defect despite repairs, the owner is entitled to a replacement or refund.

Some jurisdictions, instead of passing a lemon law, have instituted an arbitration system to resolve consumer problems out of court. For instance, in Canada, Ontario began applying this to the automobile industry in 1987. Under the Canadian Motor Vehicle Arbitration Plan, which is funded by virtually all the carmakers who do business in the country, owners of troublesome purchases can (at no cost) bring their case before a professional arbitrator who has the authority to require any rectification, up to and including the repurchase of the vehicle by the manufacturer!

With changes of laws come modifications of focus. Manufacturers and dealers, who originally seemed to perceive the customer as fair game, have increasingly tried to justify a reputation as fair, honorable, and responsive to consumers' concerns. Some are discovering that the more resources are invested in *customer service* functions (originally the complaint department), the less the legal department is needed to protect the firm.

Similarly, the design engineering objective has changed from "Let's make it *look* like it really works" to "Let's design our new model so that it gets the top rating in *Consumer Reports.*" Still, the marketing managers know that most consumers make their purchase decisions on the basis of psychological factors such as attitude, social influence, prior experience, and selective memory, attention and perception.

So far, we have been looking at research aimed at end users. Now we turn to research designed by and for academics, that is, research on consumer behavior published in academic journals rather than in lay publications.

ACADEMIC RESEARCH ON CONSUMERISM

The American Psychological Association added the Division of Consumer Psychology in 1960, the same year as the founding of the *Journal of Advertising Research.* Prior to that time, consumer psychology was a minor topic of scientific research, represented only by the *Journal of Marketing.*

By 1976, however, Jacoby reported the existence of some ten thousand consumer-related papers that had been published between 1967 and 1975. By the time of this review (Jacoby, 1976), three other journals were reporting on consumer research, the *Journal of Marketing Research,* the *Journal of Consumer Research,* and the *Journal of Advertising. Marketing Science* joined them in 1982.

In a review of the academic literature in consumer psychology, Bettman (1986) evaluated over 200 papers published between 1981 and 1984. He found that the most active research areas dealt with the determinants cf buying behavior, especially the effects of what is recalled by the buyers; the connection between affect and cognition; and the processes of persuasion. Bettman also argued that the issues involved in consumer research can serve to further the advance of psychological theory in general, because consumer choices involve basic psychological variables such as prior knowledge, information presented through various media, and the effect of other consumers.

Research in consumer psychology may be divided into a few general categories. These are (a) assessing responses to advertising, (b) measuring consumers' attitudes and opinions through surveys and (c) other measures such as projective techniques, (d) identifying organismic variables associated with specific consumer behavior, and (e) consumer product testing. The first three topics were covered in the previous chapter; in the next section, we will consider how the consumer psychologist looks at product testing.

Product-testing principles

One of the strongest expressions of the consumer movement is the recent emphasis on *consumer product testing.* It used to be one of the ironies of marketing that only the most affluent customers tended to review comparative evaluations before purchasing. Now, however, the reliance on test reports has become much more common as schools, trade unions, fraternal organizations, retirement associations, and government publications increasingly emphasize the importance of becoming an informed consumer.

Anyone can perform scientific, valid tests of consumer products. A fully instrumented laboratory is not required for testing; all that is needed is a knowledge of *testing principles.* All purchasers, from homemakers to hotels, from tradespersons to tycoons, can, with few restrictions, mount a testing project as meaningful as those published by professional testers. You yourself can perform simple product evaluations, as you are about to see.

Choosing test products

The choice of products to be evaluated is influenced by practical considerations and by one's interest. You may be fascinated by high-altitude rockets but unable to handle them; you may easily be able to test jelly beans but disinterested in them. Most people choose one brand of product in their early years and make few changes over their lifetime. It should not be difficult for you to list all such brands in your own purchasing habits; from these you should be able to select appropriate candidates for systematic evaluation.

The tested brands should belong to the same general category. Various red table wines could be compared with each other, beers could be tested against lager or ale, fresh orange juice could be matched with frozen or canned. But fruit juice would not be tested against soup; pencils should not be expected to compete with crayons.

Product-testing methodology

The test protocol, or specific testing procedure, may include objective or subjective procedures. *Objective* measures are those to which numbers can be assigned without relying on personal judgments; they usually involve laboratory procedures. If, for instance, the evaluation of dental floss included a measure of the samples' breaking strengths, this would be determined objectively.

Before *subjective* tests are initiated, you would select the group of testers (consumer jury), perhaps from volunteers among associates, classmates, colleagues, or employees. You will probably administer a pretest questionnaire to the potential jurors. Its purpose is to establish (a) past experience with the product or product type, (b) variables regarding the product category that are seen as important to the jurors, and (c) suitability of jurors to test this product. Regarding (c), take care to ensure that abstainers would not test beer, or that people allergic to nuts would not test peanut butter.

You may want to conceal some questions of interest within the questionnaire. For instance, you may want to determine whether or not people can detect potato flavor in potato chips in a blindfold test. Therefore, you would embed your questions about potato chips in a questionnaire seemingly dealing with other products, so that the jurors would not expect to be served the chips as their test item.

For a subjective test on, say, dental floss, jurors would be provided with samples and trained to evaluate them on specific criteria such as ease of use, comfort, or taste. These subjective tests should be performed under blind conditions (page 25) in which the samples are identified by codes only. Jurors should be provided with well-designed record sheets on which they note their evaluations.

The main problem in subjective ratings is the *accuracy* of the judgments. One solution is to train and test the raters beforehand. Another is to assess rater consistency during the administration of a test. This can be accomplished by repeating the trial, or by including some duplicate samples in a single trial.

The subjective dimensions on which the product is to be evaluated may be derived from the questionnaire. Accordingly, this instrument should tap not only the rater's previous experience with and attitudes to the product, but preferred brands, the reasons for the preference, and the amounts normally used.

A specific protocol is recommended particularly for consumables, that is, products that are eaten or drunk. Start with a differentiation or triangle test. Three portions are served, two of which are identical. The task is to identify which two are the same (or which is different). To take into account the fact that by random chance one-third of the jurors could be expected to guess correctly, the triangle test should be repeated at least once. (An individual's chance of guessing right *once* is one in three, but the likelihood of guessing right twice in a row is only one in nine.)

Why is the triangle test important? If you served two cups of the identical cola to jurors and asked them to choose the better one, virtually all jurors would choose one or the other rather than declare them indistinguishable. Simple statements of preference are suspect, so you must ensure that the jurors are able at least to differentiate one brand from another. Only those who pass the triangle test are entitled to proceed to the next phase, the preference test.

In the preference test, not only must you control all the obvious variables (for example, ensure that the samples are equally fresh, presented at the same serving temperature, in similar containers, with identical portions) but also you must consider the order effect. One sample, obviously, must be tried first. But the first in any series may be the automatic preference, especially if testing the product induces sensory fatigue. For instance, the first serving of hard liquor or a frozen product like ice cream could deaden the tongue; if presented with ten perfumes, jurors would have difficulty after the first few.

There are various ways of reducing the order effect. With a large number of jurors you could administer the products to each in a random order. With a small number you could ensure that each tester tries the items in a different order, preferably so that all possible orders are administered. (This is a within-between-subjects design, since the data are analyzed between subjects to measure the *treatment effect,* and within subjects to disclose the *order effect.*)

A juror can cope with the memory demands inherent in evaluating two or three samples. But how could someone deal with, say, 10 samples of lemonade or 20 brands of chocolate? How could you determine which of 6 chairs is the most comfortable, or which of 12 cameras has the best "hand feel"?

And suppose the task were not merely to determine the *best* but to rank order all of the samples, that is, to rank them in continuous order from worst to best. Knowing the *ranking* of the samples is more useful than knowing only which is the best, because some other factor, such as price, can be contrasted with the rank order to indicate which would be the best buy.

Larger numbers of samples can be assessed by the multiple paired comparisons test, (page 217) in which you compare two at a time. Paired comparisons work best when only *one* dimension of a product is being evaluated, as in which tastes better, which feels smoother, which smells more expensive. You could not ask all three questions at each pairing, although you could ask for successive pairings, one for each dimension. When running a paired comparisons test with a jury as opposed to an individual, order effect can be controlled by prescribing in advance the sample order each juror follows.

After the testing trial has been completed you collect the responses, analyze them, and record the conclusions. Your evaluation may take into account not only the test results but also variables such as price, availability, warranty, and whatever else the pretest questionnaire indicated was salient to the users (or potential users) of that product.

Sensory evaluation

Here are ten different light bulbs. Which one is the brightest, longest-lasting, and requires the least electricity? A researcher would find this type of *objective* question quite straightforward to deal with, once the necessary instruments were set up. But how would the researcher determine which bulb *looks* best?

In objective testing, the researcher selects, calibrates, and verifies the accuracy of the testing instruments. In sensory evaluation, the "instrument" is some individual's nose and tongue, sometimes the fingers or eyes. Who these individuals are, accordingly, is important. These testers, who are called consumer panelists or jurors, fall into one of three categories.

One category of possible jurors is the *untrained* person, who is considered a representative of potential users of the product. Such testers can be recruited in, for instance, shopping malls. Typically, many jurors are recruited, and there may be problems in ensuring that they all represent the target population. Such testing is usually costly and somewhat haphazard.

More pointed and controlled testing is performed in laboratory settings, on *trained* testers. Trained panelists have been themselves tested (at least for normal sensory acuity in the variables at issue), and taught to be sensitive to small differences in certain aspects of the product. They are also trained to disregard personal preferences or opinions, and to avoid communicating their judgments to other testers. Trained panelists are typically expected to participate on a long-term basis. Procedures for recruiting, training, and running them can be found in Watts, Ylimaki, Jeffery and Elias (1989).

A third category of tester is the *expert*. Experts are not only trained, but gifted and experienced in a specific domain such as wine, tea, or ice cream. They carefully prepare for the testing session, for instance, by ensuring that nothing is interfering with their palate or nose. In the session, they watch for the slightest sensory fatigue, and stop testing at that point.

It is ironic that expert testers (who are known as "noses" in the perfume, wine, and liquor industries) are generally older men. There is no evidence that men are better than women in sensory acuity, and it is established that the ability to smell and especially to taste slightly diminishes with age.

Rather, all "experts" have learned a specific and esoteric vocabulary of sensory terminology, a word list that is shared and understood by other experts in that field. It may take years of training to learn the subtle differences in terms such as, for instance, bouquet, aftersmell, resonance, aroma, nose, and presence. Perhaps that's why expert testers are rarely young.

Besides the techniques and the terminology, the expert tester must be aware of errors that can contaminate the results; we look at these next.

Sources of testing error

Positional errors result from the *order* in which samples are presented to the tester. Typically, the first in a group of samples is upgraded, and the last ones in a long series may suffer due to the tester's boredom or sensory fatigue. As a solution, the order can be randomized or varied systematically.

Consider the case where a panelist is testing the crunchiness of samples that look different, or is assessing the flavor of beverages, some of which are carbonated. If the appearance or fizziness of the samples affects the judgments, these are called stimulus errors. One solution is to ensure that irrelevant differences in the samples are eliminated; another is to conceal these differences from the tester for instance, by using a blindfold.

A specific case of order effect or positional error is the contrast error. Trying a high-rated sample would lower the rating of a slightly inferior sample that immediately follows it. Similarly, a judgment accorded to a markedly inferior sample may spill over to the next sample, which will then be unfairly downgraded.

You were introduced to the concept of *demand characteristics* in chapter 2. In sensory evaluation, this is termed expectation error. Panelists' guesses about the identity of the samples, or even about the product attributes they are supposed to detect, can influence their judgments; so can the names—or even the code names—given to the samples.

For instance, the name "Sample A" sounds better than "Sample D." For this reason, samples are commonly coded with three-digit numbers that are randomly determined. If informed that one sample is a fine French wine and the others are cheap, local ones, panelists may overrate the preferred one—or even the most unique or distinctive sample. Obviously, testers should remain as blind and neutral as possible.

Now that we have looked at the consumer movement in general, and at principles of consumer product testing, we should consider the various media that perform and publish product evaluations.

Where are test results published?

A useful starting point for any product test is an examination of product evaluations already in print. However, not every report should be accepted uncritically, as will soon become apparent.

The results of product tests may be published in a variety of media, only some of which are available to the general public. Some of these publications such as technical reports commissioned by an industrial firm or a governmental agency are restricted in circulation. Other tests are narrowly technical, and would be published only in academic or professional journals.

Much of the unpublished product testing occurs in *quality assurance* or *quality control* laboratories operated by retailers and institutions to verify the standards of items they process or resell. For example, department store and supermarket chains typically test the paint or potato chips they sell, especially if the products are sold as a generic or imprint brand. Generic means no name; imprint or store-brand items bear the name of the retailer or a brand name owned by the retailer, for example, Craftsman tools are manufactured for and sold by Sears. These test results, of course, are not circulated beyond the sponsor.

Tests of common or consumer products are reported largely in four types of publications: (a) the specialty magazine, (b) periodicals such as *Consumer Reports,* (c) the trade or professional periodical, and (d) articles in newspapers. Let's define and then review each in turn.

Specialty magazines These are periodicals that appeal to people with a focused interest. Examples of magazines aimed at the photographic hobbyist include *Modern Photography, U.S. Camera,* and *Popular Photography.* As advertisers become increasingly unwilling to pay for promotions that many readers will not be interested in, they turn to the specialty publication, where every reader is presumably a logical target. There are now specialty magazines that appeal to people with every conceivable interest, from car drivers, cooks, and card players, to travelers, toy collectors, and tennis players.

Consumer magazines Magazines such as *Consumer Reports* are published by nonprofit consumer groups. These periodicals report the results of tests on a wide variety of common goods and services. The largest by far, with a newsstand and subscription monthly circulation of 4.5 million, is *Consumer Reports,* published in the United States.

The Canadian equivalent is *Protect Yourself,* which is sponsored by the government of the province of Quebec and is available in both English and French versions. In England, the equivalent is called *Which?* These periodicals generally carry no advertising, with the possible exception of messages from consumer-related organizations.

Trade and professional periodicals Most trade and professional groups publish their own periodicals. For instance, innkeepers may receive *Motel Management,* and garage owners may subscribe to *Auto Trade.* The *Bar Association Journal* would be sent either to lawyers or bartenders. Such periodicals present product-test reports only in a peripheral manner, and the products are usually directed to the professional tradesperson. Thus, they may all present evaluations of a personal computer, each from its own standpoint. But where the publication is directed at retail merchants, there may be reports on tests of items aimed at the buying public, to help the merchant stock the most satisfactory brands.

Newspaper articles   A final source of product-test reports may be termed the "journalistic" contribution. In every large community there is invariably a publication, typically a newspaper, which runs a column with a title such as "Consumer Corner." Such columns may publish reports on consumer issues in general, they may deal with consumer complaints, or they may offer buying advice, such as supermarket specials. But some of them include product-test evaluations.

Some newspaper-like periodicals, such as weekly financial or business periodicals, offer a consumers' interest column. These columns may report on general issues, or they may offer a test report on a single brand. It appears that the authors of such columns are basically journalists who have been assigned to write a column on this topic.

The most useful index to product tests is the quarterly publication *Consumers Index to Product Evaluations*. It surveys about 100 periodicals and organizes their product reports into categories. The index provides no information on products or test results; it lists only what sort of test or analysis was performed, and where it was published. For people interested in products associated with offices, the monthly *What to Buy for Business* publishes some test reports, and numerous comparison charts dealing with business equipment and supplies. Both of these periodicals are distributed by subscription only.

Evaluating the evaluators

There are several dimensions on which product tests in one type of publication can be compared with those in another. One variable is how the sample (the item that is being tested) is obtained. For *Consumer Reports* and some other consumer magazines, the sample is purchased in the open retail market by a shopper who is *anonymous,* in that the connection between the purchaser and the testing publication is concealed.

For specialty and trade/professional publications, however, the test samples are typically provided by the manufacturer. One problem is the possibility that the manufacturer will have accorded some extra care to the test sample, even if only to ensure that it meets design specifications and works flawlessly.

A second problem is that some equipment leaves the assembly line prepared not for the end-use customer but for long-distance shipping to a dealer. It is the dealer's responsibility to perform whatever final operations are required, such as uncrating, assembly, lubrication, test operations, and cosmetic work. This dealer preparation largely determines whether the car, bicycle, tractor, or lathe operates properly or not. It is the manufacturer's responsibility to ensure that the dealer is properly trained, equipped, and motivated to perform these tasks suitably. Obviously, it is only the anonymous purchaser of a test sample who is likely to encounter deficiencies in dealer preparation.

Further variables are the decision on which brand or product to test, and the test protocol. For instance, with cars, should the tester choose a powerful convertible and measure its top speed, or should the project test a low-powered sedan for the ease of changing its tires? Do we choose a low-cost toaster and measure its electricity consumption, or should expensive toasters be measured for speed and convenience?

In making such decisions, the publications cater to their readers. The specialty magazines tend to feature the new, the technologically innovative, and the more complex and higher-priced items of interest to those already attracted. For instance, comparative evaluations of television satellite receiving systems would more likely appear in *Television Electronics* than in *Consumer Reports.*

Two problems here are that the average prospective purchaser may not be aware of these hobbyist magazines, and the publications, since they cater to a limited readership, usually lack the resources necessary to mount a substantial comparison test. On the other hand, some of these product tests are highly elaborate. As an example, some photography magazines take apart every camera they test and analyze each component.

The test protocol would, again, appeal to the enthusiast and feature the exploitation of sophisticated features, rather than casual, day-to-day use. Trade publications tend to relate the choice of test sample and test protocol to marketing variables such as anticipated demand, selling features, and serviceability.

So far, it would seem that the hobbyist publication is suspect in its method of acquiring samples, but sometimes more detailed in its examination of them. We must here consider the element of product mystique. Many industries and product groups are associated with a set of folklore-like expectations and assumptions. It would be unreasonable for a group of aficionados, no matter how objective they tried to remain, to not be influenced by the cachet of the Rolls Royce car, the Leica camera, or Joy perfume.

Psychologists have thoroughly documented the effect of experimenter bias, which is the tendency for researchers who are presumed to be objective to derive results that match their preexisting expectations or wishes. Where the tests rely on subjective evaluations, as in how the item "feels" when being operated, the potential for *experimenter bias* is obvious. Publications like *Consumer Reports* purposefully avoid examining products whose primary merit seems to be that of mystique (unless for the purpose of demonstrating the objective emptiness of mystique).

Another variable is the possible influence of advertising. Publications are supposed to maintain complete separation between their editorial and their advertising factions. In theory, then, editorial criticism of brands should never be softened by the fear of losing advertising revenue from sponsors disgruntled by an unfavorable review of their brand or their industry. However, the mass media depend on advertising for their survival, and in practice, major advertisers have been known to stifle disparaging reviews or comments. The editorial staff that drafts the wording of the product-test report on Speedy Shoes would surely be aware that the Speedy advertisements contribute to their salaries and those of their coworkers. Magazines of the *Consumer Reports* type refuse to publish advertisements, primarily to prevent the possibility of ads influencing testing or editorial decisions. In fact, one of IOCU's rules is that the publications of members may not include any advertisements.

Another difference among the product-test media is the language adopted for presenting the published report. Many specialty magazines feature breezy, imaginative, simile-laden prose, with trendy superlatives and frequent exclamation marks. By contrast, the language in magazines like *Consumer Reports* is detached, matter-of-fact, and clear.

Why should we criticize writing that tries to be entertaining as well as informative? The danger is that the style influences the content. It is possible, for instance, that a writer first concocts a good line and then searches for an opportunity (or an excuse) to use it. Also, readers may assume that inventive phrases were meant to convey emphasis, rather than simply to provide stylistic interest.

Editors of product-testing publications face a number of problems regarding the passage of time. Some products are introduced abruptly, with much publicity, and are discontinued almost too suddenly for a test report to reach the readers while the product remains available. Others undergo frequent modifications, so that by the time test results are published, that particular model has been superseded. On occasion, the article will itself result in misinformation. For instance, upon the publication of a favorable report, the product becomes unavailable due to high demand, or the manufacturer or retailer raises the price of what had been a "best buy."

Editors must consider the above complexities when they decide whether or not to rush a test into print, or to extend the testing process. Another factor is that some products cannot be thoroughly examined within a constrained time period. Should the tester examine a manufacturer's hand-built prototype in one hurried day of testing (so that the publication of the results would coincide with the release of the new model), or should there be a prolonged test of a model purchased from a dealer? Consider how the following test protocol requirements could delay publication of a car test.

If the car is a new model, the test sample must not be acquired until assemblers and dealers have become accustomed to it. The vehicle must then be subjected to at least the manufacturer's recommended "break-in" driving. The car must be operated under extremes of heat, cold, rain, and snow. And it must be operated long enough for wear defects to show up and to evaluate how warranty claims are handled.

Because of such restrictions, a *Consumer Reports* car test protocol may involve months of research. The specialty magazines, by contrast, may complete their testing, especially with a novel and newsworthy model, in a week or less.

Another problem faced by testing editors, especially those of the general magazine type, is the number of brands available. It would be impractical to test every possible brand of most products. For instance, there may be 100 brands or models of 35mm cameras available. The testing program might call for this product to be covered every three years. If only ten brands can be tested, the choices will probably be based on sales popularity. This could be unfair to a small firm with a new and superior camera.

The final variable involves the *location* of the testing. Testers who work for specialty and trade publications are routinely invited to visit the manufacturer and conduct the research there—under highly hospitable conditions.

Some major manufacturers offer comprehensive and elaborate test equipment and "proving grounds," but there are still several problems associated with a neutral tester conducting evaluations with the help of a manufacturer's facilities. One is that the test samples may not be randomly chosen and normally prepared. Another is that side-by-side comparisons with competing brands may be rendered impossible or unfair.

Further, the manufacturer may propose or devise a test protocol that gives its brand an advantage. Also, the manufacturer's representatives or engineers may be on hand to facilitate minor adjustments or to help interpret problems. Most important, the testers, by becoming, in effect, guests of the test sponsor, may have difficulty in remaining objective or neutral.

More objective evaluations can be expected when the testing takes place in specially designed facilities owned by the evaluators. The staff employed by Consumers Union, which publishes *Consumer Reports,* includes over 100 specialized engineers, who are provided with complete testing apparatus.

Specialty publications rarely employ test engineers, but rely on staff technicians who are experienced in their specialty area. Likewise, trade and professional periodicals rely on qualified editorial staff rather than on testing personnel to perform the tests. The more completely staffed and equipped the testing agency, the less it will be tempted to accept help from those who may be biased.

REMAINING GAPS

Despite the wealth of product-testing information available, there are many categories of products on which comparative evaluations are hard to come by. Heavy-duty equipment (like a transport truck) is, for obvious reasons, rarely tested. Items designed for commercial use are ignored, whether they be paints or cleaners (which probably should be tested), or pneumatic drills or rock crushers (which would not be of interest to the public).

Another category that is rarely tested is agricultural equipment, whether it be units designed for commercial use or smaller ones sold to hobby farmers.

The most expensive purchase most people make, the residential home, is not tested, at least in its entirety.

Consumer-product testing is big business. Readers look to product testers to advise them on what brand of toaster, can opener, or juicer to buy, and how to keep from being ripped off. But in making us question whether we should buy any of these items in the first place, or in telling us how to stop ripping off the environment, the testers have been remiss.

Most of the testing energy is devoted to cars, with never a thoughtful essay on *alternatives* to cars in the context of their degradation of natural resources and air quality. Some two decades ago, *Consumer Reports* pointed out that a car that gets 15 miles per gallon (mpg) costs only $100 more in fuel than one that gets 20 mpg, so if the former vehicle could save us more than $100 per year in repairs, it would be the better buy. That philosophy does not seem to have changed.

For instance, a 1990 issue of the magazine covered leaf blowers, which were accurately described as motorized rakes. Various brands were compared among each other. None, however, was compared with an efficient hand rake, which is easier to start, quieter, cheaper, and healthier to the user and to the environment.

Major electrical appliances are increasingly rated on their energy efficiency. The context, however, is cost of operation, implying that if you can afford to operate it, you need not worry about what it costs the environment to create that electricity.

Lawn mowers are rated for efficiency in bagging the clippings. The value of allowing these to remain to fertilize the grass is generally ignored. Orange juice squeezers are meticulously compared—with no mention of the health and convenience benefits of simply eating the orange.

Disposable cameras have been rated for operation and value. Rarely is a word printed about what happens to each camera after it is discarded. Packaging represents about 40 percent of our landfill, but less than one percent of the evaluative comments by testers!

In automobile frequency-of-repair records, all components are treated the same; there's no difference between a car that costs $300 in its third year for faulty air conditioners and one that costs the same for transmission repairs. Defective air conditioners can lead to the loss of freon gas, which can indirectly cause vast environmental and medical harm.

Finally, about a trillion dollars a year has been spent on military equipment. Since most victims of war are civilians, perhaps we should be grateful that much is *not* well tested under combat conditions.

The current need

By current standards most people acutely needed more consumer protection as recently as fifty years ago. Just as labor unions were needed to protect the worker, consumer activists were needed to protect the buyers and users of products and services. Now, custom and legislation give the nonunion member more protection than the unionist had a generation ago. Does this imply that today's consumer no longer needs activists for protection? Is consumerism out of date?

In some ways, the answer is yes. Fifty years ago there were considerable differences among brands. Some could be rather unsafe; others were downright dangerous. Some were totally useless; others performed as expected. Some would last a lifetime; others would collapse after the first use. Today there is far more *consistency and quality* among products. Presently, any cases of tainted food, failure-prone tires, or a new car that did not make it home from the dealership would be front-page news.

These advances are largely the result of governmental regulations. They are also due to a more elaborate manufacturing support network. That is, the same firm that offers a superior component to one manufacturer will offer it to another. A special process discovered in one industry will soon become available to others. There are few trade secrets or unique, protected formulae that cannot be unlocked and duplicated.

Superior product quality today is also the result of consumer sophistication. Fifty years ago, making a purchase was like making a bet. You might win; you might lose. Today the purchaser feels *entitled* to high quality and is likely to be quite communicative in the event of dissatisfaction.

Does this all mean that the importance of the consumer movement is muted? Does it mean that we should choose brands simply on the basis of convenience or price? In fact, the tenets of consumerism are still important for the following reasons:

- Our *expectations* are higher than ever. In previous generations, a stomach illness that afflicted an entire family would have been accepted as a fact of life. Today its cause would be tracked down and the manufacturer and seller of any tainted food would be subject to legal and regulatory action.

- The *consequences* of mediocre quality are higher. When people traveled by bicycle, at a jogging pace, a collapsed wheel might result in a scrape. In a modern racer a defective wheel could result in a serious injury.

- The *choices* before the buying public are vast, and include new types of products for which user expectations may be uncertain. When your grandfather received a year-end bonus of a week's wages, the windfall might well have gone into new shoes for the family—with little debate as to alternatives because there were so few to choose from. Many people today, with their essential needs met, choose from a wide assortment of products, some of them unfamiliar.

- In previous times, the original cost of buying an item was pretty well the entire expense. Now the purchase price is likely to be a small fraction of the cost of servicing, applying, fueling, storing, or maintaining the product. When somebody would paint your house for the price of a few meals, the main consideration was the price of the paint. Today, when it may cost you a month's wages to hire a painter, it is useful to know if an expensive paint will outlast a cheaper brand.

- Finally, today *promotional manipulation* is sophisticated to the point of being compelling. Consumers have been induced to pay about a billion dollars for drinking water, with small quantities of color, flavor, and carbon dioxide gas. Manufacturers of soda spend more for promotion and packaging than they do for ingredients.

On one level, product testing is so simple that this appendix has invited you to perform your own tests. But on another level, there are so many factors influencing any results, that ratings should be interpreted not only according to the test protocol but also according to the medium in which they were reported. On one level, the need for product testing has disappeared; on another, the need has never been greater.

Appendix B

How to conduct
a survey

As you saw in chapter 2, the survey (especially the questionnaire) has always been the most common means of gathering data in I/O psychology research. This appendix gives you tips to encourage you to take the first step in surveying people. Before conducting research that is meant to constitute much more than merely an exercise, you should consult a text on survey technique. Also, review the basic advantages and disadvantages of the interview and questionnaire in chapter 2, so that you may design yours to exploit the strong points and minimize the weaknesses.

TYPES OF SURVEYS

Surveys can be categorized in various ways; you have to decide what type you want. *Subjective* surveys generally involve an intense, probing interview of a small number of respondents. *Objective* surveys are typically questionnaires, in which the responses are converted to numbers for statistical analysis. Questionnaires can be administered *face-to-face,* as by stopping shoppers and asking them to fill out the form; to a *group* such as a college class or a factory division; or by *mail,* in which case you should expect a low return rate. Another decision to make is whether the respondents should be asked to identify themselves or whether they are to remain anonymous. Anonymity is the more common procedure, but response accuracy might be enhanced when respondents are expected to identify themselves.

SAMPLE SELECTION

Samples can be selected (a) *randomly,* by opportunity, or by "snowballing," or (b) by *quota,* or through *stratification.* Random samples are harder to obtain than you would think. After defining your population, you have to give everyone in it an equal chance of being selected as a member of the sample. Virtually all psychology students (and many professors) use an opportunity sample (people who are most conveniently at hand), and sometimes these are incorrectly referred to as random samples. In snowballing, each respondent or contact is asked to recruit others to participate.

Quota sampling requires you to decide what characteristics you want represented, and to what extent. If you're interested in, say, Alaskans, and 67 percent of Alaskans are male, you might set a quota of two out of every three participants to be male. A more elaborate form of quota sampling is *stratified* sampling. Here you establish strata or layers and choose participants from each stratum to ensure that your sample represents the population. In a given population, for example, you might select respondents on the basis of education, family income, sex, age, occupational categories, and political allegiances. The more strata you choose, the harder it is to meet them.

Students are usually concerned about *how many* respondents to recruit, and tend to strive to obtain a common sample size such as 30 or 100. This question is like asking how many rats a researcher should run. It's tempting to assume that the larger the N, the better the study, but researchers should emphasize quality over quantity. Five representative and reliable respondents, answering a well-planned and validated instrument, can tell you more about what you want to know than 500 poorly chosen respondents answering a carelessly conceived questionnaire.

A variable that helps the researcher decide the N is the diversity in the responses. This can be estimated by a small, preliminary survey called a pilot study. If your first 10 representative respondents give similar answers, little would likely be gained by surveying an additional one, and you can logically justify a small sample size. But if out of your first 100 respondents, no clear pattern of answers emerges, you may have to survey 1,000 participants to answer your research question. The higher the variability in the answers, the larger an N is called for.

ETHICAL REQUIREMENTS

Respondents should be told that their participation is voluntary, and that they can discontinue at any time. It is appropriate to let them know how they can learn about the purpose and results of the survey, such as by reading a report that you will post in a convenient location.

PLANNING

Before starting to write your questions, establish clearly in your mind the specific purpose of your survey. Every question should have a good reason for being there. Questionnaires are so easy to design, reproduce and distribute, that you may easily become mired in the resulting data. To take a small example, a simple 30-question instrument completed by 100 respondents will yield 3,000 numbers! If you wanted to intercorrelate these results, you could be occupied for a long time. Computers and calculators now make the mathematical operations almost automatic, but the results would leave you in this case with 870 correlations ($n[n -1]$) to interpret.

WORDING AND DESIGN

After drafting your questions, consider the initial, overall impression your questionnaire will make on someone seeing it for the first time. The title (and possibly the headings, if any) should make it clear to your respondent, at a glance, that your piece of paper is nothing more than a straightforward, nonthreatening survey. Rather than looking intimidating, it should appear interesting, inviting, and easy to complete. The general topic or purpose should also be apparent. Finally, the respondent may well remain anonymous, but not the person who is responsible for the survey. Your name and affiliation (such as the course you are doing the project for) should be clearly shown at the top, as well as instructions for what to do with the questionnaire when completed.

The first few questions should be drafted with particular care. People may be hesitant when asked to fill out a questionnaire, but most who start answering will continue. Some questionnaire designers plan to ignore the first item or two, the purpose of which is mostly to orient the respondent into answering the rest. (Whereas orienting the respondents is beneficial, inadvertently "leading" them should be guarded against.)

The wording of the questions should be simple and clear, and should incorporate the instructions on how to answer. "How do you feel about tests?" is less clear than "Indicate with a check-mark in the appropriate box how you feel about answering surveys: Scared   Challenged   Bored   ." (To avoid leading your respondents, you could ask, "Complete this sentence: I feel that surveys are. . . ." Before doing that, however, consider the next paragraph.)

A competent questionnaire designer should be able to prepare an instrument that can be administered to one thousand respondents and be computer scored. On such a questionnaire, the less handwriting on the response sheet, the better. A useful format is the 5-point or 7-point scale with anchor words on some or all of the numbers; an example is on page 487.

Use discretion in asking for any *demographic* information. Many people are willing to render opinions on external issues, but feel that questions on their age, religion, salary, politics, and so forth invade their privacy. If you need this information, use broad categories, for example:

CHECK ONE BOX ON EACH LINE:

Annual Income	under $10,000 ☐	$10,001–$25,000 ☐	Over $25,000 ☐
Age	under 20 ☐	21–29 ☐	30 or over ☐

Usually it's better to ask any demographics at the end, lest the respondent's self-identification affect the responses. For instance, a respondent who starts by indicating that she's a middle-aged woman might respond to questions in ways that she thinks a middle-aged woman *should* answer.

The responses will eventually have to be analyzed or interpreted. Generally your first step is to convert the responses into numerical form and to tabulate (collapse into a table) the numbers. The conversion from attitude and opinion to numbers can be less ambiguous if the respondents answer in a somewhat numerical form in the first place, such as:

CIRCLE 1, 2, or 3 ON EACH LINE:

Annual Income	**1** under $10,000	**2** $10,001–$25,000	**3** Over $25,000
Age	**1** under 20	**2** 21–29	**3** 30 or over

Questions usually attempt to tap the respondents' attitudes or opinions—for example, how employees would feel about wearing uniforms provided by the company on the job. How many choice points should there be in the answer array for each question? The advantage of providing an *odd* number of choices is that the respondent can use the center choice to denote indifference, uncertainty, or neutrality; also, a middle choice provides an anchor point for the alternatives.

The finer the respondents' ability to judge, the more choice points they should be offered. If you think that (in the above example) the employees are divided simply among those who favor uniforms, those who disapprove, and those who don't care, a 3-point selection menu would be appropriate. Conversely, if you were asking experts how they would rate a given sample on a given dimension, a 9-point scale could be used. The objective in choosing the most useful number of choices is to pick the largest number that would be answered *reliably*. The most common numbers are seven or five (page 487).

It may be advisable to ask, either as part of the question or as a supplementary question, how certain the respondent is of the answer given. Also consider offering as an answer choice, "No opinion," "Not sure," or "Not applicable."

Often, useful questions will take the form of asking the extent to which the respondents agree or disagree with a given statement. There are several possible question layouts. One format is to make them all the same, with "Disagree" at the left, "Agree" at the right. Another is to alternate or randomly mix them, to deter a respondent from indicating the same answer all the way down the list of questions.

In a 7-point question, should "1" be used for first choice, and "7" be used for least or last choice, or should "1" mean least and "7" most? To avoid deciding, an alternate format is to use "0" as a center point, with choices ranging from "-3" on one side, and "+3" on the other. In this format, the numbers themselves have a built-in, intuitive meaning. Anchor words (terms that define choice points) on some or all of the numbers can be included, if the clarity would thereby be improved. An example is shown on page 487.

You may want to mislead the respondents as to the ostensible purpose of the survey. Suppose the purpose is to determine whom to invite to serve as product-test jurors. You may want to select those with little experience with the type of product, a moderate amount of experience, or you may want to choose heavy users. If you simply ask the respondents to indicate their experience, they may overstate the truth, either because that makes them feel more important, or because they feel it may be to their advantage. ("Maybe," the respondent thinks, "they're looking for experts to try out their new car model for a year.") A useful solution is to embed your real questions in a set of misdirecting ones—which you will ignore.

The format and physical presentation should be decided with care. Where possible, design the final draft so that it does not extend beyond a single sheet. You can format about three ordinary pages of questions onto both sides of one 8.5 × 14 inch sheet; few respondents would volunteer to answer more than that. Also, single sheets increase response rates, and they decrease reproduction, distribution, and handling cost and work. Multipage questionnaires are less likely to be completed, they must be collated and

fastened together, and they cause other handling problems, all of which reduce the practical advantages of this medium for large-scale use.

Minimize clutter; for instance, don't number your questions if you do
not need to do so. Put to good use the available horizontal space (some of
which is usually wasted), and conserve the vertical space, which is usually
at a premium.

To assess response reliability in an individual's answers, *duplicate* questions
can be included. Duplicates should at first glance appear to be different questions, and they should be distanced from each other. Respondents who answer
essentially the same item differently can be eliminated from the analysis.

RUNNING

Every questionnaire should be subjected to a pilot study, in which a small
group representative of the target respondents (or other volunteers) is administered the questionnaire with the same standardized procedures and instructions that will be used on the main group. Do not allow any discussion
during the completion of the questionnaire. After completion and before collection, ask for problems, concerns, and possible improvements.

The next step is to field test the instrument. No matter how clear you
think the items are, somebody will manage to misinterpret something. So
ask a representative sample of your population to complete your questionnaire. Ask them not only to answer the questions but also to point out am-
biguities and to offer suggestions for improvements. The pilot or field test
run will allow you practice in collapsing and examining the responses.

The wording of a question, and even the order in which questions are
asked can influence the answers. Pilot study or field test respondents should
be asked what they *think* the survey is really designed to get at, and what
makes them think that. Different wordings and orders can be tried on these
groups.

Circle the number that best shows how clear you found the suggestions
in this appendix:

-3	-2	-1	0	+1	+2	+3	N/A
totally baffling and useless		hazy and confusing	passable	slightly useful		perfectly clear and helpful	not applic- able; didn't read it

INTERVIEW TECHNIQUES

Interviews are so much more intrusive than questionnaires that they should be administered to the public only by someone with the requisite skills and training. Respondents should be fully informed as to the identity of the interviewer and the purpose and nature of the interview, and they should be aware of their right to discontinue at any time.

If you administer practice interviews to classmates, as with the questionnaire, try to make the first few questions easy and convenient to answer. Word all questions so that they are not suggestive or leading, and generally avoid asking questions that can be answered with a yes or no.

Interviews can be structured or unstructured (page 43). Many are combinations, in which predetermined questions are asked, and then some or all of the answers can be probed. If the interview is not structured, proceed from the general to the specific.

Choose your interview respondents carefully. Prepare a procedure to deal with respondents who are unavailable when first approached. Also decide on the procedure for *recording* the responses, and how to condense and analyze the responses, once gathered.

Rehearse the interview on friends or classmates before approaching the target group. For instance, confirm that your questions are worded so as to invite a complete answer, but not an answer so detailed that it cannot be recorded accurately on the spot or analyzed usefully later. After the rehearsal, ask your pilot respondents for feedback on your questions and your manner in asking them. Then condense and analyze the pilot responses to get practice in this important task.

Appendix C
How to find and use the I/O academic literature

Many courses in I/O psychology require students to write a paper or essay, often to the consternation of those who are not familiar with the source material. This appendix, along with chapter 2, will familiarize you with your school's library for this purpose.

THE LITERATURE

Advances, breakthroughs, and discoveries are the stuff of progress. Yet, they are of little value unless communicated. In science, the medium of communication is known as the academic literature, or just the literature for short. The main component of the literature is a publication known as an *academic journal,* or journal for short. Journals are magazines that are published and distributed usually monthly, but sometimes weekly, quarterly, or even annually.

THE NATURE OF RESEARCH

Research was once a largely individual endeavor, in which an inventive individual conducted studies in a basement or garage workshop. You may have in your mind an image of someone waiting for a light bulb to light up overhead, or of a white-coated scientist mixing the contents of test tubes in a laboratory until a cloud of smoke signals an important discovery. In fact, research today is a methodical, plodding, systematic searching for problems and solutions.

The starting point for research is a review of what has already been found out about that topic. The primary medium for communicating past findings is the academic journal. This type of publication is devoted to only one purpose, that of disseminating what has been learned, in an orderly and systematic way.

There are some five thousand academic journals in the social sciences. Most are accorded high prestige. The articles or papers printed in them can be accessed by a number of indexing or retrieval facilities. Today, each new study plugs into some gap detected in a previous one.

I/O JOURNALS

How are students exposed to the academic literature of any discipline? Generally, the student starts with a topic of interest, either to write a paper reflecting that area of the literature, or as preparation to perform some student research. The student looks up the topic in an indexing or abstract reference, and is referred to specific titles in the literature. One problem is that the topics that come to the mind of a novice are likely to be the obvious ones. Another is that the student never becomes exposed to the vast variety of topics being explored by academics.

The following is a list of major journals that shows also the relative frequency with which each was cited in ten popular, recent I/O textbooks. Journals specific to I/O psychology are in bold type, and the date of the journal's origin is also indicated in most cases.

After the list, you'll find a recent title page from the *Journal of Applied Psychology*. This title page shows you the range of topics covered in the journal and demonstrates how the title of an academic paper is a minisummary of the entire paper.

The last item in this appendix is a paper, "Predicting Job Performance: Not Much More than *g*," that was published in the *Journal of Applied Psychology*. It gives you an idea of the content and layout of an article in an academic journal. The research method and design as well as the findings of the study are summarized in the *abstract*, the paragraph preceding the article.

Frequency of citations	Title	Year of first issue
100	*Journal of Applied Psychology*	1917
58	*Personnel Psychology*	1948
28	*The Industrial-Organizational Psychologist* (quarterly newsletter)	
21	*Organizational Behavior and Human Decision Processes*	1966
21	*Academy of Management Journal*	1957
20	*Academy of Management Review*	1976
15	Psychological Bulletin	1904
13	American Psychologist	1946
7	*Journal of Occupational and Organizational Psychology*	1975
6	Journal of Personality and Social Psychology	
6	*Ergonomics*	1957
6	*Human Factors*	1958
4	Human Relations	
4	*Administrative Science Quarterly*	1956
4	*Harvard Business Review*	1922
3	*Journal of Vocational Behavior*	1971
3	*The Personnel Administrator*	1956
3	*Personnel Management*	1969

Frequency of citations	Title	Year of first issue
3	**Training & Development Journal**	1946
2	*Journal of Social Issues*	
2	*Journal of Applied Behavioral Science*	
2	**Personnel Journal**	1922
2	**Group and Organization Studies**	1976
2	*Journal of Applied Social Psychology*	
2	**Journal of Business**	1928
2	**Journal of Management**	1975
2	**Organizational Dynamics**	1972
1	**Journal of Occupational Behavior**	
1	*Psychological Review*	
1	*Journal of Abnormal and Social Psychology*	
1	*Journal of Educational Psychology*	
1	*Psychological Reports*	
1	*Professional Psychology*	
1	**The Journal of Consumer Research**	1974
1	**Research in Organizational Behavior**	1979
1	**Personnel**	1919
1	**Applied Ergonomics**	1969
1	*Journal of Applied Behavioral Science*	

Frequency of citations	Title	Year of first issue
1	**Academy of Management Proceedings**	
1	**Journal of Organizational Behavior**	1980
1	Environment & Behavior	
1	Journal of Social Psychology	
1	**Journal of Organizational Behavior Management**	1976
1	Aviation, Space and Environmental Medicine	
1	**Training**	
.5	Advances in Experimental Social Psychology	
.5	Journal of Contemporary Business	
.5	Journal of Psychosomatic Research	
.5	**Journal of Human Ergology**	1972
.5	Science	
.5	Industrial Relations	
.5	Journal of Safety Research	
.3	European Journal of Social Psychology	
.3	Perceptual Motor Skills	
.3	The Personnel and Guidance Journal	1952
.3	Journal of Communication	
.3	**Journal of Marketing Research**	1964

One way to keep up with the literature is to browse through the title pages of those journals that are toward the top of the preceding list. (The only one not available in libraries is *The Industrial-Organizational Psychologist,* which goes only to members of APA Division 14.) Another way is to read *PsycSCAN: Applied Psychology.* This quarterly publication gives abstracts (summaries) from more than 50 journals covering organizational psychology, personnel psychology, management, ergonomics, consumer behavior, human relations, applied social psychology, and other related topics. The cost of a year's subscription ranges from $19.50 for APA members residing in the United States to $96 for foreign institutions; information is available by calling 1-800-374-2722. A one-year subscription, which has to start with the January issue, will bring you approximately 2,000 abstracts, some of them likely from periodicals your library does not carry.

Journal of

Applied Psychology

Copyright ©1995 by the American Psychological Association, Inc.

April 1995   Volume 80, Number 2

Feature Articles

Other

*These articles were accepted during the editorial term of Neal Schmitt.

Journal of Applied Psychology
1994, Vol. 79, No. 4, 518–524

In the public domain

Predicting Job Performance: Not Much More Than *g*

Malcolm James Ree, James A. Earles, and Mark S. Teachout

The roles of general cognitive ability (*g*) and specific abilities or knowledge (*s*) were investigated as predictors of work sample job performance criteria in 7 jobs for U.S. Air Force enlistees. Both *g* and *s* (the interaction of general ability and experience) were defined by scores on the first and subsequent principal components of the enlistment selection and classification test (the Armed Services Vocational Aptitude Battery). Multiple regression analyses, when corrected for range restriction, revealed that *g* was the best predictor of all criteria and that *s* added a statistically significant but practically small amount to predictive efficiency. These results are consistent with those of previous studies, most notably Army Project A (J. J. McHenry, L. M. Hough, J. L. Toquam, M. A. Hanson, & S. Ashworth, 1990). The study also extends the findings to other jobs and uses traditionally more acceptable estimates of *g*, application of effective sample size in cross-validation estimation, and new performance criteria.

Spearman (1904) proposed a two-factor theory of abilities, including general cognitive ability (*g*) and specific abilities (*s*). The relative importance of *g* and *s* in the prediction of criteria has been and remains the center of controversy (Calfee, 1993; Jensen, 1993; McClelland, 1993; Ree & Earles, 1992, 1993; Schmidt & Hunter, 1993; Sternberg & Wagner, 1993). The purposes of this study were to use traditionally accepted statistical estimates of *g*, to provide better estimates of validity by including effective sample size when computing multiple correlations corrected for restriction of range, and to extend previous research to new job performance criteria and additional jobs.

g and *s* Controversy

Early test developers, such as Binet and Simon (DuBois, 1970), were influenced by the concept of

Malcolm James Ree, James A. Earles, and Mark S. Teachout, U.S. Air Force Armstrong Laboratory, Human Resources Directorate, Brooks Air Force Base. Texas.

The opinions expressed in this article are ours and are not necessarily those of the Department of the Air Force, Department of Defense, or U.S. government.

We thank A. R. Jensen, F. Schmidt, and H. Wainer for discussions and comments on this research topic.

Correspondence concerning this article should be addressed to Malcolm James Ree, Department of the Air Force, AL/HRMA, 7909 Lindbergh Drive, Brooks Air Force Base, Texas 78235-5352.

g, but eventually the influence of multiple ability theorists such as Thurstone (1938) was pervasive. This led to the development of multiple aptitude test batteries, such as the Differential Aptitude Tests (DAT), the General Aptitude Test Battery (GATB), and the Armed Services Vocational Aptitude Battery (ASVAB). These were designed to measure specific abilities and to make specific predictions about employment or educational success. Sets of test scores would be differentially selected or differentially weighted for each situation, fulfilling a proposal by Hull (1928) that specific abilities could compensate for or substitute for general ability. The different composites of subtests used by the military for job placement (Earles & Ree, 1992) or for interpreting score profiles in counseling (McDermott, Fantuzzo, Glutting, Watkins, & Baggaley, 1992) are current examples of the application of multiple ability theory. The use of differential weighting and different composites led to multiple aptitude theory being termed a theory of "differential validity" (Brogden, 1951).

Jensen (1980) identified *s* with specific experience rather than with specific ability. In this same vein, Cattell (1971, 1987) posited his investment theory, which proposes that initially there is a general ability (called *fluid g* or *g_f*) that is invested in specific experiences and crystallizes to specific skills (called *crystallized g* or *g_c*). This means that *s* is *g* modified by experience. It implies that, for an individual, the best estimate of *g* can be made from testing content in which the individual has invested his or her ability

(g_c) or from tests that require little or no prior special experience from training. interest, motivation, or exposure (g_f, see also Jensen, 1992). An example of the former is that unsatisfactory estimates of g would be obtained by administering a French test to a sample, half of which has studied French and half of which has not. The estimates of g for the half that did not study French would be unsatisfactory; the estimates for the other half would be more satisfactory. To rectify this problem, Raven (1938), a student of Spearman, developed the Progressive Matrices Test, which measured g through a series of abstract diagrammatic problems (Vernon, 1960, p. 19) that did not require special investment of g but, rather, that g be used to solve nonverbal problems.

The primacy of g as a predictor has again become the subject of many studies. The December 1986 issue of the *Journal of Vocational Behavior* (Gottfredson, 1986) documented the renewed interest, as did the evidence emerging from validity generalization studies (Hunter, 1983, 1984a, 1984b, 1984c; Hunter, Crosson, & Friedman, 1985).

ASVAB and Validity of g

The ASVAB is a state-of-the-art aptitude battery (Jensen, 1985; Murphy, 1985) and an excellent source of data for investigating the value of g as a predictor, with about 1 million administrations and about 200,000 selections to job training each year. Although several studies have investigated the incremental validity of s beyond g, using training grades as criteria, studies relating g to job performance criteria have typically not investigated the incremental validity of s.

Jones (1988) correlated the average validity of the ASVAB subtests for predicting training performance with the g saturation of the subtests. For each subtest, she corrected the training validities for range restriction and averaged them over 37 diverse air force technical training courses. These averages were subject weighted over 24,482 technical training students. For each subtest, the g saturation was measured by its loading on the unrotated first principal component (see Jensen, 1987; Ree & Earles, 1991b). Jones found a rank order correlation of .75, demonstrating a strong positive relationship between g and predictive validity. This was found across all jobs, and comparable values were found within four air force job families: Mechanical, Administrative, General (Technical), and Electronics. Following Jensen (1980), Ree

and Earles (1992) corrected the g-factor loadings for subtest unreliability and calculated the Jones rank order correlation as .98.

Ree and Earles (1990) investigated the predictive utility of both the general and specific components of the ASVAB by regressing air force technical school grades on the unrotated principal-component scores of the ASVAB. Psychometric g was represented by the first principal component, and s was represented by the remaining principal components. Across 89 jobs (individual sample sizes ranged from 274 to 3.939), the average correlation of g and the training criterion was .76, corrected for range restriction. When the specific ($g \times$ Experience) components were added to the regressions, the multiple correlation increased an average of .02.

Using a linear models approach, Ree and Earles (1991a) evaluated the nature of the relationships of g and s to 82 air force job-training criteria. They found statistically significant but small contributions (an average gain of .02) for s to the regressions.

These three studies examined the predictive utility of g and the contribution of s, but none used job performance measures as criteria. Jones (1988) observed that although measures of job performance were the preferred criteria, they were frequently unavailable because of their cost. Several studies have used job performance measures as criteria in the evaluation of the predictiveness of g, however, only McHenry, Hough, Toquam, Hanson, and Ashworth (1990) examined the incremental validity of specific measures.

For example, psychometric g as measured by the Army General Classification Test (Stewart, 1947) was found to be related to the preservice occupations of soldiers serving in World War II. In as far as individuals sort themselves into jobs on the basis of their ability to perform, job incumbency becomes a form of job performance. Among the jobs with highest average estimated intelligence were accounting, engineering, and medicine. Jobs with middling average-estimated intelligence were police officer, electrician, and meat cutter. Jobs with the lowest average-estimated intelligence included laborer, farm worker, and lumberjack. The distribution of within-job intelligence scores did not overlap for the very highest and the very lowest jobs. This study did not consider specific or invested abilities.

Additionally, Hunter (1986) reviewed hundreds of studies showing that g predicted job performance criteria, including training success, supervisory ratings, and content-valid hands-on work samples for both civilian and military jobs. However, direct tests of the incremental contribution of s for the prediction of job performance criteria were not made.

Finally, McHenry et al. (1990) evaluated g, defined as the sum of several simple weighted composites rather than as a principal component, principal factor, or hierarchical factor—the traditionally accepted statistical estimates of g (Jensen, 1980). They also evaluated noncognitive variables, such as temperament, vocational interest, and reward preference in an incremental validity design in Army Project A (McHenry et al., 1990). For predicting core job proficiency as measured by job performance, no predictor added more than .03 to the predictiveness provided by g, about the same increment found by Ree and Earles (1991a) for training grades.

In the current study, we replicated some aspects of McHenry et al.'s (1990) study by determining if measures of g and s were differentially (Brogden, 1951) useful predictors of job performance. We extend the results to several additional jobs as well as to a new criterion measure, the Walk-Through Performance Test (WTPT: Hedge & Teachout, 1992). This study also demonstrates the use of effective sample size in estimating multiple correlations corrected for the effects of range restriction.

Method

Subjects

The subjects were 1,036 non-prior-service enlistees in the U.S. Air Force who had entered from 1984 through 1988; had tested with ASVAB parallel forms 11, 12, or 13; had completed both basic military training and technical training; and were, for the most part, working in their first term of enlistment. They were predominantly White (78.1%), male (83.2%), 17- to 23-year-old graduates of high school or better (99.1%), with an average job tenure of about 28 months.

Predictors

The ASVAB is a multiple aptitude test battery composed of 10 subtests (see Earles & Ree, 1992) that is carefully crafted to represent major cognitive abilities, which facilitates the estimation of g. The ASVAB is used for enlistment qualification and initial job assignment in the armed services. The Numerical Operations and Coding Speed subtests are speeded, and the others are power tests. The ASVAB has been used in this subtest configuration since 1980. Its reliability has been studied (Palmer, Hartke,

Ree, Welsh, & Valentine, 1988), and it has been validated for many military occupations (Earles & Ree, 1992; Welsh, Kucinkas, & Curran, 1990; Welsh, Trent, et al., 1990; Wilbourn, Valentine, & Ree, 1984).

In a reification of differential aptitude theory, the air force aggregates the subtests into Mechanical, Administrative, General, and Electronics composites (Earles & Ree, 1992).

There are three generally accepted ways of estimating g from a set of variables (Jensen, 1980). Ree and Earles (1991b) have shown that for the ASVAB, estimates of g from these three methods, principal components, principal factors, and hierarchical factor analysis all correlated greater than .996. Because of high correlations among the various g estimates and the mathematical simplicity of the principal components, the principal components were chosen to represent the g and s measures of the ASVAB. The first unrotated principal component serves as a measure of g (Jensen, 1980). Group factors from common-factors analyses often represent s, with g ineluctably distributed through them from rotation (Jensen, 1980). The g can be removed from the lower order factors through Schmid and Leiman's (1957) procedure. However, those theories that require common-factors procedures (Cattell, 1971, 1987; Vernon, 1960) do not account for all of the variance in the variables and put the specific variances at a relative statistical disadvantage in comparison with principal-components procedures, which do account for all of the variance and provide maximum advantage for s.

To determine the maximal predictive efficiency (Brogden, 1946) of s, one's best choice is the procedure that most fully represents the non-g portions. Therefore, we used the nine remaining unrotated principal components as the measures of s (s_1 to s_9). These are mathematically defined measures and do not necessarily represent identifiable or nameable psychological concepts. The principal components have the additional benefit of being orthogonal (Hotelling, 1933a, 1933b), which circumvents the problems of collinearity and enhances their usefulness in regression (Kendall, Stuart, & Ord, 1983).

Jobs

Data were collected for eight jobs as part of the joint-services (Wigdor & Green, 1991) and air force job performance measurement project (Hedge & Teachout, 1986, 1992). Each job had a minimum requirement on one of the four aptitude composites derived from the ASVAB. Jet Engine Mechanic and Aerospace Ground Equipment Mechanic were selected by the Mechanical composite; Information Systems Radio Operator and Personnel Specialist by the Administrative composite; Air Traffic Control Operator and Aircrew Life Support Specialist by the General composite; and Precision Measurement Equipment Laboratory Specialist and Avionic Communications Specialist by the Electronics composite. The Aircrew Life Support Specialist job was

Table 1
Results of Validity and Incremental Validity Analyses for the Jobs Studied

Criterion	N	r_g	r_g^a	R_{g+s}	R_{g+s}^b	R_{g+s}^a	$^{WC}R_{g+s}^{a,b}$	N_{eff}	$R_{g+s}^{a,b,c}$
				Air Traffic Control Operator					
HOPT	164	.127	.134	.328	.222	.391	.312	116	.267
INT	164	.104	.251	.302	.179	.406	.332	91	.268
WTPT	164	.141	.255	.311	.195	.407	.333	96	.279
				Precision Measurement Equipment Laboratory Specialist					
HOPT	126	.343	.691	.497	.427	.780	.757	63	.730
INT	126	.322	.752	.406	.304	.774	.751	35	.689
WTPT	126	.355	.713	.503	.434	.793	.772	51	.732
				Avionics Communications Specialist					
HOPT	74	.343	.717	.504	.369	.795	.757	30	.683
INT	74	.262	.607	.554	.443	.765	.720	39	.661
WTPT	74	.355	.713	.583	.484	.825	.793	37	.757
				Aerospace Ground Equipment Mechanic					
HOPT	211	.294	.424	.457	.411	.608	.581	120	.558
INT	211	.191	.307	.357	.289	.478	.435	118	.405
WTPT	211	.262	.384	.432	.382	.570	.539	121	.513
				Jet Engine Mechanic					
HOPT	178	.134	.251	.319	.219	.415	.350	106	.291
INT	178	.253	.429	.343	.354	.508	.462	82	.406
WTPT	178	.192	.354	.340	.250	.471	.418	93	.370
				Information Systems Radio Operator					
HOPT	111	.222	.278	.413	.296	.476	.386	84	.375
INT	111	.319	.317	.480	.391	.549	.491	85	.454
WTPT	111	.274	.341	.442	.340	.520	.444	80	.405
				Personnel Specialist					
HOPT	172	.220	.487	.323	.220	.538	.495	63	.390
INT	172	.112	.455	.308	.196	.549	.507	55	.402
WTPT	172	.206	.529	.345	.254	.595	.560	58	.465

Note. HOPT = hands-on performance test; INT = interview work sample test; WTPT = walk-through performance test; g = general cognitive ability; s = specific abilities or knowledge; r_g = correlation of g and the criterion; R_{g+s} = multiple correlation of g and s with the criterion; N_{eff} = effective sample size.
[a] Corrected for range restriction. [b] Wherry's (1975) correction for degrees of freedom was applied. [c] Effective sample size used in applying Wherry's (1975) correction.

found not to be predictable by aptitude in this and in a previous study (Teachout & Pellum, 1991). Therefore, the Aircrew Life Support Specialist Job was removed from the study.

WTPTs

The criterion measures used in the present study were hands-on performance tests (HOPTs) and interview work sample tests (INT), and their combination, a WTPT (Hedge & Teachout, 1992). For each job, there were tasks unique to the hands-on format, tasks unique to the interview format, and overlapping tasks measured by both formats. The hands-on criterion was the sum of all hands-on task scores for a job; the interview criterion was the sum of all interview task scores for a job; and the WTPT was the sum of all hands-on task scores and unique interview task scores for a job. Both formats required the examinee to accomplish the tasks, either manually or verbally, at the work site under the observation of a trained administrator, The HOPTs and INTs were constructed for each job to assess proficiency on representative job tasks. The task domains for each job were identified and defined from the Air Force Occupational Survey database (Christal, 1974). A domain sampling plan was developed, and tasks were selected with a stratified random sampling procedure (Lipscomb & Dickinson, 1988).

For each task, work sample developers used technical descriptions of work procedures (U.S. Air Force technical orders and manuals) as well as input from subject matter experts to define and describe the procedural steps required for successful task completion. The work sample tests were constructed for each task, reviewed by subject matter experts, and field tested at several air force bases.

The work sample tests were administered to the subjects and scored by active-duty or retired, noncommissioned officers with extensive job experience. The administrators received 1–2 weeks of observation and scorer accuracy training (Hedge, Lipscomb, & Teachout, 1988). Using videotapes of work sample test performance with known target scores, administrators discussed the key work behaviors to perform or avoid for successful task completion. These procedures have been shown to produce accurate and reliable work sample test ratings (Hedge, Dickinson, & Bierstedt, 1988). The raters demonstrated high average agreement ($r = .81$) and high average correlational accuracy ($r = .85$) between their ratings and videotape target ratings.

In addition, a shadow scoring technique was used during a portion of data collection on 58 subjects, requiring two test administrators to observe and rate task performance. The technique was effective in maintaining agreement in the scoring of the work sample tests. The average agreement of the scorer with the shadow scorer was 95% across the 58 subjects.

Procedures

Data collection. In a group orientation session, the research project was described and participation conditions were explained. Subsequent to the group session, job-incumbent subjects were individually administered both HOPTs and INTs. Time limits were specified for each WPTP, ranging from 4 hr to 7 hr, depending on the job.

Analyses. We used a linear-models approach. Two linear models were computed for each criterion. The first linear model used only g to predict the criterion, whereas the second used g and all of the s values to predict the criterion. This gives maximal advantage to the measures of specific ability; it was accomplished for the correlations artifactually depressed by prior selection. To make better estimates of the correlations in the unrestricted population, we also computed the regressions in matrices after multivariate correction for range restriction (Lawley, 1943). The Type 1 error rate was set at $p < .05$ for the regressions computed in the

uncorrected data. No statistical tests were performed in the regressions on the basis of the corrected correlations.

We used Wherry's (1975) procedure to adjust the observed multiple correlations, the multiple correlations after correction for range restriction, and the multiple correlations computed after estimating the effective sample size for the increase in sampling variance due to correcting the correlations for range restriction (Schmidt, Hunter, & Larson, 1988). More information on the estimation of effective sample size can be found in the Appendix.

Failure to apply Schmidt et al.'s (1988) procedure would lead to an overestimate in the Wherry-adjusted correlations. Although often called a *correction for cross-validation*, Wherry's procedure actually provides better parameter estimates of the multiple correlation. It is particularly useful in theoretically oriented studies like ours because it effectively estimates the correlation as if the population regression weights were applied in the population. The sample-weighted differences between the range-restriction-corrected correlations of g with the criteria and the Wherry-adjusted, range-restriction-corrected correlations of g and s_1–s_9 with the criteria provide the most informative outcome measure for incremental validity. These values were computed both across jobs, to yield an average for the criterion type, and within jobs across the three criteria to yield a within-job average.

Results and Discussion

These analyses indicated that g and s_1–s_9 were useful in predicting the job performance criteria. as has been found for training criteria (Ree & Earles, 1990, 1991a). As represented by the 2nd through 10th principal components, s added to the accuracy of prediction, but only by a small amount. The efficiency of the predictors (uncorrected correlations, r and R) in this study was smaller than in a previous study in which technical training criteria were used (Ree & Earles, 1991a). The sample sizes in this study were much smaller, so some portion of the increases resulting from s was likely to be the result of overfitting and, therefore, was likely to diminish on cross-validation. These regression results are reported in Table 1. The last column shows the adjusted correlations; these were estimated by Wherry's (1975) procedure, using effective sample size (Schmidt et al., 1988).

The regressions in the uncorrected correlations showed low to moderate correlations of g and s with the criteria. Results of the regressions in the corrected matrices, the better parameter estimates, were closer to previous findings indicating an increment of only .02 (McHenry et al., 1990; Ree & Earles, 1991a). The reason for the disparity between these corrected

Table 2

Averaged Results of the Validity Analyses by Job and Criterion

| Measure | Averaged within 3 criteria within job | | |
	r_g[a]	R_{g+s}[b]	Δ[c]
Averaged within 3 criteria within job			
Air Traffic Control Operator	.213	.271	.058
Precision Measurement Equipment Laboratory Specialist	.718	.721	.003
Avionics Communications Specialist	.679	.700	.021
Aerospace Ground Equipment Mechanic	.371	.492	.121
Jet Engine Mechanic	.344	.350	.006
Information Systems Radio Operator	.312	.411	.099
Personnel Specialist	.490	.418	.000
Averaged across jobs			
Hands-on performance test	.396	.431	.035
Interview work sample test	.420	.427	.007
Walk-through performance test	.441	.462	.021

Note. All averages were weighted by effective sample size. g = general cognitive ability; s = specific abilities or knowledge.
[a] Correlation of g with criterion, corrected for range restriction.
[b] Multiple correlation of g and s with criterion, corrected for range restriction and using effective sample size when applying Wherry's (1975) correction for degrees of freedom.
[c] The difference between a and b.

findings and the findings in the uncorrected (incorrect) correlations is the artifact of range restriction.

HOPTs. Across all jobs, the average observed validities of g and of g plus s_1–s_9 for the HOPT criterion were .229 and .394, respectively. Corrected for restriction of range, the average correlation of g and the criterion was .396. The average Wherry-corrected correlation coefficient estimate adjusted by Schmidt et al.'s (1988) effective sample size was .431 for the multiple correlation of g and s with the criteria.

INTs. Similar validity results were found for this criterion measure. The average observed validities were .209 and .370 for g and for g and s_1–s_9 as predictors. Corrected for range restriction, the average correlation of g and the criterion was .420, whereas the average correlation corrected for range restriction and the Wherry-adjusted correlation of g and s with the criterion was .427 when effective sample size was used.

WTPTs. The WTPT is a combination of the HOPT and the INT and provides a more thorough content sampling of the jobs' tasks (Hedge & Teachout, 1992) and higher reliability (Kraiger & Teachout, 1991). The average observed validity of g was .205, whereas the average for g and s_1–s_9 was .403. Corrected for range restriction, the correlation of g and the criterion became .441, and the average corrected and Wherry-adjusted correlation of g and s_1–s_9 with the WTPT was .462. These average coefficients are presented in Table 2.

In the current study, the difference between the average correlations of g corrected for range restriction and the criteria and the fully corrected multiple correlation of g and s_1–s_9 across all criteria and all jobs was an increment of .021. Adjusted by the Wherry (1975) procedure, the incremental validities of g plus s in the current study were very similar to those reported by McHenry et al. (1990, p. 343) for the job performance factors of Core Technical Proficiency and General Soldiering Proficiency. No increments reported by McHenry et al. exceeded approximately .03 for these job performance factors.

In previous studies (Ree & Earles, 1990, 1991a), when g and s_1–s_9 were used to predict training grades, it was found that g was the most potent predictor and that s added little to prediction. The same was true for predicting the job performance criteria in the current study.

The criterion that provided the greatest coverage of tasks and highest reliability was the WTPT. The average increment to g by measures of s was .021, about the same found in previous studies for both training criteria (Ree & Earles, 1991a) and job performance criteria (McHenry et al., 1990). It is also consistent with the estimate provided by Hunter and Hunter (1984). Finally, this difference is consistent with several related studies of incremental validity in performance prediction. Carey (1994) studied the predictive efficiency of adding new tests to a highly g-saturated test battery for the prediction of both job performance and training criteria: he found increments averaging .02 across these criteria. Likewise, Morales and Ree (1992) found similar incremental differences for predicting pilot and navigator performance that included work sample criteria. The consistency of results across these studies is remarkable.

Summary

The current study has extended the finding of statistically significant but practically small incremental validity for specific measures to seven additional jobs and to new criteria. It has also shown that the incremental value of the specific measures was small for all three criteria and has demonstrated the application of estimates of effective sample size in the computation of adjusted multiple correlation coefficients.

References

Brogden, H. E. (1946). On the interpretation of the correlation coefficient as a measure of predictive efficiency. *Journal of Educational Psychology, 37,* 65–76.

Brogden, H. E. (1951). Increased efficiency of selection resulting from replacement of a single predictor with several different predictors. *Journal of Educational Psychology, 11,* 173–196.

Calfee, R. (1993). Paper, pencil, potential, and performance. *Current Directions in Psychological Science, 2,* 6–7.

Carey, N. (1994, August). Computer predictors of mechanical job performance: Marine Corps findings. *Military psychology, 6,* 1–30.

Cattell, R. (1971). *Abilities: Their structure, growth and action.* Boston: Houghton Mifflin.

Cattell, R. (1987). *Intelligence: Its structure, growth and action.* New York: Elsevier Science.

Christal, R. E. (1974). *The United States Air Force occupational research project* (AFHRL-TR-73–75). Brooks Air Force Base, TX: Air Force Human Resources Laboratory, Occupational Research Division.

Dubois, P. H. (1970). *A history of psychological testing.* Boston: Allyn & Bacon.

Earles, J. A.. & Ree, M. J. (1992). The predictive validity of the ASVAB for training grades. *Educational and Psychological Measurement, 52,* 721–725.

Gottfredson, L. S. (1986). Foreword: The g factor in employment. *Journal of Vocational Behavior, 29,* 293–296.

Hedge, J. W., Dickinson, T. L., & Bierstedt, S. A. (1988). *The use of videotape technology to train administrators of Walk-Through Performance Testing* (AFHRL-TP-87–71). Brooks Air Force Base, TX: Air Force Human Resources Laboratory, Training Systems Division.

Hedge, J. W., Lipscomb, M. S., & Teachout, M. S. (1988). Work sample testing in the Air Force job performance measurement project. In M. S. Lipscomb & J. W. Hedge (Eds.), *Job performance measurement: Topics in the performance measurement of Air Force enlisted personnel* (AFHRL-TP-87–58). Brooks Air Force Base, TX: Air Force Human Resources Laboratory, Training Systems Division.

Hedge, J. W., & Teachout, M. S. (1986). *Job performance measurement: A systematic program of research and development* (AFHRL-TP-86–37). Brooks Air Force Base, TX: Air Force Human Resources Laboratory. Training Systems Division.

Hedge, J. W., & Teachout, M.S. (1992). An interview approach to work sample criterion development. *Journal of Applied Psychology, 77,* 453–462.

Hotelling, H. H. (1933a). Analysis of a complex of statistical variables with principal components. *Journal of Educational Psychology, 24,* 417–441.

Hotelling, H. H. (1933b). Analysis of a complex of statistical variables with principal components (continued). *Journal of Educational Psychology, 24,* 498–520.

Hull, C. (1928). *Aptitude testing.* New York: World Book.

Hunter, J. E. (1983). *Validity generalization of the ASVAB: Higher validity for factor analytic composites.* Rockville, MD: Research Applications.

Hunter, J. E. (1984a). *The prediction of job performance in the civilian sector using the ASVAB.* Rockville, MD: Research Applications.

Hunter, J. E. (1984b). *The validity of the Armed Services Vocational Aptitude Battery (ASVAB) high school composites.* Rockville, MD: Research Applications.

Hunter, J. E. (1984c). *The validity of the ASVAB as a predictor of civilian job perfor–mance.* Rockville, MD: Research Applications.

Hunter, J. E. (1986). Cognitive ability, cognitive aptitudes, job knowledge, and job performance. *Journal of Vocational Behavior, 29,* 340–362.

Hunter, J. E., Crosson, J. J., & Friedman, D. H. (1985). *The validity of the Armed Services Vocational Aptitude Battery (ASVAB) for civilian and military job performance.* Rockville, MD: Research Applications.

Hunter, J. E., & Hunter, R. F. (1984). Validity and utility of alternative predictors across studies. *Psychological Bulletin, 96,* 72–98.

Jensen, A. R. (1980). *Bias in mental testing.* New York: Free Press.

Jensen, A. R. (1985). Armed Services Vocational Aptitude Battery. *Measurement and Evaluation in Counseling and Development, 18,* 32–37.

Jensen, A. R. (1987). Editorial: Psychometric g as a focus of concerted research effort. *Intelligence, 11,* 193–198.

Jensen. A. R. (1992). Commentary: Vehicles of g. *Psychological Science, 3,* 275–278.

Jensen, A. R. (1993). Test validity: g versus "Tacit Knowledge." *Current Directions in Psychological Science, 2,* 9–10.

Jones, G. E. (1988). *Investigation of the efficacy of general ability versus specific ability as predictors of occupational success.* Unpublished master's thesis. St. Mary's University, San Antonio, TX.

Kendall, M., Stuart, A., & Ord, J. K. (1983). *The advanced theory of statistics* (Vol. 3, 4th ed.). New York: Macmillan.

Kraiger, K., & Teachout, M. S. (1991). *Application of generalizability theory to Air Force's job performance measurement project: A summary of research results* (AFHRL-TP-90–85). Brooks Air Force Base, TX: Air Force Human Resources Laboratory, Training Systems Division.

Lawley, D. N. (1943). A note on Karl Pearson's selection formulae, *Proceedings of the Royal Society of Edinburgh, Section A, 62, Part 1,* 28–30.

Lipscomb, M. S., & Dickinson, T. L. (1988). The Air Force domain specification and sampling plan. In M. S. Lipscomb & J. W. Hedge (Eds.), *Job performance: Topics in the performance measurement of Air Force enlisted personnel* (AFHRL-TP-87–58). Brooks Air Force Base, TX: Air Force Human Resources Laboratory, Training Systems Division.

McClelland, D. C. (1993). Intelligence is not the best predictor of job performance. *Current Directions in Psychological Science, 2,* 5–6.

McDermott, P. A., Fantuzzo, J. W., Glutting, J. J., Watkins, M. W., & Baggaley, A. R. (1992). Illusions of meaning in the ipsative assessment of children's ability. *Journal of Special Education, 25,* 504–526.

McHenry, J. J., Hough, L. M., Toquam, J. L., Hanson, M. A., & Ashworth, S. (1990). Project A validity results: The relationship between predictor and criterion domains. *Personnel psychology, 43,* 335–354.

Mendoza, J. L., Hart, D. E., & Powell, A. (1991). A bootstrap confidence interval based on a correlation corrected for range restriction. *Multivariate Behavioral Research, 26,* 255–269.

Morales, M., & Ree, M. J. (1992, June), *Intelligence predicts academic and work sample training performance.* Paper presented at the annual meeting of the American Psychological Society, San Diego, CA.

Murphy, K. (1985). Armed Services Vocational Aptitude Battery. In D. J. Keyser & R. C. Sweetland (Eds.), *Test critiques* (Vol. 1). Kansas City, MO: Test Corporation of America.

Palmer, P., Hartke, D. D., Ree, M. J., Welsh, J. R., & Valentine, L. D., Jr. (1988). *Armed Services Vocational Aptitude Battery (ASVAB): Alternate forms reliability. Forms 8, 9, and 11* (AFHRL-TP-87–48). Brooks Air Force Base, TX: Air Force Human Resources Laboratory, Manpower and Personnel Division.

Raven, J. (1938). *Progressive matrices: A perceptual test of intelligence.* London: H. K. Lewis.

Ree, M. J., & Earles, J. A. (1990). *The differential validity of a differential aptitude test* (AFHRL-TR-89–59). Brooks Air Force Base, TX: Air Force Human Resources Laboratory, Manpower and Personnel Division.

Ree, M. J., & Earles, J. A. (1991a). Predicting training success: Not much more than g. *Personnel Psychology, 44,* 321–332.

Ree, M. J., & Earles, J. A. (1991b). The stability of g across different methods of estimation. *Intelligence, 15,* 271–278.

Ree, M. J., & Earles, J. A. (1992). Intelligence is the best predictor of job performance. *Current Directions in Psychological Science, 1,* 86–89.

Ree, M. J., & Earles, J. A. (1993). g is to psychology what carbon is to chemistry: A reply to Sternberg and Wagner, McClelland, and Calfee. *Current Directions in Psychological Science, 2,* 11–12.

Schmid, J., & Leiman, J. M. (1957). The development of hierarchical factor solutions. *Psychometrika, 22,* 53–61.

Schmidt, F. L., & Hunter, J. E. (1993). Tacit knowledge, practical intelligence, general mental ability, and job knowledge. *Current Directions in Psychological Science, 2,* 8–9.

Schmidt, F. L., Hunter, J. E., & Larson, M. (1988, August). *General cognitive ability vs. general and specific aptitudes in the prediction of training performance: Some preliminary findings.* Paper presented at the 96th Annual Convention of the American Psychological Association, Atlanta, GA.

Spearman, C. (1904). "General Intelligence," objectively determined and measured. *American Journal of Psychology, 15,* 201–293.

Sternberg, R. J., & Wagner, R. K. (1993). The g-ocentric view of intelligence and job performance is wrong. *Current Directions in Psychological Science, 2,* 1–5.

Stewart, N. (1947). Scores of army personnel grouped by occupation. *Occupations, 26,* 1–37.

Teachout, M. S., & Pellum, M. W. (1991). *Air Force research to link standards for enlistment to on-the-job performance* (AFHRL-TR-90–90). Brooks Air Force Base, TX: Air Force Human Resources Laboratory, Training Systems Division.

Thurstone, L. L. (1938). *Primary mental abilities.* Chicago: University of Chicago Press.

Vernon, P. (1960) *Intelligence and attainment tests.* New York: Philosophical Library.

Ward, J. H., & Jennings, E. (1973). *Introduction to linear models.* Englewood Cliffs, NJ: Prentice Hall.

Welsh, J. R., Jr., Kucinkas, S., & Curran, L. (1990). *Armed Services Vocational Aptitude Battery (ASVAB): Integrative review of validity studies* (AFHRL-TR-90–22). Brooks Air Force Base, TX: Air Force Human Resources Laboratory, Manpower and Personnel Division.

Welsh, J. R., Jr., Trent, T., Nakasone, R., Fairbank, B., Kucinkas, S., & Sawin, L. (1990). *Annotated bibliography of Armed Services Vocational Aptitude Battery (ASVAB) Validity Studies* (AFHRL-TR-89–76). Brooks Air Force Base, TX: Air Force Human Resources Laboratory, Manpower and Personnel Division.

Wherry, R. J., Sr. (1975). Underprediction from overfitting: 45 years of shrinkage. *Personnel Psychology, 28,* 1–18.

Wigdor, A., & Green, B. F., Jr. (1991). *Performance assessment for the workplace* (Vols. 1 and 2). Washington, DC: National Academy Press.

Wilbourn, J. M., Valentine, L. D., Jr., & Ree, M. J. (1984). *Relationships of the Armed Services Vocational Aptitude Battery (ASVAB) Forms 8, 9, and 10 to U.S. Air Force technical school final grades* (AFHRL-TR-84-8). Brooks Air Force Base, TX: Air Force Human Resources Laboratory, Manpower and Personnel Division.

Appendix

Schmidt, Hunter, and Larson's (1988) Formula for the Estimation of Effective Sample Size

The usual formula for the standard error (SE) of a correlation is

$$SE = (1 - r^2)/(n - 1)^{1/2},$$

and application of this would typically give a smaller standard error for a corrected correlation than for that correlation's uncorrected value. (This would be so because corrected correlations typically increase and larger correlations have smaller standard errors than do smaller correlations.) However, this is neither logical nor, for that matter, empirical (Mendoza, Hart, & Powell. 1992). Therefore, for the usual standard error formula to make sense it must be assumed that the sample size (in the denominator) for the corrected correlation is smaller than the sample size for its uncorrected counterpart. It is this effective sample size that we are trying to estimate.

If the usual standard error formula (SE) is merged with the linear regression equation, that gives $(1 - r^2) = (SSE/SST)$, where SSE is the sum of squares resulting from error and SST is the sum of squares total. We then have

$$SE_r = (1 - r^2) / (n - 1)^{1/2} = (SSE/SST)/(n - 1)^{1/2}, \text{ and}$$

$$SE_{rc} = (1 - r_c^2) / (n_{eff} - 1)^{1/2} = (SSE_c / SST_c)/(n_{eff} - 1)^{1/2}.$$

There is no reason to expect that the instability of the uncorrected correlation should not carry through to the corrected correlation. If we let the inaccuracy of the prediction in the corrected variance case equal that of the restricted variance case, that is,

$$(SSE / SST) = (SSE_c / SST_c),$$

we then have

$$SE_r(n - 1)^{1/2} = SE_{rc}(n_{eff} - 1)^{1/2}, \text{ or}$$

$$(n_{eff} - 1) = (SE_r^2 / (SE_{rc}^2)(n - 1). \tag{A1}$$

Schmidt et al. (1988) proposed that this effective sample size be used with Wherry's (1975) correction. They substituted the usual formula for SE^2 and obtained

$$(n_{eff} - 1) = (1 - (r^2))^2/SE_{rc}^2, \text{ or}$$

$$n_{eff} = [(1 - r^2)^2 + SE_{rc}^2]/SE_{rc}^2. \tag{A2}$$

If several estimates of r and r_c are available, then the mean correlations would be used along with the empirical SE^2 of the r_cs.

If only one correlation is available, then (r^2/r_c^2) is used in Equation 1 in place of SE_r^2/SE_{rc}^2. This specifies that the endpoint of a confidence interval about r would be changed with the same proportional change made by correcting from r to r_c. This specifies that the endpoint of a confidence interval about r would be changed with the same proportional change made by correcting from r to r_c. Therefore, the equation for effective sample size can be rewritten as

$$(n_{eff} - 1) = (r^2/r_c^2)(n - 1),$$

or the computationally simpler

$$n_{neff} = [r^2(n - 1) + r_c^2]r_c^2. \tag{A3}$$

Received March 29, 1993
Revision received November 22, 1993
Accepted November 23, 1993

Appendix D
How to continue in I/O psychology

There are about one hundred institutions in North America that offer a program leading to a graduate degree in the topics covered in this book. The institutions are listed on the following pages.

I/O GRADUATE PROGRAMS

The minimum qualification to work as an industrial psychologist is a master's degree such as the M.A. (Master of Arts) or the M.S. (Master of Science) degree. These are known as *graduate* degrees because entry into the program requires the completion of an undergraduate degree such as the B.A. (Bachelor of Arts). The latter usually requires three or four years of college or university study. The acceptance rate for most graduate programs is typically about ten percent of applicants. A fairly high grade point average is required, but relevant experience is usually considered as well.

Of practitioners with a master's degree, most work in human service settings such as hospitals; others work in business or government positions, and in schools. A master's degree is usually the M.A., but it could be an M.S. or M.B.A. The most responsible positions are generally accorded those who hold the higher graduate degree, the doctorate. This is usually the Ph.D. (Doctor of Philosophy), but an alternate is the Psy.D. (Doctor of Psychology), or D.B.A. (Doctor of Business Administration). The doctorate requires two or three years beyond that needed for the masters, and it generally focuses on a major research project known as a dissertation.

For further information on Canadian programs, contact the institution, or visit the Reference section of any Canadian university library, where you will find the current Calendar for all other Canadian universities. For more details on American programs, you can contact the institution for a catalog. You can also obtain free of charge a copy of *Graduate Training Programs in Industrial/Organizational Psychology and Organizational Behavior* by writing to: Administration Office, Society for Industrial and Organizational Psychology, 617 East Gold Road, Arlington Heights, Illinois 60005.

This publication gives a brief description of the program, numbers of students and faculty, financial aid, and features of the program. It also outlines the requirements for admission to each program, namely, application deadlines, minimal undergraduate marks, and sometimes, minimal scores on stipulated tests, graduation requirements such as a dissertation and foreign language competence as well as complete addresses for each institution are also listed.

DOCTORAL PROGRAMS
(Psychology Departments)

Auburn University, Auburn, AL

Claremont Graduate School, Claremont, CA

University of California–Berkeley, CA

Colorado State University, Fort Collins, CO

University of Connecticut, Storrs, CT

George Washington University, Washington, DC

University of South Florida, Tampa, FL

Georgia Institute of Technology, Atlanta, GA

Georgia State University, Atlanta, GA

University of Georgia, Atlanta, GA

DePaul University, Chicago, IL

Illinois Institute of Technology, Chicago, IL

University of Illinois, Chicago, IL

University of Illinois, Urbana-Champaign, IL

Purdue University, West Lafayette, IN

Iowa State University, Ames, IA

Kansas State University, Manhattan, KS

Louisiana State University, Baton Rouge, LA

Tulane University, New Orleans, LA

University of Maryland, College Park, MD

Central Michigan State University, Mt. Pleasant, MI

Michigan State University, East Lansing, MI

University of Michigan, Ann Arbor, MI

Wayne State University, Detroit, MI

University of Minnesota, Minneapolis, MN

University of Missouri–St. Louis, MO

North Carolina State University, Raleigh, NC

University of Nebraska–Omaha, NE

Baruch College, City University of New York, NY

Fordham University, Bronx, NY

Hofstra University, Hempstead, NY

State University of New York at Albany, NY

State University of New York at Buffalo, NY

Bowling Green State University, Bowling Green, OH

Ohio State University, Columbus, OH

Ohio University, Athens, OH
University of Akron, OH
University of Tulsa, OK
Pennsylvania State University,
    University Park, PA
Rice University, Houston, TX
University of Houston, TX
University of North Texas, Denton,
    TX
George Mason University, Fairfax,
    VA
Old Dominion University, Norfolk,
    VA
Virginia Polytechnic Institute,
    Blacksburg, VA
University of Washington, Seattle,
    WA

DOCTORAL PROGRAMS
(Business Departments)

University of Alabama,
    Birmingham, AL
University of Arizona, Tucson, AZ
University of Arkansas, Fayette, AR
Stanford University, Stanford, CA
University of California–Berkeley, CA
University of California–Irvine, CA
University of Colorado, Boulder, CO
Yale University, New Haven, CT
Florida State University,
    Tallahassee, FL
University of Florida, Gainesville, FL
Georgia Institute of Technology,
    Atlanta, GA
Northwestern University, Evanston,
    IL
University of Illinois, Champaign, IL
Indiana University, Bloomington, IN
University of Kentucky, Lexington,
    KY
University of Maryland, College
    Park, MD
Harvard University, Cambridge, MA

Massachusetts Institute of
    Technology, Cambridge, MA
Michigan State University, East
    Lansing, MI
University of Michigan, Ann Arbor,
    MI
University of Minnesota,
    Minneapolis, MN
Duke University, Durham, NC
University of North Carolina,
    Chapel Hill, NC
University of Nebraska, Lincoln, NE
Rutgers University, Newark, NJ
Stevens Institute of Technology,
    Hoboken, NJ
Columbia University, New York, NY
Cornell University, Ithaca, NY
New York University, New York, NY
Rensselaer Polytechnic Institute,
    Troy, NY
State University of New York at
    Buffalo, NY
Syracuse University, Syracuse, NY
Kent State University, Kent, OH
Ohio State University, Columbus, OH
University of Oregon, Eugene, OR
Carnegie Mellon University,
    Pittsburgh, PA
Temple University, Philadelphia, PA
University of South Carolina,
    Columbia, SC
University of Tennessee, Knoxville,
    TN
Texas Tech University, Lubbock, TX
University of Houston, TX
University of Virginia,
    Charlottesville, VA
University of Wisconsin–Madison, WI

MASTER'S PROGRAMS
(Psychology Departments)

California State University, San
    Bernadino, CA

California State University, Long
Beach, CA

San Francisco State University, San
Francisco, CA

San Jose State University, San Jose,
CA

California State University, San
Jose, CA

St. Mary's College of California,
Morgana, CA

University of Colorado, Denver, CO

University of New Haven, New
Haven, CT

University of West Florida,
Pensocola, FL

Indiana University–Purdue
University, Indianapolis, IN

Emporia State University, Emporia,
KS

Kansas State University, Manhattan,
KS

University of Kansas, Lawrence, KS

Western Kentucky University,
Bowling Green, KY

University of Baltimore, MD

Central Michigan State University,
Mt. Pleasant, MI

Appalachian State University,
Boone, NC

East Carolina University,
Greenville, NC

University of Nebraska–Omaha, NE

Baruch College, City University of
New York, NY

Columbia University, New York, NY

New York University, New York, NY

Rensselaer Polytechnic Institute,
Troy, NY

University of Tulsa, OK

Lamar University–Beaumont, TX

University of North Texas, Denton,
TX

George Mason University, Fairfax,
VA

Radford University, Radford, VA

University of Wisconsin, Oshkosh,
WI

MASTER'S PROGRAMS
(Business Departments)

University of Illinois, Champaign, IL

Illinois State University, Normal, IL

University of Minnesota,
Minneapolis, MN

Polytechnic University, Brooklyn,
NY

Temple University, Philadelphia, PA

University of Tennessee, Knoxville,
TN

Texas A & M University, College
Station, TX

University of Virginia,
Charlottesville, VA

CANADA

There are few graduate programs in I/O psychology in Canada, although the area is well represented at the undergraduate level. (Of the 53 universities, 50 offer courses in the I/O area. The course titles, from most to least frequent, are Industrial [and] Organizational Psychology, Industrial Psychology, Organizational Psychology, and Applied Psychology. Variants include People, Work and Organizations; Industry and Work; Psychology of Industry; Organizational Behavior; and Personnel Psychology. Specialized courses include Consumer Psychology, Human Factors Engineering, Organizational Behavior, and Environmental Psychology.)

The following universities offer graduate programs in I/O psychology:

University	Degree	Length	Require- ments	Comments
British Columbia	M.A., Ph.D.			Personnel, Organizational
Calgary	M.Sc., Ph.D.	2 yrs	GRE, thesis, research	Co-op program in I/O and ergonomics
St. Mary's	M.Sc.	2 yrs	B average, thesis	Personnel, Organizational
Waterloo	M.A., Ph.D.		GRE	Personnel, Organizational, Human Factors Engineering
Guelph	M.A., Ph.D.	3 yrs	GRE, MAT	Personnel, Organizational, Human Factors Engineering
University of Western Ontario	M.A., Ph.D.			Personnel, Organizational
Windsor				courses only

Employment prospects for psychologists in general are good, Service jobs in general are proliferating, and a 1991 publication of the U.S. Department of Labor lists psychologists as the fifth from the top in predicted job opportunities (for occupations requiring a college degree) up to the year 2005. And within psychology, I/O is growing faster than other areas. The general public is not as aware of I/O psychology as they are of the other three "professional practice" fields (clinical, counseling, and school psychology), but in the academic and business communities it is a respected specialty, as people come to realize the importance of productivity to national prosperity, of work to peoples' lives, and of I/O psychology to the understanding of work.

Of the sixty thousand members of the American and Canadian Psychological Associations, almost 7 percent are I/O psychologists, with the proportion of women approaching 50 percent. In the United States, over one-third of I/O psychologists are employed by educational institutions, where they teach courses, perform research, write, and possibly do part-time consulting work. Just less than another one-third are in private practice, either on their own or in association with a consulting firm. One-fifth of I/O psychologists work under various job titles as full-time, salaried employees of major corporations, and others work for public organizations such as governmental or service agencies (Howard, 1990). Frizzell (1989) found that those with a master's degree are more likely to work in industry.

As for the possibility of unemployment, Jeanneret (1991) predicts that the high demand for I/O psychologists' services will continue to grow in the years ahead, despite the increase in graduates. Earlier, Stapp and Fulcher (1982) found that a minuscule 0.5 percent of people holding any graduate degree in I/O psychology were looking for work. So employment prospects are excellent, but what about the remuneration? No specialty within psychology commands higher compensation than does I/O psychology. One U.S. survey of members of the APA's Society for Industrial and Organizational Psychology (SIOP) found that the median income for an I/O psychologist with a master's degree was $51,500. Of those with doctorates, the median was $60,000, and one-tenth earned over $100,000 (Sorenson, Durand & Shaw, 1990). At the bottom end, Frizzell (1989) cited a starting salary of about $27,000 for master's degree holders.

Most important, the practice of I/O psychology is inherently rewarding. Few professions are as modern, challenging, varied, and stimulating, and few accomplish as much in making the workplace safer, more productive, and pleasant.

Appendix E
How to highlight

Maybe I'm odd, but I like worn steps. It's somehow reassuring to see signs of wear left by those who passed my way before. And sometimes my quirk proved useful. When I was an undergraduate at the University of Toronto, we had to learn the thrust of certain books in the library. I would first look at the page edges, because the edges of the pages in the heavily read sections were darker. These pages, the ones most turned forward and back by my predecessors, were the ones they deemed to be most important, so those were the pages I focused on.

That's why I sometimes glance at my students' textbooks. What do *they* consider important, I would wonder. Most used a highlighter to help them distinguish the critical from the filler stuff. Good idea. (Back in my day, there were no highlighters, so we underlined. The really serious students underlined in red.)

To my dismay, ten out of ten of my students seemed to highlight their text ineptly. Some (and this, if it's an exaggeration, is only a tiny one) seemed to randomly choose two words per page to highlight; others seemed to just highlight alternate paragraphs. A few highlighted all but a few words per page—which then were the only words that stood out! Some used a system (I guess) that I could not decipher. And nobody highlighted the critical stuff except apparently by accident. This is not good. First they took time to highlight, then they threw themselves off by highlighting badly.

Sometimes my students come to my office, quivering and sobbing about studying so hard, yet still failing. (And those are just the guys.) How could I help them? Referring them to the Study Skills counselors seemed like a cop-out. "Come back tomorrow and bring your textbook," I'd suggest. If they mis-highlighted or didn't at all, I'd show them how to highlight. Many returned later to tell me it really helped.

On the next pages, I've highlighted pages 98 through 107 of chapter 4. If you haven't done so, why don't you do it, and then compare your highlighting with mine. Don't turn this page until you highlight (or underline) at least those sections.

There's no value to highlighting unless you do it properly; this exercise may help you sharpen your highlighting skills. (If you read anything you already know, there's no need to highlight that.) While highlighting, you identify what you don't know and what is important. Prior to a test you can review the highlighted words in a moment. I think that good highlighting is more efficient than making notes.

Testing is an inescapable part of modern life. Everything you eat, wear, live in, or use in any way has probably first been subjected to a variety of tests. And you know that nobody can attain professional status without confronting a series of tests.

The most important and most widely used tool of the applied psychologist is the psychological test. Such tests are relied upon in clinical diagnosis, counseling, education, placement, and evaluation. The science of selecting, administering, and interpreting these tests is called psychometrics (literally mind measure).

In industrial/organizational (I/O) psychology the primary use of tests is for personnel selection. Students know that they are unlikely to be offered a worthwhile job without passing a test. Managers know that the optimal use of tests may make the difference between successful and unsuccessful personnel selection. And corporate lawyers know that if their firm is charged with discriminatory selection, a strong defense would be records of test scores along with data supporting the appropriateness of the testing procedure.

As you recall from chapter 1, psychological testing began with Binet's procedure for predicting the school performance of one group of French children. It's a long way from that use of tests to predicting the work performance of a group of job applicants. Are tests valid for both purposes? This is a prime consideration in the discipline of psychometrics.

WHAT IS A TEST?

The word **test**, as most commonly used in psychology, refers to a *standardized procedure designed to predict some behavior.* For instance, a school psychologist might administer an intelligence test to a child, not for the purpose of measuring intelligence per se, but to predict the child's school performance.

"Test" may have other meanings as well. In order to be admitted into an institution of higher learning such as a dental school, or to be offered employment, one typically first undergoes a selection procedure involving the administration of a test. Here the test is designed to predict the applicant's performance in dental school, or on the job. More important, the tester hopes that the score on the test will foretell the applicant's level of success as a practicing dentist, or as the employee who some day will be promoted to head the corporation.

More specifically, the test is designed to predict those aspects of behavior that are deemed to be important. Those performance variables that distinguish between success and failure—between the person who, it is ultimately decided, was admitted in error or whose acceptance, it turns out, was a correct decision—constitute the *job criterion* (page 87). In short, a *test predicts* the *criterion.*

The term **standardized** indicates that the test is administered in a uniform, proper manner and scored according to previously established **norms**, or baseline scores. The term further implies that the testees can be *appropriately* evaluated against the standardization sample on which the norms were established.

CHARACTERISTICS OF TESTS

There are six basic characteristics on which every selection test can be evaluated. A few of them will require some effort to understand, but we'll start with the simple ones.

1. The **difficulty** level of a test should be such that not one of the scores collides with the **upper or lower ceiling.** (A ceiling is the highest or lowest score that is possible on a given test. The lower ceiling is sometimes termed the *floor.*) For instance, suppose on a test, where the range of possible scores is 1 to 10, that the lowest score is 6 and that several applicants score 10. Because everyone performed well, and especially because the upper ceiling was reached more than once, we conclude that the test was too easy. If one person reached the upper ceiling, we cannot tell exactly *how much* better that person was than the others (maybe the score would have been even higher if the ceiling permitted it); if two or more did so we cannot differentiate among these top scorers.

2. The **dispersion of scores** is a simple concept. Consider two tests with maximum scores of 10. Test A yields scores ranging from 3 to 8; Test B shows a range of 1 to 9. Because Test B offers a wider range of scores it yields more dispersion in the results and hence is preferable. If the benefits of high dispersion are not clear to you, consider how useful you would find a test with zero dispersion (meaning that everyone tested achieved the same score).

Both dispersion and difficulty level are assessed in the same way, namely, empirically, by graphing the results and inspecting the graph. Figure 4.1 illustrates graphs of tests with and without problems in difficulty level; Figure 4.2 shows tests with good and poor dispersions.

3. The common meaning of reliability, as you know, is the personality attribute of dependability. In psychometrics, however, it is a technical term that means *consistency.* Let's see what this means.

Suppose you administer a test to 10 applicants and Merle leads the group. A month later, you readminister the same test in the same way, and this time Merle scores near the bottom. Although that particular test may have been ideal regarding its dispersion of scores and difficulty level, it lacked *reliability.*

Reliability is the most important attribute of a test. Regardless of its weaknesses in other dimensions, a *reliable* test may still be of use for some purpose. For instance, a test of employees' physical condition and attitudes to health that is designed to predict how long a person has to live, may prove to be inaccurate. But if the test scores show reliability, a different researcher may find that they predict something else, like heart problems. A test that lacks reasonable reliability, however, can serve no purpose whatsoever.

A perfectly reliable test would yield the same scores to the same testees, time after time. But of course it's impossible to readminister a test under identical conditions. If you do it the next day, testees will remember some of the items. If you wait a year, they will be a year older on the second administration. Hence, we never can tell the exact reliability of a test, but we can come close.

To measure test-retest reliability you administer the same test to the same group under similar conditions twice, with an intervening time gap. Each writer's score on the first administration is compared with the mark obtained on the second. The higher the correlation, the greater the test-retest reliability. The problems are the inconvenience of reassembling all the testees, and not knowing the effect of variables other than test reliability on the correlation. (These variables might include memory, practice, some kind of training or experience that took place between the two sittings, or just the passage of time.)

If a test is designed to measure a single attribute, all of its questions or items should measure the same characteristic. Hence, if there are a large number of items, your score on any half of them should be similar to your mark on the other half. One way to measure the split half or alternate form reliability is to compare your scores on the first half with those on the second (or your first and third quarters with the second and fourth). If your performance is likely to change as the test progresses—due to fatigue, practice, or a change in the difficulty of the items—the odd-numbered items could be compared with the even ones.

A third type of reliability is a statistic that measures how consistently the items are answered badly or well. Throughout all the test questions, do poor performers perform consistently badly, and do the high scorers do well in general? One statistic that measures this type of consistency is called KR20 (for Kuder and Richardson). A *KR20* of .7 and higher indicates good internal consistency.

Where scores are determined subjectively, researchers can determine interscorer reliability (the agreement between raters). No test can be expected to show perfect reliability on any of the four above measures. Rather, the test user expects a reliability coefficient much closer to 1 than to 0. Most standard selection tests offer coefficients between .6 and .9.

4. **Specificity** refers to the extent to which components of a test measure nonoverlapping attributes. Picture a test of muscle strength. Suppose its four subtests measured the strength of the left arm, right arm, left leg, and right leg. And let's assume that people's two arms are invariably the same in strength, as are their two legs.

You can see that in this case we could have assessed strength just as accurately by measuring only one arm and one leg. The two subtests for arm strength, the left arm and the right arm subtest, lacked specificity because they both measured the same attribute, arm strength.

Why is low specificity a problem? Testing is costly. It is usually expensive for the tester to choose, acquire, administer, score, and interpret tests, and it's psychologically costly for the testee to undergo them. Thus, any subtest that merely duplicates information offered by another, previously administered one, should be avoided.

Specificity is measured by correlating test scores across each other. If any two items, questions, or subtests are so highly correlated that knowing a person's score on one allows you accurately to predict the score on the other, then those two items lack specificity. The solution is to eliminate one, perhaps the one with the poorer showing on other characteristics.

5. **Validity** basically refers to whether a test does what it is supposed to. Managers want their tests to be valid just as when they pay for a raw ingredient with certain properties they expect it to possess those properties. Testees would have a great deal to complain about if they learned that a test on which their selection, promotion, or graduation were based, was invalid. And courts of law expect such tests to be valid in order to satisfy legislation regarding equal opportunity.

Doubtless because of the complexity of validity, only about five percent of companies have any kind of validity data to support their testing procedures (according to Moon, 1987), and not all of these data would be convincing in court. There are five types, the most important of which are **predictive validity** and **concurrent validity**. They should be thoroughly understood and clearly distinguished from each other.

The purest measure of whether or not a test performs as expected is its *predictive* validity. To assess the predictive validity of a test, you would administer it to *all* of the available applicants or to a group that fairly represents the applicant population. The second step consists of hiring all of those who took the test! These "new hires" are handled without regard for their test results, which should be sealed to prevent their scores from influencing any aspect of their early experience. When the work record has lasted long enough for a criterion score to be applied to each worker, this is performed. Then the test results are unsealed and compared to the criterion scores. *The predictive validity is the correlation between test score and criterion score.*

The concept of predictive validation is appealing to employees, because it democratically gives every applicant a chance. It is also appealing to employers, because once a test is shown to have high predictive validity, the firm can use it for future selection with confidence and with reasonable immunity from charges of unfair discrimination in hiring.

Despite its appeal, predictive validation is so costly that it is rarely carried out. The problem, of course, is with the second step, in which all applicants who write the test are offered the job. It rarely benefits people to hire them for work they can't be successful at. Unsuitable applicants, once hired, may complain with justification that their hopes were falsely raised, and they may prove costly to the firm and hard to dislodge.

Yet, in practice, predictive validation does have some application. Imagine a pilot plant that needs 100 employees now, and in a few years the main plant will recruit 1,000 workers. The firm has three tests that might be useful in predicting how best to select those 1,000. So the first 100 applicants for the pilot plant (which is not expected to make a profit) are all hired. All of the 100 take all three tests. It would be of inestimable value to the firm to know which, if any, of the three tests shows a high correlation with job performance.

Should *every* selection test undergo predictive validation prior to each new application? That is, if one employer finds the predictive validity of some test to be 0.7 for hiring a maintenance crew, can another firm confidently use it to select *its* maintenance staffers? Contrary to earlier assumptions, it turns out that test users can rely on a substantial degree of validity generalization. This means that once the predictive validity is determined for one use of a given test, similar applications can be expected to yield similar results. (Details on what is meant by "similar" and on the type of test with the greatest validity generalization can best be found in the arguments of Schmidt, Pearlman, Hunter and Hirsh, 1985, and in the rejoinder of Sackett, Tenopyr, Schmitt, Kehoe and Zedeck, 1985.)

Unlike reliability, predictive validity is not an inherent characteristic of a given test; rather, it is linked to the test's use. It is meaningless to ask if a certain test is "valid." One may ask only if it is valid for a specified use. A test that is invalid for one purpose may be highly valid for another.

It is more common for a firm to be faced with the same question ("Which of these three tests best predicts the criterion?") without having the ability to perform a pilot plant or other costly study to answer it. If the question were slightly reworded to ask "Which of these three tests is most highly correlated with our *present* workers' performances?" it could be answered easily. The employer simply administers the tests to the present staff, and correlates test scores with criterion scores. The best test, presumably, is the one on which the top employee gets the highest score and the worst performer the lowest. It is logical to assume that if this *concurrently validated* test is administered to applicants, it would accurately predict which applicant—if hired—would ultimately achieve the best work record. The administration of tests to *present* workers for this purpose is called *concurrent* validity because it measures the correlation of test score not with what the applicant will eventually do, but with the present or concurrent work record of the staff.

Concurrent validation is simple, easy, and inexpensive. The main cost is the interruption of production when the employees are taking the test. But there are weaknesses in this procedure. The major problem is that the present workers are a different group than the applicants. For instance, the worst performers have probably been gradually removed from the present workforce, whereas those who are potentially the worst still remain in the applicant pool. (That is, a test should identify hopeless cases as well as promising ones, but any present staff probably doesn't include dismal performers to be tested.) Similarly, predictive validation may reflect the *trainability* of workers. But the present staff has completed its training, and their experience is likely to influence their test scores in a way that is hard to detect or interpret.

The two types of validity we have just looked at, *predictive and concurrent,* are known as criterion validities because they are determined through an empirical correlation with some external criterion. (Although it would seem that *predictive* validity is to be preferred over *concurrent* validity, some data [Barrett, Phillips & Alexander, 1981] suggest that they are similar in value.) Because these determinations are based on logic, they are known as rational validities. Other types of validity, the ones outlined next, are determined only through an internal examination.

Content validity is more applicable to tests of knowledge than tests of work potential. For instance, at the conclusion of a training program trainees may be tested on the material presented. If these questions did not fairly reflect the program's content, the test would lack content validity. Content validity is assessed by comparing the topics of the questions with those listed on the curriculum. The closer the connection, the greater the content validity. This assessment is subjective.

Content validity is related to *representativeness.* The essence of any test, you'll recall, is that it calls for a *sample* of behavior or asks questions on a *sample* of the material that was presumably learned. If you were given an examination on this entire book, and all of the questions were based only on this chapter, the content of the exam would not properly represent the material of the book.

Construct validity is complex because it has to do with how a test relates to the underlying construct (page 58). Here's an example. Suppose you want to devise a test for leadership. You would first have to ask questions like these: What hypotheses derived from leadership theory relate to your new leadership test? To what extent can these hypotheses be confirmed through the use of this test, that is, to what extent does your test follow logically from—and confirm—the prevailing theories of leadership? The greater the extent, the more construct validity your test possesses. Again, the evaluation is subjective.

On a simpler level, it is possible to assess construct validity empirically. If a leadership test that is considered valid already exists, you could compare scores on this test with scores on yours. Construct validation is a normal part of the scientific process. Even existing tests should be validated insofar as the theory related to the particular construct improves.

The simplest type of validity is face validity. Most people, whether job applicants or university students, don't enjoy being tested. So if the test *appears* to be irrelevant to its apparent purpose, anger or indifference would be a likely reaction. Therefore, a test should look like it will serve the purpose for which it is being administered, and to the extent it does this, it has face validity.

To measure face validity, you could simply ask those who are being tested to state what they think the test is designed to measure or accomplish. The more accurate the guesses, the higher the face validity. It can easily be manipulated by the wording of a title or label that is seen by the testees.

Validity is a more complex issue than the above treatment indicates. Some theorists propose more divisions; Messick (1980) lists 12 types of construct validity, and Guion and Crany (1982) differentiate among 8 varieties of criterion validity. By contrast, Landy (1986) argues that criterion, content, and construct validity are the same; the 3 names merely show the 3 types of *inferences* that can be drawn from the same test score. Binning and Barrett (1989) expand Landy's position, review the historical changes in the meaning of validity, and present thoughtful arguments for a single type of validity from various contexts: scientific, practical, technical, organizational, political, legal, and professional. The 5-way division of validity presented in this chapter emphasizes the differences for clarity, and is summarized in table form as Table 4.1.

6. The last characteristic of a test is its discriminability. Suppose a city hires you to test firefighter incumbents or applicants. Somebody suggests a rope-climbing test in which the score is the height climbed and descended in ten seconds. You devise, standardize, and administer this test to your standardization sample, and find the scores look good in terms of difficulty level and dispersion. The testees like its face validity, and you are satisfied as to its construct validity. You repeat the test after a month and find high test-retest reliability. What else might you like to know about this test?

You already have other measures on the testees (various other scores on a set of applicants, and criterion measures on the incumbents). So what you'd like to know about the new test item is (a) does it discriminate between the "good" performers and the "poor" performers? (b) do the best performers (as determined by your other measures) excel in rope-climbing, and (c) do the poor performers score low on it?

You can quantify discriminability of individual test items this way. Select a percentage of the testees to define the top and bottom group. (If the N is large, you might take the top and bottom **deciles** or 10 percent to compare; if small, you could choose the top and bottom **quartiles** or 25 percent.) The better the performance of the top testees compared to the bottom on a test item, the better its discriminability. The usual statistical procedure used for determining discriminability is called *point biserial correlation.*

Glossary

I am a Bear of Very Little Brain, and long words Bother me.

A. A. Milne (1882–1956)

abilities current competence, as opposed to aptitude, which is potential competence. 111

absenteeism refers to employees' not showing up for work as scheduled; the quantification of absenteeism may focus on the *number* of missed work periods, their *duration,* and/or the *reason* for the absence. Absences resulting from, for instance, accident or illness are sometimes termed *authorized* or *involuntary.* 199

academic journal a periodical in which scholarly articles that contribute to the discipline are published. 24

accident proneness the tendency to be involved in accidents, more so than can be attributed to either chance or the work hazards. Accident proneness has been related to *experience* (the more the experience the lower the accident rate), *age* (generally, the older the worker the fewer the accidents), *personality* (particularly in regard to attitude), and *perceptual problems*. The tendency to precipitate an accident is different from the failure to avert an impending one. 314

acclimatization adaption to climatic, especially temperature change. Adaption to heat has behavioral, psychological, and physiological components, and is a slightly easier adjustment than adaption to cold. 379

accommodation in vision, the change of shape by the lens of the eye, to focus images on the retina. In employment practices and law, it refers to alterations to the work or workplace so as not to exclude or hamper employees with disabilities. In conflict resolution, it is an appeasement strategy in which one side makes a sacrifice to settle a dispute. 90, 418

achievement an *accomplishment* as opposed to an interest or an aptitude. It may be assessed through a test. 111

achievement-oriented leadership goal-directed leadership in which the leader focuses on the task at hand. The attribute that measures this aspect of leadership is called initiation of structure. 246

acquired immunodeficiency syndrome see AIDS 316

active badge a device worn by employees to track their location around a large facility and to chart this information at a central monitoring station. 212

active learning learning by doing, as in on-the-job training. 148

activities, interests, and opinions (AIOs) the characteristics of survey respondents and consumer juries that marketing researchers typically measure and then correlate with consumer-related behavior. 446

acuity the accuracy (usually in terms of fine detail) of a sense. *Minimum distinguishable visual acuity* is measured by the smallest character that can be read; *dynamic visual acuity* is the ability to see moving figures. 390

acutance the sharpness of the division between figure and ground on a video display terminal. 419

adaption in vision, the adjustment of the iris and the photoreceptors to changes in illumination intensity. In sensation and perception, it refers to the raising of the threshold through accustomation to the stimulus. 418

adaptiveness the altering of later items' difficulty level in a computerized test to match the testee's ability as shown by earlier answers. 123

adverse impact A selection procedure has *adverse impact* on members of a group if those members are generally outperformed on it by others. The more the adverse impact, the more the test should be demonstrably related to the job criterion. 121

affect (noun) emotion; the adjective form is affective. (Don't confuse affect and effect, both of which can be used as a noun and as a verb.) 221

affirmative action the preferential personnel-decision treatment (in recruitment of, and/or lowering of standards for) members of an identifiable group, generally to make up for that group's having been underrepresented (usually through discrimination) in the workforce. 90

affordance the extent to which a control affords only the correct and obvious interpretation of how it works. A simple drawer knob has high affordance; one that you have to push in to release the catch would have low affordance. 356

aided recall a means of measuring the recognizability of an advertisement. After exposure to ads, subjects indicate what they recall about them from a list of possibilities or "aids." 441

AIDS (acquired immunodeficiency syndrome) a virus-caused, essentially fatal disorder, spread through the exchange of bodily fluids. It is associated (in North America) mainly with intravenous drug use and homosexuality. A blood test for the antigen to the virus reveals whether a person has been exposed to it. Medical treatment is presently limited; the best prevention is behavior change. 316

ambient presently surrounding. You are reading this under ambient light, temperature, and humidity. 380

American Psychological Association (APA) the coordinating professional association of psychologists. It comprises 47 divisions; for example, *Industrial and Organizational Psychology* is Division 14. It publishes a number of academic journals, such as the *Journal of Applied Psychology*. 20

Anastasi, Anne earned her doctorate from Columbia University at age 21; author of influential textbooks on applied psychology and psychometrics, served as president of the APA.

annunciator a simple display, often color coded and labeled. It remains off most of the time, to indicate STATUS NORMAL, and turns on or blinks to signal STATUS ABNORMAL. 361

anthropometry [an-throw-POM-e-tree] or anthropometrics is the measurement of the physical dimensions of humans while at rest *(static anthropometry)* or in motion, as when the arms are outstretched *(dynamic anthropometry)*. 374

applied psychology deals with the practical applications of the discipline of psychology. Specialty areas include personnel psychology, organizational behavior, consumer psychology, human factors engineering, aerospace and military psychology, industrial sociology, community psychology, and environmental or ecological psychology. Applied psychology has links with social, physiological, cognitive, and clinical psychology.

applied research is performed for practical applications. 59

apprenticeship a structured training system, common in licensed skilled trades, in which a young trainee enters into a formal agreement to undergo on-the-job training with a qualified tradesperson. Apprenticeship programs are usually regulated by the government, and last two to four years. 149

aptitude an ability, predilection, or talent. Tests are available to detect mechanical, musical, artistic, clerical, and other aptitudes. See interest and achievement. 111

arbitration a system for resolving disputes in which an arbitrator hears the arguments of each side, and renders a judgment that is often binding on both sides. See conciliation. 291

archival research a study not of people themselves, but of traces of their behavior that they leave behind; for instance, an analysis of empty bottles in a garbage dump to measure drinking patterns. 45

Army Alpha a general-purpose, short, group-administered paper-and-pencil test devised by a group under Terman at the U.S. Army's request, and widely used during World War I to classify recruits for rejection/discharge, or assignment to different types of service or officer training. Subtests on this original intelligence test measured information, reasoning, and practical judgment. A later modification for civilian use was also widely used. See Otis. 18

Army Beta a version of the Army Alpha used for illiterate U.S. recruits in World War I. 18

aspect ratio ratio of height to width in a video display terminal. The most common ratio is 3:4.4. 419

attitudinal commitment a devotion to the organization reflected by high motivation to perform well, to volunteer for extra work, and to devote less attention to socializing on the job. 197

attribution theory of leadership focuses on how events are interpreted by leaders and followers. For instance, leaders may treat subordinates differently, depending on the reasons that leaders attribute to subordinates' behavior. 248

autokinetic effect the perception of motion in a stationary point (seen against a blank background) when a person fixates on it for a prolonged period. For example, a pilot gazing at a solitary star will eventually perceive it to be moving, and may assume it is a light from another aircraft. 385

autonomic nervous system the part of the nervous system that basically works automatically, rather than under voluntary control. It comprises the sympathetic and the parasympathetic nervous systems, the former responsible for mobilizing many body parts and systems for "fight or flight," the latter responsible for maintaining the same systems for relaxation and longevity. 449

autonomy self-directed, generally in the context of employees' having power or responsibility in making decisions at work. 173

balance theory a number of theories of social behavior that state that we tend to equalize ("balance") our cognitions and relationships in order to maintain a state of mental harmony. 179

bandwidth the period available for flextime employees to work daily. 331

bank (a noun or verb in ergonomics) the rotation of a vehicle about the longitudinal axis; an aircraft banks when one wing is lowered and the other raised. 372

basic research is performed for its own sake. 59

behavior modification the systematic application of learning theory to change behavior. Reinforcement is used to strengthen desirable behavior. 182

Behavioral Observation Scale a checklist of behavior examples, which provides measurable indicators of employee performance. 214

behavioral research gathers data by observing what the subjects actually do. 64

Behaviorally Anchored Rating Scales (BARS) rating scales in which the rater assigns a numerical score on given dimensions (for example, motivation or punctuality). Some of the scores are attached to descriptions of work behavior to help the rater choose an appropriate score. 215

bel a unit of relative sound intensity (loudness), named after Alexander Graham Bell, who studied sound transmission to help the deaf communicate. Sound volume is measured in decibels (one-tenth of a bel). 387

bell curve the graphical representation of a variable that is distributed *normally*. The curve is symmetrical, high in the middle and low at the outsides and therefore shaped like the outline of a bell.

between-subjects design an experimental design in which each subject receives only one treatment, and the data from one treatment group are compared with those from the other(s). Contrasting this is the within-subjects design. 49

bias a slant or leaning. Researchers guard against bias (intentional or not) affecting their procedures and results; I/O psychologists try to prevent bias from affecting personnel decisions. 51

bimetrology the use of two measurement systems. 376

Binet, Alfred (1857–1911) a versatile and insightful French academic, best remembered for designing a procedure to measure and express intelligence, which is basically used to this day. During his short life, Binet became a lawyer, studied medicine, attained a Ph.D. in science, and founded the first French laboratory of experimental pedagogy. 17

bipolar two opposites. 378

blackout blindness caused by extreme positive G force. 383

blind review reviewers are not given any information about the author of the material they are reviewing. Thus there is no possibility of bias. 25

Braille a tactile alphabet for the blind, named after its 15-year-old French inventor Louis Braille. 358

branched format a program in computer-aided instruction, in which the system varies the questions according to the learner's progress. 154

buddy system a term derived from swimming safety programs at summer camps; the linking typically of a novice worker with an experienced one for casual day-to-day advice. 279

burnout an extreme reaction to chronic job stress, marked by despondency, apathy, emotional exhaustion, withdrawal, and quitting. 321

business game a form of situational training at the managerial level. 153

candela a unit of light intensity in a given direction from the source; one candela is the light given by one candle. One candela per meter squared (cd/m^2) is the luminance leaving one square meter of surface; it is the metric unit of the foot lambert. 389

career development the planning of career moves throughout one's lifetime. 158

career planning the assessment of aptitudes, abilities, and interests, as well as available career opportunities to recommend occupational directions. 158

carpal tunnel syndrome shows as pain or numbness in the palm, wrist, or forearm. It results from compression of a nerve in the area of one of the carpal ligaments. It is a relatively common repetitive strain injury especially in women and is typically associated with the prolonged operation of keyboards or similar work tasks. 330

case method in research, the analysis of a case in point. The case method of training focuses on a real or imagined problem, typically featuring human relations challenges. 47

causality a cause-and-effect relationship. 48

central tendency error in assessment, the grading of everybody as "Average," even in the face of a wide range of performances. In statistics, it is the most representative score in the set. 218

change agent typically a consultant hired to facilitate organizational development (external), or a member of the organization in a similar role (internal). 277

character any symbol such as a letter, digit, or mathematical symbol in printing. 411

checklist a list of descriptors used for employee rating. They may be positive, negative, or mixed, and the applicable ones are checkmarked by the rater. 213

chronobiology the relation between internal clocks (natural bodily rhythms) and external time. 324

circadian disrhythmia [sir-KAY-dee-an] the result of interrupting the normal circadian rhythms. It occurs when a person makes major work shift changes such as switching from day shift to night shift, during jet travel across several time zones, or when studying through the night. It can cause discomfort and reduced efficiency. 324

circadian rhythms refer to 24-hour biological cycles of, for instance, alertness or body temperature. 324

Civil Rights Act the prime U.S. legislation, passed in 1964, prohibiting employment discrimination based on race, religion, sex, or country of origin. 22

clerical aptitude test examines the ability to perceive, remember, recognize, and manipulate printed characters, particularly numbers. A number of tests, such as the Minnesota Clerical Test, are available to measure it. 111

client lab works like a focus group, except that the participants are asked to *do* something (while being observed), as opposed to just talking. 443

clinical technique the use of in-depth diagnostic techniques originally associated with clinical psychologists. 63

clustering (ergonomics) the placement of interrelated displays close to each other to facilitate interpreting them. 358

cognitive mental processes such as thoughts, interpretations, and assessments. 177

collectivism (Hofstede) a close-knit social structure, in which all members expect to be looked after comprehensively and are equally prepared to protect other members. It is the opposite of individualism. 273

communication the transfer of information. In an organization, it may be *informal* as in ordinary conversation, or *formal* as in an official message. Communication patterns or networks have been widely studied in social psychology and sociology. The topic has recently become central within organizational and consumer psychology. 404

communications analysis the tracing of a message transmission, generally within an organization, often to detect blockages. 61

comparable worth a central concept in pay equity, referring to comparable pay for jobs entailing similar levels of training, qualifications, working conditions, and responsibility. For instance, the job of a nurse may *merit* the same pay as that of an electrician but in real life may pay less because it is associated with women's work rather than with men's work. 89

comparative analysis the contrasting of one's own workplace situation with that of comparable outside equivalents. 62

compensable job factors those aspects of a job that are used to determine its comparable worth. Typical factors are the training required, the responsibility entailed, and the working conditions. 90

compressed workweek a modification of the common, 8-hour, five-day schedule, typically into a 10-hour, four-day week. An alternative is a workshift of three consecutive 12-hour days, for full pay. The rationale for the compression may be to increase leisure time, to decrease travel time, and/or to staff an organization on a seven-day basis. See flextime. 331

computerized performance monitoring the use of recording devices as an "electronic watchdog" to record employee performance. Typical applications of CPM are for expensive machinery (for example, the "black box" installed in aircraft and transport trucks), and for keyboard-entry tasks, but it is being extended to law enforcement and other kinds of work. Critics charge that these devices can be stressful and dehumanizing; proponents argue that they provide accurate and fair records of performance, and sometimes improve safety. 212

conciliation a dispute resolution procedure in which a conciliator attempts to bring the disputants together, often by improving communication. See arbitration. 291

concurrent validity the correlation between test scores and the job criterion scores of present employees. 102

cones the photoreceptors on the retina responsible for color and form perception. They are functional when the illumination level is high. 392

confrontation meeting (usually face-to-face) to voice a complaint or resolve a dispute. 278

consideration (Halpin & Winer) the aspect of leadership that emphasizes the leader's response to needs for warmth, respect, mutual trust, communication, participative decision making, and rapport between leader and subordinate. The contrasting approach to leadership is initiating structure. 242

consolidation refers to the conversion of material temporarily stored in *short-term memory* into that relatively permanent material, stored in *long-term memory*. 135

construct concept. The force of the term is that all concepts have been constructed by the human mind. Hence, this is not a page but a collection of atoms or energy which *we* have learned to *perceive* as a page. Similarly, constructs in applied psychology such as *intelligence* and *motivation* do not exist in any external reality. We describe these constructs, devise tests to expose them, and infer from behavior how much intelligence or motivation the individual has, all within a theory of intelligence or motivation. 58

construct validity the extent to which a test is logically related to the construct underlying the attribute tested. 105

consumer jury a group of people trained to make subjective assessments of different products or media presentations according to criteria that are relevant to the marketer sponsoring the jury. 450

consumer psychology an interdisciplinary examination of the relation between people and the marketplace. It includes marketing and promoting goods and services, product perception, and purchase motivation. 438

contamination in a subjective assessment, an employer's ratings of an employee that are based on behaviors irrelevant to the actual job performance. 219

content validity the extent to which the questions on a test fairly represent the content of the material being tested. 104

contingency theory of leadership (Fiedler) states that the effectiveness of a leader is a function of the leader's nature and personal traits contingent upon the favorableness of the task or situation. 245

continuous rating scale allows for any number of gradations within the scale. 214

contrast in photometrics, the extent to which the figure stands out from the ground when considering the effect of illumination on performance. The lower the brightness the more contrast is needed to maintain the performance level in a visual task. 391

control in research, a procedure designed to eliminate the acceptance of explanations other than the hypothesized one; see experiment. In ergonomics it is the device with which the operator communicates with the machine; contrast with display. 49, 350

control discriminability exists when each control is clearly and easily distinguishable from the others. 356

control function logic exists when the movement of a control logically predicts the effect upon the equipment. For instance, a switch is moved *down* to lower a window. 353

control group in an experiment ensures that the level of the dependent variable can be attributed only to the effect of the independent variable. 49

control stereotype an arbitrary connection between the movement of a control and the response of the machine—a connection that users have come to expect. An example is an up/down switch where up is generally expected to mean on *or* off, depending on the country. 355

convection the transmission of thermal energy through the air. 379

convergence moving together. In vision, the axes of the eyes gradually converge when fixating on an object that is moving closer. 417

copy (noun) the textual, as opposed to the pictorial, part of an advertisement. 409, 454

core hours those hours during which flextime employees must be at work. 331

cornea the hard, transparent, bulging, refractive (and reflective) surface of the center of the front of the eye. 362

correlation the mathematical relation between two variables. 37

correlation coefficient the mathematical representation of the strength of the relation between two variables. 37

counseling a general term that may refer to friendly advice, or to nonintensive psychotherapy that emphasizes coping and adjusting. Many firms retain counselors to aid employees with financial, psychological, retirement, and other problems. 62

coupon a promotional device consisting of a printed form that can be redeemed, usually at the point of purchase, for a discount on the stipulated product. 450

criterion cutoff the criterion level (indecision theory) below which the management considers the employee's performance to be unsatisfactory. 123

criterion index the condensation of various elements of a job criterion into a single number. 87

criterion validity. See predictive validity. 104

critical illumination level the intensity of lighting above which no improvement in performance takes place. 390

cumulative trauma disorder an injury to a part of the body resulting from repetition of certain motions. Work-related examples are carpal tunnel syndrome in keyboard operators and white finger disease in operators of vibrating equipment. 329

cutoff the point or level at which a decision is made to discontinue a process. For example, a cutoff score on an employment test would be the minimum score an applicant needed to be considered for employment. 82

dark adaption the increased ability to see in dim light upon exposure to darkness. It takes place as a result of the activation of the photoreceptors known as the rods. 395

dark adaption curve the curved lines representing changes in the visual threshold as the eye gets used to the dark. 395

data numbers derived from a study. 52

data analysis statistical procedures to interpret data. 52

debriefing a researcher's explaining or confessing to a research participant at the conclusion of a project what the true nature of the study was, and answering any questions. 66

decibel (dB) a commonly used but complex unit of loudness, in which a whisper is rated at about 20, and loud music about 120 decibels. See sone. 387

decile each tenth of a set of scores. 107

decision theory a mathematically based analysis of decision making. 123

deficiency in employee appraisal, the failure to evaluate a sufficiently broad sampling of the work performance. 210

demand characteristics inadvertent cues that make a person assume that a certain behavior or response is called for or expected. The term derives from the concept that a given situation may implicitly "demand" a specific reaction. 41

demographic distributional statistics such as geographical location, income level, and marital, socioeconomic, and occupational status. 444

dependent variable the effect (as opposed to cause) in an experiment. It is the variable measured, as opposed to the independent variable, to which the treatment is administered. For instance, in an experiment to determine the influence of flextime on productivity, productivity would be the dependent variable. 48

design in research, the general methodology or research strategy. In ergonomics it is the application of appropriate human engineering principles. In marketing it refers primarily to the appearance of the product. 53

diary method a job analysis procedure that requires the employee to diarize the job components. 86

differential validity a characteristic of a test or other instrument that is more valid for one group or type of person than for others. 121

difficulty level of a test is reflected by how many scores are affected by the ceiling effect. 99

directive leadership in path-goal theory, the management style that focuses on the specifics of what the subordinates are to do and how. 246

discrete separate and distinct. 214

discretionary analysis an evaluation of an employee's status through the measurement of the freedom to work without direct supervision. 62

discriminability the extent to which a test item succeeds in being easy for the best overall performers, and hard for those who score lowest on the test in general. 105

dispersion the extent to which scores or data vary. 99

display a device on a machine that provides information to the operator; for example, a fuel gauge in a car. 350

display function logic shown by a display that pictorially symbolizes what it's announcing. The most common current example is the *icon* system used on some computer screens. 362

display location logic the placement of *displays* in logical proximity to their associated *controls*. For instance, a thermometer showing the oven temperature on a kitchen range should be placed close to the oven control. 362

display stereotype a *display* that people have learned to associate with some expectation (as in a *control stereotype*) or meaning. Many display stereotypes, from a police officer's uniform to computer icons, are so commonplace that we don't think of them as such. It becomes an issue in ergonomics when,

for instance, the unsuitability of red and green color coding (for example, for color-blind drivers) has to be balanced against the powerful display stereotype of these hues. 424

disposable income money left for discretionary spending after the nondiscretionary expenses have been covered. 448

distance senses vision and hearing, and perhaps olfaction. 357

distributional ratings any of several procedures for comparing the performance within a large group of workers. 217

distributive bargaining a form of negotiation over disputes in which both sides focus on their own gains. See integrative bargaining. 294

documentation the paperwork containing instructions for the operation and/or maintenance of complex equipment. 424

double-blind an experimental control procedure in which the identity of the independent variable (and its various levels) is kept from both the *recipient* and the *administrator* of the treatment. 52

downward communication/appraisal in an organization, communication or appraisal that moves from superiors to subordinates. 225, 251

Dvorak keyboard a keyboard designed by August Dvorak in the 1930s. The arrangement of keys conformed to ergonomic principles so that the most commonly used keys were struck by the strongest fingers. 412

dynamic anthropometry see anthropometry 374

dynamic visual acuity see acuity 390

dysfunctional turnover see turnover. 199

dysphemism a term designed to *lower* the esteem of the referent. See euphemism. 430

education systematic learning that is more general than training. 130

emergent leader one who assumes a leadership role in a leaderless group such as in a work team or in an informal meeting. 248

empirical observed, observable, or containing data. 37

employee assistance programs seek to identify and rectify problems that impair employees' well-being, on or off the job. The programs are funded by the employer. 262

employee comparison method any of several procedures for comparing the performance within a small group of workers. 216

empowerment the granting or achievement of *autonomy*. 223

environmental psychology a recent discipline dealing with how behavior is influenced by environmental variables such as the design of housing, hospitals, cities, and the workplace. 377

Equal Employment Opportunity Commission a U.S. federal body established in 1965 to monitor compliance with the Civil Rights Act.

equal opportunity a concept of occupational equity that generally means the elimination of bias in personnel decisions. 90

equity fairness, especially in regard to remuneration and opportunity for advancement. *Internal equity* deals with evenhandedness within a company; *external equity* looks at how employees are treated in comparison with their counterparts at comparable firms. 90

equity theory (of motivation) also known as balance theory, contends that people's *perceptions about fairness* in the workplace will influence their attitude and performance. 179

ergonomics the science of modifying equipment to suit the user. The word derives from Greek for work/measure. Synonyms are human factors engineering, man-machine engineering, person-machine engineering, biomechanical engineering, and engineering psychology. 21

euphemism a term substituted to increase the status or acceptability of the referent. 429

exclusion workplace designs that *prevent* accidents, as in a device that cuts the electrical power when an electrical access panel is opened. 315

exit interview an interview conducted by a personnel officer with a person who is leaving the firm. The purpose is to get feedback concerning the firm's strengths and weaknesses. 40

expectancy theory holds that motivation is determined by expectations of outcomes, their desirability, and the effort needed to achieve them. 177

experiment a research procedure designed to test a hypothesis by measuring the effect of one variable upon another. 48

experimental group in an experiment, the group that receives the independent variable. 49

experimenter bias the improper influence of the researcher upon the research outcome. 51

external control the influence of outside factors. An externally controlled person is more influenced by external variables. 113

external equity equity of salary levels and advancement opportunities between a firm and the competition. 90

extrinsic motivation the motivating influence of some external reward, as opposed to wanting to work for its own sake. 186

eye (movement) camera a camera that photographs reflections from the cornea while the subject tracks or views, thereby recording what was being looked at. It was devised at Purdue under Tiffin for use in instrument-scanning research. 64

eye movement control see eye movement camera 362

eyewash station resembles a drinking fountain but is designed to provide irrigation of the eye with water, so that any harmful chemicals can be flushed out without delay. 315

face validity refers to how much a test *appears* to measure what it is *designed* to measure. 105

facilitation in learning theory, is the helpful effect of prior learning or subsequent learning. 136

factor analysis a mathematical procedure (involving multiple correlations) for determining which among several variables (or clusters of them) are correlated. A cluster that is strongly correlated could likely represent, for instance, certain abilities or traits. 46

fail-safe workplace designs that reduce the *consequence* of a mishap; for example, a deadman switch. 315

false acceptance/rejection an incorrect decision, generally based on a misleading score on a test. 120

farsightedness the inability to focus the eye on near objects. 386

feedback generally, knowledge of results. It is also a communication term, sometimes applied to releasing a report, as in disclosing test results to an employment applicant. Another meaning is the sometimes subtle response of a listener to a speaker. This term originated in audio electronics, where it referred to the amplified sound from a speaker being "fed back" into the microphone. 134, 173

femininity a term used by Hofstede to describe countries or cultures where high value is placed on good relationships with and concern for other people. The opposite is masculinity. 274

field study a general term for research (experimental or quasi-experimental) that takes place out in the "field," that is, the factory, school, or hospital rather than in a laboratory. 39

field verification a step commonly associated with trying out documentation. Representative users are asked to follow the documentation. Their responses are either observed in a lab or applied in the field and communicated back to the documentation staff. 425

figure/ground respectively, the object or shape that stands out against the background or ground. 353

flat organizational structure one with minimal hierarchical or status/power levels. 268

flexitour a flextime schedule that is arranged by an employee in advance. It allows employees to vary their hours of work (usually within limits), as long as the total work hours per week remain the same. 331

flextime allowing employees to be flexible in their work schedule. 331

focus group a small group assembled by a leader to discuss a given issue in depth, generally to disclose consumer perceptions, convictions, and attitudes. 443

fog index a measure of readability; the higher the index, the lower the readability. 429

font a complete assortment of a given size and style of type, including capitals, small capitals, and lowercase, together with numerals, punctuation marks, ligatures, and the commonly used symbols and accents. 415

foot-candle a measure of illuminance. It is the light falling on one square foot from a candle a foot away. 389

footlambert a measure of luminance. It is the light reflected from a perfectly reflecting one square foot surface that is one foot away from a candle. 389

forced distribution a rating technique in which the rater must place a given proportion of individuals in each predetermined category, such as *above average* and *below average*. 217

formal communication messages that go through official channels that the organization has established for this purpose. 250

fovea a small pit at the center of the retina, in which are located densely packed cones. Its visual angle of two to five degrees is responsible for all high acuity vision. 393

frequency analysis refers to the remarkable ability of the auditory sense to distinguish one sound from other simultaneous ones, or from a background of noise. For example, if someone mentions your name at a noisy party, you'd pick it out quite distinctly. 367

frequency of repair records the record obtained from users, showing how often various brands of a product caused trouble. 272

Freud, Sigmund (1856–1919) a misunderstanding and misunderstood Austrian who turned from neurology to clinical work. His writings on personality, motivation, psychotherapy, and development have been extremely influential. See psychoanalysis. 19

functional turnover see turnover. 199

G stands for the force of gravity. On Earth, stationary objects (close to sea level) weigh 1 G. In a suddenly ascending elevator, you would experience *positive G* or higher than normal weight; when an elevator starts to drop, your environment would be *negative G*. 383

generalizable the ability to apply findings from one context to another. In research it refers to how much the findings on the sample apply to the population, and/or to how much the population studied represents the larger population. 55

generativeness (in psychometrics) the computer generation or invention of new test items appropriate to the testee's performance. 123

generic general, or without a brand name. 454

Gilbreth, Frank (1868–1924) applied the work of F. W. Taylor to his bricklaying work, and reduced the number of motions to lay a brick from 18 to 4½. As an engineer, Gilbreth developed time-and-motion studies, originating the use of photography to analyze work activities. Lillian (1878–1972) was an engineer and psychologist who, from 1904, was his partner in marriage, work, and research. As his widow, she worked for 50 years as an industrial engineer and professor, and managed their consulting firm, while raising their 12 children. 15

glare unwanted reflection, generally from a smooth surface. Discomfort glare is annoying; disability glare decreases performance. 390

gliding time allows flextime employees to choose their work hours without having to ask permission or give advance notice. 331

goal setting theory of motivation holds that performance is improved by setting goals. 180

grapevine communication channels that are informal but typically active, rapid, and unpredictable. 251

graphic rating scale a continuum along which a rating is made. 213

grayout the loss of peripheral vision due to positive G forces. 383

ground background (on which there may be a figure). 353

group test a test designed to be administered to a group rather than to an individual. 109

halo effect a form of rating bias in which one outstanding feature or generalization of (usually) a person influences and dominates the rating. 219

hard copy material printed on paper, as opposed to shown on a screen. 417

hard sell an advertisement that emphatically lauds the product's features. 453

Hawthorne effect originally referred to the improvement of employee productivity caused by the employees *assuming* that the work environment was being upgraded out of concern for their well-being. It is currently seen as a form of demand characteristics. See following entry. 19

Hawthorne studies took place in the early 1900s at Hawthorne, Illinois, a suburb of Chicago. The conclusions on the impact of employee expectations became a foundation of industrial, organizational, and social psychology. See previous entry. 19

head up display (HUD) a display of primary information in the windshield of a moving vehicle, allowing you to read the display while seeing where you're going. 363

hertz cycles per second (after German physicist Heinrich Hertz). 383

heterogeneous quite varied. Contrast with homogeneous. 55

heuristic (adjective) a fact or theory that is not so important per se, but what it *leads* to is crucial. As a noun, a heuristic is a strategy. 170

hierarchy of needs Maslow's explanation of what motivates a person. The theory states that needs are ordered in importance, such that a less important need will not influence behavior until all the more basic ones are satisfied. 167

high resolution in vision, fine detail. 393

homework work performed by an employee at home, for a firm, typically using telecommunications and/or a computer. 332

homonym (from *homos,* same, and *onyma,* name) a word that *sounds* the same as another. 406

horizontal communication messages that are sent among people who belong to the same general status level in an organization. 251

horizontal loading a form of job enrichment in which employees add earlier and later (but still similar) job tasks. For instance, instead of performing the same minute and seemingly meaningless task on an engine assembly line, the employees might start with the earliest stages of assembly, and continue until the unit looks like an engine. In vertical loading, the original job is enlarged by the addition of responsibilities formerly taken by superiors and/or subordinates. 333

hue color. 391

human factors engineering or psychology the science of improving equipment to suit the operator. The term is giving way to ergonomics. 342

humanistic management responds sympathetically to employees' feelings and aspirations. 256

human relations movement an organizational psychology concept that refers to the examination of (a) the needs and goals of individuals in relation to those of the group, and (b) interactions between and among people emphasizing relational styles such as communication, conflict resolution, and leadership in teamwork. 256

hygiene factors (Herzberg) work environment variables (such as company policy and supervision) that can lead to job dissatisfaction. 171

hypothesis a prediction. In a formal experiment, it is the hypothesis that is tested. 55

hypoxia a condition that results from insufficient oxygen to breathe. 380

Hz an abbreviation for hertz. 383

illuminance the amount of light falling on a surface per unit of area. 389

in-basket test a situational test that requires testees to demonstrate their handling of material they might find on their desk, awaiting their attention, if hired. 114

incident process a training procedure in which the group uses a problem-solving approach to a specific incident. 153

independent variable in an experiment that tests whether variable *a* causes or changes variable *b,* the independent variable is the *a* variable (which is systematically manipulated by the experimenter, often in the form of some treatment). 49

individual differences a general term that refers to defining personnel variables and measuring them, usually through selecting or devising appropriate tests. For instance, hearing is studied by cognitive, physiological, learning theory, and human factors psychologists to disclose auditory processes and thresholds, but the *individual differences* approach might be to measure hearing acuity in group of pilots or sonar operators. 76

individualism Hofstede's description of a culture in which people just look after themselves and their families, with little concern about the welfare of others. Contrast with collectivism. 273

individual tests those designed to be administered to one testee at a time. See group tests. 109

industrial history a country's development of communications and transport infrastructure, and its establishment of heavy industries, a skilled workforce and management accustomed to modern productivity. 164

industrial psychology a branch of applied psychology dealing with the connection between psychological principles and work, organizations, ergonomics, the military, and consumer behavior.

industrial revolution a sudden (in historical time), major change in the way that work takes place. Classically, it refers to the change especially in England in the 1700s from cottage production to factory production. 5

industrial sociology similar to industrial psychology but emphasizes sociology constructs and deals with large groups such as countries. 272

inferred theoretical construct a construct based on an inference that is related to a theory. All constructs of all disciplines are inferred theoretical ones. 58

informal communication the exchange of information through channels other than those established for formal communication. 251

informed consent an ethical requirement of research that the researcher makes sure that a participant understands all relevant aspects of the study and *agrees* to participate. 66

infradian [in-FRAY-dee-an] (from *infra* or below, and *diem* or day) occurring less frequently than once a day. The menstrual cycle is a typical *infradian rhythm.* 327

inhibition in learning theory, the interference of learning one task caused by the learning of another. 136

initiating structure (Halpin & Winer) leader behaviors that focus on accomplishing the task at hand. 242

instrumental conditioning a synonym for operant conditioning. 182

integrative bargaining negotiation aimed at maximizing the benefits for both sides. See distributive bargaining. 294

intelligence a generally misunderstood but commonly used descriptor of basic abilities for school work, and supposedly also for problem solving and life success in general. Operationally, it is one's score on an intelligence test. 111

intelligence test a battery of subtests designed to assess intelligence (see above). 111

interest what one *enjoys* doing, watching, or learning about. 111

intergroup problem solving a special meeting (or regular ones), often under the guidance of a change agent, designed to resolve conflicts between factions within the same organization. 278

internal control self-determination or influence by internal variables, as opposed to external motivating factors. 113

internal equity the extent to which remuneration is proportional to qualifications and responsibilities within the organization. See equity. 90

Internet a worldwide master network of various smaller computer networks. It is a medium for personal and business communication and a reference source on an immense variety of topics. 27

interscorer reliability the differences/similarities in the judgments made by more than one rater. 102

interview a meeting, usually of a personnel officer or trained staff member and a respondent who is questioned about relevant issues, most often to determine suitability for hiring. 39

intravenor a third party in a dispute, one who has the organizational power to impose a settlement but who also has the freedom not to, and who has a personal stake in the dispute. 291

intrinsic motivation the force that presumably drives activity that is conducted for its own sake. 186

ISO 9000 [eye-so] a worldwide set of standards for systems and processes prescribed in 1987 by the International Organization for Standardization, which registers firms that meet the standards. 156

job analysis an elaborate procedure designed to make an inventory of every individual element that makes up a given job. 84

job characteristics a model or theory by Hackman and Oldham specifying what a job needs (variety, identity, significance, autonomy, and feedback) for high worker motivation and satisfaction. 172

job criterion the measure of job performance. 87

job description an outline of what a job is and what it basically entails. 83

Job Descriptive Index (JDI) a measure of job satisfaction that considers the work, supervision, remuneration, promotion, and coworkers. 193

job design restructures the task to humanize it. 330

job diagnostic survey an employee questionnaire by Hackman and Oldham, which measures the relative importance of five *core dimensions*. 173

job enlargement a means of making a routine, repetitive job more rewarding by increasing its scope. Typically, an assembly line is converted into assembly bays in which teams assemble entire units, sharing or interchanging the job components. 333

job enrichment the addition of tasks involving responsibility, planning, controlling, and organizing. 333

job entitlement the conviction that an employee is, usually by virtue of precedent, *due* something. 195

job evaluation a procedure for determining the relative worth of a given job in terms of the remuneration it should command. 88

job inventory a list of the major components or tasks of a job. 131

job requirements the basic skills or attributes needed to perform the work in question. 81

job rotation the systematic exchanging of duties to provide employees with more experience or variety. 148

job satisfaction the level of contentment experienced by employees at work. 191

job shadowing a learning or experiential program in which the novice follows a mentor around, closely observing the work. 332

job title the common or official name associated with a specific job. 81

joining up process a workshop or similar meeting designed to integrate a new member of an organization. 280

just-in-time (JIT) a system for the delivery of components to an assembly operation timed so that they go directly from the receiving dock to the assembly line as needed, bypassing storage. 272

justified type type that is aligned on both sides so that margins on either side are straight. The left margin is invariably straight, so the term generally indicates a straight *right* margin. 415

kaizen [rhymes with eye-zen] a Japanese noun for improvement or reform. The verb *kaizen suru* means to improve. 11

Keplerian trajectory [kep-LAIR-ee-an] (after astronomer Johannes Kepler), the increasingly downward-curving path an aircraft follows to maintain a state of zero G. 385

KR20 (the 20th statistical formula of G. Kuder and M. Richardson, published in 1937) a reliability coefficient for test items where the responses are dichotomous (either pass or fail). It finds the internal consistency or homogeneity of the question set by intercorrelating the results. It can range from zero to one. A coefficient of 0.7 is generally considered acceptable; low coefficients indicate that the test is measuring different attributes or that a scoring error was made. 102

landscaped office an office design that is as open and natural as possible. 335

language test assumes the testee to be fluent in the language used to receive and/or answer the questions, as opposed to the nonlanguage test which is relatively free of language demands. 108

large group those who belong to an organization that is too large for members to all know each other as individuals. 239

latency the interval between stimulus and response. 414

law a statute, but in academics it's a statement or principle that is accepted to be true. 58

Leader Behavior Description Questionnaire presents to employees pairs of descriptions of managerial behavior; the employees choose the more accurate of each pair with respect to their supervisors. 243

leaderless group discussion test requires a small group to solve a problem, while individual performances are evaluated. 114

Leadership Opinion Questionnaire (E. A. Fleishman) surveys managers on their choices from pairs of alternative decisions. 243

learning curve a graph of performance over repeated attempts. It is generally somewhat S-shaped. 78

learning set a proclivity for learning a type of cognitive material, problem solution, or motor task. 136

learning theory a cornerstone of classical psychology that codifies the relationship between stimulus and response. 134

Least Preferred Co-worker Scale (LPC) in contingency theory, a scale that can be used to identify managerial or leadership style. 243

legibility the physical clarity and layout of text. 415

leniency in assessments, the tendency to rate generally too high. 218

light adaption the adjustment of the eyes to brighter light. 395

light intensity refers to what is generally thought of as brightness, but in photometry it's measured by the luminous flux from the light source, or the luminance of the light from a surface. 389

Likert, Rensis (1903–1981) taught at New York University, worked on supervision and management problems for industry and government, and founded what became the Institute for Social Research at the University of Michigan. Among his contributions were the Likert Scale, and a theory of participative management as described in his 1960s books *New Patterns of Management*, and *The Human Organization*.

linear format a sequence that follows a single path. 154

literature the published reports of a discipline's original research (primary literature), or reports of other people's research (secondary). 24

locus of control the relative susceptibility of a person to *external* as opposed to *internal* motivators. See self-monitoring. 113

long-term memory the memory system that stores memories permanently, at least relative to the short-term memory. 135

longitudinal study one which continues over a substantial period of time. 46

loop-backs refer to the provision within conflict negotiation for an examination of the outcomes of similar cases, so that both sides start with realistic expectations of equitable outcomes. 293

lower ceiling (or floor) the lowest score possible on a test. 99

luminance the intensity or brightness of light reflected or emitted from a surface. 389

luminaire light source, that is, bulb and associated housing. 391

luminance ratio the brightness of the work divided by the brightness of the surround. 391

lux a measure of illuminance. One lux is the light that falls on one square meter from a one-lumen source a meter away. 389

management by objectives (MBO) a managerial style based upon specifying goals (usually established with the agreement of all concerned). Employees provide regular feedback on their attainment of these goals. 181

masculinity Hofstede's term to describe a society in which there is a sharp division between men's and women's roles, and in which invariably men's roles involve profit making, and women's are service oriented. 274

matching (in methodology) the assigning of subjects to groups *matched* on specific variables. For instance, if age and sex were the matching variables, for every young, middle-aged, and older male and female assigned to one treatment group, a participant as equivalent as possible would be assigned to the other group(s). 50

mediation a dispute resolution procedure in which a mediator tries to improve communication between the disputants. 291

Mensa a club-like organization that requires applicants to show that their intelligence is in the upper 2 percent of the population. 107

meta-analysis the overall reanalysis of a number of individual studies to reach a more general conclusion. 60

method the research *procedure.* 36

methodology the *strategy* of research. 36

metrology the science of measurement. 376

minimum distinguishable acuity see acuity 390

Minnesota Multiphasic Personality Inventory (MMPI), revised in 1987 as the MMPI-2, a set of over 500 true-false questions, the answer pattern to which was originally analyzed to place the respondent into psychiatric categories, and which is now commonly used for psychological categorization. 116

model a simplified, smaller version of something. 56

motivation a construct in social science that explains why an individual evidently *wants* to perform a given activity. 165

motivators in Herzberg's two-factor theory, opportunities for professional growth and personal satisfaction. 170

Münsterberg, Hugo (1863–1916), earned a Ph.D. in physiology (under Wundt) and an M.D. degree. Later he chaired Harvard's psychology (then called philosophy) department, became president of the APA, and became known as a personnel and forensic psychologist. His early books on applied psychology were *On the Witness Stand,*

Psychology and the Teacher, and *Psychotherapy* (all published in 1909). His most influential book was his 1913 *Psychology and Industrial Efficiency.* 14

N is an abbreviation of *number,* usually of the sample (research subjects). 50

nAch or NACH stands for need for achievement, that is, ambition. 174

naturalistic observation research conducted so that the subjects are not influenced by being observed. It is sometimes termed field study. 39

natural work module an individual is assigned to produce a complete unit. 333

natural work team a group assigned to complete a meaningful end product; schedule and divide the work according to their preference. 333

need for achievement (nAch) Murray's term for ambition. 174

need for power (D. C. McClelland) the need for influence or domination over others. 176

needs hierarchy a listing (originally by Maslow) of needs, in order of dominance. 168

need theories of work motivation based on Maslow's needs hierarchy, which proposes that underlying the motivation to work is a set of basic needs that can be fulfilled only in order, from most basic to most complex. 174

need to avoid failure a possible motivator of behavior in people who seem achievement oriented. 175

negative affectivity (Watson & Clark) a personality type (characterized by introspection, general dissatisfaction, and concern with personal shortcomings and failures) that invites burnout in response to occupational stressors. 322

negative contrast the North American term for a video display unit with dark characters on a light background. 419

negative reinforcement a stimulus whose removal is reinforcing, leading to a greater probability that the response bringing about this removal will recur. 183

negative transfer occurs when an employee's training impedes the job. It may be proactive or retroactive inhibition. 136

nepotism originally the improper employment of a nephew, hence using favoritism in the employment of relatives and, by extension, friends. 332

noise unwanted sound. The term is also used metaphorically to mean unwanted or irrelevant inclusions in any signal. 382

nonempirical without data, as an essay or opinion. 37

nonlanguage test a test that requires no or minimal use of words by the testee. 108

nonresponder bias (in a questionnaire) refers to the difference in responses between those who returned the questionnaire and those who did not. 41

norm a general term for normal or average. In psychometrics, norms refer to standardization data. In social psychology, it refers to conventional behavior. 99

normal distribution one whose values are represented by a bell-shaped, symmetrical curve, and in which two standard deviations above and below the mean contain about 95 percent of the scores. 77

normative model of decision making (Vroom & Yetton) examines whether it is *normal* for decisions to be made by managers or subordinates. 247

objective measurements those which are measured numerically and would remain the same regardless of who made them. 209

objective scoring implies that the score data are derived free of bias. 116

operant conditioning the administration of reinforcement so as to affect behavior. It is also known as instrumental or Skinnerian conditioning or learning. 182

operational definition the definition of a treatment or construct in terms of the operations performed to apply the treatment or measure the construct. 56

opportunity bias unfairness in the evaluation of employees that fails to take into account differences in their opportunity to perform well, for example, some pilots may have better on-time records because they are assigned fair weather routes. 211

organismic variable a characteristic inherent to the organism under study (such as age or weight), as opposed to an environmental or situational variable. 50

organization (in organizational psychology) a general term for a business, corporation, or company, especially the people who make it up. 4

organizational behavior behavior of members of an organization within and in relation to it, and the influence of members upon the organization and vice versa. 238

organizational chart a diagram, traditionally as a box chart, showing the authority structure (and perhaps the communications or reporting channels) within an organization. 268

organizational culture the shared pattern of thought and action within an organization. 302

organizational development (OD) the bringing of change to an institution, often through improving communication and consideration. 277

organizational psychology an outgrowth of social psychology that focuses on behavior within organizations. 236

organizational structure the basic setup of a group. It's typically depicted in an organizational chart, which diagrams the main status hierarchy and span of control, and implies the reporting and communications channels among the various offices or levels. 268

Otis, Arthur S. (1886–1964) a Cleveland psychologist. As a graduate student of Terman in psychometrics, he originated multiple-choice and other objective types of questions, and turned his innovative, unpublished group intelligence test over to the U.S. Army, which had it modified into the Army Alpha test. He published the Otis Self-Administering Test of Mental Ability in 1929. 17

paired comparisons an ordinal scaling procedure in which a judge or rater compares each item or person with each other on some dimension. 217

paper-and-pencil test a test that requires the testee to write down the answers. See performance test. 109

parasympathetic nervous system see autonomic nervous system. 449

participative leadership a democratic form of supervision in which those affected by decisions have a voice in formulating policy. 246

path-goal theory of leadership argues for the importance of subordinates' goals and the paths they take to reach them. 246

pay equity designed to ensure that each employee is paid according to the worth and responsibility of the position, without any influence of bias. Internal equity considers the employees within the firm; external equity considers comparable employees elsewhere. 89

peak time pay extra earnings for working only short, peak hours. 331

Pearson's r see correlation. 37

peer a coworker at a similar level.

peer assessment performance appraisal conducted by one's peers. 222

peer nomination a form of peer assessment in which a group names the most outstanding member. 222

peer ranking a rating procedure in which colleagues rank-order the performance of their workmates. 222

peer rating a system of peer assessment in which peers evaluate each other according to given criteria. 222

performance standards the outcome measures by which the adequacy of work performance is judged. 83

performance test a test in which the testee responds by doing something

other than writing down the answers. See paper-and-pencil test. 109

personal space the area immediately around a person which, if intruded upon, leads to a feeling of discomfort.

personality the relatively stable aspects of your behavioral, emotional, and cognitive patterns. 112

personality inventory a test designed to measure and/or describe personality in a comprehensive way. 113

personality tests any of a large variety of tests designed to measure and/or describe personality. 112

person-job fit matching the worker's abilities, interests, and knowledge with the demands of the task. 323

person-machine engineering see human factors engineering. 344

person-machine system equipment, usually mechanical, that is designed to be operated by a person. 349

personnel the human resource in the context of work. 76

personnel psychology a branch of applied psychology dealing with recruiting, selecting and classifying, training, evaluating, and motivating workers. 13

personnel selection the procedure and practice of selecting the most appropriate job applicant. 80

phase advance the response your internal clock must make if you suddenly move to a time zone where you must set your watch ahead, as in flying from west to east. See phase delay. 328

phase delay the shift of your internal clock backward to accommodate the time change when setting your clocks back in the fall or flying to a westerly time zone. See phase advance. 328

phoneme the smallest or most basic unit of spoken sound. 404

phonetic alphabet a set of words, one for each letter of the English language alphabet. The words are designed to be spoken instead of letters, where the letters alone may not be heard clearly and unambiguously. 407

photoreceptors in vision, neuron-like cells on the back half of the retina that can transmit an electrochemical impulse in response to light. 392

physiological approach research that uses physiological techniques or theory, such as measuring changes in pupil diameter or palm sweating. 64

pictograms pictorial symbols, which are gradually becoming standardized. They were first used on traffic signs, instead of (or in addition to) words, to make recognition easier and faster. The use has spread to multilingual (or illiterate) environments and to warning symbols. The so-called icons familiar to many computer users are actually pictograms. 423

piece rate a pay system based on output or productivity. 15

pioneering advertising attempts to develop primary demand. 454

pipeline effect goods that are somewhere in the distribution system, which masks the ability to detect the immediate effect on sales of an ad campaign or other event. 449

pitch in sound physics, refers to the up-down position of a note, or the frequency of the vibration causing the sound. In vehicle movement it refers to the up-down position or direction of the vehicle. 372

planned negotiation the ongoing sharing of information, problems, and solutions within an organization, so that harmony and productivity are maintained. 278

population the group from which research subjects (the sample) are selected for study. 54

position analysis an analytic comparison of the worker's abilities and the requirements of the work. 61

positive presentation European terminology for negative contrast in a video display terminal, which is the use of dark symbols on a light background. 419

positive reinforcement the administration of a treatment that serves as a reward for the recipient and increases the likelihood of the associated behavior's being repeated. 183

positive transfer occurs when the employee's training facilitates the job. It may be proactive or retroactive facilitation. 136

power distance Hofstede's term for a culture's acceptance of the fact that power in organizations is not distributed equally. In a high power distance culture, authority and rank are emphasized. 273

power test one in which the emphasis is on the solution of difficult items with no time pressure. Contrast with speed test. 108

predictive validity the correlation between one's test score and the *subsequent behavior* which the test predicted. 102

premenstrual syndrome (PMS) the discomfort experienced by some women for a few days prior to their menstrual period. 327

presbyopia *hyperopia* (farsightedness, or inability to focus on near objects) caused by hardening of the lens, associated with aging. 386

prevention workplace designs that make accidents *unlikely,* for example, a railing at the end of a loading dock to deter falling off. 315

primacy effect the tendency to remember the first items in a serially learned list, or the most recent impression when performing a rating. 219

primary demand the promotional objective of creating demand for a new item rather than a specific brand. 454

primary reinforcement the administration of a stimulus that relates to the subject's biological needs. 183

PRNDL (for Park, Reverse, Neutral, Drive, Low) the display on the gear shift control of a car's automatic transmission. 355

proactive facilitation occurs when prior learning benefits subsequent learning. 136

proactive inhibition the interference of subsequent learning by prior experience. 136

product cycle the expected or actual duration of a rapidly changing product like computers, or the period between periodic model changeovers, as with cars. 440

programmed instruction/learning a teaching system in which material is presented (on paper or a screen) in response to the learner's progress. 154

progressive part training learning successively bigger sections of the entire unit to be covered. 135

projection a Freudian construct referring to the attribution of one's own feelings or motives to others. 188

projective tests require the testee to interpret an ambiguous stimulus—upon which, it is assumed, the testee's own personality will show projection. 113

prosody [PRAW-si-dy] the pattern of rhythm, inflection, pitch, tempo, and loudness in sounds, especially speech. 365

protective exclusion the barring of workers or applicants for their own good (and/or for the employer's legal protection), as in women of childbearing years who might be exposed to lead being barred in a battery factory. 316

Protestant work ethic a philosophy holding that hard, steady work is innately desirable. 238

pseudoscience a false or incorrect "science." 30

psychoanalysis a *theory of personality* and a *mode of psychotherapy*, both devised by Freud. 241

psychographics a research technique of consumer psychology that correlates personality or lifestyle variables with target markets. The term was coined in 1974 by Demby. 446

psychometrics the science of testing and measurement. (The synonym *psychometry* has been misappropriated by the pseudoscience of parapsychology.) 98

psychometry a synonym for psychometrics. 17

psychomotor tests examine physical coordination, steadiness, and balance. 111

psychotherapy the application of psychological techniques to alleviate symptoms, modify behavior, or cure disorders.

punishment the administration of an unpleasant stimulus so as to eliminate the associated behavior. 183

pupillometry [pupil-AH-met-ree] the measurement of pupil size in response to psychological stimuli. 449

quality circle a group, typically of several employees and a leader, who meet for the purpose of improving the output. 260

quality of work life organizational changes designed to improve the psychological climate of the workplace, and the meeting of employees' personal needs and expectations. 259

quartiles quarterly divisions of rank-ordered values; the first quartile is the highest quarter. 107

quasi-experimental design an approach to research design where the researcher simulates the logic of real experiments by using statistical methods. 54

questionnaire a survey in which the respondent writes down or checks off the answers. 39

RAD an acronym for a unit of radiation. 381

RADAR (from RAdio Detection And Ranging) a system for displaying visual (but generally out-of-sight) stimuli on a video display screen. 367

radiation the transmission of heat, as between the sun and Earth, or your face and this page. 379

random determined purely by chance. 50

ranking the placing of individuals into their *relative* standing on some dimension, such as from most to least productive. 216

rating scale any scale used for rating people or items. 213

rational validity one that can be quantified. 104

rationalization the concocting of excuses to explain something that would otherwise be unpalatable or hard to accept or explain. It seems to be a basic response of the mind's need to make sense of the world. Originally seen in the Aesop fable about the fox who decided that the grapes it couldn't reach were sour, rationalization became a major construct proposed by Freud as a mechanism used by the ego to protect its image. 298

readability the layout, print style, and spacing of text insofar as it affects the ease and accuracy with which it can be read. 415

reading field the width of a line of text that is seen by foveal vision. 415

realistic job preview an accurate presentation of the job in question, including its liabilities as well as its assets. 82

recency effect the tendency to remember the last items in a serially learned list or, when evaluating job satisfaction, the tendency to be influenced by the most recent occurrences. 194, 219

recognition tests memory by showing the subject items that have been presented before and asking questions related to these items. 442

redout the reddening of the visual field, caused by negative G forces damaging the eye. 384

reductionism the borrowing by one discipline of constructs of another discipline, the constructs of which are observed or measured more directly. An example would be using the (chemistry) construct of valence to describe the (organizational psychology) construct of leadership. 58

reflectance of a surface is the ratio of incoming light (illuminance) to outgoing light (luminance). 390

reinforcement the administration of a reinforcer or a stimulus that acts as a reinforcer; may be partial or continuous, fixed or variable ratio. 134

reinforcer a stimulus that changes the likelihood that an associated behavior will be repeated. 183

reliability in psychometrics, it means *consistency,* usually of each person's scores on a test. 99

rem a unit of radiation, standing for roentgen equivalent, man. 381

repetitive strain injury (RSI) (sometimes termed repetitive motion injury) is pain in or damage to a body part (typically the wrist area) caused by motions that are continuous or repeated, especially if also stressed. 329

replication a repetition, often used of research (although strictly speaking, perfect replication is impossible). 27

resolution acuity of perception. The term stems from vision research on the ability to "resolve" individual points or lines as opposed to seeing only a blur. 419

results oriented description a job description that includes for every major task the results expected, such as standards of performance, timeliness, quality, and quantity. 84

retroactive facilitation improvement in a previously learned task due to subsequent training. 136

retroactive inhibition a decrement in a previously learned task as a result of later experience. 136

review article a journal paper not to present the author's original research but to comment on a group of other papers on a given topic. 60

rods photoreceptors in the retina that perceive motion only, but do so under minimal light intensity. 392

roentgen [RENT-jen] X rays. Named after their German inventor, W. K. Roentgen. The term is also used as a unit of X radiation. 381

role ambiguity uncertainty about expectations associated with a given position. 320

role conflict the problem resulting from trying to fulfill the competing requirements of more than one role, as when a supervisor and subordinate are relatives. 321

role perception one's self-identification with one's position, or how you think of yourself in the context of your work (or other) role. 178

role playing trainees, antagonists, or applicants assigned to act out the role of someone else. 151

role reversal a technique of psychotherapy or counseling in which each antagonist is asked to represent the other in role-playing exercises. 151

Rorschach Test a projective test comprising ten inkblots that the testee interprets, thereby (purportedly) revealing personality "structure." 113

run (noun or verb) the administration of a trial, test, or treatment to research subjects (a verbal convention established when subjects were mainly rats in mazes). 51

S curve generally seen in a graph of learning, where performance is low and improvement gradual at the outset, followed by rapid improvement that levels off, resulting in what looks somewhat like a stretched-out letter S. 78

saccade [sak-ADD] a brief eye flick to change gaze fixation. (French for "jerky motion.") 394

safety audit an examination of a facility for the purpose of uncovering and correcting hazards, not only obvious and immediate ones but also covert and possibly long-term dangers. It is best performed by a trained safety officer; however, anyone can undertake a thorough "walk-through" to fulfill this duty. 315

sample research participants. 54

sampling error results from the selection of a nonrepresentative sample 211

sans serif characters without serifs. 416

scientific management F. W. Taylor's argument in the early 1900s for a machine-like optimization of employees. 256

Scott, Walter Dill (1869–1955) wrote books on advertising starting at the age of 23, another on public speaking in 1907, and the influential *Increasing Human Efficiency in Business* in 1910. This pioneer of personnel and consumer psychology started as a student of Wundt, the founder of psychology, and finished as the founder of industrial psychology. 14

screening test a short, rough test used for preliminary assessment. 109

seasonal affective disorder (SAD) refers to what used to be called the winter blues. Its existence is controversial. 327

secondary reinforcer a stimulus that has become a reinforcer through learning. 183

selection ratio the number of applicants divided by the number accepted. 125

self-actualization the full development and use of one's potential. 167

self-assessment allows those who are traditionally assessed by others to evaluate themselves. 224

self-efficacy one's feelings of being competent. 176

self-monitoring a personality tendency to "look good." 454

semistructured interview an interview in which the basic question wording and order are standardized; from this format the interviewer can probe further. 43

sensitivity group See T-group. 151

sensitivity training a semistructured group experience in which a leader shows participants how to increase their insight in communicating and interpersonal skills and to appreciate their impact on others. 151

sensorimotor test tests of systems or activities involving the coordination of vision (or other senses) and hand (or other body part) activity. 111

serial presented one after the other, in a series. 134

serifs the little projections on the ends of some letters in certain fonts, as on both arms and the base of this letter T. 416

short-term memory the memory system into which most of what we learn is stored only for the brief moments that it is needed. 135

sick building syndrome discomfort or illness due (medically or psychologically) to buildings being sealed off from outside air and/or the release of chemicals from sources like carpets, solvents, or photocopying equipment. 312

signal to noise (S/N) ratio the strength of the signal divided by the strength of the background noise. 367

similar-to-me error occurs when raters incorrectly assume a ratee is similar to themselves. 221

simulators complex, expensive training devices that accurately replicate critical aspects of the real apparatus. 144

single group validity validity only for one type of testee. 121

situational test an assessment procedure in which the tasks closely resemble the work being predicted. 114

Skinnerian (after B. F. Skinner) in learning theory, the influence of reinforcers on behavior. A synonym for instrumental. 182

small group a group small enough for its members to know and identify with each other, such as students living on the same dormitory floor. 239

social Darwinism argues that just as the most fit species survive, so do the most fit social structures. 238

sociometry a procedure for determining and recording relationships within a group or organization. 60

sociopathic personality (or antisocial personality disorder) characterized by persistent antisocial, irresponsible, impulsive behavior, and a lack of shame or remorse. The incidence of almost 5 percent in U.S. males is five times higher than that in females. 113

soft sell (consumer psychology) promotions that use techniques such as humor or an image. See hard sell. 453

sonar (SOnar NAvigation Ranging) operates like radar except that the signals are transmitted auditorily. 367

sone a unit of loudness that differs from the decibel in that it is a ratio scale. 388

source (as a verb) ordering raw materials or components; hence *outsourcing,* obtaining them externally. 270

span of control the extent to which one office or individual supervises others. 268

special effects (cinematographic) techniques such as zooming, subjective camera angle, and slow motion. 142

specificity in psychometrics, the extent to which every item on a test measures a single, nonoverlapping attribute. 102

spectral quality the faint hue imparted to a luminaire. 391

speed test one in which the tasks are easy, and the score is the total number completed within a limited time. Contrast with power test. 108

split half correlation the correlation between scores on any two halves of a test, reflecting its reliability. 101

split run the use of various versions of (usually) a magazine advertisement, each distributed to a different geographical area. 449

spondee [SPON-dee], a two-syllable word in which neither syllable is accented. 407

standard deviation shows the *dispersion* of scores. In a normal distribution, one SD above and below the mean contains about 68 percent of the scores. 101

standard placement controls (and possibly displays) are located similarly in all equivalent machines, to facilitate from one to another. 363

standardized a test or procedure that has established norms, or apparatus that has established parameters. 99

static anthropometry see anthropometry 374

status normal/abnormal the reduction of a *display* to the essentials of showing whether the machinery is operating within or beyond normal limits. For instance, most drivers need to know that their engine is neither too cold nor too hot, and not what the precise temperature is. 360

stereotype the attribution to all members of a group of the simplified, exaggerated, and often derogatory characteristics that supposedly set that group apart. 78

stick shaker a device that vibrates the control column of an aircraft as an emergency signal tactile display. 358

stimulus threshold the minimal detectable intensity of a stimulus. 395

stress an engineering construct that has been adopted loosely to refer to a psychological feeling of discomfort or strain. It is generally associated with occupational or social pressure. 319

stress interview one in which the interviewee is placed under pressure, to see how the stress is coped with. 43

stress test (psychometrics) a test designed partly or wholly to impart and gauge the response to pressure. 115

strictness error in rating is the assigning of lower scores than appropriate. 218

structured interview one in which the presentation does not vary from that determined on the interview form. 43

subjective camera angle the view shown by the camera (usually video or motion picture) as you would see it in real life. 143

subjective measurements those based on personal opinion only. 209

subjective scoring rating by intuition or opinion, rather than by a procedure that would yield results that are reliable within and between raters. 116

substance abuse the excessive or deleterious use of products such as alcohol or illegal drugs. 317

success ratio the number of employees who are deemed successful in their work divided by the total number of employees. 125

supportive leadership a compassionate management style. 246

surround background, as the white paper for these words. 422

survey (noun or verb) a common research procedure consisting of administration of questions to respondents, who may answer an interview orally, or a questionnaire in writing. 39

survey guided feedback a technique of organizational development in which some or all lower-level employees are surveyed for their perception of organizational problems, after which management provides feedback on the problems exposed and corrective action for them. 280

sympathetic nervous system the part of the nervous system responsible for mobilizing body parts and systems for emergency reactions: fight or flight responses. 449

syntax the rules for word order in a sentence. 409

system a group (usually) of components that work or are designed to work together.

system training trains employees whose work interacts together, usually involving person-machine interactions. 348

systemic discrimination an inept term that has acquired a technical meaning. "Systemic" is the adjective of "system"; hence, a systemic drug works throughout the entire organism. Systemic discrimination refers to bias (possibly unintentional) caused by the rules of the system. 92

tactile typewriter a device for transmitting text to visually impaired people by touch (usually vibrating pads on the skin). 358

tactile the sense of touch. 357

task analysis in personnel psychology, a simpler and less detailed form of a job analysis. In ergonomics, it is the perceptual, cognitive, and motor analysis of an operation. 131

task identity takes place when an employee performs enough job components to perceive how the tasks fit into some overall picture. 173

task significance the feeling that the job at hand has some relevance or meaning. 173

Taylor, Frederick Winslow (1856–1915) was an American industrial engineer known as the father of scientific management. As a foreman for Midvale Steel in Philadelphia from 1878 to 1890, he noted inefficient work practices, and instituted a piece-rate pay system, which he used when he redesigned the rail car loading/unloading system for Bethlehem Steel. His books *Shop Management* and especially his 1911 *Principles of Scientific Management* dealt with selection, training, and motivation. They widely influenced (and possibly misled) managers. (Bethlehem archives indicate that his often-cited story about motivating and showing a worker named Schmidt how to load 47 tons of pig iron per day is probably apocryphal, and that his piecework incentive system was not accepted by most employees, probably because it ignored group norms.) 15

tele-robotics allow the operator to control an interactive robot in a natural fashion. If the operator looks to the left, the robot's camera pans left and the operator's headset displays the camera view; if the operator raises the right hand, an arm on the right side of the robot lifts in direct response. The robot is usually distant from the operator, although (at least in futuristic motion pictures) the operator can "wear" the robotic equipment. See virtual reality. 146

tenure length of time employment lasts, or a state of basically guaranteed duration of employment. 87

Terman, Lewis M. (1877–1956) Stanford University psychometrist and educational psychologist who directed the translation and adaption of Binet's intelligence test for American use in 1916 (the Stanford-Binet), originating the concept of Intelligence Quotient or IQ. He wrote or was coauthor of a number of books on intelligence.

test a standardized procedure for prediction or assessment. 98

test battery a series of integrated tests. 107

test cutoff separates those who are accepted from those who are rejected, based on their test performance. 123

test-retest coefficient the correlation between each testee's scores on successive administrations of a test (or between different versions of the same test). It is a measure of reliability. 100

text the printed word. 411

T-group a small group that meets with a leader for sensitivity training. The T stands for Training. 151

thematic apperception test (TAT) measures personality dynamics by interpreting the stories that testees make up to describe and explain the drawings presented. See projective test. 113

theory an explanation, preferably a useful and testable one. 56

Theory X and Theory Y proposed by D. McGregor in 1957 to differentiate two contrasting approaches to management based on assumptions about human nature. Theory X sees employees as passive, lazy, and resistant to change, hence, needing strong, directive management. Theory Y assumes employees to be capable, motivated, and able to assume responsibility if managers allow and encourage it. See Theory Z. 256

Theory Z William Ouchi's recommended combination of Japanese and American approaches to industrial organization. See above. 258

therblig [Gilbreth backwards, almost] the smallest unit of observation or measurement in a time and motion study. 16

third party facilitation the use of a change agent or a trusted member of an organization to resolve conflicts, especially interpersonal ones, between two or more members. 279

threshold the minimal detectable intensity of a stimulus. 395

Tiffin, Joseph (1905–1989) largely responsible for the Purdue tests, and the author of a classic industrial psychology textbook *Industrial Psychology* (New York: Prentice Hall 1942).

timbre the difference perceived in sounds that nonetheless have the same pitch and volume. 366

time and motion study an analysis of the motions (and therefore the time) required to perform each task component, and/or an examination of how to modify the workplace so as to speed up work by detecting and reducing unnecessary motion. It was first described in 1911 publications by Taylor and expanded by Gilbreth. 15

time sampling the determination of when to make observations so that all representative behaviors are observed and the total observation time is minimized. 86

time shift the recording of television programs to watch at a more convenient time. 450

toe shaker vibrates the foot pedal (so far, only of an aircraft) to serve as an emergency tactile display. 358

trade union an association of and for employees. In Western industrialized countries, unions are formally recognized and governed by law, and are trade specific (so that automobile workers at competing companies may be members of the same union). 8

trainer a training device that is a simple, lower-cost substitute for the actual equipment; it is less elaborate than a simulator. A trainer is also a person who trains. 144

training education aimed at specific, limited skills. 130

training case group members analyze and propose solution to a realistic case problem. 153

training conference a group that solves a specific problem through discussion, guided by an instructor. 152

training group See T-group. 151

trait any stable, distinguishing characteristic of one's personality. 166

trait theories of leadership focus on the attributes that characterize leaders. 241

transfer in learning theory, the influence of one learning on another. 135

treatment variable the independent variable in an experiment. 49

turnover the ratio of new to existing employees. *Dysfunctional turnover* is the loss or replacement of employees the organization would prefer to keep; *functional turnover* is the loss of inferior employees and/or their replacement with better or more promising ones. 199

two-factor theory usually synonymous with Herzberg's motivation theory, but it could be applied to any theory which emphasizes a dichotomy. In consumer psychology, it is the two effects of repeated ads: *increased awareness* and *increased boredom*. 171

Type 1 error the rejection of a true null hypothesis, or a *false rejection*. 120

Type 2 error acceptance of a false null hypothesis. 120

ultradian [ul-TRAY-dee-an] (from *ultra* or beyond, and *diem* or day) means occurring more than once daily. Hunger is a typical *ultradian rhythm*. See infradian. 327

uncertainty avoidance Hofstede's term for the extent to which members of a culture accept risk. 274

unstructured interview an interview in which the questioner is free to modify and follow up on the questions. 43

upper ceiling the highest possible score on a test. 99

upward appraisal or assessment subordinates rating their superiors, or perhaps to students evaluating their professors. 225

upward communication the transmission of information in an organization that moves from subordinates to superiors. 251

user support the structures and processes established by a company to assist its customers. An example is a toll-free telephone line to call for solutions to problems. 426

validity the extent to which a test measures what it purports to. See concurrent, content, construct, face, and predictive validities. 102

validity generalization the extent to which a test with high predictive validity for one use will also serve for a similar application. 103

values and lifestyles (VALS) a procedure for identifying consumer targets on the basis of what motivates them to buy. It was devised by A. Mitchell in the 1983 book *The Nine American Lifestyles*. 446

variable any attribute whose value or score changes. 37

verbal test (psychometrics) a test that relies mainly or heavily on the testee's ability to understand the spoken or written instructions and to reply in spoken or written words. 109

vertical loading a form of job enlargement in which higher-level jobs are reclassified to be handled by lower-level employees. Contrast with horizontal loading. 333

vestibule school a training facility, generally a small one within a larger plant. 148

video display terminal (VDT) a computer-driven screen, on which a file is displayed. 417

virtual reality based on a simulator linked to a sophisticated computer and mechanical devices so that the operator's head and sometimes body movements are realistically represented in a visual display in the operator's headset. 146

Viteles, Morris (1898–1988) an American trained in clinical psychology who became an innovative and thoughtful applied psychologist, specializing in employee selection and accident prevention. His 1932 book *Industrial Psychology* structured the areas as they basically remain to the present. His 1953 *Motivation and Morale in Industry* introduced many present concepts of organizational psychology and the role of management in employee motivation. He taught at the University of Pennsylvania for half a century and worked in aviation psychology in World War II.

Weber, Max (1864–1970) a prolific German sociology professor. His main academic contribution was a methodology for social science; for the general public his most notable book was his 1920 *Protestant Ethic and the Spirit of Capitalism* (translated into English in 1930). He originally championed authoritarianism, later extolled the virtues of democracy in organizations.

weighted checklist a checklist on which some items are multiplied by a factor, making them more (or less) important than others. 216

whistle-blowing (a metaphor deriving from sports, in which a referee blows a whistle to stop the game and deal with an infraction of the rules), the reporting of wrongdoing, generally by an employee of a company to an enforcement agency or the public. 300

wind chill a measurement of the effects of wind velocity on temperatures. 379

wind chill index an index on which different wind velocities and temperatures could be compared. 379

withdrawal behavior apathy toward the task, or the pulling away from social relationships. 199

within-subjects design an experimental design in which each subject receives every treatment, and thus serves as its own control, in contrast to a between-subjects design. 49

work (noun) a term that generally refers to job tasks, employment, or occupation. As a verb it generally means to toil at some task, the toil usually but not necessarily being physical. 12

workforce a general term referring to employees. 24

workspace the physical area within which the worker or operator performs most or all of the assigned tasks. Examples of workspaces are desks, aircraft cockpits, and assembly-line stations. 335

workspace design the arrangement of the immediate work environment to make it more satisfactory physically and psychologically. 335

workspace envelope the space within which a person can reach and operate. 374

Wundt, Wilhelm [VILL-helm Voont] (1832–1920) a versatile, prolific German who is termed the "father (or founder) of psychology" because he established the first official psychology laboratory in 1873. 14

Yerkes, Robert (1876–1956) a versatile American comparative psychologist who, among many accomplishments, directed the Army Alpha and Army Beta tests, and wrote a massive report on them. 17

Yerkes-Dodson law states that performance is best under intermediate levels of arousal, decreasing as arousal becomes very low or high. 58

zap refers to television operation, generally with a remote control unit. Zapping is cancelling the audio of advertisements. 450

zip to change television channels. 450

zoom (noun or verb) a continuous change of a camera lens so as to make the viewer appear to move toward or away from the object photographed. 142

References

Abbott, W.L. (1977). College credits: Trend in apprenticeships. *Worklife, 7,* 27–30.

Abdel-Halim, A. (1983). Effects of tasks on subordinate responses. *Academy of Management Journal, 26,* 477–484.

Action for Children's Television (1977). *Submission to the Federal Trade Commission.* Newton, MA.

Adams, J.A. (1989). *Human factors engineering.* New York: Macmillan.

Adams, J.S. (1965). Inequity in social exchange. In K. Berkowitz (Ed.), *Advances in experimental social psychology* (Vol. 2, pp. 267–299). New York: Academic Press.

Adler, N.J. (1991). *International dimensions of organizational behavior* (2nd ed.). Boston: PWS-Kent.

Alderfer, C.P., & Smith, K.K. (1982). Studying intergroup relations embedded in organizations. *Administrative Science Quarterly, 27,* 35–65.

Anastasi, A. (1979). *Fields of applied psychology* (2nd ed.). New York: McGraw-Hill.

Anastasi, A. (1988). *Psychological testing* (6th ed.). New York: Macmillan.

Antonioni, D. (1994). The effects of feedback accountability on upward appraisal ratings. *Personnel Psychology, 47,* 349–356.

Arvey, R.D., Bouchard, T.J., Segal, N.L., & Abraham, L.M. (1989). Job satisfaction: Environmental and genetic components. *Journal of Applied Psychology, 74,* 187–192.

Atkin, C. (1978). Observations of parent-child interaction in supermarket decision-making. *Journal of Marketing, 42,* 41–45.

Atkinson, J.W., & Feather, N.T. (Eds.). (1966). *A theory of achievement motivation.* New York: John Wiley.

Axelsson, A., & Lindgren, F. (1982). Cited in R. Plotnik & S. Mollenauer, *Introduction to Psychology.* New York: Random House, 1986.

Ballentine, K., Nunns, C.G., & Brown, S. (1992). Development of the goal setting support scale GSSS: Subordinate assessment of supervisory support in the goal-setting process. *South African Journal of Psychology, 22*(4), 208–214.

Bandura, A. (1990). Self-regulation of motivation through goal systems. In R.A. Dienstbier (Ed.), *Nebraska Symposium on Motivation, Vol. 38.* Lincoln: University of Nebraska Press.

Barrett, G.V., Phillips, J.S., & Alexander, R.A. (1981). Concurrent and predictive validity designs. *Journal of Applied Psychology, 66,* 1–6.

Barrick, M.R., & Alexander, R.A. (1987). A review of quality circle efficacy and the existence of positive-findings bias. *Personnel Psychology, 40,* 579–592.

Barton, J. (1994). Choosing to work at night: A moderating influence on individual tolerance to work. *Journal of Applied Psychology, 79,* 449–454.

Barton, J., Costa, G., Smith, L., Spelten, E., Totterdell, P., & Folkard, S. (1993). *The Standard Shiftwork Index: A battery of questionnaires for assessing tolerance to shiftwork.* SAPU Memo, MRC/ESRC

Social and Applied Psychology Unit, The University, Sheffield, England.

Bass, B.M., & Barrett, G.V. (1981). *People, work, and organizations: An introduction to industrial and organizational psychology* (2nd ed.). Boston: Allyn & Bacon.

Bass, B.M., & Ryterband, E.C. (1972). *Organizational psychology.* Boston: Allyn & Bacon.

Bassani, G. (1983). NCR: From the first computer in Italy to the 1980s: Research and development on VDUs connected to EDP systems. In E. Grandjean & E. Vigliani (Eds.), *Ergonomic aspects of visual display terminals.* London: Taylor & Francis.

Bauer, D., & Cavonius, C.R. (1983). Improving the legibility of visual display units through contrast reversal. In E. Grandjean & E. Vigliani (Eds.), *Ergonomic aspects of visual display terminals.* London: Taylor & Francis.

Beatty, R.W., Schneier, C.E., & McEvoy, G.M. (1987). Executive development and management succession. *Research in Personnel and Human Resources Management, 5,* 289–322.

Beehr, T.A. (1990). Stress in the workplace: An overview. In J.W. Jones, B.D. Steffy, & D.W. Bray (Eds.), *Applying psychology in business.* Lexington, MA: Lexington.

Beehr, T.A., & Gilmore, D.C. (1982). Applicant attractiveness as a perceived job relevant variable in selection of management trainees. *Academy of Management Journal, 25,* 607–617.

Bell, J.D., & Kerr, D.L. (1987). Measuring training results: Key to managerial commitment. *Training and Development Journal, 41*(1), 70–73.

Berry, L.M, & Houston, J.P. (1993). *Psychology at work.* Madison, WI: Brown & Benchmark.

Bettman, J.R. (1986). Consumer Psychology. *Annual Review of Psychology, 37,* 257–289.

Biesheuvel, S. (1987). Psychology: Science and politics. Theoretical developments and applications in a plural society. *South African Journal of Psychology, 17,* 1–8.

Binning, J.F., & Barrett, G.V. (1989). Validity of personnel decisions: A conceptual analysis of the inferential and evidential bases. *Journal of Applied Psychology, 74,* 478–494.

Black, J.S., & Mendenhall, M. (1990). Cross-cultural training effectiveness: A review and theoretical framework for future research. *Academy of Management Review,* 113–136.

Blum, M.L., & Naylor, J.C. (1968). *Industrial psychology: Its theoretical and social foundations.* New York: Harper & Row.

Bobko, P., & Colella, A. (1994). Employee reactions to performance standards: A review and research propositions. *Personnel Psychology, 47,* 1–29.

Bongers, P.M., Hulshof, C.T., Dijkstra, L., Boshuizen, H.C., Groenhout, H.J.M., & Valken, E. (1990). Back pain and exposure to whole body vibration in helicopter pilots. *Ergonomics, 33,* 1007–1026.

Bouma, H. (1983). Visual reading progress and the quality of text displays. In E. Grandjean & E. Vigliani (Eds.), *Ergonomic aspects of visual display terminals.* London: Taylor & Francis.

Bowers, D.G. (1973). OD techniques and their results in 23 organizations: The Michigan ICL study. *Journal of Applied Behavioral Science, 9,* 21–43.

Bowers, D.G., & Hauser, D.L. (1977). Work group types and intervention effects in organizational development. *Administrative Science Quarterly, 22,* 76–94.

Bowie, N. (1982). *Business ethics.* Englewood Cliffs, NJ: Prentice Hall.

Brayfield, A.H., & Crockett, W.H. (1985). Employee attitudes and employee performance. *Psychological Bulletin, 52,* 396–424.

Brett, J.M., Goldberg, S.B., & Ury, W.L. (1990). Designing systems for resolving disputes in organizations. *American Psychologist, 45,* 162–170.

Brill, P. (1978). Work satisfaction best predictor of longevity. *American Medical News,* Dec. 1, 16.

Britt, S.H., & Morgan, Jane D. (1946). Military psychologists in World War II. *American Psychologist, 1,* 423–437.

Browne, P.J., & Cotton, C.C. (1973). Who are we? A profile of internal OD practitioners. *OD Practitioner, 5,* 7.

Brush, D.H., Moch, M.K., & Pooyan, A. (1987). Individual demographic differences and job satisfaction. *Journal of Occupational Behavior, 8,* 139–156.

Buch, K., & Spangler, R. (1990). The effects of quality circles on performance and promotions. *Human Relations, 43,* 573, 582.

Buhmann, K. (1983). Ergonomic and medical requirements in VDU workplaces and corresponding rules within the Federal Republic of Germany. In E. Grandjean & E. Vigliani (Eds.), *Ergonomic aspects of visual display terminals.* London: Taylor & Francis.

Burke, M.J. (1993). Computerized psychological testing: Impacts on measuring predictor constructs and future job behavior. In N. Schmitt, W.C. Borman, & Associates (Eds.), *Personnel selection in organizations.* San Francisco: Jossey-Bass.

Bushman, B.J. (1993). What's in a name? The moderating role of public self-consciousness on the relation between brand label and brand preference. *Journal of Applied Psychology, 78,* 857–861.

Caelli, T., & Porter, D. (1980). On difficulties in localizing ambulance sirens. *Human Factors, 22,* 719–724.

Campbell, D.E. (1979). Interior office design and visitor response. *Journal of Applied Psychology, 64,* 648–653.

Cederblom, D., & Lounsbury, J.W. (1980). An investigation of user acceptance of peer evaluation. *Personnel Psychology, 33,* 567–580.

Charland, W.A. (1992, January). Night-shift narcosis. *The Rotarian, 160,* 16–19.

Chen, M.Y.T., & Regan, T.G. (1985). *Work in the changing Canadian society.* Toronto: Butterworths.

Cherrington, D.J., & England, J.L. (1980). The desire for an enriched job as a moderator of the enrichment-satisfaction relationship. *Organizational Behavior and Human Performance, 25,* 139–159.

Christensen, S. (1980). *Unions and the public interest.* Vancouver: The Fraser Institute.

Cleary, D.P. (1981). *Great American brands: The success formulas that made them famous.* New York: Fairchild.

Cleveland, J.N., Murphy, K.R., & Williams, R.E. (1989). Multiple uses of performance appraisal: Prevalence and correlates. *Journal of Applied Psychology, 74,* 130–135.

Cohen, S., Evans, G.W., Krantz, D.S., & Stokols, D. (1988). Physiological, motivational, and cognitive effects of aircraft noise on children. In E.M. Hetherington, & R.D. Parke (Eds.), *Contemporary readings in child psychology* (3rd ed.). New York: McGraw-Hill.

Conlon, D.E., & Carnevale, P.J. (1994). Intravention: Third-party intervention with clout. *Organizational Behavior and Human Decision Processes, 57,* 387–410.

Cooke, W.N., & Blumenstock, M.W. (1979). The determinants of occupational injury severity: The case of Maine sawmills. *Journal of Safety Research, 11*(3), 59–67.

Cooper, W.H. (1981a). Conceptual similarity as a source of illusory halo in job performance. *Journal of Applied Psychology, 66*(3), 302–307.

Cooper, W.H. (1981b). Ubiquitous halo. *Psychological Bulletin, 90*(2) 218–244.

Corbett, J.M. (1994). *Critical cases in organisational behavior.* London: Macmillan.

Cronbach, L.J. (1983). *Essentials of psychological testing.* New York: Harper & Row.

Culbert, S.S., & Posner, M.I. (1960). Human habituation to an acoustical energy distribution spectrum. *Journal of Applied Psychology, 44,* 263–266.

Darke, P.R., & Freedman, J.L. (1993). Deciding whether to seek a bargain: Effects of both amount and percentage off. *Journal of Applied Psychology, 78,* 960–965.

Davis, T.R. (1984). The influence of the physical environment in offices. *Academy of Management Review, 9,* 271–283.

DeBono, K.G., & Packer, M. (1991). The effects of advertising appeal on perceptions of product quality. *Personality* and *Social Psychology Bulletin, 17,* 194–200.

Deci, E.L. (1975). *Intrinsic motivation.* New York: Plenum.

DeRuyter, R. (1994, June 28). Many companies don't put a high value on training. *The Kitchener-Waterloo Record,* p. B5.

Digman, J.M. (1990). Personality structure: Emergence of the five-factor model. *Annual Review of Psychology, 41,* 417–440.

Dobbins, G.H., Pence, E.C., Orban, J.A., & Sgro, J.A. (1983). The effects of sex of the leader and sex of the subordinate on the use of organizational control policy. *Organizational Behavior and Human Performance, 32,* 325–343.

Doran, D. (1983). CRT-keyboard VDU's: Implementing the solutions that already exist. In E. Grandjean & E. Vigliani (Eds.), *Ergonomic aspects of visual display terminals.* London: Taylor & Francis.

Dumaine, B. (1987). The new art of hiring smart. *Fortune, 16(4),* 78–81.

Dyer, G. (1985). *War.* Toronto: Stoddart.

Eden, D. (1990). *Pygmalian in management: Productivity as a self-fulfilling prophecy.* Lexington, MA: Lexington Books.

Eiband, A.M. (1959). *Human tolerance to rapidly applied acceleration.* NASA Memo 5-19-59E.

Erez, M., Earley, P.C., & Hulin, C.L. (1985). The impact of participation on goal acceptance and performance: A two-step model. *Academy of Management Journal, 28,* 50–66.

Estes, W.K. (1990). Electronic publishing: A scorecard and an agenda. *Psychological Science, 1(6),* 360–361.

Evans, F.B. (1959, October). Psychological and objective factors in the prediction of brand choice: Ford versus Chevrolet. *Journal of Business,* 340–369.

Farh, J.L., Dobbins, G.H., & Cheng, B.S. (1991). Cultural relativity in action: A comparison of self-ratings made by Chinese and U.S. workers. *Personnel Psychology, 44,* 129–147.

Farh, J., & Werbel, J.D. (1986). Effects of purpose of the appraisal and expectation of validation on self-appraisal leniency. *Journal of Applied Psychology, 71,* 527–529.

Feather, N.T. (1966). Effects of prior success and failure on expectations of success and subsequent performance. *Journal of Personality and Social Psychology, 3,* 287–298.

Feldman, D.C. (1989). Socialization, resocialization, and training: Reframing the research agenda. In I.L. Goldstein (Ed.), *Training and development in organizations.* San Francisco: Jossey-Bass.

Fidell, L.S. (1970). Empirical verification of sex discrimination in hiring practices in psychology. *American Psychologist, 25,* 1094–1098.

Fiedler, F.E. (1964). A contingency model of leader effectiveness. In L. Berkowitz (Ed.), *Advances in experimental social psychology.* New York: Academic Press.

Fiedler, F.E. (1965). Engineer the job to fit the manager. *Harvard Business Review, 43,* 115–122.

Fiedler, F.E. (1967). *A theory of leadership effectiveness.* New York: McGraw-Hill.

Fiedler, F.E., Chemers, M.M., & Mahar, L. (1976). *Improving leadership effectiveness: The leader match concept.* New York: John Wiley.

Fisher, J.D., Bell, P.A., & Baum, A. (1984). *Environmental psychology.* New York: Holt, Rinehart & Winston.

Fleishman, E.A. (1953). The description of supervisory behavior. *Journal of Applied Psychology, 38,* 1–6.

Fleishman, E.A. (1957). The leadership opinion questionnaire. In R.M. Stogdill & A.E. Coons (Eds.), *Leader behavior: Its description and measurement.* Columbus, OH: Bureau of Business Research, Ohio State University.

Folkard, S., Barton, J., Costa, G., Smith, L., Spelten, E., & Totterdell, P. (1993). The standard shiftwork index. *Ergonomics, 36,* 313–314.

Foltz, R.G. (1985). Communication in contemporary organizations. In C. Ruess & D. Silvis (Eds), *Inside organiza-*

tional communication (2nd ed.) New York: Longman.

Ford, J.K., MacCallum, R.C., & Tait, M. (1986). The application of exploratory factor analysis in applied psychology: A critical review and analysis. Personnel Psychology, 39, 291-314.

Ford, J.K., & Noe, R.A. (1987). Self-assessed training needs: The effects of attitudes toward training, managerial level, and function. Personnel Psychology, 40, 39-53.

Ford, J.K., Kraiger, K., & Schechtman, S.L. (1986). Study of race effects in objective indices and subjective evaluations of performance: A meta-analysis of performance criteria. Psychological Bulletin, 99(3), 330-337.

Ford, J.K., Smith, E.M., Sego, D., & Quinones, M.A. (1993). Impact of task experience and individual factors on training-emphasis ratings. Journal of Applied Psychology, 78, 583-590.

Forsterling, F. (1985). Attributional retraining: A review. Psychological Bulletin, 98, 495-512.

Francis, D. (1991, November 4), Unions: The new rich and privileged. Maclean's, 45, 13.

Freeman, R.B., & Medoff, J.L. (1984). What do unions do? New York: Basic Books.

Frey, A.H. (1961). Human behavior and atmospheric conditions. Psychological Review, 68, 225-228.

Fried, Y., & Ferris, G.R. (1987). The validity of the job characteristics model: A review and meta-analysis. Personnel Psychology, 40, 287-322.

Frizzell, M.L. (1989). The placement of I/O Master's degree graduates. Proceedings of 10th Annual Graduate Conference in Industrial/Organizational Psychology and Organizational Behavior.

Gallupe, R.B., Dennis, A.R., Cooper, W.H., Valacich, J.S., Bastianutti, L.M., & Nunamaker, J.F., Jr. (1992). Electronic brainstorming and group size. Academy of Management Journal, 35, 350-369.

Garfield, E. (1983). The tyranny of the horn—automobile, that is. Current Contents, 28, 5-11.

Geuter, U. (1984). Die Professionaliserung der Deutschen Psychologie im Nationalsozialismus. [The professionalization of German psychology in national socialism.] Frankfurt: Suhrkamp.

Ghiselli, E.E. (1966). The validity of occupational aptitude tests. New York: John Wiley.

Gilgen, A.P. (1982). American psychology since World War II: A profile of the discipline. Westport, CT: Greenwood.

Goldberg, H. (1985). Where are men going? [Review of The changing definition of masculinity: Perspectives in sexuality.] Contemporary Psychology, 30, 309-310.

Goldberg, M.E., & Gorn, G.J. (1978). Some unintended consequences of TV advertising to children. Journal of Consumer Research, 5(1), 22-29.

Goldberg, P.A. (1968). Are women prejudiced against women? Transaction, 5, 28-30.

Goldhaber, G.M. (1979). Organizational communication. Dubuque, Iowa: W.C. Brown.

Goldstein, I. (1991). Training in work organizations. In M.D. Dunnette & L. Hough (Eds.), Handbook of industrial and organizational psychology (2nd ed., Vol. 2, pp. 507-619). Palo Alto, CA: Consulting Psychologists Press.

Goldstein, I.L. (1993). Training in organizations: Needs assessment, development, and evaluation (3rd ed.). Pacific Groves, CA: Brooks Cole.

Goktepe, J.R., & Schneier, C.E. (1989). Role of sex, gender roles, and attraction in predicting emergent leaders. Journal of Applied Psychology, 74, 165-167.

Gordon, D.A. (1966). Experimental isolation of the driver's visual input. Human Factors, 66(2, 8), 129-137.

Goulet, Therese (1986). The visibility and health of the aged in Canadian commercials. Gerontion, 1, 21-25.

Graham, J. (1986). Principled organizational dissent: A theoretical essay. Research in Organizational Behavior, 8, 1-52.

Grandjean, E. (1983). Ergonomics of VDUs. In E. Grandjean & E. Vigliani (Eds.), *Ergonomic aspects of visual display terminals.* London: Taylor & Francis.

Green, S.G., & Mitchell, T.R. (1979). Attributional processes of leaders in leader-member interactions. *Organizational Behavior and Human Performance, 23,* 429–458.

Greenberg, J. (1994). Using socially fair treatment to promote acceptance of a work site smoking ban. *Journal of Applied Psychology, 79,* 288–297.

Griffin, R.W. (1991). Effects of work redesign on employee perceptions, attitudes, and behaviors: A long-term investigation. *Academy of Management Journal, 34,* 425–435.

Guion, R.M., & Cranny, C.J. (1982). A note on concurrent and predictive validity designs: A critical re-analysis. *Journal of Applied Psychology, 67,* 239–244.

Guion, R.M., & Gottier, R.F. (1965). Validity of personality measures in personnel selection. *Personnel Psychology, 18*(2), 135–164.

Gunning, R. (1952). *The technique of clear writing.* New York: McGraw-Hill.

Guzzo, R.A., Jette, R.D., & Katzell, R.A. (1985). The effects of psychologically based intervention programs on worker productivity: A meta-analysis. *Personnel Psychology, 38,* 275–291.

Hackman, J.R., & Oldham, G.R. (1975). Development of the job diagnostic survey. *Journal of Applied Psychology, 60,* 159–170.

Hackman, J.R., & Oldham, G.R. (1976). Motivation through the design of work: Test of a theory. *Organizational Behavior and Human Performance, 16,* 250–279.

Hahn, K. (1991). *Running out of time: The circadian factor in the occupational environment.* Paper presented at the 24th annual conference of the Human Factors Association of Canada, Vancouver, B.C.

Haire, M. (1950). Projective techniques in marketing research. *Journal of Marketing, 14,* 649–565.

Hall, D.T. (1986). *Career development in organizations.* San Francisco: Jossey-Bass.

Halloran, J. (1983). *Applied human relations.* Englewood Cliffs, NJ: Prentice Hall.

Halpin, A.W., & Winer, B.J. (1957). A factorial study of the leader behavior description. In R.M. Stogdill & A.E. Coons (Eds.), *Leader behavior: Its description and measurement.* Columbus, OH: Bureau of Business Research, Ohio State University.

Hansen, C.P. (1989). A causal model of the relationship among accidents, biodata, personality, and cognitive factors. *Journal of Applied Psychology, 74,* 81–90.

Harpaz, I. (1990). The importance of work goals: An international perspective. *Journal of International Business Studies, 21,* 75–93.

Harper, S.C. (1992). The challenges facing CEOs: Past, present and future. *Academy of Management Executive, 6*(3), 7–25.

Hart, P. (1994). Teacher quality of work life: Integrating work experiences, psychological distress and morale. *Journal of Occupational and Organizational Psychology, 67,* 109–132.

Hartley, J.H., Burnhill, P., & Davis, L. (1978). The effects of line length and paragraph denotation on the retrieval of information from prose text. *Visible Language, 12,* 183–194.

Harvey, R. (1991). Job analysis. In M.D. Dunnette & L. Hough (Eds.), *Handbook of industrial and organizational psychology* (2nd ed., Vol. 2, pp. 71–163). Palo Alto, CA: Consulting Psychologists Press.

Haynes, M. (1986). Partnerships in management: Employee involvement gets results. *Personnel Journal, 46–54.*

Hellriegel, D., Slocum, J.W., & Woodman, R.W. (1986). *Organizational behavior.* St. Paul, MN: West.

Hemphill, J.K., & Coons, A.E. (1957). Development of the Leader Behavior Description Questionnaire. In R.M. Stogdill & A.E. Coons (Eds.), *Leader behavior: Its description and measurement.* Columbus, OH: Bureau of Business Research, Ohio State University.

Henderson, G. (1994). *Cultural diversity in the workplace.* Westport, CT: Praeger.

Herzberg, F. (1966). *Work and the nature of man.* Cleveland: World.

Herzberg, F. (1974). Motivator-hygiene profiles: Pinpointing what ails the organization. *Organizational Dynamics, 3,* 18–29.

Herzberg, F., Mausner, B., & Snyderman, B. (1959). *The motivation to work.* New York: John Wiley.

Hirschman, A.O. (1970). *Exit, voice, and loyalty: Responses to decline in firms, organizations, and states.* Cambridge, MA: Harvard University Press.

Hoffman, C.C., Nathan, B.R., & Holden, L.M. (1991). A comparison of validation criteria: Objective versus subjective performance measures and self- versus supervisor ratings. *Personnel Psychology, 44,* 601–619.

Hofstede, G. (1980). *Culture's consequences: International differences in work-related values.* Beverly Hills, CA: Sage Publications.

Hofstede, G. (1983). The cultural relativity of organizational practices and theories. *Journal of International Business Studies,* 75–89.

House, R.J. (1977). A 1976 theory of charismatic leadership. In J.G. Hunt & L.L. Larson (Eds.), *Leadership: The cutting edge.* Carbondale, IL: Southern Illinois University Press.

House, R.J., & Mitchell, T. (1974). Path-goal theory of leadership. *Journal of Contemporary Business, 3,* 81–97.

House, R.J., Spangler, W.D., & Woycke, J. (1991). Personality and charisma in the U.S. Presidency: A psychological theory of leader effectiveness. *Administrative Science Quarterly, 36,* 364–396.

Howard, A. (1990). The multiple facets of industrial-organizational psychology: Membership survey results. Arlington Heights, IL: Society for Industrial and Organizational Psychology.

Howell, W.C., & Dipboye, R.L. (1982). *Essentials of industrial and organizational psychology.* Homewood, IL: Dorsey.

Hunter, J.E., Schmidt, F.L., & Jackson, G.B. (1982). *Meta-analysis: Culminating research findings across studies.* Beverly Hills, CA: Sage Publications.

Iaffaldana, M.T., & Muchinsky, P.M. (1985). Job satisfaction and job performance: A meta-analysis. *Psychological Bulletin, 97,* 251–273.

Inglehart, R., & Hildebrandt, K. (1990). Cultural change and changing worldviews. Paper presented at the annual meeting of the American Psychological Association, Boston.

Irving, P.G. (1993). On the use of personality measures in personnel selection. *Canadian Psychology, 34:2,* 208–214.

Jackofsky, E.F., Slocum, J.W., & McQuaid, S.J. (1986). Cultural values and the CEO: Alluring companions? *Academy of Management Executive,* 39–49.

Jackson, S.E., Schuler, R.S., & Rivero, J.C. (1989). Organizational characteristics as predictors of personnel practices. *Personnel Psychology, 42,* 727–786.

Jacoby, J. (1976). Consumer psychology: An octennium. *Annual Review of Psychology, 27,* 331–358.

Jaeger, A.M. (1986). Organization development and national culture; Where's the fit? *Academy of Management Review,* 178–190.

Jeanneret, P.R. (1991). Growth trends in I/O psychology. *The Industrial-Organizational Psychologist, 29,* 47–52.

Jewell, L.N. & Siegall, M. (1990). *Contemporary industrial/organizational psychology* (2nd ed.). St. Paul, MN: West.

Judge, T.A., & Watanabe, S. (1994). Individual differences in the nature of the relationship between job and life satisfaction. *Journal of Occupational and Organizational Psychology, 67,* 101–107.

Kahn, K. (1991). *Running out of time: The circadian factor in the occupational environment.* Paper presented at the 24th annual conference of the Human Factors Association of Canada, Vancouver, B.C., Aug. 28, 1991.

Kane, J.S., & Lawler, E.E., III. (1978). Performance appraisal effectiveness: Its assessment and determinants. In B.M. Staw (Ed.), *Research in organizational behavior* (Vol. 1). Greenwich, CT: JAI Press.

Katzell, R.A., & Guzzo, R.O. (1983). Psychological approaches to productivity improvement. *American Psychologist, 38,* 468–472.

King, N. (1970). Clarification and evaluation of the two-factor theory of job satisfaction. *Psychological Bulletin, 74,* 18–31.

King, W.C., & Miles, E.W. (1994). The measurement of equity sensitivity. *Journal of Occupational and Organizational Psychology, 67,* 133–142.

Kipnis, D. & Schmidt, S. (1985, April). The language of persuasion. *Psychology Today, 19*(4), 40–46.

Klein, G.D. (1986). Employee-centered productivity and QWL programs: Findings from an area study. *National Productivity Review,* Autumn 1986, 348–362.

Klein, R. & Armitage, R. (1979). Rhythms in human performance: 1½-hour oscillations in cognitive style. *Science, 204,* 1326–1328.

Klimoski, R.J., & Hayes, N.J. (1980). Leader behavior and subordinate motivation. *Personnel Psychology, 33,* 543–555.

Klinger, D.E. (1979). When the traditional job description is not enough. *Personnel Journal, 58,* 243–248.

Kornblueh, I.H., Piersol, G.M., & Speicher, F.G. (1958). Relief from pollinosis in negatively ionized rooms. *American Journal of Physical Medicine, 37*(1), 18–27.

Kronk, P.C. (1979). Role of women psychologists during the Second World War. *Psychological Reports, 45,* 111–116.

Kulik, C.T., & Ambrose, M.L. (1993). Category-based and feature-based processes in performance appraisal: Integrating visual and computerized sources of performance data. *Journal of Applied Psychology, 78,* 821–830.

Kyllonen, P.C. (1994). Cognitive abilities testing: An agenda for the 1990s. In M.G. Rumsey, C.B. Walker, & James H. Harris (Eds.), *Personnel selection and classification.* Hillsdale, NJ: Erlbaum.

Landy, F.J., & Farr, J.L. (1983). *The measurement of work performance: Methods,* theory, and applications. New York: Academic Press.

Landy, F.L. (1986). Stamp collecting versus science: Validation as hypothesis testing. *American Psychologist, 41,* 1183–1192.

Latham, G.P., & Blades, J.J. (1975). The practical significance of Locke's theory of goal setting. *Journal of Applied Psychology, 60,* 122–124.

Latham, G.P., Skarlicki, D., Irvine, D., & Siegel, J.P. (1993). The increasing importance of performance appraisals to employee effectiveness in organizational settings in North America. In C.L. Cooper & I.T. Robertson (Eds.), *International Review of Industrial and Organizational Psychology.* New York: John Wiley.

Latham, G.P., & Wexley, K.N. (1981). *Increasing productivity through performance appraisal.* Reading, MA: Addison-Wesley.

Läubli, T., Hunting, W., & Grandjean, E. (1983). Visual impairments in VDU operators related to environmental conditions. In E. Grandjean & E. Vigliani (Eds.), *Ergonomic aspects of visual display terminals.* London: Taylor & Francis.

Lawler, E.E., & Porter, L.W. (1967). Antecedent attitudes of effective managerial performance. *Organizational Behavior and Human Performance, 2,* 122–142.

Lawler, E.E., & Suttle, J.L. (1972). A causal correlation test of the need hierarchy concept. *Organizational Behavior and Human Performance, 7,* 265–287.

Lee, M. (1979). *Bookmaking: The illustrated guide to design/production/editing.* Reading, MA: Addison-Wesley.

Levin, I., & Stokes, J.P. (1989). Dispositional approach to job satisfaction: Role of negative affectivity. *Journal of Applied Psychology, 74,* 752–758.

Levine, E.L. (1983). *Everything you always wanted to know about job analysis.* Tampa, FL: Mariner.

Lewy, A.J., Sacks, R.L., Miller, L.S., & Hoban, T.M. (1987). Antidepressant and circadian phase-shifting effects of light. *Science, 235,* 352–354.

Locke, E.A. (1968). Toward a theory of task motivation and performance. *Or-*

ganizational Behavior and Human Performance, 4, 309–329.

Locke, E.A. (1976). The nature and causes of job satisfaction. In M.D. Dunnett (Ed.), *Handbook of industrial and organizational psychology.* Chicago: Rand McNally.

Locke, E.A., & Latham, G.P. (1984). *Goal setting: A motivational technique that works!* Englewood Cliffs, NJ: Prentice Hall.

Locke, E.A., & Latham, G. (1990). Work motivation and satisfaction: Light at the end of the tunnel. *Psychological Science, 1,* 240–246.

London, M. & Bray, D.W. (1980). Ethical issues in testing and evaluation for personnel decisions. *American Psychologist, 35,* 890–901.

Lord, R.G., DeVader, C.L., & Alliger, G.M. (1986). A meta-analysis of the relation between personality traits and leadership perceptions: An application of validity generalization procedures. *Journal of Applied Psychology, 71,* 402–410.

Lott, B. (1985). The devaluation of women's competence. *Journal of Social Issues, 41,* 43–60.

Louw, J. (1987). World War II, industry, and the professionalization of South African psychology. *South African Journal of Psychology, 17*(2), 33–39.

Maier, N.R.F., & Verser, G.C. (1982). *Psychology in industrial organizations.* Boston: Houghton Mifflin.

Makin, P.J., Cooper, C.L., & Cox, C.J. (1989). *Managing people at work.* Leicester: British Psychological Society.

Martin, S.L., & Klimoski, R.J. (1990). Use of verbal protocols to trace cognitions associated with self- and supervisor evaluations of performance. *Organizational Behavior and Human Decision Processes, 46*(1) 135–154.

Martocchio, J.J., & Dulebohn, J. (1994). Performance feedback effects in training: The role of perceived controllability. *Personnel Psychology, 47,* 357–373.

Maslach, C., & Jackson, S.E. (1981). The measurement of experienced burnout. *Journal of Occupational Behavior, 2,* 99–113.

Maslow, A. (1943). A theory of human motivation. *Psychological Review, 50,* 370–396.

Maslow, A. (1954). *Motivation and personality.* New York: Harper & Row.

Maurer, T.J., Palmer, J.K., & Ashe, D.K. (1993). Diaries, checklists, evaluations, and contrast effects in measurement of behavior. *Journal of Applied Psychology, 78,* 226–231.

McClelland, D.C. (1961). *The achieving society.* Princeton, N.J.: Van Nostrand.

McClelland, D.C. (1975). *Power: The inner experience.* New York: Irvington.

McCormick, E.J. (1970). *Human factors engineering.* New York: McGraw-Hill.

McCormick, E.J. (1979). *Job analysis: Methods and applications.* New York: AMACOM.

McCormick, E.J., & Ilgen, D. (1985). *Industrial and organizational psychology.* Englewood Cliffs, NJ: Prentice Hall.

McCormick, E.J, Jeanneret, P.R., & Mecham, R.C. (1972). A study of job characteristics and job dimensions as based on the Position Analysis Questionnaire (PAQ). *Journal of Applied Psychology, 56,* 347–368.

McElroy, J.C., Morrow, P.C., & Ackerman, R.J. (1983). Personality and interior office design: Exploring the accuracy of visitor attributions. *Journal of Applied Psychology, 68,* 541–544.

McElroy, J.C., Morrow, P.C., & Wall, L.C. (1983). Generalizing impact of object language to other audiences: Peer response for office design. *Psychological Reports 53*(1), 315–322.

McFarland, R.A. (1946). *Human factors in air transport design.* New York: McGraw-Hill.

McGregor, D. (1957). An uneasy look at performance appraisal. *Harvard Business Review, 35,* 89–94.

McGregor, D. (1960). *The human side of enterprise.* New York: McGraw-Hill.

McKinstry, G. (1988). Some typesetting conventions. *TUGboat: The Communications of the TeX Users Group, 9,* 236–238.

McLean, R. (1980). *The Thames and Hudson manual of typography.* London: Thames & Hudson.

McQuaig, J.H. (1973). *How to motivate men.* New York: Fall.

Meglino, B.M., DeNisi, A.S., Youngblood, S.A., & Williams, K.J. (1988). Effects of realistic job previews: A comparison using an enhancement and a reduction preview. *Journal of Applied Psychology, 73,* 259–266.

Messick, S. (1980). Test validity and ethics of assessment. *American Psychologist, 35,* 1012–1027.

Meyer, H.H. (1980). Self-appraisal of job performance. *Personnel Psychology, 33,* 291–296.

Miller, D., Kets de Vries, M.F.R., & Toulouse, J-M. (1982). Top executive locus of control and its relationship to strategy-making, structure, and environment. *Academy of Management Journal, 25,* 237–253.

Miller, G.A., Heise, G.A., & Lichten, W. (1951). The intelligibility of speech as a function of the context of the text materials. *Journal of Experimental Psychology, 41,* 329–335.

Miller, K.I., & Monge, P.R. (1986). Participation, satisfaction, and productivity: A meta-analytic review. *Academy of Management Journal, 29,* 727–753.

Milne, S.H., Blum, T.C., & Roman, P.M. (1994). Factors influencing employees' propensity to use an employee assistance program. *Personnel Psychology, 47,* 123–145.

Miner, J.B. (1992). *Industrial-organizational psychology.* New York: McGraw-Hill.

Mitchell, T.R. (1974). Expectancy models of job satisfaction, occupational preference and effort: A theoretical, methodological and empirical appraisal. *Psychological Bulletin, 81,* 1053–1077.

Mitchell, T.R. (1979). Organizational behavior. *Annual Review of Psychology.* Palo Alto, CA: Annual Reviews, *30,* 243–282.

Mobley, W.H. (1982). *Employee turnover: Causes, consequences and control.* Reading, MA: Addison-Wesley.

Moon, P. (1987). Psychological testing—cost and ethics. *The Human Resource, 3,* 16–17, 22.

Moores, J. (1990). A meta-analytic review of the effects of compressed work schedules. *Applied Human Resources Management Research, 1*(1), 12–18.

Morrow, P.C., & McElroy, J.C. (1981). Interior office design and visitor response: A constructive replication. *Journal of Applied Psychology, 66,* 646–650.

Mossholder, K.W. (1980). Effects of externally mediated goal setting on intrinsic motivation: A laboratory experiment. *Journal of Applied Psychology, 65,* 322–333.

Mottaz, C. (1986). Gender differences in work satisfaction, work-related rewards and values, and the determinants of work satisfaction. *Human Relations, 39,* 283–384.

Mowday, R.T. (1983). Equity theory predictions of behavior in organizations. In R.M. Steers & L.W. Porter (Eds.), *Motivation and work behavior.* New York: McGraw-Hill.

Mowday, R.T., Porter, L.W., & Steers, R.M. (1982). *Employee-organization linkages: The psychology of commitment, absenteeism and turnover.* New York: Academic Press.

Muchinsky, P.M. (1987). *Psychology applied to work.* Chicago: Dorsey.

Murphy, K.R., Thornton, G.C. III, & Reynolds, D.H. (1990). College students' attitudes toward employee drug testing programs. *Personnel Psychology, 43,* 615–631.

Murray, H.A. (1938). *Explorations in personality.* New York: Oxford University Press.

Napoli, D.S. (1981). The architects of adjustment: The history of the psychological profession in the United States (*Series in American Studies*). Port Washington, NY: Kennikat.

National Safety Council (1991). *Accident facts, 1991 edition.* Chicago: National Safety Council.

National Safety Council (1995). *Accident facts, 1995 edition.* Chicago: National Safety Council.

Nicholas, J.M. (1982). The comparative impact of organization development interventions on hard criteria measures. *Academy of Management Review, 7,* 534–537.

Norman, D.A., & Fisher, D. (1982). Why alphabetic keyboards are not easy to use: Keyboard layout doesn't matter much. *Human Factors, 24,* 509–519.

Offerman, L.R., & Gowing, M.K. (1990). Organizations of the future: Changes and challenges. Special issue: Organizational psychology. *American Psychologist, 45*(2) 95–108.

O'Hara, K., Johnson, C.M., & Beehr, T.A. (1985). Organizational behavior management in the private sector: A review of empirical research and recommendations for further investigation. *Academy of Management Review, 10,* 848–864.

Okechuka, C. (1994). The relationship of six managerial characteristics to the assessment of managerial effectiveness in Canada, Hong Kong and People's Republic of China. *Journal of Occupational and Organizational Psychology, 67,* 79–86.

Ones, D., Vishwesvaran, C., & Schmidt, F.L. (1994). Meta-analysis of integrity test validities. *Journal of Applied Psychology, 79,* 20–24.

Oppler, S.H., Campbell, J.P., Pulakos, E.D., & Borman, W.C. (1992). Three approaches to the investigation of subgroup bias in performance measurement: Review, results, and conclusions. *Journal of Applied Psychology, 77,* 201–217.

Orlov, M., II (1993). Definitions and doctrine: Operational language and understanding in combined arms warfare. *Monograph of the School of Advanced Military Studies, United States Army Command and General Staff College.* Fort Leavenworth, KS (AY93–94).

Ornstein, S. (1986). Organizational symbols: A study of their meaning and influence on perceived psychological climate. *Organizational Behavior and Human Decision Processes, 38,* 207–229.

Ouchi, W. (1981). Theory Z: How American business can meet the Japanese challenge. Reading, MA: Addison-Wesley.

Ozer, Elizabeth, & Bandura, A. (1990). Mechanisms governing empowerment effects: A self-efficacy analysis. *Journal of Personality and Social Psychology, 58,* 472–486.

Palmore, E.B. (1969). Physical, mental and social factors in predicting longevity. *Gerontologist, 9*(2), 103–108.

Palmore, E.B. (1971). Longevity predictors—implications for practice. *Postgraduate Medical Journal, 50*(1), 160–164.

Paludi, M.A., & Strayer, L.A. (1985). What's in an author's name? Differential evaluations of performance as a function of author's name. *Sex Roles, 10,* 353–361.

Parsons, C.K., & Liden, R.C. (1984). Interviewer perceptions of applicant qualifications: A multivariate field study of demographic characteristics and nonverbal cues. *Journal of Applied Psychology, 69,* 557–568.

Peters, L.H., Hartke, D.D., & Pohlmann, J.T. (1985). Fiedler's contingency theory of leadership: An application of the meta-analytic procedures of Schmidt and Hunter. *Psychological Bulletin, 97,* 274–285.

Phillips, J.S., & Lord, R.G. (1980). Determinants of intrinsic motivation: Locus of control and competence information as components of Deci's cognitive evaluation theory. *Journal of Applied Psychology, 65,* 211–218.

Pierce, J.L., & Porter, L.W. (1986). Employee responses to formal appraisal feedback. *Journal of Applied Psychology, 71,* 211–218.

Pinder, C. (1991). Valence-instrumentality-expectancy theory. In R. Steers & L. Porter (Eds.), *Motivation and work behavior.* New York: McGraw-Hill.

Plevel, M.J., Lane, F., Nellis, S., & Schuler, R.S. (1994). AT&T global business communication systems linking HR with business strategy. *Organizational Dynamics, Winter, 1994,* 59–72.

Premack, S.L., & Wanous, J.P. (1985). A meta-analysis of realistic job preview experiments. *Journal of Applied Psychology, 70,* 706–719.

Radl, G.W. (1983). Experimental investigations for optimal presentation-mode and colours of symbols on the CRT screen. In E. Grandjean & E. Vigliani (Eds.), *Ergonomic aspects of visual display terminals.* London: Taylor & Francis.

Ragins, B.R., & Sundstrom, E. (1989). Gender and power in organizations: A longitudinal perspective. *Psychological Bulletin, 105,* 51–88.

Rassenfoss, S.E., & Kraut, A.I. (1988). Survey of personnel research departments. *The Industrial/Organizational Psychologist, 25*(4), 31–37.

Rathje, W., & Murphy, C. (1992). *Rubbish!* New York: HarperCollins.

Reichhardt, T. (1994, October/November). The cyberspace program. *Air & Space, Smithsonian, 9,* 74–80.

Reubens, B.G., & Harrison, R. (1980). *Apprenticeship in foreign countries.* Washington, DC: U.S. Government Printing Office.

Reynolds, L. (1982). Display problems for text. In I. Jonassen (Ed.), *The technology of text.* Englewood Cliffs, NJ: Educational Technology.

Rhodes, S.R. (1983). Age-related differences in work attitudes and behavior: A review and conceptual analysis. *Psychological Bulletin, 93,* 328–367.

Rice, C.G., Hyley, J.B., Bartlett, B., Befored, W., & Hallum, G. (1968). Cited in R. Plotnik & S. Mollenauer, *Introduction to Psychology.* New York: Random House, 1986.

Roberts, T.A. (1991). Gender and the influence of evaluations on self-assessments in achievement settings. *Psychological Bulletin, 109,* 297–308.

Robertson, T., & Rossiter, J.R. (1976). *Children's consumer satisfaction.* Center for Research in Media and Children, University of Pennsylvania.

Robbins, T.L., & DeNisi, A. (1994). A closer look at interpersonal affect as a distinct influence on cognitive processing in performance evaluations. *Journal of Applied Psychology, 79,* 341–353.

Roethlisberger, F.J., & Dickson, W.J. (1939). *Management and the worker: An account of a research program conducted by the Western Electric Company, Chicago.* Cambridge: Harvard University Press.

Ruch, F.L. (1941). *Psychology and life* (2nd ed.). Chicago: Scott Foresman.

Saal, F.E., & Knight, P.A. (1988). *Industrial/organizational psychology.* Pacific Grove, CA: Brooks Cole.

Saari, L.M., Johnson, T.R., McLaughlin, S.D., & Zimmerle, D.M. (1988). A survey of management training and education practices in U.S. companies. *Personnel Psychology, 41,* 731–743.

Saavedra, R., & Kwun, S.K. (1993). Peer evaluation in self-managing work groups. *Journal of Applied Psychology, 78,* 450–462.

Sackett, P.R., Tenopyr, M.L., Schmitt, N., Kehoe, J., & Zedeck, S. (1985). Commentary on forty questions about validity generalization and meta-analysis. *Personnel Psychology, 38,* 697–798.

Salthouse, T.A. (1984). The skill of typing. *Scientific American, 250,* 128–135.

Sanders, M.S., & McCormick, E.J. (1993). *Human factors in engineering and design* (7th ed.). New York: McGraw-Hill.

Schein, E.H. (1969). *Process consultation: Its role in organization development.* Reading, MA: Addison-Wesley.

Schein, E.H. (1990). Organizational culture. *American Psychologist, 45*(2), 109–119.

Schmidt, F.L., & Hunter, J.E. (1992.) Development of a causal model of processes determining job performance. *Current Directions in Psychological Science, 1,* 89–92.

Schmidt, F.L., Pearlman, K., Hunter, J.E., & Hirsh, H.R. (1985). Forty questions about validity generalization and meta-analysis. *Personnel Psychology, 38,* 697–798.

Schmitt, N., & Lappin, M. (1980). Race and sex as determinants of the mean and variance of performance ratings. *Journal of Applied Psychology, 65,* 428–435.

Schneider, B., Hanges, P.J., Goldstein, H.W., & Braverman, E.P. (1994). Do customer service perceptions generalize? The case of student and chair ratings of faculty effectiveness. *Journal of Applied Psychology, 79,* 685–690.

Schriesheim, C.A., & DeNisi, A.S. (1981). Task dimensions as moderators of the effects of instrumental leadership theory. *Journal of Applied Psychology, 66,* 589–597.

Schriesheim, C.A., Tepper, B.J., & Tetrault, L.A. (1994). Least preferred co-worker score, situational control, and leadership effectiveness: A meta-analysis of contingency model performance predictions. *Journal of Applied Psychology, 79,* 561–573.

Schudson, M. (1984). *Advertising, the uneasy persuasion: Its dubious impact on American society.* New York: Basic Books.

Schultz, D.P., & Schultz, S.E. (1986). *Psychology and industry today: An introduction to industrial and organizational psychology.* New York: Macmillan.

Schwind, H. (1987). How well do interviews predict future performance? *The Human Resource, 4,* 19–20.

Shamir, B. (1983). A note on tipping and employee perceptions. *Journal of Occupational Psychology, 56,* 255–259.

Shepperd, J.A. (1993). Productivity loss in performance groups: A motivation analysis. *Psychological Bulletin, 113,* 67–81.

Shore, L.M., & Bleicken, L.M. (1991). Effects of supervisor age and subordinate age on rating congruence. *Human Relations, 44*(10), 1093–1105.

Simons, A.K., Radke, A.O., & Oswald, W.C. (1956). A study of truck ride characteristics in military vehicles. *Bostrom Research Laboratories,* Milwaukee, Report 118.

Sims, R.R., Veres, J.C., & Heninger, S.M. (1987). Training appraisers: An orientation program for improving supervisory performance ratings. *Public Personnel Management, 16,* 37–46.

Singh, S.N., Rothschild, M.L., & Churchill, G.A. Jr. (1988). Recognition versus recall as measures of television commercial forgetting. *Journal of Marketing Research, 25,* 72–80.

Siple, P.A., & Passel, C.F. (1945). Measure of dry atmospheric cooling in subfreezing temperatures. *Proceedings of the American Philosophical Society, 89,* 117–199.

Smith, P.C., & Kendall, L.M. (1963). Retranslation of expectations: An approach to the construction of unambiguous anchors for rating scales. *Journal of Applied Psychology, 47,* 149–155.

Smith, P.C., Kendall, L.M., & Hulin, C.L. (1969). *The measurement of satisfaction in work and retirement: A strategy for the study of attitudes.* (Chicago: Rand McNally.

Smither, R.D., (1988). *The psychology of work and human performance.* New York: Harper & Row.

Solomon, C.M. (1990). Careers under glass. *Personnel Journal, 69,* 96–105.

Sorenson, W., Durand, A., & Shaw, P. (1990). Income of SIOP members. *The Industrial-Organizational Psychologist, 28,* 21–31.

Spector, P.E., & Jex, S.M. (1991). Relations of job characteristics from multiple data sources with employee affect, absence, turnover intentions, and health. *Journal of Applied Psychology, 76,* 46–53.

Spencer, D.G., & Steers, R.M. (1981). Performance as a moderator of the job-satisfaction-turnover relationship. *Journal of Applied Psychology, 66,* 511–514.

Spilling, S., Eitrheim, J., & Aaras, A. (1986). Cost-benefit analysis of work environment investment at STK's telephone plant at Kongsvinger. In N. Corlett, J. Wilson, & I. Manenica (Eds.), *The Ergonomics of Working Postures* (pp. 380–397). London: Taylor & Francis.

Stagner, R., & Effal, B. (1982). Internal union dynamics during a strike: A quasi-experimental study. *Journal of Applied Psychology, 67,* 37–44.

Stahl, M.J. (1983). Achievement, power, and managerial motivation: Selecting managerial talent with the job choice exercise. *Personnel Psychology, 36,* 775–789.

Stapp, J., & Fulcher, R. (1983). The employment of APA members: 1982. *American Psychologist, 38,* 1298–1320.

Staw, B. (1986). *The Chronicle of Higher Education, 23*(15), 7.

Staw, B.M., & Ross, J. (1985). Stability in the midst of change: A dispositional approach to job attitudes. *Journal of Applied Psychology, 70,* 469–480.

Steers, R.M. (1975). Effects of need for achievement on the job performance-job attitude relationship. *Journal of Applied Psychology, 60,* 678–682.

Steiner, D.D., & Rain, J.S. (1989). Immediate and delayed primacy and recency effects in performance evaluation. *Journal of Applied Psychology, 74,* 136–142.

Steiner, D.D., Rain, J.S., & Smalley, M.M. (1993). Distributional ratings of performance: Further examination of a new rating format. *Journal of Applied Psychology, 78,* 438–442.

Sternberg, R.J., & Kolligian, J. Jr. (Eds.) (1990). *Competence considered.* New Haven, CT: Yale University Press.

Stogdill, R.M. (1948). Personal factors associated with leadership: A survey of the literature. *Journal of Psychology, 25,* 35–71.

Stogdill, R.M. (1963). *Manual for the Leader Behavior Description Questionnaire-Form XII.* Columbus, Ohio: Bureau of Business Research, OH State University.

Stogdill, R.M. (1974). *Handbook of leadership.* New York: Free Press.

Storey, W.D. (1979). *A guide for career development inquiry.* Madison, WI: American Society for Training and Development.

Storms, P.L., & Spector, P.E. (1987). Relationships of organizational frustration with reported behavioral reactions: The moderating effect of locus of control. *Journal of Occupational Psychology, 60,* 227–234.

Stroh, L.K., Brett, J.M., & Reilly, A.H. (1992). All the right stuff: A comparison of female and male managers' career progression. *Journal of Applied Psychology, 77,* 251–260.

Sumby, W.H., & Pollack, I. (1954). Visual contribution to speech intelligibility in noise. *Journal of the Acoustical Society of America, 26,* 212–215.

Swazey, J.P., Anderson, M.S., & Lewis, K.S. (1993). Ethical problems in academic research. *American Scientist, 81,* 542–553.

Sweetland, R.C., & Keyser, D.J. (1986). *Tests: A comprehensive reference for assessments in psychology, education, and business* (2nd ed.). Kansas City: Test Corporation of America.

Swim, J., Borgida, E., Maruyama, G., & Myers, D.G. (1989). Joan McKay versus John McKay: Do gender stereotypes bias evaluations? *Psychological Bulletin, 105,* 409–429.

Tait, M., Padgett, M.Y., & Baldwin, T.T. (1989). Job and life satisfaction: A re-examination of the strength of the relationship and gender effects as a function of the date of the study. *Journal of Applied Psychology, 74,* 502–507.

Tannenbaum, S.I., Mathieu, J.E., Salas, E., & Cannon-Bowers, J.A. (1991). Meeting trainees' expectations: The influence of training fulfilment on the development of commitment, self-efficacy, and motivation. *Journal of Applied Psychology, 76,* 759–769.

Tannenbaum, S.I., & Yukl, G. (1992). Training and development in work organizations. *Annual Review of Psychology, 43,* 399–441.

Taylor, F. (1947). *Scientific management.* New York: Harper.

Taylor, J., & Bowers, D. (1972). *The survey of organizations: A machine-scored questionnaire instrument.* Ann Arbor, MI: Institute for Social Research.

Taylor, P. (1984). *Smoke ring: The politics of tobacco.* London: The Bodley Head.

Terpstra, D.E. (1981). Relationship between methodological rigor and reported outcomes in organization development evaluation research. *Journal of Applied Psychology, 66,* 541–543.

Thomas, E.L. (1968). Movements of the eye. *Scientific American, 219*(88) 516.

Thornton, G. (1980). Psychometric properties of self-appraisals of job performance. *Personnel Psychology, 33,* 263–271.

Thornton, G.C., & Cleveland, J.N. (1990). Developing managerial talent through simulation. *American Psychologist, 45,* 190–199.

Ting-Toomey, S., Gao, G., Trubisky, P., Yang, Z., Kim, H.S., Lin, S.L., & Nishids,

T. (1991). Culture, face maintenance, and styles of handling interpersonal conflict: A study in five cultures. *International Journal of Conflict Management, 2,* 275–296.

Treece, J.B. (1990, April 9). Will GM learn from its own role models? *Business Week,* 62–64.

Trice, H., & Beyer, J.M. (1993). *The cultures of work organizations.* Englewood Cliffs, NJ: Prentice Hall.

Tully, S. (1990). The hunt for the global manager. *Fortune,* May 21, 140–144.

U.S. National Institute on Drug Abuse. (1991). National Household Survey on Drug Abuse.

U.S. Department of Labor. (Fall, 1991). Outlook: 1990–2005. *Occupational Outlook Quarterly.* Washington, DC: Bureau of Labor Statistics.

Von Baeyer, C.L., Sherk, D.L., & Zanna, M.P. (1981). Impression management in the job interview: When the female applicant meets the male (chauvinist) interviewer. *Personality and Social Psychology Bulletin, 7*(1) 45–51.

Vroom, V.H. (1964). *Work and motivation.* New York: John Wiley.

Vroom, V.H., & Yetton, P.W. (1973). *Leadership and decision-making.* Pittsburgh, PA: University of Pittsburgh Press.

Vulcano, B.A., Barnes, G.E., & Breen, L.J. (1983). The prevalence and predictors of psychosomatic symptoms and conditions among police officers. In A.J. Krakowski & C.P. Kimball (Eds.), *Psychosomatic medicine.* New York: Plenum.

Wade, C., & Tavris, C. (1993). *Psychology* (3rd ed.). New York: HarperCollins.

Wahba, M.A., & Bridewell, L.B. (1976). Maslow reconsidered: A review of research on the need hierarchy theory. *Organizational Behavior and Human Performance, 15,* 212–240.

Warr, P.B., Cook, J.D., & Wall, T.D. (1979). Scales for the measurement of some work attitudes and aspects of well-being. *Journal of Occupational Psychology, 52,* 129–148.

Watson, D., & Clark, L.A. (1984). Negative affectivity: The disposition to experience aversive emotional states. *Psychological Bulletin, 96,* 465–490.

Watts, B.M., Ylimaki, G.L., Jeffery, L.E., & Elias, L.G. (1989). *Basic sensory methods for food evaluation.* Ottawa: International Development Research Centre.

Wehr, T.A., Sack, D.A., & Rosenthal, N.E. (1987). Seasonal affective disorder with summer depression and winter hypomania. *American Journal of Psychiatry, 144,* 1602–1603.

Weick, K.E. (1987). Organizational culture as a source of high reliability. *California Management Review,* Winter, 112–127.

Wickens, C.D. (1992). *Engineering psychology and human performance.* New York: HarperCollins.

Wiesner, W.H., & Cronshaw, S.F. (1988). A meta-analytic investigation of the impact of interview format and degree of structure on the validity of the employment interview. *Journal of Occupational Psychology, 61,* 275–290.

Witt, L.A., & Nye, L.G. (1991). Gender and the relationship between perceived fairness of pay or promotion and job satisfaction. *Journal of Applied Psychology, 77,* 910–917.

Word, C.O., Zanna, M.P., & Cooper, J. (1974). The nonverbal mediation of self-fulfilling prophecies in interracial interaction. *Journal of Experimental Social Psychology, 10*(2), 109–120.

Wright, P.L. (1990). Teller job satisfaction and organizational commitment as they relate to career orientations. *Human Relations, 43,* 369–381.

Zabriskie, N.B. (1973). *How to motivate salesmen without increasing sales costs.* Chicago: Dartnell Corporation.

Zweigenhaft, R.L. (1976). Personal space in the faculty office: Desk placement and the student-faculty interaction. *Journal of Applied Psychology, 61,* 529–532.

Index

Illustration credits

All part opener photos by Harry Rinehart.

Chapter 1 3 The Bettmann Archive; 6 © Andy Sacks/Tony Stone Images; 10 Noel Malsberg; 17 Noel Malsberg

Chapter 2 35 Jon Feingersh/Tom Stack; 38 Digital Stock; 42 Pamela Carley; 65 Noel Malsberg

Chapter 3 75 SuperStock; 89 Bill Cramer/NYT Pictures; 92 Noel Malsberg

Chapter 4 97 Elizabeth Hansen; 108 Los Angeles Police Department; 115 Zypher Pictures

Chapter 5 129 SuperStock; 144 Noel Malsberg; 146 Noel Malsberg; 147 Stanley Leary

Chapter 6 163 courtesy PSE&G; 166 Jim Cummings/FPG; 175 Harvard University Press; 196 Noel Malsberg

Chapter 7 205 ©Jon Riley/Tony Stone Images; 207 Noel Malsberg; 220 SuperStock; 223 © Bruce Ayres/Tony Stone Images

Chapter 8 235 ©Frank Herdolt/Tony Stone Images; 250 Noel Malsberg; 257 © Bruce Ayres/Tony Stone Images; 259 David Bartroff

Chapter 9 267 Richard Vogt/Berlin Steel; 270 Noel Malsberg; 275 © Bruce Ayres/Tony Stone Images; 276 I. Harpaz. (1990). The importance of work goals: An international perspective. *Journal of International Business Studies*, First Quarter, 75–93; 282 Nancy Siesel/NYT Pictures

Chapter 10 311 EPA; 317 Pamela Carley; 323 © Gerd Ludwig/Woodfin Camp & Assoc.; 325 Carrie Boretz/Image Works

Chapter 11 341 courtesy Lincoln-Mercury Division/Ford Motor Company; 348 Carlos Demand; 349 courtesy Hind; 354 Noel Malsberg

Chapter 12 371 © Dennis O'Clair/Tony Stone Images; 375 Noel Malsberg; 384 courtesy Busch Gardens; 394 Noel Malsberg

Chapter 13 403 © Bruce Ayres/Tony Stone Images; 410 Digital Stock; 414 courtesy Handykey Corporation; 421 Noel Malsberg

Chapter 14 437 © Alan Levenson/Tony Stone Images; 441 Cheryl Greenleaf; 446–448 VALS 2. Copyright © SRI International. Reprinted with permission; 453 Pamela Carley; 455 Bozelle Worldwide, Inc.